Working in Microsoft Office

Working in Microsoft Office

Ron Mansfield

Osborne **McGraw-Hill**

Berkeley   New York   St. Louis   San Francisco   Auckland   Bogotá   Hamburg   London   Madrid   Mexico City
Milan   Montreal   New Delhi   Panama City   Paris   São Paulo   Singapore   Sydney   Tokyo   Toronto

Osborne **McGraw-Hill**
2600 Tenth Street
Berkeley, California 94710
U.S.A.

For information on translations or book distributors outside the U.S.A., or to arrange bulk purchase discounts for sales promotions, premiums, or fundraisers, please contact Osborne **McGraw-Hill** at the above address.

Working in Microsoft Office

1234567890 DOC 99876

ISBN 0-07-882164-9

Acquisitions Editor: Joanne Cuthbertson
Project Editors: Cynthia Brown, Kim Torgerson
Copy Editor: Jan Jue
Proofreader: Linda Medoff
Technical Editor: Eric Bowden
Computer Designer: Richard Whitaker
Illustrator: Marla J. Shelasky
Series Design: 17th Street Studio
Quality Control Specialist: Joe Scuderi

To Adam and Scott, my two terrific sons
Thanks for being so patient and supportive

About the Author...

Ron Mansfield is a microcomputer consultant and author of several best-selling computer books, including Windows 95 for Busy People *and* Excel for Windows 95 for Busy People. *He is a frequent lecturer at national computer seminars and has written hundreds of articles for industry magazines and newsletters.*

CONTENTS

Welcome to Microsoft Office

Word Processing with Word for Windows

Working with Excel

V Managing Your Data with Access

Organizing Your Life with Schedule+

Delivering Information with Microsoft Exchange

VIII   Sharing Information with OLE

Acknowledgments

Wow. It seems to take fewer weeks but more people to create a computer book these days! I'd like to thank here as many of the participants as I can name, and to thank anyone else down the line whose name I've missed or whose contribution was made anonymously. Starting at the top, I'd like to thank Joanne Cuthbertson, for keeping me in mind to tackle this large project.

Thanks also to David Krassner for his writerly expertise and his unique capacity for circumventing the laws of time and space that seem to bog down the rest of us.

Then the editors—Cynthia Brown, Kim Torgerson, Terese Tatum, Jan Jue, and Linda Medoff had the unenviable job of making sense of my misspelled instructions and keeping the project rolling and on track. Robin Merrin gets the credit for smoothing out the details in the process of adapting the book to reflect the package's integrative approach. Technical editor Eric Bowden took pains to weed out technical inaccuracies. Richard Whitaker layed out the pages, and a whole team of Production Artists, led by Marcela Hancik, pulled the parts together. Finally, Richard Shrout produced the excellent index you'll find at the back. Thanks to all.

Introduction

TODAY you can purchase several of Microsoft's award-winning programs for what any one of them would have cost a few years ago. Here's what you get when you buy Microsoft Office Professional:

- Microsoft Office Binder and Shortcut Bar
- Word for Windows
- Excel
- PowerPoint
- Schedule+
- Exchange
- Access

There's also a version of Office called "Standard version," which leaves out the Access application. You can save a little money by getting that version if you're sure you'll never need the database management tools provided by Access, but the difference in price is less than the cost of buying Access later if you find out you could really use it, so I'd suggest springing for the Professional version.

One of the best things about Office is that Microsoft has standardized the look and feel of the component applications. For instance, most of the menus and the top menu choices in Word, Excel, and PowerPoint are arranged identically. Also, all of the programs in the Office collection share common modules for things like spell-checking and special text effects. This means that you'll spend a lot less time *learning*, and a lot more time *enjoying* your new programs.

Microsoft's Object Linking and Embedding technology (OLE) makes it easy to share text, data, and graphics among the Office programs. For example, to include an Excel chart in a Word document, you need only drag it from an Excel window into the desired location in a Word window. This industry standard is evolving to also let you exchange information with other conforming programs, both Microsoft and non-Microsoft.

While it's not totally seamless, the ideal of the fully integrated Office package is getting close.

Microsoft Office also offers these benefits:

- Microsoft Office includes an Office Shortcut bar that lets you switch quickly from one program to another.

- IntelliSense technology provides Tip Wizards that "watch" you work and offer time-saving suggestions for the current context.

- Help Wizards—on-screen guides—offer basic instructions for complex tasks like charting, creating form letters, and presentations.

- If you like, you can read a new Tip-of-the-Day each time you start any of the programs. This is a painless way to gain additional skills and confidence a step at a time.

About This Book

Working in Microsoft Office covers the essential skills for using all the Office programs, separately and as a team. The examples and reference materials are designed to get you up and running in minutes. We've tried to make this book easily accessible so you can find your way around without too much trouble and also make sure that the book is complete enough to use as an everyday desktop reference.

How This Book Is Organized

This book is divided into eight parts and an installation appendix. Each part has its own thumb tab, making it easy to find the sections on the different programs.

In each part, you'll find examples of the program at work, plus step-by-step instructions for all the essential features. Part Eight of the book presents a detailed look at Object Linking and Embedding, the big hitters in the integration department.

Part One: Welcome to Microsoft Office

Part One provides the basic information you'll need to work efficiently with the Microsoft Office Shortcut bar, menus, dialog boxes, and online help. You will also learn what's available to you as an Office user for exchanging information among the applications.

Part Two: Word Processing with Word for Windows

In Part Two you will learn everything you need to know to create, format, and print documents in Word for Windows, perhaps the most important program in the Office package, and the one you'll probably consider your "home base." Version 7 of this word-processing application is a major upgrade to an already full-featured program. If you have already used a previous version, you'll find a lot here to make your work even easier and faster, including how to use Word's sophisticated autotext and file-finding capabilities.

Part Three: Working with Excel

In Part Three you will see how you can use Microsoft's latest version of Excel to compute and keep track of all sorts of interdependent data. You'll learn not only how to have Excel perform complex calculations, but also how to display your data in eye-pleasing charts and graphs. Once you've gotten the hang of it, spice up your work by including graphics and special annotations, and speed up your work with macros. Use Excel's Scenario Manager to automatically generate various "what-if" conditions, and when you've found the optimum balance, import your results into Word or PowerPoint for a polished presentation.

Part Four: Presenting with PowerPoint

There was a time when you could stand up, speak your piece, get a yes or a no, and sit down. But it's the nineties now, and you are expected to give "awesome" meeting presentations to the MTV generation. Your audience expects to be dazzled. They want to see color, motion, and special effects. To a large extent how a presentation *looks* is often as important as what it *says*.

PowerPoint is Microsoft's answer to that need. It will help you create good-looking overhead transparencies, 35mm slides, and even video slide shows. And while it is true that most of what PowerPoint does can also be done by Word and Excel, PowerPoint streamlines a few of the tasks, and provides some handy prefabricated layouts, color schemes, and font choices.

Part Five: Managing Your Data with Access

As you will see in the chapters describing Word's mail-merge features, Excel's database tools, and PowerPoint's outlining features, Office provides many different ways to collect and organize business and personal information. But while PowerPoint is fine for small projects, and Word and Excel are great for small to medium projects, you may still need the extra features, speed, and flexibility provided by a full-featured database management system. Microsoft Access Version 7 is a major package in its own right, and perhaps the main reason you bought Microsoft Office Professional in the first place. In this part of the book I'll show you how to use Access to your best advantage, with both simple and complex examples, and an eye toward cutting through the sometimes confusing terminology connected with DBMS (oh yeah, I mean, "database management systems").

Part Six: Managing Your Life with Schedule+

Schedule+ is the computer equivalent to one of those hand-held PDAs (personal data assistants). You can keep your appointments, anniversaries, contacts, and other information in Schedule+, and have it remind you of appointments, etc. What's more, you can use it to plan meetings, because you can import other people's schedules and use a special utility called Meeting Planner to come up with times that everyone is free. It's quite a nice addition to the Office suite!

Part Seven: Delivering Information with Microsoft Exchange

Microsoft Exchange makes it possible for networked users to exchange messages and files. Depending on your network, you can communicate with other users in the same department, the same building, or stretched world-wide. Here you will find out how to use Exchange to join the e-mail revolution.

Part Eight: Sharing Information with OLE

This last part of the book presents a detailed look at the opportunities and, realistically, the limits of, the two most powerful ways to share information between documents—Object Linking and Embedding. Known collectively as OLE, these techniques are available to all of the component programs of Microsoft Office. With OLE you could create a graph in Excel or Microsoft Graph and then insert it in a Word document or PowerPoint slide presentation, and if the data in the graph changes over time you can choose whether you want the graph in the Word or PowerPoint presentation to show the changes automatically or simply to serve as a snapshot of the way things were when you first inserted it. With OLE, you're not even limited to using programs from the Office package.

Conventions Used in This Book

We've used some standard conventions and typographer's tricks to make this book easier to read. While most of them will be obvious, you should scan the next few paragraphs just in case.

Keyboard Notations

To simplify instructions and make them easier to follow, we've used a special kind of shorthand notation:

- Whenever you need to hold down one key, then press another, you'll see the keys separated by plus signs. For instance, CTRL+S means hold down the CTRL key while pressing the S key.

- Boldface text usually indicates text you are expected to type.

The | Symbol for Menu Commands

As a shortcut and an eye-catcher, we've used a special convention to indicate menu commands. When we want you to choose a menu command, it will follow this pattern: *menu name | command*. For instance, "Choose File | Save" is a shorter, neater way of saying, "Choose the File command from the menu bar, then choose the Save command from the File menu." Sometimes you'll even see a sequence of commands that goes three or four levels deep into subcommands.

Notes, Tips, and Warnings

Often there are quicker, but more complicated ways to accomplish tasks. And there are always pitfalls to anything you try on a computer. So throughout the book, you'll see Notes, Tips, and Warnings to guide you along. In them, we try to anticipate ancillary questions you might have while you're working through the exercises or looking up commands. This is what one looks like:

tip *If Microsoft Office is not yet installed on your computer, refer to Appendix A for installation instructions.*

There's a lot of ground to cover, so let's get right to it! Don't forget, if you run into any difficulties, check the index to see if your topic is dealt with further elsewhere in the book. Failing that, feel free to write me, care of Osborne/McGraw-Hill, with any suggestions or (shudder) corrections. We're all trying to keep up with the latest releases, but a few mistakes might have crept in at the last minute, so let me know!

PART I
Welcome to Microsoft Office

In Part I, you will meet Microsoft Office and see how it is integrated and organized. You'll learn the names and functions of the various Office components and how to use the Microsoft Office Shortcut Bar. You will also learn how to use some of the tools shared by all Office applications, such as online Help, the Clipboard, and most importantly, OLE (object linking and embedding).

CHAPTER 1

Introducing Microsoft Office

M

ICROSOFT Office Professional is a hefty collection of programs and other files that all work together. Office includes six of Microsoft's flagship applications, as follows.

WORD   This is a full-featured word processor that you can use to create letters, memos, reports, newsletters, manuals, and just about any other kind of document.

EXCEL   This is a spreadsheet program that allows you to organize, analyze, and graph information on your computer.

POWERPOINT   This is a presentation graphics program that you can use to create slides, overhead transparencies, handouts, and speaker notes.

ACCESS   This is a powerful relational database program that you can use to store, retrieve, and organize information.

SCHEDULE+   This is a personal planner that helps you organize your schedule by noting appointments, meetings, and projects. It also contains a contacts database.

MAIL (WORKSTATION LICENSE)   This is a mail application that enables you to send and receive electronic messages.

How you use Office is, of course, up to you, but those bright young kids at Microsoft stay up nights to make your life easier, and Office reflects this. The vision at Microsoft is that people will now focus more on *what* they want to do, rather than *how* they want to do it. Hence, Office is set up so you can start new projects right away without having to stop and wonder "will it be better for me to use Excel, Word, or Access to do this?" So when you get a great idea (the one thing your computer *can't* do), all you have to do is charge ahead, like a bull in a china shop, and Office will do its best to move the china out of the way. You'll see how a little later in this chapter.

Office makes it easy to transfer information from one application to another. This means that you can combine text, data, and graphics created in different programs into a single compound document. And, since the Office applications share a common look and feel, once you've learned how to use one of the Office components, it's easy to learn the others.

You'll need anywhere from 16 to more than 70MB of hard disk space to install Microsoft Office and its components. This is over and above the disk space needed for Windows and DOS. Moreover, you'll probably need disk space for your documents, spooled files that are printing, and so forth. It is possible to do minimum installations of the Office components by eliminating advanced features, sample files, and so on. Appendix A can help you understand disk requirements, installation options, memory, and other installation considerations.

tip *If at all possible, try to make room on your hard disk for at least the "typical" installation of the Office components you've purchased. Later, after you've had a chance to experiment, you can delete things you never use.*

Besides the main components (Word, Excel, PowerPoint, Schedule+, Mail, and, if you have Office Professional, Access), Office provides smaller programs that help you organize related files into complex documents called *binders,* check spelling, evaluate a document's grammar, create drawings, and much more. And, if you've done a typical or complete installation, your hard disk will also contain sample documents provided by Microsoft, templates that speed creation of everyday documents, and even some graphic files (clip art) that you can use to embellish your work.

Overview of the Office Components

Whether you work for a multinational corporation, run a small business from home, or help in the community when not carpooling the kids, Microsoft Office can make you more productive. But first, you'll need to know all the ways it can be of assistance. So let's get a quick overview of each Office component before we settle into the specifics of the various programs. Let's start with Word.

Overview of Word

Microsoft Word is a legendary word processing program. You can use it for anything from simple, daily correspondence to impressive desktop-publishing projects. As you can see from Figure 1-1, Word is as comfortable with graphics as it is with text.

note   *Tip Wizard watches as you work and makes helpful suggestions.*

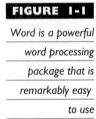

In addition to more traditional menus and keyboard shortcuts, Microsoft Word includes *toolbars*. Word's Standard and Formatting toolbars are shown in Figure 1-1. These toolbars contain *buttons* that you can click to perform common tasks like centering text or printing and saving your work. Once you've developed your own working style, you can even make *custom toolbars* like the one in Figure 1-1. You can customize menus or make new ones (like the "Ron's" menu in Figure 1-1) to make you more efficient. Word also provides a macro capability to help you automate repetitive tasks.

FIGURE 1-1

Word is a powerful word processing package that is remarkably easy to use

■

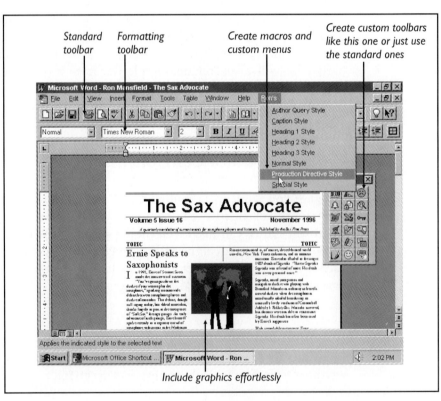

Standard toolbar

Formatting toolbar

Create macros and custom menus

Create custom toolbars like this one or just use the standard ones

Include graphics effortlessly

Word's designers have created a collection of *templates* and *Wizards* to help with everyday tasks. For instance, there are canned letters (templates) covering such topics as employee issues and overdue payments. To create a letter or memo, you can often start with one of these templates and personalize it for your needs, rather than typing the whole thing from scratch. Other templates help you create manuscripts, press releases, reports, and even a resume or thesis.

Wizards are even more powerful than templates. These assistants ask you questions about your next project and do much of the grunt work for you. As an example, you can create a 12-month calendar by answering only five questions!

Here you see the first page of a typical Wizard-created calendar. Wizards let you add graphics, change the orientation of the pages, and more. Other Wizards help create more personalized legal documents like pleadings, newsletters, meeting agendas, and so on.

January	Sun	Mon	Tue	Wed	Thu	Fri	Sat
				1	2	3	4
	5	6	7	8	9	10	11
	12	13	14	15	16	17	18
	19	20	21	22	23	24	25
	26	27	28	29	30	31	

1997

For serious publication projects, you'll want to take advantage of Word's ability to quickly create headings, a table of contents, indexes, and more. There's a spelling checker that actually checks your spelling as you work, an online thesaurus, and other authoring tools. An *AutoFormat* feature will even examine your plain text and embellish it with complementary type styles, formatting choices, and so forth. Figure 1-2 shows the same document before and after auto formatting.

Word also has a feature called *Tip Wizard,* which watches you work and makes suggestions about how you could work faster and more efficiently! It's a little spooky, but very helpful. Give it a try.

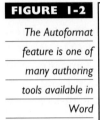

FIGURE 1-2

The Autoformat feature is one of many authoring tools available in Word

■

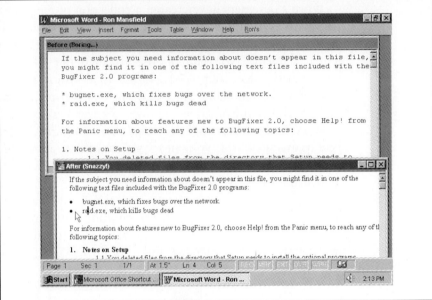

Additional features simplify the task of printing envelopes and labels. You'll find predefined settings for most common envelope sizes and label stocks. You can use onscreen addresses from your current document, or create and use stored address lists. Next time you need a single envelope or a dozen laser-printed labels, they will be only a click or two away. You might actually be able to toss out that old Selectric!

Finally, let's look at Word's *mail-merge* features. They let you do much more than send personalized junk mail. Here, too, Wizards make your life much easier, assisting in everything from setting up "data documents" (such as names and addresses), to formatting your merged documents.

Overview of Excel

Microsoft Excel was designed from the ground up for graphical (Windows and Macintosh) users. It was meant to be mouse driven, and it shows. Perhaps that's what makes Excel the premier Windows spreadsheet program. Notice the similarity between it and Microsoft Word in Figure 1-3.

Many of Excel's menus will remind you of others you'll see throughout the Office collection. Here, too, you can personalize the program to fit the way you work. Excel sports toolbars, as well. Like Word, Excel has a Tip Wizard, shown at the bottom of Figure 1-3.

Since so many spreadsheet projects involve multiple subjects, Excel lets you assign multiple sheets to a single file. When you're budgeting, for

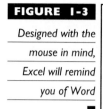

FIGURE 1-3

Designed with the mouse in mind, Excel will remind you of Word

Familiar menus and commands   Handy toolbars

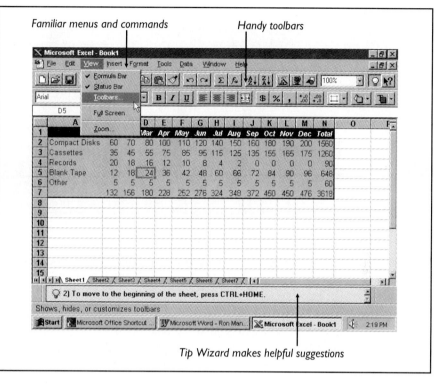

Tip Wizard makes helpful suggestions

instance, it's a snap to create a separate sheet for each branch office or department, each on its own worksheet, and then to consolidate the results.

Automatic formatting tools help you develop just the look you want for reports and presentations. There are buttons for common tasks like adding dollar signs and commas to cells. You can create borders and add shading manually or let Excel's *AutoFormat* feature take charge. Like its Word counterpart, Excel AutoFormat has a number of predefined color, shading, and font schemes that you can use as is or modify to suit your taste.

Excel sports a wealth of built-in, industry-specific *functions* that will be useful to scientists, bankers, and homemakers. Functions make quick work of setting up complex equations. There's a *Function Wizard* to help you sort this out, not to mention a massive amount of online help.

Charts and *graphs* are a snap (or perhaps a click?). The chart shown here was made by simply selecting the cells to be included and answering a few questions from Excel's *Chart Wizard*. Too bad you can't see the stunning onscreen colors the Wizard selected for the graph on the next page.

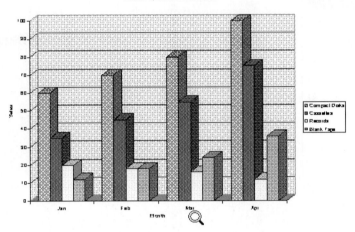

Besides including charts and graphs in your Excel spreadsheets, you can add artwork—photographs, drawings, clip art, logos, and more.

Excel includes features that help you develop and explore complex what-if scenarios. You'll be able to create cross-tab reports. Excel also offers database tools; if you have Microsoft Office Professional, though, you'll probably find Access more to your liking.

You've already seen a hint of the integration possible with Excel. It's easy to use all or part of a spreadsheet in your Word or PowerPoint documents. The reverse is also true. Access data can be exported easily to Excel, and vice versa.

Overview of PowerPoint

PowerPoint is a presentation tool that will help you capture and hold people's attention, whether in a big meeting or in a one-on-one presentation. You use PowerPoint to create *slides,* which can be arranged into *presentations.* In addition, you can print *handouts* and *speaker's notes.* Again, notice the familiar-looking menus and toolbars in Figure 1-4.

PowerPoint's designers have provided a wealth of predefined slide formats useful for 35mm slides, overhead transparencies, onscreen computer presentations, and printouts. You can use the designs as is or modify them. PowerPoint takes care of the formatting issues so that you can concentrate on the content of your presentations.

And, speaking of content, there's an *AutoContent Wizard* that helps prepare commonly given presentations. Do you need to break bad news? Run a training session? Report your progress? The AutoContent Wizard can begin the presentation, even providing outlines and major topic headings for you. All you need to do is add your own thoughts and specific facts. It's faster than microwaving frozen lasagna!

FIGURE 1-4

PowerPoint lets you quickly create compelling presentations

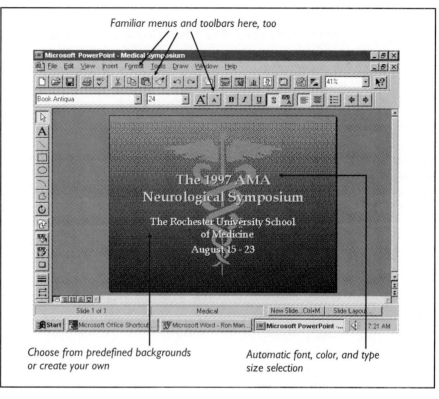

Rearranging presentations has never been easier. When you switch to *Slide Sorter view,* PowerPoint lets you drag slides around, delete unwanted slides, hide those "just-in-case" facts, and play until you are happy with the results. PowerPoint worries about the details like renumbering:

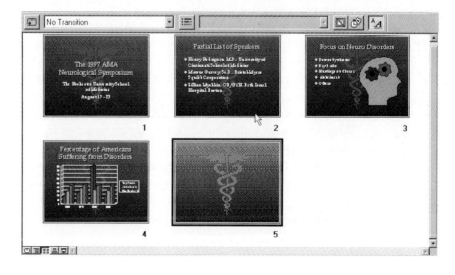

As you might have guessed, PowerPoint presentations can include elements from Word, Excel, and Access. PowerPoint supports sound objects (as do the other Office programs); so if you like, you can have your computer sing and dance. It is also a snap to *export* PowerPoint material to Word documents.

When you get ready to rehearse, watch your computer screen. PowerPoint will time your talk as you give it. You can turn your finished presentations into slides or pass them around to other computer users via disks or a network for their own private viewing. A number of third parties will convert your Power-Point files into film, often overnight if you send the files via modem.

Overview of Access

It's a simple data collector. It's a development system for hard-core consultants and system developers. Microsoft Access attempts to be all things to all people, and it's not a bad set of compromises. While there are simpler database programs, and while real computer wonks will probably find something to complain about, Access is a nice balance of power and simplicity.

As you can see from Figure 1-5, Access is a database program that helps you collect information in *tables* (collections of rows and columns) that you design. It then lets you scroll through the information onscreen, sort it, print it, and so on. You can design onscreen (and printed) forms. Reports can contain subtotals, averages, and numerous other computations. When you need to find specific information, you *query* Access. It responds by showing you just the information you've asked for in an agreeable layout that you design.

By allowing you to use *multiple tables* in the same database, Access lets you break your information up into manageable chunks, then *relate* the various pieces when it needs to be combined.

Like Word, Excel, and PowerPoint, Access has Wizards, this time helping you set up different *kinds* of databases. Wizards know a lot about databases and can provide you with suggested designs for contacts databases, customer lists, employee records, and dozens of other business and personal database applications. For example, have you ever wanted to get a handle on your garden? Ask the Wiz to help you set up a database for that purpose. Dieting? Wine collector? Video buff? Setting up an order-entry system for your new business? The Wiz has been there, done that.

You can create custom buttons and macros in Access so that even casual users can perform complex data manipulations. Naturally enough, Access knows how to import and export information. It knows how to use graphics, sound, and other 20th-century information sources.

FIGURE 1-5

Access is a relational database for both beginners and experts

Consistent menus and toolbars will make you feel right at home here, too

Create your own forms

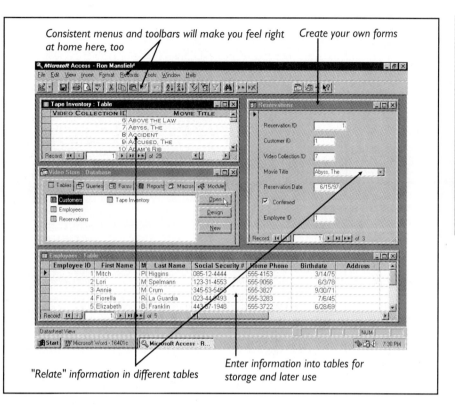

"Relate" information in different tables

Enter information into tables for storage and later use

Access is a lot like the game of chess. You can learn the basics in an evening, then spend the rest of your life exploring and discovering the Zen of it all.

Overview of Schedule+

If you've always wanted to organize your life, but never found the time, Schedule+ can do it for you. While you *will* have to fill in the things you have to do, you won't have to do much else. Schedule+ is the PDA (Personal Digital Assistant) to end all PDAs. You might want to hold on to your Sharp YO-110 for when you're on the road; but Schedule+, shown in Figure 1-6, can take care of everything for you at the office (or wherever your computer happens to be).

Offering a slew of personal management tools, Schedule+ first of all lets you quickly keep track of all meetings and appointments you have for the day, week, or month. But there is so much more. You can look at other people's schedules (if they let you!), set alarm reminders, automate entry of

FIGURE 1-6

Schedule+ helps

you plan your life

The usual menus and toolbars

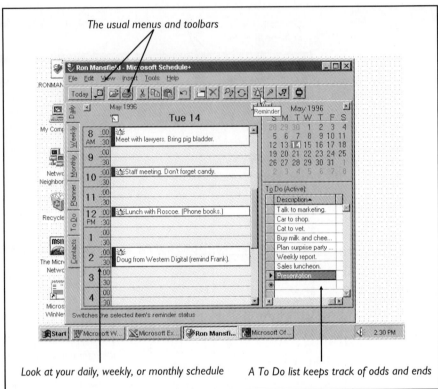

Look at your daily, weekly, or monthly schedule   A To Do list keeps track of odds and ends

recurring events (such as weekly departmental meetings), and even devise project schedules.

To make contacting people easier, Schedule+ comes complete with a Contacts utility. You can even set up appointments directly from your contacts list. A To Do list lets you note down odds and ends that you haven't gotten around to formally scheduling. Finally, as if your life weren't simple enough, Schedule+ further simplifies it by making it possible for you to export data to a Timex Data Link watch. Zowie! This process is explained fully in Chapter 41.

Overview of Mail

By now you must be dying to pick up your mouse and get clicking, so just note that Microsoft Office also comes with a Microsoft Mail license. So, if you are on a network, and you use Microsoft Mail around your shop, you can instantly become a legal MS Mail user. Office makes it easy to use MS Mail to route documents (such as Word and Excel files) to others on your network for review and comment, as you will see later in this book. But for now, since you can't pass what you don't have, let's figure out how to create some documents!

The Microsoft Office Folder

When you install Microsoft Office or any of its individual components, the Installer will suggest that you create a *Microsoft Office* folder. If you agree (which is the default and an excellent idea), you will wind up with a folder called Microsoft Office, visible in *Windows Explorer.* Icons for the smaller programs will appear in the Office folder. The principal Office programs (Word, Excel, and so on), though, will be installed in their own subfolders (called Access, Winword, Excel, and so on), where their files are also stored. If you double-click a folder to open it, you will see icons like the ones shown in Figure 1-7.

note   *For an overview of Windows techniques, see Chapter 2. There you will learn how to arrange windows and manage files.*

You probably won't be spending much time in these folders, since so much of the functionality of Office is centralized in the Office Shortcut Bar

FIGURE 1-7

Typical icons (for Microsoft Word) in an Office folder

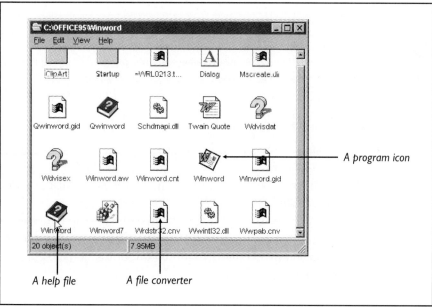

A program icon

A help file   A file converter

Welcome to Microsoft Office

(discussed next). It's good to know where these files and programs are, though.

tip *Immediately after installing Office or any new Office component, double-click on the related help icons in the folder window (Winword, and so forth) and look at the What's New subject under the help topics. Then browse the resulting screens. Right-click and choose Print from the menu to print information of interest.*

The Office Shortcut Bar

You can run the various Office components (Word, Excel, Access, and so on) without the *Office Shortcut Bar* by simply double-clicking on their program icons. But there's a better way. The Microsoft Office Shortcut Bar is a handy toolbar with menus that makes it easy to run programs. But it does more than that. You can place just about anything on the Office Shortcut Bar, from programs to documents to network connections. Furthermore, the Office portion of the Office Shortcut Bar is *task oriented*. That is, you decide *what* you want to do, and let Office worry about finding the right application. For example, if you click the Add a Contact button, Office will take you to Schedule+. If you click the Start a New Document button, Office will give you a New dialog box listing projects you can do in Word, Excel, and so forth. This approach frees you from the mundane task of trying to figure the best way to do what you want.

tip *You can easily switch from one program to another by using the Taskbar at the bottom of the screen. Just click on whatever program or document you want to see, and it will appear. The keyboard shortcut for this is ALT+TAB.*

Starting the Office Shortcut Bar

After a normal Office installation, the Startup folder menu will contain an Office Shortcut Bar entry like the one shown in Figure 1-8.

This will be in addition to the Office Shortcut Bar icon in the Microsoft Office folder.

If your Startup folder contains such an icon, the Office Shortcut Bar will run automatically each time you start Windows. (You can also run the Office Shortcut Bar manually by finding it on the Start menu.)

FIGURE 1-8

The Microsoft

Office Shortcut Bar

is a handy toolbar

for running

programs

■

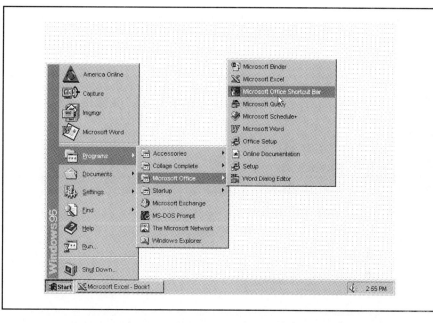

Office Shortcut Bar Appearance and Location

When you first install and run Microsoft Office, you'll see the default Office Shortcut Bar near the upper-right corner of your screen:

This is called the *Large Buttons* version of the Office Shortcut Bar. You can resize the Office Shortcut Bar and move it anywhere you like. You can even minimize it to make it run in the Windows Taskbar. Once you start to play with it, you'll find the Office Shortcut Bar to be your Houston Control in running tasks on your computer.

The number and kinds of buttons in your Office Shortcut Bar will depend upon what you have specified. By default, the Open a Document, Start a New Document, Make an Appointment, Add a Task, Add a Contact, and Answer Wizard buttons are shown. You can put anything else you want on the Office Shortcut Bar. The small icon in the upper-left corner of the Office Shortcut Bar reaches one of its menus.

tip   *If you forget the purpose of an Office Shortcut Bar button, just move the mouse pointer over the button and wait a moment. The name of the button will appear onscreen, thanks to a feature called* ToolTips.

Office Shortcut Bar Menus

One Office Shortcut Bar menu is reached by clicking on the Office Shortcut Bar menu icon with either mouse button. The other is reached by pointing anywhere on the Office Shortcut Bar except a button, and clicking with the *right* mouse button. There is some redundancy between the two menus. If you click on a button, you'll either launch an application or see a Windows menu.

warning   *Don't confuse application menus and Windows menus. Application menus are specific to a program and can only be used in that program. Conversely, Windows menus are available at all times. For example, if you point to an icon and press the right mouse button, you'll get a short list of file management commands (Close, Make Shortcut, Properties, and so forth).*

The Main Office Shortcut Bar Menu

Click the Office Shortcut Bar menu icon with either mouse button, and the main Office Shortcut Bar menu will appear:

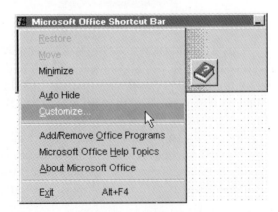

This menu offers you the following choices:

MINIMIZE   This option minimizes the Office Shortcut Bar.

AUTO HIDE   This option automatically hides the Office Shortcut Bar when other windows are active.

CUSTOMIZE   This option lets you add, delete, and rearrange buttons and menu items. You can also use this option to turn off Large Buttons. Leave things as they are for the moment. Later, when you decide to experiment, read the Customize command's online Help. (See Chapter 2 to learn how to use Help.)

ADD/REMOVE OFFICE PROGRAMS   This option lets you add or remove Office programs from your hard disk. Note that this is different from simply adding or removing programs from the Office Shortcut Bar.

MICROSOFT OFFICE HELP TOPICS   This option launches online Help for the Microsoft Office Shortcut Bar. (See Chapter 2 for more about online Help.)

ABOUT MICROSOFT OFFICE   This option tells you everything you always wanted to know about Microsoft Office, but were afraid to ask.

EXIT   This option closes Microsoft Office.

t i p   *If you double-click anywhere in the Office Shortcut Bar except on a button, you'll be taken to the Customize dialog box.*

The Right Mouse Button Menu

Unless you've swapped the functions of your mouse buttons (as many left-handed people do), clicking the right—or nonprimary—mouse button will display a menu that looks something like this:

This menu also offers you ways to change the appearance of your Office Shortcut Bar. For example, choosing any of the listed folders (Office, msn, Desktop, Favorites, Programs, or Accessories) will make Office add another small window to the Office Shortcut Bar, with icons for the contents of the selected folder. You can then zip between windows by clicking:

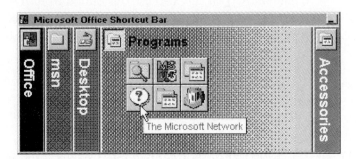

You can click these icons to go to specific files or launch specific applications, just as in the Office portion of the Office Shortcut Bar.

The Auto Hide, Customize, and Help buttons on the right mouse button menu work as described earlier. Refresh just refreshes the Office Shortcut Bar (that is, redraws it and removes any screen glitches). To move the Office Shortcut Bar, point to its title bar and drag. Reshape it by pointing to an edge; when the mouse pointer changes shape, drag the toolbar to a new shape.

tip   *Stick with the Large Buttons option in the beginning. The small ones are awfully tiny and it's hard to tell what they are. Why make it hard on yourself?*

Exiting Office Shortcut Bar

When you exit Windows, Office quits automatically. The Exit choice on the Office Shortcut Bar menu also quits Office and removes the Office Shortcut Bar from your screen. If you've displayed the regular or large Office Shortcut Bar toolbar buttons, you can exit Office.

tip   *If you exit the Office Shortcut Bar accidentally, use the Start menu to locate it in the Startup folder or the Office folder, and choose it to restart.*

The What's New Dialog Box

The first couple of times you start the Office Shortcut Bar, you will see a What's New window that will welcome you to Office and act as an online guide as you explore. It will look something like this:

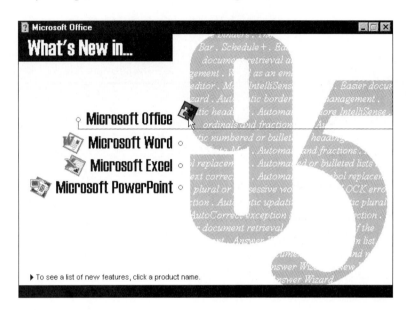

Click on the various products to learn more about Microsoft Office and the individual programs. The Back button moves you back one screen at a time. To close the What's New window, click the Close box in the upper-right corner. To visit What's New again, use the Office menu described earlier in this chapter.

The Windows Taskbar

Whenever Windows is running, you'll see the Windows Taskbar along the bottom of your screen. Clicking on the Taskbar button with the primary (usually the left) mouse button will

- Run the corresponding program if it is not already running
- Switch you to that program if it is already running

For instance, clicking on the Word button will either run Word or switch you to Word if Word is already running.

CHAPTER 2

Common Office Tools and Techniques

T H E R E are a number of common threads that run through Microsoft Word, Excel, and the other Office components. In this chapter you will learn menu, dialog box, and keyboard techniques that you can use with all the Office programs. You will also learn about the online Help system, which works similarly in all the Office applications. The small, external programs that come with Office, like Microsoft Graph and WordArt, are covered later.

Microsoft Office provides many techniques for moving information between programs. These include using the Clipboard, the Insert | File command, document scraps, and object linking and embedding (OLE). These techniques are discussed in Chapter 3 and in Part Eight.

note   *Techniques that vary among the Office applications are explained fully in the application-specific sections of this book. See Chapters 4–12 for information on Word, Chapters 13–23 for Excel, Chapters 24–28 for PowerPoint, Chapters 29–39 for Access, Chapters 40 and 41 for Schedule+, and Chapters 42 and 43 for Mail.*

Switching from One Application to Another

In Chapter 1 you learned how to use the Office Shortcut Bar and the Windows Taskbar to open and navigate between programs. Another way to switch from one application to another is by holding down ALT and then pressing TAB. When you do this, you will see the icons of all running programs in the center of your screen, with the active program's icon surrounded by a box. Each time you press TAB, the box moves to the next icon. When the box is around the icon of the program you wish to use, release ALT and you will switch over to that program.

$\int$izing and Arranging Windows

When you're working on a complex project, you may have two or more windows open on your screen at once. These can be two windows from the same program (two Word windows, for instance) or windows from different programs (such as Word and Excel). Figure 2-1 shows an example of this.

note   *Notice in Figure 2-1 how the menu bars wrap to fit inside narrow windows. You can use the horizontal scroll bars, if necessary, to see parts of your document that are hidden.*

You can use standard Windows techniques to move and resize windows (for example, drag the corners of windows). Consult your Windows documentation for additional information on this topic. To return a window to its normal, full-screen width, click the Maximize button in the upper-right corner of the window.

WELCOME TO
MICROSOFT OFFICE

FIGURE 2-1

*A Word window
and an Excel
window open on
the screen*

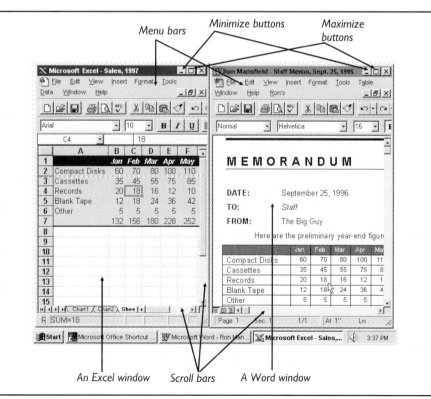

An Excel window   Scroll bars   A Word window

Working with Menus

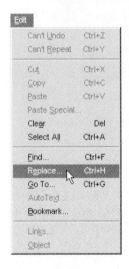

Here is a typical Office application menu.

To display a menu, just point with your mouse to a title in the application's menu bar and click your left mouse button once. In most cases, you can then execute a command by clicking on its name in the menu.

Notice that some menu commands end in an ellipsis (...). The ellipsis tells you that when you choose that menu command, you will be presented with a dialog box where you will need to make additional choices before the command can be executed. For instance, when you choose File | Print, the Print dialog box will appear on your screen, offering you a variety of Print options to choose from.

When you pull down a menu, some of the options on the menu may be dimmed or light gray. Dimmed menu choices are unavailable until you do something else. For instance, if you have not made any changes to a document, the Undo command on the Edit menu will be dimmed, because there are no changes to be undone.

Using Menus Without a Mouse

You can often make choices from menus without using your mouse. There are two ways to do this.

Some commands (like Paste, Copy, and Cut) have keyboard shortcuts. These are listed next to their names. For example, the shortcut for Cut is CTRL+X, the shortcut for Copy is CTRL+C, and the shortcut for Paste is CTRL+V. Not all menu choices have these keyboard shortcuts; however, you can assign your own shortcuts from within a program by customizing. (You'll learn about customizing in later chapters.)

If you don't mind learning some multistep keyboard shortcuts, you can reach virtually any menu option from the keyboard. This is particularly handy if your mouse dies or your aircraft tray table is too small for your portable *and* your mouse. The names of all menu choices contain an underlined letter (for example, Paste and Paste Special). You can select these options by pressing ALT and then typing the necessary sequence of underlined letters. For instance, to choose the Paste Special command from the Edit menu, you would press and release ALT, then type E (for Edit), then S (for Paste Special).

Shortcut Menus

Also available in Word, Excel, PowerPoint, and Access are *shortcut menus* that you can display by pointing to items on the screen and clicking the right (or nonprimary) mouse button. The available menu choices depend on the item you are clicking on, but usually you'll have at least Cut, Copy, and Paste. You'll learn more about these useful menus later in the book.

Working with Dialog Boxes

Many of Microsoft's dialog boxes now have handy, easy-to-use *tabs*. Simply click on a tab at the top of the dialog box to reveal additional options. For instance, the dialog box in Figure 2-2 has three tabs: Toolbars, Menus, and Keyboard.

When the Menus tab is foremost, you will see only the options relevant to menus. If you were to click on the Toolbars tab, the menu choices would drop back, and you would see toolbar choices.

You can usually TAB from place to place in a dialog box. You can also use underlined letters in dialog boxes as keyboard shortcuts.

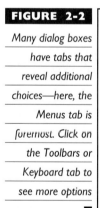

FIGURE 2-2

Many dialog boxes have tabs that reveal additional choices—here, the Menus tab is foremost. Click on the Toolbars or Keyboard tab to see more options

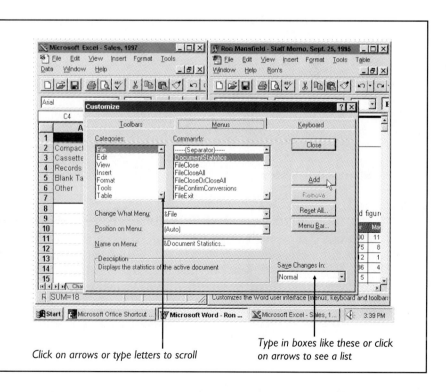

Click on arrows or type letters to scroll

Type in boxes like these or click on arrows to see a list

You can use TAB to reach the buttons in dialog boxes, too. Watch the outlines surrounding the buttons darken as you tab from one to the next. To select a button with a dark outline, press ENTER. In Figure 2-2, for example, pressing ENTER would select the Close button.

tip   *Many dialog boxes contain Description boxes like the one in the Customize dialog box shown in Figure 2-2. Look to these for useful explanations of dialog box options.*

Getting Help

It's a little ironic that Microsoft Office has so many online Help features that it takes several pages of a book to describe them. Generally, you'll find four kinds of online Help:

- Contents Help
- Answer Wizards
- Screen-element Help
- Help for users of competitive products (WordPerfect or Lotus 1-2-3, for instance)

In addition, Microsoft offers product support over the telephone, via fax, and through CompuServe and other bulletin board services. There is also TTY—assistance for the hearing-impaired. Since Word's Help feature does a good job of explaining itself, it will just be touched on in the following sections.

Starting Online Help

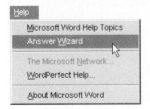

You can start online Help for a particular application from within that application by pressing the F1 function key. In addition, Office applications have Help menus. Word's Help menu is shown here.

Help menus let you search for Help on a particular topic, see previews of features, and browse an index of topics. Help menus also offer online Help for users experienced with competitive products.

The Help Contents Window

To see an overview of the online Help available for a product, choose Help | *Program Name* Help Topics and click the Contents tab if it isn't foremost. You'll see a window listing the various types of Help available. Once you're in the Help utility, you can click on tabs to see an Index of topics, go to a Find utility, or reach *Answer Wizard,* an amazing feature that seems to read your mind. Here is the Help Topics window for Word.

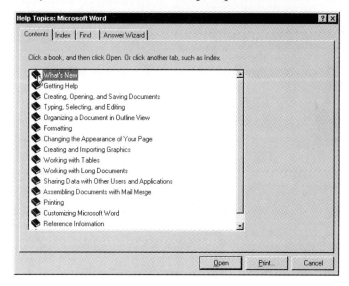

In the Contents window, you double-click icons corresponding to the category you're interested in. For example, to find out about new features in Word, you would double-click on What's New. This gives you a list of topics. Double-click on one of these to read up on the new feature.

If you've chosen to search the Index, information will come up in a regular Windows dialog box. There are three buttons along the top of the windows that you can use to move around.

HELP TOPICS   This button takes you back to the Help Topics screen.

BACK   This button takes you to the previous Help screen.

OPTIONS   This button lets you annotate, copy, or print the window.

t i p   *Some words in Help headings and Help text are underlined, and appear in a different color if you have a color monitor. Clicking on these entries will lead you to additional Help.*

Searching for Words of Wisdom with Answer Wizard

The Help | Answer Wizard command lets you enter specific words and phrases that you would like information about. For instance, to find out more about printing, follow these steps.

1. Choose Help | Answer Wizard.

2. Type the search word or phrase of interest (**print**, for example) and click Search. The Office program you are running will display a list of possible topics, as shown next. If you have chosen a rather broad topic, you may be asked to narrow it. If you have typed in an absurd topic, you might be amused by the results. For instance, *Green eggs and ham* brought up topics on tables and blue window backgrounds, among other things!

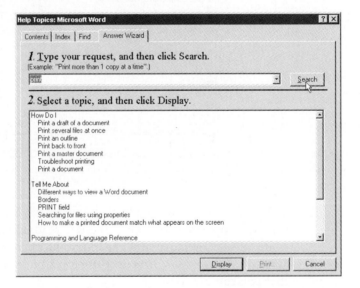

 tip   *Since Answer Wizard is really only just another tab in the Help Topics window, you can go from here to Contents, Index, or Find just by clicking on one of the other tabs.*

3. Choose a topic and click Display (or just double-click on any of the topics).

4. Answer Wizard will either display a Help window with more information or, better yet, in some cases, will offer to guide you through executing the command you have chosen. Just click Next if the latter happens.

Competitive Help

If you are familiar with WordPerfect, Lotus 1-2-3, or other competitive products, you can often get help that compares these products to their Microsoft counterparts. For instance, Microsoft Word offers help for Word-Perfect users. To access WordPerfect Help, follow these steps.

1. Make sure WordPerfect Help has been installed and enabled.

2. Choose Help | WordPerfect Help.

3. Find the topic of interest in the scrolling list, as shown here:

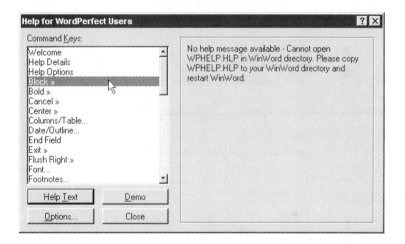

4. Point and click on a topic to read about it.

5. Use the buttons at the bottom of the window to see demos and explore other Help options. For instance, here are the Help options for WordPerfect users running Microsoft Word:

6. Press ESC or click the Close box to quit Help.

You can often get help by pointing with your mouse to items on the screen. For instance, when you point to a button in a toolbar, the function of that button will be displayed onscreen. (This is the ToolTips feature.)

You can also use the Help buttons on Office applications' Standard toolbars. The mouse pointer will change into an arrow with a question mark. When you point and click with that pointer, you get online Help. Here's an example.

1. Click the Help button on the Standard toolbar (shown at left). Your mouse pointer will become a giant question mark with an arrow. (Press ESC if this happens by mistake.)

2. Using your mouse, point to the item of interest and click. In the following illustration, the mouse pointer is pointing to Excel's Comma Style button.

3. Read the resulting Help text or click the buttons in the Help window to move around. Following is the Help screen for Excel's Basic number format codes. (You may need to scroll to read the entire text.)

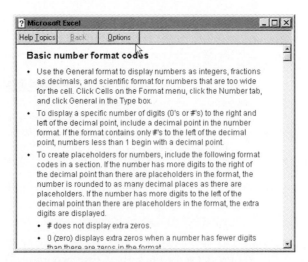

4. Click the Contents button or type **C** to see the topics list again. Or click the Close box to quit Help.

Getting Online Help in Dialog Boxes

Many dialog boxes contain Help boxes. Use these boxes when you get stumped or when you want to learn more about a dialog box's capabilities. They work just like the Help button on the Standard toolbar. When you click on the Help box in a dialog box, your cursor once again changes into a large question mark and an arrow. When you point at something and click, you'll see a brief explanation of the command or setting. For example, the Help box has been clicked in Word's Page Setup dialog box (shown as follows) to explain Header setting in the From Edge section of the Page Setup dialog box.

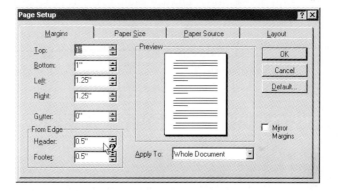

Printing Online Help

You can usually print online Help topics by selecting the Options | Print Topic command in the Help window. Make sure your printer is set up and ready.

Quitting Online Help

When you have finished using online Help, just press ALT+F4 to close the Help windows. Or you can click the Help window's Close box—the Close box found in the upper-right corner of Help windows.

Microsoft Product Support Services

When you really get stuck, Microsoft's huge technical support staff can be a big help. They provide technical note-downloading services, CompuServe forums, prerecorded voice message support, and even real, live people to answer your questions.

The first step is to "Read Your Manual." If you can't find the answers you need in online Help, in your manuals, or in books like this one, it's time to call out the big guns.

Finding Out About Tech Support Options

Microsoft is changing the way it supports users, and things that were once free are now often quite expensive. To find out more about available support options, choose Help | About Microsoft Word and click on the Tech Support button.

When you click on Tech Support, a list of support topics will appear on your screen. You can read and print these topics just as you would any other Help information.

warning   *Microsoft Technical support is not always free. Be sure you understand the costs before obtaining support.*

CHAPTER 3

Sharing Information with Microsoft Office

WINDOWS makes it possible to pass information from one program to another so you don't have to re-create the information. And Microsoft Office provides many alternatives for sharing and exchanging information. In this chapter, you'll take a look at the most fundamental methods: the Clipboard, interprogram drag-and-drop, document scraps, and the Insert File command. Later, when you've learned the basics of the individual Office applications, you can turn to Part Eight to learn about more advanced integration features, including object linking and embedding (OLE).

The Clipboard

If you've used Windows programs before, you've probably used the Clipboard to move things from place to place within a document. You can also use the Clipboard to move things *between* different programs. For instance, if you use the Windows Calculator accessory, you can copy the results of your calculations to the Clipboard, switch to Word or Excel, and paste the calculation results into a Word paragraph or an Excel worksheet cell. It is also possible to move things to and from *non-Windows* programs via the Clipboard. You can copy an entire screen's contents or just selected portions.

Since many programs use unique control codes, characters, and graphics formats, the results of pasting can be a little unpredictable at times. Windows, along with all Windows-savvy applications, does a pretty good job of minimizing these often-perplexing differences; but the farther you get off the beaten path, the more likely you are to have problems. When pasting from a non-Windows program into a Windows program, you may need to experiment, and possibly even do some manual reformatting, to obtain the desired results.

Using the Clipboard to Cut, Copy, and Paste

As you may know, you place things on the Clipboard by first *selecting* them, then either *copying* or *cutting* the selected items to the Clipboard. Once an item has been placed on the Clipboard, you can move or place a copy of it elsewhere by *pasting* it.

> **tip**   *Techniques that vary among the Office applications (such as selecting) are explained fully in the application-specific sections of this book. Please refer to Chapters 4–12 for information on Word, Chapters 13–23 for Excel, Chapters 24–28 for PowerPoint, Chapters 29–39 for Access, Chapters 40 and 41 for Schedule+, and Chapters 42 and 43 for Mail.*

The Clipboard is a *temporary* storage area, and its contents are *replaced* each time you copy or cut something new. Thus, if you are using Word and you copy something (such as a paragraph), then switch to Excel and copy something else (like a formula), when you switch back to Word, your Clipboard will contain the formula but *not* the paragraph. The paragraph will be in paragraph heaven. Even the Undo command usually can't bring it back.

Clipboard contents also disappear whenever you quit Windows or turn off your computer. Clipboard contents can be saved to disk, however. This process is discussed later in this chapter.

Copying and Pasting Portions of a Window

The steps for copying are identical in Word, Excel, PowerPoint, and other well-designed Windows applications. The same is true of cutting and pasting. You can copy or cut (and then paste) text, graphics, other objects, or combinations of them.

Start by selecting whatever it is you want to copy or cut, and then choose Edit | Copy or Edit | Cut. (The keyboard shortcuts for copying and cutting are CTRL+C and CTRL+X, respectively.) The Copy command leaves the original item(s) intact and places a copy of the item(s) on the Clipboard.

Cut removes the selected item(s), placing the item(s) on the Clipboard. (Choosing Edit | Undo *immediately* will usually restore items you've accidentally cut.)

> **tip**   *If you've accidentally cut something that is vitally important, the first thing to do is don't panic! Often a little coolheadedness can turn a major catastrophe into a minor keystroke recovery. If you haven't cut or copied anything else, just give the Edit | Undo command. If you have cut or copied, you might want to close the document without saving changes (depending upon how important what you cut was, and how much you had done—and are willing to sacrifice—since your last save). When you reopen the file, whatever you cut out will be restored.*

When you choose the Paste command (Edit | Paste, or CTRL+V), the contents of the Clipboard are inserted into the active document at the insertion point. If you are cutting or copying from one program (let's call it the *source* program) and pasting into another program (the *destination* program), you'll need to have both programs running (or at least available), and then switch from the source to the destination program before pasting. This can be as easy as pressing ALT+TAB until you see the name of the program you want to use. You can also arrange your screen so that both programs' windows show, and then just point to the one you want to paste into.

Exactly what happens when you paste depends upon a number of factors. First of all, not every application can accept everything you might place on the Clipboard. If you try to paste a graphic into a Windows program that cannot accept graphics, for instance, you will fail.

Typically, you'll want to paste things into applications that use different formats and formatting commands. Sometimes Windows and the programs you are using can work around these differences; other times they can't. Occasionally, the results are better than you might expect. For instance, when you copy a range of cells from an Excel worksheet into a Word document, Word automatically creates a table of the appropriate size to accommodate the contents of the pasted cells, as illustrated here.

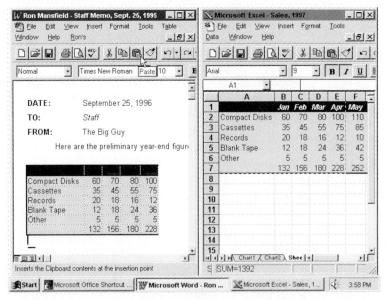

Sometimes, the results of pasting can be downright mysterious. For example, pasted items may look bizarre because they don't fit the destination document's margins or styles. Occasionally, pasted items will look fine when you view them onscreen, but then will have line- and page-ending problems when you print them. This usually happens because of differences in screen and printer fonts. Check your work after pasting and, as always, *save your work* before making major alterations with the Paste command.

t i p   *Some programs (like Word and Excel) have AutoFormat commands. Try using these to reformat items that don't look right after pasting. And be patient when you paste between programs. It can take a moment or two—your machine may only appear to be locked up.*

The Paste Special Command

While the regular Paste command is often all you'll need, sometimes the Edit menu's Paste Special command proves useful.

When you copy or cut things to the Clipboard, the source program often sends the information to the Clipboard in more than one format. When you use the Paste command, the destination application pastes the Clipboard contents using *its* default format, which is often—but not always—the best format.

The Paste Special command provides you with a dialog box containing an ever-changing list of data types. For instance, when the Clipboard contains a bitmapped graphic, you might see choices like *Picture* and *Microsoft Drawing Object*. If the Clipboard contains text, you're likely to see choices like *Microsoft Word Object, Formatted Text, Unformatted Text,* and so on.

Choosing one of these formats changes the way the item is pasted, thereby converting the Clipboard contents when you paste. Pick the desired format from the list, and then click Paste to place a converted copy of the item at the insertion point. (The Paste Link options that sometimes appear are discussed later in this chapter.)

Copying and Pasting an Entire Screen or Window

When your applications permit, you can copy the entire contents of your screen or just the contents of the active window to the Clipboard as a bitmapped graphic. This is a quick-and-dirty way to create illustrations for programming documentation. While the illustrations may lack much of the sophistication of true screen captures, you may find the trick useful.

Actual steps will vary from program to program. Generally, to begin, make sure that the screen contains exactly what you wish to capture. Next, press PRTSC (Print Screen) on your keyboard, or perhaps ALT+PRTSC or SHIFT+PRTSC on some keyboards. (Some keyboard types require SHIFT or ALT combinations, since they don't recognize plain PRTSC or ALT+PRTSC combinations.) This should capture the entire screen. Try either SHIFT+PRTSC or ALT+PRTSC to capture just the active window rather than the entire screen. To see what works, use the Clipboard Viewer accessory program, described in the next section.

Once you've placed a bitmapped image on the Clipboard, you can paste it to any application that accepts bitmaps, including Word, Excel, and PowerPoint. (Using screen dumps like these with Excel's and PowerPoint's slide show features can help you create simple training slide shows.)

The Clipboard Viewer

The Windows *Clipboard Viewer* lets you see what's on the Clipboard. You can save the Clipboard contents to disk, retrieve previously saved Clipboard files, and clear the Clipboard. The Clipboard Viewer is normally found in the main Windows folder (its icon looks like a tiny clipboard). Figure 3-1 shows how the Clipboard Viewer displays different types of Clipboard contents.

tip *If you find the Clipboard Viewer useful, consider placing it in your Windows Startup folder. That way, it will be loaded automatically each time you start Windows.*

FIGURE 3-1

The Clipboard Viewer lets you see what's in the Clipboard

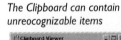
The Clipboard can contain unreocognizable items

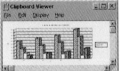

Display Clipboard contents in different formats

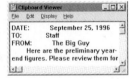

The Clipboard Viewer often distorts things

Viewing in Different Formats

The Clipboard Viewer's Display menu often lets you view text, graphics, and most other items in a variety of formats. The Owner option shows the item as it would appear in the program that created it. Other viewing options vary with the item being viewed. To return to the format that was displayed when you opened the Viewer, choose Display | Auto.

Saving Clipboard Contents to Disk

You can save Clipboard contents as disk files by using the Save As command on the Clipboard Viewer's File menu. You'll see a Save As dialog box. Get in the habit of noticing where Windows intends to save the file. Change the path if you like. Clipboard files are normally saved with the extension .CLP. It's a good idea to stick with this extension, to facilitate searches for an elusive file.

tip *If you know ahead of time that you're going to want to save what you're cutting, consider either saving it as a new file or making it into a document scrap. The latter is especially useful if you plan to paste the information a few times and then to delete it.*

Retrieving Clipboard Files

The File | Open command in the Clipboard Viewer will bring up a standard Open dialog box and let you pick files saved with the Clipboard Viewer's Save As command. When you open a saved Clipboard file this way, the existing contents of the Clipboard will be replaced with the contents of the newly opened file. You will have the opportunity to confirm that this is OK.

Clearing the Clipboard's Contents

Sometimes you'll want to clear the contents of the Clipboard. If the Clipboard contains a large item in several formats, this is a way to free up RAM.

To clear the Clipboard, first display its contents with the Clipboard Viewer. Then press DEL, or use the lonely Delete command on the Edit menu. There's no Undo command, so think twice or thrice before you delete.

tip *To remove a large item from the Clipboard without running the Clipboard Viewer, just copy something small. For example, select a single space in a Word document and copy that to the Clipboard, and it will remove whatever was there before.*

Using the Clipboard with Non-Windows Applications

It is often possible to paste non-Windows items into Windows documents and vice versa. The steps are a bit more involved than moving things between two Windows programs. You use additional commands found on the icon menu (in the title bar) when running a non-Windows program in a DOS window. For instance, Figure 3-2 uses the DOS command **type readme.txt**

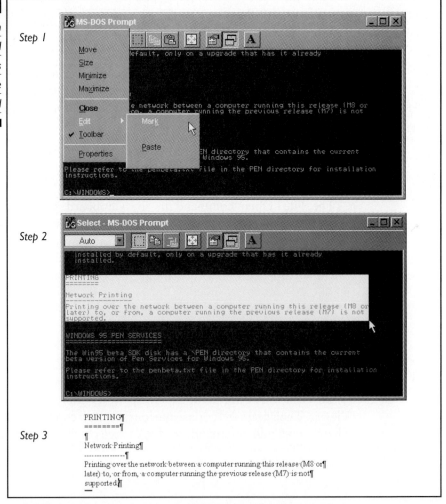

FIGURE 3-2

Often you can move things to and from non-Windows programs via the Clipboard

∎

Step 1

Step 2

Step 3

to place some DOS text on the screen in a DOS window. Then a portion of the text was copied to the Clipboard and pasted into Word for Windows. The specific steps involved are explained next.

1. Choose Edit | Mark from the icon menu.

2. Select with your mouse, and then click the Copy button or press ENTER.

3. Switch to your Windows application and paste (choose Edit | Paste or press CTRL+V).

Things pasted from non-Windows applications often have unwanted paragraph returns that you will need to remove.

Copying and Pasting Non-Windows Items into Windows Applications

Here are the general steps for copying non-Windows items into a Windows application:

1. Run the DOS program in a window (press ALT+ENTER, if necessary).

2. Choose Edit | Mark from the window's icon menu.

3. Select the item(s) in the DOS window that you want to copy.

4. Press ENTER or click the Copy button to copy the item(s) to the Clipboard.

5. Switch to your Windows application and choose Edit | Paste (or CTRL+V).

t i p   *Unless your non-Windows application uses* ALT+SPACEBAR *for something else, you can use* ALT+SPACEBAR *to bring up the non-Windows icon menu. From there you'll be able to reach the Edit command.*

Notice that when you paste, things are not always exactly as you'd like. At the bottom of Figure 3-2 the text came in just fine and was reformatted to match the Word document's current style (double-spaced Courier). But look at the paragraph marks (¶) smack in the middle of the sentence. They appear because there were carriage returns at those points in the DOS text to make it fit the DOS screen. You may need to correct such occurrences after you paste.

Enabling Non-Windows Applications for Mouse Editing

If you plan to do a lot of copying and pasting in a non-Windows application, it's a bit tedious to always have to choose the Edit | Mark command from the icon menu and then to have to remember to press ENTER to copy the selected text. It's also a pain to move around in applications that don't support a mouse. There is a way to enable non-Windows applications for editing, though. Follow these steps.

1. Click the Properties button in the non-Windows application's toolbar. This will bring up the Properties dialog box.

2. Click on the Misc tab to bring it forward.

3. In the Mouse section, click the QuickEdit option (make sure there's a check mark in the box), as shown here:

4. Click OK.

5. Now, instead of going through the rigmarole, you'll have continuous mouse highlighting capabilities, and you can use the Copy and Paste buttons on the toolbar to copy and paste things.

Copying and Pasting Windows Items to Non-Windows Applications

Not all non-Windows programs can accept formatted text or graphics. Check the documentation of your non-Windows applications or experiment on noncritical copies of your DOS files.

Here are the general steps for copying and pasting to non-Windows applications:

1. Run the DOS program in a window (press ALT+ENTER, if necessary).

2. Run the Windows program that contains the items you want to paste.

3. Place the items of interest on the Clipboard (choose Edit | Copy or Edit | Cut).

4. Switch to the DOS window and place the insertion point or its equivalent where you want the items to be inserted.

5. Choose Edit | Paste from the window's icon menu, and see what happens.

n o t e   *Some non-Windows programs might not support a mouse. This means wherever the cursor is when you switch to the program, that's where the Clipboard's contents will be pasted in. See the section called "Enabling Non-Windows Applications for Mouse Editing" to give even non-Window's applications mouse support.*

Drag-and-Drop

With Microsoft's *drag-and-drop* feature (once a Word-only tool) you can move or copy items by selecting them with your mouse and then dragging them from place to place on your screen. Drag-and-drop now lets you drag selected items from one window to another, even between applications. Here are the steps:

1. Arrange the source and destination windows on your screen so that you can see both.

2. Select the item or items you want to move or copy.

3. Point to the selected object you wish to move or copy. If you're in Excel, point to the edge of the selected area so that the mouse pointer becomes an arrow.

4. To *move* the selected item, hold down the primary mouse button and drag into the destination window. To *copy* the selected item, hold down CTRL while you drag. The mouse pointer will change

shape (it will have a small box added to it when you move, or a box and a plus sign when you copy).

5. Point to the desired destination location and release the mouse button. Be patient. In a moment the item will move.

6. Drag-and-drop will work with most applications that support object linking and embedding. It might even work with non-Microsoft programs. Try it.

tip   *Drag-and-drop is turned on when you first install most Microsoft applications, but many programs let you turn it off, since some people don't like it. Check the Options settings if you are having trouble with drag-and-drop. For instance, the Edit tab in Excel's Options dialog box contains its drag-and-drop control. Check online Help for assistance.*

Document Scraps

Extending the workplace metaphor, Windows now lets you place scraps of documents on the Windows desktop. *Scraps* are bits of text or graphics that you have copied and placed in files on the desktop. The nice part is, you don't have to do anything fancy to create them! Scraps can then be pasted into other documents or programs. The best way to think of scrap documents is as automatically saved Clipboard files. The cool thing about scraps is that you don't lose one scrap when you save another, unlike the Clipboard; also, since scraps are saved to files, you can move them around and put them in folders on disk for later use.

note   *Only programs that support OLE can make and use document scraps.*

Creating Document Scraps

Creating a document scrap couldn't be easier. Just select the text, graphics, or other data you want to save. Then drag it out to the desktop. Windows will then make a new file right on the desktop, as shown next. You can rename, delete, or move the scrap as you see fit.

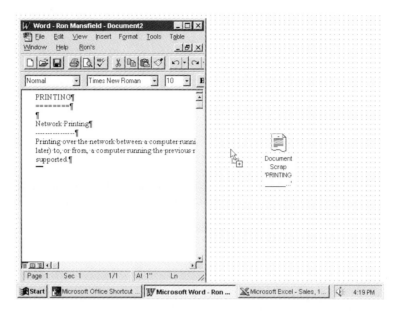

tip *You can view document scraps simply by double-clicking on them. Once they are open, you can select text and edit them just like any other document.*

Inserting Document Scraps

Once you have a scrap or two on the desktop, inserting the contents of a scrap is quite straightforward. Just click on the scrap and drag to where you want it inserted. A copy of the scrap's contents will be inserted in your destination document, leaving the original scrap untouched. This is handy, because you can repeatedly reuse a scrap.

The Insert File Command (Word)

Microsoft Word has an Insert File command (Insert | File) that lets you import documents. Imported text is placed at the insertion point in the destination file. If you have installed the necessary filters, Word will even convert non-Word documents, maintaining much of the original formatting.

Part Two

Word Processing with Word for Windows

In this part, you'll learn a lot about using Word for Windows, perhaps the most important program in the Office package. Version 7 of this word processing application is a major upgrade to an already full-featured program. If you have used a previous version, you'll find a lot here to make your work even easier and faster.

CHAPTER 4

Word Basics

Y OU'D be hard-pressed to name a word processing feature not included in Microsoft Word for Windows version 7. Usually, Word provides two or three ways to accomplish the same task. Beginners will find the program easy to use and very logically organized. Power users will discover new capabilities and possibilities each time they run it. So whether you are a first-time word processing novice or a battle-scarred WordStar and WordPerfect pro, you won't be disappointed. Let's take a look.

Starting Word

To start Word, click the Word button in the Office Shortcut Bar, or choose it from the Start menu. Figure 4-1 shows both options.

You can also use Windows Explorer and double-click on a Word for Windows *document* icon to start Word:

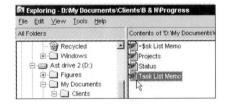

This will launch Word and immediately open the document so you can get right to work.

tip *If you always work on the same document or same type of document, put a shortcut to the document (or template) in your Word Startup folder. Then, each time you start Windows, it will start Word and open the desired document or document template.*

FIGURE 4-1

Start Word

either from the

Office Shortcut

Bar or from the

Start menu

■

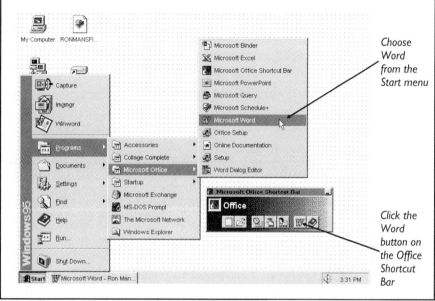

Choose Word from the Start menu

Click the Word button on the Office Shortcut Bar

Tip of the Day and Tip Wizard

You will see a Tip of the Day in the Tip Wizard each time you start Word.

Most are very useful; a few are even entertaining. Tip Wizard also watches as you work, making helpful suggestions about how you could complete tasks more quickly and efficiently. You can see such advice any time you like by displaying the Tip Wizard toolbar.

Creating New Documents When Word Is Running

Whenever you start Word for Windows, it opens a new, untitled, "normal" document so that you can begin a new project from scratch (unless you specified a Word filename or double-clicked a document icon to start Word). If you want to start a new project with Word already running, simply choose File | New. You will see the New dialog box shown in Figure 4-2. Word gives you a choice of document templates and Word Wizards designed to minimize repetitive formatting tasks. You'll learn more about templates and Wizards in Chapter 9.

FIGURE 4-2

The New dialog box

■

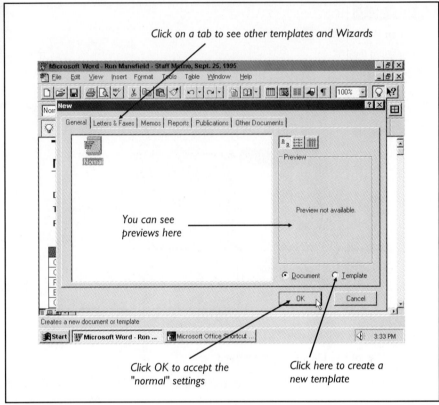

Click on a tab to see other templates and Wizards

You can see previews here

Click OK to accept the "normal" settings

Click here to create a new template

If you simply click OK, Word will open a new, untitled document window using the standard or "normal" settings. Each new window opened this way in a session is sequentially numbered (Document1, Document2, and so on).

tip *You can also open a new, untitled document window by pressing CTRL+N or by clicking on the dog-eared–document icon located on the Standard toolbar.*

Opening Preexisting Documents When Word Is Running

To open a Word document when Word for Windows is running, choose File | Open. Use the Look In list to open the appropriate disk, and then scroll through the files until you find the one you want. Double-click on the desired filename to open the document.

The Parts of a Word Window

An active Word window has standard Windows scroll bars, a title bar, zoom boxes, a menu bar, and so on. (If you are unfamiliar with these terms and concepts, take a moment to review your Windows manuals.)

In addition to the usual Windows tools, you should see a ruler, toolbars, a flashing insertion point, and possibly some of the other items shown in Figure 4-3. Word for Windows now has many toolbars, and you may see up to eight at one time onscreen (although two is more common and practical).

You may see more or fewer buttons on the toolbar than those illustrated in Figure 4-3. Don't worry. The exact size and shape of your Word for Windows workspace will vary with your screen size and other factors.

The Menu Bar

The top of your screen will probably have Windows-style menus in a menu

FIGURE 4-3

The Word workspace

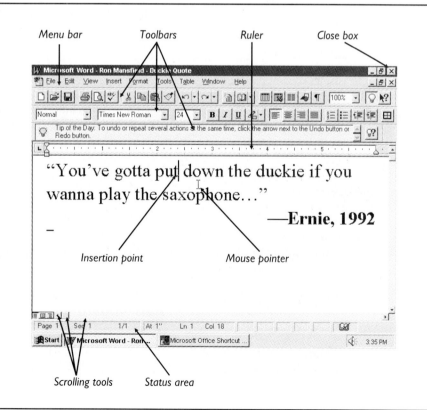

bar. When you point to a menu title with the mouse pointer and click once, the menu will drop. Clicking on the desired command in a menu tells Word to execute that command. Commands with an ellipsis (...) after their names will ask you for additional information before they go to work. Dimmed commands cannot be used until other functions have been performed.

Many commands can be executed by holding down specific key combinations (often called *hot keys*). As with other Windows programs, these keyboard shortcuts are often listed next to command names in menus. For instance, holding down CTRL and pressing P is the same as choosing File | Print.

The Mouse Pointer

Your mouse pointer should look like an I-beam, and you should be able to move it freely about the screen. The pointer will change shapes when it passes over certain parts of the Word for Windows workplace. For instance, it turns into a large arrow at the edges of Word windows.

The Insertion Point

The *insertion point* or *cursor* indicates where text, graphics, and other items will be placed when you type or insert them. The insertion point is a blinking vertical bar.

warning *Beginners sometimes forget to press the mouse button after pointing with the I-beam. Don't confuse the I-beam with the insertion point! First you use the I-beam to point to where you want the insertion point. Then you click the mouse button to place the insertion point.*

Toolbars

Word for Windows provides over a dozen toolbars, but you'll normally display only two or three at once. Microsoft's "factory settings" display only the Standard and Formatting toolbars (shown in Figure 4-3). The other toolbars include

- Standard
- Formatting
- Borders
- Database

- Drawing

- Forms

- Microsoft

- Word for Windows 2.0

- Tip Wizard

Toolbars contain buttons, drop-down menus, and other controls that help you quickly alter the appearance and arrangement of documents by executing a variety of Word for Windows commands.

For example, you can use the Formatting toolbar's Bold button to make text boldface, or its drop-down font menus to pick a font and size. Point to the down-arrow buttons next to the font and type size boxes on the Formatting toolbar to see drop-down lists of choices. You can also type font names or sizes directly into the font and size boxes.

The Show/Hide (¶) button (shown at left) on the Standard toolbar alternatively shows and hides paragraph marks, tab marks, space marks (the little dots), and other nonprinting items.

You can display a toolbar by right-clicking on any toolbar on your screen and selecting from the drop-down menu that appears.

The Ruler

Use the ruler to quickly change margins and indents. The ruler lets you alter the appearance of multiple paragraphs or just the paragraph containing the insertion point. To display or hide the ruler, choose View | Ruler.

Status Area

The *status area* at the bottom of your Word window gives additional information about your work. It's always present unless you choose the Full Screen view.

Designing Your Document

You should start each new project by thinking about the document's overall design and final appearance. Word for Windows gives you onscreen clues about how your document will look on paper. If you give Word some basic information, it can show you line endings; page ending; the relative size and placement of text, graphics, and margins; and so on. To do this, Word needs information from you—such as the paper size and the kind of printer you will be using. The Page Setup dialog box is where you give Word the information it needs.

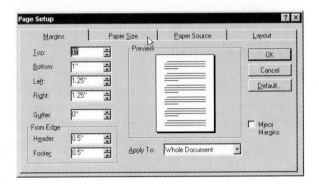

To display the Page Setup dialog box, choose File | Page Setup. Click on the tabs near the top of the dialog box to see additional choices. Type new settings in the text boxes or click on the arrows and other tools to make changes. Once you choose your settings and click OK, Word changes the onscreen appearance of margins, the ruler, and other settings to reflect your design.

tip   *It is always a good idea to input (at least preliminary) printer, paper, margin, and other document-design decisions before you start typing.*

Typing Text

Don't worry if you make typing mistakes; they are easy to fix and Word even flags words it thinks are misspelled. Watch the screen as you type. Notice that when you reach the end of a line, Word for Windows automatically begins a new line for you.

This feature is called *automatic word wrap,* and it eliminates the need to press ENTER when you want to start a new line.

Slobovia·is·restless.·In·a·recent·survey·of·10,000·Slobovians,·50%·didn't·know·what·a·survey·was,·33%·said·they·didn't·care,·9%·bit·the·survey·taker,·and·3%·would·only·bounce·up·and·down·on·a·pogo·stick·saying·"Pork!"·over·and·over·in·a·high·pitched·voice.·However,·the·5%·who·did·answer·seriously·felt·that·it·was·time·to·get·the·blood·flowing·in·Slobovia·once·again.¶

Typing Habits to Break

If you learned to type on a typewriter or even an old word processor, chances are you have established habits that will be counterproductive in your use of Word for Windows. Here are a few habits you should try to break:

- Do not use TAB or SPACEBAR to indent paragraphs. Instead, use the indent control in Word's ruler (the top "handle" at the left side of the ruler).

- Never use SPACEBAR to center or otherwise position text. Use the center-alignment button on the Standard toolbar, instead.

- Don't use SPACEBAR to make columns. Instead use tabs, Word's multicolumn features, or tables.

- Do not manually space paragraphs with carriage returns. Use Word's paragraph spacing instead.

- Do not press ENTER repeatedly to start a new page. Instead, use Word's Insert | Break command.

Selecting Text

Word lets you do a lot with text after you've typed it. You can change its appearance, move it, delete it, and copy it. The first step is *always* to tell Word which text you want to work with. This is done by selecting it. Word has many ways to select text. For instance, you can drag your mouse pointer over the text while holding down the primary mouse button. There are shortcuts for selecting individual words, lines, sentences, and paragraphs, which you will read about in a moment.

Depending on your system configuration, selected text will either change color or be surrounded by a gray or black background. That's how you know what you have selected. If you are a new Windows user, practice selecting other words, sentences, and single characters with the mouse.

Selecting with a Mouse

It is easy to select blocks of text and even graphics with the mouse. Here are the techniques.

Selecting Entire Words

Double-click anywhere on a word to select the entire word and the space that follows it.

> Slobovia·is· **restless.**·In·a·recent·survey·of·10,000·Slobovians,·50%·didn't·know·what·a·survey·was,·33%·said·they·didn't·care,·9%·bit·the·survey·taker,·and·3%·would·only·bounce·up·and·down·on·a·pogo·stick·saying·"Pork!"·over·and·over·in·a·high·pitched·voice.·However,·the·5%·who·did·answer·seriously·felt·that·it·was·time·to·get·the·blood·flowing·in·Slobovia·once·again.¶
> ¶

To select adjacent words, drag after double-clicking. Entire words will be selected when you drag this way, even if you only drag over part of an adjacent word.

Selecting Entire Lines

To select entire lines, follow these steps.

1. Move the mouse pointer to the *selection bar* (an invisible strip running down the extreme left edge of the document window). The mouse pointer will change from the I-beam to an arrow.

> Slobovia·is·restless.·In·a·recent·survey·of·10,000·Slobovians,·50%·didn't·know·what·
> a·survey·was,·33%·said·they·didn't·care,·9%·bit·the·survey·taker,·and·3%·would·
> only·bounce·up·and·down·on·a·pogo·stick·saying·"Pork!"·over·and·over·in·a·high·
> pitched·voice.·However,·the·5%·who·did·answer·seriously·felt·that·it·was·time·to·get·
> the·blood·flowing·in·Slobovia·once·again.¶
> ¶

2. Click the primary mouse button only once. The entire *line* to the right of where you've clicked will be selected. Continue dragging up or down to select additional lines.

Selecting Entire Sentences

Hold down CTRL while you click anywhere in the sentence of interest.

Slobovia·is·restless.·In·a·recent·survey·of·10,000·Slobovians,·50%·didn't·know·what·a·survey·was,·33%·said·they·didn't·care,·9%·bit·the·survey·taker,·and·3%·would·only·bounce·up·and·down·on·a·pogo·stick·saying·"Pork!"·over·and·over·in·a·high·pitched·voice.·However,·the·5%·who·did·answer·seriously·felt·that·it·was·time·to·get·the·blood·flowing·in·Slobovia·once·again.¶
¶

This also selects the sentence's punctuation mark and the space following the sentence, if there is one. Drag after you click this way to select additional sentences.

Selecting Entire Paragraphs

The quickest way to select a paragraph with your mouse is to *triple-click*. Point anywhere in the paragraph and quickly press and release the mouse button three times in succession. Use the following steps to select paragraphs using the selection bar.

1. Move the mouse pointer to the selection bar (the invisible strip running down the extreme left edge of the document window). The pointer will become an arrow.

2. Double-click. The adjacent paragraph will be selected.

Selecting Your Entire Document

To select an entire document, follow these steps.

1. Move the mouse pointer to the selection bar at the left edge of the document, and the pointer will become an arrow.

2. Hold down CTRL and click. The entire document will be selected. Alternatively, you can triple-click on the selection bar to select the whole document.

---

tip   *You can select an entire document from the keyboard by using the CTRL-A hot key combination.*

Selecting Graphics and Other Objects

Click anywhere within the graphic or other object. You'll see a border—usually with *handles* (small black boxes)—surrounding the selected object:

Selecting Variable Units of Text

Sometimes you'll want to select just a single character or parts of a text string. Here are some techniques to use.

DRAGGING TO SELECT   To select adjacent bits of text, follow these steps.

1. Point to where you want selection to begin.

2. Hold down the primary mouse button and drag in any direction.

3. When the pointer hits a screen boundary (top, bottom, or side), the document will scroll as highlighting continues.

4. Release the mouse button when you've selected the desired area.

n o t e   *Word provides an option called Automatic Word Selection. You select as many or as few characters of the first word as you want to change. Then, when you drag over to the next word, the entire second word is selected. You must hold down* ALT *to select partial words when Automatic Word Selection is on (and it is on by default). You can turn off this option in the Edit tab of the Options dialog box (select Tools | Options to display the Options dialog box).*

SHIFT-CLICKING TO SELECT LARGE AREAS   To select large blocks of continuous text, follow these steps.

1. Point to where you want selection to begin.

2. Click to place the insertion point there.

3. Move to the end of the desired area (scroll if necessary), and press SHIFT while you point and click again.

Selecting Rectangular Areas

To select rectangular areas (like columns in a tabbed list), hold down ALT while you drag the mouse.

Selecting in Tables

You can select characters, words, and other items in table cells by using Word's usual mouse and keyboard features. In addition, Word provides table-specific selection tools enabling you to choose cells, rows, columns, or areas.

SELECTING SINGLE CELLS   The area between the first character in a cell and the left edge of the cell is called the *cell selection bar*. Click on it to select the contents of the entire cell. You can also select an entire cell by dragging with the mouse. Just be sure you include the end-of-cell mark in your selection.

SELECTING COLUMNS   To select a column, move the mouse pointer to the area at the top of a column called the *column selection bar*. You'll know you've arrived when the pointer changes into a large, down-pointing arrow. Click to select the entire column.

Holding down ALT while clicking anywhere in a column will also select the entire column. Selecting the bottom or top cell in a column and dragging up or down is somewhat tedious, but will also work.

Double-clicking any cell selection bar will select the entire row. You can also select the leftmost or rightmost cell in a row and drag it.

To select groups of adjacent cells, either drag through the cells or click in one cell and SHIFT+ click in the others.

To select an entire table, hold down ALT and double-click anywhere in the table. If your document contains multiple tables and they are not separated by paragraph marks, this technique will select all adjacent tables.

w a r n i n g   *Do not use Word's Select All command to select a table, since this will also select paragraph marks and other things outside of the table.*

Selecting with the Keyboard

You can also select text with keyboard shortcuts. The following table lists a summary of the shortcuts.

To Increase a Selection	Press
One character to right of insertion point	SHIFT + RIGHT ARROW
One character to left of insertion point	SHIFT + LEFT ARROW
To start of word	CTRL + SHIFT + LEFT ARROW
To end of word	CTRL + SHIFT + RIGHT ARROW
To start of line	SHIFT + HOME
Down one line	SHIFT + DOWN ARROW
Up one line	SHIFT + UP ARROW
To end of paragraph	CTRL + SHIFT + DOWN ARROW
To start of paragraph	CTRL + SHIFT + UP ARROW
Down one screen	SHIFT + PGDN
Up one screen	SHIFT + PGUP
To document's end	CTRL + SHIFT + END
To start of document	CTRL + SHIFT + HOME
To vertical block of text	CTRL + SHIFT + F8 and arrow keys
To entire document	CTRL + A

Deleting Text

There are several ways to delete unwanted text. If you spot a mistake right after typing it, pressing BACKSPACE will remove unwanted characters and spaces. You can also delete text by selecting it and then pressing DEL, or by using the Clear command on Word's Edit menu.

Undo

Word watches as you work. It remembers which steps you last took. When asked, it can frequently undo your errors. The exact name of the Undo choice on the Edit menu changes as you work. Sometimes it says Undo Typing. Other times it says Undo Formatting or Undo Sort, or some such.

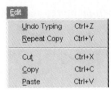

There are three ways to undo:

- Edit | Undo reverses your last action; choose Edit | Undo again to reverse the action before that, and so on.

- If you press CTRL+Z repeatedly, it will reverse previous actions.

- The Undo toolbar button and its associated drop-down list let you undo multiple actions in sequence.

To undo multiple actions or selected actions, use the drop-down list reached with the button shown at left.

Reveal the list by pointing to and clicking on the Undo list arrow. The last thing you've done will be at the top of the list.

1. Click on an item to undo it, or drag to select and undo a sequence of actions.

2. If you accidentally undo the wrong things, use the Redo list to the right of the Undo list to undo your Undo.

Redo

Use the Redo command to undo an Undo. To redo your last action only, choose Edit | Redo, press the keyboard shortcut (F4), or click the Redo button on the Standard toolbar.

To redo multiple actions or selected actions, use the drop-down list reached with the button shown at left.

1. Reveal the list by pointing to the Redo list arrow. The last thing you've undone will be on the top of the list.

2. Click on an item to redo (undo the Undo), or drag to select a sequence of actions.

3. If you accidentally redo the wrong things, use the Undo list to the right of the Redo list to undo your Redo.

Occasionally, you will see a "Can't Undo" message, indicating that your most recent action cannot be undone. That's why it is a good idea to save your work early and often.

Repeat

Sometimes, after you've done something repeatable (like formatting or typing), you will find a Repeat command on Word's Edit menu. The shortcut key is F4. Repeat watches you work and attempts to re-create your actions on demand.

Like Undo, Repeat's name changes depending on what you have last done, and it works with most Word for Windows actions immediately after you take them. Experiment.

tip *There are often better ways to repeat actions. For instance, Word provides a format "paintbrush" that you may find easier to use than the Repeat command when repeating format changes. (See Chapter 5 for details on the Format Painter feature.)*

Inserting Text

Word offers several ways to insert new text into an existing document. The most straightforward approach is to move the insertion point to the desired location and start typing. Word accommodates the new text by pushing the existing text to the right and down as necessary.

You start by placing the mouse pointer (the I-beam) where you want to begin inserting text. Next, click the mouse button to move the insertion point to the desired position.

Replacing Text

With Word, you can combine the steps of deleting, positioning the insertion point, and inserting replacement text. Highlight the unwanted text and start typing. The old text disappears and the new text snakes across the screen as you type it.

ormatting Text

Let's take a quick look at a few of Word's frequently used ways to modify the appearance of text. They include toolbars, menus, and keyboard short-cuts. See Chapter 5 for a more complete discussion of Word's formatting capabilities.

Using the Formatting Toolbar

Word's Formatting toolbar contains a number of text formatting buttons. To see a button's function, move the mouse pointer over the button and hold it there momentarily. The button's name will appear, as shown here:

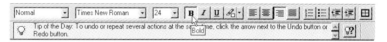

Toolbars let you make style changes by clicking buttons or pulling down single-level menus, rather than going to the more-crowded menu bar. As always, you must select text before working with it.

To change the appearance of characters (making them bold or italicized, for instance), first select them, then click the appropriate button on the Formatting toolbar.

Aligning Text with the Formatting Toolbar

Notice the group of four buttons to the right of the Underline button in the Formatting toolbar:

These let you specify left aligned, centered, right aligned, or fully justified text, respectively.

These paragraph formatting buttons and similar formatting tools work on entire paragraphs. Simply place the insertion point in the paragraph to be affected before using the button. To change multiple paragraphs simul-taneously, select them first.

Copying and Moving

Word for Windows supports all of the usual Windows techniques for copying and moving information. It also provides a feature called drag-and-drop, a one-step, mouse-assisted mover.

Using Cut, Copy, and Paste

The traditional way to move or duplicate items in Windows programs is to select them, cut or copy them to the Clipboard, move the insertion point to the new position, and paste them. You can even copy into different applications—from Word to Excel, for instance. See Chapter 3 for details.

1. Start by selecting the desired text.

2. Choose Edit | Cut or press the CTRL+X shortcut. You can also click the Cut button (shown here) on the Standard toolbar.

3. The selected text will disappear from the screen and will be placed on the Clipboard.

4. Now place the insertion point where you want the text to go (point and click).

5. Paste, using Edit | Paste or the CTRL+V shortcut. Text will flow to the right and down as the Clipboard's contents move into place. You can also click the Paste button (shown here) on the Standard toolbar.

Copying from One Word Document to Another

Since you can open and work on multiple Word documents at the same time, it is easy to move things from one document to another. First, arrange your workspace by clicking and dragging the size boxes in the lower-right corners of windows to adjust their size and shape. You can move windows around by pointing to their title bars and dragging them. Once you have arranged the windows to your liking, you can easily move back and forth simply by clicking in the window of interest (see Figure 4-4).

While it is possible to have many windows in view at the same time, you can have only one *active* window. It is easy to tell which is the active window—it's the top one with the highlighted title bar.

Using Word's Window Menu

Sometimes your screen may not be big enough to display multiple Word documents in useful sizes. Word provides the Window menu for these instances. The Window menu lists the open documents and lets you switch between them. A check mark indicates the active window. Using this menu, you can activate one window to copy information, go back to the Window menu to activate and display another window, and then paste.

tip   *The Window menu's Arrange All command will display and arrange all open windows at once.*

The contents of your Clipboard usually stay the same when you switch from program to program, as long as you do not turn off or restart your computer. Thus, you can copy information from a spreadsheet, switch to Word, and paste the spreadsheet information into your Word document. Or

WORD PROCESSING WITH
WORD FOR WINDOWS

FIGURE 4-4

Arrange windows for easy access

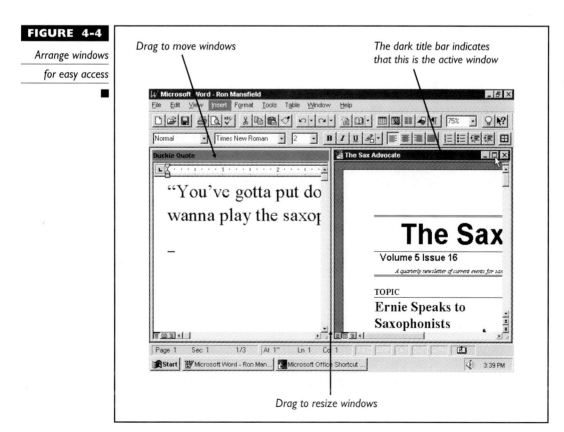

Drag to move windows

The dark title bar indicates that this is the active window

Drag to resize windows

you can use document scraps to save bits of text, data, or graphics (see Chapter 3).

Advanced users will also want to explore other pasting options such as object linking and embedding (OLE) and the Insert | File command, explained in Chapter 3. These advanced techniques make it possible to keep multiple documents up to date when data changes. See Part Eight, "Sharing Information with OLE," for more information about OLE.

Using Drag-and-Drop

Word's drag-and-drop feature lets you highlight text or other movable objects and drag them to a new location. To move text with drag-and-drop, follow these steps:

1. Select the desired text or other item.

2. Release the mouse button, if necessary; then point to the selected item(s) and press and hold down the mouse button. Watch the mouse pointer. It will change to look like the one in Figure 4-5.

3. When you see the pointer change to its drag-and-drop shape, drag the pointer while holding down the mouse button until the insertion point is at the desired location.

4. Release the mouse button. The selected item will move.

5. Undo immediately (press CTRL+Z) if things didn't go right.

tip *Drag-and-drop copying works just like drag-and-drop moving, with one exception: you hold down CTRL while you work.*

Hotspots

You can bring up dialog boxes, windows, and other tools of interest by double-clicking in areas called *hotspots*. Figure 4-6 shows many of them. There may even be undocumented hotspots you can discover on your own.

FIGURE 4-5

The drag-and-drop mouse pointer

■

Drag-and-drop insertion point

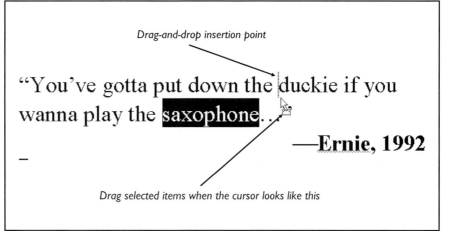

"You've gotta put down the duckie if you wanna play the saxophone...

—Ernie, 1992

Drag selected items when the cursor looks like this

FIGURE 4-6

Word's hotspots and their functions

■

Opens Page Setup dialog box

Opens Indent and Spacing tab in Paragraph dialog box

Opens Headers and Footers dialog box

Toggles split windows

Allows you to edit drawings

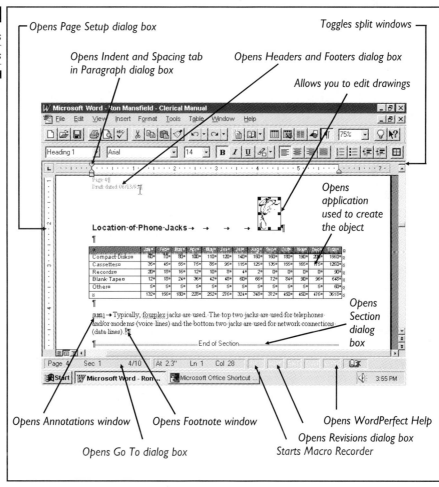

Opens application used to create the object

Opens Section dialog box

Opens Annotations window

Opens Footnote window

Opens WordPerfect Help

Opens Revisions dialog box

Starts Macro Recorder

Opens Go To dialog box

Page Setup Dialog Box Hotspot

If you click on the small box at the right end of the horizontal ruler or the top of the veritcal ruler, you'll see the Page Setup dialog box, which is used to control header, footer, and other measurements precisely.

When in Page Layout view, if you double-click in the margins at the corners of your document, you will also see the Page Setup dialog box.

Footnote Window Hotspots

To reveal a Footnote window, simply double-click on a footnote reference mark.

The Go To Dialog Box Hotspot

To bring up the Go To dialog box, useful for navigating in big documents, double-click on a page or section number in the status area at the lower-left of the document window.

Section Hotspot

Double-click on section break marks to reveal the Page Setup dialog box. It contains section break information.

Mouse Shortcut Menus

Frequently, when you point to items on the screen and press the nonprimary (usually the right) mouse button, you'll see a shortcut menu of commands that you can issue with your mouse.

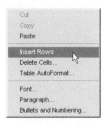

The available choices depend on what's selected and what's possible at the moment.

Navigating with Your Mouse

Word for Windows offers navigational tools that let you move quickly to the desired part of even huge documents. Several views make it easy to see what your document will look like without printing it. Other views are available to simplify and speed up the creation of rough drafts and outlines. In addition, you can hide and show elements such as paragraph marks (¶) and the little dots between words that denote spaces. Let's take a look at your scrolling options.

Scrolling in a Window

Most documents are too big to be displayed in their entirety on your screen. You reveal unseen portions of your document by scrolling to bring parts of the document into view while temporarily hiding other parts. Usually, you'll scroll up and down to see long documents, but you will sometimes need to scroll left and right to see different parts of wide documents. There are many ways to scroll.

Scrolling with the Scroll Arrows

When you click on a scroll arrow, you will see a different part of your document. For instance, suppose you are looking at page 2 of a three-page document. If you click on the up scroll arrow (located near the top-right of the active window), you will move a little nearer to the beginning of the document (see Figure 4-7). Clicking on the down scroll arrow will take you closer to the end of the document. (Typically, one click moves you up or down about one line.) The right and left scroll arrows let you see corresponding portions of wide documents.

tip   *If you click and hold down the mouse button while pointing to any of the four scrolling arrows, your document will scroll continuously until you reach the end of the document or release the mouse button. But there are better ways to scroll long distances. Read on.*

Scrolling by Clicking in the Scroll Bars

Clicking in the shaded areas of scroll bars (as opposed to clicking on the scroll arrows themselves) scrolls approximately one screen's worth. The exact scroll distance will vary with your screen and document window size. Experiment.

WORD PROCESSING WITH WORD FOR WINDOWS

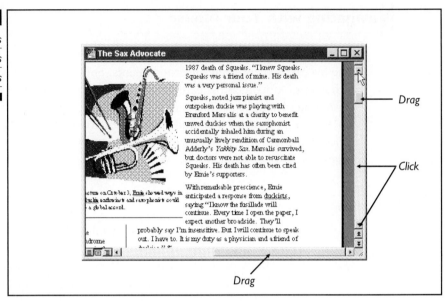

FIGURE 4-7

Use the scroll tools to view other parts of your documents ■

Scrolling with the Scroll Boxes

The square boxes in the horizontal and vertical scroll bars can be used to move great distances quickly. For instance, if you are looking at the first page of a 100-page document, the scroll box will be at the top of the vertical scroll bar. Dragging it with your mouse exactly halfway down the scroll bar will bring page 50 into view; dragging it three-quarters of the way will take you to page 75; and so forth. Horizontal scroll boxes can be used the same way to scroll wide documents quickly.

Obviously, it is difficult to drag to the exact middle or three-quarters position on the scroll bar. Use the scroll boxes to get close, and then use other scrolling tools to fine-tune.

warning *It's easy to forget to move the insertion point when you bounce from place to place in a document by scrolling or using the navigational tricks discussed in this chapter. Get into the habit of repositioning, and then looking for the insertion point before you type, paste, or do other potentially destructive things.*

Navigating with Your Keyboard

Word for Windows offers many, many keyboard shortcuts for navigating. With keyboard commands, you can just scroll or you can scroll and move the insertion point at the same time. Be sure you understand the difference!

Frequently, if you hold SHIFT down while using keyboard shortcuts, you will select text in addition to scrolling and moving the insertion point. For example, pressing CTRL+RIGHTARROW moves the insertion point to the beginning of the next word; while CTRL+SHIFT+RIGHTARROW selects the current word starting at the insertion point and the space following it.

You will probably find that, with a few exceptions, you tend to move around with the mouse, rather than with the keyboard. Table 4-1 shows some useful keyboard shortcuts for moving. If you ever memorize *all* the keyboard shortcuts, you are spending too much time with Word! Take a very long vacation.

The Go To Command

When you edit big documents, particularly when you have a marked-up paper copy, it is useful to be able to scoot quickly to a particular page or section. If you know page (and section) numbers, Word for Windows makes this easy. Word can also take you to specified lines, bookmarks, annotations,

To Move To	Press
Up	UP ARROW
Down	DOWN ARROW
Left	LEFT ARROW
Right	RIGHT ARROW
Previous Word	CTRL+ LEFT ARROW
Next Word	CTRL+ RIGHT ARROW
Beginning of line	HOME
End of line	END
Beginning of paragraph	CTRL+ UP ARROW
End of paragraph	CTRL+ DOWN ARROW
Beginning of document	CTRL+ HOME
End of document	CTRL+ END

TABLE 4-1   *Useful Keyboard Shortcuts for Moving*

WORD PROCESSING WITH WORD FOR WINDOWS

footnotes, endnotes, fields, tables, graphics equations, and objects. This is all accomplished in the Go To dialog box, reached with the Edit | Go To command or F5.

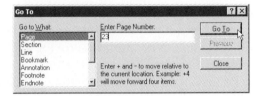

In single-section documents or documents in which page numbers do not restart in each section, just type the desired page number and press ENTER or click the Go To button. Quicker than you can say *if the crick don't rise,* Word will take you to the requested page and place the insertion point at the beginning of the first line on the page. Here are the steps:

1. Press F5 or choose Edit | Go To.

2. Type the desired page number in the Enter Page Number box of the Go To dialog box.

3. Press ENTER. Word will take you to the requested page.

4. Close the Go To dialog box with the Close button or Close box or press ESC.

5. Get back to work.

If your document is broken into sections with page numbers that restart in new sections, you must specify section numbers in the Go To dialog box. To specify a section number in the Go To dialog box, type an **S**. For instance, typing **S4** would take you to the beginning of Section 4 (assuming your document has a Section 4).

To specify a particular page and section, type **P**, the page number, **S**, and the section number. Thus, **P3S5** would take you to the third page in the fifth section. **S5P3** will do the same thing.

You can also go to a particular section by selecting Section in the Go To What list and then typing the desired section number. Once in the desired section, you can use Go To again to get to the appropriate page within the section.

You can also use the Go To command to move forward or backward a specific number of pages. And you can use it to go to the end of a document, even if you don't know the last page number. Shown next is a list of things you can do with the Go To dialog box (samples of typical entries are in parentheses).

- Move to the beginning of the document (0)

- Move to the next page (+ or leave blank)

- Move to the last page (enter any number greater than the number of pages in the document)

- Move to a specific page number (4 or P4)

- Move to a specific page within a specific section (P4S3)

- Move to the first page of a specific section (S3)

- Move forward a specified number of pages—3, for example (+3)

- Move back a specific number of pages—5, for instance (–5)

t i p   *Double-clicking on the Page Number portion of the status area will bring up the Go To dialog box.*

The Go Back Feature

Here's a handy but often-confusing gizmo. When you are editing, it is sometimes necessary to bounce from one part of a document to another part of the same document. Or, if you have two documents open, you may find yourself repeatedly moving from one document to the other.

Word remembers the last three places you have edited plus the current location of the insertion point. Go Back lets you quickly move to those edit points. Simply press SHIFT+F5 (or CTRL+ALT+Z) repeatedly to cycle through the last three insertion point locations. Go Back is not on Word's standard menus, but you can add it or even create a toolbar button for it.

n o t e   *Incidentally, simply moving the insertion point somewhere in a document does not necessarily add that point to the places in the Go Back list. Generally, you need to edit something there.*

Using Find to Navigate

Word's Find command is a great way to move to an area. For instance, if you are looking at a printout containing an error you want to fix, use the Find command to get to the right spot on your screen. Here are the basics:

1. Press CTRL+F or choose Edit | Find to bring up the Find dialog box.

2. Enter the text you want to find, and then press ENTER. Word will search (usually down from the insertion point) and show you the first occurrence of the specified text.

3. If that's not the occurrence you want, click on Next > or press ENTER to move to the next occurrence.

4. If necessary, answer Yes (press ENTER) when Word asks if it should search from the beginning of the document.

5. When you find what you need, close the Find dialog box or click in the document window to activate it.

6. Edit away.

Views

Word for Windows can show you your document with varying levels of detail to make things easier to visualize or quicker to work with. These display options are called *views*. Word provides five views:

- Normal view
- Page Layout view
- Outline view
- Print Preview
- Split screen

Switching Views

Word for Windows has a View menu that you can use to select Normal, Outline, or Page Layout views.

Three buttons in the lower-left corner of Word's status area let you quickly switch views. They are (from left to right) Normal view, Page Layout view, and Outline view. You might want to switch views as you read about them.

Switching to Print Preview either requires a trip to the File menu or the use of a not-so-intuitive keyboard shortcut (ALT+F,V).

tip   *You can switch to Print Preview by clicking the Print Preview button on the Standard toolbar.*

Normal View

Unless you are patient or have a *very* fast computer with a large screen, use Normal view for most of your heavy-duty text entry and editing. Word's other views respond noticeably slower to typing, editing, and scrolling.

Normal view keeps repagination and screen redraw delays to a minimum. It shows your text as you have typed it, and displays graphics where you've inserted them (which is not necessarily where they'll print).

This view does not show side by side column positioning, footers, headers, or the printing position of framed items. Columns are shown at their actual width, but not side by side. Automatic page breaks are shown as dotted lines. Manual page breaks, if you've defined any, are shown as darker lines containing the words "Page Break," while section breaks are double dark lines with the words "End of Section," and so on.

note   *If you have instructed Word for Windows to number lines, the numbers will not appear in Normal view. Use Print Preview to see line numbers.*

Editing in Normal View

You can create and edit text, columns, and graphics as usual in Normal view. To work on headers or footers, however, you must choose View | Header and Footer.

Page Layout View

In Page Layout view, the screen resembles a white sheet of paper, or at least a portion of a sheet.

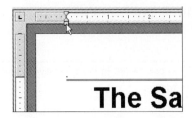

Look closely at the top and left edges of the screen in the illustration. You will see a dark background that Word for Windows places behind the "paper." On a large enough screen, you will see the whole page. On smaller screens or when you're using a large paper setting in Page Setup, you may need to scroll to see these representations of the paper's edges.

Editing in Page Layout View

Generally, you edit as usual in Page Layout view. Text and graphics are shown where they will print. Headers and footers can be both seen and edited. Click in a header, footer, or body text to position the insertion point. Page breaks, be they automatic or forced, are represented by new pages on the screen rather than by dashed lines in the text. You can scroll from page to page, as you'd expect.

Hidden Text in Page Layout View

If you have hidden text in your document and you reveal it, Page Layout view will display line and page endings adjusted to include the hidden text. This may not correspond to pages that you print if the Print tab's Hidden Text box (found in the Options dialog box) is unchecked. To see what your pages will look like without the hidden text, you must hide the text by unchecking the Hidden Text box in the Show portion of the View tab of the Options dialog box.

Headers and Footers in Page Layout View

You can see headers and footers in Page Layout view. To edit, click anywhere in a header or footer. It will "undim" and be surrounded by a dashed line. The Header and Footer toolbar will also appear if it's not already on your screen.

To add date or time entries and page numbering to headers and footers, use the buttons on the Header and Footer toolbar. You can format text in headers just as you would anywhere else in a Word for Windows document. For instance, to right align header text, place the insertion point in the text (or select multiple lines in the header) and use the Align Right button on the Formatting toolbar.

> **note**   *Unlike in earlier versions of Word for Windows, if you have requested numbered lines, the numbers will appear in Page Layout view.*

Outline View

If your document is properly formatted, switching to Outline view lets you quickly navigate and reorganize even large, complex documents. Outline view allows you to see the entire contents of the document, just chapter headings, or just section headings, and so on.

Print Preview

Print Preview is more than just another way to view documents. Choose File | Print Preview or use CTRL+ALT+I or CTRL+F2. Depending on your screen size and settings, you will see either an unreadable bird's-eye view of a page or two (like the one in Figure 4-8), or you will see a full, readable page.

For a more complete discussion of Print Preview, see "Using Print Preview Before Printing" later in this chapter.

> **tip**   *The button that looks like a magnifying glass and a piece of paper on the Standard toolbar will switch you to Print Preview mode. Use the Close button in Print Preview (or press ESC) to bring you back to whatever view you were in previously.*

Split Screen View

Regardless of which view you prefer, you can profit from using Word's split-screen feature (see Figure 4-9). You can use the split screen to view two widely separated portions of a document at the same time. To split the screen, simply point to the small rectangle in the upper-right corner of your Word document window at the top of the vertical scroll bar. The pointer will change to the Split-bar pointer. Drag the Split-bar pointer down to divide the screen.

When you release the mouse button, your screen will split into two independent windows, each with its own scroll bar. To return to a single

FIGURE 4-8

Print Preview gives you a bird's-eye view ■

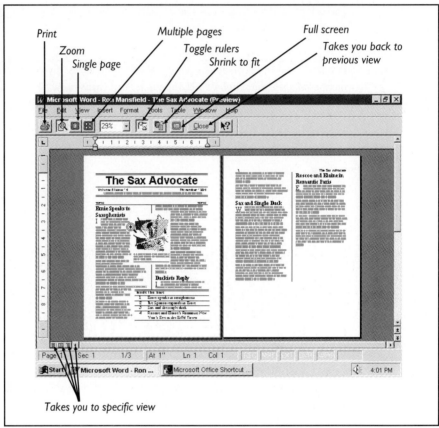

Print
Zoom
Single page
Multiple pages
Toggle rulers
Shrink to fit
Full screen
Takes you back to previous view

Takes you to specific view

screen, double-click on the Split-bar pointer. Alternatively, you can use the keyboard shortcut ALT+SHIFT+C.

tip *When you unsplit the screen, the portion that the insertion point was in becomes the only screen. This can be a nuisance if you actually wanted to be in the other portion of text! So be sure that the insertion point is in the correct pane before you unsplit.*

Why Split Screens?

With the screen split, you can see two parts of your document at once. Use this feature to refer to different portions of a document as you write, or to speed copying, cutting, and pasting. But there's another powerful reason to use split screens.

FIGURE 4-9

*Split your windows
to see different
parts of a
document*

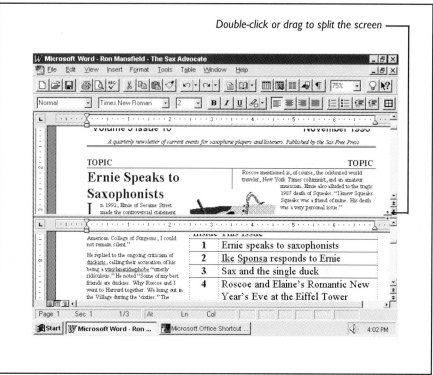

You can use a different view in each portion of the split screen. For instance, you might want to speed scrolling and editing by working in a window pane set to Normal view while watching the effects of your changes in a Page Layout view pane.

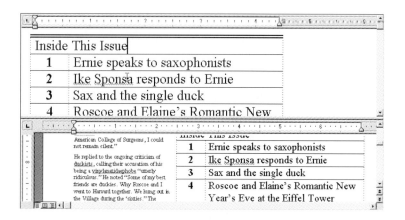

WORD PROCESSING WITH
WORD FOR WINDOWS

View Defaults

Normal view is the default for all new documents. Word does, however, remember the view you were using when you last saved a document and opens the document in that view. If you opened a new document in Normal view, did some work, switched to Page Layout view, saved, and exited, the next time you opened the document it would appear in Page Layout view.

Showing Paragraph Marks, Spaces, and More

Word for Windows can display helpful nonprinting characters to let you see what's going on. Examples include

- Paragraph marks (¶)
- Dots denoting spaces
- Arrows denoting tab characters
- Dashed lines for page breaks
- Text and graphic boundaries

I like to leave these on, although turning them off can sometimes help you better visualize the final appearance of a document. To toggle the display of these items, click the button that looks like a paragraph mark (¶) on the Standard toolbar. (It's near the right edge.)

Zooming

The little drop-down list near the right end of the Format toolbar is called the *Zoom Control*. It lets you zoom in and out to see bigger or smaller onscreen representations. It does not affect printing size. For instance, the Page Width choice lets you see both page edges.

Full Screen—Seeing Just Your Work

The View | Full Screen command, or the corresponding button that you'll find in Print Preview, removes all the usual workspace clutter and fills your screen with your current document. You'll see a very small window containing the Full button, which allows you to return to the prior view (see Figure 4-10). You can also use the ALT+V+U keyboard shortcut.

Saving Documents the First Time

When you first type and stylize a document, it exists only on your screen and in your computer's volatile RAM (random-access memory). If you were to switch off the computer or experience a power failure or other malfunction, your work would be lost forever. By saving your work to disk as you go, you can pick up where you left off, without losing your changes.

tip *Save every 15 minutes or whenever you are interrupted by phone calls or visitors. You can even set Word for Windows to do the saving for you.*

"irresponsible and insensitive to the needs of duckies." Sponsa has been a vocal critic of Ernie since the latter took up his controversial stance on saxophones and duckies in 1992.

"He says he's a friend of duckies. How could he be, though, when he continues to unabashedly advocate their being put down?" ask Sponsa in a recent press conference. "Even Roscoe finds his opinions untenable." Roscoe could not be reached for comment.

Sax and Single Duck

We've all had this experience: you walk into a music store, and see a saxophone you've just gotta have. But you know they see you coming. You know they're thinking, "Hey, this gal's a duckie; she's not going to know a saxophone from a hot roast beef sandwich." And then they try to sell you a trombone or worse, a pennywhistle. And to top it off, they try to rip you off!

Well, now it's time for you to show them who's boss, thanks to a new book by Elaine, *Sax and the Single Duck*, published by Penguin and due out early this fall. Elaine shares some of her saxophone buying nightmares, humorous anecdotes, and a few tragedies (such as the untimely death of Squeaks). But best of all, there is an entire section devoted to handy tips on how to avoid getting ripped off when you're buying instruments.

"The trouble is, most people don't take duckies seriously. They say, 'Oh, she's just a duckie; she'll be fortunate if she doesn't end up as the main course at The Four Seasons.' We've got to fight that. Knowledge is our weapon. Forewarned is forearmed, as they say."

The Sax Advocate

Roscoe and Elaine in Romantic Paris

Earlier this year, New York Times columnist and globetrotter Roscoe visited Paris with his wife Elaine and stayed for New Year's Eve. He talked to SA recently about his trip, Paris as a vacation spot, and the inherent difficulties duckies have in traveling.

"We'd always wanted to be in Paris for the New Year. You know Parisians are such a joyous bunch. Of course, the Eiffel Tower was a natural." Roscoe noted that he'd been to Paris before many times, of course, but this was the first time for a holiday.

"It was quite a display," he added. "The Rue St. Martin was alive with gaily colored banners and the festive mood was bubbling over like a glass of the fizzy stuff. They must have been drinking a lot of it, too, 'cause they were fishing them out of the Seine every ten minutes."

With all of its romance and intrigue, Roscoe says he still finds Paris to be a provincial city at heart. "You hear all about Paris being so cosmopolitan and international. But it's really just a frightened young city trying to act tough. If you want a real city, you have to go to Marseilles or Cannes."

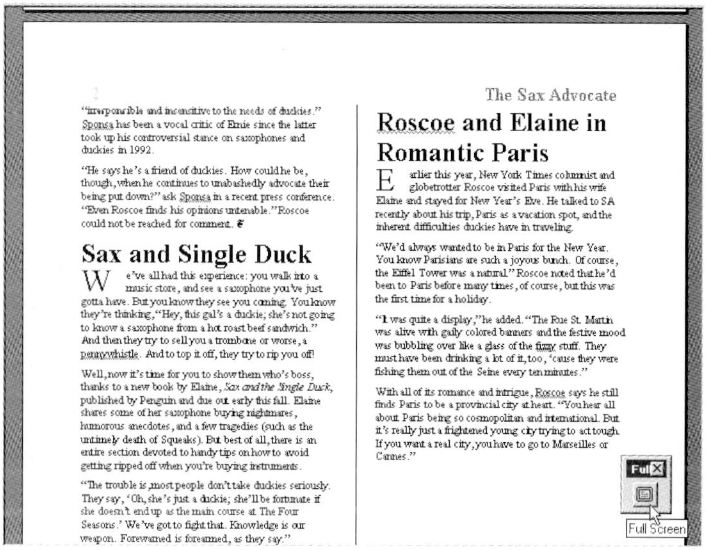

FIGURE 4-10

The View | Full Screen command fills the screen with your current document

The CTRL+S keyboard shortcut is a convenient way to save without visiting the File menu. The Save button shown at left, which can be found in the Standard toolbar, will also start the Save process.

The Save As dialog box tells you where Word for Windows plans to store your work and suggests a name for the file. It also gives you many other Save options.

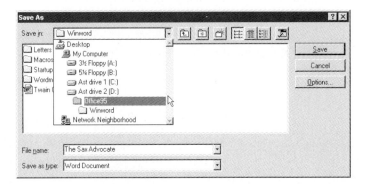

Start by noticing where Word proposes to put your document. This is a very important habit to establish.

tip *It's not a good idea to clutter up your Word for Windows directory with a lot of documents, so create some directories specifically for Word documents.*

Telling Word Where to Save Your Document

Like any good Windows program, Word lets you specify save locations. You do this by picking the desired folder in the Save In list. Use the drop-down list to switch drives, if necessary.

Naming Word Documents

Word will suggest a name. If you don't find it satisfactory, type a different name for your document in the File Name box, and then simply click the Save button. Names can be up to 255 characters long.

note *With Windows 95's ability to save longer document names, you can have nice, lengthy, descriptive names for your documents. Also, it is no longer necessary to add extensions (such as .DOC). However, if you plan to share files with those not fortunate* *enough to have Windows 95, you may want to devise standards for naming documents, such that those with earlier versions of Windows don't go nuts trying to figure out which files are which. You can force Windows and Word to show you file extensions, too, if you want to see them. Read more about these features in your Windows documentation.*

Pressing ENTER will have the same effect as clicking Save. With Word, like most Windows programs, pressing ENTER will execute the button with the bold border in the active dialog box.

One way or the other, Word for Windows will save your document and, if the Properties feature is turned on, you will see the Properties dialog box with blanks in many places. The information it collects is optional and can be added later if you like.

WORD PROCESSING WITH WORD FOR WINDOWS

Providing Properties Information

When you start a new document, you might see the Properties dialog box. If you've used earlier versions of Word, this will remind you of the old Summary Info dialog box. In fact, there is a Summary tab that contains much of the same information. If you plan to keep many documents on your hard disk, and particularly if you will be storing things on a crowded network server, it is a good idea to use this feature. It will help you quickly locate projects with the Open dialog box's Find Now button.

tip *To prevent the Properties dialog box from appearing when you save a new document, choose Tools | Options, click on the Save tab, and click in the Prompt for Document Properties box to uncheck it.*

Saving as You Work

Once you've named a document and specified a place to save it, you won't see the Save As dialog box when you save unless you request it. A quick trip to File | Save or, better still, the key combination CTRL+S, will save your work whenever you desire. So will clicking the Save button on the Standard toolbar.

Quitting and Restarting Word

There are several ways to quit Word. You can choose File | Exit or click the Close box in the upper-right corner of the main Word window.

If you have made any changes since the last time you saved, Word will ask if you want them saved. Select Yes to save changes, No to ignore the most recent changes, or Cancel to abort your exit request and return to word processing. After you have satisfied Word that you have saved everything of value, Word will quit.

warning *Word needs to do some housekeeping when you exit. For instance, Word updates its settings files and asks if you want to save last-minute changes to your documents. When you use Word's File | Exit command or attempt to exit Windows, this housekeeping will proceed smoothly. But if you use the power switch on your computer (or simply unplug it) without first exiting Word and Windows, you may damage a document file or lose valuable changes to your Word settings.*

Minimizing Instead of Quitting

You can run Word *minimized*, which gets the program out of the way without actually exiting it. See your Windows documentation for details.

Accessing Recent Projects Quickly

Once you have saved some Word for Windows documents, Word remembers their names and locations and lists them at the bottom of the File menu.

Choose the file you want, and Word will attempt to locate and load it. If you have changed the document's name or moved it since your last Word session, Word may ask for help finding it.

By default, Word lists your last four documents. To specify longer or shorter lists, choose Tools | Options, click on the General tab, and specify the desired number of entries in the Recently Used File List box.

Printing

If you have only one printer and it is properly installed and ready to go, and you just want to print a single copy of the current document, just click on the Print button, shown at left, on the Standard toolbar.

The status area will chart Word's progress as it prints. Page numbers and a little animated printer icon will tell you how many pages have been sent to the printer or to the Windows background printing feature.

While printing can be as simple as previously described, it is a good idea to get into the habit of visiting the Page Setup dialog box, and possibly the Print dialog box, whenever you begin to create a new document—particularly if you work with a variety of printers, paper sizes, and document designs. If you wait until you have finished working on your document to choose a printer, your page and line endings may change considerably from those you initially saw on your screen. This can be a minor annoyance or a major disaster.

For example, if you write a long document, create a table of contents, then change printer models or choose different printing features, you will find that line and page endings may change. This will require you to redo the table of contents. Otherwise it will not agree with the printed pages. The following printer decisions affect pagination and should be selected or determined when you begin a project:

- Page Setup options (like paper source)
- Printer model
- Paper size
- Reduction/enlargement (scaling)
- Page orientation
- Margins
- Gutters
- Larger print area
- Printing/not printing hidden text
- Printing/not printing footnotes and endnotes
- Font substitution options

Other changes affect the appearance of printed pages, but have little impact on pagination.

If you have only one printer and it works properly, you can skip ahead to the section "Choosing What to Print."

Choosing a Printer

To choose a printer:

1. Choose File | Print or use the CTRL+P shortcut. You will see the Print dialog box.

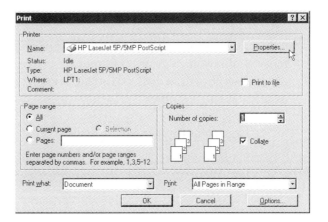

2. Click on the Name list in the Printer area to see a list of your printer models.

3. Point and click in the scrollable list to select the desired printer.

4. If the printer you've chosen has options (lighter/darker, letter quality versus draft, and so on), you can usually reach them by clicking the Properties button. This will bring up the printer's Setup dialog box.

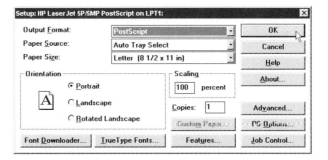

5. When you have finished making choices, click OK to verify any changes.

6. You will be returned to the Print dialog box.

Choosing What to Print

Normally, you'll want to print all or part of your document. But sometimes you'll want to print other things, such as the document's annotations or other settings information. Use the Print What drop-down list to pick any of the following options:

- Document (discussed in this chapter)

- Summary Info (discussed in the "Providing Properties Information" section earlier in this chapter)

- Annotations (discussed in the "Annotations" section in Chapter 10)

- Styles (discussed in the "Styles and the Style Gallery" section in Chapter 5)

- AutoText entries (typing shortcuts—discussed in the "AutoText" section in Chapter 10)

- Key assignments (keyboard shortcuts)

Copies

To specify more than one copy of whatever you intend to print, either type a number in the Copies box, or click on the up or down scroll arrow to choose a number.

Page Range

To print the entire page range, make sure the All button is selected (the default). Click on the little button next to All, if necessary, to select it.

To print just the page in your document currently containing the insertion point, click on the Current Page button.

To print selected text, first select it, and then bring up the Print dialog box and use the Selection button in the Page Range area. This choice will be dimmed unless you've selected something in your document.

To print a range of pages (pages 6 through 10 in a 50-page document, for instance), type the first and last desired page numbers in the Pages text box. Separate the numbers with hyphens (**6-10,** for instance).

To print specific pages, list them in the Pages text box separated by commas (**3,5,8,** for example). Ranges and single pages can be combined, so **6-10,13,19,83** also would work.

Print All, Odd, or Even

Normally, Word prints all pages in order, but if you are planning to do "manual" two-sided printing or you have other reasons to separate odd and even pages, use the drop-down Print list at the bottom of the Print dialog box to specify Odd Pages or Even Pages. For example, you might first print all odd-numbered pages, then put those pages back in the printer to print the even-numbered pages on the other side.

Print to File

It's possible to print to disk files instead of to a printer. Use this technique when you want to take a document to a service bureau for typesetting or other special services. It is a very good idea to do a test run before trying this technique for rush work, since there are many pitfalls. Consider providing your service bureau copies of the actual Word document files instead of (or in addition to) print files. Here are the steps for printing to a file:

1. Edit and polish your document as usual.

2. Consider printing a paper copy.

3. Open the Print dialog box with File | Print or CTRL+P.

4. Check the Print to File box in the Print dialog box.

5. Click OK. You'll see the Print to File dialog box.

6. Pick a destination drive and folder.

7. Name the file in the File Name box.

8. Click OK to create the file.

 tip *Print files can get pretty big, particularly if they contain graphics. Consider printing small ranges of pages to multiple files if you need to transport print files on floppies. You'll need to experiment, since the actual number of bytes per page can vary widely, even between several pages in the same document.*

Collate Copies

If you request multiple copies (five copies of a ten-page document, for instance) and you don't choose the Collate Copies option, Word will print all five page 1's, then all five page 2's, and so on. You'll need to hand-collate them to make orderly sets.

The Collate Copies option prints five "books," each one complete and in order. This may or may not increase overall printing time, depending on your printer and a number of other factors.

Choosing Your Paper Source

If your printer has two paper sources (two trays, or a tray and a "pass-through," for instance), Word can switch sources as needed. Choose File | Page Setup to reach the Page Setup dialog box. Then, use the First Page, Other Pages, and perhaps Apply To choices found in the Paper Source tab.

Other Printing Options

There are other printing options available. They can be reached by choosing the Print tab in Word's Options dialog box.

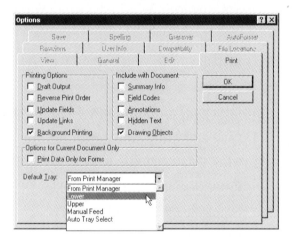

You can display the Options dialog box either by choosing Tools | Options, or by pressing the Options button in the Print dialog box. Most of these settings remain in place once you change them and are used for each new printing job until you change them.

Draft Output

This option can speed up printing. Its effect varies from printer to printer. Usually everything is printed in a single font, as efficiently as possible, and at the expense of appearance. It is often faster to print draft dot-matrix copy than fancy laser copy.

Reverse Print Order

Use Reverse Print Order when you want pages to come out last-to-first. This is handy for some printers that stack pages in the wrong order.

Update Fields and Update Links

As you learned in Chapter 3, this is how you determine when and if things get updated before printing.

Background Printing

A check in this option box causes Word to use the Windows Background printing feature. Theoretically, it lets you work on other things while your document prints in the background. In real life it often makes your computer so sluggish that you'll end up taking a break anyway. If you keep getting printing errors or low memory messages while printing, try turning off background printing.

You can turn on background printing from the Print tab in the Options dialog box.

1. Choose Tools | Options.

2. Click the Print tab, if necessary, to reveal printing options.

3. Make sure there is a check in the Background Printing box (click if necessary).

4. Click OK and print as usual. Your documents will print in the background while you're working on other things.

Include with Document

The Include with Document choices in the Print tab of the Options dialog box are pretty self-explanatory. A check causes data to be delivered with the printed pages (summary info, annotations, and so on). Click on a check to remove it and prevent the item from printing.

Options for Current Document Only

The options that appear here will vary with the contents of your document. For instance, you may be given the option to print data without printing forms.

Default Tray

Use this choice to force something other than the standard tray choice for special printing jobs (for example, a cover letter on your business letterhead). The selected printer must have more than one paper source for this to be useful.

Checking the Status of a Print Job

tip *A great Windows shortcut to know is* ALT+TAB. *If you press this key combination, Windows switches you to the next open application. If you have several open applications, repeatedly pressing* ALT+TAB *will cycle through them.*

With background printing at work, you can check and change the status of multiple print jobs. Follow these steps.

1. Click on the printer's icon in the Taskbar.

2. Click to select the job or jobs you want to cancel or reschedule.

3. Click on the appropriate button (Pause, Resume, Cancel, and so on).

4. Use the menus for other options.

5. To return to Word for Windows, hold down ALT and press TAB as many times as necessary.

For more information about background printing with Windows, use the online help and see your Windows documentation.

Aborting Printing

To prematurely stop printing, press ESC repeatedly until the printing status information disappears from your screen. Even after the printing status information disappears, your printer may print a few pages that were sent before print cancellation, since many printers contain their own memory (called a *buffer*). Check your printer manual for ways to quickly clear the printer's memory if this annoys you.

If you are using background printing, you will probably need to visit the printer itself, as described earlier in this chapter, and cancel the job there.

Using Print Preview Before Printing

You can use Print Preview to see a screen representation of your document before printing it. Print Preview will give you an excellent idea of the printed text. You can now edit this text. You will be able to see margins, as well. If your document contains headers, footers, line numbers, and other embellishments, you will see them, too. Using Print Preview will allow you to make adjustments to any of these settings *before* printing, thus saving paper and time.

The buttons along the top of the screen let you control many of Print Preview's functions. As always, if you forget a button's function, simply point to it without clicking to reveal button help. Here is a general description of each button.

Print button   This button prints a single copy of the document without taking you to the Print dialog box. (If you really want to visit the Print dialog box, choose File | Print or use the CTRL+P shortcut.)

Magnifier button   The Magnifier button lets you zoom in to better read small portions of the page and zoom out to get a bird's-eye view of one or more pages. It also toggles you in and out of edit mode, as you will see momentarily.

One Page button   This button displays a single page even if you are working with a multipage document.

Multiple Pages button   The Multiple Pages button lets you specify the number of miniaturized pages you'll see onscreen. Pressing this button reveals a matrix that you drag across to design your screen display. Choices range from a single page to 3 × 6 (18) pages.

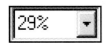

Zoom Control button   The Percentage text box and related zoom list are called the *Zoom controls*. They tell you the current zoom percentage and let you pick a variety of zoom options from a drop-down list.

View Ruler button   The View Ruler button is used to toggle the rulers that you use to see and change margin settings.

Shrink to Fit button   When you press the Shrink to Fit button, Word attempts to tighten up documents that end with a mostly white page. To undo proposed changes, use the CTRL+Z shortcut or File | Undo Shrink to Fit. Occasionally, Word can't shrink your document and will tell you so.

 Full Page button   The Full Screen button removes most of the Print Preview clutter (menu bar, status line, and so on) so you can see a bigger version of your document. Pressing the Full Screen button a second time returns the hidden controls.

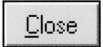 **Close button**   The Close button takes you back to the previous view.

 Help button   The Help button will turn your pointer into a question mark. Point to the item of interest (the vertical ruler, for instance) to read any available help. Double-click on the Help window's Close box or press ESC to quit Help.

Moving Margins in Print Preview

Here is a quick trick you can try in Print Preview:

1. Type some text.

2. Display the rulers if they are not already onscreen by clicking on the View Rulers button.

3. Point to the vertical ruler on the left edge of your screen. Notice how the pointer gets smaller and has an up- and down-pointing head.

4. Hold down the primary (usually the left) mouse button and notice the dashed margin line.

5. While holding down the mouse button, drag down to specify a new top margin while watching the dashed line.

6. Release the mouse button and Word will adjust the margin, moving the text down.

You can use the same basic techniques to move the left and right margins.

Leaving Print Preview

Use the Close button to leave Print Preview and return to your previous view. The three standard view buttons (Normal, Page Layout, and Outline) are also available in the lower-left corner of the status area of Print Preview.

Printing Envelopes

Word can print addresses on envelopes by looking for the addresses in your documents (the inside address of a letter for instance), or you can type an address in the Envelopes and Labels dialog box.

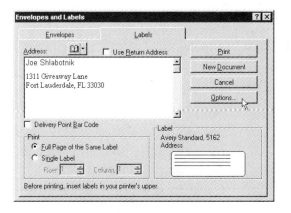

You reach the Envelopes and Labels dialog box with the Tools | Envelopes and Labels command. The dialog box lets you

■ Print envelopes containing one-time addresses that you type into the dialog box itself

■ Copy an address from your document for envelope printing

■ Type envelope addresses, then insert them into your letters or other Word documents

Including Graphics on Envelopes

You can print graphics on envelopes. It's a great way to add logos, special messages, business reply art, and so on. Here are the general steps:

1. Select the Envelope tab in the Envelopes and Labels dialog box reached with Tools | Envelopes and Labels.

2. Click on either the Add To Document or Change Document button.

3. Switch to Page Layout if not already there.

4. Paste or create a graphic and frame it (using the Insert | Frame command), and then move it into position as you would any other framed item.

5. Make any other changes that you want (rearrange or reformat lines of text in the inside address, for instance).

At this point, the envelope is one-of-a-kind, and in a separate section at the top of your current document. You can either save the document and print the envelope along with the rest of the document, or save the document as a template for repeated use. But there's one other possibility. If you want the artwork to appear on *all* of your envelopes, you can select the art and create a special AutoText entry called EnvelopeExtra 1 or EnvelopeExtra 2. (See the "AutoText" section in Chapter 10 to learn about AutoText.)

Setting Up a Return Address

If your envelopes have preprinted return addresses, you can skip this task. But if you want to use plain envelopes and have Word print your return address in the upper-left corner of envelopes, do this:

1. Choose the printer you plan to use if you have more than one.

2. Open the Envelopes and Labels dialog box by choosing Tools | Envelopes and Labels. You'll see the Envelopes and Labels dialog box.

3. Click on the Envelopes tab if it is not foremost.

4. If Word finds an address in the current open Word document, you will see it in the Delivery Address portion of the dialog box.

5. Type your return address in the Return Address box . (Word may have filled out part of the address already using your Word User Info.)

6. When you are happy with the spelling and appearance of your return address, try test printing on a plain #10 (4.25 × 9.5-inch) envelope. Word assumes that you can center-feed envelopes in your printer. If that's not possible, click on the envelope in the Feed section of the dialog box to bring up the Envelope Options dialog box.

7. Select a combination that will work with your printer, and then click OK.

8. Place an envelope in your printer.

9. Back in the Envelopes tab of the Envelopes and Labels dialog box, click Print to ensure that envelopes will print properly.

Suppressing Return Addresses

If you always plan to use envelopes that contain preprinted return addresses, you can leave the Return Address area blank. Or you can type a return address but click to place a check in the Omit box if you use preprinted envelopes sometimes and plain ones at other times.

Printing Envelopes with New Addresses

You can either type an envelope address directly into the Envelopes and Labels dialog box, or select an address in your letter or other Word document, and then open the Envelopes and Labels dialog box. Here are the general steps for envelope printing:

1. Select the address in your document if there is one.

2. Open the Envelopes and Labels dialog box by choosing the Tools | Envelopes and Labels command.

3. If you selected an address in step 1, you'll see it in the dialog box; if not, type an address in the Delivery Address box.

4. Insert an envelope in your printer.

5. Click on the Print button.

WORD PROCESSING WITH WORD FOR WINDOWS

tip *Word will often make a guess as to what it thinks should be the delivery address. Generally, it makes pretty good guesses; but if you don't have an address or if it is unclear where you want the correspondence sent, you may have to help out.*

Adding an Envelope Page to Documents

Click on the Add to Document button in the Envelopes and Labels dialog box to add an envelope page to the beginning of your document. Word takes care of all the details.

tip *Instead of adding an envelope page to your documents, you could just use the Insert Address button on the Standard toolbar, provided you have the address in your database.*

Changing Addresses

Once you've inserted an envelope page in your document, you can change the envelope and inside address at any time. Here's how:

1. Open the document.

2. Make the address change in the inside address.

Alternatively, you could

1. Open the Envelopes and Labels dialog box (Tools | Envelopes and Labels).

2. Change the Delivery Address.

3. Click the Change Document button. The envelope will be changed.

tip *If you change the Delivery Address in the Envelopes and Labels dialog box, then click the Change Document button, Word will update the envelope but not the inside address, so be careful. It's better to make the change in the document, not in the Envelopes and Labels dialog box.*

Envelope Sizes, Fonts, and Other Options

Word lets you specify envelope sizes (both standard and custom), fonts used for delivery, return addresses, and more. The options are selected in two tabs located in the Envelope Options dialog box.

Bar Codes to Speed Postal Delivery

If you are planning to send mail within the United States, you can ask Word to print bar codes on your envelopes. These will speed automated mail sorting. Two coding techniques are provided—POSTNET for regular mail and FIM-A for "courtesy reply" mail. Place a check in the box or boxes you desire. Word will do the rest.

Printing Labels

Label printing is a lot like envelope printing, except you have even more options. For instance, you can print single labels or sheets of labels. Word knows the dimensions for many different industry-standard stocks from Avery and others. For instance, you'll find Word knows how to print

- Audio tape labels
- Business card perforated stock
- Disk labels
- File folder labels
- Mailing (address) labels
- Name tags
- Postcards
- Ready indexes
- Rotary (Rolodex) cards
- Shipping labels
- Videocassette labels
- WorkSaver tabs

Simple label printing is a lot like envelope printing. Here are the general steps:

1. Select the address in your document if it has one.

2. Open the Envelopes and Labels dialog box with the Tools | Envelopes and Labels command.

3. Click on the Labels tab if it is not already foremost. You'll see some options.

4. If you selected an address in step 1 or if Word finds one on its own, you'll see it in the dialog box; if not, type an address in the text box.

5. Choose the desired options in the main Labels tab. To print a single label on a multilabel sheet, select Single Label and specify the row and column location of the label. Choose to print or not print the bar code and return address.

6. To select different label sizes, click on either the picture of a label or the Options button. You'll see the available choices.

7. Pick the label maker, label product number, and printer type. Click on the Details button to see more choices.

8. Fine-tune Top and Side margins here if your printer prints all of the labels of the current type too high or too far left or right. The other settings are probably correct if you selected the correct label type in step 6. When you have made all your choices, Click OK once or twice as necessary to return to the Label tab of the Envelopes and Labels dialog box.

9. Insert a label or sheet of labels in your printer. (Make sure the label isn't too small for your printer. Check your printer's documentation for more information.)

10. Click on the Print button.

tip *Normally, you can put partially used sheets of laser labels through your printer once or twice more, but you risk jamming and possibly damaging your printer. It's often better to print full sheets and file the unused labels for the next time you mail something to the same recipient.*

CHAPTER 5

Formatting Your Text and Documents

WORD offers almost too many ways to change the appearance of your documents. You can embellish individual characters, change the indentation of paragraphs, adjust the white space between lines and paragraphs, and much more. So far in this book, you've already done some formatting with Word's toolbars. In this chapter, we'll take a look at other techniques worth knowing.

AutoFormat

AutoFormat inspects your document and suggests formatting changes that you can accept or reject. You can use it on newly typed documents or on old Word or non-Word text files.

With AutoFormat, Word can locate and reformat headings, change straight quotes to curly quotes, and more. Here are the general steps:

1. Open or create the document you want to AutoFormat. Figure 5-1 shows an unformatted text document called City Governments. You probably have an unformatted file somewhere on your hard disk that you can practice on.

2. Choose Format | AutoFormat.

3. If you want to change the way AutoFormat works, click the Options button. Click to tell which formatting tasks you don't want it to perform. For instance, if you don't want Word to preserve any styles you've already applied, click to remove the check from the appropriate box.

4. When you have specified any changes to Word's usual AutoFormatting habits, click OK to be taken back to the AutoFormat dialog box.

FIGURE 5-1

AutoFormat inspects your document and suggests formatting changes

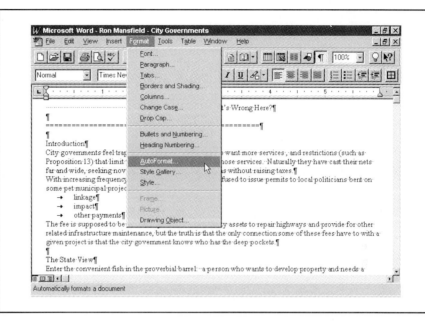

5. Click OK in the AutoFormat dialog box. Word will go to work. It can take awhile; watch the status area for a progress report.

6. You will see the changed document (notice the different appearance of the headings) and the following AutoFormat dialog box:

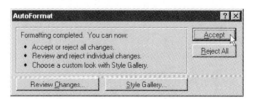

7. To see and review each proposed change, choose Review Changes. To apply different formatting via the Style Gallery, click the Style Gallery button. You can review the changes in the Style Gallery by clicking on choices in the scrolling Template list. (See the end of this chapter for more about styles.) Figure 5-2 is an example that uses the Professional Report template styles. Notice the nicely formatted title and heading.

8. Inspect your finished product carefully to be sure that you got what you wanted. You may need to polish Word's work with the

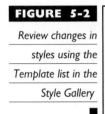

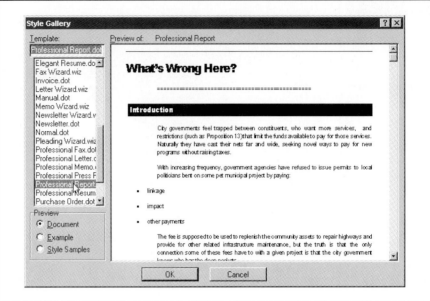

techniques described in the rest of this chapter. For instance, the Bullets button was used to create the bulleted list just shown.

tip When you type new documents, Word can automatically perform certain formatting tasks, such as creating headings, bulleted and numbered lists, and line borders. This book will explore each subject in more detail when we are dealing with it.

Formatting Characters

Word's Formatting toolbar contains a number of text-formatting buttons. There are other toolbars containing formatting buttons. (Remember, if you forget a button's function, move the mouse pointer over the button and hold it there for a moment. The button's name will appear.)

You can also use keyboard shortcuts to alter the appearance of characters. And there are dialog boxes containing character-formatting choices. The most useful is the Font dialog box (Format | Font) shown in Figure 5-3.

Changing Fonts and Font Sizes

To change fonts and font sizes, select text, and then,

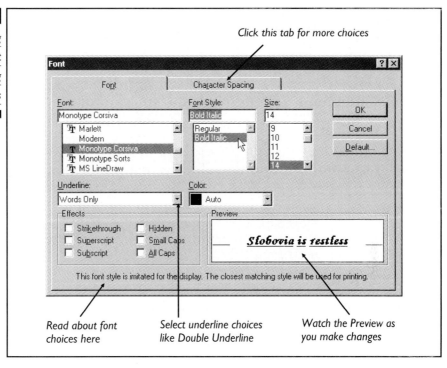

WORD PROCESSING WITH WORD FOR WINDOWS

FIGURE 5-3

The Font dialog box offers the most character-formatting choices

Click this tab for more choices

Read about font choices here

Select underline choices like Double Underline

Watch the Preview as you make changes

- Use the drop-down Font and Size lists on the Formatting toolbar, as shown in Figure 5-4.

- Type the name of the desired font or size directly into the Font or Size boxes on the Formatting toolbar, and then press ENTER.

- Choose Format | Font and select a font or size from the Font dialog box.

- Press CTRL+] or CTRL+[to increase or decrease the size one point at a time, respectively.

- Press CTRL+SHIFT+> or CTRL+SHIFT+< to increase or decrease the size by the standard increments listed in Word's various Size lists.

To Bold Selected Text

Click the Bold button on the Formatting toolbar; use one of the keyboard shortcuts (CTRL+B or CTRL+SHIFT+B); or check the Bold check box in the Font Style list in Word's Font dialog box (reached by Format | Font).

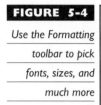

Recently used choices are at the top of the list

Use the arrows to reveal the lists

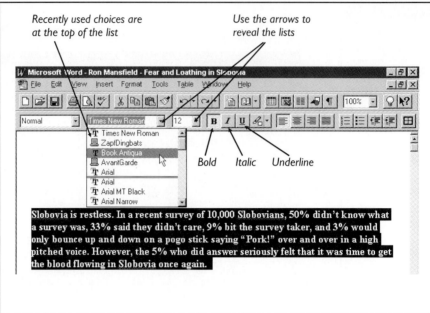

Bold   Italic   Underline

Slobovia is restless. In a recent survey of 10,000 Slobovians, 50% didn't know what a survey was, 33% said they didn't care, 9% bit the survey taker, and 3% would only bounce up and down on a pogo stick saying "Pork!" over and over in a high pitched voice. However, the 5% who did answer seriously felt that it was time to get the blood flowing in Slobovia once again.

To Italicize Selected Text

Click the Italic button on the Formatting toolbar; use one of the keyboard shortcuts (CTRL+I or CTRL+SHIFT+I); or enable the Italic option in the Font Style list in Word's Font dialog box.

To Underscore Selected Text

Click the Underline button on the Formatting toolbar (for a single, continuous underline); use the keyboard shortcut CTRL+U; or choose None, Single, Words Only, Double, and Dotted from the options in the Underline list in Word's Font dialog box.

To Highlight Selected Text

Click the Highlight button on the Formatting toolbar. You can choose a color other than yellow (hot pink, aqua, or lime) if you click the arrow. To remove highlighting, select highlighted text and click the highlight button again, or choose None from the list.

To Produce Superscripts and Subscripts

To produce superscripts and subscripts, use the shortcuts CTRL+= and CTRL+SHIFT+=, or bring up the Character Spacing tab of the Font dialog box (Format | Font) and choose either Raised or Lowered.

tip *Word lets you add Superscript and Subscript buttons to your toolbars to make this even easier. See Chapter 11 to find out about customizing toolbars.*

To Expand or Condense Selected Text

Open the Character Spacing tab in the Font dialog box (Format | Font), and choose Expanded or Condensed from the Spacing list.

Changing Case

To change case, select Format | Change Case. This opens the Change Case dialog box, which offers (and illustrates) five choices of case.

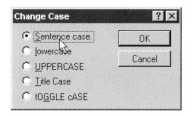

For instance, UPPERCASE changes all selected characters to uppercase letters, and the choice UPPERCASE itself appears all uppercase in the dialog box. Title Case changes the first letter of each selected word to uppercase, as illustrated in the dialog box.

The Title Case feature is not context sensitive, so it capitalizes prepositions and articles, including "of," "the," and so on. To change case with this feature, follow these steps.

1. Select the text you want to change.

2. Choose Format | Change Case.

3. Choose the desired case option.

4. Click OK.

When you change case using the Change Case dialog box, the characters themselves change to the specified case. It is just as if you had retyped them using the new capitalization scheme. Undo works here.

The All Caps Option

The All Caps feature in the Effects area of the Font dialog box changes only the appearance of letters without actually changing the letters themselves. Unlike Format | Change Case, the All Caps option lets you type in lowercase and see uppercase letters as you work. Follow these steps:

1. Select the text you want to change, or position the insertion point for typing.

2. Choose Format | Font.

3. Check the All Caps check box.

4. Click OK. Selected and/or subsequently typed case will appear in uppercase, but the underlying text will retain its actual capitalization.

Using the Small Caps Option

The Small Caps option in the Font dialog box can create some very interesting effects. Remember that applying the Small Caps formatting option to text containing Wingdings will usually capitalize the Dingbats, thereby changing the characters that appear and print. If this happens, select Dingbats and remove Small Caps formatting. Use Edit | Replace to do this if you have many changes to make.

Drop Caps

Drop caps, also called *initial caps*, are decorative first letters or words that have been stylized, and are usually bigger than surrounding text. Here's an example:

> S lobovia is restless. In a recent survey of 1
> a survey was, 33% said they didn't care, :
> only bounce up and down on a pogo stick
> pitched voice. However, the 5% who did answe
> blood flowing in Slobovia once again.

To create drop caps, select Format | Drop Caps to open the Drop Cap dialog box.

warning *Drop caps work with single-spaced text only—they won't work in tables, headers, or footers. You won't be able to see the position of drop caps or create them in Outline view. You can't place drop caps in the margins of multicolumn documents, but you can place them within text in multicolumn documents. Narrow indents sometimes mess up the automatic drop cap feature.*

That said, here are the general steps:

1. Format the body text the way you like it. Be sure you are happy with things like margins, fonts, and so on. Single-space the text.

2. Select the character or characters you want to drop, and choose the Format | Drop Cap command. If you are not in Page Layout view, Word will prompt you to switch. You'll see the Drop Cap dialog box.

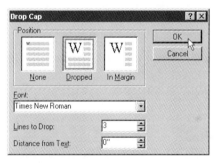

3. If you want to use a different font for the drop cap, choose it from the drop-down Font menu.

4. The Lines to Drop box proposes the number of lines the cap will drop. For instance, 3 li means that the drop cap will be three lines tall and drop alongside the first three lines of text. Pick the desired number of lines from the drop-down list.

5. In the Position area, choose the Dropped option for traditional-looking drop caps, or choose the In Margin option to place dropped caps in the margin.

6. When you click OK, Word places the specified text into a frame and positions the frame for you.

7. Use the character, frame, and paragraph tools, if you dare, to modify Word's settings.

tip   *You can use the Format | Drop Cap command to drop graphics, as well. Paste a graphic at the beginning of a line of text; drag; and, if necessary, make it reasonably small. Then, with the graphic selected, use Format | Drop Cap.*

Format Painter

Use the Format Painter to copy character formatting from place to place:

1. Select the text containing the formatting you want to copy.

2. To copy the formatting to one location, click once on the Format Painter button on the Standard toolbar. (To copy to several locations, double-click.) The mouse pointer will change to a paintbrush.

3. Select the text you want to format.

4. If you double-clicked in step 2, press ESC when you've finished using the Format Painter.

Formatting Paragraphs

Your English teachers probably taught you that paragraphs are collections of sentences on a related topic; Word uses a somewhat more liberal definition. A Word paragraph can be a single text character, a graphic, or even a blank line consisting only of the paragraph mark (¶), which appears in your document when you press ENTER. Paragraph-formatting features are an important part of Word's arsenal.

Each Word paragraph in your document can be uniquely formatted and need not contain text.

Creating Paragraphs

Each time you press ENTER, you create a new paragraph. It's that simple. When you open a new document, Word applies the default paragraph settings stored as Normal style. It formats each new paragraph the same way until you tell it to do otherwise.

Word paragraphs can be simple blank "lines" or complex collections of indentation, tab, line spacing, and other settings. A paragraph's attributes are stored with its paragraph mark. Deleting the mark removes a paragraph's formatting. To create new paragraphs, press ENTER.

To modify the appearance of a single paragraph, simply place the insertion point anywhere in the paragraph (point and click with the mouse). To modify multiple paragraphs, select all or parts of each paragraph to be changed.

Splitting One Paragraph into Two

Position the insertion point where you want to break the paragraph and press ENTER. Watch out for extra spaces!

Joining Paragraphs

Select the paragraph mark that separates them and press the SPACEBAR Look out for extra spaces or tabs.

Forcing a New Line Without Creating a New Paragraph

Press SHIFT+ENTER. This inserts a new line mark, pushing text down to the next line, but does not create a new paragraph. This can be important when you are working with sophisticated styles.

Deleting a Paragraph

To delete a paragraph, double-click in the left margin to select the doomed paragraph and press BACKSPACE. This will delete the paragraph *and* its ¶ mark.

WORD PROCESSING WITH WORD FOR WINDOWS

Alternatively, you can select all text in the paragraph except the ¶ and delete it, which will leave the ¶ mark with its formatting information.

Think twice when deleting paragraphs. You can delete just the contents of a paragraph or delete the contents and the paragraph marker. If you delete the marker, text above the old paragraph will take on the characteristics of the remaining paragraph below it. This is by design, and is not a bug. If you accidentally delete a paragraph mark and create a problem, the Undo command (Edit | Undo or CTRL+Z) will usually return your heart rate to normal.

Modifying the Appearance of Paragraphs

To modify the appearance of paragraphs, use the ruler, the Formatting toolbar, and the Paragraph dialog box; or consider using one of Word's paragraph-formatting shortcut key combinations.

To Indent Paragraphs Automatically

Drag the top half of the triangular indent marker on the ruler to the right to the desired position:

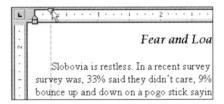

Alternatively, use the keyboard shortcut (CTRL+M), or select Format | Paragraph and enter a setting in the First Line indent box in the Paragraph dialog box.

Increasing or Decreasing Indents by One Tab Stop

Use the Increase Indent and Decrease Indent buttons on the Formatting toolbar.

Hanging Indents

To create a hanging indent (an indent that sticks out beyond the paragraph), drag the bottom half of the triangular indent marker to the left to the desired position, as shown here.

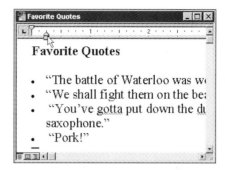

You can also use the keyboard shortcut CTRL+T, or select Format | Paragraph and enter a setting in the First Line indent box in the Paragraph dialog box that is *farther* left than the indent of the paragraph as a whole.

Indenting with Keyboard Shortcuts

Word offers various keyboard shortcuts that move the left indent marker. Some of these are additive commands and can create nested paragraphs. For example, pressing CTRL+M three times will move the indent position in three stops.

Indent Action	Keyboard Shortcut
Center	CTRL+E
Justify	CTRL+J
Left align	CTRL+L
Right align	CTRL+R
Left Indent	CTRL+M
Remove left indent	CTRL+SHIFT+M
Create hanging indent	CTRL+T
Reduce hanging indent	CTRL+SHIFT+T

Creating Bulleted Lists

Select the items in your list, and then click the Bullets button on the Formatting toolbar, which automatically creates a hanging indent and places bullets to the left of the text.

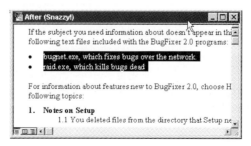

Word can also insert bullets for you automatically. If you begin a line with an asterisk (*), when you press ENTER, Word will turn the asterisk into a bullet and add a bullet to each succeeding item.

Creating Automatically Numbered Lists

Select the items in your list, and then click the Numbering button on the Formatting toolbar, which automatically creates a hanging indent and places numbers to the left of the items.

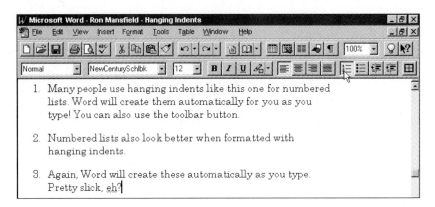

Like the automatic bullets described earlier, Word can automatically number lists. Begin a line with a number, and Word will number each successive line.

Centering, Right Alignment, and Left Alignment

Select the paragraph(s) you want to align, and then use one of the four paragraph-alignment buttons on the Formatting toolbar (Left, Right, Center, or Justify), as shown here. (Justify aligns text with both the left and right margins or indents.)

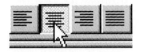

Formatting with the Paragraph Dialog Box

Choose Format | Paragraph to reach the Paragraph dialog box. (Alternatively, double-click on any indent marker.)

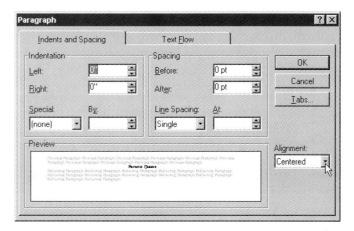

The Paragraph dialog box lets you:

- Precisely specify line spacing (single, double, and so on)
- Precisely specify paragraph spacing (space before and after paragraphs)
- Dictate exact indentation measurements
- Turn off line numbering for specific paragraphs
- Specify text alignment (left, centered, right, or justified)
- Specify text flow guidelines (widows, orphans, and so on)
- Suppress hyphenation

tip *Widows are short lines (typically a single word) at the ends of paragraphs. Orphans are the first lines of paragraphs that print by themselves at the bottom of a page.*

You can often use different units of measure for the same specification when entering measurements in the Paragraph dialog box. For instance, you can specify line height in points (pt), lines (li), inches (in), picas (pi), or centimeters (cm). Each possible numeric entry in the Paragraph dialog box has a default unit of measure that is shown in each entry box.

tip *Line spacing shows a unit of measure when you select At Least or Exactly. When you select Multiple, you can enter a number and Word will assume you mean lines (li).*

In United States versions of Word, the default for horizontal measurements, such as indents, is inches. The default unit of measure for line and paragraph spacing is points. (There are 72 points per inch.)

tip *You can make entries in the Paragraph dialog box without specifying units of measure if you know the default unit of measure for each type of entry. For instance, the default for line spacing is points. Here's the rub. If you enter **2**, Word will assume you mean 2 points, not double spacing. To specify double spacing, you'd need to enter **2 li** (or specify Double in the Line Spacing box). When you are uncertain about the default unit of measure for a paragraph specification, enter the abbreviation for the unit of measure.*

Line Spacing

Individual line spacing is easy to change. You can change the space between lines, and the space before and after paragraphs.

Adjusting the Space Between Lines

The Indents and Spacing tab of the Paragraph dialog box provides a drop-down list for simple but effective control of the space between lines under most circumstances. The Preview area demonstrates the relative effect of single, one-and-a-half, and double line spacing. Single spacing causes 12-point line spacing, $1\frac{1}{2}$-line spacing is 18 points, and double-spaced lines will be 24 points apart.

When you use these choices, Word will compensate for graphics, superscripts, and large or small type sizes. To force exact line spacing, use the At Least or Exactly choices described in a moment.

Single Spacing Text

To single-space text, follow these steps.

1. Single spacing is Word's default spacing. To reapply it to text spaced some other way, place the insertion point in a paragraph or select multiple paragraphs.

2. Press CTRL+1 or choose Single in the Paragraph dialog box's Line Spacing menu. Selected text and subsequent typing will be single spaced.

Double Spacing Text

To double-space text, follow these steps.

1. To apply double spacing to text spaced some other way, place the insertion point in a paragraph or select multiple paragraphs.

2. Press CTRL+2 or choose Double in the Paragraph dialog box's Line Spacing menu. Selected text and subsequent typing will be double spaced.

Line-and-a-Half Spacing

To apply 1½-line spacing to text spaced some other way, follow these steps.

1. Place the insertion point in a paragraph or select multiple paragraphs.

2. Press CTRL+5 or choose 1.5 Lines in the Paragraph dialog box's Line Spacing list. Selected text and subsequent typing will be 1½-line spaced.

Specifying Exact Line Heights

Word automatically sets the appropriate amount of white space between lines for you, unless you tell it to do otherwise. It even compensates for different-sized characters on the same line by setting line spacing to the tallest character.

But sometimes you'll want to specify exact line spacing for one or more paragraphs. Increasing the spacing by a nonstandard amount can help you fill unused space when your copy runs a little short. Specifying slightly less than normal space between lines can help keep text from running on to the top of an extra page.

Here's how to specify exact paragraph spacing:

1. Place the insertion point in a paragraph or select multiple paragraphs.

2. Open the Paragraph dialog box (choose Format | Paragraph or double-click on any indent marker).

3. Choose Exactly or At Least from the Line Spacing drop-down list.

WORD PROCESSING WITH WORD FOR WINDOWS

4. Enter a specification and unit of measure (**2.5li**, **26pt**, **1.5in**, **22cm**, and so on) in the At box. Watch the preview as you work.

5. Click OK to make the specified spacing change.

tip *If the tops or bottoms of characters are cut off, you may have set a line height that is too small. Revisit the Paragraph dialog box and increase the line height.*

∫pace Before and After Paragraphs

The Spacing area in the Paragraph dialog box (Format | Paragraph) lets you define the amount of white space Word places before and after paragraphs. You can enter spacing settings in points (pt), inches (in), centimeters (cm), or lines (li). Thus, 12 points would be entered as **12pt**, 25 centimeters would be entered as **25cm**, and so on.

You can give each paragraph unique before-and-after spacing if you like. One advantage to adding space this way is that the spacing before and after paragraphs does not change when you change the point size of your text. Another advantage is that you can use different spacing combinations for different purposes.

Headings often have different spacing requirements from body text, for instance. You may want to create different before-and-after spacing designs for figures and figure captions, as well.

tip *You can have Word handle line spacing and headings automatically if you like. Just type your heading text, and then press ENTER twice. Word will format your head and place the correct amount of space after it.*

As you will learn soon, you can save unique spacing specifications as part of a *style*, making it easy to keep the look of your documents consistent.

tip *If a paragraph has space added after it, and the paragraph beneath it has space added before, the white space between them will be the combination of the two settings. For example, if one paragraph has 12 points of spacing after it and its successor has 6 points of spacing before, the white space between will be 18 points.*

Adding White Space Before Paragraphs

To add a single line of white space before a paragraph, place the insertion point in a paragraph (or select multiple paragraphs) and press CTRL+0 (zero). (To remove single lines of white space originally created with CTRL+0, press CTRL+0 a second time.)

To enter a specific amount of space before a paragraph:

1. Place the insertion point in a paragraph or select multiple paragraphs.

2. Double-click on any indent marker to open the Paragraph dialog box.

3. Enter new Before dimensions in the Spacing area in lines, inches, picas, and so on, and then click OK. Selected paragraphs and subsequent ones will have additional amounts of white space before them.

Fine-Tuning Paragraph Spacing

While the ruler buttons are fine for most occasions, you may need to visit the Paragraph dialog box occasionally to get just the right look. Select Format | Paragraph, and then enter appropriate specifications in the Spacing Before and After boxes to fine-tune. You can observe the effect of your changes in the Preview box. Click OK when you are satisfied.

Space Before and Page Tops

When you print, Word ignores the Space Before setting in paragraphs that automatic pagination places at the top of a page. If you force a page or section break, however, Word retains this extra space. It will also retain the additional space if you check the Page Break Before option in the Pagination section of the Paragraph dialog box.

Margins and Gutters

The white space around the edges of a Word page are determined primarily by margin and optional gutter settings. (*Gutters* add extra white space for bound documents.) You can use one set of margin and gutter settings for an entire document, or you can define different settings for different pages in your document. Your choice of paper size, paper orientation (portrait versus landscape), margin, and gutter settings determine the size and shape of the text area of pages.

Larger margins and gutter settings decrease the available text area and increase the surrounding white space on each page.

Since margin settings (and Page Setup information) all affect pagination, it is a good idea to define these dimensions when you begin a new project. This will give you a better grasp of the page count and overall look of the document as you work. You can always fine-tune margin settings just before final printing.

When printing two-sided documents, you may want to use Word's Mirror Even/Odd margin feature and possibly add gutters to place extra white space near the center of your book. (Note that it is convention to have odd-numbered pages on the right and even on the left—just look at any book!) If you plan to have different left and right margins in a two-sided document (a wide left and narrow right, for instance), it is useful to think of these as *inside* and *outside* margins rather than left and right margins, since the wide margin will be on the left side of odd-numbered pages but on the right side of even-numbered pages.

If you use headers and footers, you will want to know how they interact with margin settings. Word makes this all fairly painless. When setting margins, bear in mind that some printers cannot print at the extreme edges of a page.

Don't confuse Word's margin settings with its paragraph indentation feature. A Word *page* can have only one user-specified left *margin* setting and only one user-specified right margin setting, but each *paragraph* on the page can have a different left and right *indentation* setting.

Indents are *added* to margin settings. That is to say, if you specify a 1.0" left margin and a ½" left indent, your text will print 1½ inches from the left margin. If you set a 1.0" right margin and indent the right edge of a paragraph 1.0", the text will stop 2.0 inches from the right edge of the page.

Changing Document Margins

Word gives you three ways to set margins. The most straightforward method is to use the Margins portion of the Page Setup dialog box, reached with the File | Page Setup command.

You can also drag margins by using the rulers in Print Preview. This lets you see the results of margin changes after a slight repagination delay.

Finally, you can drag new margins with the rulers in Page Layout view. The margin brackets are located on the ruler. Let's look at all three techniques, starting with the dialog box.

Follow these general steps to change margins from within the Page Setup dialog box:

1. Place the insertion point on the page where you want margin settings to be changed (unless you plan to use the Whole Document choice).

2. Choose File | Page Setup.

3. If need be, change paper size and orientation by using the Paper Size tab.

4. Switch to the Margins tab if it is not already displayed.

5. Current settings are shown in the various margin dimension boxes.

6. Type the dimensions you desire, or click the little triangles to increase and decrease settings. The Preview will change as you work.

7. When satisfied, click OK.

Dimensional settings in most Word dialog boxes can be expressed in inches (in), points (pt), centimeters (cm), picas (pi), and, frequently, lines (li). For instance, to set a top margin's height to 12 points, you would type **12pt** in the Top margin box; to set a 1½-line top margin, you'd type **1.5li**, and so forth.

n o t e *While you can type other measurements, Word will convert them to the default measurement when you close the dialog box. You change the default measurement in the General tab of the Options dialog box (Tools | Options).*

Dragging Margin Brackets on the Ruler

Word's new rulers display margins as dark gray areas that you can drag to change the document's margins. Don't confuse this with dragging to create indents, which is similar but has a very different effect. Follow these steps:

1. Change to Page Layout view if you're not there already.

2. If the ruler is not displayed, choose View | Ruler.

3. Point to the transition area on the ruler where gray becomes white. The mouse pointer will become a two-headed arrow.

4. Drag the margin to the desired position with your mouse. Watch the ruler's dimensions change as you drag.

Alternate Facing (Mirror) Margins

Select the Mirror Margins feature in the Margins tab of the Page Setup dialog box (File | Page Setup) when you want different left and right margin widths, and your final output will be two-sided. Word makes inside margins of odd- and even-numbered pages the same size, and does the same with the outside margins of odd and even pages. This is how you get white space on the appropriate side of even and odd, two-sided pages.

When adjusting margins in Print Preview, if you've chosen the Mirror Odd/Even feature, display two pages in Print Preview so that you can see the different margins.

Gutters Facilitate Binding

Gutter margins—additional white space in the inside margins—compensate for the paper tucked away in the binding of a two-sided book that would be unreadable. The gutter width, which you specify in the Margin tab of the Page Setup dialog box (File | Page Setup), reduces the text area. Instead of using gutters, you might simply want to increase the size of the inside margins to accommodate binding.

Printing in the Margins

You can place text, graphics, and page numbers in margins by using indent markers. You can drag indent markers into margins, and text or graphics will follow. You can also use Insert | Frame to place things in margins. (See Chapter 8 to find out how to use frames.)

To See What Formatting Choices Are at Work

Click the Help button on the Standard toolbar and point at the characters of interest. A balloon box will appear, containing information about the paragraph and character styling.

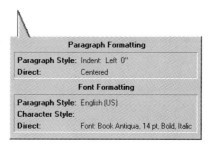

Columns

 To quickly arrange your text into columns, click the Columns button on the Formatting toolbar and drag it to select from one to six columns:

When you release the mouse button, Word automatically determines the appropriate width of columns and the amount of white space between columns based on the page and document settings (see Figure 5-5).

 tip   *To avoid unsightly column widths and spacing, change your margins, page size, orientation, indents, and related settings before you set your text in columns. For greater control over the look and number of columns, use the Columns dialog box (Format | Columns), where you can preview the results of choices made.*

Using Multiple-Column Designs in a Document

To create different columns (even on the same page), select the desired text and specify column settings with the toolbar button or the Columns dialog box. Word will apply the settings *only to the selected text* and will insert necessary breaks automatically (see Figure 5-6).

Changing Column Widths

To change column widths, drag columns to different widths using margin markers. Start by placing the insertion point in the desired column and, in

FIGURE 5-5

Arrange text into

columns using the

Columns button

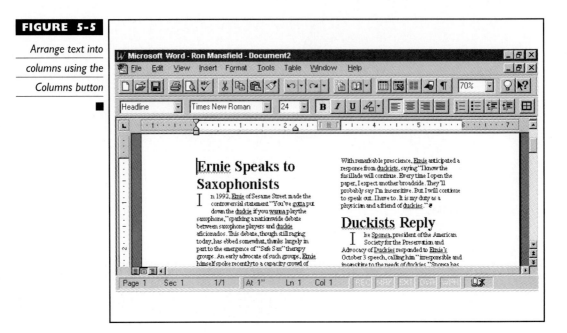

Page Layout view, display the rulers if they aren't already onscreen. Click on the Margin Marker button in the ruler to display the margin markers, then drag any marker, and the columns will adjust to their new width:

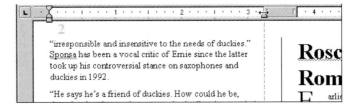

Decorative Lines Between Columns

To add decorative lines between columns, place the insertion point in a column that you want to decorate. Then choose Format | Columns to open the Columns dialog box and check the Line Between check box.

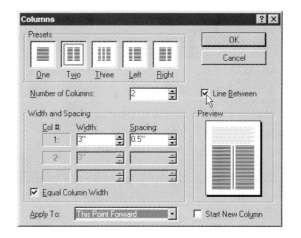

FIGURE 5-6

*Select text and
specify the desired
number of columns*

A single column

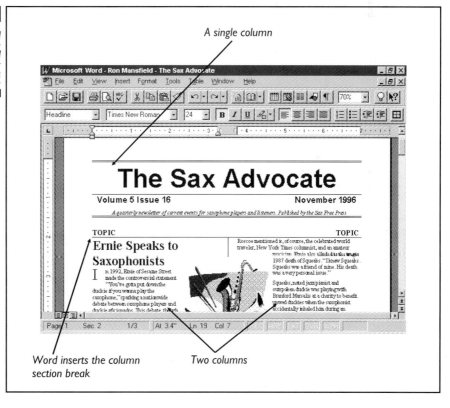

Word inserts the column
section break

Two columns

Forcing Column Breaks

Place the insertion point where you want the column break, then choose Insert | Break, specify Column, and click OK. To remove breaks, highlight them and press DEL.

To Even Out Uneven Columns

Place the insertion point after the last character in the text and choose Insert | Break. Choose Continuous in the Sections area. Then click OK and the column bottoms will align.

Removing Columns Throughout

Select all of the text, and then use the Standard toolbar's Columns button to specify a single column.

Removing One of Several Column Specifications

Place the insertion point in the unwanted column, and then use the Columns toolbar button on the Standard toolbar to redefine the number of columns.

Borders and Shading

You can apply various border treatments and shading to single paragraphs or groups of paragraphs. You can also put borders around graphics. Don't limit yourself to boxes. Use the Border feature to create lines as shown here.

Borders needn't be boxes. Use them to create lines like this one.
Lines above attract attention.
Make thick lines from thin, shaded paragraphs...
Lines below set things off
Consider leaving off left & right sides
Tables often look better with borders, too.

Creating Lines with the Border Command

Format | Borders and Shading can be used to create lines, as well as boxes. You adjust the horizontal *length* of borders or lines by adjusting a paragraph's width with indent markers or the Paragraph dialog box. It's also easy to control the distance between text and border lines. You can use borders to surround paragraphs, framed objects (like graphics), and tables.

tip   *You can have Word make borders for you automatically as you type. Just type three consecutive hyphens (-) or equal signs (=) and press ENTER. Word will convert what you've typed into a single or double line and figure the required spacing after to make it look good.*

The Border Toolbar

You can quickly add borders by using the Borders toolbar.

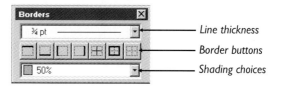

1. Place the insertion point in the paragraph of interest, or select elements to be formatted—multiple paragraphs, graphics, and so on.

2. Adjust indents if necessary to define the desired width for the borders.

3. Reveal the Borders toolbar by clicking the Borders button on the Formatting toolbar or by selecting View | Toolbars and checking the Borders check box.

4. With the Borders toolbar open, choose the desired line thickness from its drop-down list. You will see the changes in your document as you work.

5. Click on the button corresponding to the desired border (No Border, Outside, Inside, Right, Left, Bottom, or Top).

6. If you like, pick shading from the drop-down Shading list.

7. Admire your work.

You can mix line thicknesses and shading by reselecting different parts of the project and using different settings. Read on.

Custom Borders and Lines

For more complex border and shading projects, select Format | Borders and Shading, and use the Paragraph Borders and Shading dialog box.

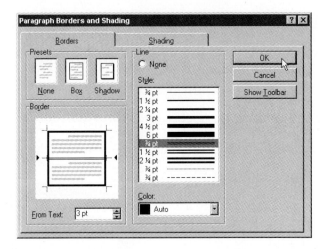

The border sample changes to represent the border you are creating. You specify lines (add and remove them) by clicking on border guides. They look like dotted *T*'s and *L*'s. Clicking on any of the three horizontal guides toggles horizontal lines on and off. Clicking on vertical guides toggles them on and off.

The *selection markers*, the little triangles that appear and disappear, show you which border lines will be affected when you click a border guide. Don't worry—this will begin to make sense when you experiment on your own.

If you've selected multiple paragraphs (or tables), you'll be able to place lines between the different paragraphs (or table rows) thanks to the center border guides. And, as you've seen in the examples, you can specify the line widths used for borders or even combine different line styles in the same project. Here are the general steps for custom borders:

1. Place the insertion point in the paragraph of interest, or select elements to be formatted—multiple paragraphs, graphics, and so on.

2. Select Format | Borders and Shading to open the Paragraph Borders and Shading dialog box.

3. Click on the appropriate border guides in the sample to turn them on or off.

4. Click on the line type or types you want. Watch your document change as you work.

Increasing the Space Between Borders and Text

To add extra space between the text contained within borders and the borders themselves, specify a measurement (in points) in the From Text portion of the Borders tab of the Paragraph Borders and Shading dialog box. You can do this when you are designing the border, or select an existing border and change the spacing later by visiting the Paragraph Borders and Shading dialog box.

Controlling Border Width

A paragraph's indents (and the document's margins) control the width of a border. To change the border, select the paragraph(s) containing the border formatting and change the indents.

Shading

You can add shading to paragraphs with or without borders. Use shading to create forms or just to add decoration. Be aware, however, that shading can look pretty raggedy on many printers. Test-print some samples before spending hours shading your favorite form or resume.

You can use either the Borders toolbar, or the Paragraph Borders and Shading dialog box to add and change shading. To add paragraph shading, pick a shading percentage from the drop-down Shading menus, or enter the first number of a percentage in the entry box. For example, to choose a 40% shading, type **4** in the shading list box and press ENTER. The smaller the percentage, the lighter the shading—100% is solid black.

For settings that begin with the same number (for example, 5 and 50), typing the number acts as a toggle. For example, typing **5** once selects 5; typing it a second time selects 50.

While you can remove borders and shading either with the Borders toolbar, or the Paragraph Borders and Shading dialog box, the toolbar's easier. Here are the general steps for using the Paragraph Borders and Shading dialog box:

WORD PROCESSING WITH WORD FOR WINDOWS

1. Place the insertion point in the paragraph of interest, or select elements to be shaded—multiple paragraphs, graphics, and so on.

2. Open the Paragraph Borders and Shading dialog box with the Format | Borders and Shading command.

3. Click on the Shading tab.

4. Scroll through the Shading list and select a percentage.

5. You will see the effects of your work in the Preview box.

6. Click OK.

7. Be sure to test print new designs.

Removing Borders and Shading

To remove borders and shading:

1. Select the objects with the borders or shading you want to remove.

2. Display the Borders toolbar (View | Toolbars).

3. Click on the No Border button (it's the rightmost button).

4. If shading has been applied, choose Clear from the Shading list, or type **c** in place of the displayed percentage and press ENTER.

Page Breaks

Page breaks are the places in your document where one page ends and a new page begins. Many things affect where page breaks will occur. Factors include the size of your paper, margin settings, paragraph formats, and section breaks. Word automatically computes and displays page breaks as you add and delete information. You can view page breaks in all views before printing. Breaks appear as dotted lines in Normal and Outline views. Since both Page Layout view and Print Preview simulate sheets of paper, page breaks are easy to see in those views, as well.

You can force your own page breaks—for instance, to start new chapters on a new page. Generally speaking, only force page breaks after you have done all of your other formatting.

Forcing Page Breaks

To force a page break, you insert manual page breaks. In Normal and Outline views, these look thicker than Word's automatic page breaks and contain the words "Page Break."

To insert a manual page break, place the insertion point where you want the break, and then press CTRL+ENTER. Alternatively, select Insert | Break to open the Break dialog box, make sure the Page Break button is selected (the default), and then click OK. You'll see a thick manual page break line on your screen. Text or graphics below the manual page break will appear on the next page of your document.

Moving and Deleting Page Breaks

You can delete manual breaks as you would delete text. (You cannot delete automatic breaks placed by Word.) Select a manual break line and press DEL. Alternatively, use Edit | Replace to search for manual breaks and replace them with nothing.

Repagination

To display and print page breaks properly, Word must recalculate page endings after you've made changes. This is done automatically in the background whenever Word can steal some otherwise unused computer time. This process is called *automatic repagination*. Since page endings affect certain other features, Word always repaginates when

- You ask it to print.
- You are in Print Preview or Page Layout view.
- You compile a Table of Contents or Index.

To turn off automatic repagination (and speed up Word on slower computers or when working on large documents), follow these steps:

1. Choose Tools | Options.

2. Click on the General tab if it's not already in view.

3. Clear the check from the Background Repagination check box. (You won't be able to do this if you are in Page Layout view.)

4. Click OK to close the Options dialog box.

5. Word will repaginate only when you are in a view that requires it. To force repagination, switch to Page Layout, Print Preview, or issue a Print request.

Sections

Word's section features can help you organize large projects this way, of course, but they do much more. Word sections are designed to let you change major formatting features at places you decide in your document.

Sections need not be used only for books or reports. It's a shame sections aren't called "zones" or something less ambiguous.

You must start a new section whenever you need to

■ Change page orientation within a document

■ Change margins in part of a document

■ Turn line numbering on or off

■ Change footnote appearance or suppress notes

■ Change the appearance of headers and footers

■ Change the format, position, or progression of page numbers

While the exact sequence of events will vary with your project and needs, in general you will

1. Place the insertion point where you want a new section to begin.

2. Select Insert | Break to create the new section.

3. Make the desired formatting and other changes for that section.

4. Perhaps create other sections farther down in the document.

You'll see practical applications of sections in a moment. There are no hard-and-fast rules about *when* to create new sections. Experienced Word users often create 10 or 20 sections in a short document. Others use a single section for an entire 100-page report.

Occasionally, Word will insert section breaks for you—when creating an automatic table of contents, for instance. Mostly, you'll insert them yourself.

Inserting Section Breaks

To insert a section break, follow these steps:

1. Place the insertion point where you want the break.

2. Choose Insert | Break. Choose one of the types of Section Breaks in the Break dialog box, and click OK.

This places a double-dotted, nonprinting line containing the words "End of Section" at the insertion point on your screen. The status area reflects section numbers as you move the insertion point or scroll to pages in the new section.

Sections as Chapter Elements

It is very common to create a new section for each chapter in a large publishing project, such as a manuscript or report. This makes it possible to change header and footer information like chapter names. If you were creating an employee handbook, Chapter 1's header might contain the words "Welcome, new employees," while the headers in Chapter 2 might say "Your health plan explained," and so forth.

Sections also make it possible to customize page numbers within chapters. Your document's front matter might be numbered in lowercase Roman numerals (i, ii, iii, and so on). Page numbers within chapters might contain chapter-related numbers that restart at the beginning of each chapter (1-1, 2-1, and so on). As you'll recall, you can use different page-numbering styles in each section of your document, and you can restart page numbering at the beginning of any new section.

Setting Sections with the Layout Tab in Page Setup

You can set sections using the Layout tab of the Page Setup dialog box.

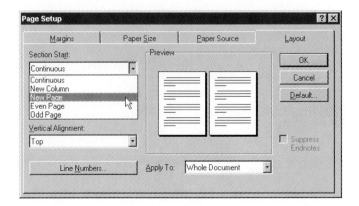

To reach the Layout tab, double-click on the section break at the end of the section you want to change; or place the insertion point in the section and choose File | Page Setup, and then click on the Layout tab.

Many of the choices in the Layout tab are covered elsewhere in this book, but the Section Start drop-down menu of the dialog box contains a number of section-specific items worth exploring.

The options listed in the Section Start drop-down menu are the same as those in the Break dialog box (reached by choosing Insert | Break).

This is how you tell Word where you want it to start printing the various sections of your document. You can make a different choice for each section. Here's what the options do:

Option	Action
Continuous (the default setting)	Text from preceding sections occupies same page as designated section, if there is enough room for text from both sections
New Column	In multicolumn formats, Word breaks column when it encounters section mark, prints subsequent text at top of new column
New Page	Starts new sections on new pages
Even Page	Starts printing new section on even-numbered page, even if it means leaving odd-numbered page blank
Odd Page	Starts new section on odd-numbered page; use to ensure new sections start on right-hand pages when designing documents for two-sided printing

The Apply To portion of the Layout tab lets you tell Word how far to go with your requested changes:

Option	Action
This Section	Changes affect only section containing insertion point
This Point Forward	Changes affect document from insertion point to end
Whole Document	Changes affect whole document

Copying Section Breaks

Section-formatting information is stored with section breaks much the same way paragraph formatting is stored with paragraph marks, and you can copy section information by copying and pasting section breaks. You can even place section breaks as AutoText items. (AutoText is explained in Chapter 10.)

Section breaks differ from paragraph marks (¶) in that a section break controls the information *after* it, while a paragraph mark controls the information that precedes it.

Click on a break to select it. An insertion point will straddle the break line. You may find it easiest to do this in Normal view. Once the break is selected, you can then copy, cut, and so forth.

Deleting Section Breaks

Select a section break as just described. Then press BACKSPACE or DEL. Text after the removed section break will take on the characteristics of the preceding material. It may take a moment for Word to reformat and repaginate the document. Watch the status line and be patient.

Changing Page Orientation with Breaks

Section breaks make it possible for you to mix portrait and landscape page orientations in the same document. For instance, you could have a three-page memo with pages 1 and 3 in portrait mode (for example, the text) and the middle page in landscape mode (for example, a wide spreadsheet).

Word flips headers, footers, page numbers, and other marginalia for you unless you override this. Therefore, if you've placed page numbers at the bottom of your pages, the landscape page(s) will have numbers at the right edge of the paper so that they read like the rest of the (flipped) text on the page(s). Here are the general steps:

1. Position the insertion point where you want the break.

2. Choose Insert | Break.

3. Choose the Next Page Option.

4. Click OK.

5. Move the insertion point to where you want the orientation to change again (if you do)—the beginning of page 3 in our example.

WORD PROCESSING WITH WORD FOR WINDOWS

6. Insert another section break there.

7. Position the insertion point in the new section you've created.

8. Visit the Layout tab in Page Setup (double-click in an unmarked part of the ruler or choose File | Page Setup).

9. Make other page layout choices in the other Page Setup tabs.

10. Preview and then print your work.

Styles and the Style Gallery

Styles are collections of paragraph and character formatting decisions that you or others make and save using meaningful names. Styles make it easy for you to reuse complex paragraph formats without laboriously re-creating them each time. Built-in styles are available in all Word documents, and each document can have its own collection of custom styles.

Applying Styles from the Formatting Toolbar

Since Word comes with built-in styles, you can easily apply them to one or more paragraphs. Here are the general steps:

1. Either place the insertion point in a paragraph or select several paragraphs.

2. Scroll through the drop-down Style list on the Formatting toolbar to pick the desired style. The available items in the list will vary from document to document for reasons you'll soon understand.

3. Click on a style name to apply it to the selected text. Your text will be reformatted using the selected style.

4. Use Edit | Undo if you don't like the results.

When the drop-down list is long, type the first letter of the style's name. The list will scroll to the proximity of your desired style.

Applying Styles from the Keyboard

A few of the commonly used styles have their own keyboard shortcuts. To use them, select text or place the insertion point in the paragraph to be stylized and use one of the following key combinations:

Style	Press
Normal	CTRL+SHIFT+N
Heading 1	ALT+CTRL+1
Heading 2	ALT+CTRL+2
Heading 3	ALT+CTRL+3
List Bullet	CTRL+SHIFT+L
Style Shown in Toolbar	CTRL+SHIFT+S

The Edit | Repeat keyboard shortcut (CTRL+Y) works when applying styles. After you apply a style once, you can move the insertion point to other paragraphs and press CTRL+Y to apply the new style where needed.

You can no longer type the first few characters of a style name to apply it as you could in earlier Word versions.

Defining Your Own Styles from the Formatting Toolbar

You can define your own styles, and many experienced users do that. But before spending hours reinventing the wheel, check out the styles already provided by Word. When you have satisfied yourself that you need something that doesn't exist, try the following steps:

1. Display the Formatting toolbar if it is not already in view.

2. Place the insertion point in the formatted paragraph whose style you'd like to capture. Make any last-minute changes in style.

Click *once* on the Style box (the name portion of the drop-down Style list). The Style box will be highlighted, indicating that you can type a new style name.

Type a meaningful style name and press ENTER. Word will save the style information and add the new name to the drop-down Style list for the current document.

Choosing Suitable Style Names

Style names can be up to 253 characters long, but shorter is often better. Names can contain any legal characters except backslashes (\), braces ({}), or semicolons (;). Word cares about capitalization in style names. For example, "Figure" and "figure" are two different names. Try to be consistent when naming similar styles in different documents.

The Style Dialog Box

The Style dialog box (Format | Style) shown in Figure 5-7 lets you define new styles and rename, explore, list, or delete existing ones.

To define a style via the Style dialog box, follow these steps:

1. Place the insertion point in or select a paragraph containing the desired format.

2. Open the Style dialog box.

3. Click on the New button.

4. Type a legal style name in the box provided.

5. Click on OK to record the style.

FIGURE 5-7

Define and explore styles using the Style dialog box

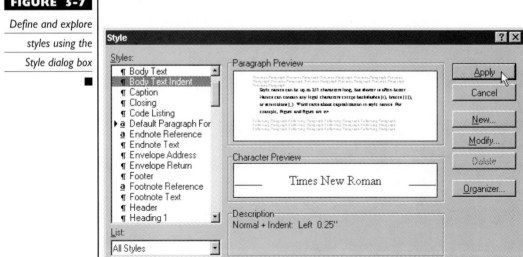

Defining Keyboard Shortcuts for Styles

Word lets you assign keyboard shortcuts from the Modify Style dialog box (reached with the Modify button in the Style dialog box). You can also use the Keyboard tab of the Customize dialog box (reached with Tools | Customize).

Basing One Style on Another

Word lets you build on styles, or base one on another. Word watches as you develop new styles and bases new styles on the styles you modify. Unless you are careful, you can create quite a chain reaction this way. Experienced users try to create one or two base styles and tie most of the rest of their styles to those base styles, rather than basing each new style on the previous style. To base styles, follow these steps:

1. Choose Format | Style to open the Style dialog box.

2. Select the style you plan to base on another.

3. Click the Modify button to open the Modify Style dialog box.

4. Choose a base style from the Based On list.

5. Make any other necessary changes in the Modify Style dialog box.

6. Click OK when you've finished.

To add a style you've created to your document's template, enable the Add to Template option in the Modify Style dialog box.

Next Style

Frequently, you can predict the order in which styles will be used. When you type letters, for instance, you know that the To style will always be used after the From style. In reports and manuals, headings are usually followed immediately by body text, and so on.

The Modify Style dialog box lets you specify which style Word will flip to when you finish typing a paragraph and press ENTER. Often, you want a paragraph to be in the same style as its predecessor (this is the default setting) when creating styles. But you can specify different next styles:

1. Choose Format | Style.

2. Select the style you plan to modify.

3. Click the Modify button.

4. When you see the Modify Style dialog box, choose a "next" style from the Style for Following Paragraph list.

5. Make any other necessary changes in the Modify Style dialog box.

6. Click OK when you have finished.

Finding Out Which Styles Have Been Used

The obvious way to sniff out styles is to place the insertion point in the text of interest and look at the Formatting toolbar indicators (the Style list, the depressed buttons, and so on). But there are several easier ways to see which styles and character formatting have been applied. The first is to print a style list.

Printing a Style List

It is often useful to have a printed list of styles and their descriptions. This can help you keep things consistent in a large organization, and it can help you troubleshoot formatting problems in complex documents. To print style information:

1. Open the document of interest.

2. Choose File | Print (or press CTRL+P).

3. Choose Styles from the pop-up Print What list (see Figure 5-8).

4. Click OK.

The Style Gallery

This new feature lets you explore the seemingly endless collection of styles provided with Word's templates. Earlier in this chapter you saw one use of the Style Gallery (previewing the effect of a template's styles on your document).

By clicking the Style Samples button in the Style Gallery, you can see examples of all of the styles for a document or template. Clicking Examples shows you how documents will look based on those styles. Check out how cool the Elegant Report looks in Figure 5-9.

If you are currently working on a project, you can also see how the project would look if you applied styles from various templates. If you like what you see, you can even have Word automatically apply the styles to your

FIGURE 5-8

Print styles and

their descriptions

from the Print

What list box

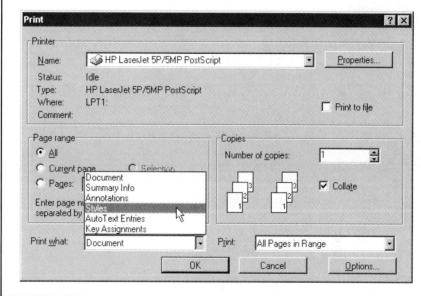

current project. You do not need to have a project in the works to visit the Gallery; but if you think you might want to reformat something, open it first and make it the active Word project before you begin. Here are the general steps:

1. Open a Word project you think you might want to reformat.

2. Open the Gallery with the Format | Style Gallery command.

3. Click the Style Samples button.

4. Pick a style from the Template list.

5. Wait a moment while Word displays the samples.

6. Choose different template names if you want to see samples of other style collections.

7. Click the Document button if you want to see the styles automatically applied to the current document you have open (your current project).

8. Click OK to close the gallery *and apply the new styles,* or Cancel to close the gallery without changing your document.

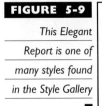

FIGURE 5-9

This Elegant Report is one of many styles found in the Style Gallery ■

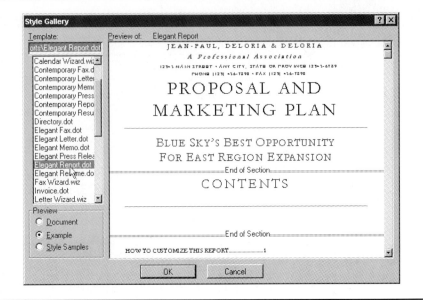

Displaying Style Names Onscreen

To keep track of which styles a document uses, you can display style information at the left edge of the screen in the *style area*:

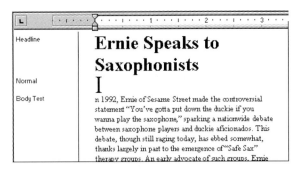

1. Switch to Normal or Outline view.

2. Choose Tools | Options and select the View tab.

3. Pick a style area width (1", perhaps) from the Style Area width section of the View tab, and then click OK. Style names will appear at the left of the screen.

4. To remove them, repeat steps 1 through 3, but choose 0 (zero) for the Style Area Width.

When and Where Styles Are Saved

Styles are saved with your document, and they are saved only when you save the document. This is yet another good reason to get in the habit of saving early and often. If your computer crashes after you've spent several hours setting up a complex collection of new styles, or if you accidentally click No in response to the "Do you want to save changes?" message box when you close a document, you will not be happy.

Word's Standard Styles

Word's designers have created hundreds of standard styles that are used by its footnote, outline, index, table of contents, page numbering, header, and footer features.

Many of the templates for letters, brochures, newsletters, and other documents have predefined styles. Open a few documents based on these templates and explore their styles. As a starter, try this:

1. Choose File | New.

2. Click the tab called Reports and choose Contemporary Report. Take a few moments to look it over. Could you use this template as is? How might you modify it to make it more useful?

Styles That Word Applies Automatically

Word applies certain styles automatically, as listed here.

Style	When Word Applies the Style
Annotation Text	Comments inserted by Annotation command
Annotation Reference	Initials of person who inserted comment
Caption	Captions and table and figure titles
Footer	In footers
Footnote Text	Text in footnote or endnote
Endnote Text	Endnotes
Footnote Reference	Numbers and characters used as reference marks
Endnote Reference	Reference marks
Header	Header info
Index I–Index 9	Index entries created with Index and Tables
Line Number	Automatic line numbers
Macro Text	Text of WordBasic macro
Page Number	Automatic page numbers
TOC I–TOC 9	Table of Contents, TOC entries
Table of Figures	Automatic figure numbering

WORD PROCESSING WITH WORD FOR WINDOWS

Reapply/Redefine Styles

If you ask Word to apply a style to a paragraph that already uses that style (applying Normal to an already Normal paragraph, for instance), you will be visited by this strange and powerful dialog box:

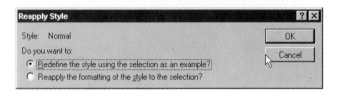

To Restore Styles

This box serves two purposes. First it lets you reapply a style to a paragraph that you have inadvertently messed up. Suppose you accidentally dragged the first line indent marker in a Body paragraph, and the paragraph no longer looks like the others. By choosing the Body style again from the Formatting toolbar, you will get a chance to reapply your Body style and repair the errant paragraph. Follow these steps to restore a style.

1. Select the paragraph, paragraphs, or characters you want to restore.

2. Chose the desired style from the Formatting toolbar's list.

3. If asked to reapply or redefine, pick Reapply.

4. Click OK.

To Redefine a Style

The second use of this dialog box is to let you quickly redefine a style. Suppose you hate the first line indent you've used for body text. Change the indent in any one Body style paragraph, and then pick Body from the Style list. Click on the Redefine button and click OK. Word will redefine the Body style using the new indent from your sample paragraph. All of your Body paragraphs will be changed. To redefine a style, follow these steps.

1. Select any paragraph or character formatted with the style to be changed.

2. Make the desired appearance changes (indents, underlining, and so on).

3. From the Formatting toolbar's list, choose the style *originally* used for the formatting.

4. When you see the Redefine/Reapply choice, choose Redefine.

5. Click OK.

Strange things sometimes happen when you redefine or reapply styles to manually embellished paragraphs, however. While the interaction of manually applied formatting and styles may seem almost random at times, it is not.

Deleting Styles

You cannot delete Word's built-in styles (Headings and Normal, for instance), but you can remove custom ones you've created and many of the fonts provided with Word's templates. To delete unwanted styles, select them in the Style dialog box and click the Delete button.

You will be asked to confirm; press OK. All paragraphs formatted with a deleted style will revert to the document's Normal style. Follow these steps.

1. Open the Style dialog box with Format | Style.

2. Click on the style you want to delete in the Styles list (scroll, if necessary).

3. Click Delete.

4. Click OK to confirm the deletion.

5. The style will be deleted from the current document.

warning   *Undo does not restore deleted styles. Thus, you cannot undo (reestablish) a deleted style, but you can sometimes work around this. Save the document just before you attempt any style deletion. Inspect the document immediately after deleting styles. Do not save the document again until you are certain that the deletion of styles hasn't caused problems. If there are problems, close the document without saving (by answering No to the "Save Changes?" prompt). Reopen the document and your styles should all be intact. Better yet, experiment on a copy of your document.*

Renaming Styles

You can rename styles in the Style dialog box:

1. Open the Style dialog box with the Format | Style command.

2. Click on the style you want to rename in the Styles list (scroll, if necessary).

3. Click the Modify button.

4. You will see the Modify Style dialog box.

5. Edit the name in the Name box.

6. Make any other desired changes while in the Modify Style dialog box.

7. Click OK.

If you change a style's name to one that already exists in the document, the style that you have renamed will take on the characteristics of the preexisting style. For instance, if you have a double-spaced style called "Draft" and you change the name of a single-spaced style from Body to Draft, all of the paragraphs formatted as Body will be double-spaced and take on any other style characteristics associated with the original Draft style.

Remember—Word cares about capitalization when you name styles. The names "Salutation" and "salutation" are not the same.

Finding and Replacing Styles

Style-change junkies rejoice. You can search for and replace styles:

1. Open the Replace dialog box (Edit | Replace or CTRL+H).

2. Place the insertion point in the Find What box.

3. Choose Style from the drop-down Format menu. You will be presented with a list of possible styles in the Find Style dialog box.

4. Pick the style you want to replace (Heading 2, for instance) and click OK. The name of the style will appear in the format portion of the Find What area.

5. Move the insertion point to the Replace With portion of the dialog box.

6. Choose Style from the drop-down Format menu again.

7. Choose the new style from the resulting Replace Style dialog box list (Heading 1, for example).

8. Click OK.

9. Tell Word if you want to search the whole document (All), up from the insertion point, or down from the insertion point.

10. Click Find Next and Replace, or Replace All, as appropriate. For instance, to replace all Heading 2 style occurrences with Heading 1 styles, you'd pick Search All and Replace All.

Transferring Styles to Other Documents

After you've spent time setting up complex styles, it would be nice to reuse them in new projects. Word provides several ways to do this. For repetitive tasks, consider setting up Template documents containing styles. If you have just a style or two you want to copy from one document (the source) to another (the destination), follow these steps:

1. Select some text from the source document containing the style of interest and paste it into the destination document needing the style.

2. Word will bring over the style with the text.

warning   *Remember that if the destination document has a style name identical to the style being copied from the source, the destination document will reformat the incoming text rather than take on the new style. Moreover, if you copy more than 50 styles at once, the source document's entire style sheet will be automatically copied to the destination document.*

You can also merge different style sheets, which copies unique styles from one document to another and modifies styles with identical names. Think of the document containing styles you want to copy as the *source* document and the document receiving the new styles as the *destination* document. Here's how to merge style sheets:

1. With styles properly named and saved, work in the destination document.

2. Open the Style dialog box with the Format | Style command.

3. Click on the Organizer button to open the Organizer dialog box.

4. Pick the Styles tab if it is not already foremost.

5. The name of the source file should appear in the In list at the left side of the dialog box, and probably the file Normal.dot will be specified as the destination or To file on the right of the dialog box. This is telling you that Word wants to copy new styles to the Normal.dot template so they will be available in each new document that you open.

6. If you want to make the style or styles you are copying globally available, leave the To setting as Normal.dot. If you want to add the style(s) to just a selected document or template, click the *right* Close File button (note that there are two). It will change to an Open File button. Choose the desired destination file using standard Windows file-opening techniques.

7. When the source and destination files have been properly identified, pick the styles you want to copy in the left scrolling list. Click to choose a single style, press SHIFT+click to select ranges, or hold down CTRL while you selectively click on noncontiguous styles.

8. With the desired styles selected, click Copy.

9. Use the Delete or Rename buttons as necessary.

10. Open other source or destination files as necessary, and then click Close when you've finished.

CHAPTER 6

Working with Headers, Footers, and Footnotes

S

OMETIMES it's helpful to print data—such as headers, footers, and footnotes—in the margins of your text. Word makes it easy for you to add these features to your documents and edit them. Read on to learn more about Word's Header, Footer, and Footnote features and how to use them.

What Are Headers and Footers?

Headers and *footers* are places to put repetitive information in a document's top and bottom margins—headers print at the top, footers at the bottom. You can use headers and footers to print something simple on each page (such as your name) or something complex (such as a graphic). Stylized text, dates, and automatic page numbering can all be included in headers and footers.

You can use identical headers and footers on all pages in your document, or you can specify different contents for each section of the document. Odd and even pages can have different designs if you wish. The first page of each document or each section can be unique.

In Word, header and footer editing always takes place in Page Layout view. You work right in the header and footer area of your document after double-clicking to undim it. You can apply virtually any paragraph or character style to your headers and footers using the Formatting toolbar and rulers. They will repeat on all pages thereafter.

Once headers and footers have been added to a document, it is possible to see and edit them in Page Layout view. They are also displayed in Print Preview; but when you attempt to open a header or footer in Normal view or Print Preview, Word switches you to Page Layout view and displays the Header and Footer toolbar.

Creating Basic Headers and Footers

To enter a header that repeats on all pages in your document:

1. Choose View | Header And Footer or double-click in the header area of the first page to be modified in Page Layout view or Print Preview.

2. Word will switch to Page Layout view if it is not already there and display the Header and Footer toolbar, shown in Figure 6-1.

3. Create and edit header text as you would any other. You can paste graphics, apply styles, and otherwise format your work normally.

4. Use the automatic page-number, time-stamping, and date-stamping features described later in this chapter.

5. Double-click in the main document to return to work there.

WORD PROCESSING WITH WORD FOR WINDOWS

FIGURE 6-1

Edit headers and footers in Page Layout view

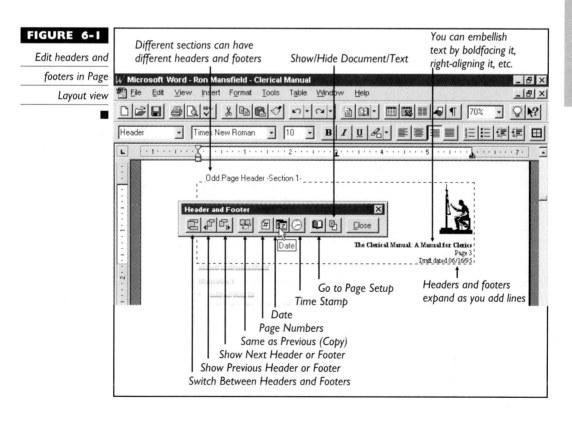

Different sections can have different headers and footers

Show/Hide Document/Text

You can embellish text by boldfacing it, right-aligning it, etc.

Go to Page Setup
Time Stamp
Date
Page Numbers
Same as Previous (Copy)
Show Next Header or Footer
Show Previous Header or Footer
Switch Between Headers and Footers

Headers and footers expand as you add lines

You enter footers the same way as headers, except that you work in a Footer window:

1. Choose View | Header And Footer or double-click in the footer area of the first page to be modified in Page Layout view or Print Preview. Word will switch to Page Layout view if it is not already there and display the Header and Footer toolbar.

2. If you chose View | Header And Footer in step 1, Word will show you the header first. Click the Switch Between Header And Footer button to view the footer.

3. Create and edit footer text as you would any other. You can paste graphics, apply styles, and otherwise format your work normally.

4. Use the automatic page-number, time-stamping, and date-stamping features described later in this chapter.

5. Double-click in the main document to continue working there.

note *You can use your regular document ruler or Formatting toolbar when working in header and footer windows. Margins, indents, tabs, and all the other tools work as you'd expect.*

Creating Different Headers and Footers for Odd and Even Pages

To create different even- and odd-page headers or footers:

1. Place the insertion point in the section where you want the odd/even effect to begin.

2. Open the Page Setup dialog box (double-click in a blank part of a ruler or choose File | Page Setup) and click the Layout tab.

3. Check the Different Odd And Even choice in the Headers And Footers area, and then click OK.

Creating Different Headers and Footers for the First Page

Word lets you create unique headers and footers for the first page of your document:

1. Place the insertion point in the section where you want the different first page.

2. Open the Page Setup dialog box (double-click in a blank part of a ruler or choose File | Page Setup) and choose the Layout tab.

3. Check the Different First Page choice in the Headers And Footers area. You'll have different header and footer areas on first pages. Their names will be visible in Page Layout view.

4. Create different headers and footers for the first page in Page Layout view.

Putting Page Numbers in Headers and Footers

Word offers a variety of tools to help you automatically number pages. You can choose from many page-numbering format and style choices and position page numbers nearly anywhere you want. Let's explore these features and discuss the effects of document sections and pagination on page numbering.

tip *If you plan to break a document into multiple sections, you may want to insert page numbers first. Otherwise, you will have to repeat the page-numbering process for each section of your document.*

Word provides two page-numbering techniques. Both have advantages and disadvantages. Normally, you will use only one for a particular document—otherwise, you might end up with two or more sets of page numbers!

Using the Header or Footer Toolbar to Add Page Numbers

To add page numbers by use of the header or footer toolbar:

1. Open a header or footer by double-clicking on it in Page Layout view.

2. Click on the page-numbering button in the Header And Footer toolbar. Word will insert a number in your header or footer at the insertion point.

3. Like anything else placed in headers and footers, page numbers can be stylized, repositioned, surrounded with borders, accompanied by text, and otherwise embellished.

Word uses the standard header or footer style to format page numbers placed there. You can override this by applying additional character and paragraph formats or by changing the standard header or footer style (see Chapter 5 to learn about styles).

Headers and footers have tab stops, which you may find useful for positioning page numbers.

Using the Page Numbers Command

Word's Insert | Page Numbers command provides a wider variety of numbering options than the header/footer toolbar offers. It reveals the Page Numbers dialog box and lets you quickly reach the Page Number Format dialog box.

1. Place the insertion point in the section you want to number.

2. Display the Page Numbers dialog box (shown here with the Page Number Format dialog box) by choosing Insert | Page Numbers.

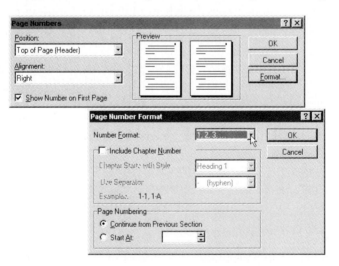

3. Word suggests placing page numbers in the lower-right corner of your document ($\frac{1}{2}$ inch from the bottom and right edges of the paper), but you can specify different positions with the Position and Alignment drop-down menus. Watch the Preview area as you work.

4. Choose whether you want a page number on the first page by clicking to add or remove the corresponding check mark.

5. Either click OK or click on the Format button to review other page-numbering options.

Using Page Numbering Formats and Styles

Word supports four page-number formats, all of which are available regardless of which page-numbering technique you use:

- Standard Arabic numbers (1, 2, 3...)—the default
- Capital Roman numerals (I, II, III...)
- Capital letters (A, B, C...)
- Lowercase formats (i, ii, iii... and a, b, c...)

To specify number formats:

1. Choose Insert | Page Numbers.
2. Click the Format button in the Page Numbers dialog box, shown earlier.
3. In the Page Number Format dialog box, choose the format you want from the drop-down list and choose OK.
4. After inserting page numbers, switch to Page Layout view and change their appearance.

You can use Word's many character and paragraph embellishment features to spruce up page numbers. Choose another font, make numbers bold, align them, or put boxes around them. You can have text appear next to the numbers (*Page-1,* for instance).

Documents containing multiple sections can have different formats in each section. That's both good and bad news. If you want all sections to have the same format, you will want to pick a format *before* you break up the document. Otherwise you must place the insertion point in each section and pick the same format for every one. Plan ahead.

Adding Chapter Numbers to Page Numbers

If you use Word's standard heading styles, and if you use one of the headings for chapter titles, you can have Word include chapter headings with your page number (*2-36,* for instance). You can specify one of five separators—hyphens, periods, colons, en dashes, or em dashes.

You set up chapter page numbering in the Page Number Format dialog box, in the Use Separator box.

Specifying the Starting Page Number

Word lets you specify the starting page number in four ways:

- You can suppress the first page number (for example, on multipage letters) but then have 2 on the second page, 3 on the third, and so forth. To do so, uncheck the Show Number On First Page check box in the Page Numbers dialog box.

- You can restart each new section in a multisection document with 1. To do so, place the insertion point in any section, check the Start At box in the Page Number Format dialog box, specify the number each section will start with, and then click OK.

- You can print your first page without a number (a cover page, for instance) and then have the second page begin from 1. To do so, uncheck the Show Number On First Page check box in the Page Numbers dialog box, and then enter 0 in the Start At box in the Page Number Format dialog box.

- You can start page numbering with a number other than 1, like 25 or 100. This is helpful when you are combining your work with other documents. To do so, enter the starting number in the Start At box in the Page Number Format dialog box.

Removing Page Numbers

To remove page numbers, simply open the header or footer containing unwanted page numbers and delete one. The rest of the page numbers in the section will disappear.

To delete all the page numbers in a multisection document, follow these steps:

1. Open a header or footer containing page numbers.

2. Choose Edit | Select All or use the CTRL+A shortcut.

3. Delete a page number. The rest will disappear.

Date and Time Entries

To insert the current date or time:

1. Position the insertion point.

2. Choose Date And Time from the Insert menu.

3. Pick the appropriate format from the scrolling list.

4. Click OK.

If the Insert As Field box is checked, Word will update the date and time entry whenever you print the document. The Header and Footer pane also contains buttons for inserting times and dates.

Creating Footnotes and Endnotes

Word lets you create *footnotes* or *endnotes* (notes appearing at the end of your document) and personalize their appearance. For footnotes, follow these steps:

1. Place the insertion point where the footnote marker is needed (after the words *without raising taxes* in our example).

2. Choose Insert | Footnote.

3. You can dismiss the Footnote And Endnote dialog box by clicking OK, since Word's defaults are fine for this project.

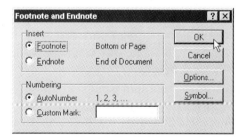

4. In Normal view, a second window pane, where you do the footnote typing, opens.

In Page Layout view, you type right where the footnote will print—usually between the text and footer.

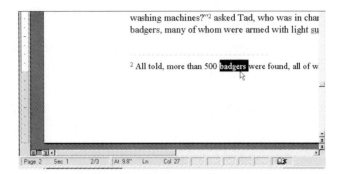

5. In either case, the insertion point automatically moves to the proper place for you to type the footnote. Type it.

6. To return to the main document, move the insertion point with the mouse or press CTRL+ALT+Z.

Viewing Footnotes

Footnotes are always displayed in Page Layout view and Print Preview. If they are not visible in Normal or Outline view, choose View | Footnotes to open a footnote window.

If you are constantly entering or referring to footnotes in Normal view, you can leave the footnote window visible while you work. Scrolling in your document will cause corresponding scrolling in the footnote window. Use the footnote scroll bars if necessary to view notes. You can resize the footnote window to suit your taste and screen size by dragging the bar separating the two windows the same way you resize other Word split screens (point to the split box and drag).

To hide the footnote window, choose View | Footnotes again or click the Close button.

Double-clicking on a footnote marker in your document will display the footnote pane and place the insertion point at the beginning of the footnote. If necessary, Word will open the footnote pane and scroll to the appropriate note. Also, moving the insertion point in the footnote pane will cause the main document to scroll to the reference.

note *Whenever you insert or delete footnotes, Word renumbers the others accordingly.*

Working with Entire Footnotes

You can copy, move, or delete entire footnotes as easily as you would a single character.

1. Select the footnote marker of interest in the document text.

2. Cut, copy, paste, or drag-and-drop the footnote mark.

3. Word does the rest. If you have Numbering turned on, Word will update the numbers in your text and in the corresponding footnotes. If you copy and paste a mark, a corresponding new footnote will magically appear in the right spot in your footnotes. Deletion works as you would expect.

Editing Footnote Text

Visit the footnote pane in Normal view, or the footnote itself in Page Layout view. Cut, paste, and drag-and-drop away to your heart's content. (Note that you cannot cut a footnote's entire text; you must cut the footnote mark in text if you wish to delete or move it.)

Personalizing Footnotes

You can personalize footnotes by using Insert | Footnote and the Note Options dialog box:

1. Choose Insert | Footnote.

2. Click the Symbol button to bring up the Symbol dialog box. Click on the desired symbol to change the footnote symbol character.

3. Click on Options to bring up the Note Options dialog box.

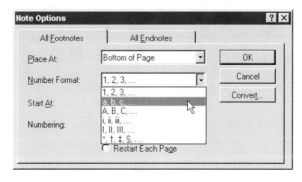

4. Click to switch to the All Footnotes tab, if necessary.

5. Specify note placement, number formats, starting numbers, and starting points.

6. Click OK.

For more ways to personalize footnotes, check the online Help.

CHAPTER 7

Tabs, Tables, and Sorting

M

ICROSOFT Office provides many ways to create and format *tabular information* (lists of items in columns). Although you can use Word as a typewriter and press TAB as needed to create columns, you can take a giant step up from that basic approach by using Word's Table features. However, note that Excel is also a possible option for such tasks. See Part Eight for details of how to use Excel tables in Word.

Tabs

Tabs are great for creating quick, relatively simple lists—and tabs do some things in Word you can't do on a typewriter. For instance, they can help you exchange Word data with spreadsheets, databases, and other programs. Each paragraph in a Word document can have the same or different tab settings. Word offers five specialized types of *tab stops:*

Left	Like the plain-vanilla ones you find on your old typewriter. Text typed at these tab stops bumps up against the left edge of the stop.
Center	Centers your text around the tab stop.
Right	Positions whatever you type to the left of the tab stop. This is a great way to type long lists of numbers and have them line up.
Decimal	Aligns columns of numbers on the decimal point—perfect for simple financial reports.
Bar	Creates nice, thin vertical lines that separate columns. These aren't actual tab stops—that is, you cannot use them to align text—but they can be placed and moved like stops. You can only specify bar tabs from the Tabs dialog box.

Each type of tab helps you align text, and they are particularly useful for making simple columnar lists. Figure 7-1 illustrates the types of tabs.

FIGURE 7-1

Tab stop buttons and the tab stops they create

■

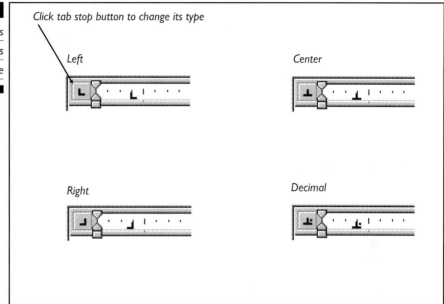

Click tab stop button to change its type

Left

Center

Right

Decimal

With Show ¶ turned on, you'll see fat arrows indicating each tab character you type:

```
Animas       →   12675·Colony·Street  →  Chino     →  CA→91710→800-800-5885¶
Apple·Credit →   440·Willow·Road      →  Pleasanton→ CA→94566→800-367-1334¶
Ashton-Tate  →   20101·Hamilton·Ave   →  Torrance  →  CA→90502→800-437-4329¶
```

Setting Custom Tab Stops

In the United States, at least, Word starts each new document by default with tab stops set at intervals. You can create custom tabs to replace these.

Tab stop information is always stored with the paragraph mark for each paragraph, thus all of the rules about paragraph markers apply. If, for example, you set tab stops once and press ENTER at the end of each typed line, each new paragraph (line) will use the same tab stops as the preceding one, until you tell Word otherwise.

Setting Tab Stops with the Ruler

You can set custom tabs as you type, or you can use the standard tabs initially and then go back to fine-tune. Here are the general steps:

1. With the ruler in view, click the button at the left edge of the horizontal ruler repeatedly until it shows the icon for the desired tab stop type (Left, Right, Decimal, or Center).

2. Click on the ruler where you want to place a tab stop. If you make a mistake, drag the stop off the ruler and try again.

3. When you type, press TAB to move the insertion point to the new tab positions.

Moving Tab Stops on the Ruler

To move tab stops before you've entered text, simply point to the stop you need and drag to the right or left.

note *If you have already entered text that uses the tab stops you want to move, first select all of that text before moving the tab stop.*

Setting Tab Stops with the Tabs Dialog Box

Although using the ruler is easy, you may want to use the Tabs dialog box (shown next) for some projects. It provides ways to set tab stops precisely and it offers some additional tab-related options. To reach the Tabs dialog box, choose Format | Tabs or click the Tabs button in the Paragraph dialog box.

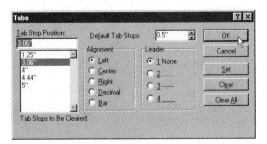

Remember to select all the intended text and paragraph markers before you move tab stops. Undo (CTRL+Z) will save you when you forget.

Units of Measure in the Tabs Dialog Box

Measurements in the Tabs dialog box are assumed to be in inches unless you type another legal abbreviation (**cm** for centimeter, **pt** for point, or **pi** for pica). As an example, **5 cm** would position a tab stop 5 centimeters from the left margin.

There is also an Alignment section in the Tabs dialog box, where you can change current tab stop types. This is the only place where you can select a bar tab.

Adding Tab Leader Characters

Leader characters make it easy to read wide, sparsely populated lines without losing your place. Word's leader characters are dots, dashes, and solid lines (see the following illustration). You set them in the Tabs dialog box.

```
                              None (Type 1)
................Dots (Type 2)
---------------Dashes (Type 3)
_____Solid (Type 4)
```

To create leaders, follow these steps:

1. Select the paragraph(s) you want to change.

2. Click on the tab where you want the leaders.

3. Choose the leader style you desire from the Tabs dialog box.

4. Click OK.

You can apply this effect when defining new tab stops, or you can double-click on existing stops to bring up the Tabs dialog box.

Default Tab Stop Positions

The Word standard settings specify tabs every ½ inch (0.5 in). You can change this for a single document by changing the setting in the Tabs dialog box. To forever change default tabs, change and save stops in the Normal template.

Clearing Tab Stops

You can drag a tab off the ruler if you don't need it. The Tabs dialog box provides facilities for clearing multiple tabs at once—you can clear all the tabs at one time by clicking Clear All, or choose a specific tab in the Tab Stop Position and click the Clear button to remove it.

WORD PROCESSING WITH WORD FOR WINDOWS

Entering and Editing Tabular Data

Once you have set up tab stops, simply press TAB to reach the stop and begin typing. Word will position the text as you type. If you are typing at a center or right stop, text will flow appropriately as you type. When you type at decimal stops, the insertion point sits to the left of the decimal position until you press the period key; then it hops to the right side. To leave an entry blank, simply tab past it by pressing TAB.

Tables

Tables help you organize complex columnar information. Use them to create such diverse documents as forms, television scripts, financial reports, parts catalogs, and résumés. You can insert tables anywhere you need them in Word documents. Word's table feature and the terminology used to describe it will remind you of a spreadsheet.

Word tables consist of horizontal *rows* and vertical *columns* (see Figure 7-2). You do the typing in areas called *cells*. Cells can contain text, numbers, or graphics. The text in cells is edited and embellished as usual with Word's Formatting toolbar and ruler.

A number of table-specific features let you control the size, shape, and appearance of cells. Border and shading features are available. It is also easy to insert and delete rows and columns.

FIGURE 7-2

Tables consist of cells arrayed in rows and columns

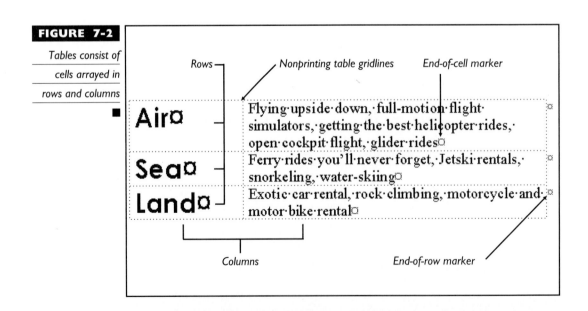

Tables can be created from existing text without needless retyping. Or, you can use the table feature to organize information and then convert your table to text. You can even import and export spreadsheet data. A feature called the Table Wizard helps you automate table creation, but this will be discussed after you understand the manual process. Because you will often want to fine-tune the Wizard's results, you'll need to become a wizard, too.

The dotted lines around each cell represent *nonprinting table gridlines*. You can add printing borders with the Format | Borders And Shading command. The larger dots are end-of-cell and end-of-row marks. Click the Show ¶ button in the Standard toolbar to reveal them.

Creating a Simple Table

To create a table with the Table button, follow these steps:

1. Place the insertion point where you want to insert a table (ideally, *not* at the very beginning of a new, otherwise empty document).

2. With the Standard toolbar in view, click the Table button, and then drag while holding down the mouse button to highlight the number of rows and columns you want in your table.

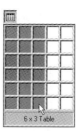

3. When the displayed grid represents the desired number of rows and columns, release the mouse button. Word will insert an empty table at the insertion point when you release the mouse button.

Creating a Table Using the Table Menu

You can use the Table | Insert Table command to create more complex tables with the Insert Table dialog box.

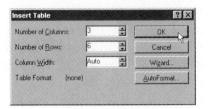

Unless you specify a column width in the Column Width box, Word computes a column width automatically, taking into consideration the available text area in your document and the number of columns you've specified. Initially, all table columns are the same width, but you can change column widths using techniques described later in this chapter.

Entering and Editing Text in a Table

With only a few exceptions, you navigate, enter, and edit table text just as you do any other Word text. Use your mouse or arrow keys to position the insertion point, and then type normally. Think of cells as *miniature pages,* and the cell borders as *margins.* Word will automatically wrap text within the cell as you reach the right edge. Rows will automatically grow taller as necessary to accommodate your typing.

To move from cell to cell within a table, either use your mouse or use TAB to go forward and SHIFT+TAB to go backward. The insertion point will move down to the beginning of the next row when you press TAB in the rightmost column (thus, it jumps from the right down to the left); and it will move to the end of the previous row when you SHIFT+TAB past the leftmost column (thus it jumps from the left up to the right). If you press TAB in the last cell of the last row, you will create a new row.

You can apply the usual character formatting to all or selected characters in a table. The familiar toolbar, ruler, and menu features all work here.

A cell can contain more than one paragraph. You create paragraphs in the usual way, and you can apply all of Word's paragraph formats to paragraphs in cells. Since cells can contain multiple paragraphs, they can also contain multiple paragraph formats. Thus, within a single cell, you can have several indent settings, tab settings, line-spacing specifications, styles, and so on.

Selecting in Tables

As you've just seen, you can select characters, words, and other items in table cells by using Word's usual mouse and keyboard features. In addition,

Word provides *table-specific* selection tools enabling you to choose whole cells, entire rows, columns, or areas.

The area between the first character in a cell and the left edge of the cell is called the *cell selection bar*. When you point to it, the mouse pointer changes directions (points to the right).

Clicking on it selects the contents of the entire cell. You can also select an entire cell by dragging with the mouse. Just be sure you include the end-of-cell marker in your selection.

To select a column, move the mouse pointer to the area called the *column selection bar* at the top of a column. You'll know you've arrived when the pointer changes into a large, down-pointing arrow.

Holding down ALT while clicking anywhere in a column will also select the entire column. Selecting the bottom or top cell in a column and dragging up or down is somewhat tedious, but will also work.

Selecting Rows

Double-clicking any cell selection bar will select the entire row. Selecting the leftmost or rightmost cell in a row and dragging will also work.

Selecting Adjacent Groups of Cells

To select groups of adjacent cells, either drag through the cells, or click in one cell and SHIFT+click in the others.

Selecting the Whole Table

To properly select an entire table, hold down ALT and double-click anywhere in the table. If your document contains multiple tables and they are not separated by paragraph marks, this technique will select all adjacent tables.

Do *not* use Word's Select All command to select a table, since this will also select paragraph marks and other things *outside* the table. Instead, use Table | Select Table or pressALT+5 on the numeric keypad (NUMLOCK has to be off for this to work).

Table Borders and Shading

An easy way to dress up a table is to add printing borders and shading, as shown next. Select the cell or cells you wish to embellish, and then use the line thickness portion of the Borders toolbar. Pick the desired combination of line thicknesses, and apply the borders just as you would add them to Word paragraphs. Add shading to some or all of the cells.

Air	Flying upside down, full-motion flight simulators, getting the best helicopter rides, open cockpit flight, glider rides
Sea	Ferry rides you'll never forget, Jetski rentals, snorkeling, water-skiing
Land	Exotic car rental, rock climbing, motorcycle and motor bike rental

Test print any shading you intend to use before getting carried away. It often looks different on paper than it does on your screen. For example, compare the 20% screen in the previous "screen shot" with this printed output of the same document:

Air	Flying upside down, full-motion flight simulators, getting the best helicopter rides, open cockpit flight, glider rides
Sea	Ferry rides you'll never forget, Jetski rentals, snorkeling, water-skiing
Land	Exotic car rental, rock climbing, motorcycle and motor bike rental

Adding Rows

To add a new row *at the end of an existing table,* place the insertion point anywhere in the last cell (the one in the lower-right corner of your table) and press TAB.

To insert a row *in the middle of a table,* place the insertion point in the row *below* where you want the new row and select Table I Insert Rows. Word will insert a new row using the styles of the cells immediately above.

Changing Row Heights

Normally, Word sets the height of each row automatically to accommodate the cell containing the tallest entry. For instance, if one cell in a row needs 2 inches to accommodate the text or graphic it contains, all of the cells in that row will be 2 inches high. All cells in a row must be the same height, but different rows can have different heights.

Dragging a Row to New Heights

To adjust the height of a row, follow these steps:

1. Click anywhere in the row you wish to resize.

2. Move the pointer to the vertical ruler at the left edge of the screen, watching the pointer as you move it.

3. When it becomes an up-and-down arrow, use it to drag the row to the desired height.

4. Release the mouse button.

Resizing Rows with Cell Height And Width

You can also overrule Word's automatic row height (and column width) settings via the Table I Cell Height and Width command. this is one way to create forms with fixed-size entry areas.

WORD PROCESSING WITH WORD FOR WINDOWS

tip *There is no standard keyboard shortcut for this command, but experienced table typists often add their own.*

To resize cells, follow these steps:

1. Place the insertion point anywhere in the row whose height you wish to specify. If you want multiple rows to share the same height, select all of them.

2. Choose Table | Cell Height And Width.

3. Click on the Row tab if necessary to reveal its choices:

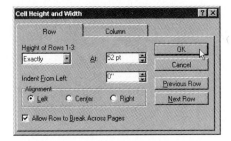

4. Use the height drop-down list to choose Auto, At Least, or Exactly.

5. Enter the desired dimension in points, inches, centimeters, and so on. (The default is points.)

6. To change settings for previous or next rows, click the Previous Row or Next Row buttons.

7. Click OK to make the change and close the dialog box.

If the exact height you specify is too small to accommodate the biggest entry in a row, the excess text or a portion of the entry will be cropped when printed. Simply increase the row height if this is undesirable.

Changing the Spacing Between Rows

To change the amount of white space between rows—not the *height* of rows—select the rows, choose Format | Paragraph, and specify the before-and-after spacing (see Chapter 5 for details).

Deleting Rows

To delete a row or rows of cells, select the row(s) to be deleted, and then use the Table | Delete Rows command. This will delete both the rows (the cells) and their contents (text or graphics or whatever). To delete the *contents* of cells but leave the cells intact, use Word's usual text-deletion tricks (select text or graphics and press DEL, for instance).

Inserting Columns

To insert a single column in the middle of a table:

1. Select the column to the *right* of where you want the new column to appear.

2. Click the Table button in the Standard toolbar (notice how its name has changed to Insert Columns) or choose Table | Insert Columns. Word will add a new column, but will not change the width of the earlier columns to accommodate it.

3. To make the enlarged table fit on your page, you will probably need to adjust margins or column widths (described in a moment), or change page orientation. New columns retain the format of the old rightmost columns, but borders will not transfer.

To insert multiple columns, select as many existing columns as you want to insert new ones to the right of the desired location of the new columns—if you want to add three columns, select the three existing columns to the right of the desired insertion point—then click on the Table button. Word will insert three columns.

Inserting Columns at the Right Edge of a Table

To insert a column at the right edge of a table, select an end-of-row marker, click on the Table button in the Standard toolbar (notice how its name has changed to Insert Cells), pick Insert Entire Column in the Insert Cells dialog box, and click OK.

Deleting Columns

To delete columns, select the column or columns to be removed and choose Table | Delete Columns.

Changing Column and Cell Widths

You can change the widths of entire columns or selected cells within columns. You can make most changes by dragging column markers on the table scale in the ruler, or you can make precision adjustments in the Table Cells dialog box.

To change the width of one or more *cells only*, select them and visit the Cell Height And Width dialog box (Table | Cell Height And Width). Specify a new width in the Columns tab.

Changing Column Widths with the Ruler

....

To change the width of an entire column:

1. Point to a column boundary so that the pointer changes shape.

2. Drag the column width marker:

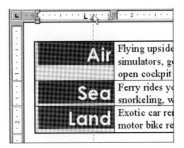

3. Watch the dotted line and ruler settings, and then release the mouse button when it reaches the desired width.

   ■ If you hold down SHIFT while dragging, the column to the right changes size to make up the difference while the table's overall width remains unchanged. (Note that this affects two columns: the one being dragged and one whose width is encroached upon.)

   ■ If you hold down CTRL while dragging, *all* columns to the right change size, but the table's overall width does not.

   ■ You can also drag the *column markers* on the ruler to change column widths. (Just don't accidentally drag the cells' indent markers instead.)

Changing Cell Widths with the AutoFit Button

The AutoFit button attempts to make cells surround their contents snugly. Use it after you've entered all the information in your table, or after you have finished adding or deleting items. Follow these steps:

1. Select the cells you want to resize (or, more often, the entire table).

2. Choose Table | Cell Height And Width.

3. Click the Column tab if it is not already in view.

4. Click the AutoFit button. Word will snug up the selected cells.

Merging Cells

Use the Merge Cells feature to combine the contents of multiple cells—for example, to make a heading in one cell span an entire table or a selected group of columns. You select the cells to merge, then choose Table | Merge Cells, and the contents of the designated cells will merge. You may need to reformat text merged this way.

Unmerging Cells

To split (unmerge) cells, place the insertion point in a merged cell and choose Table | Split Cells. you'll be asked how many cells you want after the split.

Changing the Space Between Columns

Word assigns cell widths based on the available text area and the number of columns you request. In the process, it sets aside a small amount of unprintable space between each cell (or within, actually). This space takes away from the usable cell space. For instance, a $1\frac{1}{2}$-inch column with $\frac{1}{4}$-inch column spacing would have $1\frac{1}{4}$ inches of usable space in the middle of each cell.

To change the space between columns, follow these steps:

1. Select the desired columns.

2. Select Table | Cell Height And Width to open the Cell Height and Width dialog box, and then choose the Columns tab.

3. Type a new specification in the Space Between Columns box, or use the arrows to scroll through suggested choices.

4. Click OK.

AutoFormatting Tables

Word's Table | Table AutoFormat command attempts to pick cell settings that make a presentable table. Whether it succeeds will vary with the project it's given and your definition of success. Personal taste plays a role, too.

Here are the basic steps for using Table AutoFormat:

1. Enter, edit, spell-check, reorganize, and otherwise finish with your table.

2. Save your document to disk.

3. Select the entire table (Table | Select Table or ALT+5 on the numeric keypad with NUMLOCK off).

4. Choose Table | Table AutoFormat to open the Table AutoFormat dialog box.

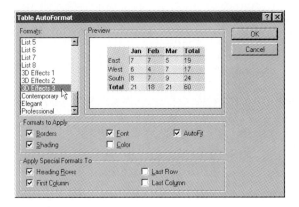

5. Preview the format choices from the scrolling list by highlighting their names one at a time. UP ARROW and DOWN ARROW are handy here.

6. Pick a style by highlighting it and click OK.

Pay particular attention to how Word handles row and column headings in the preview examples. Note that most of the canned styles assume that the top row will be column headings (months or years, for instance) and the leftmost column will be row headings of some kind (itemized expense items, for instance). Turn these effects on and off with their corresponding check boxes in the Apply Special Formats To area of the Table AutoFormat dialog box. You can also turn off many of the AutoFormat effects (borders, shading, and so on) the same way.

note   *Use Table | Table AutoFormat, not Format | AutoFormat, to format tables.*

Converting Tables to Text and Vice Versa

Sometimes you'll start a project using tabs and wish you'd created a table—or a coworker will give you some tabbed text. Other times, you will want to export things you've typed by using Word's table feature for database and other programs that expect tab- or comma-separated (delimited) input. Word has solutions for all these contingencies.

Word makes it quite easy to convert back and forth from tables to text. You may need to do some cleanup before or after conversion, though. Always work on copies of your documents when you do this!

Converting Text to Tables

To convert text to a table, highlight the text you want to turn into a table. Choose Table | Convert Text To Table, and click the appropriate option button in the resulting dialog box. Here's an explanation of the choices:

Tab	Lines of text separated by paragraph marks or line breaks will become rows in your table. Tab-separated strings of text within those lines will become cell entries in the row. Word will automatically create the columns based on the maximum number of tabs in a line.
Comma	Lines of text separated by paragraph marks or line breaks will become rows in your table. Comma-separated strings of text within those lines will become cell entries in the row. Word will automatically create the columns based on the maximum number of commas in a line. Beware of commas that might create unintentional cells.
Paragraphs	Word will propose a single column and create as many rows as you have paragraphs. Changing the number of columns will distribute paragraphs among the columns from left to right. In a two-column layout, the first paragraph would end up in the top-left cell of the new table, the second paragraph in the top-right cell, the third in the left cell of row 2, and so on.

Converting Tables to Text

To convert an existing table to text, select the table cells you wish to convert, or ALT+double-click to select the whole table. Choose Table | Convert Table To Text. Word will display a Table To Text dialog box, which asks if you want the table converted to paragraphs, tab-delimited text, or comma-delimited text. Pick one.

Choosing the paragraph option will convert each old table cell into at least one paragraph. If the table's cells contain multiple paragraphs, the paragraph marks are retained during the conversion, so some cells will create more than one new paragraph.

If you pick the comma or tab options, Word will convert each row of your table into one paragraph. Cells from the tables will be separated within the paragraphs by tabs or commas.

The Table Wizard

The Table Wizard will ask you some questions and format your table.

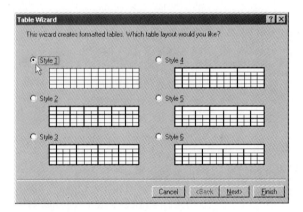

Here are the basic steps to using this Wizard:

1. Place the insertion point where you want the table. Press ENTER once or twice if you've just opened a new document.

2. Choose Table | Insert Table.

3. Click the Wizard button in the resulting dialog box. You will be presented with a number of screens asking you questions.

4. Look at each choice *carefully,* and study the examples if they are given. Don't confuse *rows* and *columns* when the Wizard gives you choices. Try to imagine *your* data in the sample table formats.

5. Click on the Next button after each choice, or the Back button to back up one screen.

6. When the Wizard runs out of questions, click Finish. You'll be presented with the Table AutoFormat dialog box (which you read about earlier).

7. Cruise the format samples until you find just the right mood, and then click OK.

Sorting

Word can sort lines of tabular text, items you've entered in tables, or even paragraphs in a document. The Sort command can be helpful when you prepare data files for Word's Print Merge feature.

warning *As with some other Word features, Sort can make substantial changes to your document (read: ruin your hard work if you didn't save it first), so save **before** you sort. **Don't** save **after** you sort until you've scanned the document to see if the sort worked as you intended. For extra security, consider running the sort on a copy of your document rather than the original.*

Sorting with the Database Toolbar

The Database toolbar contains sorting buttons, among other things. To sort rows of text, select them and click on either the Sort Ascending or Sort Descending button. Word will perform its sort based on the first letter(s) at the left of each line. If the first row (line) of text is bold or otherwise seems like it might be part of a label, Word will not move that row.

To sort items in a table with the Database toolbar, follow these steps:

1. Save your work, just in case.

2. Place the insertion point in the column that you want to use as the "sort by" column.

3. Click the Ascending or Descending sort button. This displays the Sort dialog box.

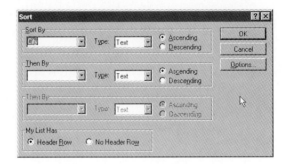

4. Word will sort the entire table (all columns), leaving labels untouched.

Sorting with the Sort Text Command

Word's Table | Sort Text command will attempt to sort selected text alphabetically, numerically, or chronologically at your request. Sorts can be up to three levels "deep." They can be used in free-form text, but are much more powerful when used with a table. To sort a table with this command, follow these steps:

1. Save your work, just in case.

2. Place the insertion point in the table you wish to sort.

3. Pick Table | Sort Text. Word will highlight (select) the entire table, and you will see the Sort dialog box.

4. If you have labels at the top of your table, choose the option My List Has Header Row. There will be up to three drop-down lists containing the column labels (if you have them) or column numbers.

5. Specify the sort order by choosing the desired column for each sort level.

6. Choose a sort order for each column.

7. Tell Word if the data in each column is text, numbers, or dates by choosing from the Type drop-down lists.

8. Click OK and Word will sort.

If you want the sort to be case sensitive, or if you are sorting things that are not in a table, click the Options button in the Sort dialog box, and make the appropriate choices in the Sort Options dialog box.

Alternatives to Word

For big sorting projects, check out Excel's database features or full-fledged databases like Access (see the chapters on Excel and Access later in this book).

CHAPTER 8

Working with Graphics

W

ORD for Windows lets you draw, place, resize, reposition, and embellish graphics. You can work with your own drawings; charts from Excel, PowerPoint, and other software packages; photos from scanners; and just about any other computer-compatible art form. In fact, Microsoft Office even comes with some clip art and a clip-art viewer you can use to get your graphics library started.

tip *Microsoft Office actually comes with two art collections—one in the Clipart subfolder (in the Office95 folder) and another collection reached via the ClipArt Gallery. You'll see how to combine the two collections later in this chapter.*

You can simply paste graphics or place them in *frames*. As you'll soon see, using frames makes it easier for you to reposition and work with graphics. OLE is also a possibility. See Chapter 3 for more information about OLE.

There are plenty of graphics buzzwords and standards to learn. In fact, another book the size of this one could be written just on those subjects. But this chapter contains all you'll need to start creating your own art and using free or low-cost clip art.

Importing Graphics

Like text, computer art can be stored in disk files. Unfortunately, different drawing packages, scanners, and other graphics tools create files in their own formats. Word for Windows comes with a number of built-in translation utilities (called *filters*) that can convert graphics from many sources, allowing you to insert them in Word for Windows documents. At a minimum, you will be able to work with the following graphic formats. (Their usual file extensions are listed after their names.)

- AutoCAD 2D (.DXF)
- Computer Graphics Metafile (.CGM)
- CompuServe GIF (.CGM)
- CorelDRAW! 3.0 (.CDR)
- Encapsulated PostScript (.EPS)
- HP Graphics Language (.HGL)
- Kodak Photo CD (.PCD)
- Lotus 1-2-3 (.PIC)
- Macintosh PICT (.PCT)
- Micrografx Designer 3/Draw Plus (.DRW)
- PC Paintbrush (.PCX)
- TIFF (Tagged Image File Format—.TIF)
- Targa (.TGA)
- Windows Bitmap (.BMP)
- Windows Metafile (.WMF)
- WordPerfect Graphics (.WPG)

If you don't see the format you need here, contact Microsoft technical support. They may be able to provide you with new filters, give you some workaround tips, or refer you to makers of graphics conversion programs.

Other Sources of Clip Art

If you don't have the time or inclination to draw your own art, you can purchase compatible clip-art disks from mail-order firms and retail software dealers. Many companies and nonprofit groups also distribute low-cost or free shareware and public-domain clip art. Check local computer user groups and online art libraries like the ones provided by America Online and CompuServe. If you have a scanner, you can convert printed images to Word-compatible art. Be sure you understand and honor any copyright restrictions when you use other people's art.

Using the Insert Picture Command

The easiest way to get hooked on graphics is to import a picture or two. Here's how:

1. Start by creating or opening a document.

2. Place the insertion point where you want the picture to appear.

3. Choose Insert | Picture to bring up the dialog box shown in Figure 8-1.

4. Click Preview to look at the pictures before you insert one.

5. Browse by scrolling until you see something you like.

6. When you find a nice graphic, click OK to insert it. Here's Elephant.wmf from the Clipart folder:

7. Reposition and perhaps resize or otherwise embellish the image. You will learn more about these options later in this chapter.

tip   *In addition to the Word for Windows clip-art folder, chances are you have other graphic images on your hard disk. For instance, your Windows folder probably has a dozen or so bitmap files (files ending in .BMP). Use the Find feature in Word's Open dialog box to locate files of interest. When you see one, click on the name to highlight it, and then click the Preview Picture button to get an idea of what it will look like. If you use graphics regularly or have a large collection, you may prefer the ClipArt Gallery, described next.*

ClipArt Gallery

The Office ClipArt Gallery is reached from the Insert | Object command. It offers categories of art and some other intriguing features.

To use the ClipArt Gallery:

1. Start by creating or opening a document.

2. Place the insertion point where you want the picture to appear.

3. Choose Insert | Object.

FIGURE 8-1

Use the

Insert | Picture

command to insert

graphics files

Click to select an image—scroll if necessary

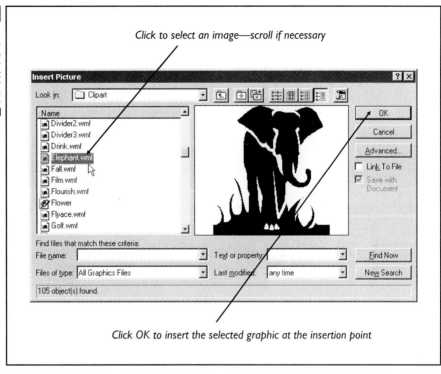

Click OK to insert the selected graphic at the insertion point

4. When you see the Object dialog box, click the Create New tab if necessary, and then scroll to pick Microsoft ClipArt Gallery.

5. Click OK. You will see the ClipArt Gallery dialog box shown in Figure 8-2.

6. Browse by clicking on categories of interest and scrolling to view *thumbnails* (miniature copies) of graphics in the gallery.

7. Double-click on a thumbnail, or click once on it and once on Insert to insert a full-sized copy of the image at the insertion point in your Word document.

THRILL SEEKERS

A Book Series Proposal

Amusement park screamers   Parasailing
Breathtaking horseback rides   Pontoon planes

8. Reposition and perhaps resize or otherwise embellish the image. You will learn more about these options later in this chapter.

Maintaining the Gallery

You can add other images to the gallery by using the gallery's Add Pictures and Update Pictures buttons in the Organize dialog box shown in Figure 8-3, reached via the Organize button. Learn more by reading the associated online Help in the Organize dialog box.

Using the Clipboard to Insert Art

If you already have a drawing program that you use to create and edit artwork, it is easy to copy your work to the Clipboard and then paste it into a Word document. Here are the steps:

1. Switch to or run the drawing program.

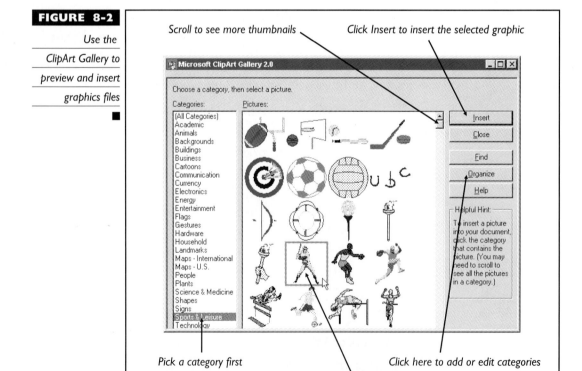

FIGURE 8-2

Use the ClipArt Gallery to preview and insert graphics files

Scroll to see more thumbnails

Click Insert to insert the selected graphic

Pick a category first

Click here to add or edit categories

Click on the thumbnail of the graphic you like

2. Select the art of interest.

3. Copy it to the Clipboard (CTRL+C).

4. Switch to or start Word.

5. Move the insertion point to the desired location in your Word document.

6. Paste the graphic with the Edit | Paste command or CTRL+V.

tip   *You can make document scraps of graphics if you want to use them more than once. Scraps can be more useful than the Clipboard, particularly if you want to use their contents frequently. Remember, the Clipboard is cleared every time you cut or copy something new. Scraps are forever (almost).*

Resizing Graphics with Your Mouse

When you click on a graphic in a Word document to select it, the picture will be surrounded by a box containing eight handles—one in each corner and one on each side of the outline box. When the mouse pointer touches one of these handles, it will turn into a two-headed arrow.

FIGURE 8-3

Add and remove gallery items with the Organize dialog box

■

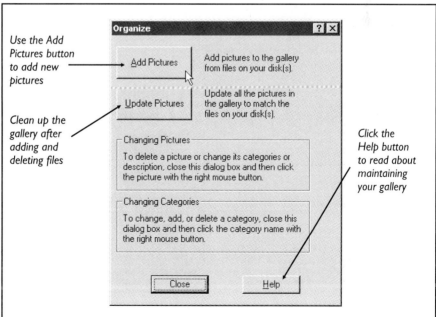

Use the Add Pictures button to add new pictures

Clean up the gallery after adding and deleting files

Click the Help button to read about maintaining your gallery

note *If you size something (a graphic, for example) proportionally, as the size changes, the width and height retain the same proportions relative to each other. That is, if the height gets three times larger, the width will get three times larger, as well.*

To increase or decrease the size of the entire graphic *proportionally*, drag a *corner* handle diagonally, releasing it when you are happy with the size.

To distort a dimension, use the handles on the *edges* of the graphic outline to stretch (distort) the graphic, as shown in Figure 8-4. Use Undo if you are unhappy with the results.

Cropping Graphics with Your Mouse

To crop a document (hide part of it), hold down SHIFT while you drag any of the handles to create the desired effect. The mouse pointer will turn into a square with a line through it.

Adding Space Around Graphics

To add space around a graphic, hold down SHIFT and drag handles away from the graphic. Use Undo to restore the original size.

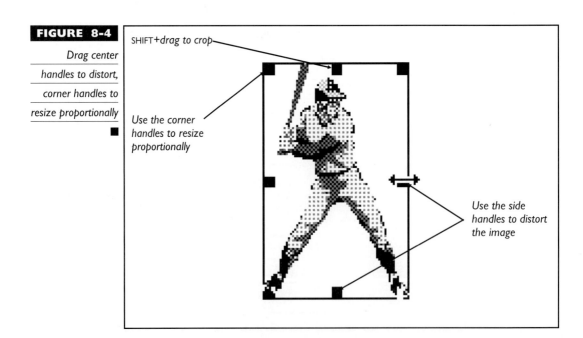

FIGURE 8-4

Drag center handles to distort, corner handles to resize proportionally

SHIFT+*drag to crop*

Use the corner handles to resize proportionally

Use the side handles to distort the image

Sizing and Cropping Graphics with the Picture Command

The Format | Picture command reveals the Picture dialog box.

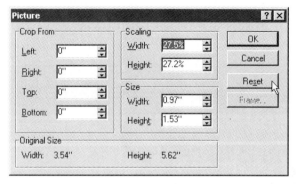

It contains information about a selected picture's original size and any cropping or resizing that's been done. You can also use this box to specify new size and cropping dimensions. The Reset button returns a graphic to its original size and uncrops it.

Using Word's Drawing Features

To create a new drawing using the Word for Windows drawing features:

1. Open a new or existing Word document.

2. Place the insertion point where you want your new art to be inserted.

3. Click on the Standard toolbar's Drawing button, shown at left. (Or, if you have a Word document containing a graphic you want to modify, double-click on the graphic.)

4. You'll see the Drawing toolbar.

You'll use a series of buttons, menu commands, and your mouse to draw, resize, and rearrange shapes, lines, and text.

tip   *You might want to reshape the Drawing toolbar to facilitate moving it around and keeping it out of the way. Drag an edge of the toolbar to change its shape from wide and short to tall and skinny, for instance, as shown here.*

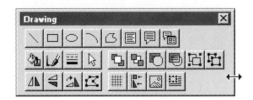

Drawing Objects

First click on a shape button or line button (line, ellipse, circle, and so on) in the Drawing toolbar, and then use your mouse to create lines or shapes. For instance, to create rectangles for an organizational chart, you would click on the Rectangle tool and drag with your mouse to create a rectangle of the desired shape and size. (Hold down SHIFT while dragging to create squares.)

Use the Ellipse tool for ovals and circles. (Hold down SHIFT while dragging to create precise circles.)

To create polygons, choose the Freeform tool, and then click and drag repeatedly until you have finished. For example, to make a triangle, you would click once to anchor the first point and drag to create the first side. Click again to anchor the second point and drag again. Click to anchor the third point, and then drag back to the starting point and click one last time to complete the triangle. Be sure not to hold down the mouse button when you are dragging. It is *very* important to end the triangle where you began it. If you miss the first anchor point, you'll end up with a big mess. Getting it right might take some practice.

tip *To change the shape of a polygon, select it using the techniques described next, and then click the Reshape tool on the Drawing toolbar. Handles will appear at each intersection of the shape. Drag them as necessary to create the desired shape.*

Selecting Objects

To select rectangles or other drawing elements (lines, text, and so on), click on the arrow button at the top of the drawing-tool stack, and then point to the item you want to move.

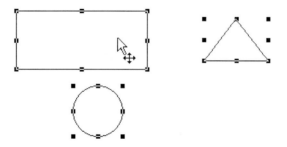

Hold down SHIFT to select multiple objects. The Edit | Select All command selects all text and pictures. Selected objects are surrounded by small handles. Click outside of any selected object to deselect all selected objects.

Text in Drawings

You can create text for drawings either in *text boxes* or in frames. Creating text in frames will be discussed later in this chapter. To create a text box:

1. Click on the toolbar's Text Box button.

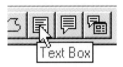

2. Drag the text box to the desired size and shape. Make it a little bigger than you think it needs to be to accommodate the text you will type.

3. Type **Marketing** (the insertion point's already in the box, so there's no need to position it).

4. If necessary, you can increase the size of a text box by dragging, just as if it were any other graphic object.

Text in boxes is automatically surrounded by lines unless you eliminate them. You will learn how to do so later in this chapter.

Embellishing Text in Drawings

You can embellish text (make it bold, center it, change type styles, and so on), and you can combine the effects using most of Word's formatting tools. For example, here's a box with two typefaces, some bold characters, and a bulleted list, created with the Bullets button on the Format toolbar.

Marketing Department
- Sandra Lexington
- William Johnson
- Karin Danialson
- Bobbi Wrightwood

More or Less Space Between Text and Text Box Lines

To increase or decrease the space between the text and text box lines:

1. Select the text box.

2. Choose Format | Drawing Object.

3. Select the Size and Position tab. You'll see the choices in the following illustration.

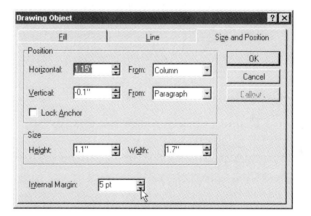

4. Specify a new internal margin by typing a new setting in the appropriate box or by using the up and down scroll arrows. For instance, here's the Marketing text box with 6 points (6pt) of internal margin:

Marketing Department
- Sandra Lexington
- William Johnson
- Karin Danialson

Eliminating Text Box Lines

To eliminate the lines surrounding the text box, follow these steps:

1. Select the box or boxes by clicking or SHIFT+clicking.

2. Use the Drawing toolbar's Line Color button to reveal the line color palette.

3. Click on None (at the top), as shown here:

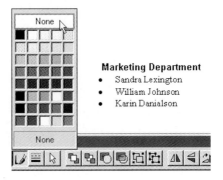

Moving Objects

To move objects, follow these steps:

1. Select the item or items to be moved.

2. Point to one of the selected items with your mouse pointer, avoiding the object's handles.

3. The pointer will change, now looking like an arrow with four heads.

4. Drag with your mouse and watch as an outline of the object(s) proposes a new location.

5. Release the mouse button to complete the move.

Gridlines

Word's drawing feature has optional *invisible gridlines* that make it easy to align objects. These gridlines make dragging a little jerky when the Snap To Grid feature is enabled. The gridlines act like magnets, and moved objects migrate to them. For precise, smooth moves, turn the Snap To Grid feature off. You can also change the spacing and origin of grids. Click the Snap To Grid button.

This will reveal the Snap To Grid dialog box, shown here.

Snap to Grid

To turn off the snap feature, click to remove the check from the Snap To Grid box. Even if the grid is turned off, you can still use it whenever you wish by holding down ALT while you drag.

Use the other settings in the dialog box to change the grid's dimensions and starting point with respect to the upper-left corner of the window.

Layers

You can construct objects from multiple elements placed near, on top of, or beneath one another. For instance, the Books.wmf file shown here contains a number of elements that you can rearrange, delete, or use separately.

Objects piled on top of each other in drawings are said to be *layered*. You can select items and use the Bring To Front or Send To Back buttons on the Drawing toolbar to arrange layers to your liking.

Grouping and Ungrouping

Sometimes you'll want to turn multiple drawing parts into a single object. This makes it easier to move and resize complex elements. Simply select all of the elements of interest by SHIFT+clicking, and then use the Group button on the Drawing toolbar.

t i p   *Only elements of drawings can be grouped and ungrouped. Bitmap images (like those found in Microsoft's free ClipArt Gallery) are not drawings.*

Henceforth, all of the items will act as a single item, as you can see here:

The items will act as a unit until you select the group and choose Draw | Ungroup.

Reorienting Objects

To flip objects, select them and choose Draw | Rotate/Flip. Choose one of the three Flip and Rotate buttons, shown here, on the Drawing toolbar.

Duplicating Objects

Once you've created an object, you can select, copy, and paste it to save time. Consider grouping complex collections of lines and shapes and text before duplicating them.

Pictures Versus Drawing Objects

There are two general types of graphic images—drawings like the ones created and discussed in this chapter, and "pictures" or "painted" images created with paint programs. Drawings are made up of individual elements— lines, circles, and so on. Painted images are generally treated as one large collection of dots. Files that end with the extension .BMP are bitmap "paintings." So are many Windows Metafiles (.WMF). Word can use both drawings and bitmaps; but if you want to edit them, you must do so in a special window. Suppose you want to change the color and shading of the Ornamnt1.wmf file in the Clipart folder. Here are the steps:

1. Position the insertion point where you want the graphic to appear in your Word document.

2. Choose Insert | Picture and locate the desired file (Ornamnt1.wmf), as shown in Figure 8-5.

3. Click OK to insert the graphic. It will appear in the Word document, but most of the Drawing toolbar buttons won't work. You can confirm this by watching the status area as you point to the various buttons.

4. Double-click on the graphic to open a picture window. You'll see the graphic, a *picture boundary*, and a small dialog box:

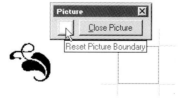

5. If the graphic isn't surrounded by the picture boundary, click on the Reset Picture Boundary button to move the picture into the boundary, as shown in the following illustration.

6. Edit the picture. SHIFT+click to select all elements and use the Fill Color button on the Drawing toolbar to choose 20% gray, as illustrated here:

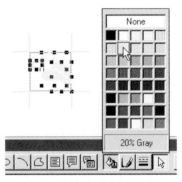

7. When you've finished editing, click the Close Picture button in the little Picture window. The edited graphic will be placed in your Word for Windows document at the insertion point.

FIGURE 8-5

To edit a graphic image you must insert it into your document

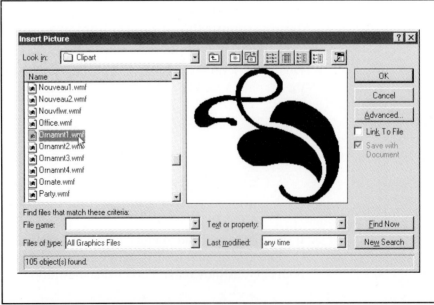

Rotating and Flipping Objects

To rotate or flip objects, select them and use the Flip Horizontal, Flip Vertical, and Rotate Right buttons on the Drawing toolbar.

note *These buttons won't work on text boxes. Use WordArt, described later in this chapter, to manipulate the orientation of text.*

Callouts

You can use callouts to label graphics in Word for Windows documents. Here are the steps:

1. Create or import a graphic.

2. Click the Callout button, shown at left, on the Drawing toolbar.

3. Click where you want the callout arrow to point.

4. Drag to where you want to position the text, and then release the mouse button. The callout will appear.

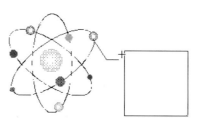

5. Type any text you want to show in the callout, and then select the text and change its appearance if you like.

6. Select the callout box and resize it if you wish.

7. Drag the box and line as desired to reposition them.

8. To change the design of the callout box, use the Callout Defaults dialog box, shown here. Reach it with the Format Callout button, shown at left.

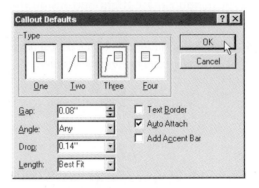

note *If you select a callout and then click on Format Callout, changes you make will affect that callout and the defaults, but not any other existing callouts.*

Filling

To fill drawn items with different colors or shades of gray, follow these steps:

1. Select the desired item(s).

2. Choose the button shown at left from the Drawing toolbar to bring up the Fill Color palette.

3. Click to select the desired fill color.

Line Colors and Shades of Gray

To change the color or shade of lines:

1. Select the desired item(s).

2. Choose the button shown at left from the Drawing toolbar to bring up the line palette.

3. Click to select the desired line color.

Line Sizes and Arrowheads

To change the size of lines and arrowheads:

1. Select the desired line(s).

2. Choose the button shown at left from the Drawing toolbar to bring up the line palette.

3. Click to select the desired line type.

4. Choose More to bring up the Line tab in the Drawing Defaults dialog box, illustrated here.

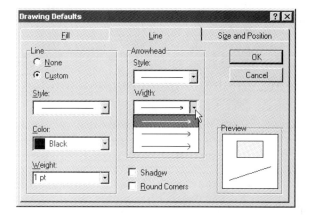

Using Frames to Position Objects

If you simply paste a graphic into a Word for Windows document (without framing it), it is treated like a character. You can place the graphic between characters, move it from one line to another, copy it, delete it, and so on. But it is a slave to elements like line and paragraph specifications, margins, indents, and such. To have maximum control over graphics and other document elements, place them in frames.

Frames can contain either graphics, text, or both. Frames let you precisely position objects virtually anywhere in your document. And you can tell Word for Windows to flow your unframed text around frames, as illustrated in Figure 8-6. Frames can contain graphics, Excel charts, Word text, or any combination thereof. In fact, it may be helpful to think of frames as pages within a page that you can move, resize, and embellish.

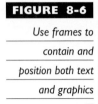

FIGURE 8-6

Use frames to
contain and
position both text
and graphics

Framed objects can span columns

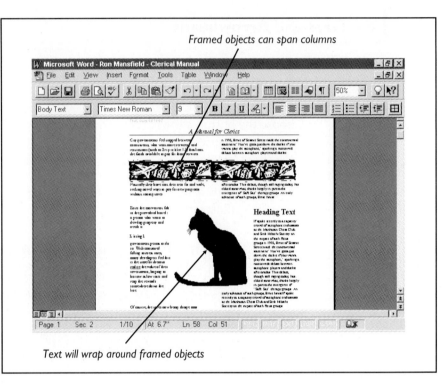

Text will wrap around framed objects

To use frames, you create them, insert objects into them, and then size and position them either with your mouse or with the Frame dialog box. Normally, you'll want to work with framed items in Page Layout view or Print Preview so that you can easily see and move them.

tip It's a good idea to turn on hidden paragraph marks when working with frames. If they are not visible, click on the Show/Hide button in the Standard toolbar. It looks like a ¶ (paragraph symbol).

Inserting Frames and Framing Objects

You can either insert an empty frame and then place something in it, or you can select something and frame it. In either case, you use the Insert | Frame command *or* the Insert Frame button, shown at left.

Inserting Empty Frames

Here are the steps for creating a new, empty frame:

1. Start by switching to Page Layout view if you are not already in it. (If you forget to do this, Word for Windows will ask if it can switch views for you.)

2. Click the Drawing toolbar's Insert Frame button or choose Insert | Frame.

3. Your pointer will change to a cross hair. Drag to create a frame of the approximate size and shape you desire, located about where you want it to be placed.

4. Shortly after you release the mouse button, you'll see a frame surrounded by a border. If you have the Show/Hide paragraph feature enabled, you will see a paragraph symbol within the frame and an anchor outside of it.

5. You can type text in the resulting frame (you'll learn how in a moment); paste things from the Clipboard; or use one of the Insert menu commands, such as the Picture and Object commands.

Framing Existing Objects

If you already have something in your document that needs framing, you can do so by following these steps:

1. Switch to Page Layout view if you are not there already.

2. Select the item or items to be framed.

3. Use either the Frame button on the Drawing toolbar or choose Insert | Frame.

4. Your selected item(s) will be surrounded by a frame, and you'll see a paragraph symbol and an anchor, as illustrated here, if you have clicked the Show/Hide ¶ button.

Framed items and their frames can be resized just as you resize graphics. Drag their handles. If you accidentally frame the wrong thing or too many or too few things, or accidentally distort the size or shape of a graphic, use Undo to reverse your mistakes.

tip *If you start the framing process (choose Insert | Frame) and change your mind, cancel it by pressing ESC.*

Positioning Framed Items with a Mouse

The simple way to position frames is to drag them with your mouse while in Page Layout view or Print Preview. Follow these steps:

1. Place the pointer anywhere within the frame and watch the pointer.

2. The pointer will change to include a four-headed arrow.

3. Press down on the primary mouse button and drag the frame to the upper-left corner of the text.

4. Release the mouse button.

5. Soon after you release the mouse button, the frame will take up residence in its new location. Text will move out of the way for the frame, and the anchor icon will move, as well.

You can continue to drag the framed graphic around to suit yourself. Switch to Print Preview and try moving it there, too. Remember—you'll need to click on the Magnifier button in Print Preview first to let you edit the document.

A frame is always anchored to a paragraph. When you position a frame by dragging it, it is initially anchored to its closest paragraph. When you move it, the anchor moves to the next nearest paragraph. To see where a frame's anchor is, select the frame and look for the anchor icon.

As you add or delete text in your document, the framed item stays with its paragraph. A frame always appears on the same page as its paragraph.

This is often the desired effect. But what if you want to keep a framed item on a particular page, or a specific distance from a particular paragraph?

Positioning Framed Items with the Frame Dialog Box

When you want to position frames precisely or force a frame to position itself relative to other things that might move, choose Format | Frame. You will see the Frame dialog box.

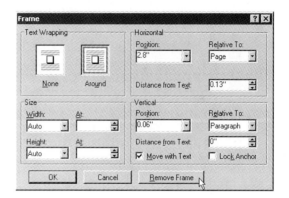

When you select a frame and open this dialog box, you will see the current size and position of the frame. You can specify new size and position settings for the frame in inches (in), centimeters (cm), points (pt), or picas (pi). You can change the units of measurement by using the General tab in the Options dialog box (reached by choosing Tools | Options).

Aligning Frames with Reference Points

The Frame dialog box also provides a mindboggling array of positioning and reference options. For instance, you can force a frame to always remain in the exact horizontal and vertical center of a page, even when you change margins or page sizes. Or you can tell Word for Windows to keep a frame a specified distance from margins or columns. Finally, you can anchor a frame to text, so when the text moves, the frame accompanies it. Place a check mark in the Move With Text box to accomplish this.

Text and Frames

Frames and text can be used together several ways. Besides framing text, you can position frames relative to text or have text flow around frames. Here are a few ways to work with frames and text.

Placing Text in Frames

You can use frames as small text windows that can be moved anywhere in your document. For instance, here the heading "Been there, done that" has been framed and moved into the document's margin. (You may want to remove the frame borders when you do this.)

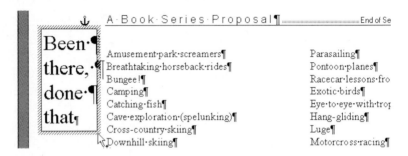

If the Move With Text option is checked in the Frame dialog box, the headings will stay with their paragraphs when your document is edited.

A quick way to create lots of marginal headings like this is to create one, and then *redefine the document's heading style(s)* on the basis of the example. All of your headings will be framed and placed in the margin quicker than you can say "Bungeeee!" When framing existing *text,* Word will make the frame big enough to accommodate all of the text you've selected. If you paste text into an existing frame, make sure the frame is big enough to prevent "weird word wrap," a problem that arises when you specify large line indents or place long words in narrow frames. If the text you insert changes into a long vertical string of characters, try resizing the frame to make the text legible.

Feel free to use all of Word's text formatting tools in Frames. You can have multiple paragraphs in frames. Word's Formatting toolbar and ruler work in frames. You can change type sizes and styles, center, justify, and otherwise fool with text in frames. Even Word's spelling checker peeks into them.

Inserting Text in Framed Graphics (Captioning)

If you want to add a caption to a framed graphic, select the frame, and then press ENTER. You'll see a new paragraph mark in the frame. Type the caption. Stylize the text if you like. The caption will stay with the frame when you move it.

How Framed Items Appear in Different Views

Framed items can be seen where they will print when displayed in Print Preview and Page Layout view. When you switch to Normal or Outline views, framed items will appear within the page boundaries where they will print, but not necessarily in their printing positions. You can easily spot framed items in Normal and Outline views.

Selecting and Deleting Framed Items

It's possible to delete frames *and their contents* simply by selecting the frame and then cutting (CTRL+X) or pressing DEL. (Select a frame by pointing and clicking with your mouse. Eight dark black handles and a black line will appear around the frame when you've selected it.)

To remove a frame but not its contents, select the frame and click the Remove Frame button in the Frame dialog box (choose Format | Frame). If you use this method to remove a frame with a printing border but not its contents, the frame's *border* will remain. Delete it or change it as described next.

Deleting or Changing Frame Borders

Frames are created without printing borders, but these can be added and altered.

1. Select a framed object in Page Layout view by clicking on the object.

2. Use the Format | Shading command to add, change, or remove the border. For instance, clicking on the None icon in the Preset area of the Border dialog box removes a frame's border.

tip   *There is also a border button on the Standard toolbar. It's on the right end and looks like a four-pane window.*

Repeating Framed Items on Multiple Pages

To repeat the same framed objects on multiple pages, create them in headers or footers.

Captions

If you write long documents with numbered figures, tables, and other elements, you will love this new feature! It automatically numbers things, lets you label them, and then renumbers them if you move them or otherwise change their sequence in a document. There are a variety of display options, as well.

Adding Captions

You can either manually caption the occasional item or turn on automatic captioning. To manually caption:

1. Select the item to be captioned.

2. Choose Insert | Caption.

3. You'll see the Caption dialog box.

4. Word proposes a caption label that you can accept as is or edit. For example, you can type descriptive text.

5. You can change the default appearance options by visiting the Position list or the Caption Numbering dialog box.

6. Click OK to insert the label. Be patient; it takes a moment.

To automatically add captions to items of a particular type (all drawings, for instance), use the AutoCaption dialog box, reached with the AutoCaption button in the Caption dialog box. Word for Windows can recognize and automatically caption the following types of files:

- Most graphic files

- Microsoft drawings

- Microsoft equations

- Microsoft Graphs

- Microsoft WordArt

- Inserted Word documents

- Paintbrush pictures

- Sounds

and much more.

To automatically caption items, follow these steps:

1. Choose Insert | Caption.

2. Click AutoCaption.

3. Pick a type of item to automatically caption. You can pick more than one type for the same caption label (for instance, you can pick Microsoft drawings and Word pictures). Inserting either will have the same effect.

4. Pick a label type from the Use Label list, or create your own with the New Label button.

5. Pick a position for the label (above or below the item).

6. Change the numbering scheme if you like.

7. Repeat steps 3 through 6 for each different type of caption you want.

8. Click OK.

After you've turned on AutoCaption and defined the appearance options, Word for Windows will automatically label any insertion that meets the AutoCaption criteria.

When you move a figure and its label, Word will not immediately update the figure labels. But it *will* update figure numbers whenever you ask to print or switch to Print Preview. To force an immediate update, select all of your text (CTRL+A) and press F9.

To revise a caption, just edit it like any other text. To change all of the captions of a given type ("Figure" to "FIG", for instance), select a caption in text, visit the Caption or AutoCaption dialog box, and pick a different label from the Use Label List.

To create new label types ("FIG", for example), use the New Label button in the Caption and AutoCaption dialog boxes.

Including Chapter and Other Numbers in Captions

You can include chapter and similar numbers in automatic captions if you like. Here are the steps:

1. Format all of the main headings (chapters, for example) as Heading Style 1.

2. Choose Format | Heading Numbering. Make sure a numerical numbering style is in use (not *Chapter One,* for instance).

3. Visit either the Caption or AutoCaption dialog box.

4. Choose the Numbering button.

5. When you see the Caption Numbering dialog box, choose Include Chapter Numbers.

6. Back out by clicking OK as needed.

CHAPTER 9

Templates, Wizards, and Sample Documents

R EAD-ONLY documents with styles and other design elements that you can use to create or restyle your own documents are called *templates*. *Wizards* are computerized assistants. Wizards also use templates to create documents, first asking some questions and making a few design decisions on their own. The following Wizards come with Word:

- Agenda
- Award
- Calendar
- Fax
- Letter
- Memo
- Newsletter
- Pleading
- Resume
- Table

In addition, some Word templates actually have instructions embedded right in the example text that tell you how to personalize them to your own ends. These are called *sample documents,* and they are excellent learning tools. If you did a complete installation, these files are in their own subfolders within the templates folder.

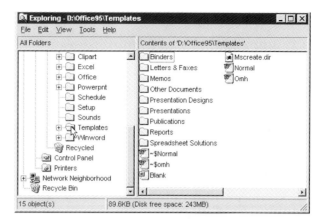

Look for the templates subfolder in your Office95 folder. Let's begin our tour with templates.

Templates

There are at least four ways to use templates:

- Start new projects based on templates shipped with Word.

- Modify projects by choosing templates and *completely reformat* your work in the template's styles.

- Copy *selected* styles from templates to use in your projects.

- Create templates, and save new templates of your own creation.

note *All new documents are based upon Word's Normal template, unless you specify otherwise. Normal includes hundreds of predefined styles, and it may suit your needs just fine. To make your documents look really professional, though, consider using Word's other templates.*

Template Types

Word's standard templates come in up to three different "flavors." Microsoft refers to these as *Template Types:*

- Contemporary

- Elegant

- Professional

Each type gives a document a different mood. For instance, the Contemporary Letter template uses Times New Roman, while Professional uses Arial. The Company Name style in the Contemporary Letter template includes shading, while the Elegant type does not, and so on.

tip   *Use Find and Replace to speed the task of changing things like product names that repeat many times in the same document.*

By always using templates of the same type, you can give your work a consistent look. And when creating other documents based on templates, you can copy the existing styles using the tricks you learned in Chapter 5.

tip   *No matter what kind of document you want to create (whether it be a newsletter, manual, invoice, time sheet, press release, brochure, and so on), chances are Word has a template for it. Since these templates were intended to be used together, some even sharing a common design, one way to ensure some consistency within your company is to standardize the use of Word's templates.*

Many templates come in the three types just discussed, but not all templates come in all types. For instance, there is only one invoice type, simply called Invoice. Here is a list of Word's templates, divided into those that are available in Contemporary, Elegant, and Professional, and those that are not.

Available in All Three Types	Only One Type
Fax	Brochure
Letter	Directory
Memo	Invoice
Press Release	Manual
Report	Newsletter
Resume	Purchase Order
	Thesis
	Weekly Time Sheet

Using Templates

Once you know what each template looks like, you can quickly start projects by picking a template. Choose File | New and click the tab you wish in the New dialog box, shown here, and then just pick the template you wish by name.

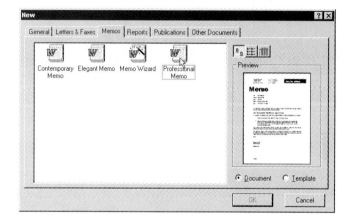

Notice that you can preview templates here. You can also start Wizards from the New dialog box. Double-click on your choice. Then simply add your own text by clicking on the appropriate areas of the template and replacing the labels with your own words.

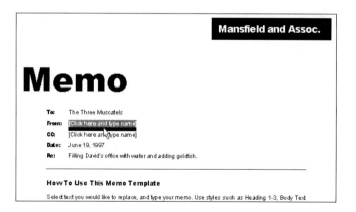

But first, it's helpful to know what the various templates look like. You could load each one and take a look, but there's an easier way.

Word Processing with Word for Windows

Exploring Templates

Use the Style Gallery, reached with the Format | Style Gallery command, to preview templates. Here are the steps:

1. Open a new document with the File | New command.

2. Choose Normal (the Default template).

3. Choose Format | Style Gallery. You will see a window like the one in Figure 9-1.

4. Pick the template that you want to see from the scrolling list.

5. Click the Example button in the Preview area to see a preview of the template's appearance.

6. Scroll to make sure you see the entire template; templates are often several pages long.

7. Click Style Samples to see the names of styles displayed in the styles themselves. Unfortunately, these are often too small to read.

8. When you have finished, click Cancel. Clicking OK copies the styles to your current document but does not load the other template elements—boilerplate text, and so on.

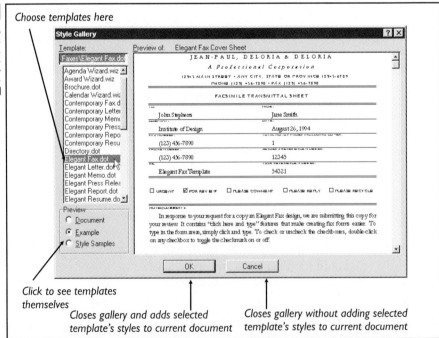

FIGURE 9-1

You can preview templates in the Style Gallery

Choose templates here

Click to see templates themselves

Closes gallery and adds selected template's styles to current document

Closes gallery without adding selected template's styles to current document

Modifying Templates

You can change templates just as you would any other Word documents. The only difference is one additional step you must take when saving your work. Suppose you wanted to update the Professional letter template to include your company logo. Follow these steps to see how:

1. Use the File | New command to open the Contemporary Letter template. Be sure you click the Template button.

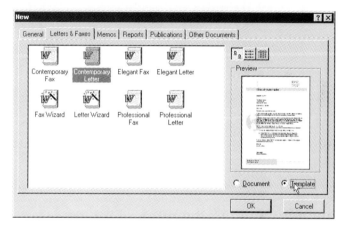

2. Make the changes, such as adding your logo and other embellishments.

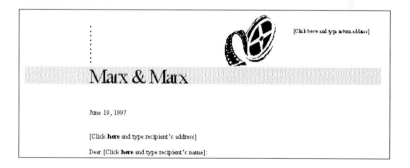

3. Print a sample and check your work.

4. When you are satisfied, choose File | Save As. You will see the Save As dialog box, shown next.

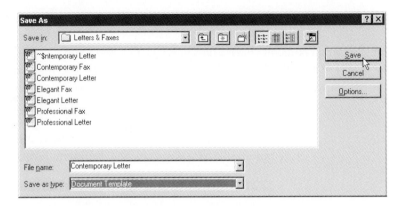

5. Type the same filename as the old template if you want to replace the old template, or type a new filename if you want to keep *both* the old and new (make sure you choose Document Template in the Save As Type box if you choose a new filename).

Prewritten Business Letters

Word comes with a number of prewritten letters for various uses.

They are generally accessed via Letter Wizard. When you elect to use a prewritten letter, you will be prompted for details specific to you and your purposes. Whether the letters will work for you is a matter of taste and circumstance.

To use the letters, replace the underlined phrases with your own information, and then delete the underlining.

tip　*Use Find and Replace to speed the task of changing items like product names that repeat many times in the same document. To remove underlining, consider using the Select All command (CTRL+A) and toggling all underlining off at once by clicking the Underline button in the Formatting toolbar.*

Word comes with over a dozen canned letters. These include

- Apology for delay
- Announcement of price increase
- Collection letter
- Complaint under investigation
- Credit report request
- Direct mail
- Lease expiring
- Letter to Mom
- Order cancellation
- Press release
- Resume cover letter
- Returned check (firm request for payment!)
- Thanks for inquiry
- Thanks for job application
- Thanks for the suggestion

Tips for Using Templates

Word often gets information from the User Information entered with the User Info tab in the Options dialog box (reached with the Tools | Options command). Make sure your info is up to date by visiting that tab.

In templates with inside addresses, signature blocks, and other multiline items, consider the SHIFT+ENTER trick to keep lines all in the same paragraph. This eliminates unwanted space before each address line, for example.

Switching types (from Elegant to Professional, for instance) can give your documents a whole new look. And you can mix and match styles by copying selected styles from other documents.

Some of the more complex templates (like Manual) use a wealth of Word features, including tables of contents and index entries.

Don't forget other time-savers such as the Tools | Envelopes And Labels command. They work with templates, too.

Wizards—The Computer Wants Your Job

Wizards ask you questions, then use your responses to design documents for you. Take the Calendar Wizard for instance. You start Wizards with the File | New command. Pick the Calendar Wizard from the Other Documents tab in the New dialog box, as shown here.

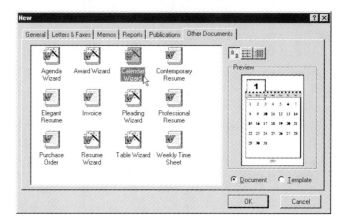

You'll be asked questions about your hopes and dreams for the new document. Do you want portrait or landscape orientation? Would you like to leave room for a picture or other graphic? Do you want fries with that? And so on.

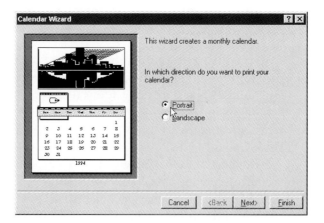

As you answer questions, Word shows you a preview, making changes so you can see the effect of your decisions. The preview allows you to try several different settings in each window to see which you prefer. Eventually the Calendar Wizard tires of this and, when you click the Finish button, it works its magic.

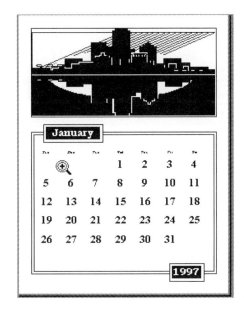

CHAPTER 10

Writers' Tools

I N this chapter, we'll cover the ways in which Word can make you a better author. If you are intrigued by what you read here, consider picking up an additional "Word-only" book such as *Microsoft Word for Windows 95, The Complete Reference* (by Mary Campbell and Gabrielle Lawrence, published by Osborne McGraw-Hill), which contains additional information and many more examples and illustrations.

Typing Symbols and Special Characters

Word for Windows makes it easy to type special characters and symbols not shown on your keycaps but available in most fonts. Use the Symbol feature or keyboard shortcuts.

The Symbol Command

This dialog box appears whenever you choose Insert | Symbol. It has two tabs.

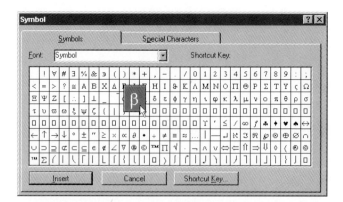

The Symbols tab shows you *all* available characters in the current font. Clicking on a symbol shows you a magnified, more readable version. Double-clicking inserts the character at the insertion point in your document. (Alternatively, you can click on a character and then click on the Insert button, but that's more work.) To see which symbols are available in different fonts, simply choose a font from the Font drop-down list in the Symbol dialog box.

tip *Once you've clicked to magnify a character in the Symbol dialog box, you can see magnified views of others by navigating with the arrow keys. This can eliminate the need for a lot of precision clicking. Also, once a character is highlighted, you can insert it by pressing ENTER.*

The Special Characters tab provides a scrolling list of commonly used symbols and characters. Here, too, double-clicking inserts the character at the insertion point. Click on the Special Characters tab to see em dashes (—), ellipses (…) the trademark symbol (™) and many other useful characters.

tip *The Special Characters tab in the Symbol window also lets you see (and change) keyboard shortcuts.*

Typing Symbols from the Keyboard

If you know the appropriate key combinations, you can enter them directly from the keyboard without having to use the Symbol feature. Different fonts sometimes have different key combinations, so consult the documentation that comes with your fonts or use the Insert | Symbol command to learn the combinations. Table 10-1 shows commonly used special characters and their keyboard shortcuts.

Wingdings and Dingbats

Use the little pictures found in the Wingdings font to embellish documents. Wingdings are great as bullets, list separators, and border decorations. Use the Insert | Symbol command to see and insert them.

International and Accented Characters

To type accented international characters (like the ñ in *La Cañada*), you use three keys. First you hold down CTRL plus a key to tell your computer which accent to apply, and then you press the character key for the character you want to accent. For example, to insert an umlaut (dieresis character) over an *o*, do the following:

1. Hold down CTRL and press the : key.

2. Release both keys.

3. Press the o (or SHIFT+O) key to get a small (or capitalized) umlauted o (ö/Ö).

Name	Sample	Keys
Angstrom	Å	CTRL+@+A
Bullet	•	ALT+0149 ‡
Cent sign	¢	CTRL+/, C
Copyright	©	CTRL+ALT+C ‡
Dagger	†	ALT+0134
Degree	°	CTRL+@, SPACEBAR
Double close quote	"	ALT+0148 ‡
Double open quote	"	ALT+0147 ‡
Ellipsis	…	CTRL+ALT+. ‡
Em dash	—	CTRL+ALT+− (numeric)‡
En dash	-	CTRL+− (numeric)‡
Function, f-stop	*f*	ALT+0131
Logical not	¬	ALT+0172
Mu (lowercase, micro)	μ	ALT+0181
Much greater than	»	ALT+0171
Much less than	«	ALT+0187
Paragraph mark	¶	ALT+0182
Plus-or-minus sign	±	ALT+0177
Pound (currency)	£	ALT+0163
Registered trademark	®	CTRL+ALT+R ‡
Section mark	§	ALT+0167
Single close quote	'	CTRL+', ' ‡
Single open quote	'	CTRL+SHIFT+', ' ‡
Trademark	™	CTRL+ALT+T ‡
Yen (currency)	¥	ALT+0165

Note: Keys marked with a double dagger (‡) (have easier AutoText shortcuts or are created automatically under normal conditions.

TABLE 10-1   *Special Characters and their Keyboard Shortcuts*

Incidentally, you can't accent just any characters. Table 10-2 shows you the possibilities and their key combinations.

Bulleted List Command

There's a button on the Standard toolbar that looks like a bulleted list. Clicking it places bullets in front of selected paragraphs and creates hanging indents. The feature uses the current font.

Bulleting Existing Paragraphs

To bullet existing paragraphs, follow these steps:

1. Select the paragraph or paragraphs you want to format.

2. Click the Bullets button, shown at left. Word will create hanging indents and insert bullets in front of each selected paragraph.

Typing New Bulleted Lists

To type new bulleted lists, follow these steps:

1. Click the Bullets button on the Standard toolbar or choose Format | Bullets And Numbering. A bullet appears.

2. Type an entry and press ENTER. A new bullet appears on the next line.

3. Repeat step 2 and continue until you've finished the list.

4. When finished, click the Bullets button to deactivate the feature.

Name	Sample	Keys
Acute	áéíóú ÁÉÍÓÚ	CTRL+', letter
Circumflex	âêîôû ÂÊÎÔÛ	CTRL+^, letter
Dieresis	äëïöü ÄËÏÖÜ	CTRL+:, letter
Grave	àèìòù ÀÈÌÒÙ	CTRL+`, letter
Tilde	ãñõ ÃÑÕ	CTRL+~, letter

TABLE 10-2 *Keyboard Shortcuts for Accented Characters*

tip *You can now use AutoText to type new bulleted lists. Just type an asterisk (*) and then type your first item. When you press ENTER, Word will turn the asterisk into a bullet, with the proper hanging indent, and will automatically bullet the rest of your list as you type it.*

Changing Bullet Styles

Word for Windows offers an astonishing array of bulleted list options. You can even choose your own, nonstandard bullet characters. Here are the steps:

1. Select your list if you've already typed it.

2. Choose Format | Bullets And Numbering.

3. Click to pick a style you like.

4. Click OK to change the style of the selected list.

5. Type additional list items or a new list, as necessary.

Smart or Typographer's Quotes

Word can automatically place curly quotes in documents when you type straight quotes. These *smart* quotes give your work a typeset look. Turn the option on before typing, since Word will not automatically change quote marks you've already typed.

1. Use the Tools | Options command to display the Options dialog box.

2. Click on the AutoFormat tab to display the AutoFormat options.

3. Enable Smart Quotes by clicking to place a check in the option box.

4. Subsequently, when you type quotes, Word will convert them to curly opening and closing quotes (assuming that your chosen font has these characters).

tip *If you are creating a document that you plan to export (for use with different word processing software, perhaps), turn off the Smart Quotes feature before creating documents containing quotes. Otherwise you risk confusing the other programs with strange codes instead of quotation marks.*

Spelling Checker

The first time you use the Spelling checker, it's a good idea to ensure that it is set to use the proper dictionary—English (US) in the United States. Here are the steps:

1. Choose Tools | Language.

2. Scroll to the desired language—probably English (US)—and select it by double-clicking or clicking once on the name and once on OK.

3. Click the Default button.

4. Answer Yes to the confirmation prompt.

5. Click on OK.

warning   *You can format certain text (foreign language or technical, for example) as "no proofing" text, which means Word will skip it during spell checks. However, if you don't instruct Word to use another dictionary (Spanish, for example), you might think it has spell-checked your document and found nothing wrong. Your only clue will be a casual note that text formatted with "no proofing" has been skipped.*

Start the Spelling checker with the F7 shortcut or by picking Tools | Spelling. The Spelling dialog box appears.

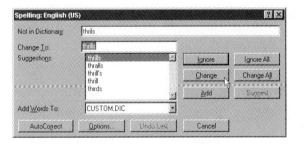

note   *If there are no mistakes in the text you ask Word to check, you won't see the Spelling dialog box—Word will pop up a message box saying "The spelling check is complete."*

Unless you've selected only a portion of your document to check, Word for Windows scans down, beginning at the insertion point, and will then ask if you want to go back to the top of the document to continue checking.

The Spelling checker looks for words that it cannot find in its open dictionaries. When it spots a word that it can't match, Word highlights the questionable characters, scrolls the document so that you can see the problem word in context, and offers you a number of choices.

tip *One of the great new features of Word is its Automatic Spellchecking. Word will actually watch as you type, and if it encounters an unfamiliar word, the checker will flag it with a red, squiggly underline. You can then check it on the fly, by right-clicking on the flagged word, or check it later using the Spelling checker. This feature can be turned off if you find it annoying. You can tell if it's on by looking at the status area. If automatic spell checking is enabled, you will see a little book icon with a red pen checking it.*

Typing Your Own Changes

If you want to change a misspelled word only once:

1. Type a replacement in the highlighted Change To box.

2. Press ENTER or click the Change button. Word will replace the problem text with the new text you have typed in the Change To box and then continue spell-checking.

To change the word throughout the document that you are checking, click Change All instead of pressing ENTER or clicking Change. If the new word you've typed is something you want Word for Windows to recognize in all of your documents, see the section "Custom or User Dictionaries" later in this chapter.

Word's Suggested Changes

If you have enabled the suggestions feature (check the Always Suggest option in the Spelling tab of the Options dialog box), Word for Windows will usually list one or more possible spellings, placing what it thinks is the best guess in the Change To box. If the default is not enabled, you can always ask for suggestions by clicking Suggest. Other suggestions, if any, will be listed in the scrollable Suggestions box. It may take a moment for Word to find alternative words. You'll know Word has finished looking for suggestions when you see either (End of Suggestions) or (No Suggestions) in the Suggestions list.

If you agree with Word's best guess, simply click the Change button to change this occurrence, or use the Change All button to change this and all succeeding occurrences of the word. The Spelling checker will replace the word and continue examining your document.

Word's best guess is usually, but not always, right. If one of the alternative suggestions is correct, simply double-click on the desired word to replace the misspelled word, or click once on the desired word in the list to move it to the Change To box, and then click the Change or Change All button as necessary.

tip   *If you have Automatic Spellchecking enabled, you can see suggestions on the fly. Just right-click on the flagged word, and a list will pop up with suggested changes. If one of them is the spelling you want, just click on it.*

Overruling Suggestions

Sometimes Word won't make correct suggestions, or you might want to correct the problem yourself without retyping the entire word or phrase. For instance, Word may spot two run-together words. When it has no suggestions, Word moves the problem text to the Change To box, where you can edit it yourself (by placing a space between the two words, for instance).

Ignoring Flagged Words

Sometimes Word for Windows will spot a word that is properly spelled but is not in Word's open dictionaries. Proper nouns, technical jargon, and typesetting codes are examples.

tip   *If you have the Automatic Spellchecking feature on and Word flags a word that is spelled correctly, just right-click on the word and choose Ignore All. You then won't be bothered again, at least not for that word.*

If you want Word for Windows to ignore the text only once, click the Ignore button. Word will leave the word or other text string as you typed it and continue to spell-check. To ignore the word throughout the document you are checking, click Ignore All. (If the word is something you want to ignore in all of your documents, you may want to add it to a custom dictionary, discussed next.)

note *If you tell Word to ignore a word in the morning, it will ignore the word all day, in each document you check, unless you exit Word or use the Reset "Ignore All" List button in the Spelling tab of the Options dialog box.*

Custom or User Dictionaries

Most of the words used by the Spelling checker are located in a dictionary that comes with your Word for Windows program. You cannot make changes to this dictionary. You can, however, maintain one or more of your own *custom* dictionaries. Word checks only open dictionaries. The more dictionaries you have open, the slower the spell-check will be.

The Standard Custom Dictionary

When you install Word for Windows, the installation program places an empty Custom Dictionary in your Windows/Msapps/Proof subfolder. The default name for the dictionary is Custom.dic. It is opened and used whenever you spell-check, unless you instruct Word otherwise. This is where you will want to keep most proper nouns, trademark names, and so on.

Word will place words in the Custom Dictionary whenever you click the Add button while spell-checking. (The first time you add a word, you may be asked to create a custom dictionary.) You can overrule this default by using the drop-down Add Words To list to specify a different dictionary.

Custom dictionaries handle capitalization as follows. If you add a word to a dictionary as all lowercase, it will be recognized later, regardless of whether it is typed as all lowercase, all uppercase, or with an initial capital letter. If you enter a word with only the first letter capitalized, Word will recognize the word when it later appears in all caps or with a leading cap, but will question the word if it is all lowercase. Unusual capitalizations like *VisiCalc* will be questioned unless they are stored in the dictionary exactly as they should appear.

Creating Additional Custom Dictionaries

If you work on unusual projects that involve technical jargon, typesetting codes, and so on, you might want to create one or more additional, specially named custom dictionaries, which you can turn on or off in the Spelling tab of the Options dialog box. To create a new custom dictionary, follow these steps:

1. Visit the Spelling tab in the Options dialog box either by choosing Tools | Options or by clicking the Options button in the Spelling dialog box.

2. Click the Custom Dictionaries button to get to the Custom Dictionaries dialog box.

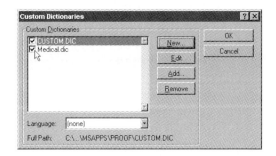

3. Click New to create a new dictionary. You will be prompted for a dictionary name.

4. Type a new name containing up to 32 characters.

5. Specify the folder where you want to store the dictionary (it is best to keep custom dictionaries with the main dictionary).

6. Click Save.

7. To tell Word to use this dictionary when spell-checking, make sure there's a check in the box next to it.

Opening and Closing Custom Dictionaries

To make a dictionary available to the Spelling checker, it must be open. Place checks next to both custom dictionaries to make both open and available for the Spelling checker to use. Click in the box next to the desired dictionary to open or close it. A check means it's open.

To open dictionaries that are not in the folder containing the main dictionary, click the Add button. Show Word where the desired dictionary is, using standard Windows folder-navigation techniques.

Editing Custom Dictionaries

To add a word to a custom dictionary, click the Add button when the Spelling checker encounters the word. You can also type a Word for

WORD PROCESSING WITH
WORD FOR WINDOWS

Windows document containing all of the words you want to add, and then spell-check the document, adding each unrecognized word.

If you accidentally add a word to a custom dictionary, it is a good idea to delete it, since extra words mean more searching time during your spell checks. And if you add misspelled words, they will no longer be challenged by the checker. Here's how to remove words from a custom dictionary:

1. Choose the dictionary you want to edit from the Custom Dictionaries dialog box (reached from the Spelling tab in the Options dialog box).

2. Click the Edit button.

3. A dialog box will appear, warning you that Automatic Spellchecking is turned off when you edit dictionaries. Click OK. Word will then close all open dialog boxes and bring up a regular document of the dictionary with all its words.

4. Edit the dictionary.

5. Save it with the Save command (CTRL+S) and close it.

6. If you want to have Automatic Spellchecking, go into the Options dialog box (the Spelling tab) and reenable it.

AutoCorrect

The primary reason for AutoCorrect is to fix typos like "teh" when you meant to type **the**. Word for Windows will watch you type and change words for you.

note *AutoCorrect moves into action every time you press SPACEBAR, TAB, or ENTER after entering a letter or a word. If the previous word is stored as an AutoCorrect entry, AutoCorrect changes it; if it is not stored as an AutoCorrect entry, nothing happens.*

You can create your own entries or use predefined entries. For instance, if you type (r) or (**R**), Word will replace those characters with the Registered symbol, ®.

To use the built-in entries, you just type along as usual. Word for Windows will make changes when it thinks they are needed. You can see a list of the current autocorrections by scrolling in the AutoCorrect dialog box (reached with the Tools | AutoCorrect command).

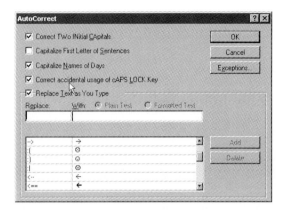

Other Uses of AutoCorrect

In addition to correcting typos, you can use AutoCorrect to convert "shorthand" into longer text strings. For instance, you could tell Word for Windows that you want it to replace "aka" with "also known as," or replace "mwg" with "Mr. William Gates," and so on. You can even insert text and graphics this way. Type **omhlogo** for instance, and insert the Osborne/McGraw-Hill logo (see "Creating Your Own AutoCorrect Entries," next).

Word's AutoCorrect feature is even more robust than before. Now, Word will even autocorrect words and retain the proper possessive case or plural. For instance, if you have the entry "mwg," Word will properly change things whether you type **mwg**, **mwg's**, or **mwgs**. Also, Word now has many more AutoCorrect symbols, including arrows and smileys!

AutoCorrect will *always* make the replacement when you type a defined string of characters followed by a space, a tab, or a paragraph mark (produced by pressing ENTER). AutoText, which you will read more about later, waits for you to press F3 or click on the toolbar button before it takes over.

Creating Your Own AutoCorrect Entries

When creating your own AutoCorrect entries, there is one potential land mine, which is that AutoCorrect will always blindly replace certain text strings with other text strings. So, try to use names that are uncommon yet easy to remember. Consider preceding all of your many entry names with some unusual character that will never appear in normal text, like a backslash (\ **add** for instance). Names can be up to 31 characters long. Here are the steps:

1. Open the AutoCorrect dialog box with the Tools | AutoCorrect command.

2. Type the *name* (the text string you want to replace) in the Replace box.

3. Type the replacement in the With box (or see the tip that follows).

4. Click Add.

5. Make any other entries or changes.

6. Click OK when you have finished.

tip *If you select the text (or graphics and other things) you want to use as the replacement item before you open the AutoCorrect dialog box, it will appear in the With portion of the box when it opens. If the items are formatted, you'll be given the choice of pasting the items as formatted or not.*

Editing AutoCorrect Entries

To modify an AutoCorrect entry, follow these steps:

1. Correct the entry in a document.

2. Choose Tools | AutoCorrect to open the AutoCorrect dialog box.

3. Type the old Replace name.

4. When the Replace button undims, click it.

5. Answer Yes to the "Do you want to redefine?" question.

6. The entry will be updated.

Deleting AutoCorrect Entries

To delete an AutoCorrect entry, follow these steps:

1. Choose Tools | AutoCorrect to open the AutoCorrect dialog box.

2. Select the victim.

3. Click the Delete button. The entry will be deleted.

Automatic Correction

In addition to fixing mistakes as you type them, you can run the Auto-Correct feature at any time to inspect and clean up documents. Use the AutoCorrect dialog box to choose the options you want Word to use.

AutoText

AutoText is the replacement for Word's old Glossary command. It's an easy way to store and retrieve boilerplate text, graphics, addresses, letter closings, memo distribution lists, tables, logos, and just about anything else that you can create with Word for Windows.

You can store AutoText entries with the Normal template so that they are always available or with other templates for specialty projects.

Creating AutoText Entries

Simply select whatever it is you want to memorialize, and then choose Edit | AutoText. If you want to store the paragraph formatting with the entry, be sure to include paragraph marks in your selection. (Even if you store an entry *with* paragraph formatting, you can later insert the entry *without* formatting if you wish.) Click Add.

tip *If you use AutoText a lot, consider adding a button to one of the toolbars or a keyboard shortcut to the menu command.*

Saving AutoText Entries

To save AutoText entries, follow these steps:

1. Before you save an entry, you are given a chance to review and change the automatic entry name assigned by Word for Windows. To change the name, just type a new one in the name box. Names can be up to 32 characters long and spaces are permitted.

2. If you want an entry to be available whenever you use Word, leave the default choice All Documents (Normal.dot) in the drop-down

"availability" list. To attach an entry to a different template, pick one from the drop-down list.

3. Click the Add button.

It is often good to select the space *after* text being memorialized as an AutoText entry (that is, the single space created by SPACEBAR, not the blank line created by the paragraph return). Then you won't have to type a space each time you insert the entry later.

Using AutoText Entries

Once you've saved some AutoText entries, you can insert them using any of several techniques. Always begin by placing the insertion point where you want the entry to be placed. If you need spaces or tabs or anything else before the entry, it is easiest to type them first. When the insertion point is properly positioned, do one of the following:

- Type all or part of an AutoText entry's name and then press F3.

- Type all or part of an AutoText entry's name and then type ALT+CTRL+V.

- Choose Edit | AutoText (you'll see a preview), and then double-click to select an entry from the scrolling name list. Instead of double-clicking, you could also click once and then click the Insert button or press ENTER.

In any event, Word for Windows will insert the entry. Edit it as you would any other text, graphic, or other document element.

Forcing Plain Text

You can have an AutoText entry take on the appearance of the text at the insertion point in the current document, even if you saved it with its own formatting. To do so, choose Plain Text in the Insert As box of the AutoText dialog box.

Editing AutoText Entries

To edit an entry, follow these steps:

1. Insert the entry in a document.

2. Edit and reformat it as necessary.

3. Select the corrected entry and any necessary punctuation, paragraph marks, spaces following, and so on.

4. Visit the AutoText dialog box (Edit | AutoText).

5. Rename the entry, if necessary.

6. Click the Add button.

7. Answer Yes to the "Do you want to redefine?" question.

Deleting AutoText Entries

Deleting AutoText entries is as simple as you'd expect (and hope). Follow these steps:

1. Choose Edit | AutoText to open the AutoText dialog box.

2. Select the doomed item from the scrolling list.

3. Look in the Preview box or insert the entry and check to be *certain* that this is the entry you want to delete.

4. Click Delete.

Grammar Checker

Word offers grammar and style checking, which is no match for a human editor, but worth mentioning nonetheless. Start the Grammar checker by choosing Tools | Grammar.

Unless you select a portion of your document, Word will attempt to check the whole thing. Working from the insertion point, Word will highlight a portion of your prose (usually a sentence) and evaluate it. There may be a slight delay. If Word spots questionable spellings, you will be given the opportunity to correct them or tell Word to ignore them. Once spelling issues have been dealt with, Word will use its Grammar dialog box to point out questionable style and grammar issues. The text being considered is listed in the scrolling Sentence box. Refer to *Microsoft Word for Windows 95, The Complete Reference* (by Mary Campbell and Gabrielle Lawrence, published by Osborne McGraw-Hill) and online Help for details.

Word Count and Other Statistics

The Word Count command is found in the Tools menu. Simply choose the command to start the process.

Tools | Word Count will scan an entire document or just text you've selected. It counts pages, words, characters, paragraphs, and lines. If you place a check in the appropriate box, it will include footnote and endnote text when counting. It does *not* count words in headers and footers. You must display invisible text to count it.

tip   *You can also see the information found in the Word Count dialog box (and a lot that isn't in the Word Count dialog box) by looking at the Statistics tab of the Properties dialog box (File | Properties).*

Tables of Contents

Word for Windows will help you create a *table of contents* (TOC) for your documents. If you format your headings using Word's standard heading styles or Outline feature, the Insert | Index And Tables command will quickly compile (create) a simple but very usable table of contents and place it in a new section at the beginning of your document.

It is also possible to manually select items to appear in your table of contents (TOC). You do this by identifying words and phrases in your document using hidden text codes called *TOC Entry* codes. You can control the appearance of the table of contents as well. Your TOC can have one or multiple levels.

The Insert | Index And Tables command and the hidden *Index Entry* codes work together to produce equally simple or distinctive *indexes* at the end of your document.

Creating a Table of Contents

To create a table of contents, follow these steps:

1. Begin by formatting your document's headings with Word's standard heading styles. (These styles can be added to your Formatting toolbar's drop-down style list by visiting the Style dialog box. Be sure to hold down SHIFT when clicking on the Formatting toolbar's Style drop-down list.

2. When you have typed and proofed your document and are happy with margins, headers, footers, and other design elements (especially those that affect page breaks), pick Insert | Index And Tables.

3. Choose the Table Of Contents tab if it is not already foremost.

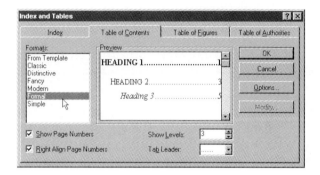

4. Preview the available formats by clicking in the Formats list and watching the Preview area. Pick a format.

5. Choose the number of levels you want to include in the TOC.

6. If you want to include a tab leader (dashes or dots, for instance), choose the style from the Tab Leader drop-down list.

7. Click OK or press ENTER. Word will compile the new TOC. It starts by repaginating your document. Then it will begin the TOC at the insertion point.

If you've already created a TOC for the document, Word will ask if you want to replace it. If you choose No, you will end up with *two* TOCs at the beginning of your document (or wherever the insertion point was). This is a way to create two levels of content detail like the "Contents at a Glance" and regular TOC at the beginning of this book.

Including Nonheading Styles in Your TOC

Word also lets you easily specify nonheading styles for inclusion in your TOC. For example, suppose you create and define a style called Chapters, and you want it to be "above" Heading 1 in your TOC. Use the TOC options to accomplish this.

1. Create and define styles for items you want to include in the TOC.

2. Format the material using these styles.

3. Open the Table Of Contents tab in the Index And Tables dialog box (reached with Insert | Index And Tables).

4. Click on the Options button.

5. You will see a scrolling list of all of the styles in the current document.

6. Assign levels to the styles you want to include in the TOC.

7. Make any other formatting choices and create the TOC as usual.

Changing a TOC's Appearance

You can edit the resulting TOC as you would any other text in your document. Feel free to boldface characters, change line spacing, and so on. As you'd expect, changing the style definitions for styles 1 through 9 will change the appearance of your TOC. Here's how to change style definitions:

1. Choose Insert | Index And Tables to visit the Table Of Contents tab in the Index And Tables dialog box.

2. Pick From Template from the Formats list.

3. Click the Modify button. You will see the Style dialog box.

4. Pick the style you want to modify by clicking on it in the scrolling list.

5. Click the Modify button. You'll see the Modify Style box.

6. Make the desired changes to the style by using the drop-down lists and the Format button (which takes you to familiar formatting dialog boxes).

7. Back out to the Index And Tables dialog box and click OK.

Some of the TOC styles apply elements like all caps and small caps formatting for different levels. Some styles include underlines. Remove one or the other format and redefine the style using standard Word techniques.

Restricting Levels

If you want to suppress the printing of all the levels past a certain point (everything after 5, for instance), specify the levels you want to print in the Show Levels portion of the Table Of Contents tab. You can also turn levels on and off with the Table Of Contents Options dialog box.

Updating a Table of Contents

You should update a TOC after you've made changes to your document. You'll be given the choice of just changing page numbers or updating the entire TOC.

Creating an Index

Automatic indexes are created using hidden codes sometimes called *XE* or *Index Entry* codes. Word for Windows compiles indexes on demand and places them at the end of your document in new sections that it creates for this purpose. Index entries can include the contents of headers and footers if you wish.

Marking Index Entries

Word makes it easy to create an index. Simple indexes can be created by selecting text, issuing the ALT+SHIFT+X keyboard shortcut, and choosing a few options. Word then compiles and stylizes an index and places it at the document's end. Here are the steps:

1. Start by making sure that you have finished proofing, fiddling with margins and page endings, and the like.

2. Select (highlight) a word or phrase you want to use as an index entry.

3. Press ALT+SHIFT+X.

4. You'll see the Mark Index Entry dialog box.

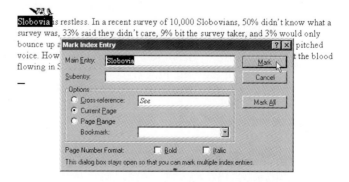

5. Click Mark to mark just this entry, or Mark All to mark all occurrences. (Word will scan the document, mark all occurrences,

and the status area will tell you how many were found.) Edit the entry and add a subentry. You can also include a cross-reference (*See...*) at this time.

6. The Mark Index dialog box remains visible so that you can scroll to other text and mark it, or simply type words to be indexed into the Main Entry section of the dialog box.

7. Repeat steps 2 through 6 until you have specified all desired entries.

8. Click on Cancel to close the dialog box.

9. Place the insertion point where you want the index (typically at the end of your document).

10. Choose Insert | Index And Tables.

11. Visit the Index tab of the Index And Tables dialog box.

12. Pick an index style using the scrolling Preview area as your guide.

13. Double-click on the name of the desired style, or click once on a style name and once on OK.

14. Word will repaginate the document and then create an index that will be placed at the insertion point.

Updating Indexes

Each time you visit and close the Index tab in the Index And Tables dialog box, Word for Windows will ask if you want to replace (recompile) the selected index. Click Yes if you do (and you probably will want to).

Here's an index-updating shortcut worth knowing:

1. Click anywhere in the index to select it.

2. Press the right mouse button to display the shortcut menu.

3. Choose Update Field. Word will repaginate and then recompile and update the index.

Formatting Indexes

The easy way to change the appearance of index entries is to pick a different index format choice from the scrolling Formats list in the Index tab of the Index And Tables dialog box. Watch the Preview area of the dialog box as you shop. It is also possible to change the standard index styles (Index 1 through Index 9).

Creating Automatic Indexes

You can have Word for Windows automatically index a document without your needing to visit the text manually. You do this by creating a list of terms you want to index (called a *concordance* list). Here are the steps:

1. Create a new document with the File | New command.

2. Insert a two-column table (with the Table button, perhaps).

3. Type all index entries in the first column. They must be identical to text Word will find in the document you intend to index. Capitalization counts. (**Network Troubleshooting** might be a typical entry.)

4. In the second column, type all index entries as you want them to appear in the index (**Troubleshooting: network**, for instance).

5. Save the document.

6. Open the document to be indexed.

7. Choose Insert | Index And Tables.

8. Visit the Index tab of the Index And Tables dialog box.

9. Click the AutoMark button.

10. Choose the concordance file from the resulting Open dialog box.

11. Click OK.

Tables of Authorities

Word can help you automatically create *tables of authorities* (TOAs). It provides commonly used categories, including

- Cases

- Statutes

- Other Authorities

- Rules

- Treatises

- Regulations

- Constitutional Provisions

You can control the appearance of the entries and the table itself. Word will even help you seek out items to be included in your table.

Creating TOA Entries

Always type a long citation as your first entry in a legal document—*Mansfield v. Numan*, **45 WN 2D 412 (1994)**, for instance. Subsequent entries can be short versions like *Mansfield v. Numan*. Once you've typed all the entries:

1. Scroll to the first long entry.

2. Select it.

3. Press ALT+SHIFT+ I to bring up the Mark Citation dialog box.

4. Type your selected text in both the Selected Text and Short Citation boxes.

5. Edit the long Citation and format it if you like; you may use only the keyboard shortcuts here (CTRL+B, CTRL+I, and so on).

6. Pick a category ("Cases", for example).

7. Edit the short Citation so that it matches those in your document, *Mansfield v. Murphy*, for instance.

8. Click the Mark button to visit each potential citation, or click Mark All to automatically mark them.

9. To find the next citation to mark, click Next Citation. Word will search for legalese (*v.*, *in re*, and so on) and display possible citations. When you find one, repeat steps 2 through 8.

10. When you've marked all the citations, click Close.

Creating the Actual Table of Authorities

To format and compile the actual table, visit the Table Of Authorities tab in the Index And Tables dialog box. Follow these steps:

1. Choose Insert | Index And Tables. You'll see the Index And Tables dialog box.

2. Pick a format from the Format list.

3. If you want Word to replace five or more page references with *passim,* choose that option.

4. Click OK. Word will compile the table.

Updating a Table of Authorities

Place the insertion point anywhere in the table of authorities, and then press F9. Word will update the table to include any recent insertions, deletions, and so on.

Custom Styles and Categories

Word lets you change the appearance of the styles used for TOAs. It also lets you create and edit category names. Consult the online Help for details.

Tables of Figures

Word will help you create tables of figures and other elements based on captions and bookmarks. Assuming you've captioned documents with the Insert | Caption command, the process is quite simple:

1. Place the insertion point where you want the table to appear.

2. Choose Insert | Index And Tables.

3. Display the Table Of Figures tab if it is not in view.

4. Select the desired caption label from the scrolling list.

5. Select a format for the table.

6. Visit the Table Of Figures Options dialog box if necessary to pick the style you want Word to use as the basis of the table.

7. Back in the Table Of Figures tab, make other option choices (Show Page Numbers, and so on).

8. Click OK. Word will compile a table and place it at the insertion point.

Updating a Table of Figures

Place the insertion point anywhere in the table of figures, and then press F9. Word will update the table to include any recent insertions, deletions, and so on.

Outlines

Word's *Outline* view, located on the View menu (CTRL+ALT+O), is really more than a view. It's a collection of tools designed to help you plan, create, and reorganize long documents. It does this by letting you expand or contract the amount of detail you see on your screen.

The lower half of Figure 10-1 shows a document in Outline view with all of the body text collapsed (not revealed). Since only paragraph headings are visible in the bottom window, it's easy to see the overall organization (the outline) of the document. Outline view lets you control how much detail you see. For instance, you can view the first line of text following each heading if you wish.

Notice also that headings in Outline view are indented, giving you a better idea of the document's organization. Each new level is indented ¼ inch from the preceding one.

It's a snap to reorganize documents in Outline view. If you want to move all of the paragraphs having to do with "Landing Gear" so they appear before "Tail," simply drag the "Landing Gear" heading using the Outline view's special pointer. This will move all corresponding paragraphs, called the *subtext*.

Finally, you can quickly promote or demote portions of your document by using the Outline view tools found on the Outline toolbar.

FIGURE 10-1

Outline view allows you to expand or contract the amount of detail on your screen

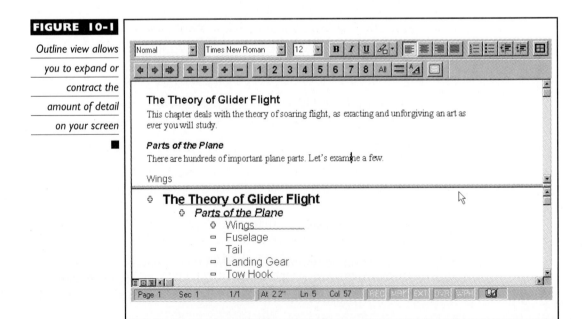

Styles and Outlines

To use Outline view, your headings need to be formatted using Word's standard heading styles (heading 1 through heading 9). If you didn't use these styles when you created a document, it is easy to reformat with them. And, as you probably know, you can change the appearance of standard headings if you don't like Word's standard styles.

The Outline View's Toolbar

Outline view provides a number of unique tools. They are found on the Outline toolbar.

There is an unusual pointer shape indicating the pointer's ability to move large collections of text. It looks like a compass.

Onscreen text in Outline view is often underlined with an unusual line style. Text that is underlined onscreen will not be underlined when printed. Rather, onscreen underlining indicates that there is collapsed subtext beneath the text.

Plus Signs, Dashes, and Boxes

Large plus signs, dashes, and boxes appear next to many headings in Outline view. Boxes tell you that you are looking at body text, pluses indicate headings containing subtext, and minuses denote headings without subtext.

Finally, Outline view includes the Outline toolbar, with its special heading and body-text symbols.

Creating and Editing Outlines

When you start typing a new document in Outline view, Word for Windows assumes the first thing you want to type is a level 1 heading. Each new paragraph you type will take on the heading level of the previous paragraph.

One strategy is to type all of your top-level headings first, and then go back and insert headings in progressively lower heading levels. Another approach is to type all your document's headings in sequence, promoting and demoting as you go. It is even possible to type the entire document (all headings and text) in Outline view, without doing a traditional outline first.

The approach you choose is largely a matter of preference. In any scenario, you will need to know how to promote and demote headings and text.

Promoting and Demoting

The two arrows at the left end of the Outline toolbar are used to promote and demote headings. Place the insertion point in the heading you want to promote or demote. Click the left arrow to promote.

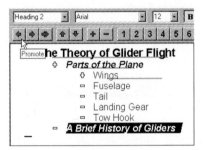

This illustration starts out with all subheadings at the same level. By selecting "A Brief History of Gliders" and clicking on the Promote button, you can change the relative importance of a heading and the underlying text. For instance, the heading has been promoted here to the same level as "Parts of the Plane."

Outlining Existing Documents

To outline existing documents, follow these steps:

1. Open your document in Outline view. You will see the first line of each paragraph.

2. Place the insertion point in each heading and promote or demote them as desired.

3. Save your work.

4. Use the viewing techniques described next to view, rearrange, and understand the organization of your document.

Expanding and Collapsing Outlines

One of the main reasons to use Outline view is to get a collapsed overview of a document's contents, such as that shown next.

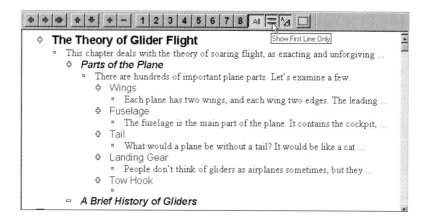

Do this by expanding and collapsing views with the numbers and buttons on the Outline toolbar.

Clicking on the various numbered buttons reveals corresponding levels of detail. For instance, clicking on the 3 button displays heading levels 1 through 3. Clicking on the 4 button reveals an additional level of detail, and so on. The All Text button reveals your whole document, and the Show First Line Only button displays the first line of text for each heading.

Split Views

You can split the screen and show your document in Normal view in one part of the window and Outline view in the other (see Figure 10-2).

To split a window this way, double-click on the Split-bar. Then drag it up or down to change the size of the two areas. Double-clicking on the Split-bar in a split window returns you to a single window. Each part of the screen has its own scroll bars.

Moving Paragraphs

With the outline collapsed, you can move collections of paragraphs (subtext) by moving their associated headings. When you move a heading, *all* heads (that is, those of lower head levels) and text below it will be moved along with it. This facilitates the movement of entire chapters without the need to highlight them. Think of this feature as drag-and-drop on steroids.

FIGURE 10-2

Splitting the

window allows you

to see both the

Normal and

Outline view of

your document
■

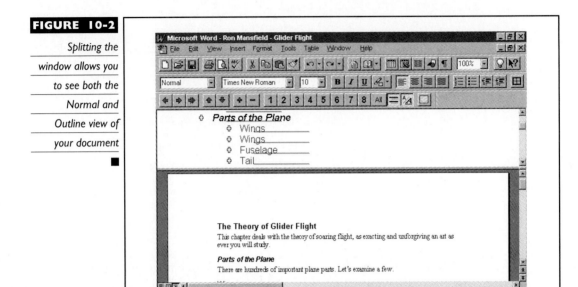

Placing the pointer over the left edge of a heading changes the pointer's shape. It will look like a compass. Click-and-drag, and a large right arrow will appear along with a dotted line. Drag the line and the pointer to where you want to move the text. Release the mouse button and the document will be reorganized.

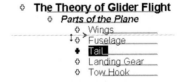

The up-and-down pointing arrows on the Outline toolbar will also move items up and down. Highlight the headings and then click on the appropriate arrow.

Dragging to Change Levels

You can also drag to change the indent level in Outline view. When you do, the pointer arrow changes and you'll see a guideline that indicates the pending indent.

Rearrange Tables by Dragging Rows

When you view a table in Outline view, it is possible to move rows by dragging. It's a great way to rearrange a table!

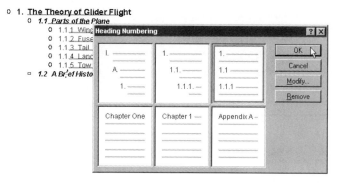

Numbering Headings in Outline View

You can number headings in Outline view just as you can in any other view. Here are the steps:

1. Choose Format | Heading Numbering. You will see the Heading Numbering dialog box.

2. Click on a sample to select the numbering format you desire, or choose Modify for custom numbering choices.

WORD PROCESSING WITH WORD FOR WINDOWS

3. Click OK. Word will renumber immediately and whenever you rearrange your outline. Whenever you add a heading it will automatically be numbered.

    ✧ 1.1<u>4 Landing Gear</u>
    ✧ 1.1<u>5 Tow Hook</u>
▫ ***1.2 A Brief History of Gliders***
▫ ***1.3 Thermals—Rising Hot Air***

Outlines and Tables of Contents

Since Outlines assign standard Word for Windows heading styles to headings, you can quickly create a table of contents based on your outline. The TOC will include each heading from the outline.

Printing Outlines

Printing in Outline view creates a document containing only the levels you see on the screen. Collapse the document to the desired level, and then use the File | Print command or the CTRL+P shortcut. Even if just the first line of text appears, Word for Windows will print the whole paragraph.

Find and Replace

Every contemporary word processing product has a way to quickly locate and replace specific text strings (collections of words, numbers, and other characters). Lawyers use these features (sometimes called *global replace features*) to do things like finding each occurrence of "Marion Morrison" in a contract and replacing it with "John Wayne."

Some typists enter shorthand or acronyms for lengthy items when they draft. Then, while polishing the document, they replace the shorthand with the actual text. For instance, you might initially type **DRD** in the draft of a government document, and then have Word find and replace each occurrence of "DRD" with "Department of Redundancy Department."

tip *If you do a lot of this, consider using Word's AutoCorrect feature instead. It will replace acronyms as you type them.*

Word provides two separate commands called Edit | Find (CTRL+F) and Edit | Replace (CTRL+H). Find is really just an evolutionary predecessor to Replace. In fact, if you are careful, you can use Replace instead of Find for everything.

With Word you can search for and then replace or remove special characters like paragraph marks, optional hyphens, or footnote-reference marks.

You can use wildcards in search requests to work around minor spelling variations. Asking Word to find "Sm?th," for instance, would find both "Smith" and "Smyth." You can search for ranges of numbers using a similar technique. Word's designers refer to this process as searching for *unspecified letters* and *unspecified digits.*

Occasionally, Word's Find and Replace features can be used to reformat documents. You might, for instance, search for all occurrences of two consecutive spaces and replace them with a single space. But Word can do much more than that. The Find and Replace commands can do the following:

- Help you find all or selected paragraphs formatted with a particular style and apply a different style.

- Find all *forms* of a particular word, saving you the effort of multiple searches.

- Remove things simply by telling Word to search for the item you want to delete and replace it with nothing.

- Search your entire document or selected portions. You specify the direction of the search (up or down).

The Art of Finding

The Find feature helps you quickly locate text, formats, special characters, and combinations thereof. It lets you search selected parts of your document or the whole enchilada. Simple Find requests can locate text regardless of format. Well-thought-out features make it easy to ask Word to search for very specific things, like occurrences of the word "Liberace" formatted in bold, blue, 24-point Playbill.

You need not limit your searches to text. You can look for section marks, graphics, paragraph marks, and more. When you use the Find command (as opposed to Replace), Word finds what you've requested, then scrolls to the found item and its surrounding text without modifying anything.

You must click in the document window to work with the found item. You can leave the Find dialog box on your screen as you work, flipping between it and your document window.

Here's a general overview of the Find dialog box. (Details will follow.) To do a search,

1. Choose Edit | Find.

2. Specify text and special characters (if any) to find.

3. Specify formatting characteristics (if any) to find.

4. Tell Word where to search and in which direction.

5. Use the Special menu to search for things like section breaks, paragraph marks, and so on.

6. Check off any special search requests like Match Case or Find Whole Words Only.

7. Click Find Next to start the search.

8. When Word finds what you want, return to the document.

9. To find again, press = (the equal sign) on the numeric pad or ENTER on the numeric keypad (if you're still in the document), or click the Find Next button in the dialog box.

Like any good computer program, Word takes your requests quite literally, so you will need to understand each Find option fully to locate exactly what you want.

For example, if Word searches using the criteria "B B King," it will find "B B King," but not "B.B. King," "BB King," or "Burger King."

There are ways to get Word to find each of these text strings, of course. Just realize that you may need to carefully formulate and test your search strategy. In some cases, you will need to perform multiple searches to find similar but subtly different text strings.

Word will automatically search in headers and footers. For multisection documents, you may need to open and search headers and footers in each section. If you plan to search for items such as paragraph marks or hidden text, the hidden text must be visible on the screen.

tip *Consider proofing your document or at least running the Spelling checker before important, major searches. If you spell "banana" correctly six times and incorrectly once, Word will find only six of your seven "banana"s...*

Finding Text

Choose Edit | Find or use the CTRL+F Shortcut. Move to the text area of the Find What box and type enough text (a maximum of 255 characters) for an accurate, unambiguous search. For instance, suppose you wanted to find the word "man." Entering **man** in Find What would cause Word to find the words "man," "Man," "Mansfield," "reprimand," "manhole," and "man" at the end of a sentence (followed by a period, question mark, and so on).

Placing a space after **man** in your find request would eliminate the unwanted "Mansfield", "reprimand", and "manhole", but would also prevent you from finding "man" at the ends of sentences because periods, question marks, and such are not spaces.

That's the reason for the Match Whole Word Only check box in the Find dialog box. If you type **man** (no space) in the Find What area and check Match Whole Word Only, Word will locate only "man," "Man," and "MAN" anywhere, including at the end of sentences.

The Match Case check box instructs Word to look for exact capitalization matches. If you type **postscript** in the Find What area and check Match Case, Word will not find "POSTSCRIPT," "PostScript," or even "Postscript" at the beginning of sentences.

The Find All Word Forms check box is a handy one. It lets you type a word and then search for all tenses and other possible variations of it. For example, the verb "to be" has dozens of different forms, depending upon tense, person, mood, and so on. If you were to type **be** in the Find What box, Word would find "is," "are," "were," "will," "am," and so on, because they are all forms of the verb "to be."

Extra spaces, nonbreaking spaces, and forced page breaks can also get in the way of searches. See the section "White Space" later in this chapter to learn how to work around this.

Finding Special Characters

The Special drop-down list is a convenient way to enter certain special characters like tab marks, nonbreaking spaces, and such when constructing a search request. Place the insertion point in the Find What box where you want the special character to go, and choose the desired character from the drop-down list.

Find requests can combine regular text and special characters. For instance, you could ask Word to search for occurrences of **Bob** followed by two tab marks. Many of the special characters in the drop-down list are self-explanatory. Let's look more closely at the ones that are not. Some are extremely useful.

WHITE SPACE   Here's one to keep you awake nights. Suppose you are searching for two words together like "Microsoft Corporation." Suppose further that sometimes you used nonbreaking spaces to separate the two words. Other times you've just typed regular spaces. Occasionally, you typed two spaces between the words by mistake. Unless you use Word's White Space feature, you will not find the occurrences of "Microsoft Corporation" containing nonbreaking spaces or two spaces!

So, to do it right, insert Word's White Space special character in your search string. In our example, you'd start by typing **Microsoft** in the Find What box. Then, without touching SPACEBAR, choose White Space from the Special menu. The White Space code (^w) will appear next to "Microsoft." Type **Corporation**. Your finished search string would be **Microsoft^wCorporation**. That should do it.

ANY LETTER   The Any Character choice lets you overcome some nasty problems, too. Suppose you've used accented characters sometimes but not always. "La Cañada" and "La Canada" are not the same thing to Word when it searches. A search for *La Ca^?ada* will find both. Enter the Any Character code from the Special drop-down menu the same way you entered the White Space character.

ANY DIGIT   This special character will sometimes help you find numbers within ranges. It might be helpful for finding specific groups of part numbers or ZIP codes.

note   *When using Any Digit once with the Replace feature, Word will find all occasions, but only highlight the first two digits. So, when you use Replace, you must handle this differently. With the Find feature, it doesn't matter.*

For instance, the search string **99#** would find any number between 990 and 999. The specification **1#** would find the combinations 111 and 11 in 111. It would also find 1000, but not 1,000, since Word treats numbers as text, not numeric values, in searches like these. Commas confuse things. Ah, computers...

Finding Soundalikes

Word can attempt to locate words that sound alike but are spelled differently ("smith" and "smyth," "but" and "butt," for instance). This is an imprecise art at best, since even words that are *spelled* the same *sound* different in various parts of any country. (If you doubt this, ask a Bostonian, New Yorker, and Chicagoan to pronounce the word "car.")

At any rate, the Sounds Like option can sometimes round up useful word variations and misspellings.

Pattern Matching

To perform advanced searches for combinations of things (such as both "bet" and "bat"), you use *operators*. For instance, to find either "bet" or "bat," you would place **b^?t** in your Find What box and check Use Pattern Matching. If you forget to check Use Pattern Matching, the results will not be what you expect. Here's the list of operators you can use with Word and what they help you do:

Operator	Lets You Find
^?	A single character: **b^?t** finds "bet" and "bat"
^*	Any string of characters: **b^*d** finds "bed," "befuddled," and "blood"
[*characters*]	Any of the characters in brackets: **b[eo]d** finds "bed" and "bod" but not "bid"
[*character-character*]	Any character in the range: **b[a-i]d** finds "bed" and "bid" but not "bod"
[!*character*]	Any single character except the one in brackets: **b[!i]d** finds "bed" and "bod" but not "bid"
(!*range of characters*)	Any single character *except* those in the specified range: **t[!a-g]ll** finds "hill" and "toll" but not "tall" or "tell"
character **{n}**	Any *n* occurrences of the preceding character: **ble{2}d** finds "bleed" but not "bled"
character **{n,}**	At least *n* occurrences of the preceding character: **b{1,}** finds "bled" and "bleed"
character **{n,m}**	The specified range of characters: **10{2,3}** finds 100 and 1000 but not 10
character **@**	One or more occurrences of the preceding character: **ble@d** finds "bled" and "bleed"
<*text***	The beginning of a word: **<man** finds "manhole" and "manage"
>*text***	The end of a word. **in>** finds "in" and "herein" but not "interfere"

tip *To search for characters used as operators ({, !, *, and so on), separate them with a backslash. For instance, to find the asterisk, search for *.*

The Art of Replacing

To replace, follow these steps:

1. Save your work.

2. Choose Edit | Replace or press CTRL+H.

3. Create search criteria using the techniques discussed in the previous section.

4. Specify the desired replacement text, formats, and so on.

5. Tell Word where to search and in which direction.

6. Click Find Next or Replace All to start the replacement.

7. Confirm the replacements.

warning   *It is a good idea to save your work before using the Replace feature. If you are working on a complex, important project, you might want to use a copy rather than the original document, since it is much easier to mess up a document with Replace than it is to repair it.*

As you can see here, the Replace dialog box looks like the Find dialog box, with additional features.

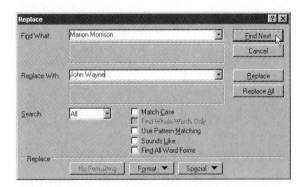

Word lets you confirm each replacement before it happens, or it will find and replace without your intervention.

Just as you can search for text, formats, styles, and special characters, you can also replace them. For instance, you could replace "Marion Morrison" with "John Wayne." (Don't you wish the Duke had kept his given name?)

Or you could change each occurrence of two consecutive paragraph marks to a single end-of-line marker, or change the style of certain paragraphs from chapter-heading style to appendix style. It is even possible to replace text with graphics. Here are examples of each technique.

Replacing Text with Text

To simply replace text (like changing "Marion Morrison" to "John Wayne") without altering formats or styles, start by entering both the text to find and the desired replacement text. For instance, you might enter **Marion Morrison** in the Find What box and **John Wayne** in the Replace With box. Follow these steps:

1. Save your work.

2. Choose Edit | Replace (CTRL+H).

3. Visit the Search drop-down menu to tell Word if you want it to search the entire document or a selected portion, and so on.

warning   *If there are any formats or styles listed under the Find What or Replace With boxes, click No Formatting with the insertion point in the appropriate place (Find What, Replace With, or both). This way, Word will not alter the style or format of the document.*

4. When the replacement instructions are complete, click Find Next. Word will search the document (or selected portion) for things matching your Find criteria and propose the next replacement. The Replace button should undim, and your document screen should scroll to reveal the first potential replacement point.

5. If you want Word to make the change it is proposing, click Replace. To skip the change, click Find Next. To make the change and let Word continue uninterrupted, click Replace All. Word will make the rest of the replacements nonstop, and probably too quickly for you to even see them. The status area in the lower-left corner of your document window will briefly flash the number of replacements made.

6. Check your work. You can use Undo if you have made any mistakes.

WORD PROCESSING WITH
WORD FOR WINDOWS

Replacing Formatting

Suppose you have italicized words scattered throughout your text and decide to change all of them to underlined words. Start by removing any text from the Find What and Replace With boxes. (This is because you want Word to find all italicized text, not just words in the Find What box that are italicized.) Then follow these steps:

1. Specify the character attributes you want Word to find (italics, for example). You can do this in several ways. Always start by placing the insertion point in the Find What entry box. Then specify the Italic format from the Standard toolbar or pull down the Format list in the Replace dialog box. From there, choose Font, and then click in the Italic option of the Font dialog box. The word "Italic" (or whatever) will appear beneath the Find What box.

2. Next go to the Replace With box and specify the new format (Underline, in our example). To prevent Word from changing the italic to italic underline, you may need to click the Formatting toolbar's italic button until the Replace With criteria read "Underline: No Italic."

3. Let 'er rip! Either tell Word to Replace All, or you can supervise by using the Replace and Find Next buttons.

tip *You can use keyboard shortcuts or toolbar buttons to specify formatting as well. It is often much quicker.*

Replacing Styles

If you want to change the style of certain paragraphs, the Replace command can help:

1. Click on the Format button.

2. Choose Styles.

3. You will see a list of your document's styles and descriptions.

4. Pick styles for both the find and replace criteria, and then proceed as usual.

In this example, paragraphs formatted with the Heading 3 style will be reformatted using the Heading 2 style.

Combining Replacement Tasks

Within reason, it is possible to combine search and replace instructions to restrict actions. For instance, assuming you had a document with appropriate styles, you could italicize all occurrences of "Gone with the Wind" in the body text of your report, while leaving the same words alone when they appear in headings, tables of contents, and indexes.

You would do this by typing **Gone with the Wind** in the Find What box and restricting the find to the body text style. Then you'd have to type **Gone with the Wind** again in the Replace With box and specify Italic as the format. (If you forget to enter **Gone with the Wind** in the Replace With box, Word will replace occurrences of "Gone with the Wind" with nothing....) Computers are very obedient but not very clever. Undo should help, but work on *copies* of important documents just in case.

Search

Word has several methods to search your document for words you want to either find or replace. These options are found under the Search drop-down menu in the Find and Replace dialog boxes. Up searches back toward the beginning of the document, while Down searches toward the end. All, as you would expect, searches the entire document.

Using the Clipboard with Find and Replace

The Clipboard can be used for several interesting Find and Replace tasks. For instance, you can copy text from your document to the Clipboard, then paste it into the Find What or Replace With boxes. This is a great way to paste long passages or obscure characters like umlauted letters or math symbols. It is even possible to overcome the 255-character limitation this way.

Word also lets you replace text with graphics if you place the graphics on the Clipboard.

1. Copy a graphic to the Clipboard.

2. Visit the Replace dialog box.

3. Enter find criteria.

4. Place the insertion point in the Replace With portion of the dialog box.

5. Choose Clipboard Contents from the Special list.

6. Replace as usual.

Replacing Tips

Here are some tips for replacing:

- The Replace command uses considerable memory if you make a lot of changes. It is a good idea to perform a normal save after assuring that your replacements are satisfactory.

- Undo will undo all changes if you used Replace All, but only your last change if you were supervising with the Find Next button.

- If you've used styles in your document, you may find it easier to make wholesale style changes by redefining or reapplying styles rather than using Replace.

- You can specify any character in Find or Replace strings by typing **n,** where *n* is the ASCII (decimal) code for the character of interest.

- Remember to click No Formatting when specifying new search criteria in the Find What and Replace With boxes.

- All of the special characters (paragraphs, tabs, and so on) are represented by two-character codes that you can enter into Find and Replace boxes from the keyboard. It's often the quick way to go. Here's a handy reference list. Notice that they must always be typed in lowercase:

Character	Code
Paragraph mark	^p
Tab	^t
Annotation mark	^a
Any character	^?
Any digit	^#
Any letter	^$
Caret	^
Column break	^n
Em dash	^+
En dash	^=
Endnote mark	^e
Field	^d

Character	Code
Footnote mark	^f
Graphic	^g
Line break	^l
Manual page break	^m
Nonbreaking hyphen	^~
Clipboard contents	^c
Nonbreaking space	^s
Optional hyphen	^-
Section break	^b
White space	^w

How Replace Interacts with Styles

Be aware that just as manually applied formatting and styles interact when you change styles or formatting yourself, they interact when the Replace command makes changes.

Annotations

Word for Windows offers several ways to annotate. Hidden text is available along with *voice annotations,* a way to record and play back sounds attached to specific locations in Word for Windows documents if your computer is sound-capable. Finally, Word's text annotation and Revisions features let you document changes as you work.

Using Hidden Text for Annotations

Authors often use hidden text to make notes to themselves or to colleagues. They leave the notes in view while working, and then hide them when they print their work. To hide text:

1. Select the desired text.

2. Visit the Font dialog box (choose Format | Font).

3. Check Hidden in the Effects area.

4. Click OK to set.

5. When printing, click on Options in the Print dialog box (Edit | Print), and check the Hidden Text option in the Include With Document section of the Options dialog box.

The keyboard shortcut to define text as hidden is CTRL+SHIFT+H. This command toggles hidden text. If you use it with hidden text, the text will revert to nonhidden text.

Showing and Hiding Text

To show or hide text, follow these steps:

1. Use the View tab in the Options dialog box (reached with Tools | Options).

2. Enable or disable the Hidden Text feature by clicking to add or remove a check.

3. Click OK.

Text Annotations

This feature lets you add reminders to yourself and notes to others collaborating on your document. The notes can be completely hidden, flagged, or displayed and printed. When you have finished with them, they can be deleted or incorporated into your final document. Annotations with Word for Windows couldn't be easier. Follow these steps:

1. Place the insertion point at the place in your document where you want to insert the annotation, or select the item you want to discuss.

2. Pick Insert | Annotation (*not* View | Annotations).

3. You'll see the annotation window pane.

4. Word will insert initials (hopefully, yours) as hidden text.

5. Type the note.

6. Either choose Close or leave the pane visible as you work.

If you don't see your initials in the document or in the drop-down From list, visit the User Info tab in the Options dialog box and type your initials in the initials area. Click OK.

Viewing Annotations

You view annotations with the View | Annotations command. (Notice that *this* command is plural, while the one on the Insert menu is singular, since you insert annotations one at a time but can view several at once.)

1. Double-click on the annotation mark of interest in your document, or use the View | Annotations command. (If you don't see marks, reveal them with the Standard toolbar's ¶ button.)

2. To view the next or previous annotations, scroll in the annotations window.

3. To filter annotations so that you see only those from a particular author, pick the initials of interest from the annotation pane's drop-down list.

4. When you have finished, close the Annotations pane with the Close button, or leave it open while you work.

If the author of an annotation highlights document text or other elements when creating the note, those items will be highlighted again when you read the annotation. This is not the same thing as selecting before editing. If you want to edit highlighted things, you'll still need to select them.

Editing and Protecting Annotations

You can change any existing annotation, even if you are not the author of the annotation. It is possible for authors to password-protect annotations (and revision marks) with the Tools | Protect Document command. Here's how to protect your annotations and revisions:

1. Choose Tools | Protect Document. The Protect Document dialog box will appear.

2. Choose the protection you desire (Annotations).

3. Enter a clever password.

4. Repeat it when Word asks.

5. Click OK or press ENTER.

6. Remember your password.

WORD PROCESSING WITH WORD FOR WINDOWS

warning *Capitalization counts when entering passwords. "watergate," "Watergate," and "WATERGATE" are all different (and dumb) passwords. Beware of* CAPS LOCK. *Since Word no longer indicates in the status area whether* CAPS LOCK *is on or off, be especially careful.*

note *Give some thought to your passwords. They should be easy for you to remember and difficult for others to guess. Your name or nickname is too easy. The word password is too obvious. Names of old flames are good, unless they're well known to would-be password breakers. Favorite TV or movie characters are good with the same cautions. If you are a Trekkie, people who know you will try words like Spock and Kirk early on in their rummaging.*

Incorporating Annotations

You can copy and paste text from the annotation pane into the document. Drag-and-drop works here, too!

Printing Annotations

To print just the annotations, visit the Print dialog box (CTRL+P), and choose Annotations from the Print What list. To print a document and its annotations, choose Document in the Print dialog box's Print What list, and then click the Options button to reveal the Print tab. Choose Annotations from the options list.

Moving and Removing Annotations

Move and delete annotations by treating their annotation marks as you would any other character in a document. Select them, drag-and-drop, delete, copy, and so on. This assumes, of course, that the document is not password-protected, or that you know the password.

Cross-Referencing

Cross-referencing lets you say things like "see Chapter 29 for details," then have Word automatically update the reference if you change the chapter number. Cross-references are not limited to chapter numbers; they can refer to just about anything, including headings, footnotes, endnotes, captions, and so on. You can cross-reference things in different documents, as long as they are in the same Master Document.

Creating Cross-References

1. Begin by typing the in-text reference followed by a quotation mark (**Parts of an Airplane**", for example).

2. Choose Insert | Cross-reference. You'll see the Cross-reference dialog box.

3. Pick the Reference Type that will tie the in-text reference to the item you want to reference. (Figure 12, for instance.)

4. Choose the item you want to reference in the scrolling For Which list.

5. Click Insert. You'll see some new information at the insertion point. This is actually a field.

6. Click Close or make other cross-references first, and then close.

Once you've created cross-references, they will be updated when you switch to Print Preview or print. To update immediately at any time, select the entire document and press F9.

If you try to delete an item that is referenced, Word will alert you.

Thesaurus

The Thesaurus command can help you add flavor and punch to your documents. Select the word you want to change, and then open the Thesaurus dialog box either with the keyboard shortcut SHIFT+F7 or by choosing the Thesaurus command on the Tools menu. You'll see the Thesaurus dialog box.

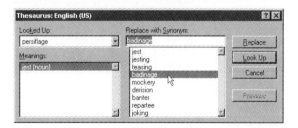

The Meanings section of the dialog box lists available meanings and parts of speech for the selected word. If antonyms (words with opposite meanings) are available, you'll see an Antonym choice as well.

1. Select the meaning of interest in the Meanings list, and you'll see a corresponding list of synonyms or antonyms in the box to the right. Click on the closest meaning or on Antonyms if that's a possibility. You'll see a list of choices in the box to the right of the Meanings box.

2. Clicking on a word places it in the Replace With box.

3. If you click the Replace button at this point, the new word will replace the selected one in your document.

4. To look for other words instead, click the Look Up button. This will display additional choices.

5. The Synonyms For list builds as you explore alternative words, and you can go back by clicking on the arrow and selecting an earlier word.

6. Clicking the Cancel button closes the Thesaurus without changing your selected word.

note *If the selected word is misspelled or unfamiliar to the Thesaurus feature, you will see a list of "close" words that may or may not be useful. You'll also see close words for some tenses of some words. For example, if you try to look up "carries," the Thesaurus will suggest "carry."*

Incidentally, the Thesaurus sometimes recognizes phrases. Look what happens when you select the phrase "about to."

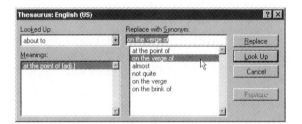

Bookmarks

Bookmarks let you name specific points or areas of your document. Use bookmarks to identify the beginning of chapters, tables, spots that need work, the place where you left off, and so on. You can mark a place, a character, ranges of characters, graphics, or just about any other element in a Word document. You can then tell Word to go to those specific points without a lot of scrolling and searching.

To use bookmarks, you simply locate things of interest, define them as bookmarks, and visit them as necessary. Here are the general steps.

Defining Bookmarks

To define a bookmark, follow these steps:

1. Either move the insertion point to the item of interest, or select the item.

2. Choose Edit | Bookmark (CTRL+SHIFT+F5). You'll see the Bookmark dialog box.

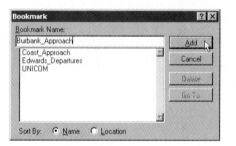

3. Give the bookmark a unique name consisting of up to 40 characters. Spaces are *not* allowed, so use an underscore instead, as just illustrated. Numbers are allowed, but not for the first character of the bookmark—that has to be a letter.

4. Click Add. (If the button is dimmed, check to see that the name is less than 40 characters long and contains no spaces.)

5. Create more bookmarks or close the box. Clicking on Add also closes the dialog box.

Going to a Bookmark

Once you've defined some bookmarks, you can go to them in one of two ways. If you select Edit | Go To, you'll see a list of bookmarks in a scrolling list.

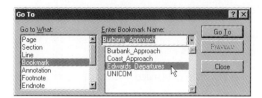

Double-click on a bookmark's name to go there. If you click the Go To button in the Bookmark dialog box, however, Word will go to the selected bookmark without displaying the dialog box.

In the Bookmark dialog box, you can sort the list either by name or by the relative location of the bookmark in the document.

Displaying and Hiding Bookmarks

You can see little in-document markers that indicate the location of bookmarks. These large, square brackets indicate the beginning and ending of a bookmarked area. For instance, the entire heading "Patch Panel" is a bookmark.

note   *If you select text before setting a bookmark, you'll get something that looks like [selectedtext]. If you don't select text, though, you'll get something that looks like a big I.*

As you can see, these markers can get in the way of the text, so you can turn them on and off by selecting or clearing the Bookmarks check box on the View tab of the Options dialog box (reached by choosing Tools | Options).

Working with Bookmarked Items

It's often easiest to work with bookmarked items and see the effect of your work if you have the bookmark markers displayed.

If you move a bookmarked item, the marker moves with it, even to another document (as long as this won't create a duplicate bookmark name in the destination document).

Deleting the entire text or other items between two bookmark markers deletes the bookmark as well. (Say that five times fast.)

To add things and have them included with the bookmark, insert them within the bookmark markers. To insert things and not have them included, place the insertion point to the right of the bookmark marker.

Deleting Bookmarks

To delete a marker but not the marked item(s), follow these steps:

1. Visit the Bookmark dialog box.

2. Choose the desired bookmark name.

3. Click Delete.

4. Click Close. The bookmark disappears and the previously marked items remain.

To delete a bookmark and the items it marks:

1. Turn on Bookmarks markers in the View tab.

2. Select the item and both bookmark markers.

3. Delete as usual (Cut, press DEL, and so on). The mark and the items(s) will disappear.

CHAPTER 11

Macros, Custom Toolbars, Keyboard Shortcuts, and Menus

MACRO

MACRO has an international status as a dirty word in computing, a reputation quite unjustified. Macros are one of the most powerful features of Word, since they allow you to customize and automate your work to a high degree. Custom toolbars and menus let you further personalize Word. You can also add or change keyboard shortcuts to speed your work.

What Are Macros?

A macro is a series of Word commands grouped together as a single command to make everyday tasks easier. You can assign a macro to a toolbar, a menu, or a shortcut key and run it by simply clicking a button, selecting a menu choice, or pressing a key combination. Macros are recorded as instructions in Word's macro language, *WordBasic*. You create a macro in two ways:

- Record a series of actions using the keyboard and mouse. This is the easiest way.

- Type a macro directly into a macro-editing window. This way you have more flexibility and can include WordBasic instructions that you can't record using the keyboard and mouse.

For complicated macros, consider combining these two ways: Record as much as possible, and then edit the result in the macro-editing window. Record further pieces, edit them, and add them as necessary.

Recording Macros

To record a macro, you start the Word *macro recorder* and record a sequence of actions. You then stop the recorder and edit the macro if need be. Then you can run the macro whenever you need to perform the same sequence of actions.

There are three ways to start the macro recorder:

- Double-click REC on the status area (at the bottom of your screen). Yes, even though REC is dim, double-clicking works.... This is the quick and easy way.

- Select Tools | Macro, and then click the Record button in the Macro dialog box. Easy but slower.

- Click the Record button on the Macro toolbar if you have it displayed.

Here's how to record a macro:

1. Start the macro recorder by double-clicking REC on the status area. The Record Macro dialog box will appear.

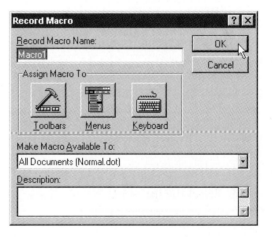

2. Enter a name for the macro in the Record Macro Name box.

3. If you don't give your macro a name, Word will name it *Macro1*, *Macro2*, and so on. No spaces, commas, or periods are allowed in the name.

4. Enter a description of what the macro does in the Description box. This is optional but highly recommended. Use up to 255 characters.

5. To assign the macro to a toolbar, a menu, or a keyboard shortcut, click the Toolbars, Menus, or Keyboard button.

6. If your current document is attached to a template other than Normal.dot, drop down the Make Macro Available To list and select either that template or Normal.

7. Click OK, and then perform the actions you want to record.

8. To stop recording the macro, click the Stop button on the Macro Record toolbar that appears when you start recording (shown here). The Macro Record toolbar will disappear.

Pausing While Recording the Macro

Word 6 allows you to suspend and resume recording a macro as suits you. If you reach some impasse in the procedure that you don't want to record for posterity, or just want to record isolated actions here and there as the fancy strikes you, here's what to do:

1. Click the Pause button on the Macro Record toolbar to pause recording.

2. Perform the actions you don't want to record.

3. Click the Pause button again to restart recording (just like a tape recorder).

Editing Macros

Here's how to edit a macro:

1. Select Tools | Macro. The Macro dialog box will appear.

2. Select the list of macros to choose from by dropping down the Macros Available In box.

3. Choose the macro you want to edit, and then click the Edit button. The macro-editing window will appear, displaying the text of the macro you chose.

4. Edit the macro.

Running a Macro

Once you have recorded your macro, you can assign it to a toolbar, a menu, or a shortcut-key combination. You can then run it as you would a normal Word command or feature.

If you don't want to assign a macro to a toolbar, menu, or key combination—perhaps you simply have too many macros, or use some of them too seldom to merit having them available all the time—you can also run a macro by choosing Tools | Macro, selecting the macro name in the Macro dialog box, and clicking the Run button.

If you've got everything right, your macro will perform the actions you taught it to do. If something is wrong, you may have to edit it.

Organizing Your Macros

Word's Organizer dialog box greatly simplifies managing your macros. You can use it to move, copy, or rename a macro.

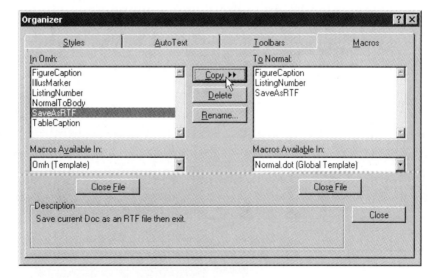

By default, macros are stored in the Global Template (Normal.dot) and so are available for use with every Word document. However, you can store them in other templates if you want. For example, if you have a macro that's only useful for annual reports, you might include it in your Annual Report template.

Copying Macros from One Template to Another

Word lets you easily copy macros from one template to another. For instance, you could record or write a macro in the Normal template, then decide you only need it in your I Am Clever template, and transfer it as follows:

1. Select File | Templates. The Templates And Add-Ins dialog box will appear.

2. Click the Organizer button to display the Organizer dialog box.

3. Choose the Macros tab.

4. If necessary, close the open file, select the Open File button, and open the template or document containing the macro.

5. Select the macro you want to copy, and then choose the Copy button.

Click the Close button when you've finished copying macros. The original remains in Normal until you delete it. You can also get to the Organizer dialog box by selecting Tools | Macro and clicking the Organizer button in the Macro dialog box.

Renaming a Macro

If you find you've given a macro a confusing name, you may want to rename it. Here's how:

1. Select Tools | Macro. The Macro dialog box will appear.

2. Click the Organizer button. The Organizer dialog box will appear with the Macros tab selected.

3. In the left list box, choose the macro to rename. If necessary, choose a different template in the Macros Available In list box.

4. Click the Rename button. The Rename dialog box will appear:

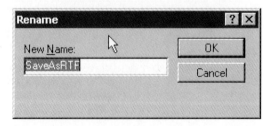

5. Enter the new name for the macro and click OK. The macro will be renamed.

Deleting a Macro

Here's how to delete a macro that you no longer need—or one that doesn't work:

1. Select Tools | Macro. The Macro dialog box will appear.

2. Highlight the macro to delete and click the Delete button.

3. Click Yes in the confirmation dialog box that Word pops up. The macro will be deleted.

4. Click the Close button to return to your document.

Word's Automatic Macros

Even if you never get deeply into writing and using macros, you should look briefly at Word's five autoexecuting macros. With only a little effort, you can use these to set and restore screen preferences, open a bunch of documents, and generally make life a little more pleasant for yourself. The five automatic macros are

Macro Name	What It Does	Suggested Uses
AutoExec	Runs when you start Word	Set general screen preferences; open a particular document
AutoNew	Runs when you open a new file based on its template	Set screen document for a particular template; change printers
AutoOpen	Runs when you open a file you created before	Return to last editing location (using GoBack)
AutoClose	Runs when you close a file (new or created before)	Prompt to back up file
AutoExit	Runs when you exit Word	Restore screen preferences for next use; reminders; valedictions

You can create automatic macros just as you do any other macros—by typing the commands into the macro-editing window (reached by selecting the Edit or Create button in the Macro dialog box), by recording a series of actions, or by a judicious mixture of the two.

The Macro Toolbar

When working with macros, you'll often want to use the Macro toolbar (see Figure 11-1). This contains 12 buttons and a name box and lets you manipulate macros in a variety of useful ways. Here's what the different parts of the Macro toolbar do.

Toolbar Item	What It Does
Macro name box	Lists the name of the macro
Record	Turns recording of macro on or off
Record Next Command	Records the next command executed
Start	Starts running the current macro
Trace	Highlights each statement as the active macro executes it
Pause/Continue	Pauses or continues running the macro
Stop	Stops running the macro
Step	Runs the active macro one step at a time
Step Subs	Runs the active macro one step at a time, considering subroutines one step at a time
Show Variables	Lists the active macro's variables
Add/Remove REM	Adds or removes a REM (remark) at the beginning of each selected line in the active macro
Macro	Runs, creates, deletes, or revises a macro
Dialog Editor	Launches the macro *Dialog Editor,* a mini-application that you can use to design dialog boxes

FIGURE 11-1

The Macro toolbar

■

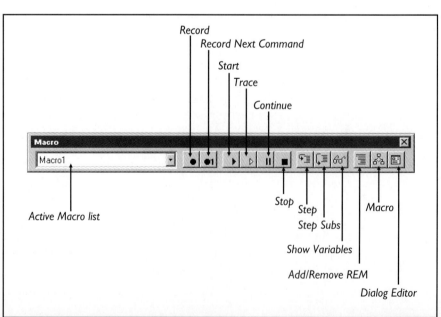

For reasons of space, this chapter has only been able to skim the surface of macros, the macro language, and the benefits they can offer you. Consult online Help and the big books for more information about macros.

Customizing Word's Toolbars

You can customize Word's toolbars to simplify the way you work. You can add and remove commands, macros, AutoText entries, and styles, and move buttons from one toolbar to another. You can even create custom toolbars. You can move toolbars to different positions on the screen or have them float freely above the document. You can move and resize a floating toolbar as if it were a window. In the following sections, we'll look at the different things you can do with toolbars.

Figure 11-2 shows a custom toolbar—a combination of Word commands and macros. The buttons are labeled in Figure 11-2 to give you some ideas for making your own toolbars.

Displaying Toolbars

To display toolbars, select View | Toolbars. In the Toolbars dialog box, check the check boxes for the toolbars you want to see and click OK.

WORD PROCESSING WITH WORD FOR WINDOWS

FIGURE 11-2

A custom toolbar

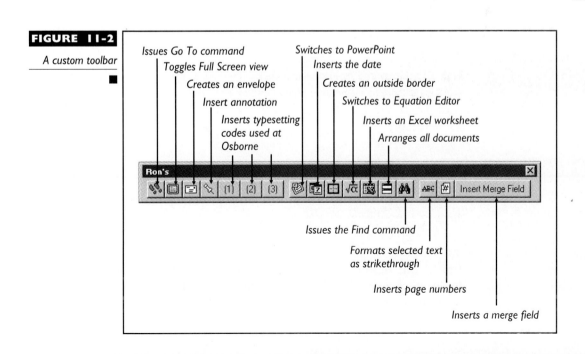

Issues Go To command
Toggles Full Screen view
Creates an envelope
Insert annotation
Inserts typesetting codes used at Osborne
Switches to PowerPoint
Inserts the date
Creates an outside border
Switches to Equation Editor
Inserts an Excel worksheet
Arranges all documents

Ron's

Issues the Find command
Formats selected text as strikethrough
Inserts page numbers
Inserts a merge field

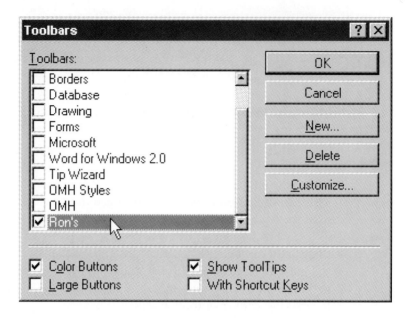

 note *You can't display the Mail Merge toolbar unless you're running a mail merge. (Select Tools | Mail Merge to fire up the Mail Merge Helper.) Likewise, with some of Word's other specialized toolbars, you can't display the Header and Footer toolbar unless you're working in a header or footer, and so on.*

To remove a toolbar from the screen, select View | Toolbars, and uncheck the appropriate check box, and then click OK.

 tip *To display and remove toolbars using the mouse, right-click on a displayed toolbar to display a shortcut menu; then click to display an unchecked toolbar or to hide a checked toolbar. Click Toolbars or Customize to display the Toolbars or Customize dialog box, respectively.*

Moving and Resizing Toolbars

You can place toolbars anywhere on your screen that suits you and resize them to a number of shapes.

To move a toolbar displayed at the top of the screen, click in some blank part of it and drag to where you want it. It'll change shape as soon as you drag it out of the toolbar area at the top of the screen. Alternatively, double-click in its blank space to display the toolbar in its last floating position on the screen.

To return a toolbar to the top of the screen, click a blank part of it and drag to the top of the screen, where it'll revert to its long and wide shape. Alternatively, double-click in its blank space to flip it back up there.

To resize a toolbar, move the mouse pointer over one of its borders so that a double-headed arrow appears; then click and drag the border to the shape you want. Toolbar shapes adjust in jumps, not smoothly, so that they're the right size and shape for their buttons.

Changing the Predefined Toolbars

If you want, you can change Word's predefined toolbars. You might want to remove buttons that you never use, or change the command that an existing button runs. Here's how:

1. Display the toolbar you want to change.

2. Choose Tools | Customize. The Customize dialog box will appear.

3. Select the Toolbars tab.

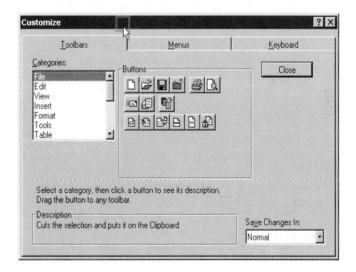

4. To add a button, select the category in the Categories box, and then drag the button or item to where you want it on the toolbar.

5. To delete a button, drag the button off the toolbar and drop it in the dialog box (or anywhere else where no toolbar is).

6. When you have finished, click the Close button.

WORD PROCESSING WITH WORD FOR WINDOWS

warning *When you delete a built-in toolbar button, it'll still be available in the Customize dialog box. But when you delete a custom toolbar button, it's gone for good. Consider creating a storage toolbar for keeping unused buttons, rather than deleting them permanently.*

Moving or Copying a Toolbar Button

Here's how to move or copy buttons from one toolbar to another:

1. Select Tools | Customize. The Customize dialog box will appear.

2. Select the Toolbars tab.

3. To move a button, drag it to where you want it on the same toolbar or on another toolbar.

tip *To move a toolbar button quickly, without opening the Customize dialog box, hold down ALT and drag the button to where you want it. To copy a button, hold down CTRL+ALT and drag the button to where you want it.*

4. To copy a button, hold down CTRL and drag the button to where you want it on the same toolbar or on another toolbar. Word will automatically close the gap (when you move a button) and shift the buttons along in the new location.

tip *To add space before a button, go to the Toolbar tab in the Customize dialog box and drag a button a little way to its right. When you have finished, close the dialog box. This seems pretty pointless unless you're megaclumsy with your mouse, and even then you'd be better off recalibrating the mouse's movements in the Control Panel.*

Resetting a Built-In Toolbar

Here's how to restore a toolbar to its original settings:

1. Select View | Toolbars. The Toolbars dialog box will appear.

2. Highlight the toolbar you want to restore, and then click the Reset button.

3. In the Reset Toolbar dialog box, select the template in which to make the change, and then choose OK.

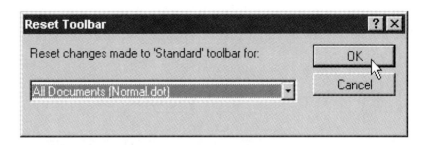

4. Click OK to close the Toolbars dialog box.

Creating a Custom Toolbar

If you find yourself using buttons on half a dozen toolbars in the course of the day's work, or if you wish there were buttons for commands, macros, templates, and other things that don't have them, you may want to create a custom toolbar that contains only the buttons you need. Here's how:

1. Select View | Toolbars. The Toolbars dialog box will appear.

2. Click the New button. The New Toolbar dialog box will appear:

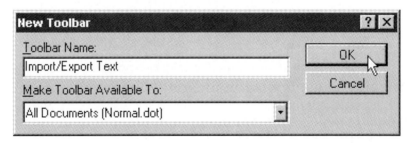

3. Type a name for the new toolbar in the Toolbar Name box.

4. Select the template in which to store the toolbar in the Make Toolbar Available To box, and then click OK. Word will display the Customize dialog box with the Toolbars tab selected and a new toolbar without buttons in its own toolbar window.

5. In the Categories box, select the category containing the first button to add to the new toolbar.

6. Drag the appropriate button to the new toolbar.

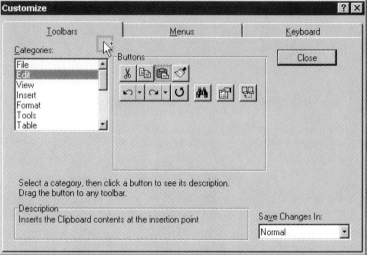

7. Add further buttons as appropriate.

8. When you have finished building your new toolbar, click the Close button.

Your new toolbar will appear in the Toolbars dialog box and in the shortcut menu produced by right-clicking a displayed toolbar.

Deleting a Custom Toolbar

When you get sick of your custom toolbars, you can easily delete them:

1. Select View | Toolbars to display the Toolbars dialog box.

2. Highlight the custom toolbar you want to delete and click the Delete button.

3. Click Yes in the confirmation dialog box.

note   *Word won't let you delete the toolbars it provides—only your custom toolbars.*

Renaming a Custom Toolbar

You can rename a custom toolbar at any point:

1. Select File | Templates. The Templates And Add-Ins dialog box will appear.

2. Click the Organizer button. The Organizer dialog box will appear.

3. Select the Toolbars tab.

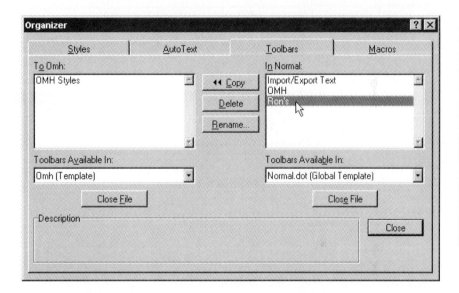

4. In the left or right box, highlight the toolbar to rename, and then click the Rename button.

5. In the Rename dialog box (shown next), enter a new name for the toolbar and click OK.

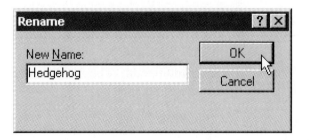

6. Click Close to close the Organizer dialog box.

WORD PROCESSING WITH WORD FOR WINDOWS

Assigning an Item to a Toolbar Button

You can assign toolbar buttons to run commands, macros, fonts, AutoText entries, or styles. You can attach toolbars to specific templates, which gives you great flexibility.

To assign an item to a toolbar button:

1. Open a document based on the template containing the item you want to assign—or open the template itself.

2. Display the toolbar you want to change.

3. Select Tools | Customize. The Customize dialog box will appear.

4. Choose the Toolbars tab.

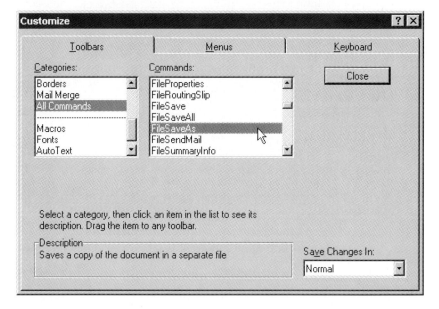

5. In the Save Changes In box, select the template containing the item you want to assign to the toolbar.

6. In the Categories box, select the category containing the command to add. (The All Commands choice will list all of Word's commands.)

7. Drag the item name from the Commands box to the toolbar.

When you choose an item without a built-in button, you'll get a blank button on the toolbar, and Word will open the Custom Button dialog box. (See the section "Creating a Custom Button," coming up next.)

8. Select a button, click the Assign button, and then click Close.

Creating a Custom Button

You can create a custom toolbar button in two ways: either create a new image in the Button Editor dialog box, or copy an image from a graphics application and paste it onto a button. The latter's more fun, so let's look at it first:

1. Create the image in your graphics application and copy it to the Clipboard, preferably in bitmap or picture format.

2. Switch to Word and display the target toolbar.

3. Select Tools | Customize.

4. In the Customize dialog box, select the Toolbars tab.

5. Right-click the toolbar button to receive the image.

6. Choose Paste Button Image from the shortcut menu.

7. Click the Close button.

If you don't have a graphics application, here's how to create (from a blank button) or modify a toolbar button:

1. Display the toolbar whose button you want to modify.

2. Select Tools | Customize. The Customize dialog box will appear.

3. Click the Toolbars tab.

4. Right-click the button you want to modify (on the toolbar, not in the dialog box).

5. Choose Edit Button Image from the shortcut menu. The Button Editor dialog box will appear.

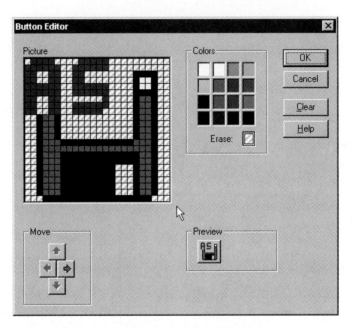

6. Change the button image to your liking. Click on the small boxes representing each pixel in the button face to add/remove or change a color. Watch the Preview box as you work.

7. Choose Close when finished.

Restoring a Built-In Toolbar Button's Image

If you don't like the changes you made to the image on a button, you can easily restore it:

1. Display the toolbar whose button you want to change.

2. Select Tools | Customize. The Customize dialog box will appear.

3. Select the Toolbars tab.

4. Right-click the button you want to restore.

5. Choose Reset Button Image from the shortcut menu.

6. Choose Close.

Enlarging Toolbar Buttons

You can enlarge the toolbar buttons to make them easier to see, or make them smaller so that more will fit on your screen. (You may want to remove unnecessary commands from the toolbars so all of your favorites will fit.)

To display large toolbar buttons:

1. Select View | Toolbars to display the Toolbars dialog box.
2. Check the Large Buttons check box, and then click OK. Your toolbars will appear with large buttons, as shown in Figure 11-3.

To restore toolbar buttons to their normal size, select View | Toolbars and uncheck the Large Buttons check box.

tip   *You can quickly resize toolbar buttons by opening the Customize dialog box, holding down ALT, and dragging on the toolbar button you want to resize.*

Customizing Word's Menus

Word lets you control the appearance and arrangement of its menus. You can add, delete, and reposition menu items. You can also change the keyboard shortcuts for most menu items. You can use this flexibility to make your copy of Word extremely easy to use or to restrict another's options. For example, you could prevent someone else from applying any formatting to your precious documents.

FIGURE 11-3

The difference between toolbars with large buttons (top) and regular ones (bottom)

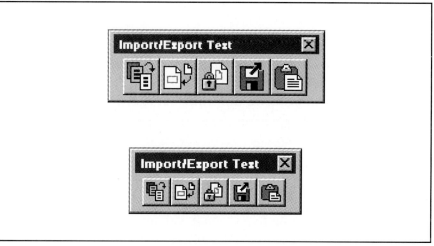

Adding Menu Items

Here's how to customize Word's menus so they contain the commands, macros, fonts, AutoText entries, and styles you need most often:

1. Open a document based on the template containing the item you want to assign—or open the template itself.

2. Select Tools | Customize. The Customize dialog box will appear.

3. Click the Menus tab.

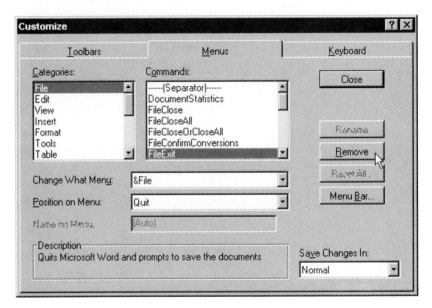

4. In the Save Changes In box, select the template in which the item is stored.

5. Select the category to which the item belongs in the Categories box.

6. Select the item you want to assign in the Commands box.

7. Choose the menu you want in the Change What Menu box.

8. In the Position On Menu box, select (Auto) to let Word automatically position similar menu items together, select (At Top) or (At Bottom) to position the item at the top or bottom of the menu, or select the item below which to position the item if you want to position it within the menu list.

9. In the Name On Menu box, either accept the default name, or type the name you want to appear. Put an ampersand (&) in front of the hot-key letter.

10. Click the Add button or Add Below button. (Word will offer you one.)

11. To close the Customize dialog box, click the Close button.

tip *To add a menu item separator bar, choose (Separator) in the Commands box of the Customize dialog box, position it as described earlier, and click the Add or Add Below button.*

Removing Menu Items

Here's the quick way to remove items you don't need from menus:

1. Press CTRL+ALT+– (that's CTRL+ALT+minus). The mouse pointer will change to a heavy horizontal line.

tip *If you change your mind, press ESC to return the mouse pointer to normal.*

2. Click the menu item you want to remove. It will disappear.

This method is much more fun than using the Tools | Customize dialog box, selecting the command to remove, and then clicking the Remove button, but that way works, too.

tip *To remove a menu item separator bar, choose (Separator) in the Commands area of the Customize dialog box and click the Remove button.*

Restoring Built-In Menus to Their Original Settings

To quickly restore all built-in Word menus to their original state:

1. Select Tools | Customize. The Customize dialog box will appear.

2. Choose the Menus tab.

3. Select the template to restore in the Save Changes In box.

4. Click the Reset All button.

5. Click Yes in the confirmation dialog box.

6. Click the Close button.

warning *Think twice before restoring all menus, especially if you've made any significant changes. Consider backing up any superb pieces of customization so you can't trash them in an instant with the Reset All button.*

Adding New Menus

Word lets you add new menus—a great feature! You can add as many menus as you want, but they may not all fit on one line of menu bar. (In case you're wondering, yes, they wrap around onto a second line of menu bar.)
To add a new menu:

1. Select Tools | Customize. The Customize dialog box will appear.

2. Choose the Menus tab.

3. Select the template for the new menu in the Save Changes In box.

4. Select the Menu Bar button. The Menu Bar dialog box will appear:

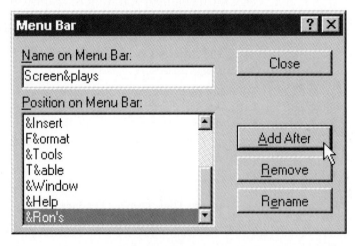

5. Enter the name for the menu in the Name On Menu Bar box. Use an ampersand (&) in front of a letter to designate a hot key.

6. Position the new menu using the Position On Menu Bar box:

   ■ To position it first, select First.

   ■ To position it last, select Last.

■ To position the menu after another menu, select the menu for it to appear after.

7. Click the Add button or Add After button (Word will offer you one, depending on your choice in step 6)to add the menu.

8. Choose the Close button to close the Menu Bar dialog box, add items to the menu as described before, and choose the Close button again to close the Customize dialog box.

Renaming Menus

You can rename a menu to suit you. Here's how:

1. Select Tools | Customize. The Customize dialog box will appear.

2. Choose the Menus tab.

3. Select the template containing the menu you want to rename in the Save Changes In box.

4. Select the Menu Bar button. The Menu Bar dialog box will appear.

5. Select the menu to rename in the Position On Menu Bar box.

6. Type the new name in the Name On Menu Bar box.

7. Click the Rename button.

8. Click the Close button to close the Menu Bar dialog box, and then click the Close button on the Customize dialog box to close that, too.

Customizing Word's Keyboard Shortcuts

You can get the most use from your keyboard by customizing Word's keyboard shortcuts. You can assign shortcut keys to commands, macros, fonts, AutoText entries, styles, and special characters. You want CTRL+A to change selected text to 40-point Desdemona? *No problemo*. You need

CTRL+SHIFT+T to type "I was quite ecstatic to see you last night, darling!"? Read on, MacDuff!

Changing Keyboard Shortcuts

Here's how to see what your current keyboard shortcuts are and change them:

1. Select Tools | Customize. The Customize dialog box will appear.

2. Select the Keyboard tab.

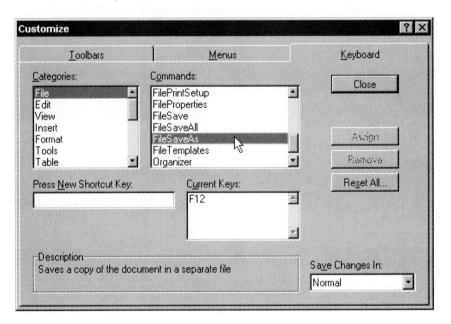

3. In the Categories box, select the category containing the items you want.

4. In the Commands box, select the command whose shortcut you want to view. The shortcut will appear in the Current Keys box.

5. Move to the Press New Shortcut Key box, and press the keyboard shortcut you want to assign. Word will display the current assignment of that keyboard shortcut.

6. Click the Assign button to assign the shortcut key to the item.

7. Click the Close button to close the Customize dialog box.

tip Here's a shortcut: Press CTRL+ALT++ (that's CTRL+ALT+PLUS). The mouse pointer changes to a command symbol. Choose a menu command or click a toolbar button. Word will display the Customize dialog box showing the command you select. Follow steps 5 to 7 of the preceding list.

Deleting Shortcuts

By deleting shortcuts, you can prevent yourself or another user of your computer from performing unwanted actions. Here's how:

1. Select Tools | Customize. The Customize dialog box will appear.
2. Choose the Keyboard tab.
3. Select the template containing the item whose shortcut you want to remove in the Save Changes In box.
4. In the Categories box, select the category containing the item.
5. In the Commands box, select the item.
6. In the Current Keys box, select the shortcut key to delete.
7. Click the Remove button.
8. Choose the Close button to close the Customize dialog box.

Reverting to Default Keyboard Shortcuts

Here's how to restore all shortcut key assignments to their original settings:

1. Select Tools | Customize. The Customize dialog box will appear.
2. Choose the Keyboard tab.
3. Select the template containing the shortcut key assignments you want to restore in the Save Changes In box.
4. Click the Reset All button.
5. Choose Yes in the confirmation dialog box that appears.
6. Click the Close button to close the Customize dialog box.

Chapter 12

Introduction to Mail Merge

ORD'S Mail Merge feature lets you quickly create personalized correspondence and other documents by combining (*merging*) information from two files. For instance, you could merge a list of names and addresses from one file (your *data document*) with a form letter in another file (your *main document*) to produce a number of personalized form letters. Or you could create catalogs, forms with variable information fields, or labels.

You insert data instructions (*fields*) in the main document wherever you want data from the data source to appear in your merged documents. For instance, for a letter, you could use fields to create suitable salutations for each one. Instead of writing plain-old, boring "Dear" to each recipient, you could have a salutation field in addition to the name field. Optionally, you could have a third field (to appear on the same line) of further greeting. This way, you could produce such salutations as "Hi, Joe Bob, how's it going?" and "My darling little Rosemary, how much you've grown this year!" as well as the staid "Dear Aunt Edna."

Once the main document and the data source are prepared, you're ready to merge them. The *Mail Merge Helper* lets you send merged documents directly to your printer or save them to a file for editing and later printing.

In either case, Word will automatically take care of things like word wrap and pagination for each new document. Figure 12-1 shows an overview of the elements in a mail merge project.

Thanks to Word's new Mail Merge Helper, merging is relatively painless, though you still need to pay plenty of attention to what you're doing. Some planning doesn't hurt either, but it's not absolutely essential. That said, let's get into it.

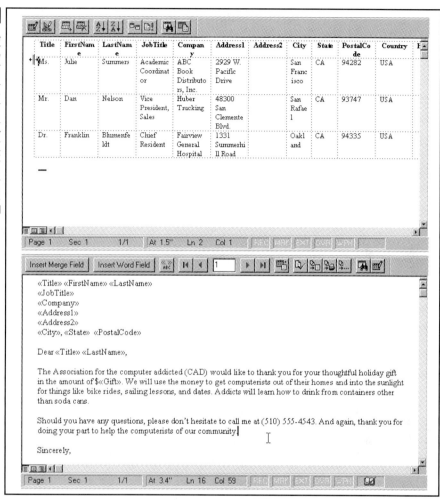

FIGURE 12-1

Mail merge projects require a data source (top) and a main document (bottom) to produce new documents that contain information from both ■

note *Unfortunately, a book this size cannot cover all the variables involved in mail merges. Sometimes you'll find it easier to copy a form letter a few times and paste in the names and addresses of the recipients, rather than perform an entire mail merge. Take a quick reality check before turning blindly to the Mail Merge Helper.*

About Data Sources and Main Documents

Data sources are organized collections of information—databases—stored as Word tables. As you'll see in this chapter, Word's Mail Merge Helper leads you step by step through the creation of a new data source.

Word can also use data from other applications, such as Microsoft Excel or Microsoft Access. All data sources, no matter where they come from, contain *records* and *fields*. For instance, an employee data source would usually contain one record for each employee. This record would contain multiple fields—one field for the employee's first name, one for the middle initial, one for the last name, one for each part of the address, and so on.

Main documents, as mentioned before, contain the text of your project (the body of a letter, for instance), fields, and merge instructions.

Using Main Documents from Earlier Versions of Word

You can use main documents from earlier versions of Word for Windows—for example, version 6.*x*—with no problem. Simply open the document in Word and proceed as normal.

n o t e *When you open a main document in Word, it will bring with it the association (to its data source) with which it was last saved. If you use a previously created main document, remember to attach to it any new data source that you want to use.*

Using Main Documents from Other Applications

You can use a main document from another application by opening the document in Word and converting its contents to Word. However, field names and formatting from some applications may not translate well into Word format. Check the fields in your main document and adjust them if necessary before completing the merge.

If you experience problems, try pasting the main document into Word for Windows as plain text, then applying the formatting and entering the field names.

Using Data Sources from Other Applications

You can use data sources from other applications in your Word for Windows merges. For example, if you have data in a Microsoft Excel spreadsheet, you can insert either the whole worksheet or just a range of cells. If you have Microsoft Access, you can open a database and insert records from a table or a selection of records defined by a query.

After opening a data source in another application, make sure that the merge fields in your main document match those in the data source.

Creating Your First Mail Merge Project

The best way to learn how to create a print merge document is to try one. Consider working along as you read the rest of this chapter.

Project Overview

For each new mail-merge project, you'll need to

- Create and proof the text of your main document
- Create a new data source
- Enter information into the data source
- Insert fields into your main document
- Check for design and data-entry errors
- Merge the data source and main document, and print the merge documents

Since data sources in Word can be documents containing tables, you can add information and edit them at any time before doing the actual merge. Once you get comfortable with merging and its possibilities, feel free to do things in any workable order that pleases you.

note   *If you already have a data source, simply open it or adapt it for the new project.*

While you don't need to type your main document first, it's often helpful to make a draft to get a sense of which information you will need from your data sources and where to insert it.

tip   *Test your new design with small data documents containing a dozen or so representative records. Try your sample data source with a number of different main documents, or have an experienced print merge user look over your new design before you spend hours entering data into your first data source. Consider keeping sample main documents and data sources at hand in a test directory, so you can perform quick tests on new merge projects you put together.*

Using the Mail Merge Helper

Word's Mail Merge Helper guides you through the steps of merging documents. The process may seem a little convoluted the first time, but it works well. Once you've tried it a few times, you'll be merging merrily with the best of them.

note *In the following sections, we'll discuss how to perform the different stages of a mail merge by using the Mail Merge Helper, since this is the easiest way to merge. We'll also indicate how you can proceed without using the Mail Merge Helper.*

To start the Mail Merge Helper, select <u>T</u>ools | Mail Merge. The Mail Merge Helper dialog box appears.

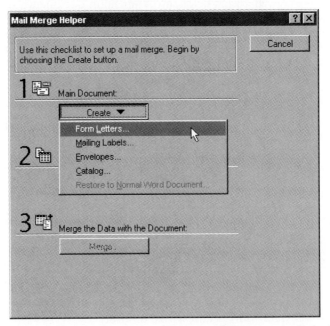

Note the instructions in the box at the top telling you to click the Create button to set up the mail merge. Watch these instructions as you proceed with subsequent stages of the mail merge. If you're ever confused about what to do next, consult this box.

The first step in the mail merge is to create your main document, since the type of main document governs the subsequent choices you can make in the Mail Merge Helper. Form Letters, Mailing Labels, Envelopes, and Catalogs have different components, so the Mail Merge Helper offers you different choices of data source.

∫tarting Your Main Document

To start your main document, follow these steps:

1. Select the Create button to start creating your main document. A list will drop down offering you four choices—Form Letters, Mailing Labels, Envelopes, and Catalog.

2. Select the type of main document you want. A dialog box will appear offering you the choice of the active window or a new main document.

3. Select the window you want to use. If you're starting from a new document, or if the active window contains information for your main document, choose the Active Window button. If your active window contains valuable information that has nothing to do with the mail merge, choose the New Main Document button. If you choose the New Main Document button, Word will open a new document. The previously active document stays open—Word does not save or close it.

Whichever button you chose, Word will return you to the Mail Merge Helper dialog box for the next stage of the mail merge, arranging the data source. You'll see that the space below the Create button now lists the information you've entered so far—the type of merge and the main document to use.

The information box at the top of the Mail Merge Helper dialog box tells you that the next step is to specify the data source. Let's do it.

Specifying the Data Source

Next, you need to specify the data source and arrange in it the fields that will be available to your main document for the merge.

1. Click the Get Data button to display a list of options for your data source.

2. If you already have a data source that you want to use, select Open Data Source. If you want to create the data source, select Create Data Source.

If you chose Open Data Source, skip ahead a section. If you chose Create Data Source, read the next section.

tip *There is another choice you can reach by clicking the Get Data button called Use Address Book. If you click this, Word will use the names and addresses you have entered in your personal address book.*

Creating a Data Source

The Create Data Source dialog box that appears when you choose Create Data Source contains a list of commonly used field names for the type of mail merge you're performing. This illustration shows the Create Data Source dialog box for form letters.

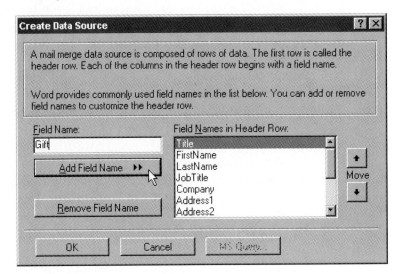

Adding a Field Name

Here's how to add field names to the list in the Field Names In Header Row box:

1. Type the name in the Field Name box.

note *Field names can be up to 40 characters long and can contain letters, numbers, and underscores (_). Field names cannot contain spaces and must start with a letter (not a number or an underscore). For example, What_We_Discussed_At_Yesterday's_ Meeting is an acceptable field name (and might remind you better of the field's purpose than MeetingTopic), but 1994_May_15_Meeting is not. Bear in mind that the ends of very long field names may not show in the Field Names In Header Row box, so it can be confusing to have long field names that differ only at their ends.*

2. Click the Add Field Name button. The new field name is added at the bottom of the list.

3. To move the new field name to a different position in the list, make sure it's highlighted and click the Move arrow buttons.

Removing or Modifying a Field Name

Here's how to remove or modify a field name:

1. In the Field Names In Header Row box, highlight the field name you want to remove by clicking it with the mouse or by scrolling to it with the scroll bars or the down arrow. Then click the Remove Field Name button. The field name will be removed from the Field Names In Header Row list and will appear in the Field Name box.

2. To modify the field name, make your changes in the Field Name box, and then click the Add Field Name button.

Rearranging Field Names

To rearrange the field names in the Field Names In Header Row box, highlight the field you want to move and click the Move arrows beside the Field Names In Header Row box to move the highlight field up or down.

Saving Your Data Source

When you've finished adding, removing, and arranging fields, click OK to save your data source. In the Save Data Source dialog box that appears, enter a name for your data source file, choose the folder where you want to save it, and select OK to save the file.

Word will save the data source file under the name you give and then return you to the Mail Merge Helper dialog box. At this point, you will be given the option of adding entries to your new data source or editing the main document.

Opening a Data Source

To open an existing data source, select Open Data Source from the Get Data drop-down list in the Mail Merge Helper dialog box. The Open Data Source dialog box that appears works just like the File Open dialog box: Select the document you want to use and click OK. Word will open the document and return you to the Mail Merge Helper dialog box.

note *If you want to use a data source from another application, such as Microsoft Excel or Microsoft Access, simply choose it at this point and select the data records you want to use.*

Editing the Data Source

Back in the Mail Merge Helper dialog box, you'll see that Word displays the name of the data source document beneath the Get Data button.

Word now checks your data source to see if it contains records. If it doesn't, Word will display a dialog box informing you of this and inviting you to edit the data source or the main document. Choose the Edit Data Source button to edit your data source.

tip *If you click Edit Main Document and then change your mind, just click the Edit Data Source button on the Mail Merge toolbar.*

Entering Your Records

In the Data Form dialog box that Word displays, enter the details for each of your records by typing text into the boxes. Press TAB or ENTER to move from field to field. To move backward, press SHIFT+TAB

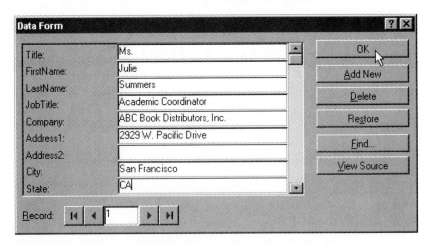

Here's how to alter the records in the Data Form dialog box:

■ To add a new record, choose the Add New button.

- To delete a record, choose the Delete button.

- If you realize you've trashed a record (by entering data in the wrong place, or whatever), click the Restore button to return its entries to their previous state.

To Find a Record

Word's database functions offer great flexibility in searching. You can search for any word or part of a word in any of the fields.

To find a record, follow these steps:

1. Click the Find button. The Find In Field dialog box will appear.

2. Type the word or words you want to find in the Find What box.

3. Click the arrow at the right end of the In Field box to drop down the list of field names, and select the name of the field you want to search.

4. Click the Find First button. Word will search for and display the first record it finds containing the word or words in the selected field.

5. If this is the record you were looking for, click Close to close the Find In Field dialog box. If not, click the Find Next button to find the next occurrence of the text.

6. When you've finished entering or updating your records, click OK to close the data source and save the changes. Now you're ready to edit your main document.

tip   *If the Find In Field dialog box is hovering annoyingly over the field you're trying to read, grab it by clicking anywhere in its title bar, and then drag it to a more convenient location on the screen.*

Editing the Main Document

Main documents contain the following:

- Text and punctuation

- Merge instructions and field names that Word uses to merge data

Here is a main document for the sample mail merge. Its elements will be discussed in detail.

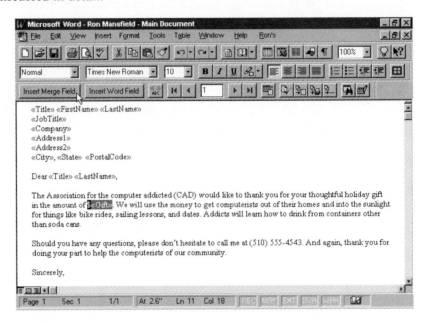

Text in Main Documents

Use Word's word processing and graphics features to create the text and design elements for your main document. Add data instructions containing field names and other merge devices inserted as needed, as explained next.

Inserting Data Instructions

The Mail Merge Helper makes it easy to insert field names and other data instructions in your main documents. Just place the insertion point where you want to insert a data instruction, then pull down the appropriate list from the Mail Merge toolbar, and pick the item to insert.

Place the insertion point where you want to insert a field name, and then click the Insert Merge Field button on the Mail Merge toolbar to display the list of field names available in the associated data source. Next select the appropriate field name to insert it into the document. (The guillemets—« »—are inserted automatically with the field name.)

tip *When preparing the text of a main document, remember to include things like spaces between field names and any required punctuation following them. Running people's first and last names together will spoil the effect of your carefully personalized letters. You'll know the feeling if you've ever been renamed by Publishers Clearing House.*

You can combine merge fields from the Insert Merge Field button and word fields from the Insert Word Field button (both on the Mail Merge toolbar) with text typed from the keyboard, to produce powerful merge instructions. You'll see how in a moment.

Testing and Proofing

Before firing up the Mail Merge Helper and churning out a whole batch of letters, proofread your work. Use Word's spell checker and grammar tools. Make any necessary corrections. Remember that Word will faithfully copy every error in your main document into every single copy it merges.

Next run the Mail Merge Helper's error-checking program. Choose the Check Errors button from the Mail Merge toolbar. The Checking And Reporting Errors dialog box will appear.

You have several choices. Word will simulate the merge or actually do a merge and report errors. In either case, Word will check your data source and main document for errors (such as missing data fields in the data source and misspelled field names in your main document). If Word finds no errors, you will see a happy dialog box telling you that no mail merge errors have been found. If errors are found, correct them.

As a final check, consider merging some or all of your documents to a file and inspecting them, rather than printing them all at once. We'll look at how to do this in just a moment. First, let's look at Word's sorting and filtering features.

Sorting Merged Documents

Usually, records are merged in the order they occur in your data source; but Word's Mail Merge Helper lets you sort the records during the merge. In addition, Word lets you use filters to restrict merging to records containing certain data. (Filtering is discussed in the next section.)

To sort records before you perform a merge, follow these steps:

1. Open the Mail Merge Helper dialog box and choose the Query Options button. The Query Options dialog box will appear.

2. Click the Sort Records tab to enter your sorting preferences.

3. In the Sort By field that you want to use, click the down arrow, and then select a field to sort by from the list that appears.

4. Select a field for one or both Then By fields if you want to refine your sort further.

5. When you've defined the sort to your satisfaction, click OK. If you mess things up, click the Clear All button to clear the fields and start again, or click Cancel to escape from the dialog box.

Filtering Merged Documents

If you're not content with sorting your records, you can filter them as well. Filtering gives you a lot of flexibility in removing from the merge records what you don't want to use. For instance, you can exclude records based on certain criteria.

Here's how to set up filtering:

1. Pull up the Mail Merge Helper dialog box and choose the Query Options button. The Query Options dialog box will appear.

2. Select the Filter Records tab.

3. In the Field column of the first row, choose the field you want to use as a filter.

4. In the Comparison column of the first row, drop down the list of filtering comparisons. This is what they do:

Comparison	Effect
Equal To	The contents of the data field you chose must match those of the Compare To box.
Not Equal To	The contents of the data field you chose must *not* match those of the Compare To box.
Less Than	The contents of the data field you chose must be less than those of the Compare To box.
Greater Than	The contents of the data field you chose must be greater than those of the Compare To box.
Less Than or Equal	The contents of the data field you chose must be less than or equal to those of the Compare To box.
Greater Than or Equal	The contents of the data field you chose must be greater than or equal to those of the Compare To box.
Is Blank	The merge field must be empty.
Is Not Blank	The merge field must not be empty.

5. In the second row, choose And or Or in the first column to include additional or complementary criteria for filtering.

6. Repeat steps 3, 4, and 5 for further rows as necessary to refine your criteria further.

7. When you've defined the filtering criteria to your satisfaction, select OK. If you mess things up, select Clear All to start again or Cancel to escape from the Query Options dialog box.

note *When you compare a data field that contains text, Word compares the sequence of characters based on the ANSI sort order. Since* antelope *precedes* zebra *alphabetically, Word considers it "less than" zebra. So if you wanted to retrieve data records for only the second half of the alphabet, you could specify LastName Is Greater Than M. If you mix numbers with letters, Word compares the numbers as though they were a sequence of text characters.*

Printing Merged Documents

When you've specified any filtering and sort-ordering that you want, you're ready to run the mail merge.

1. Start the merge process by making your main document the active document (click in it if necessary).

2. Click the Merge button in the Mail Merge Helper dialog box to bring up the Merge dialog box.

3. You can either merge directly to your printer by selecting Printer in the *Merge To:* box, or you can have Word merge to a new, untitled document that will contain all of the merge documents by selecting New Document.

4. Select the Records To Be Merged by choosing *All* or *From:* and *To:*. If you choose *From:* and *To:*, specify the record numbers for the merge to start and stop at.

5. The default is not to print blank lines when data fields are empty. If you *do* want to print blank lines when the fields are empty—perhaps you have a reason, like to show gaps in your data source—choose the "Print blank lines when data fields are empty" option.

6. When all is set to your liking, click OK. The mail merge will finally take place, and you will get something that looks like this:

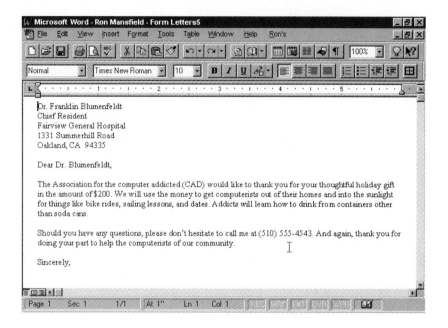

When the mail merge is finished, close the Mail Merge Helper dialog box. If you merged to a new document, it should be onscreen now. If you merged to a printer, the printer will be churning out your merged documents. Either way, check your output carefully before inflicting it on your victims. The law of mass mailing clearly states that you'll only notice an egregious error *after* you've mailed the whole batch.

If you have unsaved changes in your main document, Word will invite you to save them.

Specifying Header Options

The header row is the row of fields at the top of a data source that identifies each kind of information in the data source—the Title, FirstName, and LastName fields, and so on.

Why would you want to reuse a header? You could then use the same header source with more than one data source. If you can't change the merge fields in a data source to match the names of the merge fields in a main document (the file might be read-only), you can use a header source that contains matching merge fields.

To specify a header source:

1. Choose the Get Data button in the Mail Merge Helper dialog box and select Header Options. The Header Options dialog box will appear.

2. In the Header Options dialog box, choose Create to create a new header source. Or choose Open to open an existing header source, and then skip to step 5.

3. If you chose Create, the Create Header Source dialog box will appear. This works just like the Create Data Source dialog box we discussed under "Creating a Data Source," earlier in the chapter. Add, remove, and rearrange the fields to your satisfaction, and then click OK.

4. In the Save Data Source dialog box that appears, give your header source a name and click OK. You'll be returned to the Mail Merge Helper dialog box, and the header source you created will now appear under the Get Data button.

5. If you chose Open, the Open Header Source dialog box will appear. Select the header source you want to use and click OK. You'll be returned to the Mail Merge Helper dialog box, and the header source you created will now appear under the Get Data button.

6. Word will check the header source against the data source and warn you if the data source contains too many data fields. The Merge button on the Mail Merge Helper dialog box will be dimmed, indicating that you cannot yet run the merge.

7. If the data source contains too many fields, edit the data source or header source.

Using Word's Merge Instructions

Word provides a number of ways to change its behavior based on the contents of individual records in your data source. As you've just seen, it can eliminate unwanted blank lines in merged documents. It can insert special text if certain conditions are met, or stop during each merge to let you enter unique text from the keyboard. If you decide to use these features, be prepared to spend some time experimenting and troubleshooting. Here's a brief summary of the function of each part of the Mail Merge toolbar, shown in Figure 12-2.

WORD PROCESSING WITH WORD FOR WINDOWS

FIGURE 12-2

The Mail Merge
toolbar

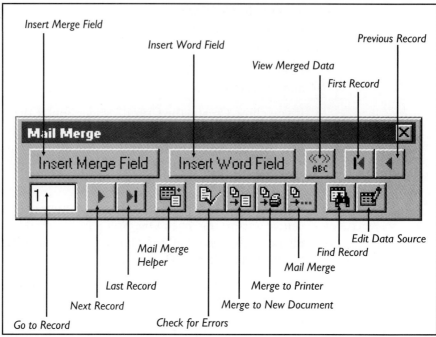

Name	Function
Insert Merge Field	Inserts a merge field at the insertion point
Insert Word Field	Inserts a Word field (e.g., ASK) at the insertion point
View Merged Data	Toggles between viewing merge fields and the data that will appear in them
First Record	Displays the first record in the data source
Previous Record	Displays the previous record in the data source
Go to Record	Enter the number of the record you want to go to in this box
Next Record	Displays the next record in the data source
Last Record	Displays the last record in the data source
Mail Merge Helper	Displays the Mail Merge Helper
Check for Errors	Displays the Check For Errors dialog box
Merge to New Document	Merges the main document and data source to a new document
Merge to Printer	Merges the main document and data source to a printer
Mail Merge	Displays the Merge dialog box
Find Record	Displays the Find Record dialog box
Edit Data Source	Displays the Data Form dialog box

Merge Printing Labels and Envelopes

You can also use Word's Mail Merge Helper to merge labels and envelopes. Since the procedures for merging labels and envelopes are very similar to those for form letters, we'll discuss them only briefly here.

Printing Labels on Laser Printers

The Mail Merge Helper makes merging labels on a laser printer dead simple. You use the Mail Merge Helper to create a main document containing a table with fixed-size cells and cell spacing that match the size and position of your blank labels, then insert merge instructions in each table cell. Here's how to do it:

1. Select Tools | Mail Merge to fire up the Mail Merge Helper.

2. Click the Create button to drop down a list of options.

3. Select Mailing Labels from the drop-down list.

4. Arrange your data source as usual. Word will then invite you to set up your main document. In the Label Options dialog box that appears, make the appropriate choices for your printer and labels:

   ■ In the Printer Information box, select Laser or Dot Matrix as appropriate. If necessary, click the arrow to drop down the Tray list and select a different tray.

tip *Consider selecting a different Tray option when printing labels on a network. That way, you might be able to avoid having someone else print a 90-page report on your precious disk labels.*

   ■ In the Label Products box, select the brand of labels you want: Avery Standard, Avery Pan European, or Other. ("Other" includes brands such as Inmac and RAJA.)

   ■ In the Product Number box, select the number for the labels you're using. If you don't know the number, consult the Label Information box to find out the size of the labels listed in the Product Number box. If you're still no wiser, measure your labels carefully and choose the closest match.

   ■ For precise layout information on the labels, choose the Details button. In the dialog box that appears, make any necessary adjustments in the labels' margin, pitch, dimensions, and layout, and then click OK.

5. When you've chosen the labels to use, choose OK to close the dialog box.

6. The Create Labels dialog box will appear. Enter the fields here by pulling down the Insert Merge Field list and selecting them in turn. Remember to include any necessary spaces and punctuation.

   ■ To include a postal bar code, click the Insert Postal Bar Code button. In the Insert Postal Bar Code dialog box, enter the Merge Field With ZIP Code and Merge Field With Street Address in the appropriate boxes, and then click OK.

   ■ Click OK when you've finished making choices in the Create Labels dialog box. Word will then enter your label fields into the main document.

7. Make any necessary adjustments to your main document (for example, adding ASK or FILL-IN fields).

8. Open the Mail Merge Helper dialog box, and choose the Merge button to merge your data source with the main document. Choose whether to merge to a new document or to the printer. (You can also use the Merge to New Document and Merge to Printer buttons on the Mail Merge Toolbar here.)

9. Save your documents with meaningful names.

Printing Addresses on Envelopes

Word offers the ability to print addresses on envelopes. This can be convenient for small numbers of envelopes; but because most laser printers require you to feed in envelopes by hand, printing large numbers of envelopes can be a slow business. Take a quick reality check before you arrange to print a whole slew of envelopes, and consider using mailing labels on the envelopes instead.

tip *Before starting to prepare envelopes, make sure your return address is correct. Choose Tools | Options to display the Options dialog box. Click on the User Info tab to view (and if necessary, change) the name and mailing address. Click OK when you've finished.*

1. Select Tools | Mail Merge to fire up the Mail Merge Helper.

2. Click the Create button to drop down a list of options.

3. Select Envelopes from the drop-down list.

4. Arrange your data source as usual. Word will invite you to edit your main document. In the Envelope Options dialog box that appears, make the appropriate choices for your envelopes:

   ■ On the Envelope Options tab, click the Font button in the Delivery Address box or the Font button in the Return Address box to change the font in which the addresses appear. If necessary, adjust the position of the delivery address or return address by entering From Top and From Left measurements in their boxes.

   ■ On the Printing Options tab, select the Feed Method and the tray to Feed From. Note that the default Feed From option is manual. For large numbers of envelopes, you'll be spending half the afternoon feeding the printer.

 note *Word displays the name of your currently selected printer in the Printing Options tab of the Envelope Options dialog box. If need be, change the printer by using File | Print and then choosing the Printer button. If necessary, click the arrow to drop down the Tray list and select a different tray.*

5. When you've chosen the envelope options and printing options, choose OK to close the dialog box.

6. The Envelope Address dialog box will appear. Enter the fields here by pulling down the Insert Merge Field list and selecting them in turn. Remember to include any necessary spaces and punctuation.

   ■ To include a postal bar code, click the Insert Postal Bar Code button. In the Insert Postal Bar Code dialog box, enter the Merge Field With ZIP Code and Merge Field With Street Address in the appropriate boxes, and then click OK.

   ■ Click OK when you've finished making your choices in the Envelope Address dialog box. Word will then enter your label fields into the main document.

7. Make any necessary adjustments to your main document.

8. Open the Mail Merge Helper dialog box and choose the Merge button to merge your data source with the main document. Choose whether to merge to a new document or to the printer. (You can also use the Merge To New Document and Merge To Printer buttons on the Mail Merge toolbar.)

9. Save your documents with meaningful names.

Creating Catalogs with Mail Merge

As mentioned at the beginning of this chapter, you can use Word's Mail Merge Helper to create catalogs. What wasn't mentioned was that to make a catalog, you follow the same procedure as for form letters. The only difference is that instead of selecting Form Letters from the Create drop-down list, you choose Catalog. Have a ball.

Restoring a Mail-Merge Document to a Normal Word Document

You can restore a mail-merge main document to a normal Word document when you've finished merging with it. This removes the association between the main document and its data source and header source (if it has one). The text of the main document does not change.

To restore a main document to a normal Word document, follow these steps:

1. Open the Mail Merge Helper dialog box by selecting Tools | Mail Merge.

2. In the Main Document section, choose the Create button to display the list of options.

3. Choose the Restore To Normal Word Document option.

4. In the Restore To Normal Word Document dialog box that appears, choose Yes. The association between the main document and its data sources will be removed.

Tips, Techniques, and Troubleshooting

To change the appearance of merged characters—to make them bold or italic, or a larger point size—format their merge instructions in the main document.

Merged characters take on the formatting of their merge instructions.

If you move your data source files, Word will ask you to relocate them before you can merge.

To print selected items from a longer data file, sort them and print just the range containing the desired records (from 10 to 30, for instance).

The following shortcut key combinations are available when merging documents using the Tools | Mail Merge command:

Key Combination	Effect
ALT+SHIFT+K	Previews a mail merge
ALT+SHIFT+N	Merges a document
ALT+SHIFT+M	Prints the merged documents
ALT+SHIFT+E	Edits a mail-merge data source

Part Three
Working with Excel

In Part Three you will see how you can use Microsoft's latest version of Excel to compute and keep track of all sorts of interdependent data. You'll learn not only how to have Excel perform complex calculations, but also how to display your data in aesthetically pleasing charts and graphs. Once you've gotten the hang of it, you can spice up your work by including graphics and special annotations, and use macros to save time on tedious tasks. Use Excel's Scenario Manager to automatically generate illustrative what-if conditions, and when you've found the optimum balance, import your results into Word or PowerPoint for a polished presentation.

CHAPTER 13

Excel Basics

I F you've been using the same old spreadsheet program for years, you're in for a pleasant surprise. Or, if you happen to be a newcomer to spreadsheets, you've made the right choice. Microsoft's Excel is a comfortable blend of old and new. Like Word, it's easy to learn and difficult to outgrow. Users of earlier versions of Excel, as well as users of Lotus 1-2-3 or other spreadsheet programs, will quickly feel right at home with Excel's familiar old features—and will grow to appreciate its powerful new ones.

The Usual Spreadsheet Features

Excel lets you create and quickly perform what-if analyses of complex, interrelated columnar reports, in workspaces called *worksheets* or *spreadsheets*. (The terms "spreadsheet" and "worksheet" are used interchangeably in this book.)

Worksheets are made up of *cells* arrayed in *rows* and *columns*—rows run across your screen and columns run down. You type or otherwise enter things like labels, numbers, and dates into cells. Excel rows are usually identified with numbers, and columns with letters. The *address* of a cell is a combination of the row and column labels. Thus, cell B5 would be the fifth cell down in the second column from the left of the worksheet.

You also create *formulas* (sometimes called *equations*) in cells. For instance, you might enter five different numbers in cells A1 through A5, then place a formula in cell A6 that adds those five numbers and displays the results in cell A6. *AutoCalc* even lets you total the numbers *without* having to create a totals column. Excel helps you quickly build formulas using your keyboard and mouse. Excel also provides toolbar tools, menu choices, and functions you can employ to create and use complex formulas.

An almost overwhelming array of formatting features lets you dress up and print your final work product. A Chart Wizard quickly converts your worksheet numbers and cell labels into all manner of impressive pie charts, line graphs, bar charts, three-dimensional charts, scatter charts, and other visual aids. There's even a way to create automated, onscreen slide shows displaying spreadsheet data and charts, complete with audio and special effects!

Windows Savvy

Because Microsoft designed Excel from the ground up as a Windows product, the program offers Windows features you've already learned about in other parts of this book. You edit Excel worksheet text by using the same techniques you learned for Word. Many of the commands you'll use are located on the same menus as they are in Word. In addition, Excel offers impressive compatibility with other Windows products. For instance, it's easy to insert graphics from most other Windows programs into Excel worksheets. It's also easy to paste Excel worksheet data and charts into PowerPoint or Word documents. Data collected in Excel worksheets can be used to create Word mail-merge data files, for example.

For most people, the real Excel advantage is its ease of use. Microsoft has created powerful tools to speed spreadsheet construction, formatting, and use. Let's get an overview in this chapter, then create a first worksheet.

Overview of Excel Features

Figure 13-1 illustrates some of the important new features in the current version of Excel.

ANSWER WIZARD   Like Word, Excel has a new feature called Answer Wizard. This addition to the Excel Help system uses "intellisense" to determine what kind of help you need, based upon your questions. What's really nice is that you can type your questions in regular English sentences. No arcane worksheet jargon is required. You reach the Answer Wizard by choosing Help | Answer Wizard. Joe Bob says, check it out!

AUTOCALC   You've probably had to create temporary formulas to quickly check totals. Well, you won't have to do that anymore, thanks to AutoCalc. All you have to do now to sum a group of numbers is select them. Their sum will automatically appear in the status area. You can even average or count the numbers by right-clicking in the status area.

AUTOCOMPLETE   Ever eager to read your mind, Excel now uses IntelliSense to anticipate what you are going to type! Based upon entries you've already made, AutoComplete will try to figure out what you intend to type, once

FIGURE 13-1

Excel offers a

number of new

and improved

features

Choose an entry from the AutoComplete list

Use the Data Map button to insert great-looking maps

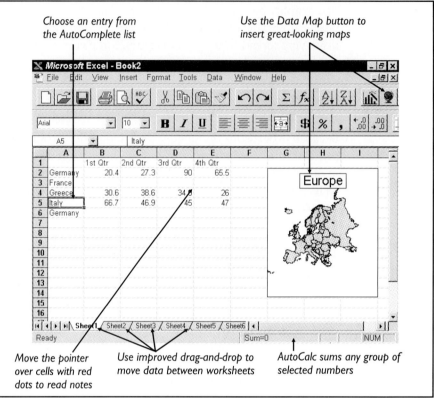

Move the pointer over cells with red dots to read notes

Use improved drag-and-drop to move data between worksheets

AutoCalc sums any group of selected numbers

you've entered a few letters. You can even choose from a list of entries you've used already, because Excel makes this list for you automatically. You reach it with the right mouse button.

AUTOCORRECT   Like Word, Excel can now automatically correct mistakes. These include the same features you're used to in Word: not allowing two consecutive initial caps, capitalizing names of days, and so on. Like the Word feature, it can be turned on or off, and you can even create your own AutoCorrect entries.

AUTOFILTER WITH TOP TEN   As Rocky the Flying Squirrel says, now here's something you'll really love! AutoFilter is a shortcut to sorting data. Just select a column or row and choose Data | AutoFilter. Excel will find the top-ten highest or lowest values, depending upon your settings. These can be monetary values, percentages, or anything else you can think of.

BETTER DRAG-AND-DROP   Do you want to move a group of cells? Excel's drag-and-drop feature lets you reposition selected portions of your spreadsheet by simply dragging them with your mouse, just as you do in Word. Properly written equations automatically adapt themselves to their new locations. It almost makes budgeting fun. You can even drag-and-drop between worksheets or workbooks.

CELL TIPS AND SCROLL TIPS   To help you get around better with the mouse, Excel now includes *Scroll Tips*. When you click and drag a scroll bar, a small window tells you what row or column you are heading for. This is great for large worksheets. In addition, you can use *Cell Tips* to read notes you've made for yourself in cells. This is a good way to remind yourself of important points regarding your data.

DATA MAP   If you do business over large regions, including foreign countries, Data Map will be a boon to you. You can use it to actually make maps of your regions of business by country. This can be quite impressive in presentations. Excel even comes with demographic statistics, so you can correlate the success of your business to the demographics of a region.

EASIER DOCUMENT RETRIEVAL AND MANAGEMENT   Like Word, Excel has now greatly streamlined file management. You can quickly find worksheets with Fast Find, and you can easily delete or rename files right in the Open dialog box. You can even preview files before opening them.

NUMBER FORMATTING   It's easy to format numbers with Excel's new number-formatting feature. Select your numbers and choose Format | Cells. In the Number tab, choose the number style you want to use. There are many formats here, including telephone numbers, dollar amounts, and dates.

SHARED LISTS   You can now have worksheets that are shared *simultaneously* over a network. What is the technology behind this? Who knows. But it works like this. You simply save your file as a shared list. Then anyone on the network can open it and work on it. This is also known as *multiuser editing*. You have the options of saving or rejecting your own changes or anyone else's.

TEMPLATES AND TEMPLATE WIZARD   Excel's template facility has been greatly enhanced. You can choose from a variety of elegantly designed templates for your home or business. You can even have Template Wizard link your worksheets to a database. Then, when you make changes in the database, your worksheet can be updated automatically.

Getting Started

The obvious way to start Excel is to choose it from the Start submenu. Or, you can click the Excel icon in the Office Shortcut Bar. You can also double-click the Excel icon in Windows Explorer, but this takes longer. Starting in any of these ways opens a new, untitled workbook.

You can also start Excel by double-clicking Excel worksheet icons and related files (files with the extensions .XLA, .XLB, .XLC, .XLL, .XLM, .XLS, .XLT, or .XLW, and possibly others). This starts the program and displays the worksheet whose icon you clicked.

Parts of a Worksheet

As you can see in Figure 13-2, Excel follows most of Microsoft's Windows conventions. There are scroll bars, control boxes, menu bars, and so forth.

FIGURE 13-2

Choose Excel from the Start menu or from the Office Shortcut Bar, or double-click an Excel file icon

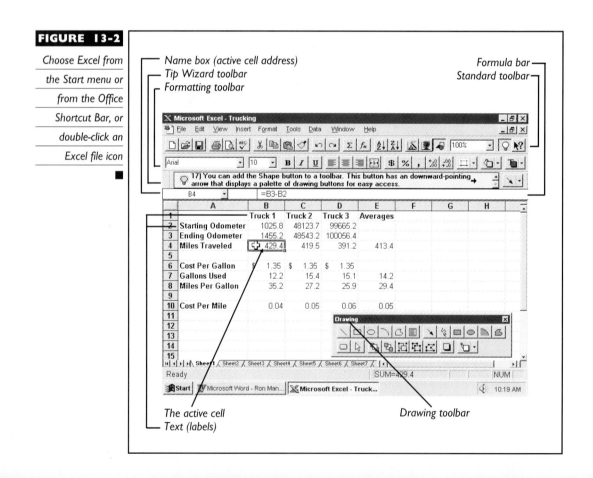

Name box (active cell address)
Tip Wizard toolbar
Formatting toolbar
Formula bar
Standard toolbar

The active cell
Text (labels)
Drawing toolbar

There are some new tools in Excel windows as well. See if you can find them in Figure 13-2 as they are described here. (Your screen may look different, especially if someone else has used the program before you. That's because users have considerable control over the appearance of the workspace.)

Normally, you will see at least one or two toolbars (probably the Standard and Formatting toolbars shown at the top of Figure 13-2). You might also see other toolbars at the bottom or even in the middle of your worksheet. For instance, that's the Tip Wizard toolbar beneath the Formatting toolbar, and the Drawing toolbar in the lower right of the window.

By now you should know that worksheets consist of horizontal, numbered rows and of vertical columns identified with letters. The resulting boxes are called *cells,* and the cell where you're working is called the *active cell.* It has a dark border around it, or sometimes appears ghostly white when you select cells around it. In Figure 13-2 cell B4 is the active cell. Notice that the address of the active cell is displayed in a box above the left edge of the worksheet.

When you type text or *formulas* (instructions Excel uses to compute results), you'll see your characters scroll across the *Formula bar* and in the active cell. There's normally a status area at the bottom of your Excel window.

Looking at Sample Worksheets and Demos

Excel comes with a folder called Examples that contains some sample worksheets. These are primarily devoted to Solver sample files, though, not to general Excel use. Users of earlier Excel versions can skip the basics and go right to "What's New?" Lotus 1-2-3 converts have their own tutorials in Excel, complete with demos.

Using Excel's Online Help

Like many other Windows programs, Excel offers extensive online Help. Reach it either with F1 or from the Help menu. Navigate the Help files as described in the Word section of this book.

tip *By far the slickest online Help can be had from the Tip Wizard. Click on the light-bulb button in the Standard toolbar, and keep one eye on the resulting Tip Wizard toolbar as you work. It will give you tips on new ways to do what you do while you do it.*

WORKING WITH EXCEL

Help for 1-2-3 Users

As mentioned earlier, 1-2-3 users can get oriented quickly by choosing the Lotus 1-2-3 option on the Excel Help menu. (If you don't see this choice, rerun the Excel Setup program and add it to your installation of Excel.)

Creating a New Worksheet

The best way to learn Excel is to use it. If you haven't already done so, start the program. You should see a blank worksheet.

Page Setup First

Since Excel can show you page endings, as well as how much information will fit on each page as you work, it's a good idea to make Page Setup decisions as soon as you start a new project and sometimes a new worksheet in a project. Use the Page Setup command located on Excel's File menu. Page size, orientation, and header and footer dimensions are just a few of the things you can control with Page Setup. For your first project you may want to stick with Excel's default settings, but as a rule you will want to get in the habit of changing Page Setup settings when you start new worksheets. The tabs on Excel's Page Setup dialog box will remind you of others that you've seen, except you'll be given options such as whether to print gridlines, the printing order of pages in reports that won't fit on one page, and so on.

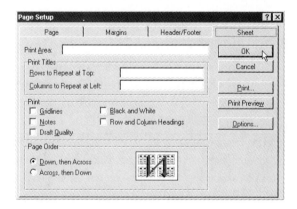

Use online Help to learn more.

Selecting Cells

Before entering or editing cell contents, or before you can format or move cells, they need to be selected. You can select single cells or *ranges* of cells.

Selecting Cells with a Mouse

To select a single cell, simply point-and-click in it. It becomes the active cell. The following techniques, illustrated in Figure 13-3, are for rows, columns, and ranges:

- Click on a row number to select the whole row (see Figure 13-3a).

- To select an entire column of cells, point to the column's heading (see Figure 13-3b).

- Click-and-drag to select a range of cells (see Figure 13-3c).

- Click on the empty button at the top-left corner of the workbook to select the entire worksheet (see Figure 13-3d).

To select noncontiguous (nonadjacent) cells, or groups of cells, hold down CTRL and do any of the aforementioned selection tricks. For example, to select rows 2 and 4 but not row 3, click on the number for row 2, then CTRL+click on 4.

Selecting Cells with the Keyboard

While you will probably want to use your mouse for most selections (it's speedier), there are many keyboard selection tricks.

- If you've already selected a range of cells, SHIFT+SPACEBAR selects the entire row or rows in which the cells are located.

- CTRL+SPACEBAR selects an entire column.

- CTRL+SHIFT+SPACEBAR selects the entire worksheet.

To *extend* selections in any direction, hold down SHIFT and press the appropriate arrow key. The other navigational keys can be used to extend selections also. For instance, SHIFT+CTRL+END extends the selection to the end of your worksheet.

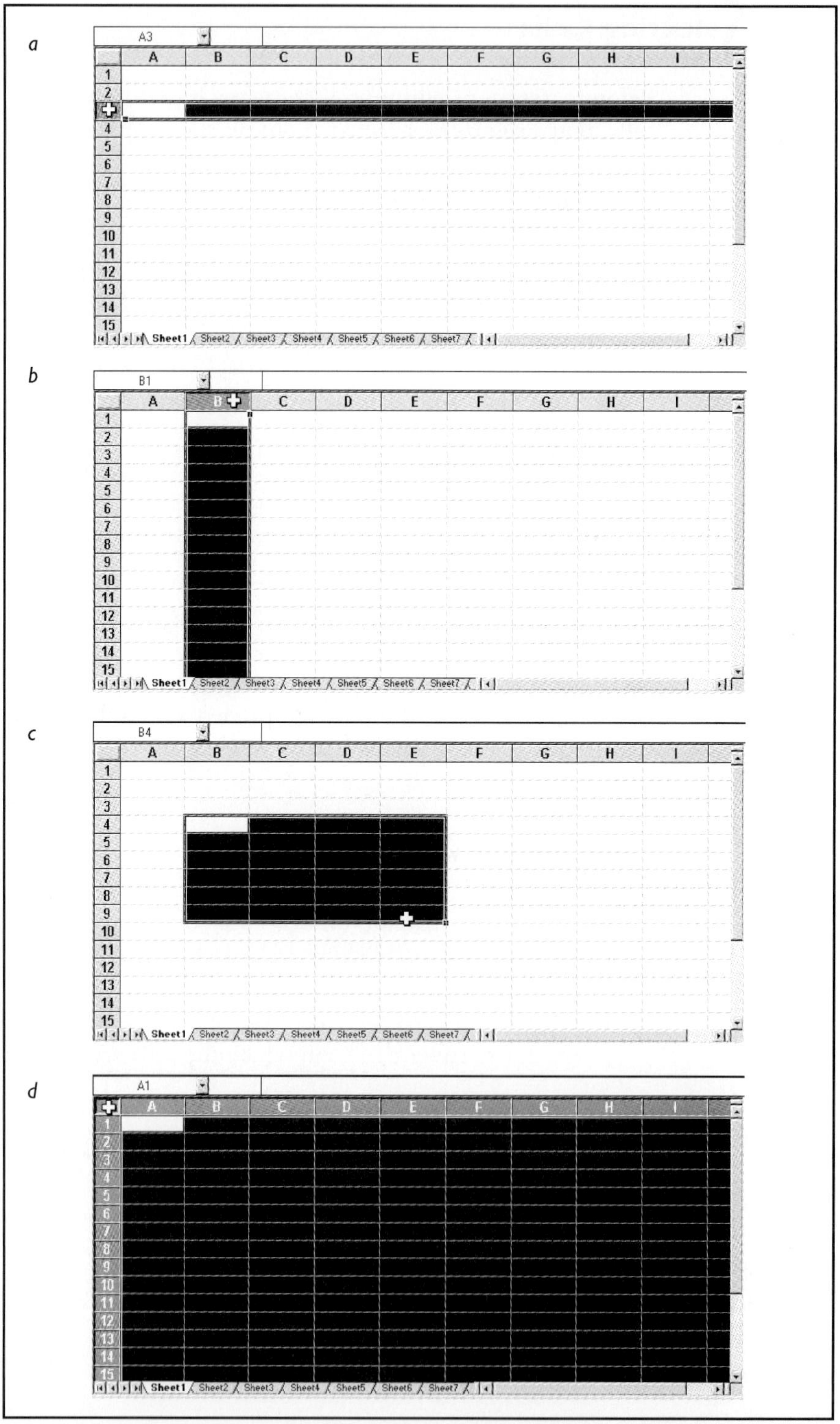

FIGURE 13-3

It's easy to select
rows, columns, or
ranges with the
mouse

Navigating with the Mouse and Keyboard

Use the same navigational tools presented earlier in this book to move around in large worksheets. Scroll with the scroll bars, and use PGUP HOME, and related keys.

The Edit menu offers a number of other navigational aids. For instance, there is a Find command that will remind you of Word's—it lets you search for text strings, formulas, and other items of interest. You can name areas of your spreadsheet by choosing Insert | Name | Define and use the Go To command to quickly find them.

Navigating with the Go To Command

The Edit menu's Go To command can be used to find areas you've named. This makes it easy to jump around in large sheets. For instance, the sample worksheet shows the names of two data-entry areas in the Go To dialog box.

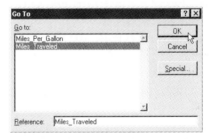

You'll learn more about labeling areas later in the Excel section of the book. For now, it's enough to be aware that it is both possible and handy to be able to name selected parts of a worksheet.

The Go To Special Button

The Go To Special dialog box (reached by choosing the Special button in the Go To dialog box) lets you select cells meeting specific criteria. For instance, you can specify all notes, formulas, blank cells, the last cell, and so on. To inspect only a certain range of cells, first select only the cells of interest before using the Special button. To search the entire worksheet, select any single cell before using the button. Here is the Go To Special dialog box.

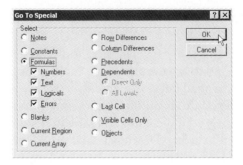

Entering and Editing Text

To enter the text used to label things in your worksheets, simply activate the cell where you want the text to appear (point to it and click), and then begin typing. (When you enter text into a cell this way, the text is sometimes referred to as a *constant value,* since you want it to remain the same until you change it yourself.)

As you start typing, the text will appear in the active cell *and* in the Formula bar. Pressing ENTER or clicking the Checkmark button in the Formula bar concludes the text entry and places the text in the active cell. If you change your mind before you press ENTER, you can press the ESC key or click on the X button in the Formula bar to cancel the entry. Figure 13-4 illustrates this.

You can type up to 255 characters per cell. After you've entered text, you can easily increase cell sizes later or word-wrap text to accommodate the entries, as you'll see in a moment.

FIGURE 13-4

Type in the Formula bar; click the Checkmark button or press ENTER to accept the entry; click the X button or press ESC to cancel

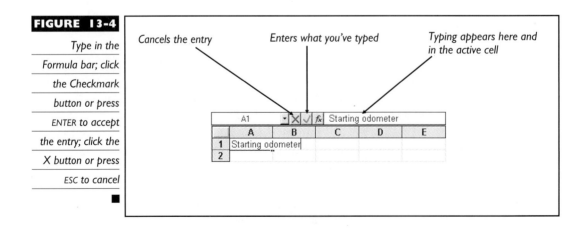

Editing Text

If you spot an error while entering text, simply backspace to correct it. If you see an error after finishing the entry, activate the cell and edit the text—you can do this in the cell itself or in the Formula bar. Use your Windows text-editing skills here: Drag over the text you want to delete or correct, or double-click it, or select it using the keyboard. Move the insertion point around in the text on the Formula bar as necessary. When the corrections have been made, press ENTER or click the Checkmark button.

Replacing Text

If you activate a cell containing text, then type new text and press ENTER or click the Checkmark button, the new text will replace the old text.

Styling Text

You can change the appearance of both text and numbers in cells (make things bold or bigger, change fonts, and so on). Normally, all the text in a cell is affected, but you can choose to modify only portions by selecting them.

Use the buttons on the Formatting toolbar and additional choices reached through the Cells command on the Format menu. The process of embellishing cell appearance is described in more detail later.

tip   *The Format Cells dialog box can also be reached by right-clicking on the cell, and choosing Format Cells from the resulting menu.*

Text Boxes

Besides typing text into cells, you can create *text boxes* and place them anywhere you like on your worksheets. They are a kind of graphic object. It's even possible to rotate text in text boxes, and draw arrows from text boxes to things the text describes. To create a text box, click the Text Box button, then use your mouse to drag a box of the desired size. Release the mouse button and type. You'll learn more about text boxes later.

Text Notes

Text notes are used to hold notes that you don't want to display on your worksheets. The notes are attached to cells, and can be viewed onscreen by you or others.

Creating Notes

To create a note, start by selecting the appropriate cell. Then choose Insert | Note or press SHIFT+F2. Excel will display the Cell Note dialog box.

A red dot appears in the top-right corner of a cell that has a note attached to it.

Type the note in the Text Note box. Click Add or OK to attach the note to the cell.

Displaying and Printing Notes

Select the cell of interest, then press SHIFT+F2. You'll see the Cell Note dialog box. To print notes, visit the Page Setup dialog box, click on the Sheet tab, and select the Note option box.

Sound Notes

If you have a multimedia-equipped computer, you can record and play back audio notes by using the Sound Note buttons in the Cell Note dialog box.

Checking Spelling

Once you've entered the worksheet headings and other text (like chart labels), Excel's Spelling command on the Options menu will launch the spelling checker, as will the Spelling button on the Standard toolbar.

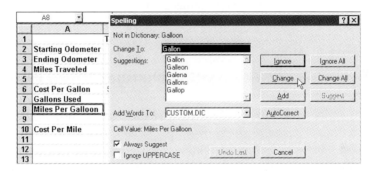

This feature is similar to the Word spelling checker, though not identical. If you have a custom Microsoft *Word* dictionary called CUSTOM.DIC in the default location—the Msapps/Proof subfolder of your Windows folder on your hard disk—Excel will also use this custom dictionary. Otherwise, it will create its own.

Running the Spelling Checker

To check the spelling of your entire worksheet, run the spelling checker *without selecting a range of cells.* This checks labels, cell notes, embedded charts, text boxes, headers, and footers. It does *not,* however, check text created by formulas.

To check a small portion of the worksheet, select the appropriate range of cells. To check a single word, highlight it in the Formula bar and run the checker.

You can accept Excel's spelling suggestions, ignore them, type your own changes, or add words to the custom dictionary as you do in Word.

Undoing and Repeating Actions

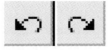

Excel's Edit menu contains Undo and Repeat commands similar to Word's. There are also the familiar Undo and Redo buttons on the Standard toolbar.

Usually, if you catch a mistake, a trip to the Undo command or use of the CTRL+Z shortcut will fix it. The Repeat command was designed to duplicate your last action. On the Edit menu, the exact names of the Undo and Repeat commands change, based on your prior actions—for example, they may say Repeat Paste and Undo Paste. Sometimes you'll see gray "Can't Undo" or "Can't Repeat" commands, indicating that Excel is unable to undo or play back your most recent type of operation, at least under the current circumstances.

Entering and Formatting Numbers

Numbers are the raw materials for spreadsheets. They are often referred to as *constant values,* or simply *values.* You type numbers into the active cell by using either the number keys above the letter keys on your keyboard, or by using the numeric keypad in NumLock mode. Pressing NUMLOCK toggles the numeric keypad between number and cursor-movement mode.

In addition to the numerals 0 through 9, you can enter the following special symbols when typing numbers:

```
+ - ( ) , . $ % E e
```

Excel ignores the plus sign in numeric entries and considers a number to be negative if you precede it with a minus sign or hyphen, or enclose it in parentheses. It treats commas and dollar signs correctly, and accepts numbers entered in scientific notation (**2.5E+2**, for instance).

When you enter dollar signs, percentages, or commas, Excel changes the number's *format.*

Number Formats

Within limits, Excel stores and calculates numbers at the precision you type them, but may display them slightly differently than you typed them. For instance, if you type

3.141592654

in a cell, that's what will be *stored* in the cell, even if you *see* something else. For example, if you place that entry in a narrow cell, you might see *3.141593*. In this case, Excel displays the number at the maximum possible precision under the circumstances and rounds it up to display it. The actual appearance of the number changes with the *number format* defined for the cell. (Normally this affects neither the value itself nor other computations based on the number.)

You can control the precision with which numbers are displayed. All new worksheets start out with all of their cells formatted in *General* format, which attempts to show as much precision as possible. You can force cells to use other formats designed by Microsoft, or you can create your own formats.

Sometimes, the entry techniques that you use change the cell's number format automatically. For example, if you activate a cell in the General format, then type a number with a dollar sign, the cell's format will change from General to a currency format.

Typing a percent sign changes a cell's number format to a percentage with two decimal places (*10.05%*, for instance). There are scientific and fractional number formats as well. You can specify the number format for a cell or group of cells from the Number tab in the Format Cells dialog box, shown here.

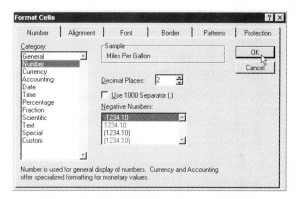

Reach it from the Cells command on the Format menu. Choose a category to reduce the number of formats displayed.

When Numbers Are Too Big for Their Cells

When a number is too big to be properly displayed in its cell, Excel often displays a series of pound signs (######) instead of the number. Other times, Excel will switch to scientific notation to accommodate a large number.

Making the column wider by use of techniques described in Chapter 15, or by use of a shorter number format, will solve the problem. For instance, when dealing with large sums of money, you can often save room in cells by using number formats that don't *display* pennies and decimal points, even if you enter them. They will still calculate correctly.

tip *A quick way to increase or decrease the number of displayed decimal places is to use the toolbar buttons called Increase Decimal and Decrease Decimal. They are located on the Formatting toolbar and contain zeros, decimal points, and arrows. Each time you click, display precision is incremented or decremented one decimal place.*

Entering and Formatting Dates and Times

You enter dates and times by typing them in most commonly accepted American formats. These include, but are not limited to,

11/7/97
11-Nov-97
Nov 7, 1997
8:10 PM
8:10:12 PM
20:10
20:10:12
11/7/97 20:10

You can even create your own date formats. For instance,

mmmm d, yyyy

will display November 7, 1997.

Excel will *store* entries like these as dates or times, and then *reformat* and *display* them using one of several predefined date formats.

How Excel Stores Dates and Times

Date and time entries are a slightly confusing topic, made tougher by Excel's desire to be all things to all people. If you ever plan to enter dates into cells, you should know the following.

T.S. Eliot's Prufrock measured out his life with coffee spoons. Excel uses *serial numbers,* so that it can perform date-and-time math (determine the number of days between two dates, or the number of hours between two time entries, for instance). It *stores* dates and times as serial numbers using January 1, 1900, as the starting date. Here's how it works:

The serial number 1 represents January 1, 1900; the serial number 2 stands for January 2, 1900. This chapter was written on serial number 34,892. Is this starting to sound like *Star Trek* yet?!

If you *reformat* a cell containing a date and display it as a number, you will see the serial number instead of the date. Excel will still treat the cell's contents as a date for computations (but the cell will *look* strange to you).

Alas, not all computers use 1/1/1900 as the starting point for their date serial numbers. For example, Excel for Macintosh computers uses 1904. Excel usually converts dates from Macintosh spreadsheets properly when importing and exporting, but check carefully when moving worksheets containing dates from one platform to another.

Forcing Numbers to Be Treated as Text

If you want Excel to treat numbers, time entries, or date-like entries as text instead of numbers, you need to tell it so. Suppose, for instance, you want to enter the part number **12/63**. Excel would try to treat this as a date, and instead of seeing your part number in the cell, you'd see **Dec-63** after you finished the entry. To prevent this, precede such entries with ' (the apostrophe or single quotation mark), which will not display or print. Alternatively, since Excel treats any cell containing nonnumbers as text, the entries **#12/63, 12/63B,** and even numbers preceded by a space (**12/63**) will be treated as text.

Entering and Editing Formulas

Formulas get the work done. When you want to add a column of numbers and see the results, or divide one number by another, or do any other computation, you must create formulas. Formulas are sometimes even used to manipulate text in worksheets.

Usually, you place the formula in the cell where you want to see the results. You type formulas in the Formula bar. Excel formulas always start with = (the equal sign), although diehard Lotus users can cheat and use & (the ampersand) instead.

Remember the sample miles-per-gallon worksheet at the beginning of this chapter? It contains formulas to compute miles traveled by three trucks, miles per gallon, and averages.

D13	▼			
	A	**B**	**C**	**D**	**E**
1		Truck 1	Truck 2	Truck 3	Averages
2	Starting Odometer	1025.8	48123.7	99665.2	
3	Ending Odometer	1455.2	48543.2	100056.4	
4	Miles Traveled	=B3-B2	=C3-C2	=D3-D2	=(B4+C4+D4)/3
5					
6	Cost Per Gallon	1.35	1.35	1.35	
7	Gallons Used	12.2	15.4	15.1	=(B7+C7+D7)/3
8	Miles Per Gallon	=B4/B7	=C4/C7	=D4/D7	=(B8+C8+D8)/3
9					
10	Cost Per Mile	0.04	0.05	0.06	=(B10+C10+D10)/3

The mileage formula in cell B4 subtracts the starting odometer reading (located in cell B2) from the ending reading (in cell B3) to compute and display the mileage. Notice that the formula does this by referring to the two cell addresses B3 and B2. Whenever the contents of B3 or B2 change, Excel will automatically compute a new answer and display it in cell B4. That's the essence of worksheet computations! Formulas tell Excel what to do whenever the contents of specified cells change.

Use the View tab in the Tools | Options dialog box to show all of your worksheet's formulas at once:

---

tip *The shortcut for displaying and hiding formulas is CTRL+´.* **That's** *CTRL plus the grave accent mark, usually located on the same key as the ~ (tilde) symbol. It toggles between displaying formulas and their answers.*

Creating Formulas

If you've never used a mouse to create formulas before, you might want to fire up Excel and follow along with this description.

Start by activating the cell where you want to place the formula (point to B4, for instance). Next type either an equal sign or an ampersand to tell Excel you want to create a formula.

You can then either type the formula one character at a time, or *assemble* it using your mouse and keyboard. For instance, you could type **=B3–B2** and press ENTER to create the formula in B4—but it's often better to reach for the mouse. You could type the equal sign, then point to and click on cell B3 with your mouse. Cell B3 will be surrounded by a dashed outline (which looks like marching ants). The cell's address will appear in the Formula bar. This makes it unnecessary for you to *type* the address with the keyboard. Next, you'd type the minus sign for your equation, then point to and click on cell B2 with the mouse. Pressing ENTER finishes the formula. If you have entered values in cells B2 and B3, they will be subtracted from each other, and their difference appears in cell B4.

Excel's Formula Operators

The *operators* you use in a formula tell Excel what you want to do (add two numbers, or compare things, for instance). For purposes of explanation, Excel operators can be divided into four general categories—*arithmetic, comparison, text,* and *reference.* Most of the time you will use arithmetic operators. The others can be useful for more complex projects.

Arithmetic Operators

You've already seen two arithmetic operators at work—the slash symbol **/** (division) and the hyphen or minus sign **–** (subtraction). Here's the standard collection:

+	Addition
–	Subtraction
*	Multiplication
/	Division
%	Percentage
^	Exponentiation

Simply include these at the appropriate places in your formulas to perform the desired calculation. For instance, the formula **=B5*10%** would compute 10 percent of the contents of cell B5. The equation **=B5^2** computes the square of cell B5's contents.

More complex formulas, like

```
=E6*B2-(B3*10%)
```

can be created by combining operators and using parentheses.

Comparison Operators

Comparison operators let you inspect two values and come to a conclusion about their relative values. They are usually coupled with Excel's *logical functions* (discussed in Chapter 17).

The operators are

=	Equal
>>	Greater than
>>=	Greater than or equal to
<<	Less than
<<=	Less than or equal to
<>	Not equal to

Here is an example of comparison operators at work with the logical function IF. Suppose you wanted to display an error message whenever the ending odometer reading in cell B3 was *smaller* than the starting reading in B2. The formula

```
=IF((B3<<B2),"Bad OD!",B3-B2)
```

would compare the contents of cells B2 and B3. If B3 is less than B2, the text "Bad OD!" is displayed instead of the negative (wrong) numeric mileage value. If the odometer readings pass the comparison test, the math is performed (B3–B2). (As mentioned earlier, the topic of logical functions will be taken up more fully in Chapter 17.)

Text Operator

Excel's only text operator is the ampersand (&). It is used to combine text. For instance, if you had the word "aero" in cell C7 and the word "plane" in C8, the formula =C7&C8 would create the text string "aeroplane."

Reference Operators

Finally, Excel offers reference operators. The most common reference is to a range of cells. For instance, the expression B1:C3 refers to cells B1, C3, and all the cells between them. You'll learn more about ranges later in this chapter.

Referencing Cells

When creating a formula, you will frequently refer to a *single cell*. For example, in a miles-per-gallon formula, you might refer to the cell containing miles traveled. Other times it is useful to refer to *ranges* of cells. In an annual budget, you might have 12 cells, each containing totals for a different month. It's possible to refer to individual cells or to all the cells in the range.

You often specify references by clicking or dragging with your mouse (clicking on cell A1 or dragging from cell B1 to B4, for instance). Alternatively, you can type references directly into formulas (like **A1** or **B1:B4**). When you create and duplicate formulas, Excel makes some assumptions about which cell or cells you want to reference. You can often overrule these assumptions as you'll see in a moment. References can be *absolute, relative,* or *mixed.* Let's consider a simplified budget exercise designed to illustrate various reference types and referencing techniques.

	A	B	C	D	E	F	G	H
1	Proposed increase:	10%						
2								
3								
4	**Item**	Last Year	This Year	Next Year				
5	Payroll	$525,000	$600,000	$660,000				
6	Benefits	$50,000	$70,000	$77,000				
7	Recruiting fees	$6,000	$1,000	$1,100				
8	Total emp. costs	$581,000	$671,000	$738,100				
9								
10	3-Year Non-Payroll Costs	$205,000						
11								
12								
13								
14								
15								

Sheet1 / Sheet2 / Sheet3 / Sheet4 / Sheet5 / Sheet6 / Sheet7 /

Single-Cell References

Single-cell references refer to a specific cell. For instance, if you were building a new formula, and you wanted to include the 3-Year Nonpayroll Costs from the example, you could either click on cell B10, or type **B10** in the new formula. An important variation on this technique creates absolute references and will be discussed momentarily.

Range References

To refer to a range of cells, you can either drag over the desired cells, or type the beginning and ending cell addresses in the range using colons to separate the beginning and ending cell addresses. For instance, to specify the group of six cells containing nonpayroll costs in the example, you would either drag from cell B6 to D7 or type **B6:D7** into your formula. Incidentally, you can give *names* to ranges of cells like these and refer to the names in equations. For instance, you could name cells B6 through D7 *Nonpay* and place the range name **nonpay** in your formulas. This approach often makes it easier to understand and troubleshoot complex worksheets. Read more about this technique in Chapter 16.

tip *To reference an entire row, type its number twice, separated by a colon (**2:2**, for example). To specify an entire column, type the column's letter twice with a colon (**A:A**, for instance).*

Absolute Versus Relative References

Sometimes you'll want to specify an exact cell not only for the first formula you create, but for others that will be modeled after it. This is particularly important when building formulas that you plan to copy. Suppose, in the example, you want to create a formula that increases Payroll expenses by a specified percentage over last year's spending. You could just include the cell address containing the percentage increase (B1) in your formula:

D5		f_x =(C5*B1)+C5		
	A	**B**	**C**	**D**	**E**
1	Proposed increase:	10%			
2					
3					
4	Item		Last Year	This Year	Next Year
5	Payroll		$525,000	$600,000	=(C5*B1)+C
6	Benefits		$50,000	$70,000	$77,000
7	Recruiting fees		$6,000	$1,000	$1,100
8	Total emp. costs		$581,000	$671,000	$738,100

This would work fine until you tried to save some time by copying the formula for other rows using the techniques discussed later in this chapter, or rearranged the worksheet. While *copying* the formula, Excel would increment (adjust) the reference to B1 as shown here. Thus the first formula would work, and the others won't because they refer to cells other than B1:

D6		f_x =(C6*B2)+C6		
	A	**B**	**C**	**D**	**E**
1	Proposed increase:	10%			
2					
3					
4	Item		Last Year	This Year	Next Year
5	Payroll		$525,000	$600,000	$660,000
6	Benefits		$50,000	$70,000	=(C6*B2)+C
7	Recruiting fees		$6,000	$1,000	$1,100
8	Total emp. costs		$581,000	$671,000	$731,100

You'll learn more about this when you learn to duplicate formulas later, but here's the solution if you are familiar with the problem and just can't wait. To assure that formulas always refer to a specific cell (like the one containing the markup percentage in the example), it is wise to make an *absolute* reference. Absolute addresses use dollar signs before both the row and column address. For instance, to create an absolute reference to cell B1, you would type **$B$1**.

Mixed References

Finally, note that you can create mixed references that point to a specific column and a relative row (like **$A1**), or a specific row and a relative column (like **A$1**), or a specific worksheet and relative row and column. Again, this will make more sense when you start copying formulas.

Named References

As you'll see in Chapter 16, you can assign names to cells or ranges of cells. When you do that, you can use the names in your formulas. For instance, if you had a column named QTY and a column named Price, you could create a formula like **=QTY*PRICE**. Read more about this in Chapter 16.

Changing Reference Types in a Formula

Naturally, you can edit the reference by typing directly in a formula (to add or remove dollar signs, for instance). But there is an alternative:

1. Select the cell containing the formula to be changed.

2. In the Formula bar, select (highlight) the reference to be changed (**B1**, for example).

3. Press F4 repeatedly, watching the reference change until you see the desired effect (**$B$1**, for example).

4. Press ENTER or click the Checkmark button to change the formula.

Changing Reference Style

By default, Excel uses letters for column references and numbers for row references (A1, for instance). It is possible, however, to use "R1C1" style referencing, as illustrated here:

WORKING WITH EXCEL

R5C4	▾	=(RC[-1]*R1C2)+RC[-1]			
	1	**2**	**3**	**4**	**5**
1 Proposed increase:		10%			
2					
3					
4 Item		Last Year	This Year	Next Year	
5 Payroll		$525,000	$600,000	$660,000	
6 Benefits		$50,000	$70,000	$77,000	
7 Recruiting fees		$6,000	$1,000	$1,100	
8 Total emp. costs		$581,000	$671,000	$738,100	

Notice that there are numbers both for columns and rows. Inspect the formulas in the example, as well. When you choose this option, row references in formulas must be preceded with the letter R and column references with the letter C.

This is a method used in some other spreadsheet programs like MultiPlan, so if you find it easier to use (or if your organization uses this method), it's easy to change over to this reference style.

1. Choose Tools | Options.

2. Bring the General tab foremost if it is not already in view.

3. Choose R1C1 on the Reference Style area of the dialog box.

4. Click OK. Excel will adjust all of your formula references automatically.

To switch back to "normal" Excel referencing, repeat steps 1 through 5, choosing A1 in step 3.

Order of Evaluation in Formulas

Whenever you add more than one operator to a formula, Excel must decide which operation to perform first. Moreover, the position of the elements in your formula plays a part. For example, the formula =5+2*10 yields **25**, while =10*5+2 yields **52**; which makes sense when you understand the order in which Excel performs operations. In the first example, Excel adds five to the product of 2 times 10. In the second example, 10 is multiplied by 5 and its product (50) is added to 2, since addition occurs after multiplication. Here's a list of Excel's operators in the order Excel uses them:

Operator	Function
:	Range specifiers
(Space)	Intersection (see online Help)
,	Union
–	Negation (creating a negative number by using only one operand)
%	Percent
^	Exponentiation (raising to a power)
* or /	Multiplication or division
+ or –	Addition or subtraction
&	Joins text
= or <> or <= or >= or <>	The comparison operators

As you may recall from algebra class, you can often use parentheses and other tricks to force the correct order of evaluation. For instance, $=10*(5+2)$ returns 70.

Built-In Functions Versus Hand-Built Formulas

Excel provides a number of built-in functions that automate otherwise time-consuming common tasks. For instance, there is a function that computes monthly loan payments given a loan amount, interest rates, and the length of your loan. Another function computes averages for specified groups of numbers. Other functions perform engineering or statistical tasks. There is also a Function Wizard to help you sort out all the details. You'll learn more about functions in Chapter 17. But there is one worth learning about now. It's called the *SUM* function, and it can be reached with the Summation or AutoSum button on the Standard toolbar.

Suppose you wanted to add the column of numbers shown at the top of Figure 13-5. You *could* type the equation

=A2+A3+A4+A5

But the SUM function is a better way to get the sum of those figures.

As you can see at the bottom of Figure 13-5, clicking the AutoSum button caused Excel to propose a range of cells to include in its range (cell E1 through cell E4). "Marching ants" surround the cells to be included. The SUM equation also appears in the Formula bar, where you can accept or edit

A5	✕ ✓ fx	=A1+A2+A3+A4

	A	B	C	D
1	10			
2	25			
3	65			
4	40			
5	=A1+A2+A3+A4			
6				

E
10
25
65
40
=SUM(E1:E4)

it. Pressing ENTER or clicking on the Formula bar's Checkmark button will accept the proposed formula and display the answer in cell E5. The AutoSum button and related SUM function work on rows, columns, or arrays (described next).

tip *If you just need a quick sum, and don't particularly need to have it appear in your worksheet, Excel has a new AutoCalc function that calculates the sum of any numbers selected and places the result in the status area.*

Arrays and Formulas

Formulas can include references to *arrays*, which are contiguous (adjacent) groups of numbers. For instance, in the following example, the SUM function will add up all the numbers in the six-cell array B2:C5.

When using the SUM function and similar tools to specify arrays, you can drag the marching ants with your mouse to include or exclude cells.

Lookup Tables

Lookup tables are special arrays that you create to provide the contents for other cells. For instance, you could create a lookup table like the one in cells A3 through B5 here:

B9	▾	=LOOKUP(A9,A		
	A	**B**	**C**	**D**
1				
2	Qty	Price		
3	1	$ 1.00		
4	100	$ 0.90		
5	1000	$ 0.85		
6				
7				
8	110	$ 0.90		
9	1600	$ 0.85		
10	1	$ 1.00		

This lookup table consists of the range A3:B5. Cells A3 through A5 contain quantities for each of three price breaks. Cells B3 through B5 contain the prices. To demonstrate this lookup table at work, there are identical sample formulas in cells B8, B9, and B10. (The formula for cell B9 is shown in the illustration's Formula bar. It was created by use of the Insert Function command and resulting Function Wizard.) You'll learn more about functions in Chapter 17.

Cells A8 through A10 contain order quantities. As you can see from the illustration, the LOOKUP functions in the formulas consult the lookup table for the quantities that have been entered in the cells A8 through A10. Then the functions enter the appropriate prices in cells B8 through B10. You can specify exact lookups or have Excel find the closest match, as illustrated in this example.

Incidentally, you can use lookup tables with text as well as numbers. Here, Excel inserts different words based on order quantities:

B9	▾	=LOOKUP(A9,$A$3:$B$5		
	A	**B**	**C**	**D**
1				
2	Qty	Price		
3	1	Small Order		
4	100	Standard Order		
5	1000	Large Order		
6				
7				
8	110	Standard Order		
9	1600	Large Order		
10	1	Small Order		

The cell *contents* in B3, B4, and B5 were replaced with text. That's the essence of table lookups. Consult the big books and online Help for more information.

tip *Lookup tables need not be on the same page or even the same sheet with the cells containing lookup formulas. Consider putting your lookup tables out of sight.*

Controlling Recalculation

Normally, Excel recalculates each time you change any number in the worksheet. And, unless you instruct it otherwise, Excel always recalculates before saving. You can overrule these automatic recalculation options and others from the Calculation tab in the Options dialog box, reached with the Calculation tab in the Tools | Options dialog box.

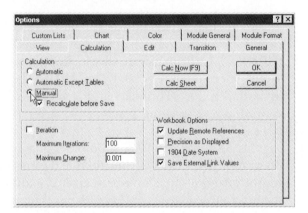

When working on large, complex projects, consider shutting off automatic recalculation if lengthy recalculation delays bother you. Just remember that once you disable automatic recalculation, you become responsible for telling Excel when to recalculate. If you make changes to your worksheet and forget to recalculate manually, one or more cells containing equations may contain old, incorrect answers. To recalculate the worksheet manually, press F9. Stick a note on your monitor to remind you to recalculate before you save the worksheet, or use the Recalculate Before Save option.

Copying Entries and Equations to Minimize Typing

When you create a large worksheet, it is time-consuming to type the same values over and over and over again. Why do it when Excel can do this for you? And, when you create similar formulas in different cells, sometimes the only things that change in the formulas are cell references. For instance, if you create an equation like $=A1-A2$ in column A, you often want a similar equation like $=B1-B2$ in column B and $=C1-C2$ in column C. Excel provides a number of powerful features to minimize mindless typing like this. But you need to use these power tools with care! Take a look.

AutoFill

AutoFill is a tool that lets you select cells of interest and make relative copies of them in adjacent cells. While often used to create tables and forecasts, AutoFill can also be used to copy formulas. Figure 13-6 shows an example of AutoFill at work.

To use AutoFill, simply highlight the cell(s) of interest, then drag the *fill outline* using the square handle (called the *fill handle*) at the bottom corner of the active cell outline. Your pointer turns into a large plus sign, as shown in the *top* screen of Figure 13-6, when it is able to drag the fill handle (when the pointer is pointing at the lower-right corner of the last highlighted cell).

The *middle* screen of Figure 13-6 shows the results of autofilling. Excel has cleverly guessed that the second truck should be labeled **Truck 2** and the

FIGURE 13-6

Features like AutoFill minimize mindless retyping, but they must be used with care—always inspect your work

	A	B	C	D
1		Truck 1		
2	Starting Odometer	1025.8		
3	Ending Odometer	1455.2		
4	Miles Traveled	=B3-B2		
5				
6	Cost Per Gallon	1.35		
7	Gallons Used	12.2		
8	Miles Per Gallon	=B4/B7		
9				
10	Cost Per Mile	=$B$6/B8		
11				

	A	B	C	D
1		Truck 1	Truck 2	Truck 3
2	Starting Odometer	1025.8	1025.8	1025.8
3	Ending Odometer	1455.2	1455.2	1455.2
4	Miles Traveled	=B3-B2	=C3-C2	=D3-D2
5				
6	Cost Per Gallon	1.35	2.35	3.35
7	Gallons Used	12.2	13.2	14.2
8	Miles Per Gallon	=B4/B7	=C4/C7	=D4/D7
9				
10	Cost Per Mile	=$B$6/B8	=$B$6/C8	=$B$6/D8

	A	B	C	D
1		Truck 1	Truck 2	Truck 3
2	Starting Odometer	1025.8	1025.8	1025.8
3	Ending Odometer	1455.2	1455.2	1455.2
4	Miles Traveled	429.4	429.4	429.4
5				
6	Cost Per Gallon	$ 1.35	$ 2.35	$ 3.35
7	Gallons Used	12.2	13.2	14.2
8	Miles Per Gallon	35.2	32.5	30.2
9				
10	Cost Per Mile	0.04	0.04	0.04

WORKING WITH EXCEL

third **Truck 3**. It has noticed a trend. Not knowing any better, it has *copied* the beginning and ending odometer readings so that all three trucks have the same readings, and thus identical mileages. This is easy to fix by typing corrected odometer readings. (This problem could have been avoided altogether by placing zeros in column B before AutoFilling.)

The *bottom* screen in Figure 13-6 illustrates automatic equation modifications accomplished by AutoFill and other Excel equation-copying tools. Switching to Display Options displays the formulas created by AutoFill shown here. Notice the formulas in row 4. Excel has altered the cell references in each column so that the formulas subtract the appropriate numbers in each column, because of the *relative referencing*. Remember, if you don't want Excel to do that for you, use *absolute referencing* instead, as discussed earlier.

More AutoFill Examples

AutoFill knows a number of tricks, and you can teach it others. Take a look at this sampling, which will be discussed next.

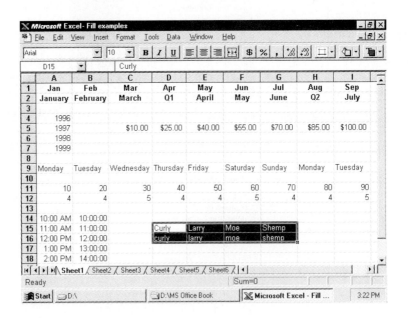

AutoFilling Days, Months, and Years

Notice the months in rows 1 and 2 of the Book5.xls example. **Jan** and **Feb** were typed in row 1, then AutoFilled, producing the rest of the months without typing them.

In row 2, typing **January, February, March,** and **Q1**, then AutoFilling, produced long versions of the rest of the months and appropriate quarters (Q2, Q3, and so on). Yes, you can enter years with your dates and they will change as necessary. So, when you extend *November 1997, December 1997,* the next cell will read "January 1998." Include just as much of the date as you want to see (just years, months, days, and so on). Row 9 shows what happens when you type just days. International date formats work here, as well.

Notice how Excel duplicates the formatting used in the sample cells (Bold and Centering in rows 1 and 2).

Dates (and other things) can be AutoFilled down also. You can see an example of this in cells A4 through A7.

AutoFilling Time

Type the first two or more time examples, and Excel will follow. That's plain-old American time in A14 through A18, and 24-hour time with seconds, to the right.

AutoFilling Numbers

The example also shows some AutoFilled numbers. Rows 11 and 12 show an example of linear forecasting. Supply a few numbers to illustrate the trend, drag away, and Excel will extend the forecast on your behalf. Here, too, formatting gets noticed. Since cells A, B, and C12 were left aligned, so are their offspring. Look carefully at row 12. It's been *filled* with the numbers 4, 4, and 5 (handy if working with budgets where you care about the number of weeks in a month). You *can't* just type **4, 4,** and **5** in the first three cells, then AutoFill, however. This would produce a forecast along the lines of 5, 5.33333, 5.833333, and so on. To prevent forecasting (and to force filling) hold down CTRL while dragging. The mouse pointer should contain an extra little + as you work.

Creating Custom Fill Lists

Excel's not a mind reader (although if you watch the Tip Wizard long enough, you'll begin to wonder). So, you might want to create some custom lists that Excel can use whenever it recognizes your request. For example (and with apologies), check out rows 15 and 16.

After a custom list was set up, Excel knew to add "Moe" and "Shemp" whenever "Curly" and "Larry" were typed and then AutoFill was chosen.

A better use for this feature might be to AutoFill department names, employee names, and so on. Here are the general steps for creating your own custom lists:

1. Choose Tools | Options.

2. Click on the Custom Lists tab if necessary to bring it foremost.

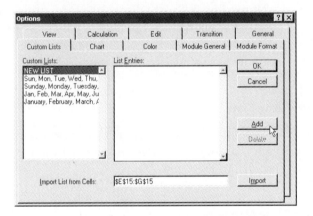

3. Click on New List in the Custom Lists area.

4. When the insertion pointer moves to the List Entries area, type your list in the desired order:

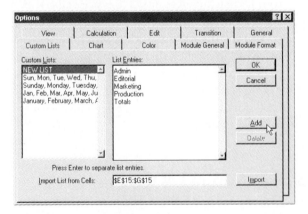

5. Click OK when you have finished.

6. The next time you type the first two or more items in your list and select AutoFill, the rest will follow (assuming you drag far enough to include all the items in your list).

tip *Ever desiring to please, Excel can now read minds a little better than before. If you are typing the same things over and over in a column or row, Excel will keep track of them for you. You can choose from this automatic list by clicking the right mouse button and choosing Pick From List. A list will drop down from which you can choose your entry.*

Excel handles capitalization quite cleverly. If you capitalize, it follows your lead—check out rows 15 and 16 in the AutoFill example.

tip *You can use an existing sample to create a list by typing its range in the Import List From Cells portion of the Custom Lists tab. For example, if you have a list of product numbers in cells A1 through A10, you could enter $A$1:$A$10 to capture them without retyping.*

Filling Right or Down

In addition to AutoFill, Excel offers a variety of fill commands on the Edit menu. You can use these to copy values or formulas in much the same way that you use AutoFill. Select the cell(s) to copy, and then drag to highlight destination cells. This time, don't drag the Fill handle. Pick the appropriate fill method from the Edit | Fill submenu, as illustrated here.

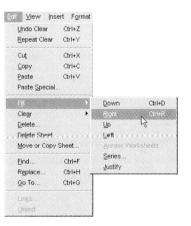

Protecting and Unprotecting Documents and Cells

Sometimes you'll want to prevent others from gaining access to a worksheet (say, a worksheet with your employees' salaries). Other times you'll want to let people see, but not change, your work—to prevent yourself or someone else from accidentally destroying a cell's formula or other contents with an inadvertent entry. Or you may want to authorize the changing of some cells but not others. These features will be discussed next.

Preventing Others from Opening Your Documents

You can assign a password to an Excel document to prevent unauthorized access. This is done with the Save Options dialog box reached by choosing the Options button in the Save As dialog box (choose File | Save As):

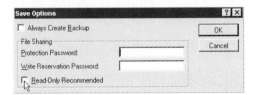

You can completely prevent unauthorized opening of documents from this dialog box, or you can permit people to open and even change things in a worksheet without allowing them to save the changes. It is also possible to let others save changes, but only after a warning.

warning   *Excel's passwords are case sensitive. That is to say, if you assign* **Mickey** *as the password, Excel will not accept* **MICKEY** *or* **mickey** *or any other variation. You are asked to confirm each password assignment by typing it a second time before it becomes "official."*

Cell Protection

It is sometimes desirable to protect portions of your worksheets even from your own mistakes. For instance, it is very easy to accidentally enter a value into a cell containing a formula. When you do this, the formula is destroyed, and your worksheet will no longer function properly.

For this reason, it's often a good idea to protect cells containing formulas and labels after you are happy with the functioning and appearance of your worksheet. See online Help and the big books for details.

CHAPTER 14

Rearranging Worksheets

REGARDLESS of how carefully you plan a project, inevitably you'll wish you had put things in a slightly different order. You'll want to insert extra rows or columns, move things around, or just plain delete them. You'll be able to use Windows and Word skills learned earlier in this book to do this in Excel. You can use the cut-and-paste and drag-and-drop features, for instance.

warning   *When you move, insert, and delete cells, formulas are sometimes affected. The end of this chapter explores these issues.*

Moving Cells

Moving the contents of a cell or cells and other items can be as simple as selecting the cell or cells, cutting with Edit | Cut, and pasting with Edit | Paste. Any existing Clipboard contents will be replaced by the data you cut. You can also use the keyboard shortcuts CTRL+X for cut and CTRL+V for paste, or the toolbar buttons. (To see these and other shortcuts, use the right mouse button to reveal the shortcut menu.) Excel does not warn you if your pasting will overwrite the contents of a cell, so keep your eye on the screen. If you use Undo in time, you can undo any accidental overwrite.

You can also move cells, rows, and columns by selecting them and using drag-and-drop. Here is an illustration of the basic process.

4	Miles Traveled	429.4	429.4	429.4
5				
6	Cost Per Gallon	$ 1.35		
7				
8	Gallons Used	12.2	13.2	14.2
9	Miles Per Gallon	35.2	32.5	30.2

Follow these steps:

1. Highlight cells you want to move.

2. Drag at their edges with the arrow-shaped pointer.

3. Release the mouse button to drop the selected items at the outlined position.

Unlike cut-and-paste, drag-and-drop *does* warn you if you are going to overwrite nonblank cells. Click OK to replace the previous cell contents with whatever you are dragging, or choose Cancel to abort the dragging and dropping.

warning *Normally, when you move the contents of cells, you also move their notes, formatting information, and equations if the cells contain them. Unless you've used absolute addressing (discussed in Chapter 13), the references in the moved cells will change. Cutting and pasting causes references to adjust to fit the new location; copying and pasting does not adjust references.*

Copying Cells

To copy cells, select them, then copy with Edit | Copy and paste with the Edit | Paste command. Any existing Clipboard contents will be replaced by the data you copy. You can also use the keyboard shortcuts CTRL+C for copy and CTRL+V for pastes, or the toolbar buttons. Excel does not warn you if your copying or pasting will overwrite the contents of a cell, so keep your eye on the screen. If you use Undo in time, you can undo any accidental overwrite.

You can also copy with drag-and-drop, as illustrated here.

	A	B	C	D
1		Truck 1	Truck 2	Truck 3
2	Starting Odometer	1025.8	1025.8	1025.8
3	Ending Odometer	1455.2	1455.2	1455.2
4	Miles Traveled	429.4	429.4	429.4
5				
6				
7	Cost Per Gallon	$ 1.35		
8	Gallons Used	12.2	13.2	14.2
9	Miles Per Gallon	35.2	32.5	30.2
10				
11	Cost Per Mile	0.04	0.04	0.04

1. Select the cells of interest.

2. Hold down CTRL while dragging. The mouse pointer will have a small plus sign next to it.

3. When you release the mouse, the selected cells will be copied to the new location.

4. Excel will ask you to confirm the copy if it will cause cells to be overwritten. Click OK to confirm the changes.

Sorting Cell Data

You can sort groups of cells in ascending or descending order, using up to three sort keys at once. Excel will even use headings in your worksheet to "name" the sort keys. For instance, if you had a spreadsheet containing first names, last names, and test scores, you could simultaneously sort on scores (descending, so that high scores are first), then last names, then first names, so that students with the same scores and last names would appear alphabetically by first name within their score group. Figure 14-1 illustrates this.

warning *Sorting in a spreadsheet is risky business.* **You must remember to select everything you want to sort, and nothing else.** *For instance, in Figure 14-1, if you select everyone's first and last names but forget to select their scores, the scores will not move, but the names will, giving some people wrong scores. You can use Undo to fix this; but you should save before you sort, so you can close a messed-up worksheet without saving, if necessary. Then you can reload the good, unsorted version (or make a copy and try your sort on it).*

FIGURE 14-1

Excel lets you sort on up to three keys at once

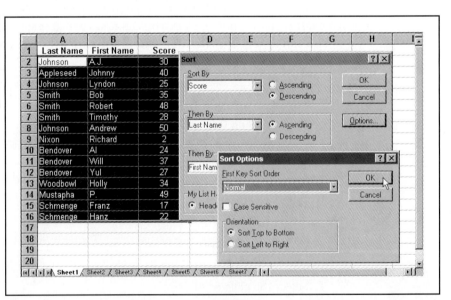

That said, here are the steps for sorting:

1. Select just the cells (or rows or columns) you want to sort. Include headings if you wish.

2. Choose Data | Sort.

3. Specify row or column sorting in the Sort Options dialog box (Data | Sort | Options).

4. If you want to use headings as sort keys, pick that option in the dialog box.

5. Pick the first sorting key. If you use headings for keys, you'll see them listed in drop-down lists.

6. Next, tell Excel whether you want the sort to produce ascending or descending results. (In Figure 14-1 we wanted the high scores first, so a descending sort was specified for scores, but ascending was used for the others.)

7. If you want to do additional sorts, move to the next key box and repeat the process. Do it again, if necessary, for a three-level sort.

8. When you've set up the sorting specifications, click OK and inspect the results.

	A	B	C
	Last Name	**First Name**	**Score**
1	**Last Name**	**First Name**	**Score**
2	Johnson	Andrew	50
3	Mustapha	P.	49
4	Smith	Robert	48
5	Appleseed	Johnny	40
6	Bendover	Will	37
7	Smith	Bob	35
8	Woodbowl	Holly	34
9	Johnson	A.J.	30
10	Smith	Timothy	28
11	Bendover	Yul	27
12	Johnson	Lyndon	25
13	Bendover	Al	24
14	Schmenge	Hanz	22
15	Schmenge	Franz	17
16	Nixon	Richard	2

tip *The Utility toolbar contains two sort buttons—Sort Ascending and Sort Descending.*

Inserting Rows

It's easy to insert additional rows in a worksheet. One way is to select the entire row *below* the place where you want a new blank row. For example, click on the row number at the left edge of row 4 to select row 4. Then choose Insert | Rows. You will see a new, blank row 4, and the old contents of row 4 will become row 5. All of the rows that follow will also be pushed down and renumbered. Formulas will usually accommodate insertions like this, but, as always, check your work.

tip *The mouse shortcut menu offers a quick way to insert rows or columns into your worksheet: Click the right mouse button and choose Insert from the shortcut menu to display the Insert dialog box.*

To insert multiple rows, *select* multiple rows before issuing the Insert command. For instance, to insert three rows in the earlier example, you could select rows 4, 5, and 6.

Inserting Columns

To insert a column, point to the label of the column where you want the new column to appear. For instance, if you want a blank column at column B, select it. Use the Columns command on Excel's Insert menu, or click the right mouse button and choose Insert from the shortcut menu. You will see a new, blank column B, whereupon the old contents of column B will become column C. All of the columns that follow will also be pushed right and renamed. Formulas will usually allow for insertions like this, but check your work to be sure.

To insert multiple columns, select multiple columns before using the Insert command. That is, to insert three columns in the example, you could select columns B, C, and D.

Inserting Cells

You can insert empty cells into an existing worksheet, thereby pushing existing cells either to the right of the insertion point or down from the insertion point. Highlight the area where you want to insert new blank cells and then use the Insert menu's Cells command (or click the right mouse button and choose Insert from the shortcut menu that appears). The Insert dialog box comes up, asking you if you want to shift cells right or down, or insert an entire row or entire column. This pushes cells as you might expect, although it can ruin the appearance of your worksheet. Use Undo if you are unhappy with the results.

Inserting as You Paste

Sometimes you'll want to make room for items as you paste them. If so, select the items to be pasted, then copy or cut them to the Clipboard. The Insert Cut Cells command will appear on the Edit menu. Activate the cell, row, or column where you want to insert the Clipboard contents, and choose the Insert Cut Cells command. Check the effect upon formulas and the overall worksheet appearance after pasting this way.

Deleting Parts of a Worksheet

Edit | Delete is used to delete unwanted rows, columns, or cells. This places them on the Clipboard and closes up the space made by the deletion. For example, if you select all of column B and use the Edit menu's Delete command, the contents of column C will shift left and become column B, D will become C, and so on, almost to infinity (or the maximum width of the worksheet).

The same basic process occurs when you delete rows. Deleting row 4 moves row 5's contents up, making those cells the new row 4, and so on.

tip   *The mouse shortcut menu offers a quick way to delete rows or columns from your worksheet: click the right mouse button and choose Delete from the shortcut menu.*

If you select an irregular collection of cells (something other than a complete row or column), Excel will ask how you want remaining cells to move when they fill in the newly emptied space.

Deletions of rows, columns, or cells can affect formulas, particularly if you remove cells that are referenced by formulas. Check your work.

Clearing Parts of a Worksheet

Clearing removes cell contents but does not move the contents of other cells to fill in the newly emptied space. Highlight the cell or cells you want to clear, then press DEL or use one of the Clear command choices on the Edit menu. You can clear every aspect of the cell or just selected features like formats, formulas, or notes.

How Formulas React to Worksheet Design Changes

The potential problems with formulas when you modify worksheet designs have been discussed, but it's worth recapping them here. Some changes can have a profound effect on formulas, others are benign. But whenever you fiddle with a cell that is referenced in a formula (even if the formula is in some other worksheet or file), there is the potential for trouble. This is particularly true when you

- Insert rows, columns, or cells

- Delete rows, columns, or cells

- Move cells, rows, or columns referred to by formulas

- Clear cells referred to by formulas

- Change the data type of a cell (for example, numbers to text)

Careful planning at the beginning of your projects, Excel's good nature, and its helpful instincts should minimize problems. But you need to anticipate the effects of changes, then test modified worksheets carefully. Let's take the issues one at a time, using the small payroll budget as an example. The command Tools | Options has been used and the Formulas option checked in the View tab to display the formulas in their cells, making it easier to see what's going on:

	A	B	C	D
1	Proposed increase:	0.1		
2				
3				
4	Item	Last Year	This Year	Next Year
5	Payroll	525000	600000	=(C5*$B$1)+C5
6	Benefits	50000	70000	=(C6*$B$1)+C6
7	Recruiting fees	6000	1000	=(C7*$B$1)+C7
8	Total emp. costs	=SUM(B5:B7)	=SUM(C5:C7)	=SUM(D5:D7)
9				
10	3-Year Non-Payroll Costs	=SUM(B6:D7)		

Effects of Inserting Rows

Inserting rows and columns can be either very straightforward or fiendishly tricky. For instance, if you were to insert a row between Payroll (row 5) and Benefits (row 6), the SUM formulas that calculate total employee costs would automatically change to include the newly inserted row.

	A	B	C	D
1	Proposed increase:	0.1		
2				
3				
4	Item	Last Year	This Year	Next Year
5	Payroll	525000	600000	=(C5*$B$1)+C5
6				
7	Benefits	50000	70000	=(C7*$B$1)+C7
8	Recruiting fees	6000	1000	=(C8*$B$1)+C8
9	Total emp. costs	=SUM(B5:B8)	=SUM(C5:C8)	=SUM(D5:D8)
10				
11	3-Year Non-Payroll Costs	=SUM(B7:D8)		

This is probably, but *not always*, what you want. In this example, if you are adding a new expense line like *Relocation costs,* perhaps you are OK, since the SUM formulas are computing *total costs*. But, suppose you inserted the new row because you plan to put some nonexpense items in the new row, like the percent of change in the payroll costs. In that instance, you wouldn't want those newly inserted percentages to be included in your subtotals below, where they would erroneously increase the subtotals. And, there's another potential gotcha. Can you spot it?

The formula that finds three-year nonpayroll costs (in what is now cell B11) does not automatically refer to the newly inserted cells after you insert the row! So, if you *do* put additional nonpayroll employee costs in the newly inserted row, they will be ignored by the formula in B11, making for a too-small result. You need to modify the B11 formula.

tip *Use named ranges to minimize insertion problems like the one in cell B11. For example, if you were to create a named range for the original nonpayroll cells (named* **Non_Payroll***, let's say), and use the range name in the B11 formula instead of the cell numbers—* **=SUM(Non_Payroll)** *instead of* **=SUM(B7:D8)***, for example—changes in the size and shape of the range would be reflected in the formula (assuming, of course, that you redefine the range when necessary). Learn more about names at the beginning of Chapter 16.*

Check out the formulas in D5 through D9. As we already discussed, D9's references have changed to automatically include the new row. The formulas in D5, D7, and D8 now refer to cells C5, C7, and C8, respectively, properly reacting to the insertion. Because we used absolute addressing each time we specified cell B1, all three old formulas got that right, too. Had we not used absolute addressing here, that might have been a problem, however. Check your work!

There is no formula in cell D6 and it needs one. It can be copied (or filled down) from D5, or copied or filled up from D7. Alternatively, you can just type a new formula from scratch.

Inserting at the Tops and Bottoms of Lists

Although inserting new rows in the middle of areas serviced by a range reference includes the new row in most formulas, inserting at the top or bottom does not. Take a look at this:

	A	B	C	D
1	Proposed increase:	0.1		
2				
3				
4	Item	Last Year	This Year	Next Year
5				
6	Payroll	525000	600000	=(C6*$B$1)+C6
7	Benefits	50000	70000	=(C7*$B$1)+C7
8	Recruiting fees	6000	1000	=(C8*$B$1)+C8
9	Total emp. costs	=SUM(B6:B8)	=SUM(C6:C8)	=SUM(D6:D8)
10				
11	3-Year Non-Payroll Costs	=SUM(B7:D8)		

If you insert a new row directly above the Payroll line (row 6 in the illustration), Excel will not include it in things like the SUM formulas used to create totals. You can see this by examining the formulas in B9 and B11. You'll have the same problem if you insert a row or rows between the SUM formula line and the old *last* row.

Effects of Inserting Columns

Excel reacts about the same way when you insert columns as it does when you insert rows. Insertions in the middle of ranges are usually included in references to the range, those on the left and the right are not. Check your work carefully.

Effects of Moving Rows, Columns, or Cells

Excel does a pretty good job of keeping track of things when you move them around on the same worksheet. For example, you just saw Excel adjust formulas when things got moved down during a row insertion. Even absolute addressing can be maintained when referenced cells are moved. Here, the contents of cell B1 were cut, then pasted into cell A2. Notice that the absolute address references in cells D5 through D7 were automatically modified, and are correct even after the move:

	A	B	C	D
	A2		10%	
1	Proposed increase:			
2	0.1			
3				
4	Item	Last Year	This Year	Next Year
5	Payroll	525000	600000	=(C5*$A$2)+C5
6	Benefits	50000	70000	=(C6*$A$2)+C6
7	Recruiting fees	6000	1000	=(C7*$A$2)+C7
8	Total emp. costs	=SUM(B5:B7)	=SUM(C5:C7)	=SUM(D5:D7)
9				
10	3-Year Non-Payroll Costs	=SUM(B6:D7)		

However, this will not work if you cut from one sheet and paste to another sheet in the same workbook or to a different file. If you do move referenced items off a worksheet, you'll often see the error message "#REF!" in cells referencing the "lost" item. (This is when you're in normal view mode, not when you're viewing the formulas—if you're viewing the formulas, they'll look all right.) For example, here the percentage information from B2 has been moved to Sheet2. Notice the error message in each cell that depends upon the moved cell that was B2.

	A	B	C	D
1				
2				
3				
4	Item	Last Year	This Year	Next Year
5	Payroll	$525,000	$600,000	#REF!
6	Benefits	$50,000	$70,000	#REF!
7	Recruiting fees	$6,000	$1,000	#REF!
8	Total emp. costs	$581,000	$671,000	#REF!
9				
10	3-Year Non-Payroll Costs	#REF!		

To remedy this, you simply need to show Excel the way to the missing data. Here are the general steps:

1. Select a confused formula (D5, perhaps).

2. Select the "#REF!" error message in the Formula bar (including the # and !):

	D5	▾ ✕ ✓ ƒₓ =(C5*#REF!)+C5			
	A	**B**	**C**	**D**	**E**
1					
2					
3					
4	Item	Last Year	This Year	Next Year	
5	Payroll	$525,000	$600,000	=(C5*#REF!)+C5	
6	Benefits	$50,000	$70,000	#REF!	
7	Recruiting fees	$6,000	$1,000	#REF!	
8	Total emp. costs	$581,000	$671,000	#REF!	
9					
10	3-Year Non-Payroll Costs	#REF!			

3. Either type the correct cell address (including sheet name, and so on), or click on the new cell location—which is often much easier than typing the whole address. The Formula bar of this example shows what happens if you switch to Sheet2 and click on cell B1 there.

	B1	▾ ✕ ✓ ƒₓ =(C5*Sheet2!B1)+C5			
	A	**B**	**C**	**D**	**E**
1	Proposed	10%			
2		✛			
3					

4. Switch back to the original worksheet by clicking on the original worksheet tab, and save the formula changes by clicking the Enter box or pressing ENTER.

5. Inspect the results from the new formula. If the problem is resolved, change other references as necessary.

Note that you may not need to correct each formula containing the "#REF!" error message. This message will also appear in any cell affected by the results of another troubled cell. In the example, for instance, fixing the trouble in cells D5 through D7 will clear up the problem in B10.

Effects of Deleting Rows, Columns, or Cells

The major problem with deletions is the obvious one. If you delete rows, columns, or cells that are referenced in formulas, the formulas may not work. Or worse yet, they may still work but use different, incorrect data—thereby providing incorrect results.

Effects of Data Type Changes

Formulas expect to see a specific type of data in cells. If you place text in a cell that is supposed to contain a number, for example, Excel will ignore the text when doing math and you will see "#VALUE!" in the cell(s) containing the formula. See Excel-specific books and online Help for details.

Auditing Tools Help Spot Potential Problems

Before you insert, delete, or move things around, you can use several of Excel's auditing tools to help you see which cells are affected by each other. This can make it easier to understand what might happen if you redesign a worksheet. For example, by selecting the B1 cell in this example and choosing Tools | Auditing | Trace Dependents, arrows will radiate from the selected cell(s) to dependent cells:

	A	B	C	D
1	Proposed increase:	10%		
2				
3				
4	Item	Last Year	This Year	Next Year
5	Payroll	$525,000	$600,000	$660,000
6	Benefits	$50,000	$70,000	$77,000
7	Recruiting fees	$6,000	$1,000	$1,100
8	Total emp. costs	$581,000	$671,000	$738,100
9				
10	3-Year Non-Payroll Costs	$ 205,100		

To see how a cell gets its results, you can use the Precedents command (Tools | Auditing | Trace Precedents) to see the other cells involved in the conspiracy. Here, Excel tells you that cells B1 and C6 are involved in the results being displayed in D6:

	D6		=(C6*$B$1)+C6		
	A	**B**	**C**	**D**
1	Proposed increase:	10%		
2				
3				
4	Item	Last Year	This Year	Next Year
5	Payroll	$525,000	$600,000	$660,000
6	Benefits	$50,000	$70,000	$77,000
7	Recruiting fees	$6,000	$1,000	$1,100
8	Total emp. costs	$581,000	$671,000	$738,100
9				
10	3-Year Non-Payroll Costs	$ 205,100		

You can use these commands repeatedly. The arrows will remain onscreen *and print on your printouts* until you choose Tools | Auditing | Remove All Arrows. To learn more about auditing, read Chapter 23.

That's the short course on rearranging worksheets. Practice on copies or expendable projects. Save before making big changes. To learn more, you should check with online Help or the book *Excel Made Easy* by Martin S. Matthews (Osborne/McGraw-Hill).

Next stop: formatting tips and techniques.

CHAPTER 15

Excel Formatting Tips and Techniques

EXCEL provides many formatting features that can enhance the appearance of your worksheets. Some of them will remind you of Microsoft Word's formatting tricks for characters, paragraphs, and tables. Others are unique to Excel. You'll be amazed at how quickly column widths and row heights can be adjusted with a simple mouse click or drag. And Excel's AutoFormat feature can make it look as if you've spent all day on a project, when all you did was make a menu choice. Even if you've used other versions of Excel, be sure to read this chapter carefully. There is plenty of good material here, including a way to center headings over multiple columns.

Excel Page Setup

Just a reminder—as with other Windows programs, it's a good idea to make at least preliminary printer and Page Setup decisions when you start a new project. This way you'll be able to see onscreen how your document will look when printed. If you have more than one printer, pick the one you'll be using for the project.

1. Choose File | Page Setup to get to the Page Setup dialog box.

2. Make any known changes to settings in the Page, Margins, Header/Footer, and Sheet tabs. (At a minimum, make preliminary page size, orientation, and margin settings.)

3. Later you can revisit Page Setup and fine-tune the settings to improve the final appearance of your document.

Changing Column Widths and Row Heights

Sometimes you'll need to change the width of columns or the height of rows. For instance, Excel often displays a series of pound signs (#####) when the results of a calculation won't fit the cell width.

If an entry is too big to fit a cell, you *could* switch to a smaller font or otherwise change the cell's content and format. But frequently you'll want to increase the size of the cell instead. Excel offers a number of ways to adjust column widths and row heights. You can adjust a single row or column, or select multiple rows or columns and change them simultaneously. You can make size changes by double-clicking or dragging, or you can visit dialog boxes. Figure 15-1 illustrates the various approaches, described next.

Using Best Fit to Automatically Adjust Columns and Rows

When you place the mouse pointer on or near the right edge of a *column label* (like the one between columns A and B in Figure 15-1a), the pointer changes into a thick black bar with arrows pointing left and right. If you double-click, Excel's *Best Fit* feature will automatically make the left column (column A in the example) wider or narrower as necessary to accommodate the longest entry in that column. When you select multiple columns before double-clicking, *each* selected column will switch to its best fit, potentially making every column a different width.

Row heights automatically increase to accommodate the tallest character in a row. In addition, heights can be changed using techniques similar to the ones used for column widths. You can change single or multiple rows at once. Pointing to a row label changes the pointer to a thick horizontal bar with up- and down-pointing arrows. Double-clicking results in a best fit (taller or shorter rows).

While the mouse tricks just described are the most convenient way to adjust column widths and row heights, you can also use the AutoFit choices on the Row and Column submenus reached via the Format menu.

If you make changes to the contents of cells later (add or remove characters, for example), you may need to use AutoFit again, since the column widths will not automatically readjust.

Use Undo (CTRL-Z) to restore column widths and row heights. Incidentally, AutoFits are computed using *screen fonts*. As a result, you may occasionally need to readjust columns and rows manually before printing. To see if this will be necessary, use Excel's Print Preview feature.

WORKING WITH EXCEL

FIGURE 15-1

*Double-click, drag,
or use the Column
and Row dialog
boxes to change
column widths and
row heights* ■

a

Double-click or drag for best fit, or
just drag to change column width

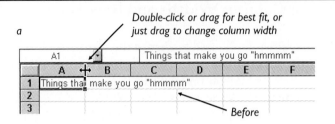

Before

b

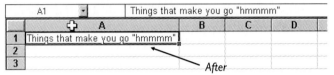

After

c

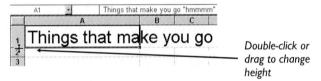

Double-click or
drag to change
height

d

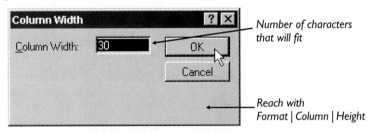

Number of characters
that will fit

Reach with
Format | Column | Height

e

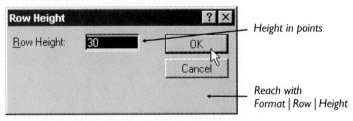

Height in points

Reach with
Format | Row | Height

Dragging to Change Row and Column Sizes

If you'd rather make your own manual column width and row height decisions, drag with the pointers rather than double-clicking. As with the Best Fit trick, when you place the mouse pointer on or near the right edge of a row label (like the one between columns A and B in Figure 15-1a), the pointer changes into a thick black bar with arrows pointing left and right. Dragging displays a light line showing the column width that will result when you release the mouse button. If you've selected multiple columns, dragging one will make all of them the same width. You can also drag to define your own row height using similar techniques.

Row Height and Column Width Submenu Commands

The Row | Height and Column | Width choices reached with Row and Column commands on the Format menu let you see and specify row heights and column widths. Column Width statistics refer to the number of characters that will fit in a cell, assuming they are formatted in "Normal" style. For instance, in Figure 15-1d the column will hold 30 characters. Row heights are displayed and entered in points. In Figure 15-1c the row height is also 30 points.

AutoFormat

Excel's AutoFormat feature uses *Table Formats,* which are predefined collections of number formats, fonts, cell alignments, patterns, shading, column widths, and row heights to embellish ranges of cells you specify. You can use these formats as-is, or overrule some of their characteristics.

warning *Because automatic formatting is sometimes difficult to undo, you should save worksheets before experimenting with the automatic formats. Then use the Save As command to save differently named copies as you experiment. Print before settling on formats, and don't forget to add format style names to the headers or footers or write them on each printout until you can recognize the styles on sight.*

Choosing Formats

To choose a format, follow these steps:

1. Start by selecting the range of cells you wish to format. Typically, this is the entire worksheet, but it could be a small range of adjacent cells if you so choose.

2. Choose Format | AutoFormat to reach the dialog box shown in Figure 15-2.

3. When you first open the AutoFormat dialog box, you'll see the short version, illustrated at the top of Figure 15-2. Click the Options >> button to show these extra check boxes.

4. Scroll through the list of table formats and click on the names in the list to see them demonstrated in the Sample window.

5. When you find a format of interest, click OK to apply it. (Use Undo to remove the formatting.) In formatting your document this way, Excel sometimes changes decisions you've made. For instance, if you've made some cells bold, Excel may change them back to plain text or italicize them instead.

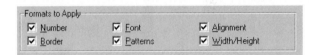

6. To remove some aspect of a Table Format (borders, for example), remove the corresponding check from its name in the Formats To Apply section of the enlarged AutoFormat dialog box. The sample box will show you the effect of these changes as you experiment.

7. Click OK to do the actual formatting.

How Excel Makes Automatic Formatting Decisions

If you have only one cell selected when you issue the AutoFormat command, Excel looks for what it thinks is a logical range of cells to format. It will highlight the proposed range. If you want to format a different range, cancel AutoFormat and select the desired range before trying again.

Different formats look for—and change—different things when formatting. For instance, the classic formats seek out cells containing totals and subtotals, which receive special formatting. The list-type formats use shading and patterns to make lists more readable. Excel considers outline information while formatting, if you've outlined your worksheet. (See Chapter 16 for more about outlines.)

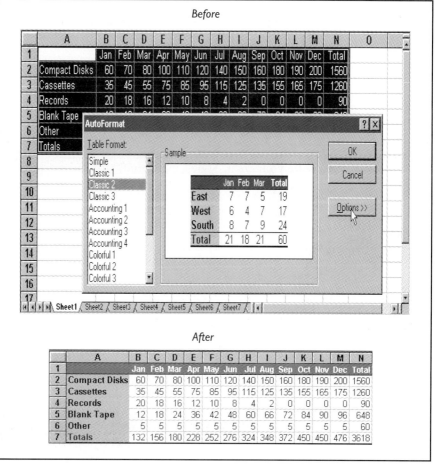

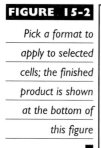

FIGURE 15-2

Pick a format to apply to selected cells; the finished product is shown at the bottom of this figure

■

Manual Formatting

You can make many common formatting changes from the Standard toolbar, from the Formatting toolbar, and with your keyboard. For instance, to make selected text bold, you can click the Bold button (B) on the Formatting toolbar or use the CTRL+B keyboard shortcut. The table at the back of this book lists Excel's buttons and their names and functions. Remember, you can see a button's name by simply sliding the mouse pointer over it and waiting a moment.

Remember to select all the cells you want to affect before using these buttons and keyboard shortcuts. Some style changes will affect the size of cell contents, which may necessitate subsequent changes in column widths, cell heights, and so on. For instance, if you increase a cell's font size and make it bold, text or numbers may be too big to fit within your current column width.

Using Styles

Styles are collections of formatting decisions that might include a number format, alignment instructions, border specifications, pattern selections, and cell protection decisions. Styles need not specify all of these. For instance, a style might consist of just a number format and bold character formatting.

Excel provides a number of standard styles for things like currency. Don't confuse styles with number formats, which only specify commands, decimal places, currency symbols, and the like. You can use Excel's predefined styles or create your own. Styles are stored with the worksheets themselves. You can create new styles, edit existing ones, and copy styles from other worksheets.

Applying Styles

To apply an existing style, follow these steps:

1. Select the cell or cells you want to format.

2. Choose Style from the Format menu.

3. Pick the desired style from the drop-down Style Name list in the resulting Style dialog box.

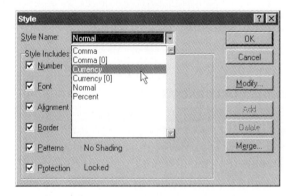

4. Click once on the name and once on OK to apply the style.

tip   *If you find yourself using styles frequently, you may wish to install a style list on one of the toolbars.*

Normal Style

Excel's Normal style displays and prints numbers using the General format, 10-point sans-serif type, no borders, and no shading. It is possible to redefine the standard style just as you can redefine any other style using the steps described next.

Creating Styles

The easiest way to create a new style is to format a cell to meet your requirements (number format, font, borders, and the like) and then name it. Here are the steps:

1. Format the cell to your liking.

2. With that cell still the active cell, choose Style from Excel's Format menu.

3. Type a new style name in the Style Name portion of the Style dialog box. Click the Modify button to set changes.

4. Click OK to save the style, which will be added to the drop-down list and saved with your document.

Modifying Styles

Modifying an existing style requires a visit to the Style dialog box and some typing:

1. Modify a cell containing the style of interest.

2. Choose Format | Style to open the Style dialog box.

3. Click the drop-down list button to display the drop-down list and choose the old style name from it. Alternatively, type the old style name in.

4. Excel may ask if you want to redefine the style based on the changes you've just made. Answer Yes to redefine the style. Choose No or Cancel to leave the style unchanged.

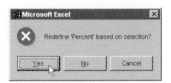

For instance, if you were to activate a cell formatted with Percent style (named "Percent"), italicize the contents of the cell, type **Percent** (the name of the old style) in the drop-down Style list area, and then press ENTER, you would be asked if you wanted to modify the Percent style.

When you redefine a style, all of the other cells formatted with the style change, too. In the example, that would mean that all existing and new cells formatted with the Percent style would be italicized.

The Style dialog box lets you see which style elements are used by the style—number formats, borders, patterns, and so on. It also lets you change these style elements by clicking the Modify button and visiting the appropriate tabs in the resulting Format Cells dialog box.

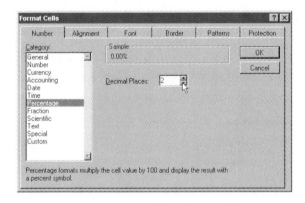

For example, to change font characteristics, click on the Font tab and make the desired choices here:

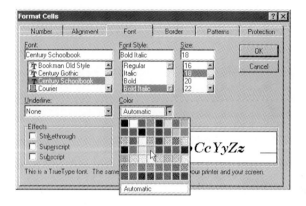

Use the entry boxes, scrolling lists, and drop-down menus to pick font characteristics. No check next to an item indicates that the style currently does not include that characteristic (perhaps no superscripting has been specified, for instance). To include previously unspecified style attributes, click to place a check in the appropriate option box.

How Styles Affect Manual Formatting

Styles usually overrule manual formatting, with important exceptions. For example, if you use a style that specifies bold characters, cells that were originally not bold but were italicized will *become* bold and *not* italicized. You can go back to cells thus altered and manually apply (or reapply) characteristics like italics.

Format Codes Alter a Number's Appearance

As you've seen, you can use *styles* to alter a number's appearance (add commas, dollar signs, and so forth). Styles use *format codes* to determine how numbers will appear. *You* can apply format codes directly to selected cells without using styles. And, you can alter existing format codes or create your own. Let's take a look.

WORKING WITH EXCEL

Applying Format Codes

Excel comes with a variety of format codes organized by type. You can get a sense of this from the list of code categories in the Format Cells dialog box. There are codes used to format percentages, other codes for currency, and so on. Here are the steps to apply a code:

1. Select the cell or cells to be reformatted.

2. Choose Format | Cells or use the CTRL+1 shortcut.

3. Bring the Number tab forward if it's not already on top by clicking on the Number tab.

4. Click on a category to display the available format.

5. Double-click on a format code to use it, or click once on the name of the code, and once on OK.

6. Reformat the columns if necessary to accommodate changes in the numbers' widths.

Creating and Modifying Format Codes

Suppose you want to display numbers in a format not offered by Excel. For example, suppose you wanted to format dollars with dollar signs before and the letter *K* after to signify thousands of dollars, like this:

	A	B	C	D
1	Proposed increase:	10%		
2				
3				
4	Item	Last Year	This Year	Next Year
5	Payroll	$ 525 K	$ 600 K	$ 660 K
6	Benefits	$ 50 K	$ 70 K	$ 77 K
7	Recruiting fees	$ 6 K	$ 1 K	$ 1 K
8	Total emp. costs	$ 581 K	$ 671 K	$ 738 K
9				
10	3-Year Non-Payroll Costs	$ 205 K		
11				

Pretty slick, huh? Here are the steps.

1. Select the cell or cells to be formatted.

2. Choose Format | Cells or use the CTRL+1 shortcut.

3. Bring the Number tab forward if it's not already on top by clicking on the Number tab.

4. Click on a category to display the available format choices.

5. Either select an existing format to use as a jumping-off place, or type your own in the Type text box. This example shows a Custom currency format selected, and the letter *K*, with a leading space, added twice.

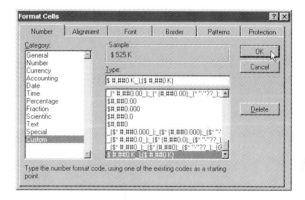

6. When you have finished, click OK. The new format codes will be saved in the list and you'll be returned to the worksheet. Selected cells should be formatted to your liking. If not, repeat steps 1–5. You can delete unwanted attempts by selecting them in the dialog box and using the Delete button.

To learn more about the various formatting symbols (#, 0, ?, _, and so on) check the Number Format Codes topic in online Help or crack the Excel-specific books.

warning   *Remember, you are altering the appearance of the numbers here, not their actual values. Thus, if you format the number $1.00 with the K format trick, it will look like $1 K. There's a big difference! Unless you are consistent in the entry and formatting of numbers, you can get into big trouble this way.*

Format Painter Speeds-Up Format Copying

The Format Painter lets you quickly copy a cell's format (size, color, bold, format codes, and so on), then spread it around elsewhere. For example, suppose you wanted to use your new "K style" number formatting in the rest of the Payroll example. Here are the steps:

1. Select the cell containing the desired formatting (click in it).

2. Click on the Format Painter button. It looks like a paintbrush.

3. The mouse pointer will change to a cross and a paintbrush. Drag with it to select the cells to be reformatted:

Last Year	This Year	Next Year
$ 525 K	$ 600.00	$ 660.00
$ 50.00	$ 70.00	$ 77.00
$ 6.00	$ 1.00	$ 1.10
$ 581.00	$ 671.00	$ 738.10

4. Release the mouse button.

5. Paint other cells, as needed.

6. Adjust column widths if necessary.

Copying Styles to and from Other Workbooks

You can either copy individual styles from one workbook to another, or you can merge all of the styles from one workbook with those of another. In either case, start by opening and (optionally) displaying both workbooks. (Use the Arrange command on the Window menu to tile both workbooks if you like.)

To copy a single format from one workbook to another, with both workbooks open, copy a cell containing the desired style to the Clipboard, then switch to the destination workbook and paste the cell into it. The copied style will appear in the Style list and therefore become available in the destination workbook. If you don't want to paste a cell's contents—just formats, for instance—you can choose the Paste Special command from the Edit menu and specify Formats only.

To copy *all* of the styles from one workbook to another, do the following (practice on *copies* of important workbooks):

1. Switch to the workbook that is to receive the new styles (click in it or pick it from the Window menu).

2. Open the Style dialog box (use the Style command on the Format menu).

3. Use the Merge button to open the Merge Styles dialog box.

4. Select the name of the workbook containing the desired styles from the scrollable list in the Merge Styles dialog box.

5. Click OK to merge the styles of the selected workbook with the destination workbook.

Use Care When Merging Styles

Be warned that if the destination workbook and the source workbook have styles with identical names, Excel will want to replace the destination styles with the source styles. Excel will caution you about this and will give you a chance to keep all of the existing styles or to cancel the Merge command. You will be warned only *once*—even if you have more than one identical style name!

Deleting Styles

When you delete unwanted styles, all cells formatted with the deleted style revert to the Normal style for the worksheet. You will not be able to use Undo here. Use care or, better still, save your worksheet before deleting styles, so that you can close the clobbered worksheet without saving and then reload the unmodified version. To delete styles, do the following:

1. Open the Style dialog box (use the Style command on the Format menu).

2. If necessary, select the name of the style you want to delete from the drop-down Style Name list in the Style dialog box.

3. Click the Delete button. Use care since you won't be asked to confirm the deletion.

Changing Font Sizes and Attributes

Use the Formatting toolbar's drop-down font name and size lists to change those font features. Use the Bold, Italic, and Underline buttons to add those attributes to your worksheet.

For more advanced formatting options, use the Font tab in the Format Cells dialog box (reached with Format | Cells or the CTRL+1 shortcut).

Adjusting Alignment

A number of alignment buttons are available on the Standard and Formatting toolbars. Use these to shift the horizontal position of cell contents flush

WORKING WITH EXCEL

left, flush right, or to the center of cells. In addition, the Alignment tab in the Format Cells dialog box offers the choices shown here.

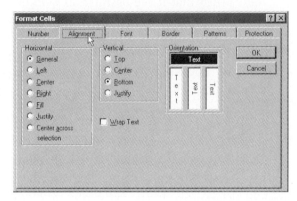

From here you can also specify how text and numbers will be positioned vertically within selected cells. For instance, you can center short type in tall rows. Text can be flipped with the Orientation buttons, so that it runs top to bottom or bottom to top within cells. The buttons illustrate their effects. The Wrap option, also found here, is discussed next.

Wrapping Text in Cells

Words can be made to wrap to fit the width of columns. Choose the Wrap Text option in the Alignment tab of the Format Cells dialog box.

Centering Text Across Columns

Sometimes you'll need to position a cell's contents to float across more than one column. Here are the basic steps.

1. Activate the cell you want to float.

2. Drag to select adjacent cells in the columns of interest, as shown in Figure 15-3. Don't AutoFill by mistake!

3. Click the Center Across Selection button, shown here, on the Formatting toolbar. Alternatively, you can use the Center Across Selection option in the Alignment tab of the Format Cells dialog box. The text will center itself across the cells. Thereafter, if you change column widths, the text recenters properly.

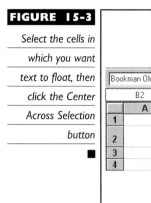

FIGURE 15-3

Select the cells in which you want text to float, then click the Center Across Selection button ∎

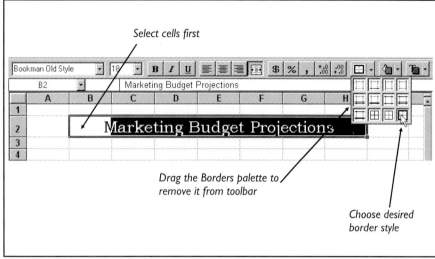

Select cells first

Drag the Borders palette to
remove it from toolbar

Choose desired
border style

Using Border Buttons and Commands

Borders can be used to set apart related worksheet sections and to emphasize totals and subtotals. Or use them just for decoration, to enhance the worksheet's appearance.

Borders can be created by using buttons on the Formatting toolbar:

1. Start by selecting the cell or cells you want to embellish.

2. To outline selected cells with a border on the four extreme sides, simply click the Border button arrow, shown here, on the Formatting toolbar. The keyboard shortcut is CTRL+SHIFT+&.

3. Pick the desired border setting by pointing to the desired border style in the palette containing border choices, shown here.

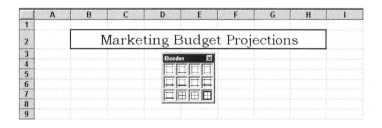

You can drag the palette off the toolbar and leave it displayed if you wish. This is handy if you will be creating numerous borders.

You can also construct custom borders in the Border tab of the Format Cells dialog box using many of the same techniques you learned in Microsoft Word.

1. Select the cells you want to enhance.

2. Open the Style dialog box and click Modify.

3. Click the Border tab, shown here.

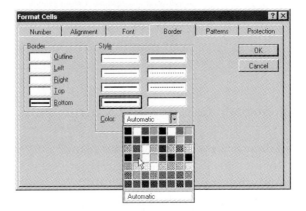

4. Click to pick a border element (left, right, and so on).

5. Pick line types (thick, thin, single, double, or whatever).

6. Repeat steps 4 and 5 until you are satisfied.

7. Click OK.

To remove all the borders from a selected range or cell, you can use the CTRL+SHIFT+underline (_) keyboard shortcut, or choose the No Borders choice in the Borders palette.

Changing Colors and Shading

You can change the color of selected text, cell shading, and other items with the Color button and Text Color button (and their drop-down palettes) found on the Formatting toolbar.

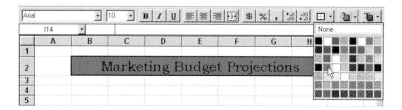

In addition, you can use the Patterns tab in the Format Cells dialog box. Watch the sample in the dialog box while you tinker away.

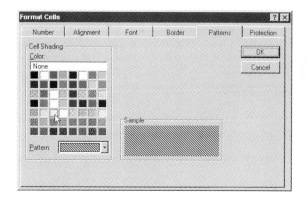

Inserting and Removing Page Breaks

Excel makes page break decisions automatically, but sometimes you'll want to force new pages elsewhere. Do this by activating the cell beneath and to the right of where you want a page break, and then choose Set Page Break from the Insert menu. Dark dashed lines will mark the new page breaks. Figure 15-4 illustrates this.

To remove breaks, activate the cell below and to the right of the break lines and choose Remove Page Break, the command that replaces Page Break on the Insert menu.

Hiding Rows and Columns

You can hide rows or columns without destroying their contents, then reveal them later when you want to see or edit them.

WORKING WITH EXCEL

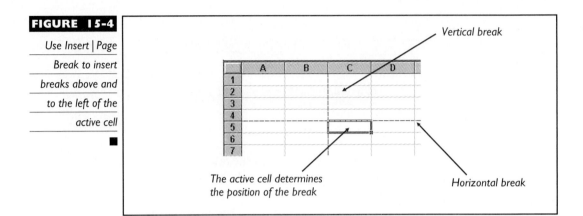

Vertical break

The active cell determines the position of the break

Horizontal break

1. Select the row(s) or column(s) you want to hide.

2. Choose the appropriate Hide and Unhide commands on the Format menu's Row and Column choices, shown here.

You can also play hide-and-seek with your mouse, but it takes a steady hand and some practice. If it's morning and you haven't had your second cup of coffee yet, forget it.

To hide rows with the mouse, select the row or rows of interest:

1. Place the mouse pointer beneath the heading of the row or rows you want to hide. For instance, if you want to hide rows 3 and 4, select both rows.

2. Point beneath the appropriate number at the left edge of the worksheet.

3. You'll see the pointer shape that indicates your ability to change row height.

4. Drag up until the rows are so thin that they disappear. The line between the visible and invisible row labels will become darker than the rest, and the row numbers will no longer be consecutive (row numbers will jump from 1 to 5, for instance).

Use the same basic approach to hide columns, but drag to the right on column letters. To bring back hidden rows or columns, slowly move the pointer over the dark lines in row or column labels (indicating hidden rows or columns). Watch the pointer carefully. At some position, the dark bar between the two arrowheads will split, indicating that you can drag the rows or columns back to a useful size. Alternatively, you can select the columns or rows to either side of the hidden column or row and use the Unhide button in the Column Width and Row Height dialog boxes.

Time to Experiment

Go forth and multiply (numbers, that is). You now have the basic skills needed to create and format powerful, great-looking spreadsheets. The chapters that follow deal with tools for managing large projects, charting, and other advanced topics. This would be a good point to create some of your own worksheets before continuing.

WORKING WITH EXCEL

CHAPTER 16

Organizing Large Projects

P

ROJECTS take many shapes and sizes. Sometimes you'll need to deal with a few big worksheets. Other times you'll need to work with lots of little ones. Excel offers a number of features to help you view, edit, navigate, and consolidate big projects. This chapter introduces you to them. You'll read about naming things in such a way that you can quickly locate and refer to them. You'll see how to split windows to make it easier to view widely separated parts of a document. Just as outlines can help you view and rearrange Word documents, they can also change the way you look at big Excel worksheets. And you'll see how those tabs at the bottom of workbook windows can help you keep related Excel information together, within easy reach.

Using Names

You can name ranges of cells, formulas, and more. Sometimes naming things this way makes it easier to refer to them. The names appear in the Name box on the left side of the Formula bar. Named items are also easy to find with the Edit | Go To command or by using F5 (Go To).

Names can be up to 255 characters long. The first character in a name must be a letter or the underline character. Names cannot look like cell references (A$1, for instance).

You can *define* names yourself, or let Excel *create* names for you by using labels in your worksheets. Let's start by seeing how Excel can automatically *create* names.

Asking Excel to Create Names

Excel can create names for selected cells based on row and column headings. Take a look at Figure 16-1.

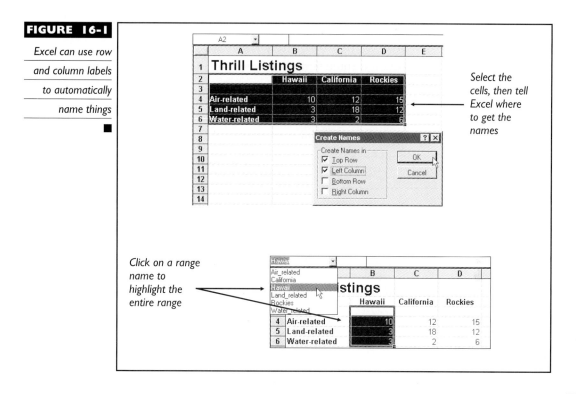

WORKING WITH EXCEL

In this instance, Excel will use the selected column labels for columns A, B, C, and D, plus the selected labels for rows 2, 3, 4, 5, and 6 to name ranges of cells *automatically*. Excel ignores empty cells when naming this way, and it "cleans up" names so that they conform to naming rules. Therefore, the resulting ranges will be labeled Air_related, California, Hawaii, Land_related, Rockies, and Water_related. Here are the general steps:

1. Select cells you want to name. (Include their headings.)

2. Choose Name from the Insert menu.

3. Choose Create from the resulting submenu. You'll see the Create Names dialog box shown in Figure 16-1.

4. Choose the label locations you want to use as names. Excel will use those labels to assign names automatically, modifying them as necessary to fit the naming rules.

5. Repeat the steps as often as necessary to name different areas. The F4 (Repeat) shortcut works great for this.

Defining Names Yourself

Suppose you wanted to define something manually—like the range of cells containing all of the listing numbers in our example. You could use the following general steps:

1. Select cells you want to name (just the listing numbers, in the example).

2. Choose Name from the Insert menu.

3. Choose Define from the resulting submenu.

4. You'll see the Define Name dialog box.

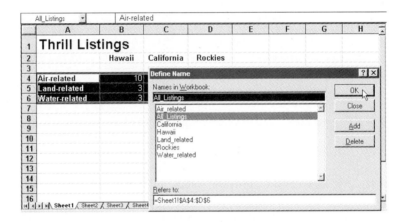

5. Excel proposes a name if it can. In this case it cannot.

6. Click OK to accept the proposed name, or type a name (**All_Listings** in this example), and then click Add or OK.

7. Repeat the steps as often as necessary to name different areas. The F4 (Repeat) shortcut works great for this.

warning *It is **very** important to **thoroughly** test your work when using names, since they won't always do what you'd expect. Consider, for example, how you selected ranges when naming them in the last example. If you later add numbers in row 3, they'll be included in the Hawaii, California, and Rockies ranges, but **not** in the All_Listings range. Why? Because you didn't include row 3 in your selection when you named that range. Folks lose their jobs when things like this happen in the real world.*

Seeing Named Items

It is important to understand what's included in a named item or range. The easy way to do that is to pick a name from the Name Box's drop-down list on the left side of the Formula bar. Picking a name causes Excel to select (highlight) the named item or range in the worksheet. For instance, here is what happens when *Land-related* is chosen.

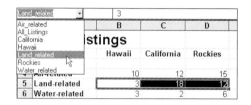

Referring to Ranges by Name

Once you've created named items, they can be used in many ways. For instance, you can create equations like the one in cell B8, as illustrated here.

	A	B	C	D
1	**Thrill Listings**			
2		Hawaii	California	Rockies
3				
4	Air-related	10	12	15
5	Land-related	3	18	12
6	Water-related	3	2	6
7				
8	Air-related	12%	15%	19%
9	Land-related	4%	22%	15%
10	Water-related	4%	2%	7%
11				

B8 · =B4/SUM(All_Listings)

As you can see, the formula

`=B4/SUM(All_Listings)`

works in place of the traditional

`=B4/SUM(B4:D6)`

or the awkward

`=B4/(B4+C4+D4+B5+C5+D5+B6+C6+D6)`

It reads better, too, don't you think?

While the example is obviously overkill, you can see how constructing formulas this way in complex worksheets might make it easier to create and troubleshoot complex projects.

tip *There's another reason why a named range is better here than something like (B4:D6). Can you see it? Here's a hint: If you had used that range and then copied down the formula, what would happen? Disaster, that's what! You'd have to use absolute cell references for the range to ensure that Excel didn't increment the values. Now isn't the named range method a lot easier?*

Inserting Names

You can type out names longhand or visit the Paste Name dialog box reached via the Insert menu:

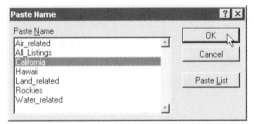

But the easiest way to insert names is to pick them from the Name Box's drop-down list in the Formula bar. Here are the general steps for all three techniques:

1. Activate the cell where you want to insert the name.

2. Construct the equation, pausing whenever a name is required.

3. Either type the name, pick it from the Name Box's drop-down list, or open the Paste Name dialog box (Insert | Name | Paste) and double-click on the name in the list. Excel will place the name at the insertion point in the equation.

4. Finish the equation (inserting other names if you wish).

Splitting Windows and Fixing Titles

Excel document windows can be split into two or four separately scrollable panes that make it easy to see different parts of your worksheet at the same time. Figure 16-2 illustrates this.

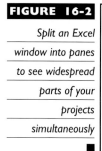

FIGURE 16-2

Split an Excel window into panes to see widespread parts of your projects simultaneously

■

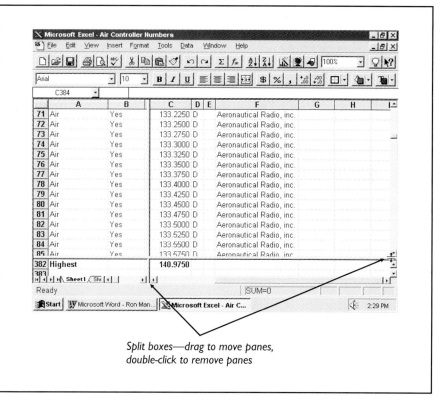

Split boxes—drag to move panes,
double-click to remove panes

Use the *Split* command on the Window menu to create four panes in the neighborhood of the active cell. Each pane will have its own scroll tools, which can be used to position each pane's contents independently. Use the *Remove Split* command that appears in Excel's Window menu whenever a window is split.

Alternatively, you can drag to create panes exactly where you want them. Here's how: In a single-pane worksheet, there are thick black lines just above the top of the vertical scroll arrow and to the right of the right horizontal scroll arrow. These are called *split boxes*. Drag on either one or both to create panes. Double-clicking on a split box removes its pane. The Window menu's Remove Split command also removes panes you've created by dragging.

Outlining Your Worksheets

Excel's *Outline* feature lets you expand and collapse large worksheets. For instance, you could create an annual budget containing annual totals, and monthly and quarterly subtotals, then collapse it to view and print quarterly subtotals and annual totals. You could collapse it further to show only annual totals. You'll see an example of this in a moment. Moreover, once items have been collapsed, all formatting, cutting, pasting, and similar activities affect all of the subordinate (hidden) detail.

To create outlines, all of the references in your formulas must point in the same direction (for instance, every row's sum ranges should be either left to right, or right to left).

Automatic Outlines

Excel will automatically outline for you, or allow you to define your own levels of detail. To outline automatically:

1. Start by selecting any *single* cell in the worksheet.

2. Use the Data | Group And Outline | Auto Outline command as shown here:

3. Excel will look for subtotals, titles, and other recognizable elements; create an outline; and display the worksheet with additional outline tools (the little buttons and sliders at the top and left edge of the window) as shown in Figure 16-3.

Viewing, Printing, Promoting, and Demoting

Once you've outlined a document, you'll see outlining tools along the top and left edges of the worksheet. (These can be hidden with the Outline Symbols choice in the View tab of the Tools | Options dialog box.)

In the preceding illustration you saw the worksheet at its full level of detail. Row-level and column-level symbols in the upper-left corner of the work-

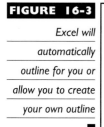

FIGURE 16-3

Excel will

automatically

outline for you or

allow you to create

your own outline

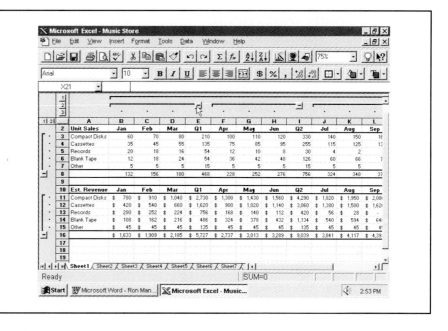

sheet tell you that there are two levels of detail in this worksheet. It is possible to have up to eight levels.

Click on the column- and row-level buttons to show or hide detail. Hidden details don't print.

Manually Outlining

Although automatic outlines are much easier to create, you can use the Utility toolbar to outline manually. Consult the big books and online Help for details.

Clearing Outline Structures

If you don't mind keeping the outline levels, but don't want to see the outline symbols because they rob some of your screen space, turn them off using the CTRL+8 keyboard shortcut. Pressing CTRL+8 toggles the display of outline symbols, saving you a trip to the Options dialog box.

To actually clear (remove) outline levels from a worksheet without otherwise changing the contents of the worksheet, use the Clear Outline command found on the Group And Outline submenu of the Data menu.

WORKING WITH EXCEL

Working with Multiple Worksheets

There are many reasons to work with multiple worksheets. You might need to combine departmental budgets into a company-wide total budget, for instance. Or you might have separate and detailed payroll, sales, and other budget worksheets containing totals that need to be included as line items on a summary worksheet for the top brass. Other times, colleagues might send you their budgets on disk or over a network, and you might need to combine them to work with them.

Each new project can have multiple worksheets. That's what the tabs at the bottom of your screen indicate.

If you've ever worked on projects requiring dozens or even hundreds of related worksheets, you'll enjoy Excel's ability to "round up" related files even if they're in different workbooks. Ultimately, you may save a great deal of time as well.

Linking Worksheets

It is possible to *link* the contents of one worksheet with another, regardless of whether the worksheets are in the same workbook. For instance, if you have a worksheet containing product prices, then decide to create a second worksheet in a different workbook containing unit sales forecasts and revenue projections based on the number of units sold times the prices on the pricing spreadsheet, you could link the two worksheets. Then, whenever you change prices on the pricing worksheet, the revenue forecasts will change on the forecast worksheet. Figure 16-4 shows a simplified example of this process.

Here are the general steps:

1. Open both workbooks, if necessary, and switch to the appropriate worksheets.

2. Select and copy the cell or cells containing the numbers you want to link (cell B2 in the Prices, 1997 worksheet in the example).

3. Switch to the worksheet where you want to paste the numbers (cell B11 in the Music Store worksheet in the example).

4. Select Edit | Paste Special and choose the Paste Link option. The path to the linked item will appear in the Formula bar. Henceforth, any change you make to the Prices worksheet will be reflected on the Music Store worksheet.

FIGURE 16-4

When you use
Paste Link, changes
on one worksheet
are updated on
other linked
worksheets
■

B11	▼	=B3*'[Prices, 1997.xls]Sheet1'!$B$2

Music Store

	A	B	C	D	E	F
11	Compact Disks	$ 780	$ 910	$ 1,040	$ 2,730	$ 1,300
12	Cassettes	$ 420	$ 540	$ 660	$ 1,620	$ 900
13	Records	$ 280	$ 252	$ 224	$ 756	$ 168
14	Blank Tape	$ 108	$ 162	$ 216	$ 486	$ 324
15	Other	$ 45	$ 45	$ 45	$ 135	$ 45

◄ ◄ ► ►◄ **Sheet1** ╱ Sheet2 ╱ Sheet3 ╱ Sheet4 ╱ Sheet5 ╱ Sheet6 ╱ Sheet7 ◄

Prices, 1997

	A	B	C	D	E	F
1						
2	Compact Disks	13				
3	Cassettes	12				
4	Records	14				
5	Blank Tape	9				

Cell B11 in Music Store changes when cell B2 in Prices, 1997 changes

note   *In this example, the material was pasted, and then the other information was typed. You cannot Paste Link data into the data entry area. You can, however, "show" Excel what you want inserted. All you do is start your formula; then, when you get to the point where you need to insert the cell reference, just click on the item to be linked. Even if it is in a different workbook, Excel will properly enter the cross-reference, and you're all set!*

If you open a document that references a link (Music Store, in the example), but the referenced document (Prices, 1997) is *not* open, Excel will ask whether you want to update from the unopened document. Range names also work for linking (and, remember, you can link things besides numbers—text, graphics, charts, and so on).

Using Multiple Worksheets in a Workbook

When you use the New command (CTRL+N), Excel always opens a new workbook containing 16 worksheets. (You can change the actual number of worksheets created in new documents in the Option dialog box's General tab.)

WORKING WITH EXCEL

To switch from worksheet to worksheet, click on the desired worksheet tab at the bottom of the workbook window, as shown in Figure 16-5. Use the scroll arrows if necessary to see the rest of the tabs.

Naming Worksheets and Tabs

To name a worksheet, double-click on its tab. You'll see the Rename Sheet dialog box.

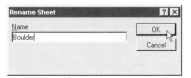

Type any name up to 31 characters, including spaces. The tab will display the new name.

Moving Worksheets Within a Workbook

To change the order of sheets in a workbook:

1. Click on the tab you wish to move. The mouse pointer will change shape, and a tiny black triangle will appear as shown here:

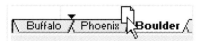

2. Drag the tab with the mouse while watching the little black triangle.

3. Release the mouse button when the triangle is pointing at the desired new tab location. The sheet and its tab will move.

FIGURE 16-5

Click on a tab to pick a different worksheet or on a scroll arrow if you need to see the desired tab

■

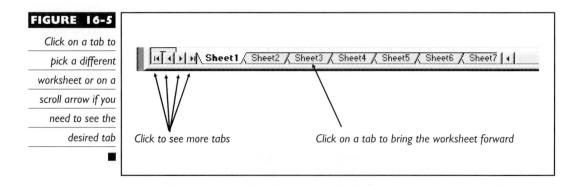

Click to see more tabs   *Click on a tab to bring the worksheet forward*

Copying Worksheets Within a Workbook

It's often handy to copy a worksheet's contents. For instance, you could set up a sample budget on worksheet 1 and then copy it to worksheet 2, worksheet 3, worksheet 4, and so on.

1. Create the first worksheet.

2. Click on the tab for the worksheet you want to copy.

3. Hold down CTRL. The mouse pointer will change shape (it will look like the Move pointer with a plus sign inside). You'll also see a tiny black triangle like the one you see when moving sheets.

4. Drag the tab with the mouse while watching the little black triangle.

5. Release the mouse button when the triangle is pointing at the desired insertion tab location. Excel will insert a new copy of the worksheet, and uniquely name the new tab:

Notice that this adds an additional sheet to your workbook. To change the tab's name, double-click and proceed as previously discussed.

Copying and Moving Worksheets to Other Workbooks

Use the Move or Copy dialog box to copy or relocate selected worksheets to another workbook. Here are the general steps:

1. Open the workbook containing the sheets to be copied or moved.

2. CTRL-click to select each sheet to be copied or moved. Selected tabs will be lighter than the others.

3. Choose Move or Copy Sheet from the Edit menu.

4. If you want to copy rather than move worksheets, be sure to select the Create A Copy option.

5. Choose the destination book and the desired insertion point as shown here. To copy or move sheets to a new workbook, choose *(new book)* from the To Book list.

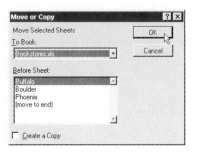

Viewing Multiple Windows

Sometimes it is useful to see more than one sheet or more than one workbook onscreen. Use these general steps and techniques:

1. Choose New Window from the Excel Window menu for each additional window you want to display.

2. Choose Arrange from the Window menu and make your desires known in the Arrange Windows dialog box. For example, the windows here are tiled. Experiment.

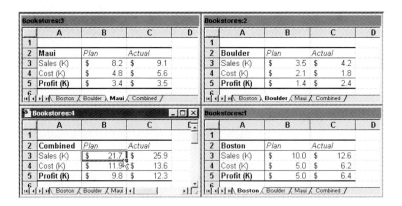

3. Drag the window borders or corners with your mouse if you want to fine-tune.

Summarizing Information from Multiple Worksheets

Often, when you have a workbook containing a sheet for each of many offices or departments, or several workbooks containing related information, you might want to create a "top" summary sheet containing company-wide totals. This is often called *summarizing* or *consolidating*. In this book we will provide an overview of this complex topic and a simple example of one consolidation technique. Consult the big books and test your work if you need to consolidate important data!

Defining References to Multiple Worksheets

One way to consolidate information is to create an additional worksheet with equations that sum the data from the others. For instance, suppose you had stores in Boston, Maui, and Boulder. You've created a *profit and loss (P&L)* statement for each store on a separate sheet in the same workbook. The preceding illustration showed this.

You might decide to create a *fourth* sheet that consolidates the data for the three stores. Here are the general steps:

1. Create the new sheet that will be used to contain the consolidated numbers (perhaps by copying one of the others to save some time and give the project a uniform look).

2. Activate a cell needing an equation in the consolidation sheet (B3 in the lower-right sheet shown earlier).

3. Type an equal sign (=) to begin the equation.

4. Continue the equation until you need to refer to a cell. (This example uses the SUM function.)

5. When it is time to refer to a cell, click on the tab for the first sheet to be included in the consolidation (let's do Boston first).

6. Click on the cell to be included in the equation (B3 in this case).

7. SHIFT-click on the tab for the last sheet to be included in the consolidation (Maui).

WORKING WITH EXCEL

8. Finish the equation back in the consolidation sheet. It should look like the following illustration:

	B3		=SUM(Boston!B3+Boulder!B3+Maui!B3)			
	A	B	C	D	E	F
1						
2	Combined	Plan	Actual			
3	Sales (K)	$ 21.7	$ 25.9			
4	Cost (K)	$ 11.9	$ 13.6			
5	Profit (K)	$ 9.8	$ 12.3			
6						

9. Test the equation. In this example, cell B3 in the consolidated sheet should equal the sum of all of the stores' B3 cells. A change in cell B3 for any of the stores should properly update the consolidation.

10. Copy the working equation to establish other 3-D sums if desired (cells B3 through C5 in our example).

11. Test again, then save your work.

12. From now on, changes in any store's P&L will update the consolidated sheet.

There are many, many variations on this theme. You can use named ranges instead of cell addresses, for instance, and OLE will let you link cells or ranges in other workbooks. Again, check online Help and the big books when you get stuck. Check your work carefully.

Printing Tips for Large Excel Projects

Excel's Print dialog box (CTRL+P, or File | Print) offers choices specific to spreadsheets. For instance, you can choose to print just selected cells, selected sheets, or the entire workbook:

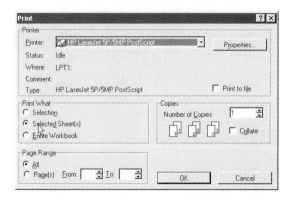

It is possible to have a different page setup for each sheet in a workbook, but that's not usually what you'll want. To change the page setup for a single sheet, click on the worksheet's tab to bring it forward, and then choose Page Setup from the File menu.

To affect the page setups for multiple (or all) sheets, SHIFT-click on the sheet tabs before visiting the Page Setup dialog box.

Use the Orientation and Scaling choices in the Page tab of the Page Setup dialog box to have Excel automatically adjust the size of images so that your work will fit on the desired number of pages.

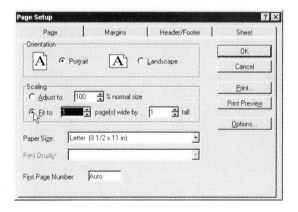

Use the Sheet tab in the Page Setup dialog box to specify printing ranges (using either cell addresses or names).

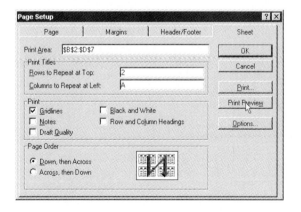

In addition, the Sheet tab lets you specify the printing of repeating rows, columns, and more.

Use Print Preview before beginning large printing jobs. It can be a real time saver. If you find yourself creating complex reports containing just selected parts of your workbook, it would pay you to explore Excel's Reports features described in online Help and in the bigger books.

CHAPTER 17

An Introduction to Functions

E

XCEL'S worksheet functions are power tools that help you perform complex computations. Excel has hundreds of functions that facilitate engineering computations, manipulate text, and do much, much more. In addition, Excel offers over 400 macro functions, which are discussed briefly in Chapter 20. This chapter deals only with *worksheet* functions.

Worksheet functions can often be used by themselves as stand-alone formulas, or they can be built into more complex formulas of your own creation. For instance, the SQRT( ) function finds the square root of a positive number. In the simplest case, you could type the formula **=SQRT(9)** into a cell and see the results (3). Or you could include the square root function in a more complex formula like **=SQRT(9)*9**.

Functions can often refer to other things in your worksheet. For instance, **=SQRT(A2)** would compute the square root of the contents of cell A2. If you use named items in your worksheets, functions can sometimes refer to them as well. For example, **=SQRT(SPEED)** might be a legal formula if your worksheet contains a positive number named SPEED or some other equation that computed speeds.

Some functions *inspect* things and take action based on what they find. For example, the function ISNONTEXT( ) can check a cell and tell you if the cell contains text or not. Other functions *convert* things. The text function LOWER( ) converts text to all lowercase, for instance. The engineering function CONVERT( ) transforms values from one unit of measure to another (Fahrenheit to Celsius, feet to meters, and so on). Most functions are already installed with Excel. Others (like CONVERT) may need to be installed as *add-ins*. You'll see how that is done later in this chapter.

Parts of a Function

Functions consist of *function names* and (usually) *arguments*. For instance, SQRT is the function name, while the value (the positive number) being evaluated is the argument. As you saw earlier in the square root example, arguments can be values, references, or names. They can also be text, logical values (TRUE and FALSE), or arrays. A function's *syntax* is illustrated by listing in the documentation, as well as in Excel's Help windows, all the function's *argument names* in the order they should be used. For example, you might see the functions and their arguments expressed as

```
SQRT(number)
```

or

```
SUM(number1,number2
```

or

```
FV(rate,nper,pmnt,pv,type)
```

Notice that in the FV example some of the arguments are boldface and others are not. This is how some documentation differentiates between *required* and *optional* arguments. Often, if you don't provide an argument, Excel uses the default argument for that function. For instance, the function

```
DOLLAR(number,decimals)
```

converts numbers into text with dollar signs and, optionally, decimal places for cents or pennies. The expression

```
=DOLLAR(10)
```

would yield *$10.00.* (Notice the default decimal point and two places for pennies even though no second argument was supplied.) The expression

```
=DOLLAR(10,1)
```

would create the text string *$10.0,* and

```
=DOLLAR(10,)
```

would yield $10 (neither decimal point nor pennies). In the first case, leaving out the optional second argument *and the comma* that separates it causes Excel to use the default argument (a decimal point and two places, in this case). In the second example, the comma separates the second argument, which specifies the number of decimal places (1). In the third example, where there is a comma and no second argument, the comma suggests to Excel that there *is* a second argument (an argument specifying neither decimal point nor decimal places). The lesson here is that commas are important in functions, and that sometimes there is a big difference in the results if you delete a comma instead of leaving it and not entering an argument after it.

You can frequently use *other functions* as arguments. For instance, you could combine the ROUND and SQRT functions to compute the square root of a number, then round the results. The formula

=ROUND(SQRT(A1),2)

would compute the square root of the contents of cell A1, then round the answer to two decimal places.

Functions Requiring Add-Ins

Some functions require an *add-in*—additional software (such as a utility program) that is provided with Excel, but not automatically loaded when you run Excel. When you attempt to use functions that require add-ins, Excel loads the add-ins automatically for you. For example, the BESSELI statistical function needs the Analysis ToolPak. If Excel can't load the required add-in, it may be because you chose not to install add-ins when you initially installed Excel on your hard disk. Try rerunning the installer program to add these features.

Online Function Help

If each Excel function were described in detail here, the book's size would double, and its title would need to be changed to *Working with Excel's Functions with an Appendix on Microsoft Office*. Fortunately, you won't need to lug around 600 extra pages of function trivia. Excel's extensive online Help feature and the Function Wizard will let you find and explore just the functions you're interested in. To expedite your searching, worksheet functions have been divided into nine categories:

- Database
- Date and Time
- Financial

- Information

- Logical

- Lookup and Reference

- Mathematical and Trigonometric

- Statistical

- Text

Use the Help menu's Microsoft Excel Help Topics command to get to the Index tab of the Help window. Then type **functions, worksheet** and double-click on About Worksheet Topics to get to this screen:

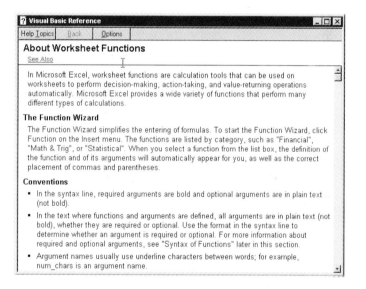

This tells you all about functions. If you want to find out more about a specific function, go to the Answer Wizard tab of the Help Topics dialog box and type the name of the function. For instance, if you want to learn more about the SUM function, you could type **sum** in the Search dialog box, pick the help topic *SUM* in the scrollable topic list, and go to that topic.

If you'd rather browse, start with a general topic like "functions," then pick a function category like "Financial" or "Statistical." This works either in Answer Wizard or in the Index tab.

Since some of the help provided for functions is often fairly detailed and complex, you might want to print the information that you find. Use the Help window's Options | Print Topic command to do so.

The Function Wizard

Excel's Function Wizard greatly simplifies the use of functions. It leads you through the necessary steps, shows the results as you work, and even provides examples of the functions in use.

1. Start by activating the cell where you want to paste the function.

2. Begin the formula with an equal sign (=), and place the insertion point where you want to insert the function.

3. Click the Function Wizard button on the Standard toolbar, or choose Insert | Function. The Function Wizard's Step 1 window appears.

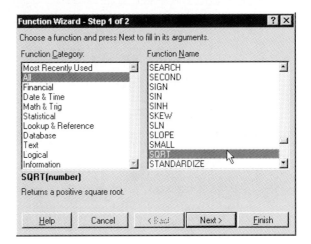

The Wizard lists functions within the nine categories mentioned earlier (Database, Date and Time, and so on). In addition you'll see the *Most Recently Used* and *All* options.

tip   *The keyboard shortcut for the Function Wizard is SHIFT+F3.*

4. Pick a category from the list on the left, then scroll in the list on the right to find the desired function.

5. Click to pick the function. Its name is displayed in the Name box on the Formula bar, and its name and arguments show near the bottom-left corner of the Paste Function dialog box.

6. Read the Wizard's description of the function to be sure it's the one you want.

7. Click the Next button and you will see the second Wizard dialog box.

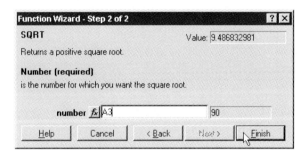

Here you see a list of arguments that are required and possibly some that are optional (and labeled as such). The arguments are explained onscreen, and the Help button provides real-life examples.

note   *Each dialog box is different and depends upon the function for its appearance and content. For instance, SQRT has only one argument, while PV has many.*

8. You can type directly in the Wizard's entry boxes or use your mouse to point to cells containing the data you wish to use as arguments.

tip   *Entries can be the actual data (like the number 90), or cell addresses (like A1), or names (like SALES), or even other functions.*

9. As you work, the Wizard will show the results of its calculations in the Value area at the top right corner of the dialog box.

10. Click Finish when your formula is complete. As you can see in Figure 17-1, when you click Finish, the Wizard pastes the function into the active cell and displays the results of the current arguments in the cell. You'll see the equation in the Formula bar.

Examples of Functions by Category

The best way to learn about functions is to experiment with them. Here are a few examples to get you started.

FIGURE 17-1

A function at work

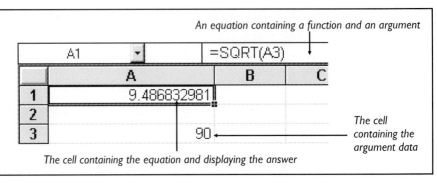

An equation containing a function and an argument

The cell containing the argument data

The cell containing the equation and displaying the answer

Date and Time Functions

Some of the Date and Time functions simply *return* the current date and/or time. Others do date-and-time math. Let's first look at a function that finds and reports the current time—the NOW( ) function. When you use it, NOW( ) inserts (returns) a new serial number corresponding to the current date and time whenever the worksheet is recalculated.

For example, if you simply paste the formula =**NOW**( ) into a cell, it will display the current date followed by the current time, then update the cell's contents every time the worksheet is recalculated (and *only* when it is recalculated).

The actual *appearance* of cells containing the NOW( ) or other Date and Time functions can be changed by using different date and time *types* found in the Number tab of the Format Cells dialog box, reached by choosing Format | Cells. For instance, Excel's Date format will display date and time in the format

```
m/d/yy h:mm
```

or in a number of other variations with or without the time. If you want to see only the *time* portion of a date serial number, format the cell(s) with one of five predefined Time formats, or create your own.

Other Date and Time functions *compute* things using date serial numbers. For instance, the DAYS360 function computes the number of days between two dates assuming a 360-day year (used by many accounting folks).

When you do any kind of date math, check your work very, very carefully. It is quite easy to produce technically correct answers that are not the ones you need. For instance, when computing working days, Excel does not automatically know that December 25th is a holiday for many. Your equations will need to take things like this into consideration.

Engineering Functions

Engineering functions are available, but require the Analysis ToolPak add-in macro, which you will probably need to install manually (that is, get out your installation disks) if you didn't opt to install it when you first installed Office. Consult online Help and the big books for details.

Financial Functions

Excel's many financial functions are well documented with online Help. Many of them can be used together, or can be included as arguments, one within the other.

Here's an example of one way to use *PMT,* Excel's payment function. Officially, this function "Returns the periodic payment of an annuity based on constant payments and a constant interest rate." In other words, it will tell you what your payments will be, given the loan amount, number of payments, and a fixed rate of interest. The function's syntax is

PMT(rate,nper,pv,fv,type)

This image illustrates PMT at work.

B6		=PMT(B3/12,B4,B5)

	A	B	C
1	Loan Payment Calculator		
2			
3	Interest Rate	10.50%	
4	Number of Loan Payments	360	
5	Loan Amount	$ 100,000	
6	Monthly Payments	($914.74)	
7			

rate is the interest rate *per period.* For instance, if you borrow at an annual fixed interest rate of 10.5% and then make *monthly* payments, the interest rate is 10.5% divided by 12. That explains the division portion of the preceding formula.

The argument *nper* needs the *total* number of payments. Thus, if you are borrowing for 30 years, and make monthly payments, you'll make 30*12 or 360 payments. *pv* is the present value, or total amount that the series of payments is worth now—the loan amount, in this case. Notice that in the example the optional *fv* (future value) and *type* arguments were omitted. Future value is a desired cash balance after the last payment is made. *type* is either 0 (zero) or 1. Omitting the *type* argument or entering 0 indicates that you will make payments at the end of each period. Entering **1**, on the other hand, tells Excel that the payments will be made at the beginning of the period.

Related financial functions include FV, IPMT, NPER, PPMT, PV, and RATE as separate functions.

Information Functions

Some functions inspect things and report back. For example, ISNON-TEXT( ) will let your formulas know if a cell entry is not text. Other information functions can check things external to Excel, like the amount of RAM in your computer, or which DOS version you are using. Here is INFO( ) at work. Its syntax is INFO(*type*).

B2	▼	=INFO(A2)

	A	B
1	Argument	Results
2	directory	D:\OFFICE95\EXCEL\
3	memavail	1048576
4	memused	120504
5	totmem	1169080
6	release	7.0
7	recalc	Automatic
8	numfile	16
9	origin	$A:$A$1
10	system	pcdos
11	osversion	Windows (32-bit) 4.00
12		

Cells B2 through B11 each have the same formula that refers to corresponding cells in column A, which contain the arguments that produce the results you see.

Logical Functions

You use logic all the time. Chances are, you say things like "If the fruit at the market looks good, please pick up some peaches or grapes, if grapes are less than a dollar a pound." You can use logic in Excel, too. Take the IF function demonstrated in Figure 17-2. Its syntax is

```
IF(logical_test,value_if_true,value_if_false)
```

In this example, the IF( ) function checks to see if the ending odometer reading is greater than the starting reading. If it isn't, chances are that the

FIGURE 17-2

Excel's IF function

tests for conditions

and responds

accordingly

■

B4	▼	=IF(B3>B2,(B3-B2),"Check OD")		
	A	**B**	**C**	**D**
1		Truck 1	Truck 2	Truck 3
2	Starting Odometer	1025.8	1025.8	1025.8
3	Ending Odometer	145.2	1455.2	1455.2
4	Miles Traveled	Check OD	429.4	429.4
5				
6				
7	Cost Per Gallon	$ 1.35		
8	Gallons Used	12.2	13.2	14.2
9	Miles Per Gallon	#VALUE!	32.5	30.2
10				
11	Cost Per Mile	#VALUE!	0.04	0.04
12				

The equation for cell B4 displays the message text only if the logical test is false

user has made a typographical error when entering readings. Or perhaps the odometer has reached its limit and "rolled over" to start again at zero. If the readings look okay, the IF function causes Excel to subtract the beginning from the ending readings (B3–B2). If there seems to be an error, the function displays text (*Check OD*) in the cell.

Lookup and Reference Functions

Like explorers, Lookup and Reference functions go to places that you send them and return with answers. They can be used to create invoices that look up and insert different unit prices based on quantities purchased, for instance. These features can inspect *rows*, *columns*, or *arrays*. Here is a simple example.

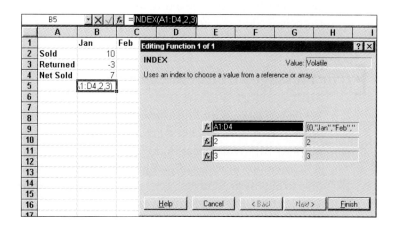

The INDEX( ) function here has been asked to go to the array bounded by cell addresses A1 through D4, then get the value stored in the cell two rows down and two columns across.

Lookup and Reference functions can refer to ranges, names, specific cell addresses, or row and column counts.

Math and Trig Functions

You've already seen several of the Mathematical functions in action—SQRT( ) and SUM( ), for example. There are many others, enough to make an eighth-grade math teacher weep with joy. Most are quite straightforward and well documented with online Help. Math and Trig functions can refer to cell references, names, or plain old numbers.

Two of the Math and Trig functions simply produce *numbers* whenever a worksheet recalculates. RAND( ) produces evenly distributed random numbers greater than or equal to 0 (zero) and less than 1 each time you recalculate—handy if you play the lottery or need to check probabilities. The PI( ) function inserts 3.141592654.

Statistical Functions

Pollsters and statisticians will want to check out the many statistical functions, from AVDEV( ) to ZTEST( ).

Text Functions

To manipulate or analyze strings of text in cells, use text functions. For example, CLEAN( )will strip away any nonprinting characters stored in a cell. UPPER( ) converts text to all uppercase. DOLLAR( ) converts numbers to their spelled-out dollar equivalents and formats them in currency format.

Error Messages from Functions

When you leave out or misuse arguments in functions, you will sometimes see cryptic error messages like "Error in formula," or a message like "#NAME?" or "#NUM!" will appear in the cell containing the flawed argument.

It is common to get messages like these when you work with names or text strings as arguments. Text strings *must* be enclosed in quotation marks, while names (references to areas, for instance) must *not* be in quotes. For instance, suppose you are using a math function like SQRT. If you enter the formula argument **=SQRT(SALES)**, Excel expects to be able to find a named numeric value or range of cells in your worksheet called SALES. If it can't, you'll get the message "#NAME?" in the cell containing the formula. If you *do* have a positive numeric value named SALES, the formula will use its contents as the function's argument. If the value of SALES is negative, you'll see the error message "#NUM!" Suppose you accidentally enclose the name *SALES* in quotes, then try to use it as an arithmetic argument. The expression **=SQRT("SALES")** will produce the error message "#VALUE!" since SQRT needs a numeric value to do its thing, and material in quotes is treated as *text*.

To Learn More About Functions

There is clearly much more to know about Excel's functions. While you can learn a lot by experimenting and exploring Excel's online Help, you may also benefit from seeing them all in one place—for which you should check out the *Microsoft Excel Function Reference* (at 500-plus pages) shipped with the program. Or for a tutorial approach to the entire topic of functions, check out *Excel Made Easy* (Martin S. Matthews; Osborne McGraw-Hill).

WORKING WITH EXCEL

CHAPTER 18

Excel's Chart Features

EXCEL helps you create charts in two or three dimensions based on data in a worksheet. You can take almost complete control over every aspect of your chart's appearance with Excel's Chart toolbar and menu choices, or you can let Excel's Chart Wizard make most of the decisions for you.

Once you've created a chart, you can print it, hide it, spell-check it, modify it, or even include it in your non-Excel projects (such as Word or PowerPoint documents).

Whenever you change data in a worksheet, Excel will update (or at least offer to update) charts that are linked to the changed data.

Chart Parts and Terminology

It's possible to fumble along without knowing the names of Excel's chart parts, and there is plenty of online Help available while you create and edit charts. But you'll be much more productive if you take a moment to understand just a few concepts and terms.

Chart Data Series

A *chart data series* is a collection of *related* values that are plotted on the chart. For instance, in the chart in Figure 18-1 there are two one-data series—the numbers 300, 907.7, and 3330 make up one data series, while 133.8, 355.4, and 320 make up the other series.

Data Markers

Data markers are the bars, pie wedges, dots, pictures, or other elements used to represent a particular data point (a single value in a series). For instance, the six shaded columns in Figure 18-1 are each separate data markers.

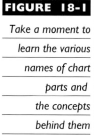

FIGURE 18-1

Take a moment to learn the various names of chart parts and the concepts behind them

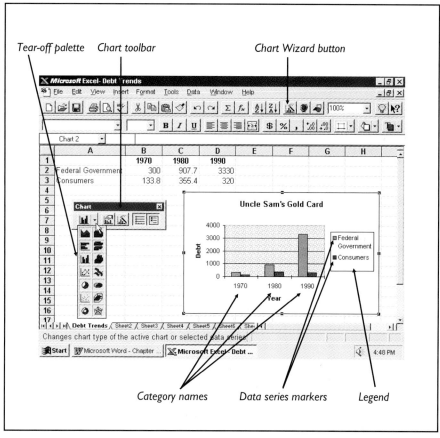

When charts have more than one data series, the markers for each series usually look different. This is also illustrated in Figure 18-1, where the consumer debt columns are one color (or shade of gray, or pattern), while government debt columns are another.

It is also possible to use different *types* of markers for different series in the same chart. You might, for instance, use *columns* for one series and *lines* for another. Think of data markers as the columns, bars, pie wedges, lines, and other elements used to represent values on a chart.

Axes

An axis is a reference line denoting one of the dimensions of a chart. Excel can plot up to three axes: X, Y, and Z. Usually the X axis runs horizontally (left to right) and the Y axis runs vertically (bottom to top). For instance, in Figure 18-1 the years run along the X axis and the billions of dollars run

WORKING WITH EXCEL

along the Y axis. In three-dimensional charts, the Z axis runs vertically, and the X and Y axes are at angles to display perspective.

Category Names

Category names usually correspond to worksheet labels for the data being plotted along the X axis (horizontally along the chart). For instance, in Figure 18-1 the category names are 1970, 1980, and 1990. Chart Wizard identifies and includes category names when it creates a new chart. Some chart types (like bar charts) place category names on the Y axis.

Chart Data Series Names

Chart data series names usually correspond to worksheet labels for the data being plotted on the Y axis. For instance, in Figure 18-1 the chart has two data series names, one for each series. Data series names are usually displayed in a box (called a *legend*) alongside a sample of the color, shade, or pattern used for each data series. Chart Wizard automatically identifies category names and creates legends.

Tick Marks and Gridlines

Tick marks are short lines that intersect an axis to separate parts of a series scale or category. You can also add optional, longer gridlines in any of a chart's dimensions by selecting them and using Format | Selected Grid Lines. Horizontal gridlines are illustrated in Figure 18-1.

Chart Text

The Chart Wizard automatically adds text for things like chart and data labels. It is also possible to add your own text, like text boxes containing notes. Chart text is discussed later in the chapter, because by now you must be itching to create a chart. Let's cut to the chase.

Instant Charts with the Chart Wizard

Chart Wizard looks at the data you've selected to plot. It also watches as you drag to define the size and shape of the desired chart area. Next, it offers you a number of chart styles, and even lets you define chart titles. Faster than you can say, "Next year let's reduce the deficit," you'll have a great-looking chart. Here are the steps for a simple column chart, plus some insights into the other options you'll encounter along the way.

Starting and Assisting the Wizard

1. Start by creating a worksheet containing the data you want to chart. In Figure 18-2, the cells A1 through D3 contain the necessary data and labels for a multiseries chart.

2. Select the data to be included in your chart (drag to highlight the relevant cells). Don't include empty rows or columns. In the sample chart, cells A1 through D3 are surrounded by marching ants, indicating that they have been selected.

3. Click on the Chart Wizard button, shown at the left.

4. Marching ants surround selected cells, and your pointer turns into cross hairs with a little chart attached.

5. Drag with it, as illustrated in Figure 18-2, to define the size and shape of your new chart. To create a square, hold down SHIFT while you drag.

FIGURE 18-2

Start a worksheet, and then let the Chart Wizard help you size and shape it ∎

Select cells first

	A	B	C	D	E	F	G	H
1		1970	1980	1990				
2	Federal Government	300	907.7	3330				
3	Consumers	133.8	355.4	320				
4								
5								
6								
7								
8								
9								
10								
11								
12								
13								
14								
15								
16								
17								

Debt Trends / Sheet2 / Sheet3 / Sheet4 / Sheet5 / Sheet6 / She

Then drag to select chart size and shape

WORKING WITH EXCEL

6. When you release the mouse button, you will see the first of five Chart Wizard Step dialog boxes, illustrated here:

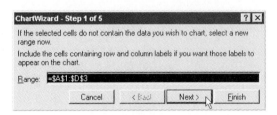

7. This box shows you the range of the data to be charted and gives you a chance to alter the selected range.

8. Normally, you'll click the Next > button at this point, taking you to Step 2 of 5.

Picking the Right Chart Type

Chart Wizard can create many *chart types* and many *formats* for each of those types. The Step 2 window, shown here, illustrates all the chart types and proposes one (Column, in the example).

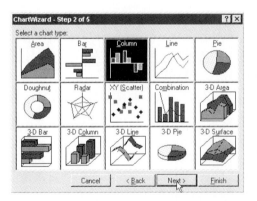

It's usually obvious from the chart samples which ones are best for various projects. You can also just experiment, or read online Help for each chart type. Use Help's Search feature to find information by chart type name (Radar, for instance).

When you've decided on a chart type, click its sample to highlight it, and then click the Next > button to continue. Don't worry if you pick the wrong type; you can easily change it later.

Once you've chosen a chart type, Chart Wizard presents a Step 3 dialog box showing various *formatting* options, which are different for each chart type. Here are the formatting options for column charts.

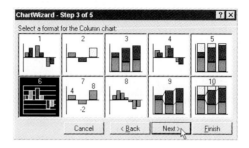

Don't lose any sleep over these choices, either. Formats can be tried on later like hats or mittens. Start with the choice the Wizard suggests, and experiment after you've seen those results. Click the Next > button to continue.

In Step 4, you'll see the beginnings of your chart design in a *Sample Chart* box. If you like what you see, forge ahead. Don't worry about the actual shape of the chart at this point, and don't be alarmed if your labels are temporarily truncated (shortened) or replaced with words like "Series 1" and "Series 2."

---

t i p   *Watch the preview as you work. Think about the general presentation of the data at this point. Does the chart help you understand the data? Do you have the appropriate data on the right axis? Do you like the chart type? If not, you can use the < Back button to return to the earlier steps and pick a different chart type or format. Sometimes the option buttons in Step 4 can improve your chart. Experiment.*

As you'll soon see, the settings proposed by the Chart Wizard are just fine for this sample project.

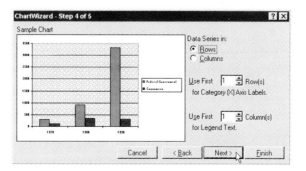

You're almost finished. Click Next > again. Step 5 gives you a chance to add chart titles for the chart itself, and for each axis. You will see the titles

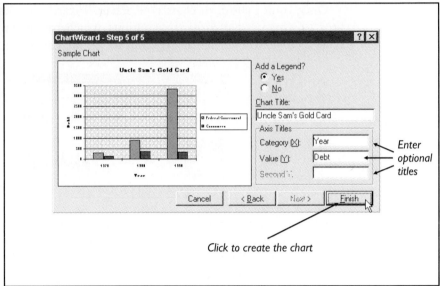

Enter
optional
titles

Click to create the chart

appear in the Sample Chart area as you type. The "Add a Legend?" option turns legends on and off. Figure 18-3 shows the Step 5 dialog box and the resulting chart.

If you get cold feet before you click Finish, you can still go back to choose other options. When you click Finish, Excel will create a chart worksheet quicker than you can say "1040EZ."

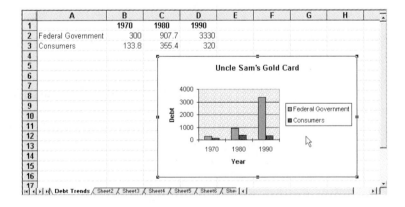

Creating Charts on Separate Worksheets

Excel charts can either be an integral part of your current worksheet, or they can be separate *chart worksheets* in the workbook that are *linked* to selected worksheet data. Chart Wizard usually creates chart objects on your current worksheet. The whole process is simple, clean, and automatic. But if you like, you can place charts on their own worksheets within a workbook.

Separate Chart Worksheets

To create a new chart on a separate worksheet:

1. Select the data to be charted.

2. Choose New (Chart) option from the Insert | Chart | As New Sheet command.

3. You'll see the Chart Wizard. Use it as previously described.

4. The Wizard will create a new sheet with a tab containing the word "Chart" and a sequential number.

5. Each new chart you create this way gets its own worksheet in the current workbook, and thus its own tab. Rename tabs just as you do any others—double-click on the tab.

Resizing and Moving Charts

You may need to change the size or shape of a finished chart, which is easily done by dragging the little handles that surround a selected chart like the one shown in Figure 18-4.

Besides making room for previously cramped labels, resizing charts changes their size and shape, and thus the appearance of the chart markers and other chart elements. Resizing is particularly useful if your data labels are invisible or all scrunched up. As you can see in Figure 18-4, though, resizing a perfectly nice chart can make it unreadable!

Adding Chart Notes and Arrows

Often it's nice to be able to draw attention to, or explain, certain items on your chart. The boxed note shown next is an example of this.

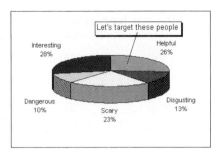

To create boxed text:

1. Click on the Text Box button, shown at the left. You'll find it in Excel's Drawing toolbar.

2. Drag to create the outline of a text box in the approximate desired size and shape.

3. Type and edit your note using text-editing techniques that should be familiar to you by now.

Restyling and Resizing Text Boxes

To resize the box or move it, point and click on any edge. The outline will thicken and you'll see eight size handles. Drag and resize this outline as you do any similar Windows object.

To embellish text, select it and use the Standard toolbar or text-related menu commands. For instance, you might select text and then use the Bold Toolbar button to make it bold.

FIGURE 18-4

Resizing charts

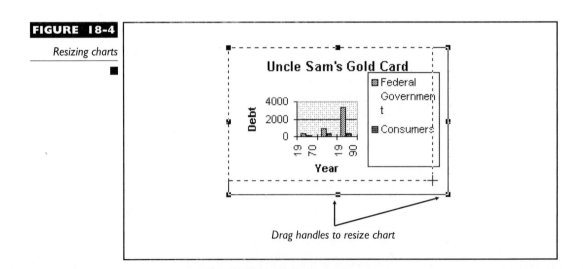

Drag handles to resize chart

To change the outline or fill pattern used for the box, or to add a drop-shadow effect like the one shown earlier, double-click on the edge of the text box. You'll see the Format Object dialog box shown here:

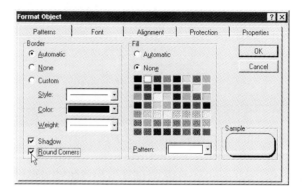

tip *If you really want a drop shadow, an easy way to make one is to select the text box and click the Drop Shadow button on the Drawing toolbar.*

Choose the desired tab and options within the tab. For instance, the example shows the rounded corner and shadow options being added via the Patterns tab.

Drawing and Formatting Arrows

To draw an arrow:

1. Click the Standard toolbar's Drawing button (shown left) to display the Chart toolbar.

2. Click the Drawing Toolbar's Arrow button, illustrated at left.

3. When your pointer turns into cross hairs, point where you want the arrow to start, and drag to the ending point.

4. When you release the mouse button, an arrow will appear. You can drag either end of selected arrows to reposition them and/or change the length of the line.

Double-click exactly on an arrow to bring up the Format Object dialog box, which lets you define arrow styles, line thicknesses, colors, and much more.

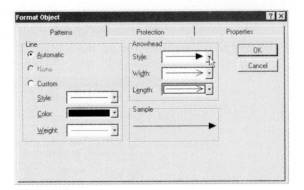

This changes only the arrow that you've double-clicked upon. To reformat other arrows immediately afterward, select them (by SHIFT+clicking, perhaps), and use the Repeat Format Object command on Excel's Edit menu.

Editing Charts

You could either get a life or spend the rest of your life exploring Excel's chart options. These are nearly endless. It's possible to change chart types and formats, embellish text, choose patterns or colors, add gridlines, insert notes with arrows, and much more. Here's the quick tour of Excel chartology.

Changing Chart Types and Formats

Once you've created a chart, you can quickly change its type by clicking on the chart type list on the Chart toolbar. This provides a palette of chart choices that can be "torn-off" if you like and moved to a convenient spot on your screen for repeated use.

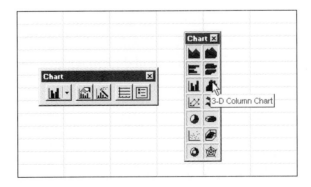

tip *The right mouse button reveals a number of chart-related choices if you point and click on a chart. This is often the quickest way to edit charts.*

Changing Data Series Ranges

There are several ways to change the data series ranges. One is to select a chart, then click on the Chart Wizard button. You'll see Step 1 of a two-step procedure, which will let you specify a new data range by typing it or dragging with your mouse. The second step lets you change the appearance of the chart.

Selecting and Editing Chart Components

You can edit specific parts of a chart, like text, gridlines, the shading used for markers, and so on, by either single- or double-clicking on them. For instance, to change the appearance of a chart title, you would double-click on it to bring up the Format Object dialog box.

To edit the content of the title object, click once to select the object, and then select the text by dragging or waiting a moment before clicking or double-clicking on the text.

To select a *data series,* click on any marker in the series. For instance, to select the government spending series in your sample chart, you could click on any of the government columns in any year. You would then see a description of the data series in your Formula bar, where you can edit the series definition if you choose.

To select a *single data marker* (like the 1990 Federal borrowing column marker in your sample chart), hold down CTRL while pointing.

To select a *gridline,* click exactly on a gridline. Clicking on any axis selects it. To select just the *plot area* (the columns without their category names, for instance), click in any part of the plot area not occupied by other things like gridlines or markers. To select the *entire chart,* click anywhere outside of the plot area, but not on other items like titles or legends.

General Formatting Techniques

Frequently, you can double-click on chart elements to quickly bring up relevant formatting options. If you double-click on a data marker, for instance, you'll soon see a Patterns dialog box that will let you select a new color or pattern for the marker. Double-clicking on a legend takes you to a dialog box where you can rearrange the appearance of the legends, and so on.

The other general editing technique is to select something, and then use the appropriate menu commands and toolbar buttons.

Rotating 3-D Charts

As you experiment with 3-D graphs, you will find that in some instances tall parts of a chart will obscure inner details. Other times you'll just want to tilt or rotate a 3-D object to get a more dramatic effect. In either case, select a 3-D chart, and then choose 3-D View from the Format menu. You'll see a dialog box like the one in Figure 18-5. Use the Elevation buttons to tilt the chart and the rotation buttons to rotate it. Use the Apply button to preview your changes without closing the dialog box. Clicking OK applies the latest changes and closes the box.

FIGURE 18-5

Try a 3-D chart to reveal inner details or to achieve a special effect

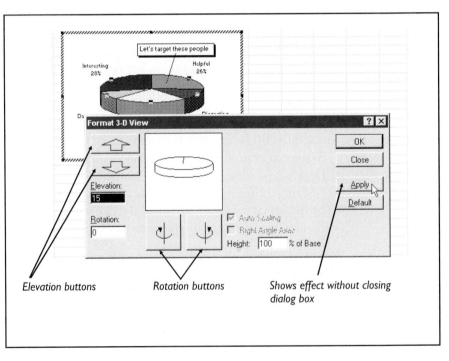

Elevation buttons   Rotation buttons   Shows effect without closing
                                                 dialog box

Changing Worksheet Values by Dragging Chart Parts

Here's a neat way to "what-if," or to make your data fit a desired scenario:

1. Create a worksheet and a chart—your Debt worksheet, for instance.

2. Click once on the data marker you wish to resize, the 1990 Federal Government bar in this example, and then wait a second or two so as not to make Excel think step 3 is a double-click.

3. Click once again (after that brief pause just mentioned).

4. Just the data marker you clicked upon will be selected. And it will have some small, black selection markers.

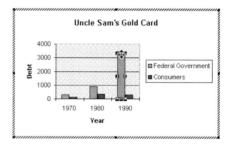

5. When you *drag* on the top center black marker, you will be able to move that selected part of the chart *and* automatically change the numbers in the corresponding worksheet cell(s)!

Hear the voice of corporate America now... "Jones, make the report say we did 26 percent of our sales in February, truth be damned."

Printing Charts

Unless you tell Excel to do otherwise, it prints all charts. To display but not print an embedded chart, select the chart, then remove the check mark from the Print Object option on the Properties tab of the Format Object dialog box. Reach this box by choosing Format | Object.

If a chart is a separate worksheet, print it like any other Excel worksheet. Remember to update it before printing if that's what you want. Use the Page Setup and Print Preview features to format these documents, add headers or footers, and so on.

Deleting Charts

To delete charts, simply select them and press DEL, or use the Clear command on Excel's Edit menu. Undo works here if you act promptly.

Delete separate *chart worksheets* as you would any other unwanted Windows worksheet. (Use Excel's Delete Worksheet command on the File menu.)

Setting the Default Chart Type

Chart Wizard and the New Chart (F11) command normally create new charts by using the Column chart type and format 1. This is the default *preferred chart style*. You can define a different preferred style this way:

1. Select a chart from the current worksheet that you would like to use as the default.

2. Select Options from the Tools menu.

3. Click the Chart tab.

4. Click on the Use The Current Chart button in the Default Chart area.

5. Give the chart a custom format name in the resulting dialog box.

Controlling Which Series Is on Which Axis

Excel considers the numbers of rows and columns you've selected when determining how to plot your data. While space prohibits showing each chart type and examples of the results with different row/column combinations, it's easy to watch the sample as you work with the Chart Wizard, and change the outcome. For example, look at the following illustration:

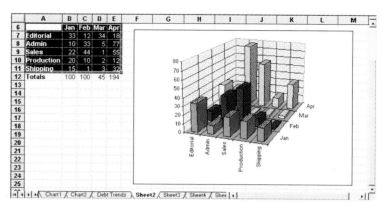

As you can see, Excel has plotted the months on the X axis and the departments on the Y axis because of the number of rows and columns selected. To overrule this choice, simply change the Data Series In choice from Columns to Rows in Step 2 of the Chart Wizard. You can either do this while you are creating the chart, or later select the chart, click on the Chart Wizard button, and choose the Next > button to visit Step 2. Here is the same data plotted with the Data Series set to Rows.

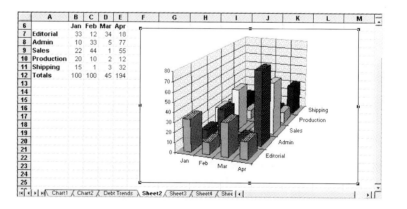

Adding Overlay Charts

Sometimes you'll want to overlay one kind of chart data on another. For instance, you might want to add a projected income line to a bar chart as shown next.

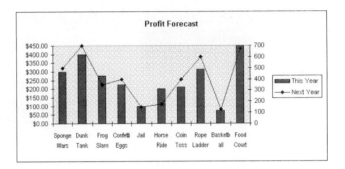

The easy way to do this is to choose the Combination chart type. It creates two *layers* on the chart, displaying half of the layers as bars and the other half as lines. If there is an uneven number of series, the extra series is plotted as bars.

Creating Trendlines

Trendlines are used to plot the direction of data in a series. It's easy to add trendlines to Excel bar, column, area, and scatter charts. To create trendlines on charts, follow these general steps (a simple exercise will demonstrate the technique):

1. Double-click on a chart object if necessary to select it.

2. Select the data series for the trendline by double-clicking on one of its markers.

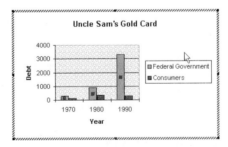

3. Choose Insert | Trendline to display the Trendline dialog box.

4. In the Trendline dialog box, pick a Trend/Regression type, as shown next.

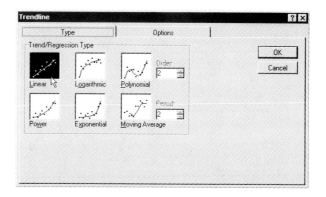

5. If necessary, click the Options tab of the Trendline dialog box and change options. For example, this extends the trendline for two periods to create a forecast:

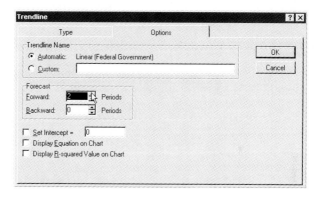

6. Click the OK button and admire your work.

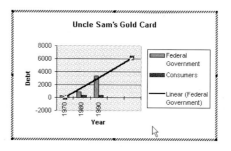

Here is a projection for the federal deficit. Not very pretty, is it?

Data Map

Here's one guaranteed to knock their socks off in the board meetings. Excel has a terrific new feature called Data Map, which allows you to insert actual maps into your spreadsheets in lieu of the informative, but not quite as snazzy, charts and graphs. Figure 18-6 shows the Data Map window.

You can add titles, adjust shading, even draw demographics data from files on disk. Follow along here to learn how to make a data map.

Using Data Map

To map data, follow these steps:

1. Select the data you wish to make into a map, and click on the Data Map button in the Standard toolbar.

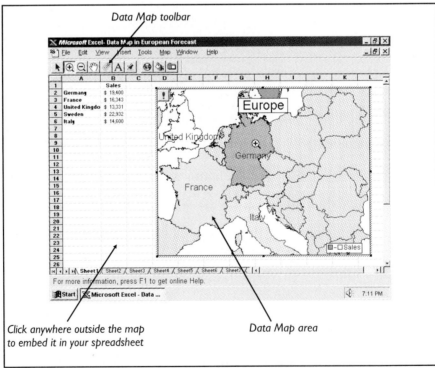

FIGURE 18-6

The Data Map

window

Data Map toolbar

Click anywhere outside the map
to embed it in your spreadsheet

Data Map area

2. Show Excel where you want your map to go by clicking and dragging.

3. After humming and whirring for a bit, Excel will open a new window and attempt to create the map, given the locations you have specified in your data.

4. Often Excel will have more than one map to choose from. You might be asked to choose a map. Notice there is a different toolbar in the Data Map window. If you use a country name that Excel doesn't know, you'll have the option to tell it the correct one.

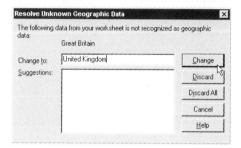

5. Excel will then place your map where you have specified and bring up the Data Map Control dialog box, where you can change shading along with many other options.

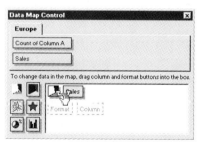

6. You now can accept the map as-is or do a bit of editing, as explained in the next section. When you are satisfied with the map, click anywhere outside of it to embed it in your document.

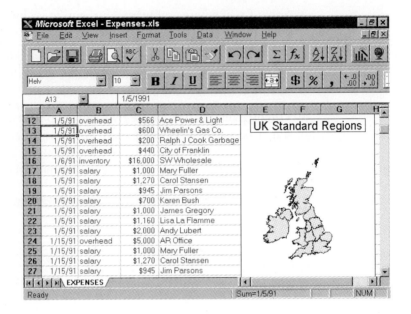

Editing Maps

To edit a map, use any of the following techniques.

■ Choose Insert | Data to bring up the Data Map dialog box. Here you can specify what data should be included in the data map.

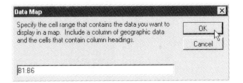

■ You might want to have a closer view of your map, in which case, you can click on the Zoom button in the toolbar and click in the map.

■ You can refresh the map at any time by clicking the Refresh button in the toolbar.

■ To change the shading or format of a column's data, drag the column into the format box of the Data Map Control dialog box, and click on the appropriate button.

■ To edit an existing map, just double-click the map to get back to the map window.

Using Demographics Info

You can link your maps to demographics data that comes with Excel in the file called Mapstats.xls, found in the Datamap folder. You can then use this information along with your own sales results to monitor trends and predict demand. See the big books for more details.

Tell Me More

These are the basics of Excel charting, and, as you can see, skills you learned in Windows and practiced in Word are often called for and applied in Excel. Many times, just reading the menu, dialog boxes, or the status area will show you how to do new and useful things.

But there may be other charting details that are not so obvious. For instance, you can link a chart's text with worksheet cells so that chart notes or labels change when worksheet cells change. You can sometimes plot nonadjacent data. There is more to know about forcing axis values than you've read here. If you don't find the answer to questions like these in Excel's online Help, check out the hundred-plus pages on charts in your Excel manual.

WORKING WITH EXCEL

CHAPTER 19

Working with Graphics in Excel

Y

O U can apply many of your Windows graphics skills to Excel worksheet projects. Worksheets can include imported graphic images, items you draw yourself, arrows, text boxes, and so on. You can use graphics to dress up the appearance of a document or as an integral part of a presentation. Figure 19-1 is an example of a worksheet drawn from many sources: The computer is from the ClipArt folder, the price tag was drawn using the Drawing toolbar, prices of the individual options are entered into worksheet

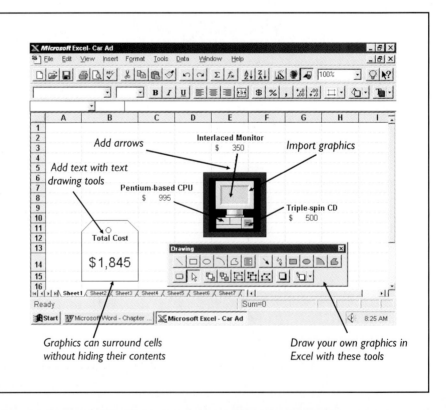

FIGURE 19-1

Excel worksheets can include imported graphics or graphics you create using Excel's drawing tools

Add arrows

Interlaced Monitor
$ 350

Import graphics

Add text with text drawing tools

Pentium-based CPU
$ 995

Triple-spin CD
$ 500

Total Cost

$1,845

Drawing

Graphics can surround cells without hiding their contents

Draw your own graphics in Excel with these tools

cells, and the Total Cost figure of $1,845 in the price tag is a worksheet cell containing a formula that adds up all the items.

Creating and Placing Graphic Objects

You can place graphics anywhere on a worksheet. Select graphics to move, resize, and restyle them. Copies of graphics can be pasted from your Clipboard into a worksheet or *linked* with the original objects so that changes in the original are reflected on the worksheet.

Importing Graphics

As a general rule, if you can get a graphic onto your Clipboard, you can paste it into an Excel worksheet. Sometimes it pays to visit Excel's Paste Special command rather than using the basic Paste command or the CTRL-V keyboard shortcut when inserting graphics into Excel worksheets. For instance, if the source program supports object linking and embedding (OLE), you might want to Paste Link rather than Paste.

Any of Microsoft's object-creating tools (WordArt, the ClipArt Gallery, and so on) can provide graphic fodder. Simply use the Insert Object command to bring up the available list of object creators, shown here:

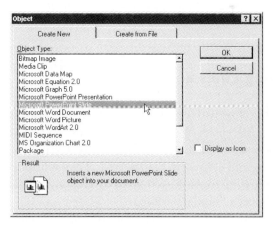

Then go for it.

Exporting Excel Graphics

You can also paste parts of your Excel worksheet into other types of documents. For instance, you can copy an Excel drawing or chart to your

WORKING WITH EXCEL

Clipboard, then switch to another program and paste (or Paste Link) the Clipboard contents either as a picture or often in other formats. The type of pasting that you do and the program you paste into determine how the pasted items will both appear and behave in the destination document.

Resizing Graphics

Chances are, you already know how to resize Excel graphics:

1. Select a graphic by pointing with your mouse.
2. When the handles appear, drag on a handle to resize the graphic.
3. To change both dimensions at once, drag the corner handles.

Positioning Graphics on Worksheets

To move an object, select it and drag with your mouse. To move more than one object, SHIFT-click on each of them. Drag them all at once with your mouse and release. To align a graphic object's border with the worksheet cell grid, hold down ALT and drag one of the object's corner handles. You can also select graphics, copy or cut them to the Clipboard, and paste them elsewhere.

Drawing Lines and Shapes

 Excel provides a number of drawing tools that will remind you of the ones in Microsoft Word's Draw feature, as well as the Windows drawing packages described earlier in this book. Excel's tools were used to create the price tag and arrows in Figure 19-1. They work like most similar Windows-savvy drawing tools. Reach them by clicking the Drawing button, shown here, on Excel's Standard toolbar.

Since you've probably used similar drawing tools by now, let's not waste paper here covering familiar ground. If you forget what a tool does, point to the tool in question, and read its description in Excel's status area.

Incidentally, the polygon and oval tools were used to create the price tag in Figure 19-1.

Examples of Graphics in Excel

You can create invoices and other forms that include logos, as illustrated here:

The same basic technique could be used to place illustrations in order forms. And how about this? Excel makes a great teaching tool. Set up some spreadsheets that illustrate concepts and let students explore, as illustrated here:

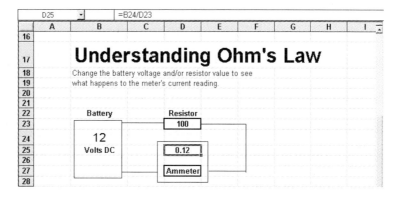

How about sprucing up those budgeting exercises by creating "Org chart-like" top sheets like the one here.

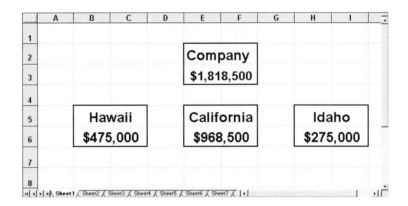

Link them to the detailed numbers using OLE.

Possible Sources of Excel Graphics

Here are just a few potential sources of Excel graphics and how to get them into your worksheet:

Graphic Source	How to Import
Bitmap graphics	The Windows Clipboard or OLE
WordPerfect Graphics files	Insert Picture command or OLE
Encapsulated PostScript files	Insert Picture command or OLE
Tagged Image File Format files	Insert Picture command or OLE
Macintosh PICT graphics	Insert Picture command or OLE
Computer Graphics Metafiles	The Windows Clipboard or OLE
PC Paintbrush files	Insert Picture command or OLE
CorelDRAW 3.0 files	Insert Picture command or OLE
HP Graphics Language files	Insert Picture command or OLE
Lotus 1-2-3 Graphics	Insert Object command or OLE
MS ClipArt Gallery items	Insert Object command or OLE
MS Graph graphs	Insert Object command or OLE
MS Org Charts	Insert Object command or OLE
MS Word Pictures	Insert Object command or OLE
MS WordArt	Insert Object command or OLE
Micrografx Designer/Draw files	Insert Object command or OLE
MS PowerPoint objects	Insert Object command or OLE

Excel Slide Shows

Excel no longer has the Slide Show utility. Since you are probably a Microsoft Office owner, though, check out Part Four: Presenting with PowerPoint. PowerPoint is a powerful presentations package that should be adequate for your presentation needs. You can use OLE to include Excel information in your PowerPoint presentations.

WORKING IN MICROSOFT OFFICE

CHAPTER 20

Introduction to
Excel's Command Macros

J

UST as Microsoft Word lets you create macros to automate repetitive tasks, Microsoft Excel will record and play back *command macros*. When you record a series of steps, Excel watches you work and converts your actions into *Visual Basic*—a computer programming language that describes what you've done. You can then save this information as a named macro and run it whenever you wish.

For instance, if you find yourself continually creating 12 centered and bold column headings (**Jan, Feb,** and so on), you can record your typing, AutoFilling, and formatting tasks *once,* and then use the resulting macro in the future. Or you can use a macro to update past-due amounts in invoice worksheets.

There are several ways to run macros. You can assign keyboard shortcuts to macros. You can even create *macro buttons* or place macros on menus, as you will see in this chapter.

Advanced users can write and modify macros by working directly with the hundreds of macro functions (called *programming commands*) described in the *Microsoft Excel Visual Basic User's Guide* that comes with your Excel program. For now, let's stick with macros that don't require any programming skills, because you can accomplish quite a lot without knowing anything about ABSREFs or ZTESTMs or HENWAYs. (Don't ask.)

Recording Your Own Macros

Follow these steps to create your own macros.

1. Start by practicing what you intend to do a few times so you know what steps to take and are assured that they will work.

2. When you have finished rehearsing, choose Tools | Record Macro | Record New Macro. You'll see The Record New Macro dialog

box; click the Options button to see the "big" version of the dialog box.

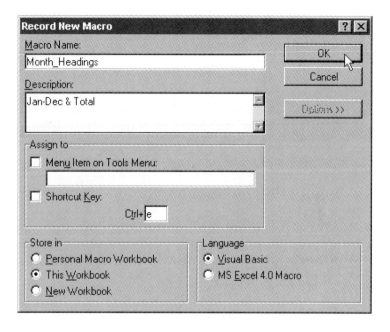

3. Excel will suggest a macro name that you will probably not like. Type a new name if you wish. Macro names must start with a letter, cannot contain spaces, and should not look like a reference (no A$1 names, for instance). In place of spaces, use an underline character (**Month_Headings**, for instance).

4. Add a note in the Description box if you like. It will help you remember what the macro does.

5. Decide where to save your macro—in the current workbook (the default), a new workbook, or a personal collection of macros. (Stick with the current workbook at first.)

6. Excel proposes a keyboard shortcut that you can use in combination with CTRL, and sometimes SHIFT, to execute macros. In the preceding illustration, it is proposing CTRL+E. Excel differentiates between upper- and lowercase keyboard shortcuts, so you can use both a CTRL+E and a CTRL+SHIFT+E combination. Excel will not propose key combinations that are already used by Excel itself or by the open macro sheet.

7. You can also add the macro to your Tools menu by checking the Menu Item On Tools Menu choice and typing a menu item name in the menu item box.

8. Once you have named the macro, chosen a key combination for it, and told Excel where to store the macro, click OK to begin recording.

9. Live it up! Click, drag, format, enter text or values, construct formulas, use functions, and so on. When you have finished, click the Stop Recorder button, shown here.

Running Macros

Once you've recorded a macro, use either the keyboard shortcut, the Tools menu choice if you've added one, or the Macro command on Excel's Tools menu. If you use the keyboard shortcut, it will run immediately. The Macro command provides a list of macros.

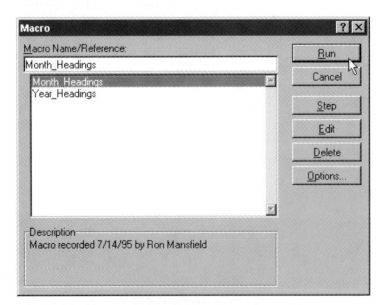

Pick the one you want—either double-click on it, or click once to select and once on Run.

Any way you start your macro, Excel will repeat your recorded steps, sometimes with surprising results. Remember that you may need to prepare your worksheet before running a macro. If a macro expects cell A1 to be the active cell, you may not like the results if Q7 is the active cell. And when you want your macro to sort a table of cells, there had better be the right data in them.

warning   *There is no short list of macro "gottas," as you will learn the hard way. And, as you will also discover, Undo may not always completely rectify the results of a macro's rampage. You should save your work before running powerful macros.*

When you want to give some input into what Excel does when you start a macro, you can use Visual Basic to create dialog boxes, test for specific conditions, and much more. You can even create your own online Help for macros.

Assigning Macros to Buttons

If you have a favorite macro or you want to make a complex task easy for other users, consider creating macro buttons. The process is surprisingly simple.

1. Start by displaying the Drawing toolbar. (Use Excel's Toolbars command on the View menu or the Drawing button on the Standard toolbar.)

2. Click the Create Button button.

3. When you click on the button tool, your pointer turns into cross hairs. Drag to create a button large enough to contain a descriptive label.

4. When you release the mouse button, you'll see a rectangle like the one shown here. The box will contain the word "Button".

5. Excel will then present a list of macros. Pick the one you want to assign to the button (double-click on the macro's name in the scrolling list).

6. Click on the button name and change it to something meaningful.

> Past Due

Click on the button to run your macro. To move, resize, or otherwise change a button *without* running the macro, hold down CTRL when you point to the button. The button will take on a by-now-familiar outline that will remind you of a graphic (it will be outlined with size handles). You can reposition a selected button by dragging with the pointer shaped like an arrowhead. You can edit the button's size, shape, or name by holding down CTRL while you click on the button. (This selects the button without activating it.) Use Excel's formatting commands and tools to change the button's font, type size, style, and other text attributes. Drag the button as you would any other graphic object to change its size and shape. (See how this all starts to tie together?)

To delete a button (to free up some screen space, perhaps), select it (CTRL-click), and then use DEL or the Edit menu's Clear command. Deleting a button does *not* delete the macro that it is assigned to. To delete the macro, open the Macro dialog box (reached with Tools | Macro), select the macro to be deleted, and click the Delete button.

To Learn More About Macros

You now know enough about macros to be dangerous. Through online Help and trial and error, you will learn a lot more. Also check out the *Excel Users Guide 2* and *Excel Function Reference* that are packaged with your Excel program, or try *Excel Made Easy* (Martin S. Matthews, Osborne).

If you are just curious about what the instructions look like for a macro, check out Figure 20-1.

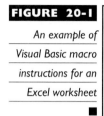

FIGURE 20-1

An example of

Visual Basic macro

instructions for an

Excel worksheet

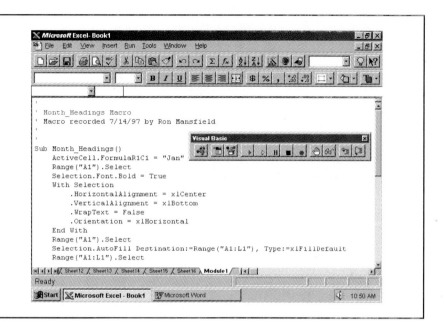

Alternatively, you can use the Macro dialog box to select a macro, and then click the Edit button to see the Visual Basic programming instructions created by the recorder.

CHAPTER 21

Using Worksheets as Databases

W

HEN you get a new hammer, the saying goes, everything looks like a nail. Perhaps that's why many users (to say nothing of spreadsheet manufacturers) turn to spreadsheet packages when they really need a database-management program. It is true that Excel has a number of database *features*. It is also true that you can use these features to manage a Print Merge mailing list, to control your inventory, or to do a statistical analysis of complex opinion surveys. But *should* you?

Most spreadsheet programs, including Excel, have limits that can frustrate database users. For instance, you can only have 16,384 *records* in a single Excel worksheet. If you keep 16,385 people in your mailing list, you'll have a problem (though not an insurmountable one).

In any one field you can have a maximum of 245 *characters*. So, if you want to collect quotations from famous people in an Excel database, they had better not be quotes from long-winded speakers. (This paragraph contains more than *245* characters, for example, so it would not fit in an Excel database field.)

Excel limits you to three *sort levels* at any one time; so if you want to sort a list of employees by division, department, last name, and then first name, you will need to take extra (and sometimes confusing) steps.

The biggest concern about using spreadsheets as databases has to do with how easily the *integrity* of your data can be corrupted. For instance, in a worksheet, it is *far too easy* to sort a list of employees and their salaries only to find that you've given each worker someone else's earnings! You'll see an example of this later in the chapter. It's also pretty easy to think you've added records to an Excel database when you haven't.

Nonetheless, there *are* times when Excel's database features can be lifesavers: you can use them to extract interesting reports from budgets and other "legitimate" spreadsheet data. The moral of this sermon is this: before you spend hours entering a mailing list into a worksheet, consider whether you wouldn't be better off with a real database program, like Microsoft

Access. But if you have a large budget or other worksheet, Excel's database features can sometimes help you find and manage that information.

Database Concepts and Terms

You'll need to know several database terms to make sense of this chapter. Even if you've used "real" database programs before, it's worth browsing the next few topics, since Excel adds a few new wrinkles to "databasics." For instance, the Excel documentation often refers to databases as *lists*. Here are some other terms worth knowing.

Database Range

Even though your database might be a small part of a larger worksheet, Excel will often automatically define likely database ranges, like cells A2 through E8 in Figure 21-1.

Records and Fields

Excel treats the contents of each *row* of a database range as a *record*. In Figure 21-1, row 4 is Ringo's record, row 5 is Paul's record, and so on. The

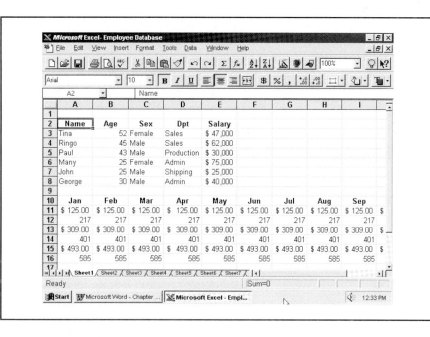

FIGURE 21-1

Excel can often find and define database ranges, like cells A2 through E8 in this example

first row of any database range (row 2 in Figure 21-1) must always contain *column labels,* which Excel will use as *database field names.* These field names can contain spaces. The field name Annual Salary would be permitted, for instance.

Microsoft calls each *column* in a database a *field,* and *individual cells* in a database are also referred to as *fields.* You can enter text, numbers, dates, functions, and formulas in cells. When a field contains a function or formula, it is referred to as a *computed field.* For instance, if you had a **Quantity Ordered** field and a **Unit Price** field, you could create a **Total Cost** field containing a formula that computes total cost based on the other two fields.

Creating an Excel Database

When creating a database, set up a separate field (column) for any item you'll want to refer to separately. For instance, if you want to sort on first and last names separately, create a field for each. This is particularly important to remember if you plan to sort on, or search for, things like ZIP codes.

Set column widths right at the start, or change widths after you've entered the data by dragging or by using Column Width features (Best Fit, for instance).

Entering Data

You can enter, edit, and format the data in a database just as you would any other Excel cell contents, or you can use Excel's Data Form feature, which is described later in this chapter. Regardless of which method you use, there are some cautions worth mentioning.

- Excel does *not* let you specify "field types," so it's possible to enter a number or text or a date into any field. This can cause problems when entering numbers that you plan to display and sort as text. For instance, Excel strips off leading zeros in numeric entries. But some ZIP codes start with zero. If you want to see those "leading" zeros in ZIP codes, you'll need to enter each ZIP code as *text,* not as a number. To do this, you must type an apostrophe before each ZIP code—or any number you intend to enter as text. If you want ZIP codes to sort the way you normally expect to see them, you'll *always* need to enter *each* ZIP code this way.

■ Unlike fancier database products, Excel will *not* challenge you if you mix text, numeric, and date entries. Usually, you can see if there is a problem by looking at the appearance of the entries. For instance, unless you format them otherwise, text entries in cells will be left justified, and general numeric entries will be right justified.

Adding Records to a Database

Normally, you'll add new records beneath the last record in your database. You can either do this the way you add regular worksheet data (by activating cells in the next empty row and typing), or you can use a database *form* that "prompts" you for data entries and automatically places new records beneath your last record.

It is also possible to make space for records in the middle of your data range (insert empty rows), then make *mid-database* entries. There are advantages and disadvantages to each of these approaches. To weigh their pros and cons, you must understand what Excel does when new data won't fit in the data range you've defined. Read on.

Excel will automatically accommodate the addition of new records if it can—which brings us to the second problem:

If you plan to have anything in rows directly *beneath* the database cells, you will be inconvenienced when you have more data than will fit in the previously defined data range. Suppose, for instance, that in Figure 21-1 you've placed a worksheet equation in cell B11. If you used the data form to enter a new record, you'd get the message "Cannot extend database," since the data form feature will not write over or push down cell contents. (If the equation was in cell F10, however, you *could* continue appending records, since the equation would not be directly beneath the data range.)

In cases where there is insufficient room to easily extend the database, either you can opt to manually *insert* additional records mid-database, pushing everything else down, or you can insert blank lines at the end of the database range to *extend* it. Check your worksheet for formulas that no longer work as a result of your pushing things down this way.

You can also add fields to an existing database. For example, if you wanted to add a Last Name field in column F, you could simply type the field name in cell F2, then enter last names in cells F3 through F8. If you decided to insert a Last Name field between Name and Age (by selecting column B and using the Edit menu's Insert command), Excel would extend the database range for you.

Working with Data Forms

Data forms are handy for data entry, record viewing, and searching. A data form is automatically created whenever you choose the Form command on the Data menu. You can see the form by choosing Data | Form. As you can see from Figure 21-2, data forms are dialog boxes containing field names, text entry boxes, and buttons.

Unfortunately, it is possible to design databases with so many fields that they won't all be visible on your form. You *cannot* scroll to overcome this. And, if you place multiple-line entries in fields by using the old CTRL+ENTER trick, you'll only see the first line of those entries in your form.

The width of the text areas in a data form (and the width of the dialog box itself) is based on the widest field (column) in your database. Thus, if you have an 80-character field in your database, you'll see a pretty big data form.

Use the scroll arrows to view different records. Enter and edit text in the data form's text boxes as you'd expect. You can use TAB to move from text box to text box (and to the buttons) in your data form. SHIFT+TAB moves you backward.

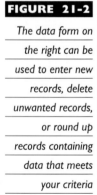

FIGURE 21-2

The data form on the right can be used to enter new records, delete unwanted records, or round up records containing data that meets your criteria

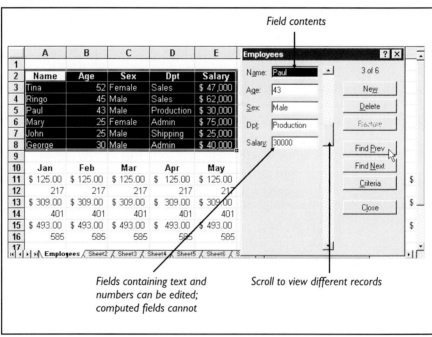

Fields containing text and numbers can be edited; computed fields cannot

Scroll to view different records

Adding and Editing Records with the Data Form

To add a new record with the data form, click the New button, or scroll to the last record, which should be empty. Type as usual, making sure you put the right data in the right fields. Feel free to leave fields empty.

To edit records using the data form, scroll to (or otherwise locate) the record of interest and edit in the text boxes using standard Windows techniques (select and change). Computed fields *cannot* be edited. You cannot *format* text in a data form (the Bold and Italic toolbar buttons won't work here, for instance). Instead, format text in the worksheet itself.

Changes and additions made in the data form aren't reflected in the database until you move to a different record or close the data form.

warning   *Even when changes have been made in the database, they reside only in your computer's RAM until you save the worksheet. Save early and often to avoid datus interruptus.*

Deleting Records with the Data Form

To delete a record with the data form, bring the record into view and click the data form's Delete button. You will be asked to confirm the deletion. You cannot undo deletions performed from the data form. (If, instead, you delete directly in the database by using Excel's Edit menu, then act immediately, you can undo those deletes.) To delete multiple records, it's usually best to round them up with AutoFilter (described in a moment) and then to delete the records found.

Search Criteria

You can use the data form to create and then scroll through collections of records that meet specific criteria (for instance, all the women earning more than $50,000). Start by choosing the Criteria button in the data form. You'll see a dialog box like the one in Figure 21-3.

In this example, Excel will gather up just female employees who earn in excess of $50,000. Notice that dollar signs and commas are ignored, so you only need to enter **>50000** for the Salary criterion.

FIGURE 21-3

Specify search

criteria to see a

filtered list

of records

■

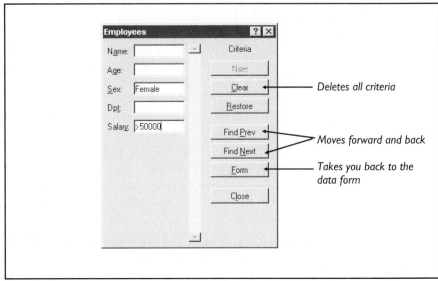

— Deletes all criteria

Moves forward and back

Takes you back to the
data form

warning   *If **none** of your records meet your criteria, frequently Excel will go ahead and display a record that does **not** meet the criteria.*

This data form search feature can locate character strings (text), and it can locate records that fall within ranges of numbers or dates.

The comparison operators are

=	Equal to
>	Greater than
<	Less than
>=	Greater than or equal to
<=	Less than or equal to
<>	Not equal to

When you use an equal sign with nothing after it as the single search criterion, only records with blank entries will appear.

These comparisons only work with numbers and dates, not with text. Thus, a search for ZIP codes entered as text, like >80000 or >"80000", won't work.

Using Wildcards

You can use asterisks (*) and question marks (?) as wildcards. But note that Excel adds an invisible asterisk to the end of any search criterion that uses wildcards. For instance, **Sm?th** finds *Smith* and *Smyth,* and also *smithereens.* The search criterion **Jo*** will find *John* and *Job* and *joke,* but then so will the string **jo.** The criterion ***mary** will find *Mary* and *Queen Mary,* while the criterion *** mary** (note the space) will find *Queen Mary,* but not *Mary* as the first name in a field.

To find an exact text match, that is, a match of the same length (for example, *John* but not *Johnny*), precede the search string with an equal sign: **=John.** By now you might suspect that search criteria searches are *not* case sensitive. You're right. The search criterion **=John** will also find *john.*

Use the Find Next and Find Previous buttons to review multiple found records.

Filtering—A Better Way to Find

Excel now offers a powerful database function that is a big improvement over the search criteria method just described. It comes in two flavors—Auto Filter and Advanced Filtering. Let's stick with AutoFilter here and leave Advanced Filtering to the bigger books.

When you choose Data | Filter | AutoFilter, Excel zips through your database looking for each unique entry in each column. For example, in the sample database it would find *four* unique departments in the Dpt column—Admin, Sales, Shipping, and Production. In the Sex column it would find *two* unique entries—Male and Female. It does this for each column and creates drop-down lists for each column, like the one shown here.

	Name	Age	Sex	Dpt	Salary
3	Tina	52	Female	(All)	$ 47,000
4	Ringo	45	Male	(Top 10...)	$ 62,000
5	Paul	43	Male	(Custom...)	$ 30,000
6	Mary	25	Female	Admin / Production	$ 75,000
7	John	25	Male	Sales	$ 25,000
8	George	30	Male	Shipping / (Blanks)	$ 40,000
9					

The lists contain all the unique values for the column plus the choices (All), (Top 10), (Custom), (Blanks), and (Non Blanks).

When you drop down one of these menus and make a choice, Excel will *filter* (hide) all records not containing the chosen value. For instance, if you choose Sales from the Dpt column, you will see only records that contain sales values in their Dpt field, as shown here. (The other records are not deleted; they are just temporarily hidden from view.)

1					
2	Name ▾	Age ▾	Sex ▾	Dpt ▾	Salary ▾
3	Tina	52	Female	Sales	$ 47,000
4	Ringo	45	Male	Sales	$ 62,000

tip   *You can tell when there are hidden records by looking at the row numbers. On some machines, they are blue (your color might be different) where records have been filtered. You can also tell what fields the records have been filtered on by looking at the drop-down arrows; the guilty party will be blue (or perhaps a different color).*

The choices (Blanks) and (Non Blanks) show records with either blank or nonblank entries, respectively. In other words, choosing (Non Blanks) will display (not filter out) any records that have something (anything) typed in the field.

The (All) choice filters nothing for that column. In other words, if you choose (All) in every column, you will see all of your records. A less robust version of (All) is (Top 10), which filters out all but the "top-ten" entries. For instance, you could filter out all but the top-ten highest salaries or ages.

You can combine filters. For instance, to find all of the males in the Production department, you could choose Male in Sex and Production in Dpt.

There is one advanced filtering capability worth noting here. It's the (Custom) choice in the drop-down menus. With it you can specify *ranges* of things you want to see. For instance, to see all of the employees that earn over $26,000, you could

1. Choose (Custom) from the Salary drop-down list to bring up the Custom AutoFilter dialog box.

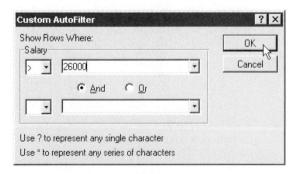

2. Specify Greater Than by picking the **>** operator from the drop-down list.

3. Enter the dollar amount (dollar signs and commas are optional).

4. Click OK. Excel will filter out (hide) records for employees earning less than $26,000.

There are many more custom filtering features. For example, you can specify ranges like "greater than 26,000 *and* less than 50,000." There are also text string specifiers. They work like those in the Criteria dialog box described earlier.

Showing All Records After AutoFiltering

There are two ways you can show all records after AutoFiltering. If you want to leave the drop-down lists in place for future use, you can display all your records by choosing Data | Filter | Show All.

Removing AutoFilter Lists

To remove the drop-down filter lists and redisplay all of your records, choose the AutoFilter choice from the Filter submenu a second time. This removes the check mark next to the menu choice, deletes the drop-down menus, and redisplays all records.

Sorting Excel Databases

It's time to turn to sorting. Here is a column typically chosen for sorting—the ages of your company's employees.

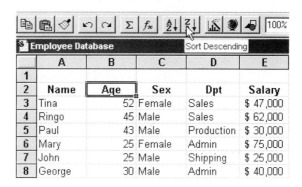

If you only have one database defined on your worksheet, sorting can be quite easy:

1. *Activate* any *one* cell in the field you want to use as the sort key (*Age*, in the example).

warning *If you **select a range of cells**, rather than **activating a single cell**, only those selected cells will be sorted. If you leave columns out when you select prior to sorting, they will not be rearranged. So, if you selected everything except column F in the sample database, most of your employees would end up with someone else's salary after the sort, and you could have a riot on your hands. This sort error is very easy to make if you have wide worksheets with fields that you can't see. Out of sight, out of mind, as they say.*

2. With either a single cell or everything you want to sort selected, click either the Sort Ascending or Sort Descending button on the Standard toolbar.

Excel will sort, leaving the labels at the top of the list where they belong.

In the preceding example, the data will be sorted in descending order, based on employees' ages, resulting in the oldest person being first in the database and the youngest at the end. You could just as easily sort the list by department, using cell D3 as the key.

Multilevel Sorts

Suppose you had a bigger database and wanted to sort it by department to see staffers listed alphabetically *within* their departments. You could do this in one pass by using the Sort dialog box (reached with the Sort command on the Data menu).

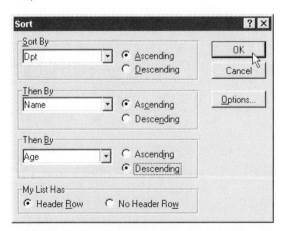

You would make *Dpt* the first sort key (Sort By) and *Name* the second sort key (Then By). Pick names from the drop-down lists or specify cell addresses.

In a still-more-complex database, if you have several people with the *same names* in the *same department*, you could use age or sex as the tie-breaker by specifying one of those criteria as the third sort key (Then By).

Incidentally, you can choose to sort by column instead of row, which is one way to rearrange the order in which fields appear in your database. If you rearrange a database this way, be sure to include the field names in the selection so that the names move with the data.

note   *Excel ignores capitalization when sorting text. Furthermore, numbers entered as numbers sort before numbers entered as text. (International versions of Excel may use slightly different sort orders.)*

Cross-Tabulating Databases

"How many women do we have in each department? How do salaries break down by sex around here?" If you ask, or are asked, questions like these, you may want to check out Excel's PivotTable Wizard. With a minimum of groaning, you should be able to create cross-tabulated tables like this one.

	A	B	C	D	E	F
1	Count of Dpt	Dpt				
2	Sex	Admin	Production	Sales	Shipping	Grand Total
3	Female	1	0	1	0	2
4	Male	1	1	1	1	4
5	Grand Total	2	1	2	1	6

Complex cross-tabulation can also be performed on budgets and other large documents.

The PivotTable Wizard is a big improvement over the Crosstab Wizard from earlier versions of Excel. It is quick, intuitive, and powerful. It seems more reliable than its predecessor, too. Just the same, save your work before using PivotTable Wizard.

1. After saving your work, click anywhere in your database.

2. Choose PivotTable from Excel's Data menu.

3. Specify a data source. (You can use your Excel database or external sources.)

4. Drag items in the PivotTable Wizard Step 3 of 4 dialog box to set up the report. By default the Wizard counts things; but if you double-click on an item, you can choose other actions such as sums (totals). Figure 21-4 shows a typical report and the settings that produced it.

FIGURE 21-4

Use the PivotTable Wizard to set up reports like these

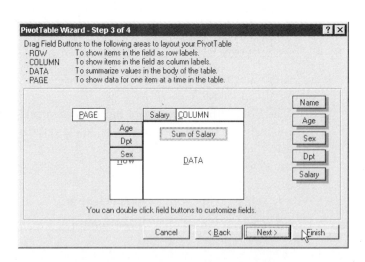

	A	B	C	D	E	F	G	H	I	J
1	Sum of Salary			Salary						
2	Age	Dpt	Sex	25000	30000	40000	47000	62000	75000	Grand Total
3	25	Admin	Female	0	0	0	0	0	75000	75000
4		Admin Total		0	0	0	0	0	75000	75000
5		Shipping	Male	25000	0	0	0	0	0	25000
6		Shipping Total		25000	0	0	0	0	0	25000
7	25 Total			25000	0	0	0	0	75000	100000
8	30	Admin	Male	0	0	40000	0	0	0	40000
9		Admin Total		0	0	40000	0	0	0	40000
10	30 Total			0	0	40000	0	0	0	40000
11	43	Production	Male	0	30000	0	0	0	0	30000
12		Production Total		0	30000	0	0	0	0	30000
13	43 Total			0	30000	0	0	0	0	30000
14	45	Sales	Male	0	0	0	0	62000	0	62000
15		Sales Total		0	0	0	0	62000	0	62000
16	45 Total			0	0	0	0	62000	0	62000
17	52	Sales	Female	0	0	0	47000	0	0	47000
18		Sales Total		0	0	0	47000	0	0	47000
19	52 Total			0	0	0	47000	0	0	47000
20	Grand Total			25000	30000	40000	47000	62000	75000	279000

PivotTable Wizard - Step 3 of 4

Drag Field Buttons to the following areas to layout your PivotTable
- ROW   To show items in the field as row labels.
- COLUMN   To show items in the field as column labels.
- DATA   To summarize values in the body of the table.
- PAGE   To show data for one item at a time in the table.

PAGE

Salary COLUMN

Age
Dpt
Sex
ROW

Sum of Salary

DATA

Name
Age
Sex
Dpt
Salary

You can double click field buttons to customize fields.

Cancel | < Back | Next > | Finish

Whenever you change data in your database, you'll need to *refresh* the data. The easiest way to do this is with the Refresh Data button on the Query and Pivot toolbar, which appears when you are working with PivotTable Wizard:

It is very easy to receive far more detail than you need; so get in the habit of visiting the Options dialog boxes, where you can customize your reports to show desired cross-tabs only, ranges instead of each specific value, and so on.

Adding Subtotals to Databases

While many Wizards automatically create subtotals for you, Excel's Subtotal command on the Data menu lets you add your own subtotals to any sorted list of data. Subtotals will be created each time the data in a specified row differs from that in the row above. For example, you could sort your sample employee database by department and get salary subtotals by department. Here are the general steps for creating subtotals:

1. Sort the data in an order that will produce the subtotals you desire; this example sorted on Dpt.

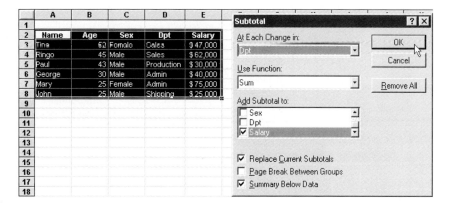

2. Choose the column to be monitored for changes (Dpt in this example).

WORKING WITH EXCEL

3. Choose the function to be used (typically SUM for numeric subtotals or COUNT for counting things).

4. Choose the columns you want to subtotal (Salary in this example).

5. Choose the other appearance options you desire. The defaults are shown in this example.

6. Click OK.

7. Reformat the columns if the subtotals exceed the old column widths (a common occurrence).

8. You should see subtotals that look something like these.

1 2 3		A	B	C	D	E
	1					
	2	Name	Age	Sex	Dpt	Salary
	3	Tina	52	Female	Sales	$ 47,000
	4	Ringo	45	Male	Sales	$ 62,000
	5				Sales Total	$109,000
	6	Paul	43	Male	Production	$ 30,000
	7				Production Total	$ 30,000
	8	George	30	Male	Admin	$ 40,000
	9	Mary	25	Female	Admin	$ 75,000
	10				Admin Total	$115,000
	11	John		25	Male	Shipping	$ 25,000
	12				Shipping Total	$ 25,000
	13				Grand Total	$279,000

9. You can show or hide detail with the new outline controls that appear on the left of the worksheet. For example, here, only totals and subtotals are displayed.

1 2 3		A	B	C	D	E
	1					
	2	Name	Age	Sex	Dpt	Salary
	5				Sales Total	$ 109,000
	7				Production Total	$ 30,000
	10				Admin Total	$ 115,000
	12				Shipping Total	$ 25,000
	13				Grand Total	$ 279,000
	14					

Removing Subtotals

To remove all subtotals, select the data of interest, and use the Subtotals command on the Data menu. (You can select just part of a worksheet if you only want to remove some of the subtotals.) Click on the Remove All button.

CHAPTER 22

Automating What-If Projects

YOU know the drill. "What are the effects of changing sales commissions to 3 percent, 2 percent, or 4 percent?" Or "What if mortgage rates fall to 7.25 percent?" It is questions like these that inspired someone to invent computerized spreadsheets. But the process of preparing them can be pretty tedious, particularly when you're juggling multiple variables. Excel provides a number of features designed to speed up complex what-if questions. They include the *Scenario Manager, What-If add-in macros,* the *Solver,* and related *reporting features*. This chapter introduces you to these tools. Excel's online Help, sample worksheets shipped with the program, and the documentation or bigger books can fill in the details.

General Organizational Tips

When you design worksheets that will be used regularly, it is a good idea to organize them logically, in a top-down manner. Place introductory text and instructions at the top, followed by the assumptions you'll most likely want to change. Label them clearly. This makes it easy for other people to see and understand your methodology.

If colleagues will be changing or examining your formulas, consider using names (like SALES and COMMISSION) rather than more obscure cell references (like B14 or $Q$13). As you will see, this can also automatically improve the appearance of your reports.

Protect essential equations so that people don't accidentally overwrite them. Consider breaking complex formulas up into smaller, easier-to-understand parts that display helpful intermediate answers. Test. Test some more. Test again. Dust off that pocket calculator.

$\int$cenario Manager

Scenarios are named sets of assumptions (inputs) and the resulting computations (results) that you ask a worksheet to compute. For instance, suppose you wanted to explore the impact of interest rates on mortgage payments and total interest paid. You might also want to see the effect of borrowing for 15 rather than 30 years. Scenario Manager can make short work of this and can even create nice summary reports.

Defining Scenarios

Select or CTRL+select the cells that you want to be able to change in the scenario. In the following example, you want to be able to explore changes in interest rates, the number of payments, and the loan amounts; so cells B2 through B4 have been selected. (To select nonadjacent cells, use CTRL+click.)

With the appropriate cells selected, choose Tools | Scenarios. You'll see the Scenario Manager dialog box telling you that no scenarios have been defined yet. Click the Add button to define some. You'll see an Add Scenario box something like the one in Figure 22-1.

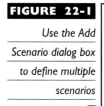

FIGURE 22-1

Use the Add Scenario dialog box to define multiple scenarios

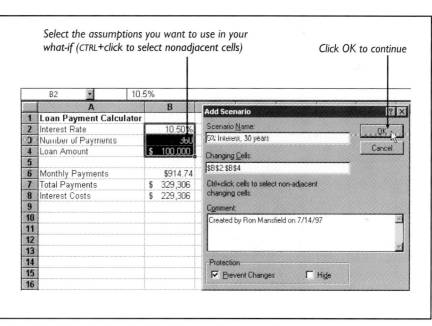

Select the assumptions you want to use in your what-if (CTRL+click to select nonadjacent cells)

Click OK to continue

Create as many named scenarios as you want by typing distinct scenario names and different values (in the Scenario Values dialog box) for one or all of the assumptions in each scenario. Click Add each time you want to save a scenario. The Scenario Values dialog box then pops up, letting you adjust numbers based upon the original selection. If you want to add more scenarios, click Add. When you have finished adding scenarios, click OK. You will again see the Scenario Manager dialog box.

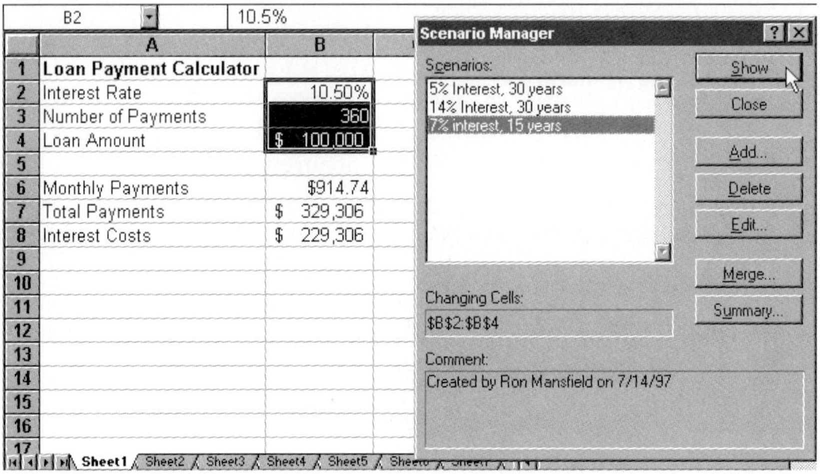

Viewing Scenarios

In the preceding illustration, there are three possible scenarios for cells B2 through B4: 5% Interest 30 Years, 14% Interest 30 Years, and 7% Interest 15 Years. To see the effect of a scenario, select it from the list and click Show. Your worksheet will reflect the chosen assumptions.

Obtaining Scenario Summaries

It is also easy to obtain summary reports that show the assumptions for each scenario and the results of each scenario. The following illustration is an example of this.

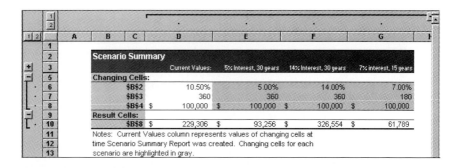

Start by clicking the Summary button in the Scenario Manager dialog box. Excel asks you to define the changing cells to be displayed. It proposes a range for you.

The proposed range usually contains formulas that refer to the changing assumption. You can keep the suggested range or define your own. Click OK when you are satisfied with the results range.

You can ask Excel to create a summary report (the default) or, by clicking on the appropriate button, request a Scenario Pivot table. (See Chapter 21 for more about PivotTables.)

Excel then creates and formats a report (as a separate worksheet in your workbook, actually), showing the various scenarios and their results. Notice that Scenario Manager labels rows with cell addresses ($B$2, $B$3, and so on). It makes for pretty obscure reading. You can overcome this by *naming* cells back in your model worksheet. (Use the Insert I Name I Define command to do this.) The names will appear in the reports.

WORKING WITH EXCEL

1 2		B	C	D	
	2	**Scenario Summary**			
	3			Current Values:	5% Int
	5	**Changing Cells:**			
	6	Interest_Rate		10.50%	
	7	Number_of_Payment		360	
	8	Loan_Amount	$	100,000	$
	9	**Result Cells:**			
	10	Interest_Costs	$	229,306	$
	11	Notes: Current Values column represents values of changing cells at			
	12	time Scenario Summary Report was created. Changing cells for each			
	13	scenario are highlighted in gray.			

Notice also that Excel may not propose all of the result cells that you'll want to see. You can overrule the proposed range by entering your own.

Changing Scenarios

Visit the Scenario Manager dialog box to add, delete, or edit scenarios. You cannot undo scenario deletions.

Finding the Right Number with Solver

Solver helps you find combinations that reach a goal. For instance, have you ever said, "If interest rates are 7 percent, and I can afford monthly payments of $1,000 a month, how much can I borrow?" Or have you ever needed to find the most profitable product mix, or examine sales commission scenarios to find the mix that is most profitable? Excel's Solver add-in program can assist you. Tell it your goals, and it does backflips to help you reach them.

Suppose you know you can spend $1,000 per month for 360 months, and you know that interest rates are 7%. Solver will help you determine the maximum loan amount.

1. Start by constructing and testing your model (a worksheet built around Excel's PMT function in this case).

B6		=-PMT(B2/12,B3,B4)	
	A	B	
1	**Loan Payment Calculator**		
2	Interest Rate	6.00%	
3	Number of Payments	360	
4	Loan Amount	$ 100,000	
5			
6	Monthly Payments	$599.55	
7	Total Payments	$ 215,838	
8	Interest Costs	$ 115,838	

2. When you know the model works right, save it.

3. Choose Solver from Excel's Tools menu. Because it's an add-in, the command may take a moment to load itself the first time you use it each session.

4. Soon you'll see a Solver Parameters dialog box.

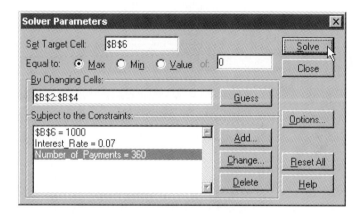

5. Tell Solver which cell you want to solve for (enter **Monthly Payments**, or **$B$6** in this example). Then define the *constraints*, or the rules to be used. For instance, you know you don't want to spend more than $1000 per month, and you don't want Solver to change the interest rates or number of payments, so you must add constraints for all three items. Create each constraint separately by using the Add button to build constraints like the one shown here:

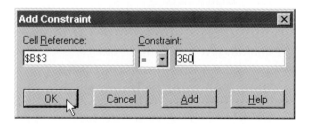

Constraints can refer to cell locations ($B$6, for instance), or to names if you've defined them (like Interest for cell B2).

6. When you've created all the appropriate constraints, use the Solve button to search for a solution. Eventually the hourglass that pops

WORKING WITH EXCEL

up will disappear. If your model worksheet is in view, you'll
see a solution:

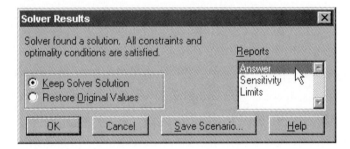

and you will see a Solver Results dialog box like this one:

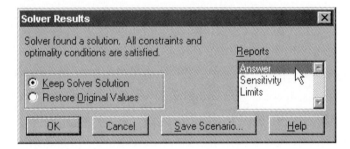

7. Choose Answer in the Reports list to see a report like the one in
Figure 22-2.

Solver lets you view your solutions, change the rules, and create reports.
You can save solutions for later reuse.

FIGURE 22-2

The Answer report created by Solver for the preceding exercise ■

Microsoft Excel 7.0 Answer Report
Worksheet: [Can I Afford a House.xls]Sheet1
Report Created: 7/14/97 16:23

Target Cell (Max)

Cell	Name	Original Value	Final Value
$B$6	Monthly Payments	$1,000.00	$1,000.00

Adjustable Cells

Cell	Name	Original Value	Final Value
$B$2	Interest Rate	7.00%	7.00%
$B$3	Number of Payments	360	360
$B$4	Loan Amount	$ 150,308	$ 150,308

Constraints

Cell	Name	Cell Value	Formula	Status	Slack
$B$6	Monthly Payments	$1,000.00	$B$6=1000	Not Binding	$0.00
$B$2	Interest Rate	7.00%	$B$2=0.07	Binding	0.00%
$B$3	Number of Payments	360	$B$3=360	Binding	0

To Learn More About Solver

This chapter illustrates a very simple Solver example that admittedly could be accomplished other ways. But it illustrates the concepts nicely. To see Solver at work on a bigger problem, open the Solverex.xls worksheet found in your Excel\Examples\Solver subfolder.

WORKING WITH EXCEL

CHAPTER 23

Auditing and Troubleshooting Worksheets

N

OTHING is more embarrassing than handing someone an important worksheet page containing an error or omission. Blunders can be expensive, both financially and personally. But errors are inevitable, particularly on large worksheets or in projects in which one worksheet refers to another. Excel will help you catch some errors, while others can lurk undetected for years. Make it a habit to test new worksheets using real data. Do the numbers look *reasonable* under a wide range of conditions? If you have time, set the work aside for a day or two and revisit it when you are fresh. Ask a knowledgeable associate to inspect and test your worksheet. Sometimes people get so close to a project that they overlook obvious problems.

Incidentally, just because a worksheet is operating properly on the day you create it does not mean it always will. It's very easy, for instance, to replace a formula with a value accidentally. This is particularly common when you share worksheet files with people who didn't create and don't fully understand them. That's why it is an especially good idea to protect your worksheets—and your formulas in particular—by using the techniques described earlier in this book.

tip *Remember, you can protect cells by selecting them, choosing Format | Cells, and visiting the Protection tab. To protect a whole worksheet or workbook, choose Tool | Protection, and then make the appropriate choice from the submenu.*

Excel provides a number of devices designed to help you locate and stamp out errors whenever they crop up. These include *error values*, *iteration*, the *Info window*, and *Auditing tools*.

Using Error Values to Locate Problems

Occasionally you will see the following error values in cells. They always start with the pound sign (#):

#DIV/0!
#N/A
#NAME?
#NULL!
#NUM!
#REF!
#VALUE!

These values appear both in cells *containing* erroneous formulas and in cells with formulas that *refer* to the erroneous formulas. Thus, you may need to inspect more than one cell to find the real source of the problem. Although they should never be *completely* ignored, error values like these sometimes appear simply because you are not finished creating the worksheet. For instance, if you create a formula that performs division using the contents of a cell as the divisor, and if that referenced cell is empty because you haven't entered a value into it yet, you'll see Excel's #DIV/0! value. The error value should disappear when you place an appropriate divisor in the referenced cell.

Let's look at each of the error values and consider what they mean and what to do when you see them.

#DIV/0!

You'll see this error when Excel tries to divide by zero, or if a referenced cell is blank when it needs to contain a divisor. Some Excel functions return the value of zero under certain circumstances. If your division formula looks to a cell containing a function for a divisor, then the function itself (or one of its arguments) may be causing the problem. Fix the formula if it is referring to the wrong cell, or fix the cell being referenced or the erroneous function or argument.

#N/A

N/A stands for "No Value Is Available." Under certain circumstances, Excel inserts this error value in cells (when you've improperly used certain function arguments, for instance). Other times, you may want to type **#N/A** into cells yourself as a reminder that you need to obtain and enter missing data. Suppose, for instance, that you were creating a worksheet that computes sales commissions for many salespeople and that the commission percentages were still being negotiated for some of them. You could enter **#N/A** as the commission percentages for the "problem" reps. Then, any formulas that rely upon those missing percentages will display #N/A. The #N/A will "ripple through" the rest of your worksheet and be seen in any cell that can't be computed properly without the missing data (totals and subtotals of sales commissions, for example).

#NAME?

The #NAME? error message usually appears because you've referred to a *named item* improperly. For instance, if you define a cell name **Sales** and create a formula like **=SQRT(Sails)**, you'll get the #NAME? error message. (Unless, of course, you also have an item named *Sails* in your worksheet, in which case Excel will attempt to find the square root of *it*.)

If you name an item, then delete or change its name, you will also get the #NAME? message. Solution: either rename the item or fix the affected formulas.

You might also see #NAME? if you enter a *function's* name improperly. For instance, the formula **=Sqr(9)** will produce a name error.

Forgetting to place a colon between cell addresses in a cell range will make Excel think you are referring to a name rather than a range. For example, **=SUM(B1B3)** will make Excel think you meant an item named B1B3 instead of the range B1:B3.

#NULL!

The #NULL! message means that you've specified the intersection of two areas that don't intersect, usually in a range specifier. For example, the formula **SUM(A1:D1 A3:D3)** produces a null error. Use a comma to separate referenced areas that don't intersect. For instance, **SUM(A1:D1,A3:D3)** is permitted.

#NUM!

You will see the #NUM! error value for several reasons. Unacceptable numeric arguments in functions will produce the error. For instance, trying to find the square root of negative numbers will produce the #NUM! error value.

When worksheet functions that use iterations to solve problems can't reach a workable result, you will also see the #NUM! error value. See the section "Using Iteration to Solve Circular References" to learn more about iteration.

#REF!

The #REF! message is commonly seen after you delete something to which other formulas refer. For instance, if you delete rows or columns containing things that remaining formulas need, you'll see the #REF! value in all affected formulas. Either use Undo to restore the deleted items or fix the formulas.

#VALUE!

You'll get a value reminder whenever you use the wrong type of argument, value, or operand. For instance, if you have a cell named Sales and you type the formula ="**Sales**"*2, Excel will see the quotation marks and treat sales as text rather than a name.

Sometimes, however, Excel will convert text automatically. For instance, if you make the cell entry '**10.5** (notice the leading apostrophe) in cell A1, the entry will be formatted and entered as text. You can tell this because it will be left-justified. If you then type the formula =**A1/2** in another cell, Excel will continue to display and treat cell A1 as text, but will convert it to a number for purposes of the formula. Thus, the formula will return the answer 5.25.

Using Iteration to Solve Circular References

It is not uncommon to see a dialog box warning that Excel "Cannot resolve circular references." That's not completely true. Excel *can* resolve circular references; you just need to use iteration (multiple passes) to do it. First, here's a review of what a circular reference is. Take a look at this error message.

A circular reference is a bit like a catch-22—for example, telling a young actress you'll give her a role in your play if she has experience, but she can't gain experience until she gets her first role.

In worksheet terms, suppose you wanted to pay sales commissions based on company profitability, and wanted to include commissions as one of the expenses affecting profit. You might create a profit formula in cell B3 that subtracted the contents of both cells B2 and B4 from the gross sales cell (B1). This would result in a circular reference, since profit will change when sales commissions change. Since commissions change with profit changes, commissions will need to be changed again, and so on. The first time you create a formula like this, and each time you load (open) a worksheet containing such a circular reference, you will see a warning like the one just shown.

There are several ways to work around circular-reference problems. One way is to redesign the worksheet (and perhaps your commission policy) so that there is a precommission profit line, then a commission line, then an actual profit line that takes commissions into consideration.

Another approach is to use iteration to resolve the circular reference.

1. Start by selecting the cell containing the circular formula (B4 in the example).

2. Choose Tools | Options.

3. Choose the Calculation tab in the Options dialog box.

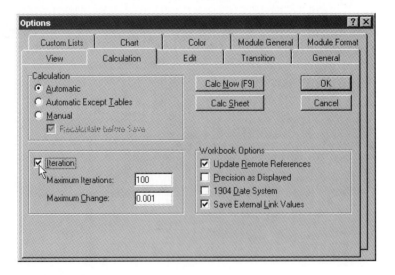

4. Choose the Iteration check box, and specify the Maximum Iterations and the Maximum Change options if you don't like the values shown.

5. You can see the results without closing the Calculation Options dialog box by using the Calc Now button or F9. Clicking OK will also run the iteration routine and display an answer in the affected cell(s).

Using the Info Window to Find Errors

The Info window gives you another useful troubleshooting tool. It can tell you a lot about the active cell. Here's how to open and use the Info window:

1. Activate the cell of interest.

2. Choose Tools | Options.

3. Click on the View tab if necessary to bring it topmost.

4. Choose the Info Window option in the Show area.

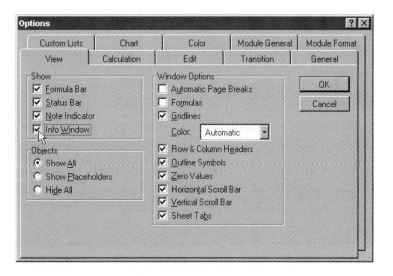

5. Click OK.

6. Visit the Windows menu and choose Arrange.

7. You'll see an Info window containing information about the active cell. Resize and move the window as you would any other.

Book2						
	A	B	C	D	E	F	G
1	Gross Sales	$ 100,000					
2	Total Costs	$ 50,000					
3	Profit	$ -					
4	Commision	$ 9,000					
5							
6							
7							
8							

Info [Book2]Sheet1

Cell: B3
Formula: =B1-(B2+B4)
Note:

Most of the displayed items are self-explanatory. What you see varies with the cell contents. "Cell" is the cell reference of the active cell, for instance. "Formula" shows the formula, and so on. In this case, the selected cell is within the same worksheet. If the cell were linked to another worksheet, you would see the path to the other cell—for example, C:\Windows\ [Forecast]Prices'!$B$5, or some such.

"Precedents" lists all the cells referred to by the formula in the active cell. "Dependents" lists all other cells containing formulas that rely upon the contents of the active cell. This is particularly useful information when you are working with multiple worksheets that are consolidated. To display things like precedents and dependents, go to the View menu and select the items you want to see.

To print information about a range of cells:

1. Select all cells of interest.

2. Open or activate (click in) the Info window.

3. Choose File | Print.

Using the Auditing Command to Troubleshoot

Errors can be particularly elusive in large worksheets. Get in the habit of double-checking your work, and don't forget to expand outlined worksheets when examining them. You can also use Excel's Auditing command to help you. Among other things, it can show you which cells are used by which others.

Do you remember the bookstore workbook with three store worksheets and a summary worksheet? Here it is again.

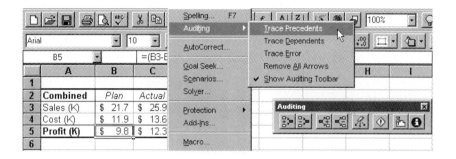

The Auditing command can find all of the cells referenced by the summary equations—including the ones in other worksheets.

To try auditing on your own, open a worksheet and follow these steps:

1. Choose Tools | Auditing | Trace Precedents (or Trace Dependents).

2. Excel will show you cells that depend upon (or affect) the active cell. You'll see an arrow as well. Notice that if the cells are in another worksheet, there will be a little worksheet icon at the start of the arrow.

3. To visit the cells, double-click on the arrowhead; if the cells are in the same worksheet, you will be taken there. If they are in another worksheet, you will get a list of possible places to go in the Go To dialog box:

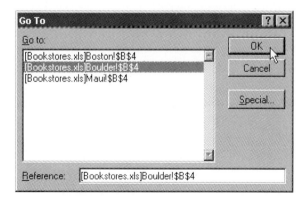

4. Double-click on the location of interest.

Finding the Source of Error Messages

The Trace Error choice on the Auditing submenu will take you to the worksheet and cell containing the equation responsible for an error message. For instance, if you are looking at the "combined" bookstore worksheet and see an error like #####, choose Trace Error to take you to the offending cell (B4 in the Combined worksheet):

	A	B	C	D
1				
2	Combined	Plan	Actual	
3	Sales (K)	$ 21.7	$ 25.9	
4	Cost (K)	#######	$ 13.6	
5	Profit (K)	#######	$ 12.3	
6				

Part Four
Presenting with PowerPoint

There was a time when you could stand up, speak your piece, get a yes or a no, and sit down. But it's the nineties now, and you are expected to give "awesome" meeting presentations to the MTV generation. To a large extent, how a presentation looks is often as important as what it says. PowerPoint is Microsoft's answer to that need. It will help you create good-looking overhead transparencies, 35mm slides, and even video slide shows. And while it is true that most of what PowerPoint does can also be done by Word and Excel, PowerPoint streamlines a few of the tasks and provides some handy prefabricated layouts, color schemes, and font choices. Let's take a look.

CHAPTER 24

PowerPoint Basics

P

OWERPOINT helps you quickly create, update, and sort "slide-based" professional-looking presentation materials, even if you are not a graphic arts designer.

PowerPoint is no replacement for multimedia development programs, and it is probably not the tool you should choose for creating a brochure or proposal booklet; it does not have the page layout capabilities of Word. Rather, PowerPoint is a program that helps you quickly create

- Black-and-white overhead transparencies
- Color overhead transparencies
- 35mm slides
- Computer screen and video slide shows complete with special effects
- Presentation files that you can send to coworkers for their review, even if they don't own PowerPoint
- Printed meeting handouts
- Detailed speaker's notes
- Printed and onscreen presentation outlines

Figure 24-1 shows an example of items you can create using PowerPoint.

While creating and modifying your presentation materials, you will use techniques that should be familiar by now, because PowerPoint "behaves" much like Word and Excel. Moreover, you can use cut and paste or use OLE to include Word and Excel information such as worksheets, charts, and text in your presentations.

PowerPoint provides rehearsal tools that let you practice your presentation at your desk. It lets you quickly rearrange presentation materials by dragging them around on your screen with your mouse. It also offers "drill-down" capabilities that let you pull up supporting documents. For

FIGURE 24-1

An example of

presentation

materials

PowerPoint can

help you create

■

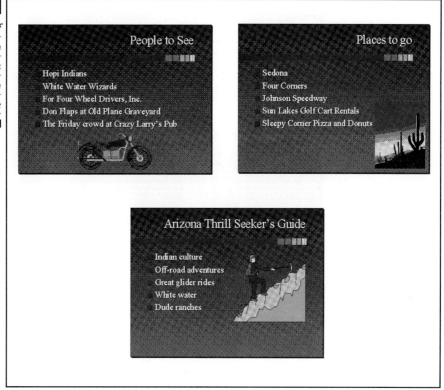

example, if you are presenting a budget summary, PowerPoint makes it easy to pull up the supporting detail numbers from a worksheet or other source. This assumes, of course, that you have your computer with you and that it has the necessary data on it. And, as you will see if you experiment with this feature, there may be quicker ways to accomplish the same thing.

Terminology

You can't have a new program without some new buzzwords, now, can you? Here's everything you need to know about PowerPointSpeak.

Slides

You create and edit individual pages called *slides*. For instance, in a sales presentation you might have a slide titled Competition, another called Pricing, and so on. For example, here are six typical PowerPoint slides.

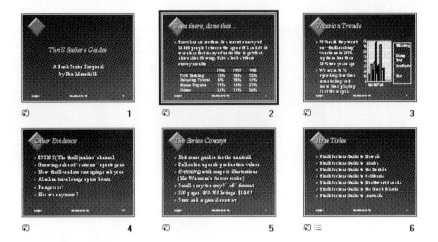

Speaker's Notes

Use speaker's notes when you present. They are usually printed on paper and can be either the exact text of the speech, reminder notes, backup information, or combinations thereof. Here is an example of speaker's notes.

Handouts

Handouts are paper copies of all or some of the slides to be given to the audience. They can be one per page or reduced so that three or six fit on a sheet of paper. Figure 24-2 shows a typical handout. Notice how PowerPoint will place up to six slides on a single sheet of paper.

FIGURE 24-2

Print handouts for your audience and perhaps for yourself
■

Thrill Seekers Guide

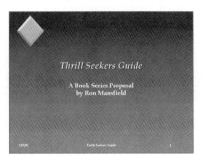

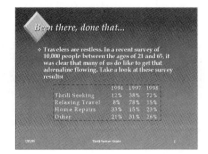

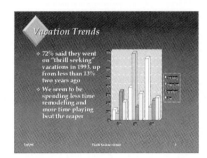

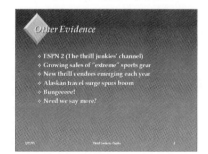

Presentation Files

All of the PowerPoint slides for a particular project (a sales pitch, for instance) are kept in a single PowerPoint file called a *presentation file*. These presentation files normally end with the extension .PPT (Sales.ppt, for example).

note *As discussed earlier, you often will not see these extensions; this does not mean they aren't there, though. It's just that Windows 95 hides extensions by default. PowerPoint will show you (in the Open and Save dialog boxes) all files it thinks are PowerPoint presentation files; but if you are going to be doing a lot of work with other computers that will not be running Windows 95, you might want to limit yourself to the eight-character filename convention.*

A presentation file might have just a few slides or many. If you've recorded sounds as part of your presentation or added speaker's notes, those presentation elements will also be stored in the presentation file. In other words, each presentation consists of only one file, making it easy to copy and pass around presentations.

Masters

You create *masters* (also called *master slides*) to hold information that will appear on multiple slides in your presentation. For instance, if you wanted to put your name, company logo, or some other decoration on each slide, you'd add it to the master for that presentation.

You can also create separate masters for handouts and speaker's notes within each presentation. PowerPoint comes with a variety of preprogrammed masters to get you started. You can use these as-is, modify them, or create your own masters from scratch. Here is one master—designed to make it easy to create slides with bulleted lists.

Color Schemes

PowerPoint lets you define rules used for applying colors or shades of gray to the various components of your presentation. For instance, you can specify a slide's background colors, the colors used for major headings, and so on. PowerPoint comes with many predefined color schemes, which you can use as-is or modify to taste. Chapter 30 explores colors and shades of gray in more detail.

PowerPoint Templates

A PowerPoint *template* consists of a master and a color scheme. PowerPoint comes with 160 predefined templates. For example, this slide was created with a template that includes a diamond-shaped graphic and changes the colors of headings and bullets.

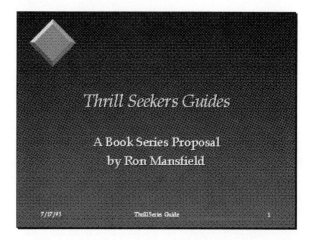

If you've created presentations containing your own custom masters and color schemes, you can use these as templates. To change the *look* of a presentation, you need merely apply a different template to an existing presentation to completely change the presentation's appearance. Power-Point makes all the necessary changes in colors, fonts, and so on. (You'll see how this all works in Chapter 26.)

Getting Started

No surprises here: Start PowerPoint as you would any other Office program. One way is to choose PowerPoint from the Start menu. It will be on the Programs submenu. As always, you can double-click the program icon or a document icon in Windows Explorer, too. You can also click on the PowerPoint button, shown next, in the Office Shortcut Bar:

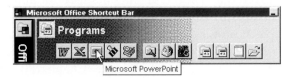

tip   *If you create and show onscreen presentations, you may find that the Office Shortcut Bar gets in the way of the presentation. To get it out of the way, consider minimizing it by clicking its minimize button.*

Unless you turn this feature off, you will be greeted with a PowerPoint Tip of the Day.

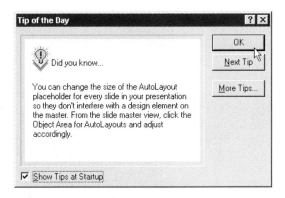

When you dismiss the tip dialog box by clicking on the OK button, you will see a second dialog box.

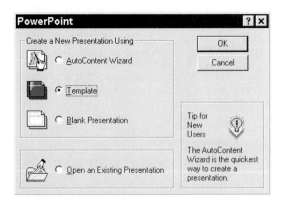

It wants to know if you'd like to create a new presentation or work with an existing one. Notice that, if creating a new presentation, you have the options of using several Wizards and template choices. Chapter 25 will explore these choices in detail.

Views

Like other Microsoft Office products, PowerPoint offers different views for entering, editing, and previewing your information. For instance, Power-Point's Outline view is handy for entering text and for rearranging the text in a given slide; but once you have done the bulk of the typing, you'll want to switch to other PowerPoint views. They include

- Slide view
- Slide Sorter view
- Notes Pages view
- Slide Show view

Switching Views

You can switch views by using the View menu or the view buttons (shown next) at the bottom left of the PowerPoint window. You may want to try switching views as you read about them.

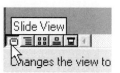

The buttons are named (from left to right) Slide View, Outline View, Slide Sorter View, Notes Pages View, and Slide Show View.

Outline View

It's easy to rearrange the individual line items while in Outline view. And you can collapse items in this view so that you can see just headings or just the names of each slide. For example, to show just the title for each slide, you could use the Show Titles button shown next.

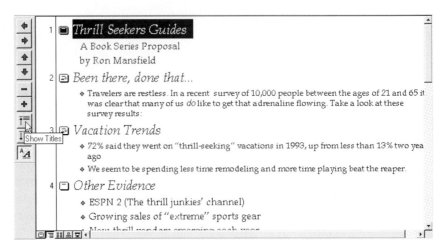

It's easy to move collapsed slides to different places in your presentations. You work with outline buttons in much the same way you do in Word's Outline view. Chapter 27 has the details.

Slide View

Slide view shows you how your finished slides will look. You'll see the backgrounds, colors or shades of gray, and so forth. Here is a typical slide in Slide view.

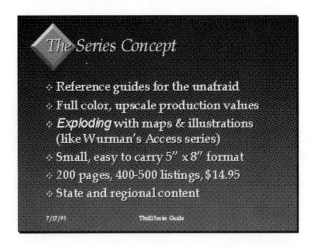

Notice that PowerPoint has wrapped long lines whenever necessary. You can move from slide to slide with PAGE UP and PAGE DOWN or the scroll box.

You can edit text and other slide elements while in Slide view, as you will learn in Chapter 26.

Slide Sorter View

Slide Sorter view lets you see *thumbnails* (reduced-size slide images) like those shown in Figure 24-3. While in Slide Sorter view, you can drag slides to move them. Chapter 27 shows how this is done. The Slide Sorter view is also where you specify types of slide transitions. For example, you can make one slide dissolve into another, or make slides appear and disappear using venetian blind effects. You can also specify how individual bullet points on a slide are revealed to the audience (all at once or one at a time). Slide Sorter is an excellent view to use for this purpose because you get a preview of the effects as you choose them.

FIGURE 24-3

Slide Sorter view

lets you see

reduced-size slide

images

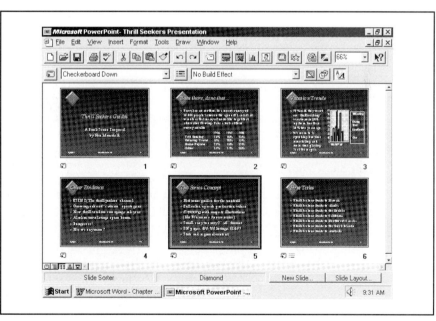

Notes Pages View

Use the Notes Pages view to create and see notes to the presenter. It shows a miniature slide image and provides a text area for presenter's notes.

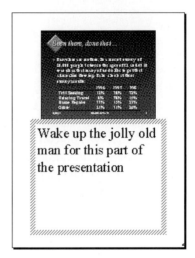

To enter a note:

1. Click in the text area beneath the slide. The box outline will change appearance.

2. Type and edit in the note box as you would any other.

As you will see in Chapter 28, you can print these notes if you like.

Slide Show View

Use Slide Show view to help you rehearse, or for actual video presentations of finished shows. It removes all of the PowerPoint clutter and places a small icon in the lower-left corner of the screen.

When you switch to Slide Show view, shown in Figure 24-4, you'll see the slide you were working on in the previous view. To move forward (to see higher-numbered slides), press SPACEBAR, click the primary mouse button, or use RIGHT ARROW. Use LEFT ARROW to move backward.

Use Slide Show

view for rehearsals

or actual video

presentations

■

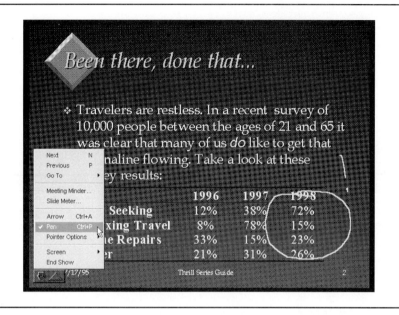

t i p   *You can see this menu at any time by right-clicking. This is handy if you've chosen to hide the icon (which you do from the pop-up menu).*

If you click on the little icon, a menu will pop up with a lot of nifty options. Among them, you can opt to have a "pen" at your disposal. Using the mouse to write with this pen, you can draw temporary lines on the screen, emphasizing things as you talk. These lines are not saved with the presentation, and might remind you of chalk marks—visible only during the current presentation or rehearsal.

You can also use this menu to change the color of the pen, to go to a particular slide, or to make the screen black.

To leave Slide Show view, press ESC or choose End Show from the pop-up menu. You'll be switched to the previous view you were using. You'll learn more about slide shows in Chapter 28.

CHAPTER 25

Creating Presentations
the Easy Way

I'S the Wizards, templates, layouts, and masters that put the *power* in PowerPoint. While you *could* format each slide manually, the combination of wizardly automation and predesigned layouts greatly simplifies the task. There's even a Wizard called "AutoContent" that will help you develop a presentation's content and organization. So let's get off on the right foot by looking at automation first. You'll learn about manual techniques in later chapters.

AutoContent Wizard

The AutoContent Wizard asks you several questions and then uses a predefined template containing suggested topics and tips to help you tell your story. There are templates for

- Breaking bad news
- General presentations
- Progress reports
- Sales presentations
- Strategy meetings
- Training sessions

When you start PowerPoint and dismiss the Tip Of The Day, you will be presented with the PowerPoint dialog box. It offers a number of choices. If you want help with the content of your presentation, click on the AutoContent Wizard button and then on the OK button to get started.

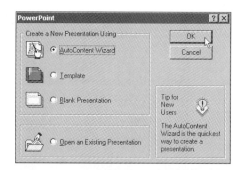

tip   *You can start a new Wizard-driven presentation at any time by choosing New from the File menu.*

After you read the Wizard's greeting, click the Next > button (or press ENTER). You'll see the second dialog box.

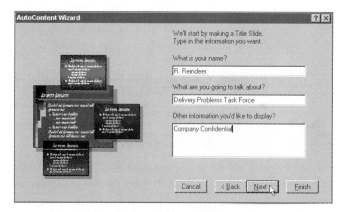

Here, you are asked to provide information for the title slide (the opening slide in your presentation). Change the name in the name box if necessary, type a topic, and place other text in the "Other information you'd like to display?" text area, if you wish. When you click Next >, you will see a list of presentation types (Recommending a Strategy; Selling a Product, Service or Idea; Training; and so on). A summary of each choice appears on the right side of the dialog box as you click on a presentation type. For instance, the following illustration shows the Communicating Bad News choice.

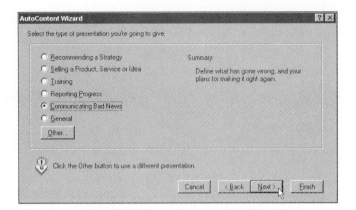

tip *If you are using your own computer, the name in the "What is your name?" box should be correct. PowerPoint gets this information from the registered user's name.*

When you settle on a topic (Communicating Bad News in this example), click the Next > button to move on. You will see a dialog box that lets you make a few more decisions about your presentation.

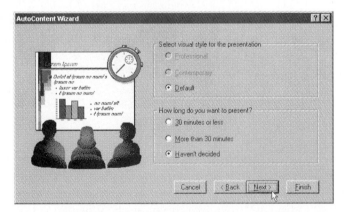

You can also tell AutoContent how long you want your presentation to run, in this dialog box. Click Next > when you are satisfied with the settings.

tip *If you know what the rest of the dialog boxes do and their settings are acceptable, you can click Finish at any time to create the presentation.*

The penultimate AutoContent box is where you specify what kind of output you want. You can also tell the Wizard whether you want handouts of your presentation.

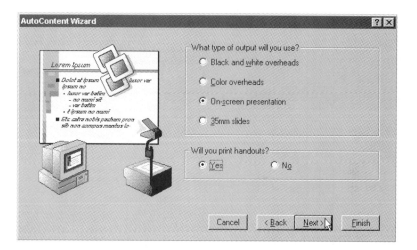

Click Next > when you're ready to move on. You will get the racing flag dialog box (the last box). Click Finish to begin to create the actual presentation. Click the outline button to see an outline of the presentation. Figure 25-1 shows the beginning of a Communicating Bad News presentation.

The Wizard no longer automatically switches to PowerPoint's Outline view, but it's a good idea to visit the outline first. Click on the outline button if you aren't already in Outline view. You will see a number of slides. In Outline view, the slides are numbered along the left edge of the windows. Notice that the Wizard has already edited the title slide for you. It inserts the topic and presenter's name information that you typed earlier (**Delivery Problems Task Force** and **R. Reindeer** in Figure 25-1).

Editing the Wizard's Work

Edit PowerPoint text just as you do Word or Excel text. As you can see in Figure 25-1, the PowerPoint window has scroll bars, toolbars, and all the other things you've come to expect. Select text to edit or replace it. Figure 25-2 shows some edited text.

You already know the important text editing techniques well if you've ever used another Windows program. Here's a brief review. (Details can be found in Chapter 26.)

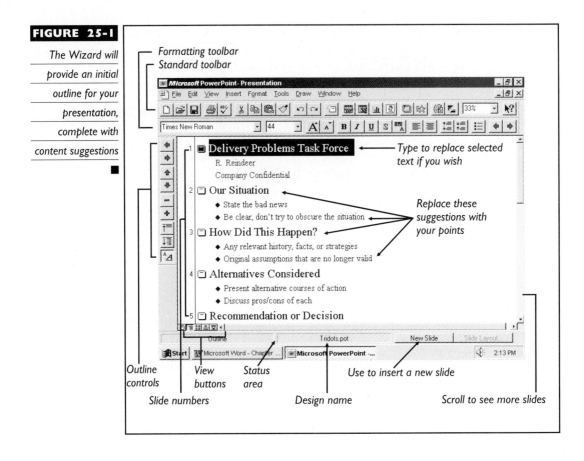

FIGURE 25-1

The Wizard will provide an initial outline for your presentation, complete with content suggestions

- Select text by dragging or double-clicking.

- Type to replace selected text.

- Use toolbar buttons and drop-down lists to embellish (bold, underline, and so on).

- To insert text, point and click to move the insertion point, and then start typing.

- Press ENTER to insert new bullet items.

- Use DEL to remove text and bullets.

- Most other tools (like drag-and-drop or cut-and-paste) work in PowerPoint.

FIGURE 25-2

*It's easy to edit
text in PowerPoint's
Outline view*

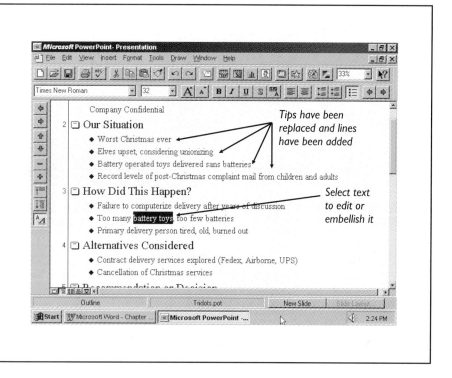

Using Design Templates to Automate Wholesale Design Changes

You can *manually* change the background, type styles, and other design elements on slides by using techniques discussed in Chapter 26. But when you want to change the look of *all* the slides, it is better to change master slides. This changes design elements for all the slides in a presentation. PowerPoint's *design templates* make this easy to do. You can change the design template at any time on an existing or new presentation, making it easy to try multiple looks on the same presentation until you find the one you like.

tip   *You can open the Apply Design Template dialog box by double-clicking on the design name in the status area.*

1. Begin by opening the presentation you want to improve.

2. Choose Format | Apply Design Template (you can also click the Apply Design Template button on the Standard toolbar). The Apply Design Template dialog box will appear.

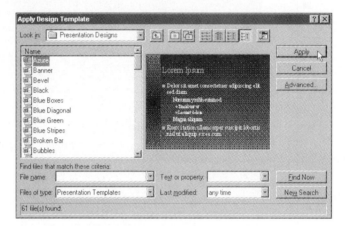

3. Scroll to see additional template designs. As you click each template, you'll see a thumbnail of the resulting look in the preview area at the right of the dialog box. It will give you a general idea of what to expect.

4. To locate other templates of interest, the Apply Design Template dialog box behaves like the Open dialog box (select a disk drive, then a folder, and so on).

5. When you find a look you want to try, click Apply.

6. You'll be returned to your presentation, and there will be a heart-stopping pause while the Wiz thinks this all over. In a moment (sometimes after a "kilomoment") you will see one of your slides, such as the one shown in here, strutting the new look.

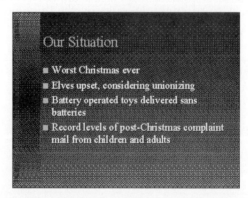

tip *If you've created presentations with looks that you like, you can locate and preview those in addition to PowerPoint's predefined looks.*

The font(s) may have changed. If the template calls for shadowed text, you'll see shadows. The type of bullets might have changed in bulleted lists.

warning *Occasionally, all of the Wizard's font changing, margin changing, and other remodeling will cause some problems. Slide headings that once fit on a single line now might take two lines. Text that fit on the slide may fit no longer. Graphics inserted by the new template may obliterate something important on one or all of your slides. Therefore, it is very important that you inspect each slide in Slide View or with the Slide Show feature after applying a new design template!*

Masters

Masters make it easy for you to specify common design elements that you want to include throughout your presentation. Masters can contain elements like backgrounds, logos, font choices, color schemes, date and time stamps, page numbers, and so on. Each presentation has a master for

- Slides
- Outlines
- Handouts
- Speaker's notes

PowerPoint comes with a variety of predefined masters. They are stored in templates. You can pick the masters you want to use for each presentation and even change to different masters after you've created your presentation, as described earlier.

Changes that you make to masters in a presentation affect all of the slides or pages in your current presentation. For instance, if you add a big logo to a presentation's slide master and a little logo to the presentation's handout master, the big logos will appear on all of your slides and the small logos will print on handouts, but not on the outline or speaker's notes.

You can "overrule" master settings for individual slides (or printout pages). PowerPoint will remember these exceptions even if you switch masters in a production.

PRESENTING WITH POWERPOINT

Typical elements of a master include

- Title text

- Body text (in a variety of indent levels)

- Color schemes

- Background shading and other "wallpaper" art

- Presentation title or other marginal text

- Date stamp

- Time stamp

Figure 25-3 shows a typical slide master.

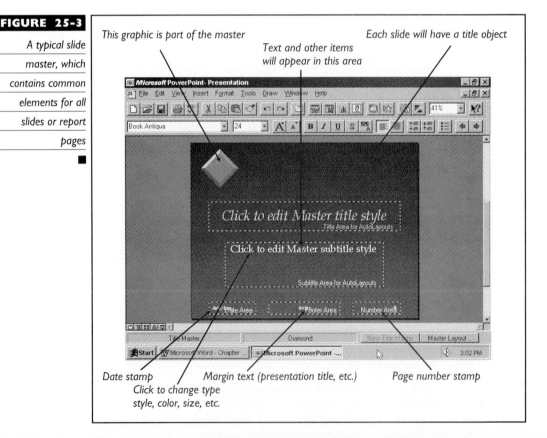

This graphic is part of the master

Text and other items will appear in this area

Each slide will have a title object

Date stamp
Click to change type style, color, size, etc.

Margin text (presentation title, etc.)

Page number stamp

Editing Your Masters

To change something in a master, follow these steps:

1. Open the presentation.

2. Choose View | Master | Slide.

3. Make changes as you would in most Microsoft Office programs. For instance, to change the font of the title style, click on the master's title and choose a new font from the Formatting toolbar.

4. To move items on a master, click to select, and then drag them with the mouse pointer. Notice how the border surrounding the object changes appearance when selected. Figure 25-4 illustrates this.

5. To *resize* master elements (like the areas that contain text and cause it to wrap), select the object as in step 4, then drag the *black handles* to change the object's size and shape.

6. View *all* the slides in your presentation to see the effect of the changes.

FIGURE 25-4

You can drag master elements after selecting them

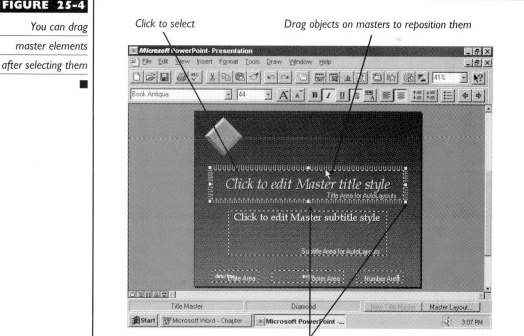

Click to select

Drag objects on masters to reposition them

Drag handles to resize

warning *If you've spent a long time creating a presentation and then decide to make major changes to the masters for that presentation, experiment on a **copy** of your presentation (made with the Save As command) rather than working on your original presentation file. It's often easier to abandon an experiment and revert to the old file than it is to undo everything.*

Adding Slides

You can add (insert) new slides while in the Outline, Slide, or Slide Sorter views. The new slides can be created by inserting an AutoLayout to help with the format and then typing, or you can insert slides from other presentations. Moreover, by using OLE and other techniques, you can insert elements from other programs including Word outlines, Excel charts, and much more. You'll learn more about this in Chapter 27. For now, let's stick with manually inserting and typing slides.

Specifying the New Slide's Insertion Point

New slides are always inserted *after* the current slide in a presentation. The easiest way to see this is in Slide Sorter view, but the concept is the same in Slide and Outline views. Here are the steps:

1. Switch to one of the three views (Slide, Slide Sorter, or Outline view).

2. Click to select the slide just before the point where you want the new slide. For instance, to place a new slide after slide 2 here, you would click on slide 2 to select it.

tip *To insert slides while in Outline view, simply click on the slide icon next to the slide you want to select.*

3. Choose Insert | New Slide (or click the Insert New Slide button on the Standard toolbar).

4. If you are in Outline view, PowerPoint inserts a new slide that uses the same layout as the preceding slide. (You'll learn more about layouts in a moment.) If you are in Slide view or Slide Sorter view, you will be presented with the New Slide (AutoLayout) dialog box, which will be explained in a moment. Select an AutoLayout and click OK.

5. The new slide will be inserted, and the slides following it will be renumbered.

     1   2   3   4

AutoLayout—Simple Slide Design

Chances are, your presentations have many things in common with those of other people. *You* need a title slide, *they* need a title slide. You create bulleted lists, they need bulleted lists. They show graphs with some explanatory text and so do you. Organizational charts are often important in presentations, as are photos, clip art, and other embellishments. Knowing this, Microsoft has developed a number of *slide layouts* for common slide-making tasks. These layouts have text boxes, places to insert graphics, bullet list formatting, and so on. AutoLayout takes care of things like margins, line spacing, and so on. Each slide in a presentation can use the same or different layout.

There are two very similar dialog boxes to help you automatically lay out slides. You see the New Slide dialog box automatically when you insert new slides in Slide and Slide Sorter views, or you can call for the Slide Layout dialog box, shown in Figure 25-5, by choosing Format | Slide Layout while in Slide view.

Except for one button, these two dialog boxes are identical. In both instances, each AutoFormat choice is illustrated in a thumbnail example. You can select a layout by clicking on its thumbnail. This surrounds the thumbnail with a dark border. The text box in the lower-right corner of the dialog box contains a brief description of the selected layout.

Scroll to see the rest of the AutoLayout choices. Click on different choices to read about them.

FIGURE 25-5

The Slide

Layout (New Slide)

dialog box

■

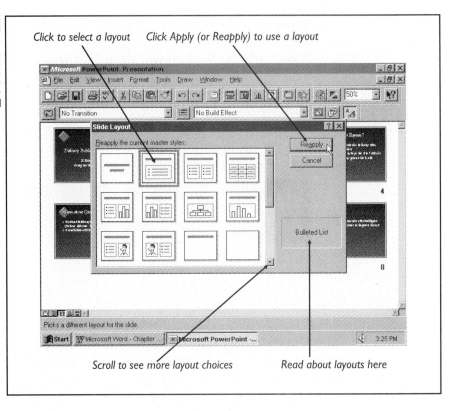

Click to select a layout   Click Apply (or Reapply) to use a layout

Scroll to see more layout choices   Read about layouts here

t i p   *To see which layout was used for a particular existing slide (in someone else's presentation for instance), select the slide in any view, and then choose the Slide Layout command. The Slide Layout dialog box will open with the current slide's layout thumbnail selected (surrounded by a dark border).*

Click on the Apply button in the New Slide dialog box or on the Reapply button in the Slide Layout dialog box to apply the chosen layout to the current slide in your presentation. Let's see an example of this at work.

Using AutoLayout When Inserting a Slide

Suppose you wanted to add a new slide after slide 10 in an existing presentation. The slide will contain a bulleted list and some clip art. Here's one way to do that:

1. Open the presentation.

2. Switch to Slide view (or Slide Sorter view), and go to the slide just before the insertion point (slide 10 in your example).

3. Choose Insert | New Slide or click the Insert New Slide button on the Standard toolbar.

4. Peruse the AutoLayout choices until you find one that offers a design layout you like—a combination of text and clip art in your example. (Notice that there are *two* layout choices in this instance.)

5. Click on the desired choice to select it, and then click OK.

6. PowerPoint will insert a new empty slide and renumber the slides that follow it.

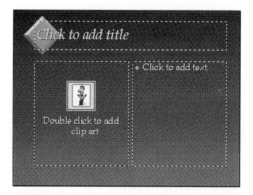

7. The new slide will take on the general characteristics of the current presentation, including things like marginal text, page numbering options, and so on.

8. Click in the various areas of the slide blank to add and edit things, or double-click if that's what the onscreen instructions say to do. For instance, to add a title, click in the title area and start typing. To create a bulleted list, click in a text area and type. Pressing ENTER will start a new bulleted line.

9. Save your presentation (CTRL+S) when you are happy with the changes.

tip   *Some layouts (including the one in the example) facilitate Object Linking and Embedding (OLE) and the inclusion of graphics—topics covered in more detail in Chapter 27. OLE is also discussed in Part Eight, "Sharing Information with OLE."*

Deleting Slides

To delete an unwanted slide, select it in any view and then choose Edit | Delete Slide.

warning   *You won't be asked to confirm slide deletions, and Undo will only work if you catch your mistake immediately.*

CHAPTER 26

Working with Text in PowerPoint

POWERPOINT does a pretty good job of formatting text for you. But if you get the urge to one-up your copresenters, you can reach deeper into PowerPoint's bag of tricks. In fact, you could probably fritter away days playing with type styles, shadow effects, and more.

Fundamentals first, though—nothing's worse than spotting a five-foot-tall misspelling. That's why it's a good idea to let PowerPoint check your work *before* you present.

tip *PowerPoint now comes with a Style Checker and improved AutoCorrect, in addition to your old friend, the Spell Checker.*

Last-minute changes in content and organization are a snap with Power-Point's outlining and text-editing features. Most of the techniques will seem familiar if you've already used Microsoft Word. Oddly, there are text tools in PowerPoint you'll wish you had in Word (like the Periods command), and some tools in Word that you sure could use in PowerPoint (like Insert Symbol).

Editing and Moving Text

As you've already seen, PowerPoint requires familiar text-editing skills. Text is kept in things called *title objects* and *body objects*. These objects are rectangular areas surrounded by nonprinting lines. First you select an object, then you select text within the object to work with it. Work in Slide view, Outline view, or Note Pages view.

Inserting Text

Point and click within a title object or body object to move the insertion point to the place in the text where you want to make the addition. Begin typing. Text to the right of the insertion point will be pushed forward and down.

w a r n i n g   *Unlike Word, PowerPoint does not automatically scroll text onto the next "page" (a new slide) if you run out of room on the current slide, so watch the screen as you type.*

Keep your writing terse. Insert additional slides if necessary. While you *can* decrease type sizes and line spacing to make things fit, you shouldn't make text too much smaller or tighter than the AutoFormat defaults; if you do it will be difficult for audiences to read your words of wisdom.

Inserting New Bullet Items

Place the insertion point where you want the new item and press ENTER. PowerPoint will add a new line preceded by a bullet, as shown in Figure 26-1.

Remember, since PowerPoint won't add new pages or "spill" text onto slides that follow, your bulleted line insertion can force text to fall outside of the body object. You'll need to create additional slides or use other techniques in this chapter to make the words fit.

Deleting Text

Select the unwanted text and press DEL. Text below will snake up to take its place. To delete bullets, select them and delete them like other text. Alternatively you can use the Edit menu's Cut command (CTRL+X) or the scissors-like Cut button on the Formatting toolbar.

Moving Text

The technique you use to move text will vary depending upon how much you need to move, and how far you want to move it. When you reorganize multiple items, it is often best to work in Outline view (using techniques described in a moment). But for minor alterations, like moving a little text from one point in a title or body object to another place within the same

FIGURE 26-1

Press **ENTER** to

insert a new

bulleted line

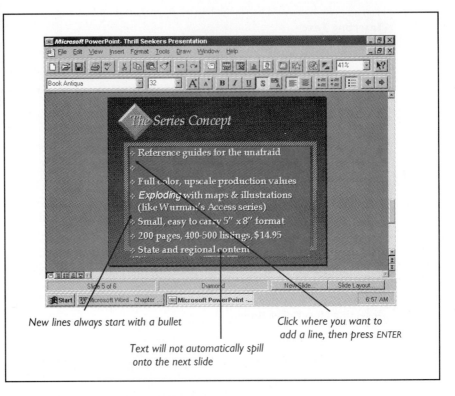

New lines always start with a bullet

Text will not automatically spill
onto the next slide

Click where you want to
add a line, then press ENTER

object, you can work in Slide view. Simply select text, and then drag and drop as in Microsoft Word.

To move a little text to other objects, to other slides, or even to other presentations while in Slides view, it is best to

1. Select the text to be moved.

2. Cut it (CTRL+X).

3. Switch to the destination slide if it's not the current slide.

4. Select the title or body object to receive the text.

5. Click to position the insertion point where you want to place the incoming text.

6. Paste (CTRL+V).

tip *Double-clicking on a word selects the entire word. Dragging after double-clicking selects subsequent words.*

Working in Outline View

Outline view is *the place* to make major renovations to the content and organization of your text. It will remind you of Word's Outline view, but there are differences. Figure 26-2 shows a typical presentation in Outline view.

Outline view lets you see all text or just selected heading levels. You can rearrange the order of slides by dragging them from place to place. You can move text around on its slide or move text from one slide to another. Let's take a closer look.

FIGURE 26-2

Work in Outline view when reorganizing or making major revisions

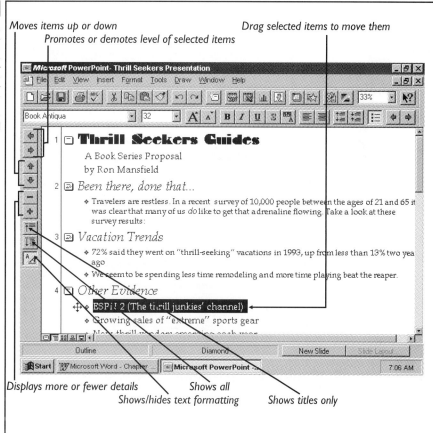

Expanding and Collapsing Outline Views

You can increase and decrease the amount of information displayed by clicking on the buttons on the left edge of the Outline view screen. For example, to hide all the text and show just slide titles, you'd click the Show Titles button as illustrated here.

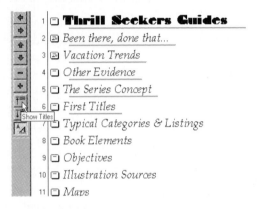

To reveal all the text, click on the Show All button (just beneath the Show Titles button). This will bring all the text back into view.

To expand or collapse details for selected slides only (or even portions of slides):

1. Select the slide or slides, or portions thereof (SHIFT+click to select multiple slides or lines).

2. To expand (reveal) information in the selected area, use the Expand Selection button (the plus sign):

3. PowerPoint will expand the selected area so that you can see additional detail.

4. To collapse (hide detail), use the Collapse Selection button (the minus sign).

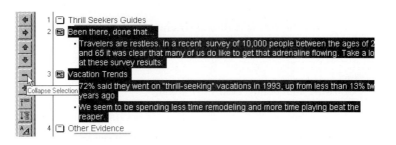

Promoting and Demoting Headings

Like Word headings, PowerPoint titles and headings can have different levels. These let you quickly create multilevel indented lists like this:

> ☐ *About the Author*
> > ✦ Ron has written 16 books
> > ✦ Is a columnist
> > ✦ Has appeared on CNN
> > ✦ Has traveled to:
> > > ↦ 49 States
> > > ↦ Europe
> > > ↦ Japan
> > ✦ Is a glider pilot
> > ✦ Is a photographer

The top level is the slide title itself. The next level is for the usual bullet lists, and the next indent ("49 States," "Europe," and "Japan" in this example) are the next level down. As you saw in Figure 26-2, different levels have their own appearance (different type size, fonts, and so on).

To move items from one level to another, follow these steps:

1. Select an item to promote or demote.

2. Point at the left edge of the item. The mouse pointer will change to a four-headed arrow.

3. Drag left to promote or right to demote the selected item.

4. A vertical line will appear to show you the pending new level of the item being dragged.

5. Release the mouse button. The item will take on its new indent level and appearance.

You could also just select the item to promote or demote, and then click on the up or down arrowheads in the Outlining tools collection on the left side of the screen.

Showing and Hiding Text Formatting

Sometimes it's desirable to see Outline views without text formatting. You can get more information on the screen this way, and it may speed scrolling. Use the Show Formatting button to toggle onscreen text formatting. It's the bottom button in the Outlining toolbar collection.

Spell-Checking

PowerPoint's spelling checker dialog box should look familiar. It's a lot like those in Word and Excel, though not identical. The PowerPoint Spelling checker shares dictionaries with your other Office applications. It doesn't, however, let you check just selected parts of your presentation. It always checks all of the words in your slides, notes, and other printouts—with one important exception: it will not check words in your drawings.

You can work in Outline or Slide view when checking spelling. To start the checker, press F7, use the Standard toolbar button, or choose Tools | Spelling. The checker will scan your whole presentation looking for unfamiliar words (unrecognized collections of text surrounded by spaces, actually). When it finds one, it will highlight it in your presentation and place it in the Not In Dictionary section of the Spelling dialog box, as shown in Figure 26-3.

You can accept PowerPoint's suggestions, type a correction of your own, add the unfamiliar word to a custom dictionary, or skip the word by clicking the appropriate buttons. When making changes, you can have PowerPoint always make the same correction without asking you again whenever it occurs later in the same spell-checking session, by selecting Change All.

tip *Run the checker after you've entered all your text but before doing your final formatting, and before changing Design Templates, and so on, since some corrections will change line endings, affecting the amount of room available on a slide, and so on.*

Finding and Replacing Text

PowerPoint lets you do basic text searching and replacement, though not to the degree that Word permits. (Wildcards are not supported, for instance.)

FIGURE 26-3

The Spelling

checker highlights

unfamiliar text

strings and offers

suggestions

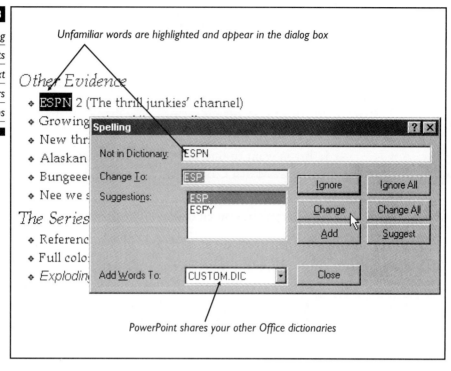

Unfamiliar words are highlighted and appear in the dialog box

PowerPoint shares your other Office dictionaries

The Edit | Find command lets you search for text, and the Edit | Replace command lets you search for and change text. The usual cautions apply here. Automatic replacements can make guacamole out of a great presentation, so save your work before replacing, then check to see how it went.

Replacing

Replacing is pretty self-explanatory. For instance, to replace all occurrences of *Travelled* with *Traveled* you would

1. Save your presentation.

2. Choose Edit | Replace.

3. Enter **Travelled** in the Find What box.

4. Enter **Traveled** in the Replace With box.

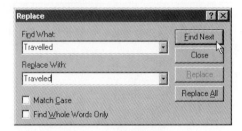

5. If you want to find only words with matching capitalization, choose Match Case.

6. To find only exact word matches (*Ron* but not elect*ron*ic, for instance) choose Find Whole Words Only.

7. Click Find Next. PowerPoint will search for a match.

8. Click Replace to replace the first match, and Find Next to continue, or Replace All to replace all occurrences.

9. Check your work.

Finding

Finding is actually a subset of replacing—the Find dialog box in Power-Point includes a Replace button if you decide to expand your Find operation into a Replace operation.

1. Choose Edit | Find.

2. Specify the text you are looking for.

3. Specify any restrictions (Match Case or Find Whole Word Only).

4. Use the Find Next button to find matches or Close to quit.

If you want to replace a word after finding this way, click the Replace button. You'll see the Replace dialog box, discussed in the preceding section.

note   *As you'll see in Chapter 28, PowerPoint does not have a Go To feature like Word or Excel's. Find can be of some help here, though: enter things like slide titles or unique text that you know is on a particular slide, and you can scoot from place to place that way.*

Adding and Removing Periods in Sentences

Here's a trick Word can't do that PowerPoint can—and it's a nice one. Maybe you can never decide whether to end each bullet list item with a period. Or perhaps you are combining the works of multiple authors with different styles. Either way, the Periods command can help.

1. Select the text you wish to conform.

2. Choose Periods from the Format menu.

3. Choose Add Periods or Remove Periods to suit your taste.

As illustrated in Figure 26-4, you should check your work after using this command. After all, computers are just dumb servants. They will obediently remove periods even after abbreviations like *etc.,* so you will have to put those periods back in after running the Periods command.

Formatting Text

While PowerPoint automatically chooses fonts, colors, character sizes, and the like, you can overrule these choices on individual slides and reports or for entire templates. You use toolbars, menu choices, and dialog boxes that will seem familiar from your work with other programs in the Office package.

Changing Fonts and Sizes

You have the usual tools at your disposal:

- The Formatting toolbar buttons
- Keyboard shortcuts
- The Font command
- The Replace Font command

FIGURE 26-4

You can quickly

add or remove

periods at the end

of bulleted lines

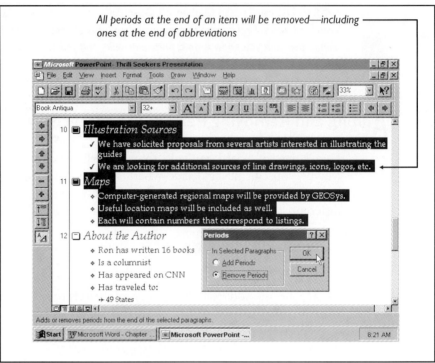

Select the text of interest and then apply the desired formatting. Power-Point will tell you if you need to switch views. Here are some examples of the less obvious formatting choices.

Shadow Effects

Perhaps you've noticed those shadow effects applied by some of the Microsoft AutoFormat features. You can also add them manually. Work in full-size views (choose 100% on the Standard toolbar) to get the best understanding of the effect:

1. Select the text.

2. Click the shadow button on the Formatting menu for default shadow effects, or choose Format | Shadows.

3. Make your choices in the resulting Shadow dialog box. Usually just a few points of Offset is all that's required.

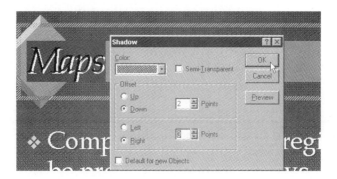

4. Click OK. You may need to deselect the text to see the results.

5. Experiment with different amounts of Offset.

warning *Moderation is a good thing when applying shadows. Nobody likes a show-off, and too much shadow effect makes text difficult to read.*

Embossing Text

Select the text and choose Emboss from the Font dialog box.

Underlining Text

To underline text, select it and use the Formatting toolbar's Underline button or the CTRL+U keyboard shortcut.

> ❖ <u>Travelers are restless</u>. In a recent survey
> 10,000 people between the ages of 21 and
> was clear that many of us *do* like to get t
> adrenaline flowing. Take a look at these
> survey results:

You may notice that the Underline feature in PowerPoint uses a continuous underline by default (that is, it includes the spaces and any punctuation between words). To underline single words, you must select and underline them one at a time.

---

tip   *These commands toggle; using them on underlined text removes the underline.*

Font Colors

Here are the steps for changing the color of text in PowerPoint:

1. Select the text.

2. Either click the Text Color button or choose Format | Font.

3. In the dialog box that appears, click on the Color list arrow.

4. Choose one of the basic colors shown on the palette, or choose Other Color.

> Automatic ☐
>
> Other Color...

5. If you chose Other Color, click on the desired color in the Colors dialog box.

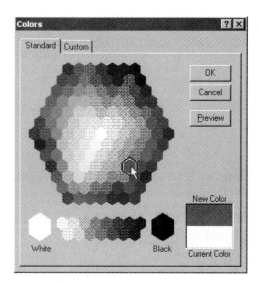

6. Click OK to finish up. You may need to deselect the text to experience the resulting show of color.

tip   *In the Colors dialog box, you can either choose a color shown or create your own on the Custom tab.*

Incidentally, you need not have a color display to use color. If you plan to print your output on a color printer, or send files to a slide-making company, you can specify colors on your black-and-white screen and get color output.

warning   *Picking colors for slides and overheads can be tricky. That's why PowerPoint makes many of those choices for you. If you plan to get creative, test your work using the output device and preferably the projection system you plan to use in your final presentations. The wrong color combinations can make things hard to read, and might make things seem to disappear entirely.*

Changing Case

PowerPoint lets you change the case of selected text. For instance, you can switch all text to uppercase, or automatically create "capitalized" sentences. Use the Format | Change Case command to do this. The resulting dialog box illustrates the effect of each available choice (including the rather interesting "tOGGLE cASE").

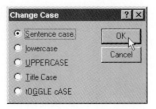

Alas, there is no Small Caps option; and this feature cares not a whit about the content of your document. So if you select a sentence containing acronyms like ASAP, you'll end up with things like asap or Asap, so check your work.

Replacing One Font with Another

When you change design templates, PowerPoint automatically changes fonts for you. You can also choose fonts on your own by using the Tools | Replace Fonts command.

1. Choose Tools | Replace Fonts. The Replace Font dialog box will appear.

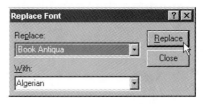

2. Choose the font that you wish to replace from the drop-down list, or type the font name.

3. Choose the replacement font from the second list, or type its name.

4. Click OK.

Behold. Check your slides; you may need to reformat some things (perhaps enlarge a title or body object here and there, or tighten line spacing to make things fit). If you hate the results, just replace the new font with the old font and try something else.

Line and Paragraph Spacing

You can change the amount of space between lines, and before and after paragraphs, in body objects and title objects. You can change all of the paragraphs in a text object, or just selected lines.

1. Select the line(s) or text object(s) you want to reformat.

2. Choose Format | Line Spacing.

3. Use the Line Spacing dialog box to specify new settings in either lines or points.

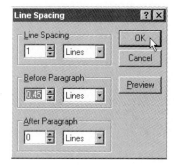

4. Click Preview to see the effect of your choices.

5. Click OK to make the changes.

Copying Text Styles

There are two ways to copy text formatting. One uses the Pick Up and Apply commands on the Format menu; the other uses a toolbar button. To copy text formatting with the menu commands:

1. Select the text containing the formatting you'd like to copy.

2. Choose Pick Up Text Style from the Format menu.

3. Select the text you want to reformat.

4. Choose Apply Text Style from the Format menu. (This choice is visible only after you've picked up some formatting.) The selected text will be reformatted.

If you don't select multiple words for reformatting, only the word containing the insertion point will be reformatted.

To use the Format Painter toolbar button on the Formatting toolbar:

1. Select the text containing the formatting you want to copy.

2. Click on the Format Painting toolbar button. It looks like a paintbrush.

3. The mouse pointer changes shape. (It will look like a paintbrush also.)

4. Click the text you want to reformat. The selected text will be reformatted.

Picking Bullets for Lists

You can use virtually any character from any font as a bullet in the bullet lists. You have control over the size and color of bullets as well.

1. Select the bulleted items you want to modify.

2. Choose Format | Bullets to open the Bullets dialog box.

3. Choose a font to explore in the Bullets From list.

4. To get an enlarged view of your candidates while still in the dialog box, click on individual symbols.

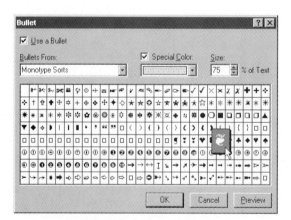

5. Specify a different color if you like.

6. Click the Preview button to see the proposed changes at work.

7. The size of the bullets is specified as a percentage of the text size. Use the Size text box to change this percentage if you like.

8. Click OK to make the change or Cancel to abort.

Aligning Text

You can right align, left align, center, or justify text just as you would in Word. There are even similar-looking toolbar buttons. Start by selecting text, then apply the desired formatting.

The Format menu's Alignment command offers the most options—found on a submenu, as illustrated in Figure 26-5.

Alternatively, you can use the Left and Center toolbar buttons, labeled in Figure 26-5.

Here, too, temperance is called for. PowerPoint does a pretty good job of aligning text all on its own. But excessive white space between justified words bothers some people.

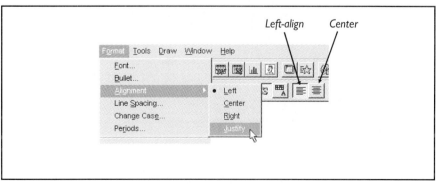

You can manually hyphenate words to minimize this.

FIGURE 26-5

First select the text to be aligned, and then use the Format | Alignment command or toolbar buttons to align it

CHAPTER 27

Working with Graphics and Multimedia in PowerPoint

T H E S E days, what's a presentation without graphics? In a PowerPoint presentation you can include virtually any graphic created with other programs. Examples include

- AutoCAD (.DXF) images
- Clip art from the ClipArt Gallery
- Computer Graphics Metafiles (.CGM)
- CompuServe .GIF images
- CorelDraw! (.CDR) files
- Excel charts (.XLS)
- Encapsulated PostScript (.EPS) images
- HP Graphics Language (.HPGL) images
- Joint Photographic Experts Group (.JPG) images
- Kodak Photo CD (.PCD) images
- Lotus 1-2-3 (.PIC) files
- Macintosh (.PICT) pictures and drawings
- Micrografx Designer/Draw (.DRW) images
- Microsoft Organization Chart 2.0 objects
- PC Paintbrush (.PCX) pictures
- Pictures created with Word's Drawing features
- Scanned images
- Tagged Image File format (.TIF) images
- Targa (.TGA) pictures

- Windows bitmap images of all kinds
- WordPerfect (.WPG) images
- And more...

Moreover, PowerPoint has a nifty AutoShape feature that can make anyone seem to draw like an artist. If you can draw, you'll find the usual collection of more traditional tools in PowerPoint, as well. Let's take a look at the various options.

Importing Images from the Outside World

The general steps for importing, sizing, and positioning images for use with PowerPoint are pretty straightforward. Here they are in a nutshell, followed by a couple of examples.

1. Open the PowerPoint presentation needing a graphic image.

2. Go to the slide needing the image or insert a new slide to receive the image. (Choose a slide layout specifically designed for graphics or any other.)

3. Use any of these commands: Insert | Picture, Insert | Clip Art, or Insert | Object.

4. Choose the type of graphic element you want to import, if more than one type is offered (PhotoCD, .TIF, bitmap, and so on).

5. Choose the filename of the desired image.

6. Click OK and PowerPoint will insert a full-size copy of the chosen image, converting its file format, if necessary.

7. Use your mouse to resize and reposition the graphic as desired.

8. To edit the image, you can just double-click on it.

With those general steps in mind, let's see some actual examples. We'll start with inserting clip art from Microsoft's ClipArt Gallery.

The ClipArt Gallery

Suppose you wanted to add some clip art to this slide.

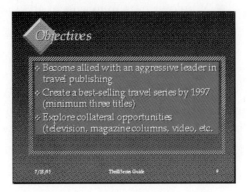

1. After switching to the slide and perhaps dragging the text object's bottom edge up to make room for the graphic on the slide, you could click on the George Jetson–looking Insert ClipArt button, shown at left, on PowerPoint's Formatting toolbar.

2. You'll see the ClipArt Gallery.

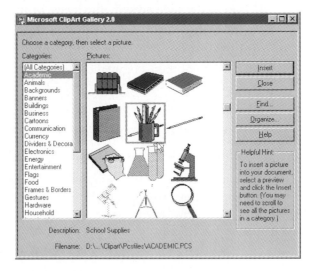

3. Browse the various categories and images, and double-click on the chosen picture. A copy of the picture will appear on your slide.

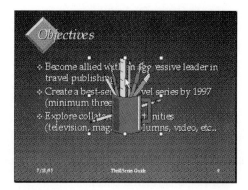

4. Drag a corner of the image to reduce its size, then drag the image itself, if necessary, to reposition it. Here, the image has been resized and repositioned.

5. Later, if you want to substitute a different image from the ClipArt Gallery, simply double-click on the graphic in your slide. This will bring up the Gallery. When you choose a *new* image from the Gallery, it will automatically shrink and position itself as a replacement for the old one. Too easy!

tip *There is a nifty feature called AutoClipArt, which you can turn on and off from the Tools menu. When activated, this feature will seek out and find appropriate clip art for your slides. Think of this as a high-tech golden retriever!*

Drawing in PowerPoint

There are a number of drawing tools available in PowerPoint. Use View | Toolbars to turn on the Drawing toolbar, Drawing+ toolbar, or both. The toolbars can be reshaped and moved, as is always the case.

Most of the drawing tools and concepts should be familiar to you if you've read Parts One and Two of this book, or used other Microsoft Windows programs. Others may not be as clear.

Manually Drawing Shapes and Lines

You've already learned how to use some Microsoft drawing facilities in Chapters 8 and 16. It's enough to know that you can follow these steps:

1. Switch to a slide where you want to insert a drawing or insert a new slide. If you use the Insert New Slide command, choose an AutoLayout that includes an object area and double-click in it.

2. Use the resulting dialog box to choose your favorite object type and related tools (PaintBrush, Word Picture—whatever). Some of your options are shown here.

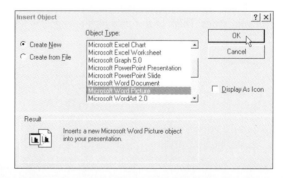

3. If you click Microsoft Word Picture, you will be taken to Word's drawing utility. Draw using the line, shape, text, and other drawing tools, as shown in Figure 27-1.

4. When you close the drawing window (by clicking Close), your masterpiece will be inserted into the slide, where it can be resized and moved with your mouse.

5. To edit the drawing, just double-click on it.

FIGURE 27-1

Draw shapes and lines using a variety of tools

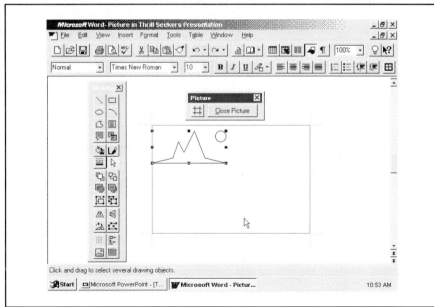

AutoShape for Everyday Objects

PowerPoint offers a nifty AutoShape drawing feature that's worth a look. It's less complicated than Draw and combines a small collection of clip art with some text tools.

1. Switch to the slide needing artwork or insert a new slide.

2. Choose View | Toolbars to display the AutoShapes toolbar.

3. Pick a shape from the AutoShapes toolbar (such as the Balloon Tool cartoon balloon).

4. Drag with your mouse to define the desired size of the chosen graphic.

5. Position the graphic by selecting it and then dragging it.

6. Use the toolbar's text tools to add text, then use the Formatting toolbar to embellish the text, if you like. For instance, the example shows centered bold text in the balloon graphic.

7. Resize them if necessary to make things fit by dragging on handles.

8. Group the text and graphic if you like, to make them easier to move simultaneously.

9. Drag the drawn object and/or text objects to move them.

Inserting Photos in Your PowerPoint Presentation

You can insert scanned photos into PowerPoint slides, but there are some things you should know.

First of all, photos take *lots* of disk space, particularly if the images are large and in color. This is particularly important to know if you plan to pass around your PowerPoint presentations on floppies.

Photos slow down the loading of slides and the process of switching from slide to slide in an electronic presentation, particularly if you are using a slow machine. Rehearse on the machine you'll use for the presentation to see if this will be a problem.

Large photos can also slow you when editing a presentation, since it takes time for the photos to be displayed. Consider leaving "holes" where the photos will go, and then insert the actual images at the end of your creation process.

Photos may *print* better than they look *onscreen* if you do not have a high-resolution monitor. For instance, look how dark this onscreen image is:

This image can be found on the office CD in Fun Stuff/Pictures.

This is not a big problem unless you plan to give onscreen presentations. If you do, consider investing in a high-resolution monitor and display card. Preview before the audience arrives to see what to expect.

Save early and often when working with photos. The memory gods will get you sooner or later. In fact, this happened even as these words were written....Fortunately, the presentation had been saved before the printing attempt.

It takes a long time to print slides containing photos. Leave yourself plenty of extra time for printing if your presentation has photos.

Inserting Videos in Your PowerPoint Presentation

If pictures are good, moving pictures must be even better, right? PowerPoint lets you add videos to your presentations to wow people even more. Here are the steps:

1. In Slide View, switch to the slide needing the video or insert a new slide.

2. Choose Insert | Movie to display the Insert Movie dialog box.

3. Double-click a movie from the list to insert it.

4. Right-click on the movie to bring up the pop-up menu and choose Animation Settings.

5. In the Animation Settings dialog box, in the Play Options list, click on Play (Don't Play is the default). Then click OK.

6. Go to Slide Show view to preview your movie.

7. Movies work as if they were extra slides, a lot like a build (discussed earlier). When you reach a slide with a video, press SPACEBAR to play it (see Figure 27-2).

8. You can stop, pause, or replay the video at any time by using the video controls. You can advance to the next slide by pressing SPACEBAR, or navigate in your slide show using any of the usual techniques.

Inserting Sound in Your PowerPoint Presentation

You can add sound to your PowerPoint slides, in addition to the transition sounds, by following the same steps just outlined for movies. When you get to step 2, just choose Insert | Sounds rather than Insert | Movie. All the other steps are the same.

FIGURE 27-2

You can play videos in PowerPoint. Wow!

■

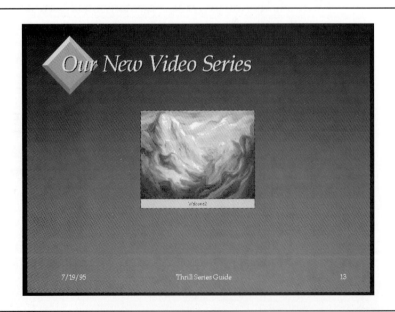

CHAPTER 28

Showtime!

I T'S almost time for those sweaty palms. You've combined your greatest thoughts with wonderful graphics and a color scheme that yells "promote me, now!"

But before you jump into the spotlight, it might be worth taking some extra time to polish your work, rehearse, prepare for unexpected questions, and create some handouts. That's what this chapter is all about.

f We Can Put a Man on the Moon...

Why can't a presentation be given without some kind of audio-visual equipment meltdown? You've seen it. Rhodes scholars, Nobel-laureates, doctors, lawyers—all looking like idiots because their slide show's messed up.

Chances are they all have one thing in common. They didn't rehearse with their final material in the room where the presentation was to be given on the equipment that was to be used for the real show (preferably on the *day of the show*).

Of course, you can't always do that. But whenever possible, *try*. Some projectors don't throw certain colors very well. If you are using someone else's computer for an electronic presentation, does it have enough RAM for that beefy slide number 12 with the full-color photo, or will it lock up? Does the borrowed or rented computer have the proper fonts, or are you headed for disaster? The *only* way to minimize embarrassment is rehearsal. There. Enough said.

Arranging, Previewing, and Rehearsing

The sequence of information in a presentation is often as important as the content itself. PowerPoint makes it easy for you to try different slide sequences by yourself or with friendly coworkers in rehearsals. Start with a desktop slide show, then switch to the Slide Sorter to move things around, or even to delete unnecessary slides. Here's how.

tip *PowerPoint was created by programmers who built in features that not even the program's designers know about. These are not always obvious, though; so next time you're making a presentation, keep an eye on tasks that are taking you a long time. Chances are there's a quick work around that's not in the documentation. This book does its best to tell you about things here, but there's no substitute for experience...*

Desktop Slide Shows

Unless you have a monster monitor on your computer, desktop slide shows are best for rehearsing and for very small group huddles. Here are the steps to present a desktop slide show.

After opening the presentation file, switch to the first slide. You can do this in any view, but the technique varies:

■ In *Slide Sorter view,* click on the first slide.

■ In *Outline view,* click on the first slide's icon.

■ In *Slide view,* drag the scroll box at the right of your screen all the way to the top. Watch the slide numbers that appear as you drag.

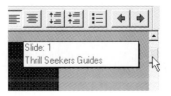

Begin the slide show either by picking Slide Show from PowerPoint's View menu, or by clicking on the Slide Show button illustrated in the margin.

All of PowerPoint's familiar menus and other tools will disappear. If you've been running the Office Shortcut Bar, it will still be visible. To remove it, choose Exit from the icon menu.

In the bottom-left corner of the slide show screen you'll see a button used to access a pop-up menu. Here you control whether you have a piece of electronic "chalk" with which you can scribble temporary onscreen lines while presenting:

tip *You can erase anything you've written by pressing E. Also, you might find it easier to write from top to bottom of the screen; you'd probably do this anyway, but it's worth mentioning!*

To enable the pen, either click on the button or right-click, then choose Pen from the menu. To draw, just use your mouse and mouse buttons.

The scribbles do not permanently scar your masterpieces. Press E on your keyboard to erase all onscreen marks. And, when you switch to another slide, the drawings will vanish. That's the good news and the bad. If someone "chalks" something important, *make notes*, because the electronic chalk marks will be squirted like watermelon seeds out of the universe when you change slides. Chalk it up to experience...

tip *You can also use your mouse pointer while presenting. Move it around the screen to point to things you want to emphasize. To hide the mouse pointer (and the little drawing button) press A or the equal sign (=).*

Manually Advancing Slides

To manually move from slide to slide during a slide show, you can do any of the following:

- To advance to the next slide, press SPACEBAR, click the primary (usually the left) mouse button, or press N, RIGHT ARROW or DOWN ARROW, or PAGE DOWN.

- To go back one slide, press BACKSPACE, click the nonprimary (usually the right) mouse button, or press P, LEFT ARROW or UP ARROW, or PAGE UP.

- To go to a specific slide, type the slide number, and press ENTER. For example, to go to slide 5, you'd type 5 and then press ENTER.

- To go to the first slide in your presentation, simultaneously press and hold *both* mouse buttons for at least two seconds, and then release them both.

- To quit a slide show and return to the previous view, press ESC, CTRL + BREAK , or either of your computer's minus keys.

tip *If a slide is distracting your audience and you want to temporarily hide it without advancing to the next slide, press B to blacken the screen or W to make the screen all white. These choices toggle, so pressing B when the screen is black or W when the screen is white will bring your slide back into view.*

Transition and Build Effects

You know those fancy video transition effects weather forecasters use on the television news? Some remind you of venetian blinds, others look like confetti....Or a nearly blank slide fades up, then lines of text reveal themselves one at a time to *build* the completed slide. PowerPoint provides its own suite of transition and build effects, which you can add to your onscreen shows. Here's how.

Transitions

Transition effects dictate how one slide leaves the screen and how the next arrives.

1. Switch to Slide Sorter view.

2. Select the slide that you want to transition *from* (or pick the first slide if you want to transition *into* your presentation).

3. Pick a transition effect from the drop-down list.

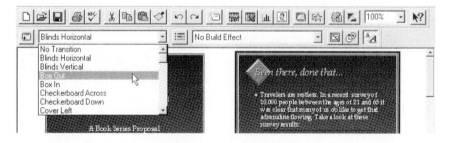

4. Watch the *selected slide* in Slide Sorter view as you pick the effect. It will demonstrate the transition for you.

5. Select the next slide and choose another effect.

6. You may need to switch to Slide Show to understand the full impact of these transitions, then switch back to Slide Sorter and try other effects until you see one you like. Some combinations work well together on adjacent slides, like Cover Right and Uncover Left. Experiment.

tip *You can select multiple slides and apply the same effect to all of them at once. Simply hold down SHIFT while you click on each of the slides you want to influence.*

Removing Transitions

To remove transitions, select the slide or slides of interest, and choose No Transition from the transition list.

Changing the Speed of Transitions

To change the speed of transitions, use the Transition button (next to the transition list) to reveal the Transition dialog box. The preview box shows you what the transition will look like. Here's one in mid-transition!

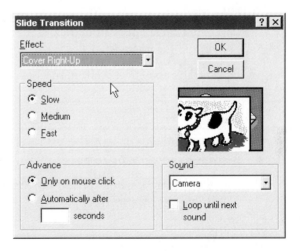

Pick Slow, Medium, or Fast from the Speed section. Faster is usually better. Another neat trick is to add sound to the transition. You can choose among a number of sounds from the Sound list. Want applause? a camera click? breaking glass? an explosion? Any of these is only a mouse-click away.

tip *If you don't like any of the sounds that come with PowerPoint, you can use ones that you've created. Just choose Other from the Sound list to reach a standard Windows Open dialog box and round up the usual suspects.*

Automatically Advancing Slides

While most speakers like to manually advance slides in order to maintain full control over their presentations, you can ask PowerPoint to change slides at timed intervals. This works well for trade shows where you want to let a presentation run continuously and unattended, or when you have a precise presentation time limit that you cannot exceed.

Even when you let PowerPoint advance slides at timed intervals, you can intervene. Here's how automatic advancing is accomplished:

1. Open your presentation in Slide Sorter view.

2. Click or SHIFT + click to select the slide or slides for which you plan to specify an onscreen time.

3. Click on the Transition button to reveal the Transition dialog box illustrated a moment ago.

4. Click in the box next to the word "Seconds" and enter the desired onscreen time. (The Automatically After button will automatically be selected for you.)

5. Pick a transition effect while in this dialog box, if you haven't already.

6. Click OK.

7. To rehearse, run the slide show and see how the timings feel to you. Remember, you can always use the keyboard and mouse buttons to advance or go back.

8. There's another keyboard trick worth knowing: to pause the automatic advance feature, press S.

tip *If you forget the keyboard controls while presenting in Slide Show mode, press F1 for an onscreen list of shortcuts. Don't be embarrassed. Remember: nobody else in the room can run "AV" equipment either. Click OK or press ENTER to make the help screen disappear.*

Running a Presentation Continuously

To run a presentation nonstop (in a trade show booth, for instance):

1. Open the presentation.

2. Make sure all your slides have transition times assigned to them.

3. Choose View | Slide Show. You'll see the Slide Show dialog box.

4. Select the range of slides to be shown (or use the All default).

5. Select Use Slide Timings in the Advance section of the Slide Show dialog box.

6. Click the Show button.

7. The show will run continuously until you press ESC (but watch it in its entirety before going on that coffee break, just in case).

8. Move the keyboard and mouse out of sight and out of reach to frustrate the mischievous, but *don't* (even though the Microsoft manual suggests this) unplug the keyboard and/or mouse with your computer running.

tip *Notice that in the Slide Show dialog box, you can control the color of the pen. This is very useful if you know you'll be highlighting things that have a light background, for instance, because you'll want a dark pen.*

Changing Slide Timing

After you've rehearsed or presented a show a few times, you may decide to tweak slide timing. In fact, PowerPoint can watch you give the show and learn the timings. (Just don't stop to answer the phone while doing this.)

1. Choose View | Slide Show.

2. Pick Rehearse New Timings from the Advance options.

3. Click the Show button. A little clock/button appears in the lower-left corner of the screen.

4. When the current slide's been onscreen long enough, click the clock/button to advance to the next one.

5. Continue this way through the entire show. At the end of the show, PowerPoint will tell you the total running time, and ask if you want to save the timings:

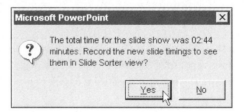

6. If you switch to Slide Sorter view, you'll also see the times. (You can change individual times here, as well.)

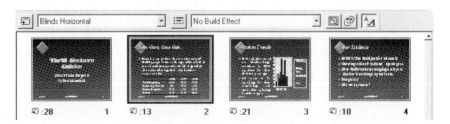

Using Build Slides

Don't you hate when you project a slide and half the room reads ahead and then interrupts with questions on topics you were going to cover in a moment anyway? Build slides can help you avoid this.

The quickest way to specify builds is to select the material that you want to reveal in a series of steps, then click the Build button illustrated at left. It's located on the Slide Sorter toolbar.

For example, suppose you wanted to reveal a list of book titles one at a time.

1. Click on the slide of interest in Slide Sorter view.

2. Choose a build effect from the Text Build Effects list.

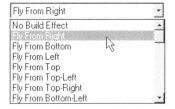

3. Switch to the Slide Show to see the build effect.

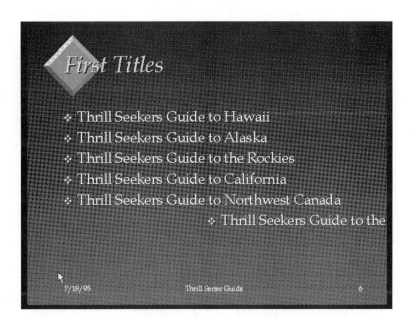

tip *If you wish to add different effects to each individual object in the box, see the section "Using Other Animation Special Effects," next.*

Each time you advance one "slide" (by clicking, using SPACEBAR, and so on), the screen will contain an additional bulleted line, until the entire build is complete.

Using Other Animation Special Effects

PowerPoint now comes with a wonderful array of animation effects. You can make text pinwheel in, drive by, drop in, and so on. These effects are incredibly cool. You apply these animation effects as follows:

1. Click the Animation Effects button on the Standard toolbar. This brings up the Animation Effects toolbar.

2. Find the slide to which you want to apply effects in Slide view.

3. Click the objects you want to emphasize.

4. Then click the appropriate button on the toolbar.

5. You can also choose an option from one of the Tools | Build Slide Text submenus. If you choose Tools | Build Slide Text | Other, the Animation Settings dialog box appears.

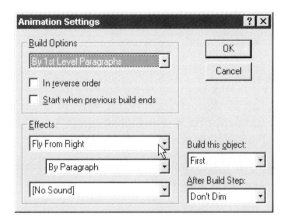

6. Here you can make all sorts of adjustments to how your animation works. You can even specify what should happen to items after the build (for example, fade, become a certain color, and so on).

Hiding Slides

Slides can be included in your presentation file but not shown in the presentation. Simply select the slide or slides in Outline, Slide Sorter, or Slide view, and then choose Tools | Hide Slide.

There's also a Hide Slide button in Slide Sorter view, illustrated to the left.

warning   *Hidden slides don't get displayed in your shows unless you force them, but the slide numbers do not change, so savvy audience members may notice that your onscreen slide numbers jump from 10 to 12, and challenge you. Be ready to show the hidden slide or explain why you're not showing it.*

You can display a hidden slide at any time by typing its number and pressing ENTER. Pressing H will also reveal a hidden slide; you press H while viewing the slide preceding the hidden one.

$\int$howing Slides Out of Order

From time to time you may need to present slides out of sequence (*branch*, in PowerPoint parlance) in response to questions from your audience or to reiterate a point, or you might want to resequence your show entirely because you've discovered a better way to present your information. These are standard orders of business for any good presentation package, and Power-Point makes it easy to do both.

Branching and Drilling Down

During your presentation you can branch to a slide out of sequence whenever the need arises by simply typing the slide number and pressing ENTER. Alternatively, you can right-click and choose Go from the menu. You can also *drill down*—branch to another application to show an embedded object—to reach the source of the information on the current slide if you've included linked, embedded objects (like Excel worksheets, Word tables, or PowerPoint slides from other presentations). Simply double-click on them to bring up the source document. Alternatively, you can use the Drilling Down button on the Standard toolbar. (This assumes, of course, that the source document is on the computer being used for the presentation.) Realize, too, that the process can sometimes be painfully slow. So rehearse first if you plan to show off this way in a big meeting.

Resequencing

To change the order of slides permanently:

1. Switch to Slide Sorter view or Outline view.

2. Point to a slide (or its icon in Outline view).

3. Hold down the mouse button and drag. The mouse pointer's shape will change, and you'll see a line indicating the proposed new position of the slide.

4. Release the mouse button when the line indicates the correct slide position. The slide will move and be renumbered automatically along with those that follow it.

Deleting Slides

To delete a slide or slides:

1. Switch to Slide Sorter view or Outline view.

2. Click to select the slide (or its icon in Outline view).

3. Press DEL or choose Edit | Delete Slide.

To delete multiple slides at once, SHIFT + click to select them, and then press DEL .

warning   *You are **not** asked to confirm the deletion of slides. Use of Undo will restore something you've just deleted, but be careful!*

Printing Presentation Elements

PowerPoint's Print dialog box offers choices not found in other Office applications.

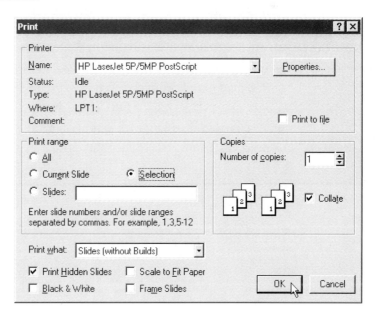

You can access the Print dialog box choosing File | Print, the CTRL+P shortcut, or the Print toolbar button.

Most of the choices are pretty obvious. Select the desired item to be printed from the drop-down Print What list (slides, handouts, and so on). Here are some printing tips:

- You can specify a range of slides either by typing the numbers in the range (**3–6**, for instance), or by selecting slides in Sorter or Outline view and then specifying printing of selected items.

- If you are making overhead transparencies and plan to mount them in cardboard or plastic frames, be sure the frames won't cut off information in your slides. If necessary, change the margins in the slide master to make the images fall within the frames' openings.

- When you print handouts of slides, you can request reduced size copies (2, 3, or 6 slides per page) from the Print What list, as shown in Figure 28-1. The Handouts (6 slides per page) choice usually provides very legible results and saves some paper.

- Multiple sets will come out of the printer faster if you don't ask the computer to collate. Then you'll need to hand collate, so only you can decide which approach is quicker overall.

- If you pick the Slides [Without Builds] choice on the Print dialog box's Print What drop-down list, you'll get *one* copy of build slides, containing all the slide's lines. Choosing Slides [With Builds] will give you multiple copies of the slides, one at each build stage.

- When printing handouts or overhead masters from presentations designed with 35mm slide settings, use the Scale To Fit Paper option.

- To change the orientation and margins of slide, outline, and note printouts, choose File | Slide Setup. You'll see the Slide Setup dialog box.

Printing six slides

to a sheet can

save paper while

still providing

legible results

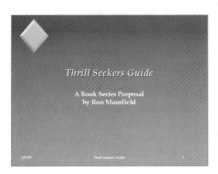

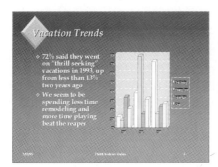

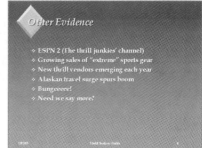

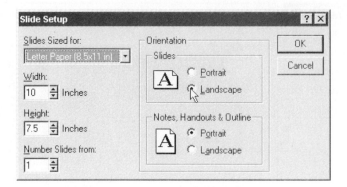

Creating Overhead Transparencies

A number of companies sell overhead transparency materials for laser and inkjet printers. Since not all transparency materials work in all printers, do some research ahead of time. Test print and test project, if possible. Follow the printer and material manufacturers' suggestions for loading transparency material. There is usually only one side of the material that is designed to accept an image.

note *Consider whether you want your hidden slides to be included in handouts. If you want to print hidden slides, check the Print Hidden Slides choice in PowerPoint's Print dialog box before printing.*

Obtaining Color 35mm Slides

Many service bureaus can convert PowerPoint files into 35mm slides. In fact, PowerPoint comes with special GraphicsLinksoftware for use with Genigraphics slide delivery services. Expect to pay around $9 per slide for non rush service, more if you are in a panic. It's even possible to send PowerPoint files to Genigraphics through your modem, and get the slides back the next day via express courier. Your PowerPoint software came with a brochure explaining these services. If you need more information or assistance, you can contact Genigraphics at 800-638-7348.

Here are the general steps for using the Genigraphics driver; refer to the Genigraphics literature for details.

1. Open the presentation and select the first slide.

2. Choose File | Send To Genigraphics.

3. Follow the instructions.

4. Click OK to print the slides to disk or to use the modem connection, depending on which you've selected in the Send Via area of the dialog box.

tip *It's a good idea to do a test run with your slide-making vendor before sending a large, important project. And be sure you understand all of the costs involved (one-time setup fees, costs for duplicates, dial-in surcharges, and so on).*

Sharing Presentation Files with Others

You can share your presentations with other computer users in several ways. The most obvious is to play "pass the floppy," or to send a copy of the presentation file via network or modem. These straightforward approaches will work if the other user has the same version of PowerPoint on his or her computer, along with all the fonts you've used in your presentation.

If you've used only TrueType fonts in your presentation and think the recipient might not have the fonts, you can send them along with your presentation by clicking the Embed TrueType Fonts option in the File Save dialog box:

Sending along embedded fonts can greatly increase the size of a presentation file, so do it only when necessary. Not all TrueType fonts can be embedded this way. Experiment.

tip *When sharing presentations with others on a network, it is sometimes possible to share "downloadable" fonts stored on the server. Check with your network administrator or help desk for assistance.*

Obviously, if you plan to exchange presentations on floppy disks, they'll need to fit, or you'll need to use some file compression or backup-and-restore scheme. For instance, the main 12-slide Thrill Seeker example shown in this book is about 1.2MB in size, due mainly to the map and small grayscale photo at the end. If you added another large graphic or embedded fonts, it would be too big for most floppy formats.

note *Users without PowerPoint on their computers can play your presentations (but not edit them) if you send along the Viewer. You'll need one 1.44MB floppy for the Viewer and its installer, and another disk or disks for your presentation. See online Help for details.*

PART 5

Managing Your Data with Access

As you have seen in the previous chapters, Office provides many ways to collect and organize business and personal information. But while Word and Excel are fine for small to medium projects, you may need the extra features, speed, and flexibility provided by Microsoft Access for larger jobs.

Access is an integral part of Microsoft Office Professional; if you have the Standard version of Office, you can purchase Access separately and add it to the Standard version. We'll take a look in these next few chapters at how this database management system can help you collect, find, and use mountains of data.

CHAPTER 29

Introduction to Access

MICROSOFT Access is a fully featured *database management system (DBMS)* that lets you collect, organize, find, display, and print information about your personal and business life. The amount and variety of information it can deal with is staggering. Since folks at Microsoft have done much of the setup work for a variety of common database management tasks, it's easy for you to start working with simple, professional-looking information systems in a matter of moments. Access comes with Wizards and a variety of predefined database elements that let you keep track of the following common information with only a few clicks of your mouse:

- Asset tracking
- Book collection
- Contacts lists (personal and business)
- Donations
- Event management
- Expenses
- Household inventories
- Inventory control
- Ledgers
- Memberships
- Music-collection inventories
- Order-taking and -tracking systems
- Payment-tracking systems
- Picture libraries
- Recipes

- Resource scheduling

- Service call management

- Student and class records

- Time and billing

- Video collection inventories

- Wine lists

- Workouts

Of course, you can create your own tools, or modify any of these for your own situations. Moreover, you can combine tools to form complex systems. For instance, while the video collection tools in Access were designed for personal use, they can quite easily be combined with other elements like reservation and invoicing tools to run a video rental store. You'll see examples of this shortly.

But we are getting ahead of ourselves. Let's start with some basics.

Access System Requirements

Let's face it. Computer programs are getting bigger and slower. (But then, aren't we all?) Access is no exception. Here are Microsoft's minimum and recommended system configurations for Access:

Component	Minimum	Recommended
Computer	80486 SX or greater	Pentium or greater
RAM	8MB	16MB
Hard disk space (for programs)	5MB (minimum installation)	19MB+ (typical installation)
Monitor	EGA	VGA or higher
DOS version	DOS 7.0	Current MS-DOS version

In addition, you'll need a mouse or other compatible pointing device (like a trackball), and plenty of hard disk space for your database files. Access works with virtually all printers supported by Windows. A tape drive or other device capable of backing up large files would also be a good idea.

Upgrading from Earlier Access Versions

While version 7 can open and use databases created with earlier versions of Access, the reverse is not true. And, since once you've used an old database with version 7, you won't be able to open it directly with earlier Access versions, eventually you'll probably want to convert all of your databases (and coworkers) to version 7. Think of it as contributing to the economy, at least in and around Redmond, if that makes the investment in new software less painful.

tip *Hard disk space permitting, if you have an earlier version of Access installed on your PC (Access 2.0 or 2.1), you might initially want to keep it installed, and place Access version 7 in a separate directory. This is particularly important if you share databases over a network with people who have not yet upgraded to version 7.*

Access Concepts and Terms

Microsoft has its own take on certain standard DBMS terms and has added a few new terms to the database world; so even if you're a seasoned pro, you should skim this next section.

Database

A *database* is simply a collection of useful data. The phone book is an example. So is your office filing cabinet, or a Rolodex full of cards. Access databases include such objects as tables, queries, forms, and more.

Tables

In Access-ese, *tables* are collections of *similar data*. For instance, if you ran a videotape rental store, you might have an Access table that collects information about each tape you own (title, running length, date purchased, tape inventory number, and so on). A portion of it might look like this:

	Video Collection ID	Movie Title	Subject	Rating	Length	Y
▶						
	1	Thelma and Lassie	Our heroes take a trip	NC-17	120	1ξ
	2	The Clinton Election	A stranger comes to town	PG-13	240	1ξ
	3	Bad Day at Blackrock	A stranger comes to town	NR	90	1ξ
	4	My Amazing String Collection	A boy and his string	G	45	1ξ
*						

Tape Inventory : Table

Record: 1 of 5

You might also have a *different* table that collects customer's names, phone numbers, membership numbers, addresses, and so on:

Customer ID	Last Name	First Name	Phone Number
1	Rather-Knot	Ide	(818) 555-9392
2	Gone	Hellen	(310) 555-3400
3	Sea	Abee	(310) 555-1124
4	Foolzday	April	(818) 555-9043
5	Reed-Moore	Wanda	(213) 555-3367
6	Johnson	J.J.	(818) 555-3392

There might be yet another table where you keep information about which customer has reserved which tape for which night, and so on. With Access, all of these tables would be organized differently, and contain mostly different information; but they'd all be in the *same* database file.

For instance, you might have a database file called *Video Store* containing tables named *Members, Tapes, Reservations,* and so on. These tables are stored in the same database file because they are often used together to create reports, to help you fill out onscreen forms, and so forth. The following illustration shows how parts of a simple Access video store database might look as separate tables.

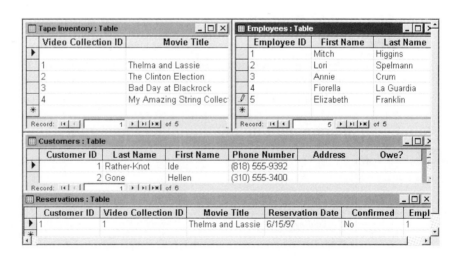

Relational Databases

Access is a *relational database,* which means that it allows data that has been stored in different places (normally in various Access tables) to be *linked.* (The "relational" part of the term actually refers to a class of operations described by a branch of mathematics called *set theory* rather than from the relationships between data, but that needn't concern us here.) For instance, whenever your video store employee enters a customer's phone number into an onscreen invoice form, Access could look up the customer's name, address, and membership number from the tables that contain that data.

You'll learn more about this concept in Chapter 35. For now, it's enough to know that relational database tools like Access can help you manage information in three important ways. They can

- Reduce redundancy
- Facilitate the sharing of information
- Keep data accurate

All of these will be discussed in the upcoming chapters.

Records

A *record* is all the information contained in *one row* of an Access datasheet table. In the video store example, the store's employee records might include a row (a record) for each employee, as shown in Figure 29-1.

Fields

Fields are places in a table where you store individual chunks of information. If you look at Figure 29-1, for instance, you'll see that there's a field called Employee ID, another called First Name, and so on.

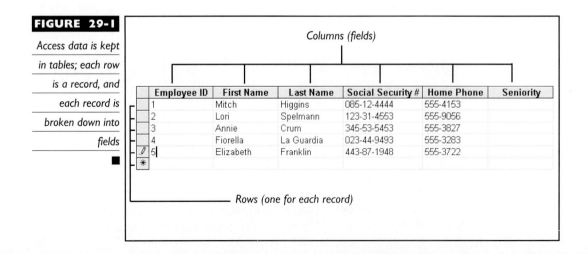

FIGURE 29-1

Access data is kept in tables; each row is a record, and each record is broken down into fields ■

Columns (fields)

Employee ID	First Name	Last Name	Social Security #	Home Phone	Seniority
1	Mitch	Higgins	085-12-4444	555-4153	
2	Lori	Spelmann	123-31-4553	555-9056	
3	Annie	Crum	345-53-5453	555-3827	
4	Fiorella	La Guardia	023-44-9493	555-3283	
5|	Elizabeth	Franklin	443-87-1948	555-3722	

Rows (one for each record)

Primary Key and Other Indexed Fields

Access uses *key fields* and *indexing* to help speed many database operations. You can tell Access which fields should be key fields, or Access can assign them automatically. You'll learn more about these later.

Controls and Objects

Controls are Access *objects* that help you display, print, and use your data. They can be things like field labels that you drag around when designing reports, for instance. Or they can be pictures, or titles for reports, or boxes containing the results of calculations.

tip   As you'll see, Microsoft refers to a rather confusing collection of things as controls and objects. Even though the terms are not synonymous, often the terms are used interchangeably in Microsoft's documentation. Don't fret. Such terms will make more sense later.

Queries and Dynasets

When you request a list of all videotapes that were due back yesterday and did not arrive, that's a *query*. Queries are *requests* to Access for information. When Access *responds* with its list of overdue tapes, that response constitutes a *dynaset*—a dynamic set of data meeting your query criteria.

Because of the way Access is designed, dynasets are updated even after you've made your query. So, if your video store has networked computers, and if you display a list of overdue tapes, and someone checks in an overdue tape on another computer, your dynaset will *automatically* update to reflect the returned tape. (This works in theory, anyway. In practice it seems to make a difference just how your machines are networked. In some cases you have to *ask* Access to update your dynaset, by pressing SHIFT+F9.)

Forms

Forms are onscreen arrangements that make it easy to enter and read data. You can also print the forms if you want to. You can design forms yourself, or let the Access *AutoForm* feature do it for you. Here's a sample AutoForm for the Reservations table in the video store database:

Reports

Reports are (usually) paper copies of dynasets. You can also print reports "to disk," if you like. Here, too, Access can help create the reports. There are even Wizards for complex printouts like Crosstab reports—reports in which the data is cross-tabulated. You'll learn much more about reports in Chapter 34.

Properties

Properties are the specifications (or characteristics) you assign to parts of your database design. For instance, each field's properties can include things like the type of data (text, numbers, and so on) and the format of the data (number of decimal places, type style, color, and so on). You can define properties for fields, forms, controls, and most other Access objects.

Calculations, Expressions, and Functions

If you own a store and decide to give certain customers a discount on rentals, you can have Access do the calculations as required. You instruct Access to perform specific calculations by building *expressions* using built-in *functions* (which will remind you of those in Excel). You'll learn how in Chapter 36.

Wizards

Unless you've just picked up this book, you've already met some *Wizards*. These are built-in assistants that know how to guide you through steps necessary for common tasks.

Access Wizards can help you create

- Queries
- Tables
- Forms
- Reports
- Macros
- Mailing labels
- Modules
- Controls and buttons

Like Word, Excel, and PowerPoint, Access also has an Answer Wizard, which can answer questions that you type in real English. For instance, you could ask "How do I create a form?" and the Wiz, all knowing, would tell or show you.

Macros

Macros are tools that can help automate complex or time-consuming repetitive manual tasks. Consultants and advanced users often set up macros to help simplify things for less experienced users and to make databases "bullet-proof." You get an introduction to macros in Chapter 36.

Command Buttons

Command buttons are onscreen objects that you can click on to run macros. You'll get a chance to create your own buttons in Chapter 36.

Modules and Access Basic

Modules are programs that advanced users create with *Access Basic,* a programming language. These programs can perform complex operations not possible with Access alone or even Access with macros. While a full treatment of Access Basic is beyond the scope of this book, you'll get a glimpse of how it can be used with macros in Chapter 36.

∫tarting and Quitting Access

Enough theory, let's process some data! Once you've properly installed Access (see the installation instructions in Appendix A, if necessary), you start it in the usual ways. That is, with Windows already running, do one of the following:

■ *In the Office Shortcut Bar,* click on the Access button (the one with the image of a key):

■ *Or, from the Start menu,* choose Access from the Programs submenu:

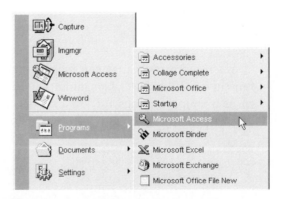

■ *Or, in Windows Explorer* (or any open window), double-click on the Access icon:

Microsoft
Access

■ *Or, in Windows Explorer* (or any open window), double-click on an Access database file:

Video Store

Quitting Access

Always use the Exit command on the Access File menu (or ALT+F, X) to quit Access. This provides for an orderly shutdown and will prompt you to save any recent changes to database elements.

If you attempt to quit Windows with Access still running, Access will also prompt you for any necessary saves, then shut down properly.

The Access Workspace and Tools

In addition to the usual Windows tools (a menu bar, control boxes, and so on), the Access window (shown in Figure 29-2) contains some other items of interest.

The Access Window

The Access window contains the menu, toolbars, and other windows you use to create and use data.

The Database Window

The Database window lets you both create and see database elements (tables, queries, forms, and so on). In Figure 29-2 you can see the Database window for the video store example. Clicking on the various tabs in the

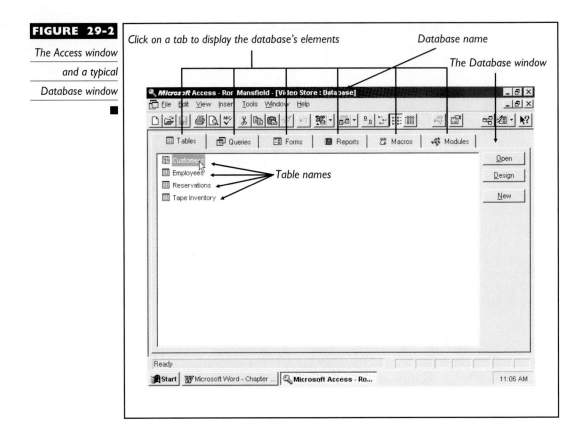

FIGURE 29-2

The Access window
and a typical
Database window

window reveals lists of the various tables, forms, reports, and other elements that have been created for the database.

The Status Area

As with other Microsoft applications, get in the habit of checking the status area at the bottom of the Access window. It can often tell you what's going on, what the tool you are pointing to will do, or what's going wrong.

Menus

Menus work as you'd expect, but they change quite often in Access, depending on what you are doing at the time. As in other well-behaved programs, there are keyboard shortcuts (like CTRL+S for Save); the shortcuts are displayed on the menus. There are mouseless ways to issue virtually all the menu commands.

Shortcut Menus

In most situations, holding down the nonprimary mouse button (usually the right one) produces a short list of actions that can be taken at that time.

For example, if you right-click on a table name in the Database window, you'll see a menu that allows you to rename the table, print its contents, and so on:

Toolbars

Access has toolbars galore, many of them appearing automatically when you need them. You can resize and reposition them by dragging, as with other Microsoft applications. Moreover, you can customize them just as you can with the other Office programs.

Views

The term *views* can be a little confusing in Access, because there is so much onscreen commotion. The three "official" views are *Datasheet view, Design view,* and *Form view.* They all have to do with the way the data you're looking at is arranged onscreen. Unfortunately, there is also a View menu, which has to do with the different lists of database objects (Tables, Queries, Forms, Reports, and so on) that you can see in the Database window. The View menu lets you switch these lists; but since the tabs along the side of the Database window do the same thing, you won't be losing anything if you conveniently forget that the View menu exists.

In any case, Access usually switches views for you as needed anyway (when you click on a particular toolbar button, for instance).

Online Help for Access

The usual, comprehensive Microsoft online Help is available in Access, and it's described in Chapter 2, so it won't be redescribed in detail. Like the Help menu in the other Office programs, the Help menu in Access offers an index and allows you to search by keywords using the Answer Wizard. You can also obtain information about Microsoft's technical support programs. This is also where you go for the About Microsoft Access command, which provides version, owner, serial number, and system information.

In addition to the Help menu, the *Access Help button* lets you explore the various Access tools by pointing and clicking. As a review, in case you've forgotten how this works in other programs:

1. Click on the Help button (at the right end of the Database toolbar).

2. Click on the onscreen item of interest.

3. Read the resulting onscreen help.

4. Close the Help window by picking Exit from Help's File menu or by clicking on the Help window's close box; or use the key sequence ALT+F, X.

Microsoft's Sample Databases

Access comes with three sample database files worth exploring. These are Nwind.mdb, Orders.mdb, and Solution.mdb. They can be found in the Samples subfolder of the Access folder. If you are new at database management, let the Cue Cards walk you through Nwind.mdb, a collection of information used by a fictitious worldwide gourmet food company.

Experienced database users will also want to poke at the Orders and Solution database files to see what makes them tick.

When you're ready to create your own database, turn the page and let's get started.

CHAPTER 30

Creating a Simple Database
and Tables

T

ABLES are key ingredients to an Access database. In this chapter you'll first see how to create a new database, and then you'll use a Wizard to create a new table. Next, you'll learn how to create a table from scratch without the Wizard. Once you've got that under your belt, you'll learn about field properties, and how to view and print detailed design descriptions.

Exercise: Creating a Contacts Database with the Wiz

If you are near your computer, work along with this exercise.

1. With Access running, choose File | New, use the CTRL+N keyboard shortcut, or click the New button on the Database toolbar.

2. In the New dialog box, double-click on Blank Database.

3. When you see the File New Database dialog box, shown here, type a filename. There's no need to add the file extension .MDB since Access will do this for you, and it will probably be hidden by default anyway. Let's call the exercise database **Friends**:

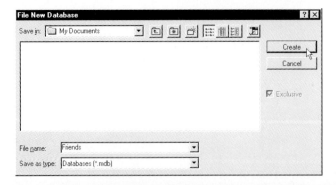

4. Notice where Access plans to store your new file. Like all good Office programs, it stores things in the subfolder My Documents by default, wherever that may be. It starts out life in your Windows folder; but if someone has moved it or changed the default folder, your computer might store it somewhere else. Change the drive and/or folder in the usual way, if necessary.

5. Click Create.

6. Soon you'll see a new, empty Database window like this one:

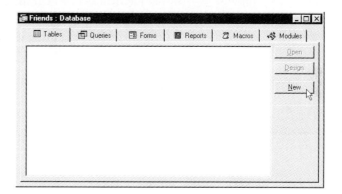

7. Click the New button. You'll be offered a number of choices. Select Table Wizard and click OK:

The Access Table Wizard

Before you can enter data into a database, you must set up a field in which to store it. In Access, these fields will become *columns* in your database *tables*. The Table Wizard already knows how to create a bunch of tables for various tasks. These sample tables have been subdivided into Business and Personal categories, but the distinctions often blur.

When you activate the Table Wizard (as you did earlier in step 7), you'll see a dialog box like the one in Figure 30-1. Yours may differ, depending upon which Sample Table you choose.

To use the Table Wiz:

1. Select either Business or Personal. (Click on the appropriate button.)

2. Scroll the Sample Tables list to see the available table types.

3. Click once on a table of interest to select it, and view the sample field in the Sample Fields list. For example, in Figure 30-1, the Personal category in the Friends sample table has been chosen; you can see some of the fields for that table in the Sample Fields list. Scroll if necessary to see all the fields in the list.

4. After you've had a chance to browse the available tables and their fields, make your screen look like Figure 30-1. That is to say, when you find a table you like (Friends in the example), click to select it.

5. To add fields from the Sample Fields list to your new table, you can either double-click on a field name or click on the > button between the two windows. To add *all* of the fields from the Sample

---

FIGURE 30-1

The Table Wizard knows how to design many useful tables

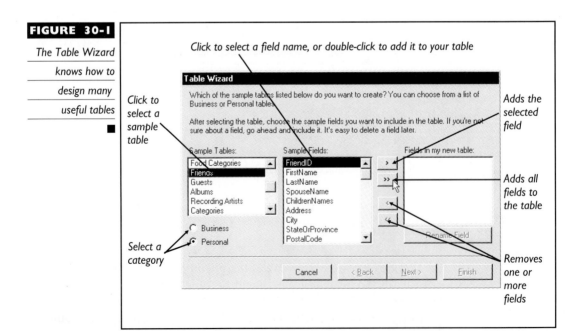

Click to select a field name, or double-click to add it to your table

Click to select a sample table

Select a category

Adds the selected field

Adds all fields to the table

Removes one or more fields

Fields list to your table, click on the **>>** button. Add all of the fields now. Your screen should look like the following illustration:

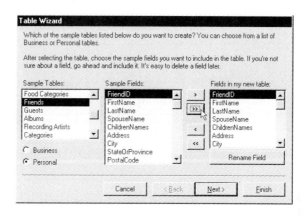

6. To remove a field from your table, scroll up or down to it in the rightmost list, click to select, and then click on the **<** button. For example, here the MobilePhone field is being removed from the table:

Clicking on the **<<** button—you guessed it—removes all of the fields from your table.

tip *You can use fields from different sample tables by clicking on different sample table names while building your new table.*

7. When you are satisfied with the new table list, click on the Wizard's Next > button to continue.

8. You'll be asked to name your table. Here you can use longer names that include spaces. The Wizard proposes **Friends,** which is fine, but suppose you and a spouse want to keep separate friends tables in the *same* friends database? You could both have your own tables. So let's personalize your table's name. Type the new name

as shown here (**Ron's Friends**). Table names can be up to 64 characters long and can include spaces.

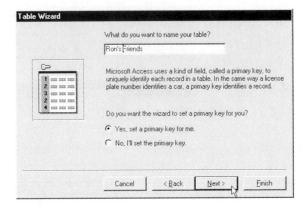

9. Access databases always need a *primary key,* which you'll learn about later. For now, leave well enough alone, and let the Wiz create the primary key by clicking on the Next > button.

10. At this point, you *could* start entering data right into the table that the Wiz will create, but you can also have the Wiz create an onscreen *form* for data entry. Since there's no extra charge, what the heck? Click the Enter Data Into The Table...choice as shown here, and then click the Finish button.

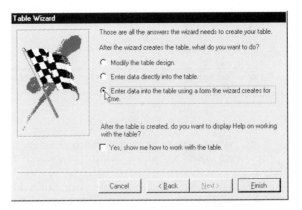

11. In a moment (or in a flash if you are a Pentium junkie) you'll see a form, and under that form, the Database window has been updated to include the name of your first table. Drag things around if necessary to see what the Wiz has done. Slick, no?

12. Save the form by clicking on it to select it if it isn't already the active window, then choose File | Save, click the Save button on the Standard toolbar, or use the CTRL+S shortcut. Form names, like table names, can be up to 64 characters long and can include spaces. (You'll learn all about forms in the next chapter.)

tip   *You can add your own favorite table designs to the Wiz by using the techniques outlined in Chapter 38.*

Creating Databases Without the Wiz

Designing tables from scratch requires considerable attention to detail. You'll need to decide which information to collect and what names to give each field, and you'll need to specify the types of fields you'll be using, and their properties, among other things. So before you can create your own table, you'll need to know about these concepts.

note   *If this is your first-ever database, or if you like to take things slowly, you might want to jump ahead now to Chapter 32, and return to the remainder of this chapter and Chapter 31 only when you need to know how to mess with table designs, or how to create your own tables and forms without the Wizard's help.*

Plan Ahead

Still here, gluttons? Start by trying to imagine all of the ways you plan to use the data. Sketch out *all* of the screens and reports you hope to create. Pretend you are creating a paper, computerless system. Pencil it out. What would each of the blanks on the forms contain?

If you are creating a mailing list, for instance, will you need to sort by postal code? If so, you'd better have a separate field for that piece of information rather than one big field that holds the recipient's name, address, city, state, and ZIP as one block of information.

Database designing is an art, and there are many books and seminars on the subject. Before you spend hundreds or even thousands of hours entering data into a huge database, learn the basics. Start small and experiment. Talk to others about blunders they've made.

Designing Your Table

When you are ready to take a stab at designing a table without the Wizard:

1. Open the database that needs a new table, or create a new database (CTRL+N).

2. If necessary, click on the Table tab to bring it to the forefront.

3. Click the New button in the Database window.

4. Click on Design View in the New Table box and click OK.

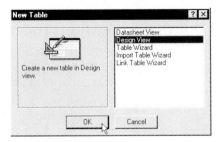

5. You will see an *empty* table window like the one used to create Figure 30-2. It is here that you type field names and put into effect other design decisions. Notice how properties change with different field types.

To create a table, follow these general steps (the specifics will be discussed in a moment):

1. Type a field name.

2. Pick a data type.

3. Specify any necessary properties. (You may need to save the table first.)

4. Repeat steps 1 through 3 for the remaining fields.

5. Save the table if you haven't already done so.

Field Names

Field names can be up to 64 characters long, and include spaces and numbers. Simply click in the first empty field name box and type a unique, meaningful field name as illustrated in Figure 30-2.

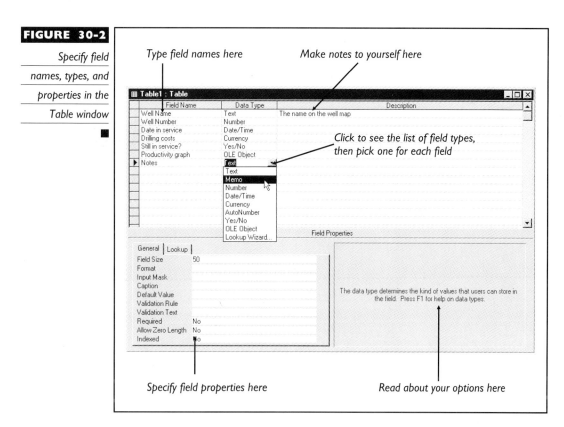

FIGURE 30-2

Specify field names, types, and properties in the Table window

tip *Shorter field names without spaces are often better, particularly if you are planning to write expressions that refer to field names, or are planning to use SQL (Structured Query Language) statements or Access Basic.*

Data Types and Properties

Access offers eight *data types* for its fields, and each type offers a variety of options called *properties*. It is important to understand what the different types and properties do—and when to make which choices. Sometimes the answers are not obvious. For example, although postal ZIP codes are numbers, you'll probably *not* want to put them in a numeric field. Same goes for telephone numbers, part numbers, Social Security numbers, and so on. Read on to find out why.

You choose a field's data type by clicking on the little arrow in the current field's Data Type column. This displays a list, from which you choose an appropriate type. You can see this list back in Figure 30-2, where a data type is being chosen for the Notes field.

Once you've chosen a field's *data type,* its *property list* is displayed in the bottom half of the dialog box. Different data types offer different properties.

Properties let you specify things like the maximum length of entries, how the entries will be formatted, whether an entry is required, and so on. For example, in the following illustration, the Unit Price field is a *Number* data type with properties that specify a Currency format and a default value of 0. Moreover, the number entered must be a positive number (as you can see from the >0—greater than zero—requirement in the Validation Rule property). If the user forgets to enter a unit price (or enters an invalid value, such as zero or a negative number in this case), Access will display the text "Please enter a valid unit price."

▦ Table1 : Table		
Field Name	**Data Type**	
⚷ ID	AutoNumber	
Order ID	Number	
▶ Unit Price	Number	

Field Properties

General │ Lookup │

Field Size	Double
Format	Currency
Decimal Places	Auto
Input Mask	
Caption	
Default Value	0
Validation Rule	>0
Validation Text	Please enter a valid price unit
Required	No
Indexed	No

The error r
the

Properties can also force things like all uppercase letters. And you can use properties to insert characters for you, like the hyphens in Social Security numbers or slashes in phone numbers.

tip   *Explore the field types and properties assigned in Microsoft's NWIND and other sample databases to see which choices the pros have made. You'll learn how to do this in a moment.*

Here's an overview of the various data types, their properties, and examples of their applications.

Text Fields

Text is the default data type. You use the Text data type when you need to store words, obviously. But it is also a good type to use for fields that will contain part numbers, Social Security numbers, or ZIP codes. Why? When you enter numbers beginning with zeros into an Access *Number* field, Access strips off the leading zeros, and doesn't like hyphens or other nonnumeric characters. So when you enter a Social Security number like 085-98-9999 into a numeric field, it becomes 85989999—the zero disappears! Likewise, the ZIP code 01234 becomes 1234. You can avoid such potential disasters by using the Text data type.

Text fields can be *indexed* (a process you'll learn about later), so that Access can find pieces of it quickly. Unfortunately, a Text field cannot contain more than 255 characters; for longer text entries, you must use the Memo data type (described in a moment).

There are ten possible Text field properties. You do not need to specify them all. They include

- Field Size
- Format
- Input Mask
- Caption
- Default Value
- Validation Rule
- Validation Text
- Required
- Allow Zero Length
- Indexed

Field Size

The Field Size of a Text field can be anything from 1 to 255 characters. Smaller sizes save disk space, but you shouldn't make the setting too small, unless disk space is at a premium. Also, be careful when changing the length of a Text field to smaller values after data has been entered into your table. You run the risk of *truncating* (shortening) long entries.

tip   *If you expect that in some cases you will be filling a field with just a phrase or a few words, while in other cases you will fill the same field with whole lines or even paragraphs, use a Memo field instead of a Text field for maximum flexibility. A Memo field will "shrink to fit" each entry on a record-by-record basis. If you opt for a Text field,* *remember that you have to define a Text field at the largest size you estimate any of the field's entries to be (and no greater than 255 characters).*

Format

The Format property forces entries to appear according to the characteristics you specify. For instance, to force all text to uppercase, regardless of how it is entered, you can place a > (greater-than sign) in the space next to Format. Conversely, a < (less-than sign) forces all text to lowercase.

To force a specific character to appear in a particular place (for example, a hyphen after the second digit of a six-digit part number, perhaps), use the @ sign as a placeholder for the digits and type the special character itself in the position where you want it to always appear, for example, @@-@@@@.

Use an & character to tell Access that text is not required. Check out the examples in online Help to see how this works.

Input Mask

Input masks provide things like parentheses around area codes in telephone numbers, time and date formats, and so on. The Input Mask Wizard can help you pick and experiment with predefined masks:

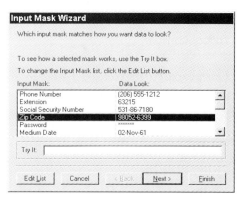

The Wizard will launch when you click on the small button at the right edge of the Input Mask property box as shown here:

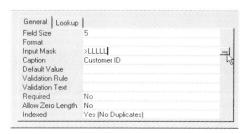

note *You will need to save the table at least once before you can use the Wizard and will be prompted to do so if necessary.*

Caption

The Caption property lets you specify replacement text for the name of the field as it appears *onscreen*. Captions thus have the same effect as *labels*. For instance, if you have a field named "PostalCode," you might want the onscreen caption or label to read "ZIP Code." Type the desired label in the space for the Caption property.

Default Value

This property lets you specify a value that will be automatically entered into the field whenever you create a new record. For instance, if you want the word "Member" to appear in the field, you would type **Member** in the space for Default Value. Although the default entry will then appear automatically whenever a user is entering new records, the user can edit, replace, or delete it.

Validation Rule

This property lets you specify error checks. For instance, if an entry must be at least 12 characters long, you can create an expression here to check for this. See the online Help and Chapter 36 for details.

Validation Text

Place your desired error message here, like "Oops! Part numbers are always 12 characters in length." When an entry violates the validation rule, the error message text will appear onscreen.

Required

Use this Yes/No field to tell Access if an entry is required in the field you are designing. You can change the setting here by clicking on the space next to Required and then picking Yes or No from the drop-down list.

Allow Zero Length

As any homicide detective will tell you, there's a big difference between "nothing" and "I don't know." Sometimes, when entering data, users leave a field empty because there is no data for that particular field in that particular record. Other times users leave a field empty because they don't know the correct data to enter. For example, when entering data in an employee database, you might leave a particular field empty for one employee—say a field for Assigned Parking Space—either because she does not have an assigned space or because you don't know her parking space number. In databases, this subtle but important difference, between "None" and "I don't know," is frequently distinguished as follows:

- For "None," the user enters a *zero length*, or *null*, character by typing two double quote marks with no spaces between them ("").

- For "I don't know," the user simply skips the field.

Although there are other ways, like simply entering **None** for "None" and **Unknown** for "I don't know," many of your users may already be familiar with the traditional DBMS approach outlined here. To make Access recognize the "" choice, set the Allow Zero Length option to Yes, the Required option to No, and leave the Default Value option blank. Then instruct your users to enter the "" null character when the value for the field is none, null, not applicable, or whatever. See online Help and the bigger books if this intrigues you.

Indexed

Use this Yes/No field to tell Access if a field is to be indexed for speedy lookups. (See "Indexing Fields" later in this chapter or online Help for details.) You can change the setting here by clicking on the space next to Indexed and then picking Yes or No from the drop-down list. You can also choose to permit or prohibit duplicate records.

Memo Fields

A field of the Memo data type can hold up to 64,000 characters. However, it can't be indexed, so use it only for data that will exceed 255 characters per entry.

Other than maximum character counts and the fact that it does not offer an Input Mask property, the Memo field's property options are identical to those of the Text field.

Number Fields

The Number data type should be used

- When you are collecting data to be used in computations
- When you want to require someone to enter only numbers (as opposed to letters)
- When you want to format entries with things like decimal places and currency symbols

Number field properties affect both the precision of numbers *and* their appearance.

Field Size

The following table summarizes the available Field Size choices and their specifications. As you can see, some field sizes use more disk space than others, with a resulting increase in precision:

Field Size	Notes
Double	The default; stores numbers with 15 digits of precision, from $-1.79769313486232E308$ to $+1.79769313486232E308$, in 8 bytes
Single	Stores numbers with 7 digits of precision from $-3.402823E38$ to $+3.402823E38$ in 4 bytes
Byte	Uses 1 byte to store whole numbers (no fractions) from 0 to 255
Integer	Uses 2 bytes to store whole numbers (no fractions) from $-32,768$ to $+32,767$
Long Integer	Uses 4 bytes to store whole numbers (again, no fractions) from $-2,147,483,648$ to $+2,147,483,647$
Replication ID	Used to generate unique numbers automatically to identify records

tip *When you want to change the way numbers are stored, change the Field Size setting. To change how a number appears on the display and in printouts, change the Field Format, which is discussed next.*

Field Format

The Field Format property lets you choose the onscreen and printed appearance of numbers. This does not change the internal precision of the numbers, thus it does not affect things like storage and computations.

There is a drop-down list that lets you see and pick the desired formats, which include commas, currency symbols, scientific notation, and so on. You can also define your own formats. See online Help and the bigger books for details.

Decimal Place

This property tells Access how to *display* numbers. For example, with the Format set to Fixed, if you enter **1.1234** in a field and the Decimal Place option is set to 1, Access will only display "1.1." This does not affect the precision of data or computations the way choosing a Field Size does. Leave the default Auto setting, type a number from 0 to 15, or pick a number from the available drop-down list.

Input Mask

Although Input Mask appears as a property option in Number fields, it only applies in Text and Date/Time fields. Access will remind you of this if you forget.

Other Number Properties

The remaining number properties (Caption, Default Value, Validation Text, Validation Rule, Required, and Indexed) are identical to those previously described under "Text Fields."

Date/Time Fields

The Date/Time data type lets you enter dates and times in a variety of formats as illustrated here:

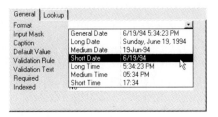

 note *Although Access supports a wide range of date and time formats, the options available are based on the International settings in your Windows Control Panel.*

Available Date/Time properties include many you will recognize from earlier field types:

- Format
- Input Mask
- Caption
- Default Value
- Validation Rule
- Validation Text
- Required
- Indexed

Since the features and functions of most of these properties have already been discussed in this chapter, let's avoid a rehash.

Use the Input Mask Wizard if you want users to enter dates and times in predefined formats. Here's how:

1. Click on the button next to the Date Field's Input Mask property.

2. Answer Yes if asked to save the table first.

3. Pick the desired date format in the resulting dialog box:

4. Try entering a date if you like, by clicking in the white part of the "Try it:" portion of the dialog box.

5. If you want to personalize the input mask, click the Next > button; otherwise, click Finish.

Currency Fields

Use the Currency data type when you want to store information about money. The options listed are based on the International settings found in your Windows Control Panel.

Standard American currency options include General Numbers, numbers with dollar signs, and so on, but you'll probably want to leave it at the default setting (which provides dollar signs, commas, and two decimal places). If you like, you can create your own custom settings.

You can have Access worry about decimal place location in displays and printouts, or you can specify a decimal position in the Decimal Places section of the Field Properties list.

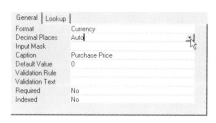

MANAGING YOUR DATA WITH ACCESS

To choose a specific decimal setting, either type the desired number of decimal places to replace the default setting Auto, or click on the drop-down list to see the options available.

The rest of the Currency field properties (Caption, Default Value, and so on) work as you'd expect.

AutoNumber Fields

To have Access automatically number each record as you add it, use the AutoNumber data type. Many users define the Primary Key field as an AutoNumber field. (In fact, Access does this automatically if you let it create the Primary Key field for you.)

AutoNumber field properties include Format, Caption, and Indexed. Normally you'll leave them alone, except, perhaps, for the Caption property.

Yes/No Field

Use the Yes/No data type when you want to give users a field with only two entry choices, like Yes or No, On or Off, or True or False, or perhaps Male or Female, Paid or Unpaid—in short, any either/or value you want. You can specify a default answer (like No).

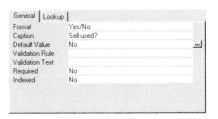

In addition, you can specify a caption for the field if you don't want to use the field name as a caption. Validation rules are possible.

You'll see Yes/No fields at work later in this chapter.

OLE Object Field

Finally, you can define a field as an OLE Object field. This makes it possible to round up and use OLE objects like video clips, audio clips, graphs, and so forth. See Chapter 37 for details.

Adding or Deleting Fields in Tables

Even the best-designed tables will need an additional field occasionally. Or you may want to delete an unnecessary field. Access makes it easy to do this.

Adding Fields

Begin by opening a table (if it's not already open), then switch to Design View, and add or delete the necessary field, and/or field properties. Here's a specific example of that process:

1. Open the appropriate database with File | Open.

2. Open the table you want to alter. Your screen will look something like this.

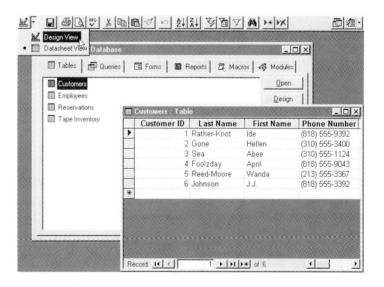

3. Click on the Design View button at the left edge of the toolbar. Your table will disappear and the field list will appear in its place (resize this window, if necessary).

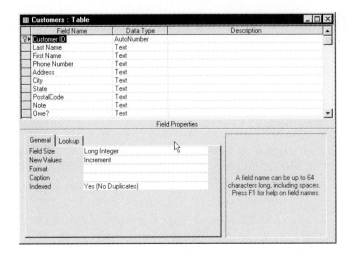

4. To add a field, scroll through the field list until you see an empty Field Name row, then type your new field name (**Send Mailings?** in this example):

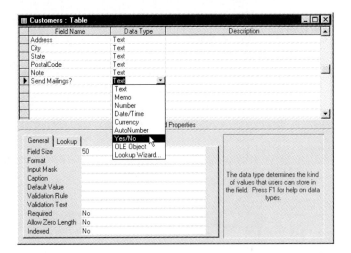

5. Tab to the Data Type area (or click there), and then click on the arrow button to reveal the field type list.

6. Pick the appropriate type from the drop-down list.

7. Make any necessary changes to the field's properties.

8. If you want to add additional fields, repeat steps 4 through 7 as necessary.

9. Click on the Datasheet View button on the toolbar when you have finished.

10. You'll be asked if you want to save the table changes. Agree to do this, if that's what you want.

Renaming Fields and Their Captions

When you change a field *name*, you actually change the way Access internally refers to the field. When you change a field's *caption*, however, you only change the onscreen and report labels for the field.

While the process of *renaming* a field is quite easy, it can have far-reaching effects. For instance, if you've created expressions that reference the field (see Chapter 36), or if you have a database using multiple tables (discussed in Chapter 35), changes to field names may require changes in the expressions and/or related tables. That's why it's a good idea to leave the field *names* alone whenever possible, and change the field *captions,* instead.

Changing Captions

Begin by opening a table (if it's not already open), then switch to Design View, and change the entry in the Caption area of the Field Properties list. Here's an example of that process:

1. Open the appropriate database with the Open Database command on Access's File menu.

2. Open the table you want to alter.

3. Click on the Design View button at the left edge of the toolbar. Your table will disappear and the field list will appear in its place.

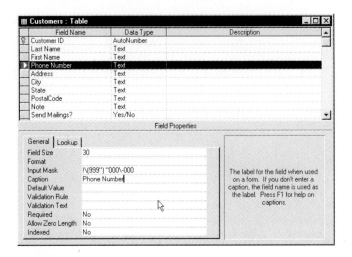

4. Scroll in the field list if necessary until you see the field whose caption you want to change. Click on that field name. You'll see a black triangle at the left edge of the selected field.

5. Click in the white Caption area of the Field Properties section of the dialog box. (This should select the current caption if there is one.)

6. Type a new caption.

7. Make any other necessary changes to the field's properties.

8. If you want to change captions for additional fields, repeat steps 4 through 7 as necessary.

9. Click on the Datasheet View button (far left in the toolbar) when you have finished.

10. You'll be asked if you want to save the table changes. Agree to do this, if that's what you want.

Changing Field Names

Begin by opening a table (if it's not already open), then switch to Design view, and change the field name in the Field Name column of the dialog box. Here's a specific example of that process:

1. Open the appropriate database with File | Open.

2. Open the table you want to alter.

3. Click on the Design View button at the left edge of the toolbar. Your table will disappear and the field list will appear in its place:

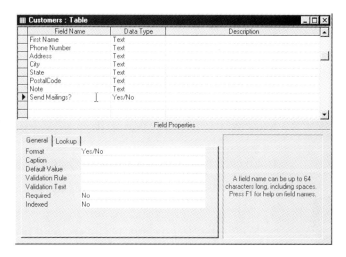

4. Scroll in the field list if necessary until you see the field whose name you want to change. Click on that field name. You'll see a black triangle at the left edge of the selected field.

5. Select all or a portion of the field name in order to edit or delete it, and make your changes.

6. Make any other changes you need to the field's properties (a new caption, perhaps?).

7. If you want to change field names for additional fields, repeat steps 4 through 6 as necessary.

8. Click on the Datasheet View button (second from the left on the toolbar) when you have finished.

9. You'll be asked if you want to save the table changes. Agree to do this, if that's what you want.

Moving Fields (Rearranging Tables)

To rearrange the order of fields in tables, you can simply switch to the table of interest, view it in Design view, select the field you want to move, and then drag it to the desired location. Suppose, for instance, you want to move the Note field so that it is last on the list:

1. Open the appropriate database with File | Open.

2. Open the table you want to alter (Customers in this example).

3. Click on the Design View button at the left edge of the toolbar. Your table will disappear and the field list will appear in its place.

4. Scroll in the field list if necessary until you see the field you want to move. Click to the left of that field name. You'll see a white triangle at the left edge of the selected field.

5. Click a second time on the left edge and hold down the mouse button. You'll see a new pointer shape (the drag-and-drop pointer).

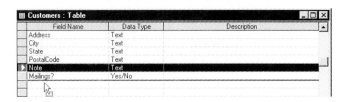

6. Drag the field to a new location in the field list and release the mouse button.

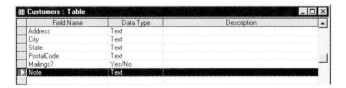

7. Click on the Datasheet View button (second from the left in the toolbar) when you have finished.

8. You'll be asked if you want to save the table changes. Agree to do this, if that's what you want.

Deleting Fields in Tables

Deleting fields in tables should not be taken lightly. When you delete a field, you also delete all of the information in that field for each record in your database. For example, if you have 100 employees, and you delete the Social Security Number field in your employee database, you will delete all 100 Social Security numbers! While Undo can save you if you catch your mistake in time, use caution, and whenever possible, back up your database before deleting things!

Also, realize that if you delete a field that is related to other tables (see Chapter 35), or a field that is referred to in expressions (see Chapter 36), you may cause additional problems that will need to be solved somehow. That said, here are the steps:

1. Open the appropriate database with File | Open.

2. Open the table you want to alter (Customers in this example).

3. Click on the Design View button at the left edge of the toolbar. Your table will disappear and the field list will appear in its place.

4. Scroll in the field list if necessary until you see the field you want to delete. Click to the left of that field name. You'll see a white triangle at the left edge of the selected field.

5. Press DEL.

6. Access will ask if that's what you really want to do.

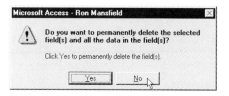

7. Click on the Datasheet View button (second from the left in the Datasheet toolbar) when you have finished.

8. You'll be asked to save the table changes. Agree to do this, if that's what you want.

Resizing Fields

There are several field-sizing concepts worth understanding. Here are a couple of basic ones.

First, there is the actual size of the field you define in the Field Properties area of a table in Design view. For instance, Text fields can have a maximum field size of 255 characters, but you may define smaller sizes (like 10 characters) if that's all you ever want users to enter into a particular field. This offers two benefits:

- Access will warn users if they attempt to enter more characters than the defined field size permits.

- Smaller fields take up less disk space and may improve the speed of certain database tasks.

Second, sometimes you'll want to leave the definition of a field's size large (20 characters, for example) but *display* only a smaller portion of the available field size when viewing the table in Datasheet view.

Let's start by reminding you how to change a field's size by altering the field's Size property.

Changing a Field's Size Property

warning   *If you reduce the size of a field using the steps that follow, you may truncate (lose) any portions of your data that exceed the new field length. For instance, if you shorten a field from 20 to 15 characters, and have already entered items that are 20 characters long, the last 5 characters of those long entries will be deleted. However, Access will remind you of this potential problem when you attempt to save the changed table.*

1. Open the appropriate database with File | Open.

2. Open the table you want to alter (Employees in this example).

3. Click on the Design View button at the left edge of the toolbar. Your table will disappear and the field list will appear in its place.

4. Scroll in the field list if necessary until you see the field you want to resize. Click to the left of that field name.

5. Click in the white area next to the Field Size property in the dialog box.

6. Enter a new field size (that is, type a number).

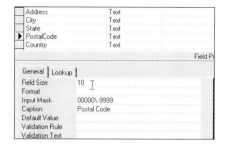

7. Click on the Datasheet View button (second from the left in the toolbar) when you have finished.

8. You'll be asked if you want to save the table changes (and warned if your changes may cause problems). Agree to save the changes, if that's what you want.

Changing Column Widths in Tables

As mentioned a moment ago, sometimes it's useful to change the *display* of column widths in your tables without actually changing the field properties of the table. For instance, if you want to keep the Middle Name field, but can get by with seeing only middle initials (to make more room on the screen for other items of more interest), you can drag the column widths much as you do in Excel:

1. Open the appropriate database with the Open Database command on Access's File menu.

2. Open the table you want to alter (Employees in this example).

3. Scroll in the table window if necessary until you see the field you wish to resize (Middle Name in this example). Point at the right edge of the heading of the field to be changed, and watch the pointer change to a two-headed arrow:

Employee ID	First Name	Middle Name	Last Name
1	Mitch	Philip	Higgins
2	Lori	Meredith	Spelmann
3	Annie	Marie	Crum
4	Fiorella	Rinzoni	La Guardia
5	Elizabeth	Barbara	Franklin
(AutoNumber)			

4. Drag the two-headed arrow to change the column width to the desired size.

	Employee ID	First Name	社† Last Name
▶	1	Mitch	Pl Higgins
	2	Lori	M Spelmann
	3	Annie	M Crum
	4	Fiorella	Ri La Guardia
	5	Elizabeth	B: Franklin
*	(AutoNumber)		

5. Here, the column has been made so small that only the first character or two can be seen. *The data's still there, it is just hidden.*

6. Next time you attempt to close the table, you'll be asked if you want to save the table changes. Agree to do this, if that's what you want.

Increasing a Column's Width to "Autofit"

To avoid wasting screen space while still being able to see all of the characters of the longest entry (record), try this simple trick:

1. In Datasheet view, place the pointer at the right edge of the field to be resized (Movie Title in this example). The pointer shape changes to a double-headed arrow:

2. Double-click on the line between the two columns. The Field will expand or contract just enough to display the longest entry (or just enough to show the full field name if it's longer than any of the entries):

3. You may need to do this again later if you add or remove long entries.

Changing the Appearance of Text in Tables

You have some control over the appearance of text in tables, via the Access Format menu. For instance, you can change the font used for all columns by using the Format | Font command. Here's what 10-point Copperplate Gothic Light looks like.

VIDEO COLLECTION I[	MOVIE TITLE	ACTORS ID	ACTRESS ID	DIRECT
5	ABBOT AND COSTELLO MEET FRANKENSTEIN			

Access will adjust row heights to accommodate new fonts and font sizes, but you may need to change the widths of columns.

tip   *Rather than changing the appearance of your tables, consider creating different forms for different uses, as described in the next chapter.*

Freezing Columns

Sometimes it is useful to freeze one or more columns so that they stay in view when you scroll through the rest of the table. For instance, here the first two columns (ID and Movie Title) are selected and Format | Freeze Columns is chosen, so that these two columns will stay in view when you scroll to see the columns for other fields:

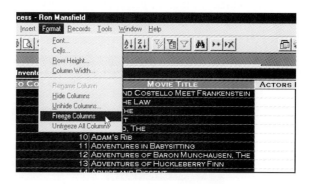

Primary Key Field(s)

Access needs a unique way to identify each record in your tables. To do this, either you or Access must create what is called a *primary key*. There can only be one primary key in a table, but a primary key can use multiple fields. (This will make sense in a moment.)

If you let Access automatically create the primary key for you (a good idea, particularly for beginners), Access will add an AutoNumber field that will assign a unique number to each new record that you create. If you like, you can sometimes rename (or at least recaption) this field and use it for additional purposes. For instance, in the video store example, you could take the numbers generated by Access in the Primary Key field and print them on the tapes themselves as "inventory control numbers."

Defining Your Own Primary Key Field

If you're bold and decide to create your own primary key (or change the existing primary key to some other field), here are the general steps:

1. Open the appropriate database with File | Open.

2. Open the table you want to alter (Employees in this example).

3. Click on the Design View button at the left edge of the toolbar. Your table will disappear and the field list will appear in its place.

4. Scroll in the field list if necessary until you see the field you want to define as the primary key (Social Security #, perhaps). Click to the left of that field name. You'll see a white triangle at the left edge of the selected field.

5. Click on the Set Primary Key button on the toolbar, as shown here, or, if you'd rather, choose Edit | Primary Key:

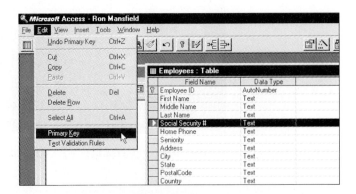

6. A little key icon will appear next to the new field, indicating that it is now the primary key:

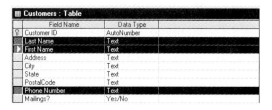

7. When you get around to closing the table or switching to Datasheet view, you'll be asked if you want to save the table changes. Agree to do this, if that's what you want.

Creating Multiple-Field Primary Keys

Sometimes you'll want to create a primary key by using multiple fields (First Name, Last Name, and Phone Number, for instance). To do this:

1. Select multiple fields by holding down CTRL while clicking on them.

2. Click on the Set Primary Key button from the toolbar or choose Edit | Primary Key as you did in the last section.

3. Notice that the key icon now appears next to all the fields you selected:

4. Save or cancel the table changes when asked to do so.

Indexing Fields

Often, you can speed up searches (queries) and reporting by telling Access to *index* certain fields. Indexing is the procedure by which Access orders a field's entries in some way that makes it easier to search. For example, it can find text entries faster if it keeps track of them alphabetically than if it keeps them in the more or less random order in which users enter them. There's a trade-off to indexing, however: indexes sometimes slow the data-entry process.

Access always indexes the primary key field(s). You can specify other fields for indexing. Don't do that, however, until you are unhappy with the speed of things like finding and sorting information (discussed in Chapters 33 and 34). When you are ready to experiment with field indexing, follow this example:

1. Open the appropriate database (Video Store in this example) with File | Open.

2. Open the table containing the field(s) you want to index (Tape Inventory in this example).

3. Click on the Design View button at the left edge of the toolbar. Your table will disappear and the field list will appear in its place.

4. Scroll in the field list if necessary until you see the field you want to move (Movie Title in this example). Click to the left of that field name. You'll see a black triangle at the left edge of the selected field.

5. Click in the Indexed area of the Field Properties list. You'll see an arrow button indicating that there is a list of choices for this property.

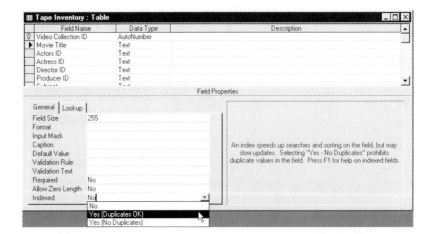

6. Click on the button to reveal the indexing options and pick one.

7. Click on the Datasheet View button (second from the left in the toolbar) when you have finished.

8. You'll be asked if you want to save the table changes. Agree to do this, if that's what you want.

Viewing a List of Database Properties

To see a detailed description of your tables and their field properties:

1. Open the database whose properties you want to see.

2. Choose File | Properties. The Properties dialog box will appear.

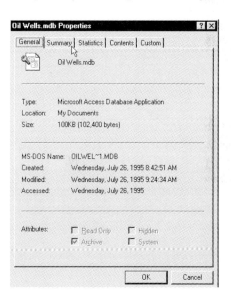

3. Click on the other tabs to see additional information.

Where to Go from Here

If you feel you are ready to enter a little data and experiment with some simple tables, you should still at least skim Chapter 31 to learn something about forms in Access, and then jump into Chapter 32 where you'll learn how to enter and edit data. You can return to Chapter 31 later after you get some experience playing with the program.

If you are already a database pro and want to get going in a hurry, take a few minutes first to check out Chapter 38, which shows you how to use existing data from other databases like dBASE and Paradox.

Because forms are such a powerful and attractive part of Access, it's suggested, regardless of your ability, that you read the following chapter sometime. It will make a difference in your work.

CHAPTER 31

Forms

I N their simplest implementations, forms are designs (layouts) you create to improve the appearance of data from your tables. Although forms can be both displayed and printed, the main use of forms is onscreen, to improve the interface for data entry. You can add graphics to them, and specify shading, colors, type styles, and more. Access forms will often remind you of paper forms. For example, you might have a form that you use for the onscreen entry and editing of employee records:

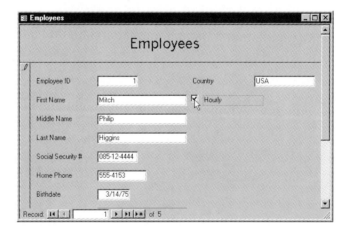

Or, you might create a form that is used onscreen to make and check videotape reservations. Notice how this form provides a drop-down list of movie titles:

As you will see in Chapter 35, forms can use information from multiple tables. So, when designing a video-store system, you might combine information from the Reservation table, Tape Inventory table, and Customer table to create a single onscreen form and perhaps a report or two. It's even possible to combine information from different databases on the same form. And as you'll learn in Chapter 36, you can compute and control things in your forms by means of expressions and other forms of automation.

tip   With Access, you can limit access—you can control how much information your users can see on your forms, permitting them to see only information that they need to know. For example, you might want to lock out all but selected employees from forms that display confidential salary information. You'll learn how in Chapter 39.

Let's start off slowly in this chapter. If you've already created a database, you may want to open it now and work along as you explore the basics.

The Form Wizard

Fortunately, there are Wizards and other tools to help you create forms. It's a good way to get started.

The Form Wizard asks you questions, then helps you to create good-looking forms. You can run the Form Wizard at any time after creating a new table. In this example you'll see how to create a couple of forms from a database called Contacts:

1. Open the database of your choice (Contacts, in this example), and click on the table you want to create the form from.

2. Click on the Forms tab, if necessary, to bring it forward. Unless you've already created some forms for this database, you'll see an empty list like this:

3. In any case, click the New button in the Forms window.

4. Select Form Wizard, be sure you've chosen the table from the drop-down list, and click on the OK button as shown here:

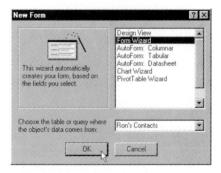

5. You'll be given the opportunity to choose which of your tables' fields will appear on the new form. To choose fields, select them in the Available Fields list (the one on the left) and click on the >> button between the two lists, or double-click on the fields. To remove fields from the Selected Fields list, on the right, double-click on them or use the << button.

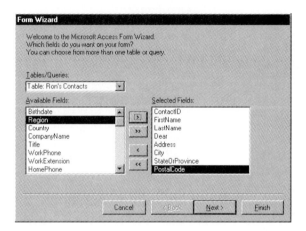

6. When you've moved all of the desired fields to the Selected Fields list, click on the Next button to continue. For this example you'll be making a Birthday Reminders form by choosing the field for birth date and the fields necessary for first and last names, phone numbers, CompuServe ID, mailing address info, and notes.

7. You'll be presented with a choice of three layouts. You can click once on a layout's name to display a brief description of its function at the bottom of the dialog box. For this exercise, click on the *Tabular* layout. When you've made your choice, click Next > to continue.

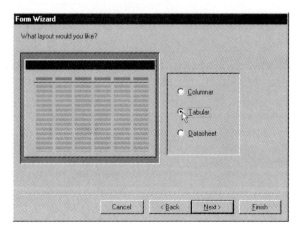

8. The Wiz will offer some predefined style choices. They are chosen by clicking on the appropriate radio button. Chosen styles are demonstrated in the upper-left corner of the dialog box. Explore them all, if you like. Then choose one and click on the Next > button.

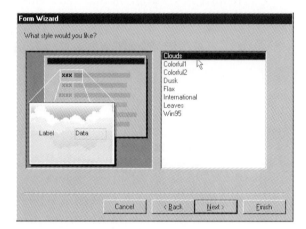

9. You'll be presented with the Wizard's final dialog box, which gives you a chance to modify the form or see it with your contacts data. This is also where you create a title for your form. Access proposes a title that you can edit. This title has been changed to "Birthday Reminders."

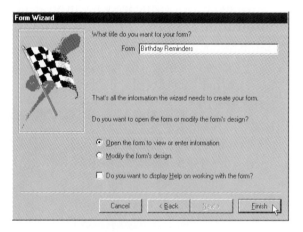

10. After you've titled yours, be sure the choice Open The Form To View Or Enter Information is marked (click on it if it's not), and click on the Finish button.

11. In a moment you'll see your new Birthday Reminders form with your Contacts data displayed in it. Here's an example that uses the Clouds style from step 8.

Birthdate	First Name	Last Name	Home Phone
11/5/51	Ted	Bravin	(555) 555-12?
12/31/50	Karen	Shewood	(800) 123-45?
7/26/56	Bryan	Hannison	(805) 555-11?
/_/_			

Record: |◄ ◄   4   ► ►| ►* of 4

note   *Using familiar Windows tools, you can resize the window that contains a form so that it reveals more or less information, and you can scroll to see additional fields that are currently out of view. Navigation keys, like PAGE UP, PAGE DOWN, and HOME, work as you'd expect in form windows*

∫aving Forms

It's a good idea to save new forms right after you create them *and* after you modify them. Use the Save command, or the Save As command. If you want to clone a form before modifying it further, give the form a different name when you save it.

warning   *Experiment on **copies** of your favorite forms, keeping the original in its unmodified state. It's often easier to delete an unsuccessful form and start over with the original than to manually undo a lot of changes. Use Save As to do this.*

Modifying Forms

Alas, Form Wizards are not perfect, nor are they mind readers (thankfully). Inevitably, you'll want to do some fine-tuning. For instance, some find the space that separates records in multirecord reports a little wasteful. That can be fixed easily. But in the Birthday Reminders form there are more subtle problems, as well. For instance, birthdays appear in an almost useless order. Using the Sort button in the toolbar to sort by year won't help; you really don't care much about the *year* someone was born. You want a list sorted by *month* then by *day* so you can buy birthday cards, make phone calls, and send e-mail on time. Looks like you need to take things into your own hands. Before you can, you'll need to know some more buzzwords.

Design View

You modify forms in *Design view,* which you can reach by clicking on the Design View button. The button contains a little ruler, a drafting triangle, and a pencil. Cute.

Clicking on the button displays the underpinnings—the controls and objects—of your current form. You can mess with these controls and objects to get the desired effect. Figure 31-1 shows what an example Birthday Reminders form looked like immediately after the Wizard created it. (Notice the toolbar that also appears when you switch to Design view.)

Forms are broken down into three sections:

- Header
- Detail
- Footer

It's pretty obvious which section does which jobs. Headers and footers contain things like form titles, page numbers, and so on, at either the head or foot of the page. The Detail section is where you specify which fields will be displayed, what they will look like, and so forth. You can also place labels (captions), graphics, lines, and other design elements in any of the three section types.

You move things around by selecting and dragging them. (See "Moving Items in Forms," following.) There are alignment tools to help. While the editing techniques are not identical to those used in other Office programs, working in Design view will probably seem familiar, and often intuitive.

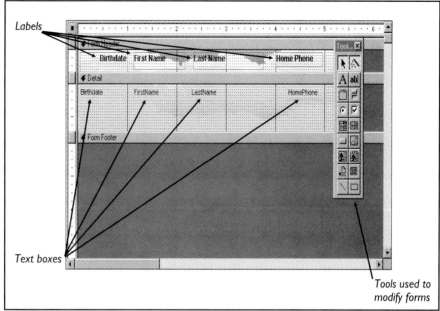

FIGURE 31-1

Forms contain header detail and footer sections

Labels

Text boxes

Tools used to modify forms

tip *Alas, some things like page numbering and adding dates are not as familiar and intuitive as they could be. You'll learn about them in Chapter 36. Perhaps the designers of Access, Word, and Excel should have lunch together more often...*

Moving Items in Forms

The brute-force method of moving things in Design view is to select an item (or SHIFT+select multiple items), then drag the selected item(s) with your mouse:

tip *To select multiple, adjacent items (controls), drag with your mouse to form a rectangle around the desired controls. You'll see a rectangle as you drag. Items within the rectangle will be selected when you release the mouse button.*

Notice how the mouse pointer turns into a little hand when it can move things. Keep an eye on that mouse pointer when working in Design view—it goes through a lot of changes.

There are grids to help you keep things lined up, and a variety of alignment tools that can be used to put multiple items on the same, straight line. For example, to align the bottoms of multiple labels, you can SHIFT+click to select them, then choose Format | Align | Bottom:

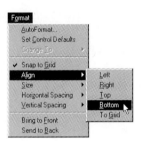

Changing the Appearance of Text in Forms

As you'd expect, you can change the appearance of text by selecting items, then using the available arsenal of menu choices, buttons, and keyboard shortcuts to embellish text. For example, to change the font used to display birth dates, names, and other data, you might select all of the boxes containing text you want to reformat:

Then make new font, size, and alignment choices from the toolbar and menus. If the new font choices make text considerably larger or smaller, you may need to resize the objects by using the techniques discussed next.

Resizing Items in Forms

To resize something, select it (and items related to it, like lines or shadow boxes) and drag the appropriate handles. For example, here's how to make the FirstName box and the white and black special effect lines smaller:

1. Drag to select the FirstName box *and* the white and black lines that are beneath it:

2. With the necessary items (and nothing else) selected, drag on one of the end handles with the cursor shaped like a two-headed arrow.

3. If necessary, resize related items (like LastName) by repeating the preceding steps. For instance, here's an example of the box for FirstName shorter and LastName longer:

4. To see how things are going, switch back to Form view from time to time, by clicking on the Form View button.

Colors and Patterns in Forms

Use the Back Color, Fore Color, Border Color, Border Width, and Special Effect buttons to bring up palettes of colors, shading, borders, and so on. Here's what the Back Color palette look like:

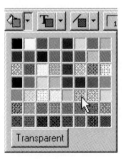

The settings for the selected object will be the default setting shown on the toolbar. For example, by selecting the Birthdate text box, you can see its choices in the toolbar:

Back color   *Fore color*   *Border color*   *Border width*   *Special effect*

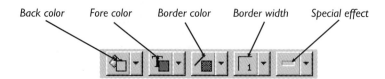

Notice how the background is clear (letting you see the form's background), the foreground color is black, the text border is light gray, the border width is 1, and the special effect is flat. You can explore other sample forms this way to see how the pros create their effects.

Select some objects on your form and experiment with the palette. Be sure to try the Normal, Raised, and Sunken Appearance options available from the Special Effects button. These are nifty effects. Incidentally, Undo is available if you hate what you've done; but as mentioned before, you should experiment only on copies of your favorite forms.

Lines and Boxes in Forms

You can draw lines and rectangles using the Line and Rectangle tools in the Design toolbar. You'll learn more about this in Chapter 37.

Adding Fields in Forms

To add additional fields to a form, drag them from the field list. Here are the specific steps:

1. Open the form if necessary and switch to Design view.

2. Click on the Field list button in the toolbar. A field list will appear.

3. Scroll in the Form window to the area where you want to insert the new field, as shown in Figure 31-2.

4. Click on the desired field name (scroll to see it if necessary), and then drag it to the place on the form where you want the field to reside.

Your mouse pointer will take on a rectangular shape as shown in Figure 31-2.

5. When you release the mouse button, the field will take up residence.

6. Use the techniques described in this chapter to resize and reformat the field and its caption if necessary. Chances are, the field will have a pretty strange name (such as "Text60:"). Don't worry about that. Just highlight to replace weird names.

Learning More About Form Design

There is much more to know. Most of the upcoming chapters in this book discuss form design topics as they arise. You can also learn a lot from online Help, and by examining some of the sample forms Microsoft has provided.

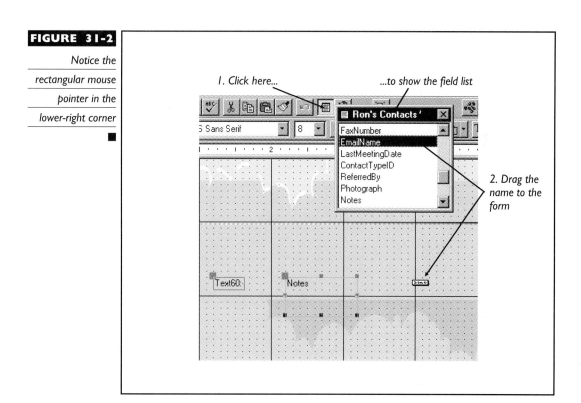

FIGURE 31-2

Notice the rectangular mouse pointer in the lower-right corner

1. Click here...

...to show the field list

2. Drag the name to the form

CHAPTER 32

Entering and Editing Data

I N this chapter you'll see how easy it is to enter, save, and edit new records using your keyboard. Many of the techniques will be familiar if you've used other Microsoft Office products like Word or Excel. You'll need the skills presented in this chapter to help you add new records and edit information in your databases.

tip   *Before spending hours retyping information you've already entered into your computer (dBASE files, or Word or Excel tables, for instance), at least skim Chapter 38. You may avoid a lot of retyping by importing or attaching data from existing files.*

Typing

There aren't many surprises here. You can enter and edit text directly in tables in Datasheet view, or you can enter and edit in forms you have created (from scratch or with the Wizard).

If you've been working along with the Contacts database exercise, you might want to continue to do so in this chapter.

Adding Records

To add records to a table:

1. Open the database and the table of interest (in this example, the "Ron's Contacts" *table* in the more general Contacts *database*).

Mailing List ID	Prefix	First Name	Middle Name	Last Name	Suffix	Nickname
1		Ted		Bravin		
2		Karen		Shewood		
3		Karen		Fries		
4		Bryan		Hannson		
5		Riva		Lesonsky		
6		Brad		Chase		
7	Mr.	Mike		Slade		
8	Mr.	Bob		Randall		
9	Ms.	Jody		Snodgrass		
10		Karen		Meredith		
11		Doug		Mahan		
12		Art		Schumer		
13	Ms.	Nina		Andro		
14	Ms.	Christy		Lemma		
15		Phil		Chase		

Record: 7 of 15

2. Choose Data Entry from the Records menu. You'll see a blank row with a triangle at its left edge, indicating that the empty row is the *current record*. You may also see "(AutoNumber)," indicating that Access will be automatically assigning a record number for possible use as the primary key.

Mailing List ID	Prefix	First Name	Middle Name	Last Name	Suffix	Nickname
(AutoNumber)						

3. Tab to the first field into which you want to enter something. Watch the flashing insertion point as you do this. It will tell which field you have activated. When you get to the desired field, start typing. Press TAB or ENTER to move to the next field of interest (or to skip a field without placing anything in it). (Incidentally, pressing SHIFT+TAB will move you *back* one field each time you do it.)

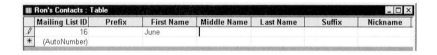

Mailing List ID	Prefix	First Name	Middle Name	Last Name	Suffix	Nickname
16		June				
(AutoNumber)						

4. When you reach the last field in the last record and press TAB or ENTER, Access will take you to the first field in a *new*, blank record. Or, also from the last record, you can start a new record by clicking anywhere in the row beneath the current record. Or, you can click on the New record button in the toolbar. All three techniques are illustrated in Figure 32-1.

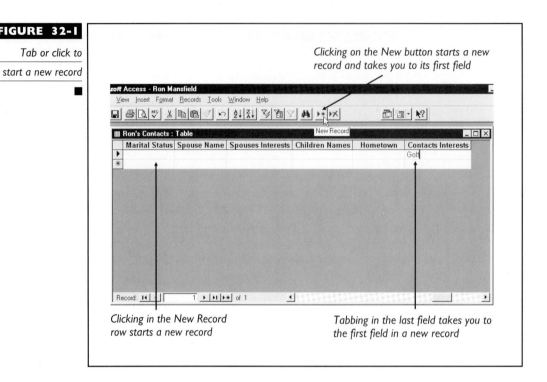

FIGURE 32-1

Tab or click to start a new record

Clicking on the New button starts a new record and takes you to its first field

Clicking in the New Record row starts a new record

Tabbing in the last field takes you to the first field in a new record

The Current Selection Symbols

By now you may have noticed two of the three little icons Access places at the left of tables to indicate the status of a record:

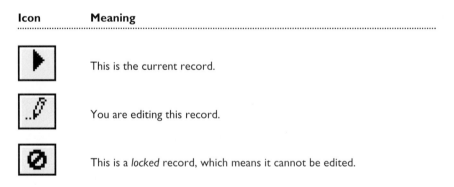

Icon	Meaning
▶	This is the current record.
✎	You are editing this record.
∅	This is a *locked* record, which means it cannot be edited.

Once you know their purposes, the visual meanings of these icons are fairly obvious. If you see a "record locked" symbol and you think you should be able to edit the record, check Chapter 39. It deals with security issues.

t i p   *When entering data into new records, it is often best to use the table's
Datasheet view or a form that includes all fields, so that you don't forget to enter
something. By the same token, if you find yourself entering or editing just the same few
fields in a table with many fields, you may want to create a small form containing only
the necessary fields, to reduce onscreen clutter. Remember, forms needn't contain all of a
table's fields.*

Entering When Fields Have Masks

Some fields may have *input masks*. Masks, which are common for entries
like phone numbers, part numbers, and so on, help force consistent entries.
You'll normally see the mask when you activate a field. For instance, most
date fields created with the Access Wizards contain masks. The Birthdate
field is an example:

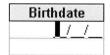

When you encounter fields like these, there is no need to add slashes,
dashes, or parentheses. When you type a date in the Birthdate field, for
instance, you can just type **110747** and Access will add the slashes to produce
11/07/47.

Entry Error Messages

You'll often be expected to enter data in a specific way, and Access may
scold you if you try to break an entry rule. For instance, here's what happens
if you commit the crime of trying to move on before adding the year:

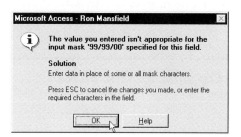

Sometimes the rules are imposed by the type of field you've specified (you
can't type letters in number fields, for example). Other times, rules are added
by the database designer. You'll see this in action in Chapter 36. Just follow
the rules and you won't get hurt. (They're usually meant to help you.)

Seriously, if the Wiz or some database designer sets up masks and rules you dislike, you might be able to change them using the information in Chapter 36 or by consulting online Help and rummaging the bigger books. Rule and mask changes are risky, however; changing rules and masks can create seemingly mysterious problems in things like expressions, searches, and sorting.

Duplicating Previous Entries Without Retyping

Sometimes, when you're entering or editing multiple records, it's nice to be able to duplicate previous entries without retyping them. For instance, suppose Ron was getting ready to type his dog Murphy's last name into his Contacts table, since he didn't want to forget her birthday:

Mike	Townes
June	Mansfield
Adam	Mansfield
Scott	Mansfield
Murphy	

He could *retype* Mansfield, of course, but the key combination CTRL+' (CTRL + apostrophe) will duplicate the data from the field above (Mansfield, in this case).

Switching Out of Data Entry Mode

When you're working in Data Entry mode, you see only the new records you've just added. Eventually, you'll want to leave Data Entry mode and see your entire table again (to edit old records, for instance). To do this, choose Show All Records from the Records menu.

When Do Entries Get Saved?

Entries and edits get saved automatically when you move to the next record. The record you were last working on will also get saved if you use the Show All Records command. There is no need to do anything special.

If it makes you feel better, however, the keyboard shortcut SHIFT+ENTER saves the current record without switching to another record.

note   *As you will see when you learn more about relational databases and "relational integrity," sometimes it is desirable to force automatic updates (or deletions) in other tables when you make changes in the current table. For now it is enough to know that you can do this. You'll learn how in Chapter 35.*

Undo

There are a number of Undo choices that may be available on the Access File menu when you are entering and editing records. These choices and their keyboard shortcuts include

Undo Typing	CTRL+Z
Undo Current Field	ESC
Undo Current Record	ESC
Undo Saved Record	CTRL+Z

Unfortunately, Access Undos are not as intuitive as, say, those in Word's drop-down Undo list. However, you will usually be given a chance to cancel an Undo, or undo the Undo if that's your wish. Obviously, when choices are dimmed or invisible they are unavailable.

Correcting Entries

You can correct entries with the usual Windows text editing techniques. Select the text to be edited or replaced and "have at it." For instance, to replace all or part of an entry, select some or all of the old entry, and then type the replacement text.

To add information to an existing text entry, click at the desired insertion point and begin typing. The mouse pointer becomes a text editing I-beam at the insertion point, unless you've landed it in a field that is protected or can't be edited.

BACKSPACE munches characters to the left of the insertion point, and Copy (CTRL+C), Cut (CTRL+X), and Paste (CTRL+V) commands work both within Access and between applications, just as you'd expect based on your

Windows experience. For instance, you can Copy text from a table in Word or Excel and then Paste it into an Access table.

tip *As mentioned earlier, there's a great shortcut for entering duplicate data (use this if you're entering the same city's name in a number of records, for example): Press CTRL+' (CTRL and an apostrophe) to copy the data from the same field in the previous record.*

Global Replacements

There are several ways to make replacements in multiple records. Some of the more powerful techniques require the creation of expressions, so they will need to wait until Chapter 36. But suppose you wanted to do something simple, like replace all those politically incorrect "Miss" prefixes with "Ms." in your Contacts database. You could use the Replace command to do that.

1. Click anywhere in a field to select it (for instance, the Prefix field in your Contacts database).

2. Choose Replace from the Access Edit menu.

3. When you see the resulting dialog box, enter the text string you want to find, and the replacement string (Miss and Ms., perhaps). Be sure to include spaces and punctuation as needed.

4. Tell Access if you want to search and replace in just the selected field (the default) or tablewide.

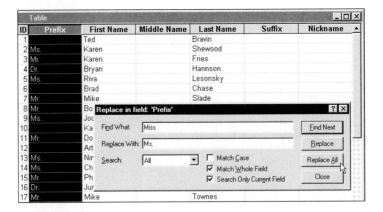

5. If you want to force Microsoft Access to change only those entries that have exactly matching capitalization, choose Match Case.

6. To force changes only when the text string exactly matches the field's *entire* contents, choose the Match Whole Field option. (This will prevent things like changing "Mississippi" to "Ms.issippi," which would also be considered politically incorrect.)

7. When you are ready, click Find Next.

8. Access will highlight the first proposed change. Click Replace to make the change, then Find Next to continue.

n o t e   *When you select Replace All, Access will make all changes, but will display a warning: "You won't be able to undo this replace operation. Do you want to continue?" Select Yes or No at that point to seal your fate.*

Moving from Record to Record in a Table

The bottom of a table window provides some handy arrow buttons that can make it easy to move from record to record—that is to say, to make a different record the *active* record. Figure 32-2 illustrates them.

In addition, there are keyboard shortcuts for locomotion:

To Make . . .	Do This . . .
The next record down the active record	Press DOWN ARROW.
The next record up the active record	Press UP ARROW.
The next window full of records appear	Press PAGE UP or PAGE DOWN.
The first field in the first record active	Press CTRL+HOME.
The last field in the last record active	Press CTRL+END.
A specific record active	Click in the ID field, press F5, type the record number, and press ENTER. Or—it may be faster, especially if you want to remain in the same field—to select the current record number, type the record number you want to see, and press ENTER.

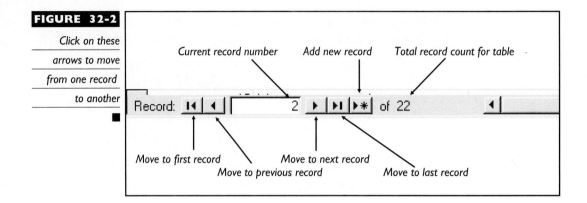

FIGURE 32-2

Click on these
arrows to move
from one record
to another

Entry and Navigational Shortcuts

There are a number of *entry* shortcuts and *navigational* shortcuts that will bounce you around more quickly from field to field within a record. Here is a table listing those shortcuts:

To Do This . . .	Do This . . .
Move to the next field	Press TAB, RIGHT ARROW, or ENTER.
Move back one field	Press SHIFT+TAB or LEFT ARROW.
Move to the current field in the next record	Press DOWN ARROW.
Move to the current field in the previous record	Press UP ARROW.
Move to the current field in the last record	Press CTRL+RIGHT ARROW.
Move to the current field in the first record	Press CTRL+LEFT ARROW.
Scroll right	Press CTRL+PAGE DOWN.
Scroll Left	Press CTRL+PAGE UP.

What Now?

Since the next exercise will involve searching for and sorting data, you might want to practice what you've learned in this chapter by typing a few of your favorite names and addresses before continuing.

CHAPTER 33

Finding, Sorting, and Displaying Data

M

ICROSOFT Access lets you search for, sort, and display data in a variety of ways. To minimize needless repetition, you can even save commonly executed searches for later reuse. In this chapter you'll learn about these features. But first, a few more buzzwords.

Queries and Dynasets

It seems everybody in the DBMS business feels compelled to invent fancy new words for age-old concepts. Not wanting to be outdone, Microsoft has coined a few new phrases, too.

Queries are simply requests you make when searching your data (for instance: show me all employees who make under $50,000).

Access responds to queries by corralling and displaying all of the records that match your query (a collection of everybody making less than $50,000, for example). These results are called *dynasets* (see Chapter 29). When you *query* Access, you'll receive a *dynaset*. If you are on a network and someone changes a record that affects your query, you will see the change as soon as the network gods decide to pass it along.

"What kinds of queries are there, and how do I query?" Well, campers, there are six kinds:

Type	Use
Select	Lets you specify desired search criteria (like all the records with a last name of Schnicklegruber).
Parameter	Displays a dialog box prompting you for information. Use as the basis for forms and reports.
Crosstab	Lets you see data with row and column headings—like a breakdown of voters by age and sex, with age in rows and sex in columns.
Action	Lets you automate tasks you do frequently. These queries change or delete records meeting your criteria. (See Chapter 36.)

Union (SQL)	Takes a 15-minute coffee break every four hours. (Actually, Union queries are those that can span multiple tables.)
Pass-through (SQL)	Sends commands to SQL databases (see Chapter 38).
Data-Definition (SQL)	Is another type that's SQL-related (see Chapter 38).

If you've entered some records into your Contacts database, run Access now and open the Contacts database if you'd like to follow along. Otherwise, just keep an eye on the illustrations.

Creating and Using Select Queries

Suppose you wanted to locate and display a list of all immediate family members and their birthdays from your Contacts database. You'd start by building the query in something called the Query by Example (QBE) grid. Here are the general steps:

1. Open the appropriate database (Contacts in this example) if it's not already open.

2. Switch to the appropriate table (Ron's Contacts, for instance).

3. Click on the New Query item as shown here:

4. Choose New Query from the resulting New Query dialog box:

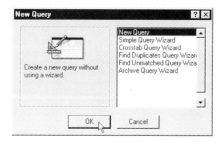

5. This will bring up a large dialog box (containing the QBE grid) where you will both design the query and enter your search criteria as illustrated in Figure 33-1.

6. Add fields you want to include by scrolling through the field list and double-clicking on each field you want to display in your results. (Alternatively, you can click once on a field name and drag it to the desired position in the grid.)

7. Be sure to include the field or fields you want to use to specify search criteria, and any additional fields you'll want to look at when Access finds the records of interest. For example, Figure 33-1 includes the Last Name field since that's what will be used to tell Access to display only records with the same last name as the author's. Figure 33-1 includes First Name and Birthdate fields since that information is also desired in this example.

8. Specify sorting options, if you wish. For example, to see your list sorted by first names (in this exercise this is important because all the last names will be identical), add a sort request to the First Name field. Do this by clicking in the Sort row in the First Name column. Pick Ascending (or another option) from the drop-down list that is revealed when you click on the arrow box:

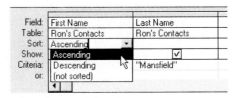

9. If you want to limit the display of records to only those meeting search criteria (last names of *Mansfield,* for instance), type the search criteria in the appropriate Criteria box. Access will add quotation marks to your entry. For this exercise, **Mansfield** is in the Last Name box:

10. Once you've completed your query, click on the Run button (which looks like an exclamation point) to run the query and display the resulting dynaset:

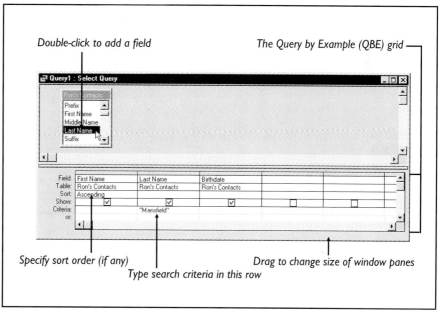

tip *When building a query, instead of double-clicking on field names, you can click and then drag them into position. To select multiple fields, CTRL-click to select before dragging. If you want to add all fields to a query, either CTRL-click on all of the field names (the suggested method) or double-click on the asterisk (*) at the top of the field list. Alternatively, you can click and select from drop-down lists in the fields themselves. This is often the quickest way.*

FIGURE 33-1

Design your query and enter search criteria in this dialog box

■

Double-click to add a field   The Query by Example (QBE) grid ─

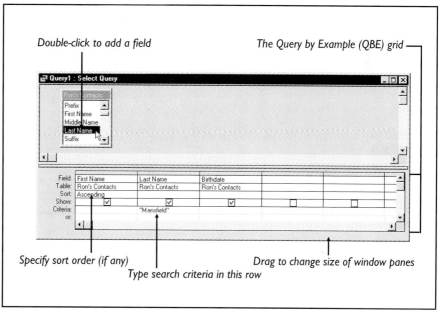

Specify sort order (if any)   Drag to change size of window panes

Type search criteria in this row

There's good news and bad. The query produced a list of Mansfields, but birth dates for everyone haven't yet been entered. This missing information is easily added, since you can type directly into the dynaset. Except in special cases (discussed in Chapter 35), changes that you make in a dynaset update the table(s) from which the dynaset was built. So you can type in the dates now or later.

note *If you use the asterisk shortcut, you might not be able to sort or specify search criteria for fields added via the asterisk trick. On the other hand, if you add fields this way, then change the design of the underlying table(s), those changes will be reflected in the query. That is, if you CTRL-click to add all of a table's fields, then add fields to the table later, those new fields won't automatically show up in the query.*

There are a few other things to fix first, however. None of the extended family members are listed, for example, since their last names are different from Mansfield. And there are some duplicate records (two "Scott"s and two "Murphy"s). Finally, in an informal list like this, there really is no need to display the last names—since first names are good enough identifiers—but you need the Last Name field to do the searching. Let's tackle one problem at a time.

Returning to the Query Design

To modify the query, you need to return to Design view by clicking on the leftmost toolbar button, which contains the ruler, pencil, and triangle. Let's modify this query to explore additional tools and techniques.

Multiple Search Criteria

To search for multiple matches (like two or three different last names), you can simply add the desired search criteria in the query as shown here:

Field:	First Name	Last Name	Birthdate	
Table:	Ron's Contacts	Ron's Contacts	Ron's Contacts	
Sort:	Ascending	Ascending		
Show:	✓		✓	
Criteria:		"Mansfield"		
or:		"Chernus"		

w a r n i n g   *Carefully check your specifications and the results they produce! In the example, Access will display records with last names of "Mansfield," "Chernus," and "Frederick," but not variations like "Chernus-Mansfield." See the next section, "Finding Incomplete Matches."*

Finding Incomplete Matches

Suppose you have a database containing film names, and you want to find a film with the word "town" in its title, but you don't remember the exact title. With some DBMS products you could just enter the text string **town** and you'd see all the near matches. Not so with Access.

Instead, entering **town** is liable to turn up absolutely nothing! So, you need to use the little-known asterisk trick.

To find text even if you don't know the exact field contents, precede and follow the text with a single asterisk. Thus, you'd type ***town*** in the example.

When you type asterisks into a search criterion this way, Access converts the criterion to a "LIKE" statement, which it then uses to find your stuff. Figure 33-2 shows an example of this. It was created by typing ***town*** in the Movie Title Criteria box.

FIGURE 33-2

Surround partial

text strings with

asterisks, and

Access will find the

strings

■

This criterion . . .

Field:	Movie Title	Subject	
Table:	Tape Inventory	Tape Inventory	
Sort:			
Show:	☑	☑	
Criteria:	Like "*town*"		
or:			

. . . finds these records

Query1 : Select Query

Movie Title	Subject
▶ Chinatown	Jack gets a bloody nose to go
On the Town	Bill Gates and wife go out to dinner
Our Town	Bill Gates and wife like the town so much they buy it
Out-of-Towners, The	Still more strangers come to town
Town Called Alice	The town that called Alice when she was in the tub
Diggstown	Bill and wife enjoy their town
Campbletown, The	Adventure, good times, and violent death on the high seas

Record: ◄◄ ◄   1 ► ►► ►* of 7

You can look in more than one place this way. For example, to find occurrences of "town" in either the Movie Title or Subject field, you could type *town* twice—once in the Movie Title Criteria box, and once in the Or box under Subject. (You'll learn more about advanced searching techniques like this later in the chapter.)

Using Wildcards in Queries

Besides using the asterisk wildcard character just described, you can include other wildcard characters in your search criteria. For example, the criterion **R?n** will find "Ron," "run," and "ran."

If you've ever used wildcard characters with computer programs (or even DOS) before, they will seem familiar. The asterisk (*), question mark (?), number sign (#), exclamation point (!), hyphen (-), and brackets ([ ]) are all Access wildcard characters.

You can use wildcard characters in queries, commands, and expressions; you can also use them to further refine searches.

Wildcard	Sample	Notes
*	***all** finds "ball," "call," and "squall"	The asterisk matches any number of characters. You can use it as the first or last character in the character string, or you can use one on each end of the text string.
?	**b?ll** finds "ball," "bell," and "bill"	The question mark matches any single character. You can use more than one question mark; for instance, **b??k** will find "beak" and "book."
#	**2#4** finds *204, 214, 224*	The pound sign matches any single digit.
[<~>]	**b[ae]ll** finds "ball" and "bell" but not "bill"	This wildcard combination matches any single character (and only the characters) placed within the brackets.
!	**b[!ae]ll** finds "bill" and "bull" but not "bell"	The exclamation mark means *not;* in the combination shown it matches any character *not* in the brackets.
-	**b[a-c]d** finds "bad," "bbd," and "bcd"	The hyphen indicates a range of characters; in the combination shown, it matches any one of a range of characters from A through C.

To search for the wildcard characters themselves—that is, the * (asterisk), ? (question mark), # (number sign), and [(opening bracket) characters—enclose them in brackets. For example, to search for an asterisk, you would type [*].

Requesting Ranges of Records

You can Request ranges of records, like "all the customers over 25 years old but under 40," or "all past-due payments that are more than 60 days late," or "all the names of customers after 'Smith' in the alphabet." You do this by using *expressions* in your search criteria. And, while you'll be spared the gory details of expressions until Chapter 36, a few simple examples are in order here.

Suppose, for instance, your video store took a straw poll to see who liked VHS, 8mm, and laser-disc formats. People as young as 22 and as old as 49 responded. After entering the data, you want to see how people over 25 and under 40 voted. You could create a query like the one in Figure 33-3 to find the answers.

All that was necessary was to type **>25 and <40** as the age criterion. Access added the quotation marks and capitalized the word "and."

The > symbol before *25* tells Access to find souls whose age is *greater than* 25 years, and <40 stands for *less than* 40. These and other operators used

FIGURE 33-3

You can include

ranges in queries

■

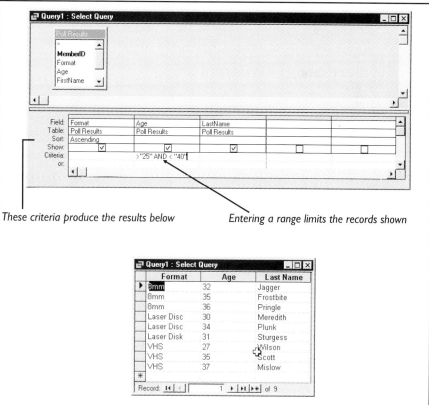

These criteria produce the results below   Entering a range limits the records shown

in expressions will remind you of those found in Excel and in Word's Print Merge features. Check online Help and Chapter 36 for details.

Hiding Columns

To hide a column (so that you can use it to generate a query, but not display it in your dynaset), click to remove the check from the appropriate "Show" box.

When you've finished changing the query, click the Run (!) button again to see the results.

There you have it, a list of family members sorted by first name and displayed without last name.

Reformatting Dynasets

You can reformat dynasets in much the same way you change the appearance of Access Tables or Excel worksheets. Here are some commonly used techniques.

Column Widths and Heights

Double-click on the lines separating columns to "autofit" column widths, or drag to set widths manually. (The mouse pointer's shape will change when you have pointed to the correct spot.)

The same basic technique works for row heights. Point to the lines separating rows at the left edge of the dynaset, and either double-click or drag when the pointer shape changes.

Moving Columns

To move a column:

1. Click once on the column (Field) name to select the entire column.

2. Click again and hold down the mouse button. The pointer shape will change to include a box:

3. Drag the column to its new location and release the mouse button.

4. The column will move:

Changing Fonts

While dynasets are not usually meant to look pretty (you'll use reports and forms to keep up appearances), you can change the font and size for the entire dynaset by using the familiar Format | Font command.

Freezing Columns

When a query reaches epic proportions and exceeds your screen width, it is often useful to nail down (freeze) the first column or two, so that the data there can be used as labels while you scroll horizontally. See, for example, the videotape list in Figure 33-4.

To freeze columns, select one or more columns (fields), and then choose Format | Freeze Columns. The Unfreeze Columns command returns things to normal.

Multilevel Sorts

Access lets you do limited—but useful—multilevel sorts in queries. For instance, if you wanted to sort a query so that it broke out people by sex, then, within that, by age, you might set up a query like this:

Field:	Sex	Age	Last Name		
Table:	Ron's Contacts	Ron's Contacts	Ron's Contacts		
Sort:	Descending	Ascending			
Show:	✓	✓	✓	☐	
Criteria:					
or:					

Since Access *always* uses the *leftmost* sort request (Sex in this example) as the first sort level, be sure to arrange the query with this in mind.

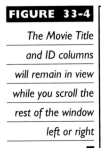

FIGURE 33-4

The Movie Title and ID columns will remain in view while you scroll the rest of the window left or right

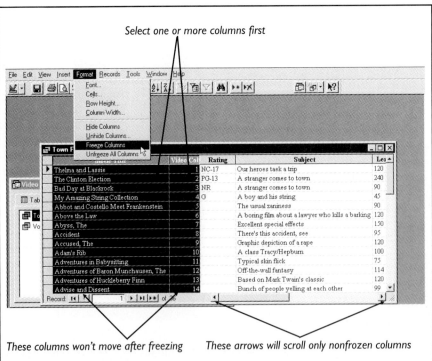

Select one or more columns first

These columns won't move after freezing   These arrows will scroll only nonfrozen columns

Remember, you can rearrange the location of the fields in the dynaset if you want to. Here are the results of a two-level sort with sex as the top level and age as the next level:

Sex	Age	Last Name
M	12	Bravin
M	12	Townes
M	13	Schumer
M	13	Mansfield
M	13	Mansfield
M	22	Hannson
M	27	Randall
M	32	Mansfield
M	35	Chase
M	36	Slade
M	42	Mahan
M	43	Chase
M	44	Mansfield
F	35	Fries
F	26	Shewood
F	23	Frubble
F	24	Lemma
F	45	Lesonsky
F	49	Snodgrass
F	55	Mansfield
F	55	Mansfield

Age and Sex : Select Query   Record: 1 of 25

You could easily add another layer of sorting to this query to make the names alphabetical within each age group, and so on. Remember, this does not affect the order of the records in your table, it just specifies the way they will be displayed for this query.

Showing All Records After a Query

Eventually you'll want to see all of your records again as opposed to just those in your query. Don't panic. Unless you've deleted them while querying, they are there, albeit sometimes a little hard to find. You just need to switch from the Query window to the Table window. If you are lucky, you can just choose the table from the Access Window menu.

In some cases you may need to choose the database from the Window menu (since the table may not be listed there if you've closed it). In this case, choose the database name from the Window menu, then click on the Tables tab in the Database dialog box, and then click on the table of interest.

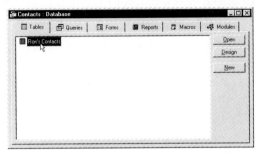

If you have a big enough screen, you can display the Database window, the table, and the Query window all at once with the Window Tile command, as shown here.

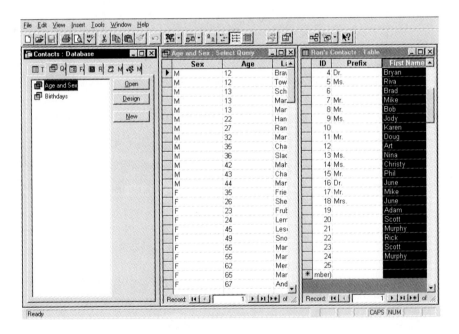

You can tile either vertically or horizontally. This shows vertical tiling.

ℐaving Queries for Later Reuse

One of the nice things about queries is that, after you spend time creating them, you can easily save them for use again and again. There is only one very important "gotcha," which deserves mentioning:

warning *Never (ever, **ever**) give a query the same name as a table when you are saving the query. If you do, it is likely that the query will replace the table—and records not meeting the query criteria will be squirted like watermelon seeds right out of the universe. Gone. Lost. Think of those watermelon seeds whenever you get ready to save a query, and then pick a clever, distinct name. Access will warn you about using the same name—don't try it!*

That seed planted, here are the steps for saving and reusing queries:

1. Switch to the Query window if you are not already there.

2. Choose File | Save or use the CTRL+S shortcut. (Sometimes you may see the command Save Query listed instead. It's the same thing.)

3. If you want to save the query to the same database, type a unique query name:

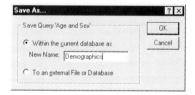

4. If you want to save the query to an external database, click the radio button and you will be shown the Save Query *name* In dialog box, which you can use to find the database where you want to save the query.

5. Click OK.

6. The query will be saved.

Crosstab Queries

Sometimes it is nice to see the results of queries summarized or arranged into meaningful groups. Crosstab queries can do this. Remember the videotape customers who voted on which formats they liked? Crosstab queries can help you see data like that in a whole new light. For example, here are the voting results in a Crosstab table that illustrates format preference broken down by age and sex:

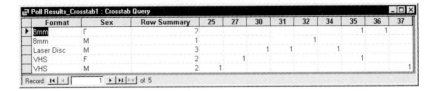

Format	Sex	Row Summary	25	27	30	31	32	34	35	36	37
8mm	F	2							1	1	
8mm	M	1					1				
Laser Disc	M	3			1	1		1			
VHS	F	2		1					1		
VHS	M	2	1								1

Record: 1 of 5

Each age is listed along the top of the dynaset. Formats and sexes are listed along the left. (Notice that there is no row for female voters for laser discs, since no women voted for that media format.) The Row summary adds up all of the entries for each row. For instance, three men chose laser disc.

This intriguing dynaset was created with the Crosstab Query Wizard. Here is the QBE (Query by Example) the Wizard created:

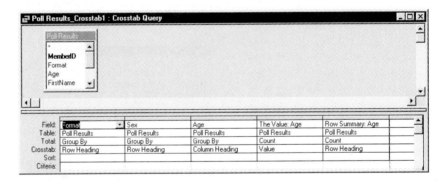

Field:	Format	Sex	Age	The Value: Age	Row Summary: Age	
Table:	Poll Results	Poll Results	Poll Results	Poll Results	Poll Results	
Total:	Group By	Group By	Group By	Count	Count	
Crosstab:	Row Heading	Row Heading	Column Heading	Value	Row Heading	
Sort:						
Criteria:						

Let's walk through the steps for using the Wizard:

1. Start a New Query using the database of interest (click on the Queries tab, and then click the New button):

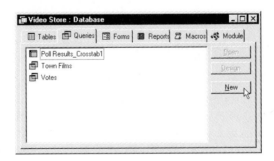

2. Pick Crosstab Query Wizard (double-click on the choice).

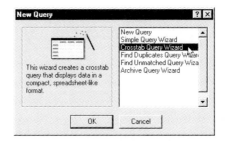

3. Start reading the Wizard dialog boxes, as shown here, making choices and watching the example develop.

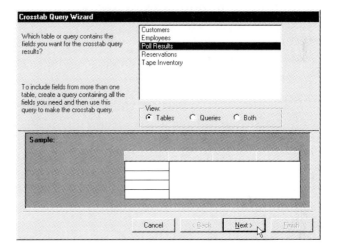

4. Pick the field or fields to be shown at the left edge of the dynaset (double-click or click once and then use the > button). Watch the sample area of the dialog box change as you work. Try to imagine how the data will look given the choices you are proposing. Remember you can use the < Back button to reverse earlier decisions. When you have finished, click Next >.

5. Specify the field type you want to use to create columns (Age, in this example). Double-click to select it. Click Next > when you're ready to move on.

6. You now must decide what you want calculated. Click on Age again and then turn to the list of function choices (Count, Average, and so on). Pick one. If you want Summary rows (like the ones in the example), be sure there's a check in the "Yes, include row sums" box, as shown on the following page, and then click Next >.

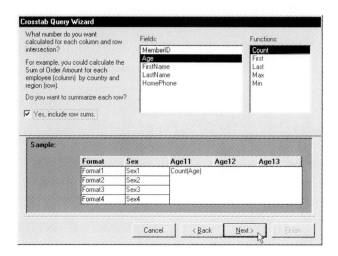

7. Name the query if you like, and then click Finish.

8. This will create the basic dynaset, which you will then probably want to embellish. (In the example, the column widths were changed and a sort request was added so that the Female and Male choices were clustered together.) Click on the Design View toolbar button to get to the QBE where you can do the fiddling.

Find and Replace

The Find command (located on the Edit menu) lets you locate text and numbers in tables. It is particularly helpful when you have lots of data. For example, here, the Find command has been asked to locate the text string "Riva" in the First Name field. It has located and highlighted (selected) the first occurrence:

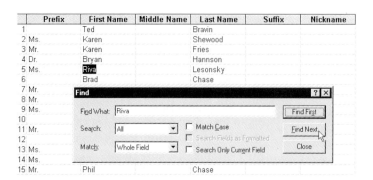

The Replace command takes things one step further and lets you change found items. For instance, you could change "Mrs." to "Ms." with the Replace command.

These commands will remind you of their counterparts in Microsoft Word. By default, Access searches only the current field (the selected field or field containing the insertion point), so click in a field to select it before finding or replacing. While it is possible to search entire tables with the All Fields option, this can be slow going.

note *You may see the term* filter *in the Microsoft documentation and online Help. Filters are simple queries that apply to a single open table. Filters can be applied to forms, however, which may be based on more than one table.*

CHAPTER 34

Printing Reports, Forms, Letters, and Labels

ACCESS provides a number of ways to put data on paper. Some of these options include

- The Print command in Table view
- The Print command in Form view
- The Print command in Query view
- The Print command in the Database window
- The AutoReport feature
- The Report Wizards (for common report and label types)
- The exporting data capabilities (for use with Word's Print Merge features)

Simple Table, Form, and Database Printing

The Print command, available in Table, Form, and Query views, and in the Database window, is great for quick-and-dirty tree killing. Basically, you put what you want to print on your screen and print it. Access even adds page numbers, dates, and a title. The general steps are almost self-evident:

1. Visit Page Setup and pick the desired page size, orientation, and other available printing options. (You can't do this in the Database window.)

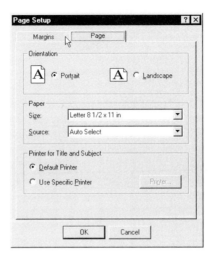

2. Open the Form, Table, or Query window from which you plan to print.

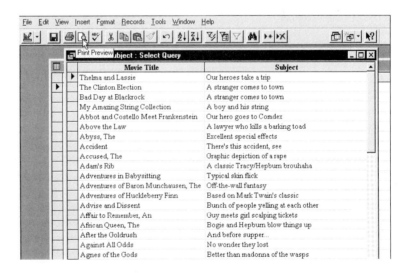

3. Make any necessary changes to the onscreen layout (column widths, locations, font choices, and so on).

4. Use the Print Preview command to save a tree.

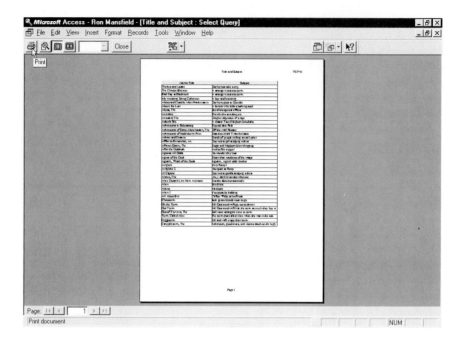

5. When you're happy with your decisions, click the Print button, or choose Print from the File menu, or press CTRL+P.

6. Make any last-minute choices (number of copies, and so on).

7. Click OK and let 'er rip. The table printed using these steps appears in Figure 34-1.

AutoReport

AutoReport is another quick way to create basic reports containing headings, page numbers, and so on. Choose AutoReport from the toolbar.

Your satisfaction with this feature will depend upon the type of data you work with and how agreeable you are to having machines run your life and arrange your printouts.

FIGURE 34-1

Actual unretouched result from the preceding step-by-step instructions ■

Movie Synopses	4/28/96

Movie Title	Subject
12 Angry Men	Lots of strangers come to town
18 Again!	Wishful thinking
2001-A Space Odyssey	Wishful thinking
39 Steps, The	Last one's a killer
400 Blows, The	Kid spray paint cars and really pays!
48 Hrs.	42 jokes
5 Corners	A war movie
8 1/2	The manuscript schedule
9 1/2 Weeks	How long it actually took
9 to 5	The odds of finishing this manuscript on time
99 Women	More wishful thinking
Abbott and Costello Meet Frankenstein	Our heros visit a book publishing convention
Above the Law	Our hero takes a trip while a stranger comes to town
Abyss, The	Bad guys sweat a lot while heros patch things up
Accident	It was just waiting to happen...
Accused, The	Larry Parker gets a stranger $3.7M
Adam's Rib	Adam opens a BBQ restaurant
Adventures in Babysitting	Kids get a much buffer babysitter than I ever had
Adventures of Baron Munchausen, The	Actors have some of what the director's having...
Adventures of Robin Hood, The	Its only a bloody brook...
Bad Day at Blackrock	A stranger comes to town
Chinatown	Jack N gets a bloody nose to go
Diggstown	Bill and wife enjoy their new town
On the Town	Bill Gates and new wife go out to dinner
Our Town	Bill Gates and new wife like the town so much that t
Out-of-Towners, The	Still more strangers come to town
The Clinton Election	A stranger comes to town
Thelma and Lassie	Our heros take a trip
Town Like Alice, A	The town really likes Alice

Page 1

For example, Figure 34-2 shows one page of an AutoReport created using the same query that created the previous example. Notice how *this* layout adds a lot of white space and creates many more pages per table or query than the regular old Print command.

Go ahead and experiment. Just get in the habit of checking Print Preview when you do.

FIGURE 34-2

A page of an AutoReport using the same query that produced the previous table printout

■

Movie Synopses

28-Apr-96

Movie Title: 12 Angry Men
    Subject: Lots of strangers come to town

Movie Title: 18 Again!
    Subject: Wishful thinking

Movie Title: 2001-A Space Odyssey
    Subject: Wishful thinking

Movie Title: 39 Steps, The
    Subject: Last one's a killer

Movie Title: 400 blows, The
    Subject: Kid spray paint cars and really pays!

Movie Title: 48 Hrs.
    Subject: 42 jokes

Movie Title: 5 Corners
    Subject: A war movie

Movie Title: 8 1/2
    Subject: The manuscript schedule

1

Defining Advanced Reports

While the Print commands and AutoReport feature are fine for basic reports, eventually you'll want to create fancy ones like the list of expenses, sorted by expense category (Account) and Payee, shown in Figure 34-3.

FIGURE 34-3

A fancy report with various type sizes and line weights, created with help from the Report Wizard

Accounting

28-Apr-96

Account	Date	Payee	Amount
Auto: Fuel	3/21/92	RMI (TEXACO)	($30.15)
	1/30/92	UNOCAL 76	($70.00)
	2/26/92	UNOCAL76	($110.90)
	3/21/92	UNOCAL 76	($200.00)
			($411.05)
			0.37%
Auto: Registration	6/26/92	DMV	($367.00)
			($367.00)
			0.33%
Capital	4/22/94	Background Engineers	($529.86)
	11/16/93	CS	($2,478.93)
	5/28/93	ST Research	($1,500.00)
	7/22/93	The Computer Store	($393.61)
			($4902.40)
			4.43%
Charity	12/7/93	American Red Cross	($50.00)
	2/11/94	KLON	($50.00)
			($100.00)
			0.09%
Credit Pay	1/15/92	AMERICAN EXPRESS	($48.04)
	2/14/92	AMERICAN EXPRESS	($151.87)
	3/21/92	AMERICAN EXPRESS	($428.41)
	4/15/92	AMERICAN EXPRESS	($241.82)
	5/27/92	AMERICAN EXPRESS	($170.05)
	6/12/92	AMERICAN EXPRESS	($430.73)
	7/11/92	AMERICAN EXPRESS	($395.12)
	8/21/95	AMERICAN EXPRESS	($88.11)
	9/17/92	AMERICAN EXPRESS	($207.60)
	10/12/92	AMERICAN EXPRESS	($420.39)
	12/11/92	AMERICAN EXPRESS	($172.95)
	1/14/93	AMERICAN EXPRESS	($216.74)
	2/12/93	AMERICAN EXPRESS	($738.40)

1

There are subtotals and the percentages have been calculated. There are nice lines and boxes of different weights used to separate the various groups, titles, dates, and page numbers. The best part is that it was all done with a Wizard. Here are the general steps:

1. Open (or simply select) the desired database and table.

2. Choose New Report from the toolbar.

3. Make sure the desired table or query name (Accounting in this example) is selected in the dialog box. Click on Report Wizard and click the OK button.

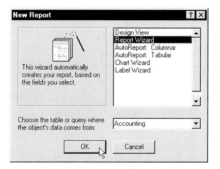

4. Choose fields you want to appear on your report. When you have finished, click Next >.

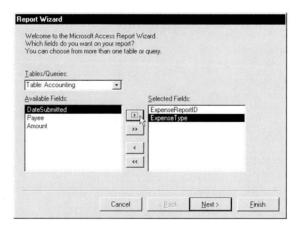

5. You will be asked how you want the report grouped. You may also need to decide how to group data in each field. Click Next > when you're ready to move on.

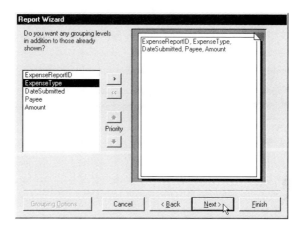

6. Next, you will be asked to choose a layout for your data. You can choose Vertical or Tabular, Portrait or Landscape. Here, Tabular and Portrait have been chosen. Click Next > to continue.

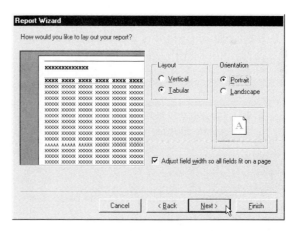

7. In the Style dialog box, click on each button and watch the example change until you find the one you like. The Compact style is handy for financial reporting and was used for the example. When you've chosen an appropriate style, click Next >.

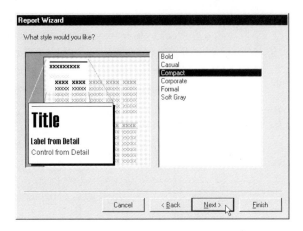

8. Give your report a meaningful title. When you've finished, click on the Wizard's Finish button and Print Preview the work.

Manual Reporting and Modifying

While it is nice to let Access handle the details for you, you'll eventually want to mess with them yourself. Or perhaps your boss will ask for something the Wizard can't deliver. That's when you will need to dig into the report design itself. Space prohibits a complete treatment of report features in this book, so let's look at the general principles. You can either experiment, use online Help, or crack the bigger books on Access for additional wisdom.

tip *You can also learn a lot about reporting by peeking behind the scenes in the sample reports supplied with the Nwind database in the Access\Sampapps subfolder.*

You make changes to reports by adding or deleting report sections and controls, and by changing their properties.

1. Begin by switching to the Database window. Click on the Reports tab, and then on the Design button.

2. Your screen will erupt with graphical nonsense as you enter Design view.

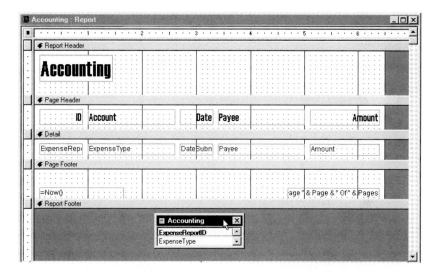

3. Take a deep breath and a long look. The Design View window is divided into many *report sections* (five, in this example—other reports will have more or fewer sections). Each section contains *controls* like text boxes, expressions, and so on. You make changes to the report by altering these controls and their properties.

Let's take a look at the various sections that were set up by the Wizard when you asked for that Accounting report.

Report Header

The report header contains a label with the report's title, and often other controls.

Page Header

Page headers contain information that will repeat on every page—like column headings. In the example there are the bold headers ID, Account, Date, Payee, and Amount.

Detail Section

The detail section contains labels and field controls (Date, Payee, and Amount) that specify which data will be printed. Don't confuse the field controls with labels.

Group Footers

There's no group footer in the example, but they are used to specify things like subtotals. These frequently use expressions—like **=sum([Amount])**. You'll learn more about expressions in Chapter 36. Depending upon your report design, you may have more than one group footer or none at all.

Page Footer

The page footer contains text and expressions that print on each page. In the example, there's an expression (**=Now( )**) that prints the current date. You could just as easily have labels that say "Confidential" on each page. There are other expressions worth exploring for page footers; you may want one that prints the message "page *n* of *x*" (see Chapter 36).

Report Footer

The report footer contains items that appear only at the end of a report, like grand totals or instructive text like "Please report all errors to EX 251."

Modifying Section Contents

By now you have most of the skills necessary to modify report sections. You can increase and decrease the height of a section by dragging on its top and bottom boundaries. To change the size of control boxes, click on them and drag their handles. To move text boxes and other controls, click to select them, and then drag with the mouse when the pointer looks like a little hand.

To change the appearance of text in a report, select the control box or boxes of interest, and then choose new settings from the toolbar and menus. For instance, to change the font(s) used in a report you might

1. Choose Edit | Select All to select all controls, or SHIFT+click to select just a few controls.

2. Choose a new font from the drop-down Font Name list in the Report Design toolbar. Here, just the controls in the Page Header have been selected and the font is being changed:

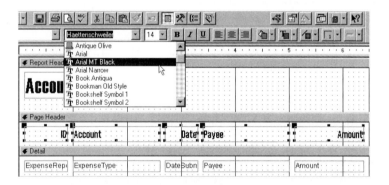

3. To accommodate the font differences, you might need to resize some or all of the control boxes by dragging. Here, since four controls are selected, resizing one resizes all four (notice the shape of the mouse pointer—it's over the leftmost control):

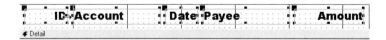

4. Move controls by dragging them to tighten things up or to make more room as necessary. Slide the mouse pointer around a selected

object until the pointer turns into a small hand, indicating that you can move objects. Again, if multiple items are selected, they will all move in unison. This is a handy way to move entire rows or columns. Here, both the heading in the Page Header section and the field control in the Detail section will move as one:

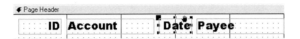

Incredibly, you can use the choices on the Format menu to alter the appearance of selected items.

Properties in Reports

There are many, many *properties* (characteristics) in reports. There are report-wide properties, section properties, and properties for individual controls. When you use a toolbar to change the font used in a control, or if you drag a control with your mouse to move it elsewhere on the screen, or if you change the source of the data to be printed, you are changing properties.

In general, to see (and perhaps to change manually) a property, select the item (the control) of interest and use the Properties command on the View menu, or click on the Properties button. Here as an example are the properties for the page-numbering control:

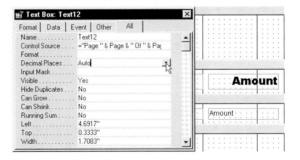

To change a property, click in the white box next to the property you want to change, and either type a new property or choose one from the resulting drop-down list. To add a normal black border around the date field, for example, you'd choose Normal from the Border Style list, and pick Black as the Border color if that's not already chosen.

You can sometimes watch the effect of property changes as you work. For instance, here the page number has been changed so that it has a shadow box effect:

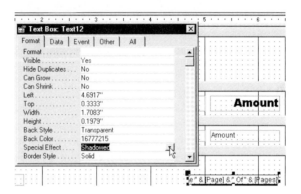

Click on the toolbar buttons to change these options.

Online Help is available to assist you with changing properties, and the bigger books review the mind-boggling options in detail.

Saving Report Formats for Reuse

Once you have a report that you like, use the Save command to save it. Report names can be long and have spaces.

To make variations on the same report, use the Save As command.

Printing Mailing Labels

Access provides a Mailing Label Wizard that can speed the creation of all kinds of labels. Don't be fooled by the Mailing Label Wizard's name. You can use it for creating name tags, file folder labels, floppy disk labels, video tape and audio tape labels—you name it.

---

tip *If you like Word better than you like Access, you can make mailing labels in Word, too. Some people even claim that Word is easy to use . . .*

Since the Wizard knows the standard layout sizes for many commercially available labels (Avery and others), you can often get the labels you need with one or two dozen mouse clicks. Here are the general steps, using mailing labels as an example:

1. Open the desired database (let's use Contacts for this example, in case you want to follow along on your own).

2. If necessary, create a Query that rounds up just the records for which you want labels (a newsletter subscribers' query has been invented here).

3. Start a new report with the New Report toolbar button shown to the left.

4. Click on Label Wizard and click OK.

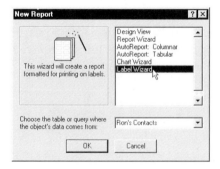

5. First, you are asked what kind of label you'd like to produce. Make your decision and click Next >.

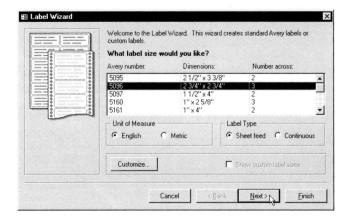

6. In the next dialog box, you are given a chance to specify the font and size of your text. You know the routine:

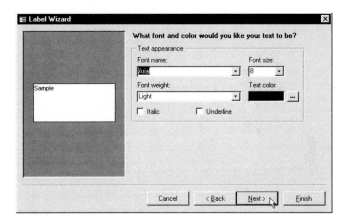

7. Select the fields that will appear in your labels, and add text or punctuation in the dialog box shown in Figure 34-4.

Now build the label design by clicking on the desired elements and pressing keys. For example, to construct a full name line from the fields Prefix, First Name, and Last Name, you'd double-click on the Prefix field, press the spacebar (to place a space between the Prefix and First Name), and then double-click on the First Name field name, or select a field and press the > key, press the spacebar again, and double-click on the Last Name field.

FIGURE 34-4

Pick label fields

and add

punctuation and

text here

■

Double-click to add a field to the label

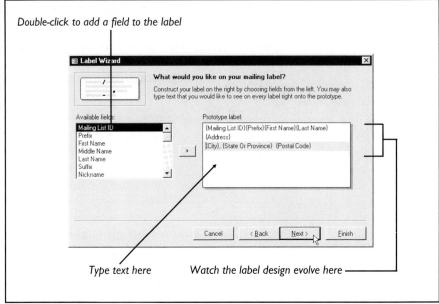

Type text here   *Watch the label design evolve here*

■ To add punctuation, press the desired character keys (comma, period, and so on).

■ To add repeating text (like "Your subscription is about to expire"), type it in the long white text box, and then click on the Text > button.

8. When you are happy with your label, click on the Next > button.

9. You'll be asked to pick fields for sorting. This example specifies a two-level sort starting with the postal code and using street address as the tie-breaker:

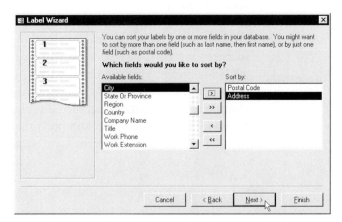

10. Click Finish when you are ready to preview your new label layout.

11. You'll see (an often uninspired-looking) print preview, as illustrated here.

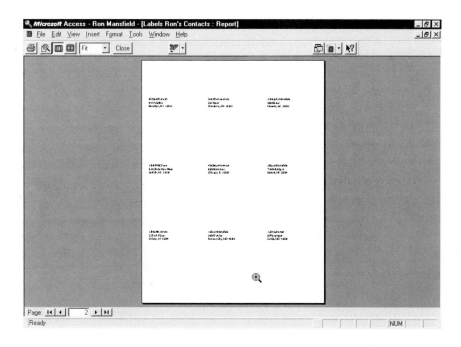

12. Use the Zoom button to take a closer look, or click on the Print button to see how the design looks on paper.

13. Save the label design the way you would any other report, with the Save command. Label report names can be long and can include spaces.

tip *Always print at least a reasonable sampling of your labels (perhaps 20 percent of them) on cheap, plain, white paper **before** you print on the more-expensive label stock. Check for things like horizontal and vertical alignment problems, fields that have been truncated, and so on.*

Changing Label Designs

To embellish your labels (by adding a logo, changing type styles, and so on), you'll use techniques that will probably seem familiar by now.

1. Open the label design by switching to the Database window, clicking on the Reports tab, selecting the desired label "report," and then clicking on the Design button:

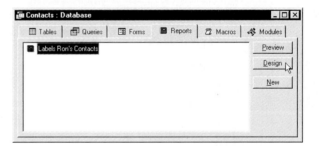

2. When you see the report design, it will contain controls for each line of the label (a control for the first line, another for the second, and so on). The Wizard constructs these controls using your specified desires and expressions (as discussed in Chapter 36). You can change these controls and their properties. (This takes some care and some knowledge, so make sure you have a backup copy before you begin.)

3. Select a control by clicking on it, and then change properties with toolbar tools or menu choices. Or, select a control, choose View | Properties, and make changes using the property editing techniques discussed earlier in this chapter.

4. You can add art, repeating text, and so on, to your report. For instance, the following illustration shows a label logo under construction. It is being created by inserting a graphic object from the ClipArt Gallery, a label, and in a moment you can add a line and some text. (You already know how to create text objects in Access reports, and you can probably figure out how to insert graphic objects and lines from your previous Windows experience. If not, turn to Chapter 37, where you'll play with graphics and lines.)

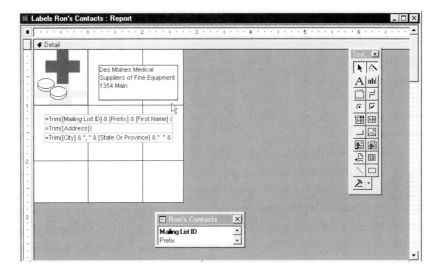

5. Save the changes when you are happy with them.

tip *When you experiment with redesigning reports, use the Save As command to save the new designs. Then you'll have copies of both the old design and the new ones. If you don't like the new ones, you can always go back and use the old design.*

On the next page a print preview of the finished label masterpiece.

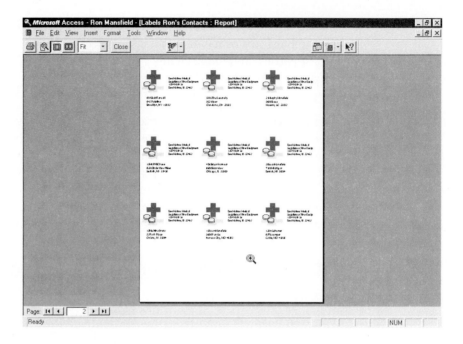

Using Access Data with Word's Mail Merge

One of the Report Wizard choices is *Microsoft Word Mail Merge.* You can use it to link data from your database to a new or existing MS Word Mail Merge document. Simply save your query or Access table with the Save command, and then run the Access Report Wizard, choosing MS Word Mail Merge when the choice is offered. Follow the resulting dialog boxes and obtain online Help if necessary. The Wizard will launch Word as needed and will lead you through the appropriate steps. Unless you have a fast computer with plenty of RAM, this can take a while. Be patient.

Other Printing Topics to Explore

There is more to know about Access printing, of course; but if you've read this chapter and have used other Windows programs, you already have the skills necessary to create impressive reports.

Many of the things you'll learn in Chapters 36 and 37 will also be useful when printing. For example, you can use expressions to control printing. You can use macros to automate printing tasks, and so on. But next, let's turn briefly to relational databases.

CHAPTER 35

Relational Databases

T H E R E are three general ways to organize databases: as flat files, as a hierarchy, or as relational databases. This chapter explores the relational approach.

Flat Versus Relational

If you keep all of your information in one table in a single database file, it is called a *flat file*. Simple projects like a personal collection of names and addresses are often good flat-file candidates. Flat files are easy to maintain. There is very little chance of misplacing or duplicating data.

Other times, however, it is wise to put data in different tables or even different database files, and then to create links between the tables or database files. These multiple tables and database files, when used together, create a *relational database*.

Relational databases allow you to store and use large amounts of data efficiently. Frequently used information like the names, addresses, and phone numbers of your customers can be stored in one table, while other information—data concerning orders, for example—is stored in another table. This way, there's no need to keep the name, address, and phone number of each customer as part of the record for each order; instead, a link between the two tables allows that data to be stored in one table and accessed for use in the other. A third table, for invoices, could then be linked so it could pull data from each of the first two tables.

This not only minimizes the amount of storage needed for large, complex databases, but can also minimize retyping of frequently used information, and reduce the chance that you'll use out-of-date information or make typographical errors. Good database designs like this break complex collections of data into chunks that can be managed by different groups of people and used by everyone.

As you may recall, in the sample video store database (Video Store) you created the four tables illustrated here.

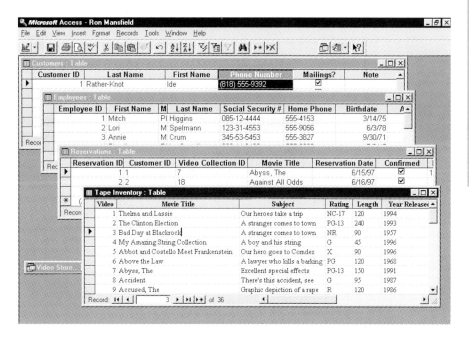

One table is called *Customers*. It contains each customer's name, address, phone number, customer ID number, and so on.

Another table is called *Tape Inventory*. It's a list of tapes, containing each tape's (movie) title, a unique number to identify each copy of that title, a brief plot description (subject), and so on. There's another table that tracks which tapes have been reserved by which customers. This table (called *Reservations*) collects reservation dates, tape numbers, the ID of the employee making the reservation, and so on.

Finally, there is the *Employees* table containing employee ID numbers, names, and the other usual data contained in employee records.

As you probably know from your trips to the video store, employees routinely call customers from lists (printed or onscreen) to confirm reservations, to ask for overdue tapes, and so on. Linking these four tables in the Video Store database means that the parts become more than the whole. For instance, looking at all four tables long enough, you *could* figure out that Ide Rather-Knot (Customer 1) reserved the film *The Abyss* (Tape ID 7) for 6/15/97; and you'd know that the employee Mitch Higgens (Employee 1) made the reservation. This takes a lot of hunting through different windows and lots of irrelevant data, though, a process that can eventually make you blind or crazy.

Obviously, you could have employees type the full names of everything in each table, but there is a better way. You can create queries, reports, and data entry forms that compile the data into meaningful information and display it in a more usable fashion. For instance, here's a query that uses not only the four tables in the Video Store database, but an external table from another database:

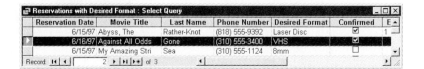

Ah, much better! Those shorthand numbers for tapes, customers, and employees have been replaced by real names. And the customer's phone number has been pulled from the customer file, so there's less chance of a typo. Notice the column *Desired Format*. It contains information from that separate Voters database you explored earlier. It collected customers' last names and their preferred media types. While, as you'll see later, it isn't always good database design to relate things this way, this example makes an important point: you can relate multiple *database files* to form relationships between them when the need arises. Sometimes, you can even use non-Access database files.

Once you've properly established links to form relationships between tables, you can create a variety of reports and queries. For instance, here's a report showing who has which tape and when it is due back. Notice that first names have been added here:

Tape ID	Due Back	Movie Title	Last Name	First Name	Phone Number
7	6/17/97	Abyss, The	Rather-Knot	Ide	(818) 555-9392
18	6/18/97	Against All Odds	Gone	Hellen	(310) 555-3400
4	6/17/97	My Amazing String	Sea	Abee	(310) 555-1124

Note that this report uses the short date format; if you prefer, you can use the long date format, which includes the names of days, and different headings (captions) for some of the fields (columns). Remember, once you understand how to change field properties, you can make these and other changes in reports, queries, and elsewhere.

How Relationships Work

This is one of those chicken-and-egg things. It's hard to understand how relationships work until you know how to create them, and it's hard to create them until you understand them. So, let's look at the insides of the Video Store relationships, and then you can try one or two of your own. Don't worry if this Video Store tour doesn't make complete sense. It will after you create your own relationships. Let's look at the "Who has the Videos" query first. It's pretty straightforward.

When you design a query or report, you start by opening the various tables you want to use. (You will learn how later.) For the first example you'll need the tables Tape Inventory and Customers.

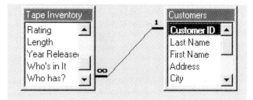

You need the Tape Inventory table because it contains, among other things, a field that tells you who has which tape. This information is stored in the field called "Who Has?" When a customer picks up a tape, the store's employees enter the customer's ID number into this field.

Obviously, a customer could pick up one tape, or many tapes, but no two customers can have the same tape at the same time. If more than one tape is rented by the same customer, the customer's ID number is placed in each appropriate tape record.

The Customers table has a field that corresponds to (is related to) the Who Has? field in the Tape Inventory table. The field is called "Customer ID." This table contains a single, unique number for each customer. No two customers have the same ID number.

The numbers in the Customer ID field and in the Who Has? fields *match*. That is, they are *related*. Access has been informed about this relationship by use of a simple technique you'll soon use yourself. Since the two fields in the example have already been related, Microsoft Access has drawn a line between them. For extra credit: look back at the diagram to see if you can figure out why there is a *1* at the Customers end of the line and the infinity sign (signifying many) at the Tape inventory end of the line. The answer in a moment.

Once you've established one or more relationships like this, you can use them to create meaningful reports and queries. For example, take a look at the design for the "Who Has the Videos?" query:

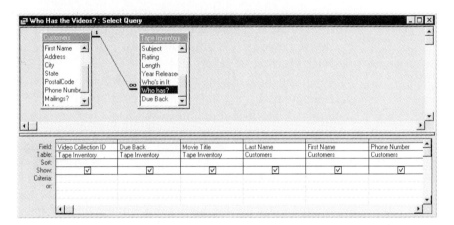

Access has been told to display information from the two tables. The first field that will be displayed is from the Tape Inventory table. It's the tape ID number. The next two fields are also from the Tape Inventory table (Due Back and Movie Title).

The next three fields to be displayed (Last Name, First Name, and Phone Number) are from the Customers database. The last field is Who Has?. Notice that the related fields (Who Has? and Customer ID) won't even show up on the screen! In this case, they do their work of linking the tables in the background.

In other words, when you run this query, Access looks for all tape records that have a customer ID in the Who Has? field. Whenever it finds one, it displays the requested tape information (Video Collection ID, Due Back, and Movie Title) *along with the requested information from the Customers table* (names and phone numbers). It matches the numbers in the Who Has? field with the numbers in the Customer ID field to know what to display in the name and phone fields.

Take a peek at some more complex relationships before you create one of your own.

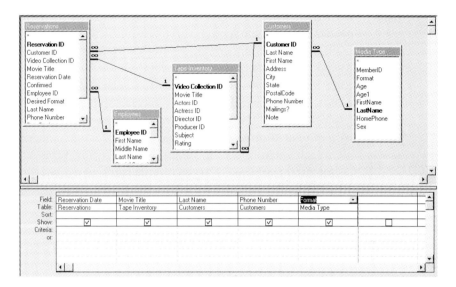

Holy cow! Actually, this is easier than it looks. There are *five* tables this time, four from the Video Store database, and the fifth (Media Type) from the Voters database.

The relationship formed by the link between the Employee ID in Reservations and Employee ID in Employees will be used to look up and display the employees' first names (First Name) in a query.

The two Video Collection ID fields in Reservations and Tape Inventory will be used together to display the Movie Title field contents from the Tape Inventory database. The relationship between the two Customer ID fields in the Reservations and Customers tables will be used to display the customers' last names and phone numbers. These relationships were made all the easier to see and understand by naming the fields in the different tables with the same names (Customer ID in Reservations and Customer ID in Customers, for example). That's a good habit to establish.

Finally, the risky step has been taken of relating the Customers table in the Video Store database with the Media Type table from the Voters database. The theory is, if customers voted in the imaginary straw poll, you could learn and display their preferred media type by relating their last names from the Customers list with the last names from Voters.

Besides illustrating the point that data from outside databases can be related, this presents an opportunity to point out the pitfalls of sloppy relationships. First, what happens if you have two customers with the last name Smith? Or what if a visiting nonmember votes? What if two members of the Smith family vote for different media types? People will find the darnedest ways to screw up seemingly wonderful database designs. The proper way to include such survey results is to ask customers to write down their customer numbers, and enter those into a Customer ID field in the Media Type table of the Voters database, or have an employee look up and enter ID numbers after the survey has been conducted.

Forcing *referential integrity* is another step you can take to minimize the risk of events like this. Basically, you ask Access to enforce the validity of data in related tables. For instance, if you change, add, or delete something in one table that affects another table, you want Access to at least warn you of potential problems. This technique is discussed later in this chapter.

Exercise: Creating a Simple Relationship

Let's create a simple relational database. How about a Little League Roster and some stats?

1. With Access running, start by closing any database you might have open with the Close Database command, and then pick New Database from the File menu (or use the CTRL+N keyboard shortcut).

2. Pick a name and location for the new database. Let's say the team's going to be the 1997 Buellton Pirates, so you can call the file **Pirates, 1997** and store it in the folder My Documents. Access will take care of adding the filename extension. Click Create to create the database.

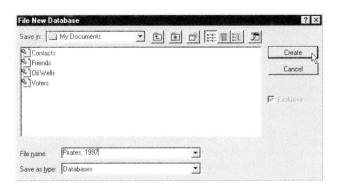

3. Now you need a couple of tables. Let's start with a Players table. When Access displays the empty Database window, click the Tables tab if it isn't already foremost, and then click the New button to create a new table.

4. Why not create your own here, without the help of a Wizard. Double-click on Design View.

5. Create a Player Number field and a Name field, specifying the appropriate data type for each:

6. Make the Player Number field the primary key by clicking in the field name and then choosing Edit | Set Primary Key or clicking the Primary Key button on the toolbar:

7. To enter a few player numbers and names, you will need to switch to Datasheet view by clicking on the Datasheet View toolbar button, but you'll be asked to save the table when you switch views.

8. Enter a few uniform numbers and names. To do this, tab from field to field, typing in the appropriate information in each field. (Notice

that Access won't let you assign duplicate player numbers, since this is the Primary Key field.) You can adjust the column widths if you like.

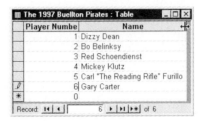

9. To create a second table to use for collecting game stats, select File | New | Table or choose New Table from the toolbar drop-down list.

10. Double-click on Design View to create the table.

11. Include a numeric field for the Player Number field, a Date/Time field for Game Date, a text field for What Happened, and a numeric field to collect Runs Batted In (RBI).

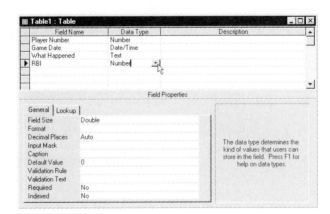

12. Save the table as Game Stats. Let Access create an index field for you when it asks permission.

13. Make four or five entries like those shown here:

ID	Player Number	Game Date	What Happened	RBI
1	1	5/4/97	2-4, Triple	0
2	2	5/4/97	1-4	2
3	3	5/4/97	3-4, Home Run	3
4	8	5/4/97	0-4, 3 K	0
(mber)	0			0

Record: 14 ◄ 4 ► ►I ►* of 4

tip *To enter today's date without typing it, use the key combination CTRL+; (CTRL+semicolon).*

Now that you have two tables with some data, let's relate them while creating a simple query.

1. Choose New Query from the drop-down list in the toolbar.

2. Click on New Query and click OK.

3. You'll see the beginnings of a query, probably with only the Game Stats table in view:

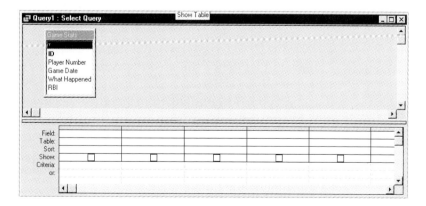

4. To add a table to the query design, click its name (Pirates in the example) and click Add or double-click its name in the Show Table dialog box:

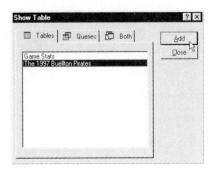

5. Now click the Add button, and the Pirates table will appear in your Query window. Close the Show Table dialog box by clicking the Close button.

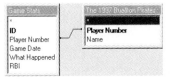

tip *You can drag the corners of the tables to resize them if you like. Dragging on the table titles will move the tables.*

Look at that! Since you used the same field *name* and field *type* in both tables, Access has inferred a relationship, which it has indicated by drawing that line representing the link from Player Number in Game Stats to the other table. You can create additional relationships by pointing to one field in a table and dragging to a field in another table, drawing new relationship lines in the process. But don't do that now, since none of the other fields should be related. For now, you've done what you came to do. You have created a relational database!

Let's check out this relationship by creating a query that shows events from Game Stats with players' names from the Pirates table.

1. To include the players' names in the query, double-click on "Name" in the Pirates table:

2. Next, add other fields you'd like to see in your query (perhaps Game Date, What Happened, and RBI).

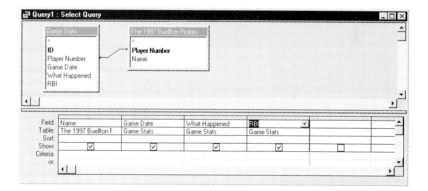

3. Save the query, if you like, by clicking on the Save button in the toolbar or by using the CTRL+S shortcut. Long spacey names are OK (for example, "Player Performance").

4. Click on the Datasheet View toolbar button to see the results of your first query:

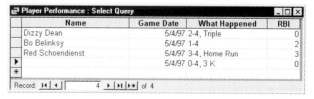

That's pretty neat, but perhaps you've noticed a problem. There were *four* entries in your sample Game Stats table, but only *three* names are showing in the query. What gives? Looking at the data in both tables together will shed some light:

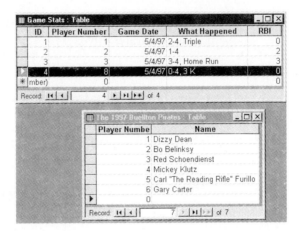

One of the Game Stats is credited to a player number 8, but there is no player number 8 in the Pirates roster (the 1997 Buellton Pirates table). Since the player struck out three times, you can understand his desire for anonymity, but Access has no mercy. What happened was you didn't enter one of your heavy hitters—Reggie Jackson. With Reggie in the table, the query produces the desired results.

The lesson is *check your work*. Get in the habit of knowing how many items you should be seeing when you perform a new query or create a new report, and consider building in data-entry *tests* that will warn you if entries are out of range. (This is discussed in Chapter 36.)

You can also minimize the chances of problems like the one that just occurred by defining *relationship types* and using Access's ability to enforce *referential integrity*. So, this near-disaster you just experienced is a good excuse to explore these concepts.

Types of Relationships

Let's look at the types of relationships first, and then learn how to specify them. The three types of relationships are (take notes, this'll be on the test):

- One-to-many
- Many-to-many
- One-to-one

Here are examples of the different types of relationships and why you would use them.

One-to-Many

One-to-many is the most common type of relationship. The Pirates database includes what should be a one-to-many relationship. Each player listed in the Pirates table has a unique Player Number. Any given Player Number can be found only *once* in the Pirates table. That is to say, there are never duplicate player numbers in the Pirates table.

In the Game Stats table, however, there can be *many* entries containing the same Player Number, because players make many plays each year. (By the way—there can be only one Player Number in any single game stat.)

...Got all that? To summarize:

- There must be one and only one player number for each player in the Pirates table—no duplicate player numbers are permitted in this table.

- Many entries in the Game Stats table can contain duplicate player numbers since one player makes many plays.

- Only one player number is stored in any one Game Stats record since there is only one field to hold a player number in a Game Stat record.

That's a classic one-to-many relationship. There are other examples of one-to-manys in the Video Store example. Each tape can only be rented by one person at a time, but one person can rent many tapes at the same time. One employee can make many reservations, but each reservation can be taken by only one employee, and so on.

Whenever possible, it's a good idea to create one-to-many relationships (as opposed to many-to-many relationships, which are discussed next).

Many-to-Many

If you are a novice database user, you may want to skim this section, and then study it along with bigger books on the subject if you ever need to set up a complex database.

Occasionally, many-to-many relationships are unavoidable, or at least troublesome to do without. A classic example of a many-to-many relationship is illustrated in the sample Microsoft Northwind Traders Orders database that is shown on the following page.

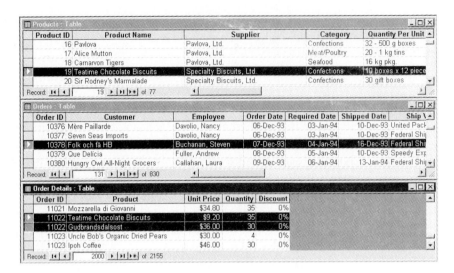

The Orders *table* (yes, it's confusing; there's an Orders table in the Orders database) collects things like Order ID numbers, Customer ID numbers, Employee ID numbers, Shipping addresses, and so on. There is only one record for each order. Each has a unique order *number*.

In addition, there's a second table called Order Details. Here, each row (record) contains the details of a single item that has been ordered by a customer. As you can see, this table has multiple rows (records), with each record containing a customer's purchase order number, the part number (Product ID) for the ordered item, the quantity ordered, and so on. Some records have the same Order ID numbers. You might have thousands of these records with many records for each purchase order number (back to this table in a moment).

Finally, you see a table called Products. It contains product information, with one and only one record for each product. Each record has a field for Product ID, a description, unit pricing, and so on.

The Orders table and the Order Details table have a one-to-many relationship. That is, there can only be a single Order ID number in each record in the Orders table, but it's OK to have more than one record in the Order Details table with the same Order ID number. Take a moment to look at the illustration. There are two highlighted items in the Order Details table. They both have the order number 11022. Since there can be only one Order ID entry in a record in the Order Details table, the relationship is one-to-many. (Or maybe one *too* many, at this point.)

The Products table and the Order Details table also have a one-to-many relationship. Each line item in the Order Details table can have only one

Product ID, but there can be many different line items with the same Product ID in the Order Details table, making this a one-to-many relationship.

The many-to-many relationship is developed because there can be many Order IDs in the Order Details table that match Order IDs in the Orders table, and many Product IDs in the Order Details table that match entries in the Products table.

The advantage to this arrangement is that you needn't bog down tables with needless repetition. You could live without the Order Details table, and clutter up your Products table with an entry each time someone ordered the product. Or you could clutter up the Orders table with a lot of repetitive product descriptions and such. But this way is cleaner.

Again: Don't try to figure this out for the first time by yourself a few hours before an important deadline. It takes time to develop, test, and trust complex relationships. Doesn't it?

One-to-One

This section discusses one-to-one relationships; but if you are clever, you'll probably never use them. In a one-to-one relationship, there can be only one matching record in each of the related tables. For instance, in the Video Store and Voters example, if you had a Customer ID field in both Video Store and Voters, there should probably never be multiple occurrences of a customer's ID in either table (assuming of course that customers only vote once, know their customer ID numbers, and that noncustomers don't vote). In such an unlikely case, Customer ID 1 would occur only once in the Customer table and only once in the Voter table, forming a one-to-one relationship.

When you spot potential relationships like this, consider adding a field to an existing table rather than creating a new table. For instance, it would probably be better to add a Media field to the Customer table rather than to create that whole Voter table just to capture customer media preferences.

Viewing Relationships

The types of relationships between tables are graphically indicated by special symbols in Relationships tables.

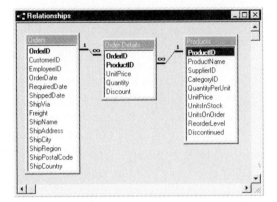

The one-to-many relationships have a number *1* at one end and the infinity sign at the other, indicating many. As you will see when you get to referential integrity, the thick connecting bars have a special meaning.

You can view relationships by following these steps:

1. Open the Database of interest (Nwind, in this example).

2. Click the Relationships toolbar button as shown here:

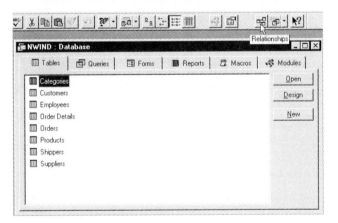

3. When you see the Relationships window, click on the Show All Relationships button.

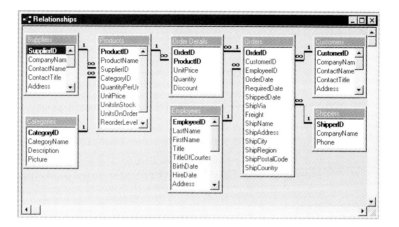

4. If necessary, drag to resize and rearrange the table lists so that the lists don't clutter or cover lines and obscure your understanding of the relationships.

5. Click once on a relationship line to select (darken) the line.

6. Double-click on a selected line to display the Relationships dialog box, which is where you can view and modify relationship settings. (You'll actually do this with your Pirates database in a moment.)

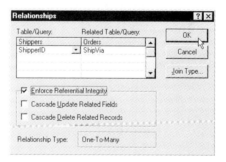

7. When you've finished, close the Relationships dialog box (if it is open) by clicking its close box. Close the larger Relationships diagram window in the same way.

Defining and Redefining Relationships

You'll frequently need to define or modify relationships. For instance, the relationship Access established automatically when the Buellton Pirates database was created needs some work. That's because Access failed to establish a one-to-many relationship, and it doesn't do an integrity check that would be helpful.

In general, you create the links that represent relationships by dragging new lines from a field name in one table list to a field name in a different table list. The first field (where you start dragging) is referred to as the *primary key field*. The second (the one you drag to) is called the *foreign key field*.

You edit a relationship by selecting the relationship's line, double-clicking on the line (this makes a total of three clicks), and then changing the rules in a dialog box or two.

This next bit is going to take some concentration. Take a break if that will help. Then let's experiment:

1. Open your Pirates database and use the Relationships toolbar button to open the Relationships window:

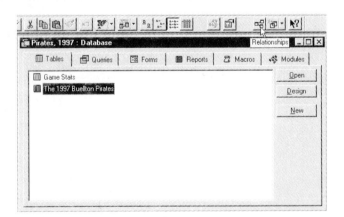

2. You should see both tables in the Relationships window and a line indicating the relationship between the two Player Number fields. Your screen arrangement may look a little different from the one shown here, but you should see all three of these elements:

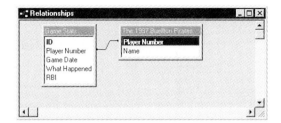

3. If you don't see all of the tables you want to work with, use the Show Table toolbar button to bring up the Show Table dialog box. Double-click on the names of tables you want to add to the Relationships window, and then close the Show Table dialog box. (You actually should not have to do this for the current exercise.)

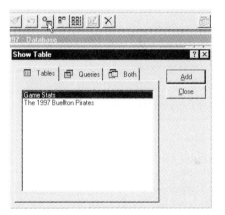

Deleting Relationships

In a moment you are going to add—and then modify—a relationship in the Pirates database. But first it's time for a brief side trip.

From time to time you'll need to delete relationships. For instance, Access might create unwanted relationships when you set up a new database, or you might try to change a field type (from number to text or from one number type to another, for instance), only to find that relationships exist and that they will have to be deleted before you can make the type changes.

To delete a relationship:

1. Display the Relationships window showing the relationship(s) to be deleted.

2. Click once, carefully, on the relationship line to select it. The line will thicken when you hit the hot spot:

3. Press DEL to remove the relationship. You will be asked to confirm the deletion. The line should disappear.

Try deleting the relationship in your Pirates database if you haven't already done so.

Creating Relationships

The process of creating links to form relationships is also called *joining*. The actual steps for joining will vary based on the *type* of relationship you want to establish, and the *source* of the tables and databases you need to relate. You'll also need to give some thought to which will be the *primary field* and which will be the *foreign field*. Sometimes you'll need to tell Access what to do when there are, or are not, matches between the two tables. Finally, there are ways to ask Access to help you maintain the integrity of your database. Here are the general steps for enforcing integrity, using a Pirates relationship as an example.

1. Open the Relationships window for the database of interest and make sure all of the necessary tables are visible.

2. Decide which field you want to be the primary key field and locate it in the field list (by scrolling, if necessary). In the Pirates example, you'll want to use the Player Number field from the Pirates table.

3. Decide which field you want to be the foreign key field and locate it in the field list (by scrolling, if necessary). In this exercise let's use the Player Number field in the Game Stats field list.

4. To begin the actual joining process, click on the primary field name (the Player Number field from the Pirates table), and hold down the mouse button. The mouse pointer will change into a rectangle. If you look carefully, you can see the funny new pointer shape hovering over the Player Number field name here:

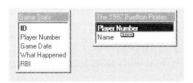

5. Hold down the mouse button and drag until the pointer is over the field name in the destination table (the Player Number field in the Game Stats field list). It's OK that the mouse pointer changes shape while moving between table lists.

6. When you reach the destination field (the Player Number field in the Game Stats field list), release the mouse button. You'll see a Relationships dialog box:

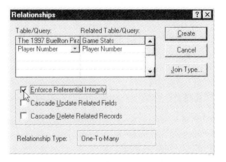

7. The Relationships window displays the primary table and field on the left and the foreign table and field on the right. (If you've made a mistake and pointed to the wrong field, you can use the drop-down lists to choose different field names.)

With the desired field names showing in the Relationships window, clicking Create will establish a one-to-many relationship between the two tables. But don't click Create if you are following along with the Pirates exercise. To define the *type* of relationship you want to establish, you must first specify whether to enforce referential integrity and pick a relationship type. Read on.

Referential Integrity

When you choose the Enforce Referential Integrity option in the Relationships window, you tell Access that there must be appropriate matches between the two tables. This is one way to prevent things like that missing player problem discussed earlier in the chapter. In that example, if the relationship between the Player Number fields in the roster and Game Stats tables had been defined as "one-to-many with enforced referential integrity," you would have seen an error message when trying to enter a game stat for an undefined player. That is, you can force Access to make sure there is a match in the primary key field for entries in the foreign key field, by demanding the enforcement of referential integrity.

Here are the steps for establishing this kind of relationship in general, using the Pirates database as an example:

1. With the Relationships window open for the relationship of interest (the two Player Name fields in the example), choose the Enforce Referential Integrity option.

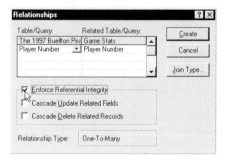

2. You will be faced with the one-to-one versus one-to-many choice. Pick one or the other radio button. In the case of the Pirates database, you want one-to-many, since there can be only unique Player Numbers in the Pirates table, but many of the same Player Numbers in the Game Stats table. Click on the Many button.

3. To create the actual relationship, click the Create button in the Relationships window. This will establish the relationship and close the Relationships window.

4. Notice that the relationship is now graphically represented with thicker lines, indicating enforced referential integrity, and that the indicators for a one-to-many relationship appear.

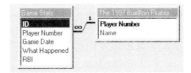

To test the results of your work, switch back to the Game Stats table and try to enter a record using a player number that you've not defined in your other table:

1. Choose Pirates, 1997: Database from the Window menu to make the Pirates Database window active.

2. Click on the Tables tab, if necessary, to see the list of tables.

3. Double-click on the Game Stats table to view it.

4. Try to enter a record with a Player Number that has not been defined yet in the 1997 Buellton Pirates table (Player Number 16 in this example):

5. When you try to leave the record, Access will display an alert telling you about the integrity problem. You can correct the Player Number in the Game Stats entry, or you can switch to the Pirates table and add a player with the number causing the problem.

Troubleshooting

It's common when setting up new relationships or changing field types to be scolded by Access for type mismatches. Access expects that if you are going to relate two fields from different tables, both fields have compatible definitions (both number fields with double field sizes, or both text fields 50 characters in length, for instance). That's why it is a good idea to plan ahead when you are creating tables. Think about the potential relationships before defining fields.

What Next?

There's much more to know about relationships if you plan to develop databases; so if that's the case, you'll need to grab some books devoted to Access. You might try *Access for Busy People* by Alan Neibauer (Osborne McGraw-Hill, January 1996).You can then begin experimenting on some small databases of your own, and you can always check out the sample databases in the Access\Sampapps directory.

You'll also need a firm understanding of expressions and other Access automation tools. These are the topics of the next chapter.

CHAPTER 36

Expressions, Macros, and Other Automation

D ATABASE management often requires a number of specific steps that must be carried out in a definite order. Access provides tools that can be used to automate these complex tasks, making experienced users more productive, and enabling novices to accomplish things with a minimum of technical expertise.

There are risks, of course. Computers take their instructions quite literally; they are famous for their lack of good judgment. When you automate your databases, it is your responsibility to anticipate (and test for) all the things that can and will go wrong.

Let's take a look at expressions, macros, action queries, the Toolbox buttons, and other forms of Access automation.

Expressions

You use *expressions* every day when you ask questions or give instructions, like

- Let's raise prices on all accessories by 10 percent.
- Who are the top-ten salespeople?
- Be sure to get each customer's phone number, including area code.
- If customers want to purchase more than ten of those, sell them for $1.50 each.
- Change the vendor name for "Air-O-Mass" products to "Aeromass" throughout the database.
- You need a list of all the customers who purchased propellers with serial numbers in the range of 11198 to 11225.

Access lets you create computerized expressions analogous to the ones just listed. These expressions can be used in reports, forms, queries, and even while creating new fields in tables. They let you find or compute information. For example, expressions let you

- Change property settings based on calculations or validation rules

- Enter and use calculations in queries and filters

- Set the stage for different actions in macros

- Add arguments to Access Basic procedures

- Change properties in SQL queries

If you've worked with Excel, Access's expressions will remind you of formulas. Unfortunately, Access expressions and Excel formulas are not identical. Neither are the buzzwords used to describe their parts.

Parts of an Expression

Access expressions always begin with an equal sign (=) and are entered into text boxes or directly into property sheets, as you'll see in a moment. Expressions contain some or all of the following parts:

- Control names (names of text boxes, buttons, and so on)

- Operators (+, –, *, AND, OR, <, >, and so on)

- Identifiers (field and table names)

- Function names (DATE, SUM, and so on)

- Literals (numbers, dates, or text strings)

- Constants (unchanging values)

- Criteria (>10, and so on)

Control Names

A *control name* is a name you define for the control that will contain the results of your formula. For example, if you create an expression to compute a 10 percent discount on list prices, the control name might be **Discounted Price**, and the expression could be **=[List Price]*.9**. When Access uses this expression, it will place the results of the computation in the Discounted Price control.

Operators

Operators do the necessary calculations and comparisons. For instance, you might use a > operator to find all the records with a price of *greater than* $1, or you might use the * operator to *multiply* the contents of one field by another. Online Help along with the examples in this book and the Microsoft sample databases will help you explore the categories of Access operators, which include

- Arithmetic

- Comparison

- Concatenation

- Logical

- Pattern matching

- Miscellaneous

The following are listings of all the operators by group:

ARITHMETIC OPERATORS   Arithmetic operators let you perform computations like addition and subtraction.

Operator	Operation
^	Exponentiation
*	Multiplication
+	Addition
-	Subtraction
/	Division
Mod	Modulo arithmetic
\	Integer division

COMPARISON OPERATORS   Comparison operators let you determine relative values, posing questions like, Is the number greater than 10? Less than another?

Operator	Meaning
<	Less than
<=	Less than or equal to
<>	Not equal to
=	Equal to
>	Greater than
>=	Greater than or equal to

CONCATENATION OPERATOR Use the concatenation operator to manipulate text strings.

Operator	Operation
&	Used for text string concatenation (for example: **FirstName & ", "&LastName**)

LOGICAL OPERATORS Use logical operators when building logic statements.

Operator	Operation
And	Conjunction
Eqv	Equivalence
Imp	Implication
Not	Negation
Or	Disjunction (inclusive Or)
Xor	Exclusion (exclusive Or)

PATTERN MATCHING OPERATOR The Pattern Matching operator is used for text searching.

Operator	Operation
Like	String comparison

MISCELLANEOUS OPERATORS The remaining operators perform a variety of functions.

Operator	Description
!	Separates parts in an identifier; tells Access that the object name that follows it refers to a user-defined object
. (dot)	Separates parts in an identifier; precedes the name of the object, method, or property
Between…And	Determines whether the value of an expression lies within a specified range of values
In	Determines whether the value of an expression is equal to any of several values in a specified list
Is	Used with the reserved word "Null"; determines whether an expression is Null

Using Operators

You can use operators in reports, property statements, and many other places. For example, in the Voters database, adding the simple expression **>17** to the Age field's property sheet will check to make certain that voters are 18 or older, as shown here.

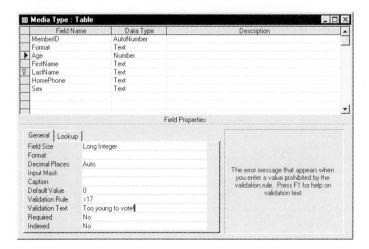

Notice that the text "Too young to vote!" has also been added to the Validation Text box. This text will be displayed in a dialog box whenever someone attempts to enter an age of less than 18.

Identifiers: Field and Table Names

Identifiers help you point Access in the direction of the desired data. Identifiers might be the name of an object or collection of objects, a form name, a table name, a property name, and so on. You must enclose an object's name in brackets when typing it in an expression; **[Unit Price]** is an example. See online Help and the big books for more about identifiers.

Functions

Functions are built-in tools that can be used for specific, often complex tasks. For instance, there's a function that computes the square root of a number you specify. Other functions simply return current information, like the present time or date.

Functions fall into four categories:

- Conversion
- Date/Time

■ Math

■ Text

Conversion functions do things like convert numbers to integers, or days of the week like Sunday to their numeric equivalent (1), and so on.

Date and Time functions either perform date and time computations, or they return current system dates and times. For instance, the function **=Now( )** uses or returns the current date and time from your computer's built-in clock/calendar. Math functions let you perform calculations, like adding sales tax to an invoice. Text functions let you find and manipulate text. For instance, you can use them to change all of the characters to uppercase in a specified field.

Literals

Literals are values you type into expressions not for the purpose of computing, but rather to be taken literally. For instance, in the expression **=[Price]*1.065**, the number 1.065 is a literal. In that case, the price is being multiplied literally by the number 1.065. Text is also permitted as a literal; for example, the text "Too young to vote!" (which you saw typed into a Validation Text box a few paragraphs ago) is a literal.

Criteria

Criteria tell Access which records are of interest. You enter criteria in queries, reports, and expressions. For example, **="Springer"** means you are interested in records that meet the criteria "Springer."

Using Expressions in Reports

Most reports contain expressions. Either you put them there, or a report Wizard does it for you. Take a look at the following report, for instance.

Accounting

ID	Account	Date	Payee	Amount
1	Auto: Fuel	3/21/97	RMI (TEXACO)	$30.15
2		1/30/97	UNOCAL 76	$70.00
3		2/26/97	UNOCAL 76	$110.90
4		3/21/97	UNOCAL 76	$200.00
5	Auto: Registration	6/26/97	DMV	$367.00
6	Capital	4/22/97	Background Engineers	$529.86
7		11/16/97	CS	$2,478.93
8		5/28/97	ST Research	$1,500.00
9		7/22/97	The Computer Store	$393.61
10	Charity	12/7/97	American Red Cross	$50.00
11		2/11/97	KLON	$50.00
12	Credit Pay	1/15/97	AMERICAN EXPRESS	$48.04
13		2/14/97	AMERICAN EXPRESS	$151.87
14		3/21/97	AMERICAN EXPRESS	$428.41
15		4/15/97	AMERICAN EXPRESS	$241.82
16		5/27/97	AMERICAN EXPRESS	$170.05
17		6/12/97	AMERICAN EXPRESS	$430.73
18		7/11/97	AMERICAN EXPRESS	$395.12
19		8/21/97	AMERICAN EXPRESS	$88.11
20		9/17/97	AMERICAN EXPRESS	$207.60
21		12/13/97	AMERICAN EXPRESS	$420.39
22		12/11/97	AMERICAN EXPRESS	$173.95
23		1/14/98	AMERICAN EXPRESS	$216.74
24		2/12/98	AMERICAN EXPRESS	$738.40

Thursday, July 27, 1995   Page 1 Of 1

Two expressions from the Page Footer section were used to create the Accounting report.

The first expression, **=Now( )**, appears in the Page Footer section of the report. It tells Access to insert the current date whenever it creates a report.

There's a similar expression, **=[Page]**, in the Page Footer section of the report. It simply tells Access to place a page number in the footer. A variation of this expression will produce page numbers in the format *Page 1 Of 5*. That expression is **"="Page "&[Page]&" Of "&[Pages]."**

Using Expressions in Queries

You can also add expressions to queries, or let Wizards add them for you. For instance, the "Like" expression shown next will round *up* only those records with the text string "phone" in the Account field.

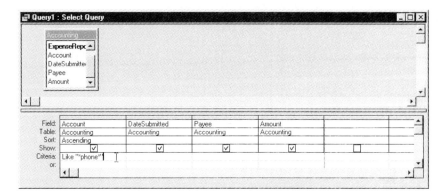

Running the query produces results like these:

Note that Access will sometimes insert the necessary Expression minutia for you. In the last example, if you had just typed *phone* in the text box, Access would have taken the initiative to change it to =Like"*phone*".

Using Expressions in Forms

Forms can also contain expressions, which are often added to the form's text boxes. In the following illustration, for instance, a field will use the current date as the default entry whenever a new entry is made (thanks to the =Now( ) function in the Date field's Default Value property):

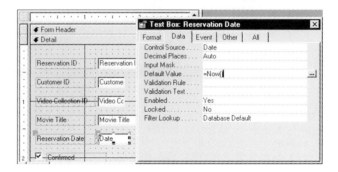

Expression Builders

While you can build expressions by simply typing them, you may want to use an *Expression Builder*. These often-cluttered dialog boxes contain lists and buttons offering available options for use in expressions. For example, here is the Expression Builder you'll see if you click on the Build button on a properties sheet like the one for the Date field previously discussed.

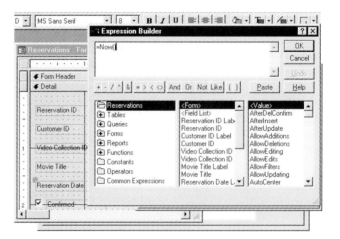

This Expression Builder lets you construct expressions either by typing them directly, or by clicking on the desired operators, field names, and so on. To open a list, double-click on the leftmost choice of interest. For instance, to see a list of the fields available in a table, double-click first on the Tables choice, then on a table. Here, the contents of the Accounting table are visible:

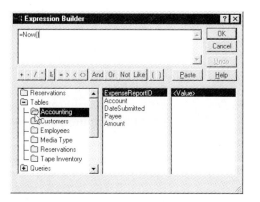

tip   *The Expression Builder can be a little confusing. Don't forget to use the Help button if you get stuck.*

Option Groups, Check Boxes, and Option and Toggle Buttons

Access lets you create a variety of buttons on forms and in reports that make it easy for users to make choices. In addition, you can add, delete, and modify toolbar buttons. Toolbar buttons will be discussed in Chapter 39. For now, let's look at option groups, check boxes, and option and toggle buttons.

Buttons

Suppose you were designing an onscreen form that permitted users to choose their favorite media for watching home videos (VHS, laser disc, and so on). Instead of having users type their choices via the keyboard (using lord-knows-how-many different spellings of "laser disc"), you could provide them with onscreen buttons like the following.

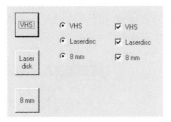

The buttons on the left are called *toggle buttons*. The center controls are called *option buttons*. The rightmost controls are called *check boxes*. Toggle buttons can include graphics; here, for instance, pictures are displayed instead of text on the toggle buttons. (You will learn how to do this in Chapter 37.)

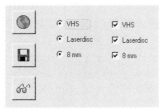

Access toggle buttons, option buttons, and check boxes should seem familiar. They all behave like their Windows counterparts. When you click on a toggle button, it depresses, indicating that you've activated the choice. A check in a check box or a dot in an option button indicates that it's activated.

When selected or deselected, these items *all* indicate yes/no decisions (or, in other words, true/false conditions) to the program. To use these items effectively (and before you can add them to your database), you must understand option groups, so that's the next stop.

Option Groups

Option groups provide users with a finite number of choices. Option groups consist of a *group frame*, which contains the buttons or boxes used to make the choices, and a *frame label*.

You can create option groups yourself, or get some help from a Wizard. Option groups are often *bound* to a particular field, but they need not be.

(This should make sense in a moment.) You manipulate the properties of groups, buttons, and fields to get the desired effects. This, too, should make sense after you've defined a group or two of your own, so let's try it.

Creating Button Groups with the Wizard

Suppose you want to create a form containing buttons to be used for tracking daily exercise and workout progress. Using a Wizard to set up this form is easier than doing it by hand, but let's try the latter first.

1. Start by opening the appropriate database (Exercise in this example).

2. Choose the Forms tab.

3. Click the New button (or select a form to which you want to add buttons):

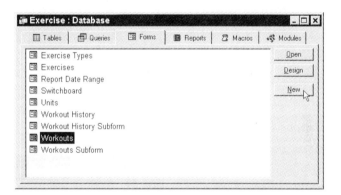

4. Select a table or query (Workouts, perhaps).

5. Choose either the Form Wizard or Design View option (Design Form for this example) and click OK. You will see a new, blank form window (or you'll see an existing form you'll modify, if that's what you are doing).

6. Make sure the Toolbox is showing. If it is not, choose Toolbox in the View menu, or click on the Toolbox button.

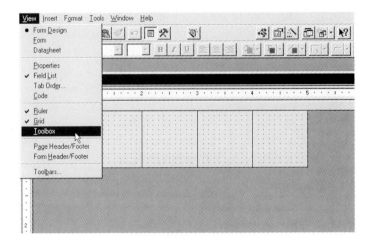

7. Click the Option Group button.

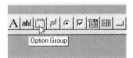

8. Point to one corner of the area where you want to create the options group, and drag to outline the approximate desired size and shape of the group as shown here. Notice the new mouse-pointer shape as you drag:

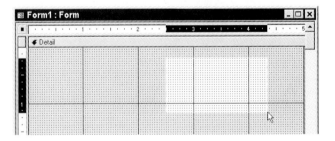

9. Type the list of options you want to display, tabbing to move from one row to the next; then click the Next > button.

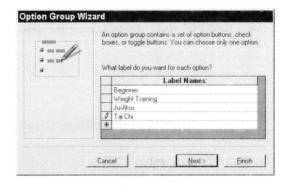

10. Pick a default entry choice if you want one, or just click Next > again, as shown in the following illustration.

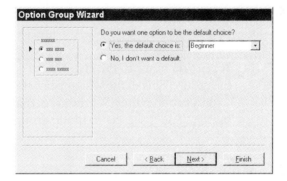

11. The Wizard suggests values for each choice. Sometimes you can change these depending on the type of field being used. Usually the Wiz will display suggested numbers for each choice—the best (and often only) way to go. Either accept the suggestions or attempt entries of your own by typing changes in the appropriate boxes. Click Next > when you're ready to continue.

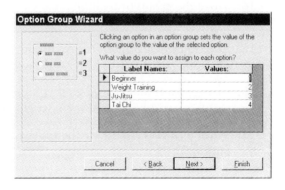

12. Indicate what you want to do with the value of the selected options. Here, the Workout ID field will be updated. Click Next >.

13. Design the appearance of the new buttons and related elements by making the desired choices. Watch the sample change as you experiment:

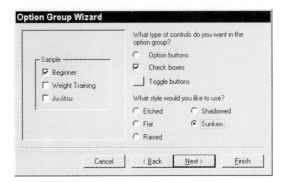

14. When you move to the last Wizard screen, you'll be asked to name the group. This name will appear at the top of the group frame. Type a group name (**Workout,** perhaps), and click the Finish button. You'll see the resulting group:

15. To change things in the group (like a misspelling), select the item of interest and change its properties. While you are at it, you can change other properties, like color, and so on.

16. Move the group or its individual elements by selecting one or more items and dragging.

17. Add other fields to your form if you like, as described in earlier chapters.

18. Change fonts and type sizes if you desire. Maybe you could include graphics (as described in the next chapter).

19. When you're ready to see the finished form, click the Form View button.

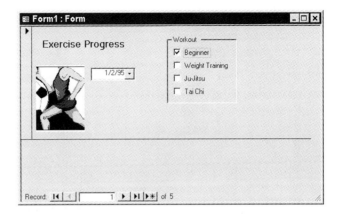

20. Make some test entries and check the table you expect to be
    updating to make sure everything is working properly.

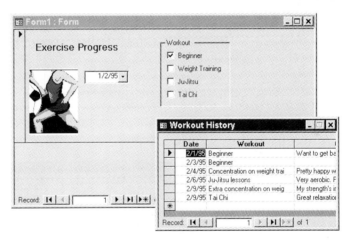

You might want to create a second, related table that contains the entries
and their meanings, and then use that table to add additional descriptive
comments about your workouts, so you can keep track of how you are doing.

List and Combo Boxes

Another way to automate choices is to provide lists from which users pick.
This is particularly useful when there are more choices than will fit on the
screen if you devote button space to each. For example, the following
illustration shows a version of the Exercise Progress data entry form with a
list box containing different types of exercises.

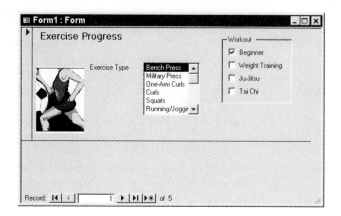

Creating List Boxes

To enter an exercise, the user scrolls to the exercise and clicks. There's a Wizard that helps you create lists like these. Here's how a list like the Exercise Type list is created:

1. Switch to the Design view.

2. Click the List Box button, as shown here.

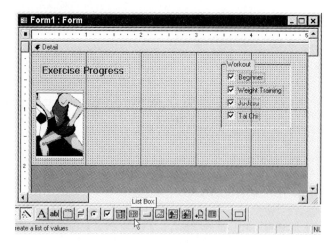

3. Drag to indicate the approximate desired size, shape, and location of the list box. Notice the unique mouse pointer shape as you drag.

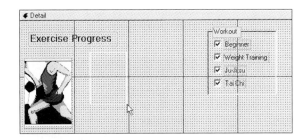

4. The Wizard asks if you want to type entries or to use values in an existing table or query to create the drop-down list. Here, an existing table will be used:

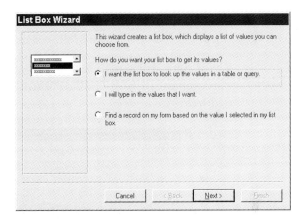

5. Specify the table or query that will be the source of the items in your list:

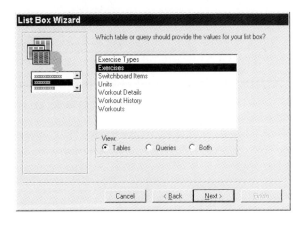

6. Choose the fields that you want to *see* in the list. More than one field can be displayed side by side:

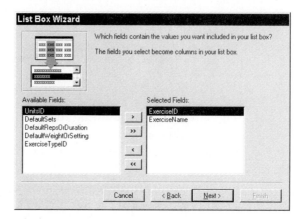

7. The Wizard will show you samples of the list and ask you to size the columns. Drag or double-click to specify the desired relative widths.

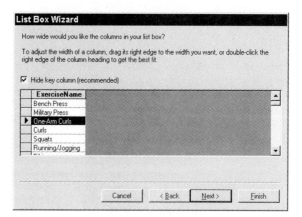

8. Access needs to know what to do with the data. Here it will be the Workout ID field.

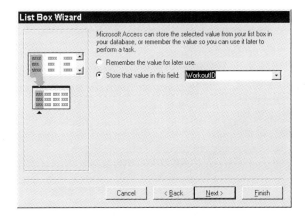

9. Finally, you'll be asked to name the list. You can leave the proposed name or type one of your own; then click Finish.

10. The Wizard will switch to Design view and create a list object. Either change its location, shape, and appearance, or switch to Form view to test it.

Creating Combo Boxes

Combo boxes provide drop-down lists like this one:

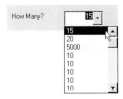

The entry is visible in a small box, and the arrow can be used to reveal a drop-down list from which to pick. Combo boxes are created by using techniques that are almost identical to those used for list boxes. The only difference is that you use the Combo Box button to the left of the List Box button in the toolbar.

Command Buttons

Command buttons let you make it obvious how to perform tasks necessary for your application. This often makes things easier for novices and pros alike. A Wizard can lead you through the steps necessary to create command buttons.

For instance, suppose you wanted to add a button to the Exercise Progress data-entry form that would create a new record each time someone clicked on it:

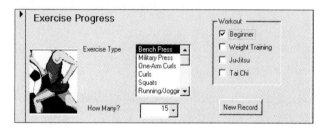

1. In Design mode, click on the Command button. Use the new mouse pointer to drag a button shape to the desired location on your form. The beginnings of a new, numbered button will appear, and you'll see the first Wizard dialog box:

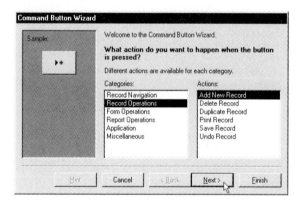

2. Choose the category of action you want the button to perform (Record Operations in the example), and the action from the displayed list for the chosen category (Add New Record in this example). Click Next >.

3. You will be asked to specify a button name or a graphic to use on the button's face. Explore the picture options first; and if you don't

find one that screams the function the button will perform, consider using text, as illustrated here.

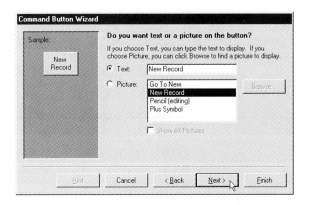

4. You will be asked to give your button a meaningful name (like New Record) or accept the automatic, incremental name (Command34, for example). Descriptive names are nice if you want to reuse the button design later. Click the Finish button to see your masterpiece in place.

5. Move it, resize it, change its priorities to alter the appearance, or just leave it alone.

6. Switch to Form view and test the button.

To learn more about buttons, consult online Help and the bigger books.

Action Queries

Action queries do things like delete records or make new tables, or update one field when criteria in another field are met. There are Wizards for some, and you can write your own.

warning   *You can screw up big time when using action queries. There is a warning that lets you cancel an action query, but lots of people fall into the habit of clicking right through the warning without looking at it. To safeguard your data, work only on **copies** of your important databases. Then if you accidentally delete a truckload of records, you'll be able to keep your job.*

Finding Duplicates with a Query Wizard

One common desire in database management is to locate duplicate (or potentially duplicate) records. Access provides an Action Query Wizard that can help you do this. It's called the *Find Duplicates Query Wizard*.

1. Begin by opening the database of interest and switching to the Queries tab.

2. Click on New, pick Query Wizard, and then click the OK button:

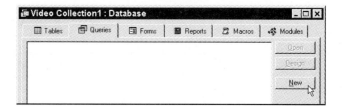

3. Double-click on Find Duplicates Query Wizard.

4. The Wiz will ask which table to examine (Videotapes in this example).

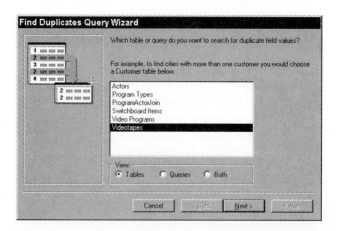

5. Tell Access which field(s) to check for duplicate entries (Description in this example).

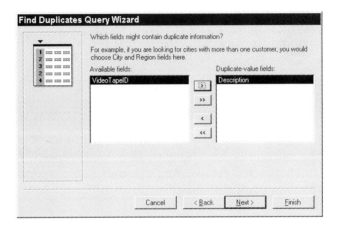

6. Ask to see additional fields in the report if they will help you determine true duplicates from similar but not identical records. For instance, The VideoTape ID numbers would help here:

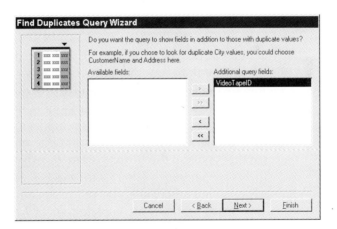

7. Click Finish, and Access will display possible duplicates, as shown next.

Description	Video Tape ID
Douglas is Sleeping	11
Douglas is Sleeping	10
Killer Frogs	9
Killer Frogs	3
Step Aerobics	8
Step Aerobics	5
	(AutoNumber)

As you can see by this example, Access sometimes collects records that are not exact duplicates. That's why it is important to specify enough fields to narrow the search. Eliminating duplicates always requires some careful inspection and hard work. There is no perfect automated solution. Even the pros get it wrong sometimes. Have you ever received two or more invitations from the Publishers Clearinghouse?

Other Action Queries

Other action queries you can perform include appending records to a table, creating a new table, deleting groups of records, and updating groups of records. Search online Help for the topic "Action," or check the bigger books for details. And remember to practice on backup copies of your important databases!

Macros

Macros are like miniprograms that record and automate repetitive database tasks. When you create a macro, Access will watch you work and record the steps you take to accomplish something. Then when you run (play back) the resulting macro, it will repeat the steps. Macros are just dumb servants, so if you don't anticipate all of the possible variations in a day's work, some mighty strange things can happen when you or others run poorly designed and untested macros. Be patient, and repeat the process you went through to create the macro; it should all work out in the end.

Sometimes, Access creates macros behind your back without you realizing it. For example, command buttons like the ones you just read about run macros that you and the Wizard create together.

Much of what can be done with macros can also be accomplished by cleverly applying other skills you've learned already (like properly designed queries). Space prohibits a complete tour of Access macro capabilities and the underlying *Access Basic* language used to create macros, but a few highlights seem in order. Then, if you get bitten by the macro bug, and have plenty of time to invest, check out the big (really, really big) books for details.

A Sample Macro

Suppose your Video Store database includes a query called Old Tapes that searches the Tapes Inventory table for tapes that were purchased more than a year ago. Suppose further that when rental tapes get to be a year old, you want to make them available for sale. You *could* use the existing query to find the old tapes, then change the contents of each "OK to Sell?" field from No to Yes manually. Or, you could create a macro to do that for you. Before you deal with the mechanics of a macro, think about the manual steps you would follow:

1. You'd open the Old Tapes query (which would locate just the old tapes).

2. You would choose Edit | Replace to bring up the Replace dialog box.

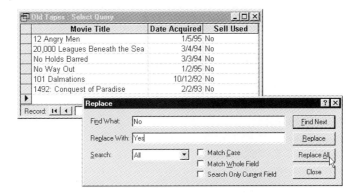

3. Using the Replace dialog box, you'd tell Access you want it to search for "No."

4. You'd tell Access you want to replace "No" with "Yes."

5. You'd tell Access where to search.

6. You'd click the Replace All button to start the process.

7. You'd inspect the results. (You would, wouldn't you?)

You can write an Access macro to do the first six of those seven steps for you. As is often the case, there are even many versions of a macro that will do the same thing. Computer lovers often spend hours finding the most elegant solutions to problems. For this exercise, however, let's use the brute-force approach, just to make it easier to see what's going on. In the process you'll see some potentially nasty problems.

Here are the steps for creating a macro:

1. Open the database, click on the Macros tab (if necessary) to bring it foremost, and click on the New button.

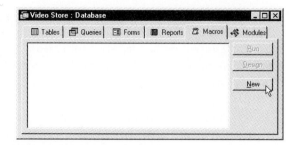

2. You'll see an empty, two-column list into which you'll place commands and optional notes of explanation.

3. Click in the first Action cell, and choose the first desired action. In the example, the first thing you want to do is open a query:

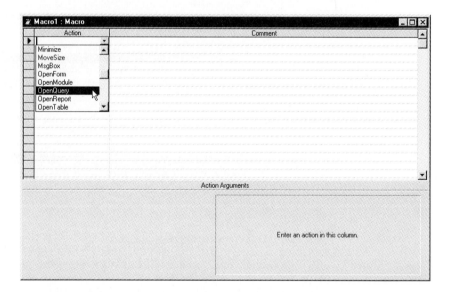

4. Action arguments will appear in the bottom half of the dialog box. The actual choices available will change with the type of action you have selected. In this case, you need to select a query from the resulting drop-down list.

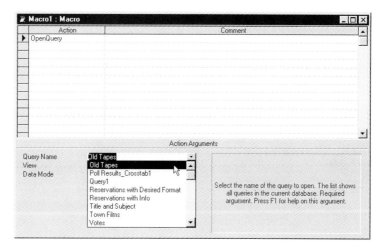

That's the essence of macro building; you can add additional steps, arguments, and (optionally) notes to build a reliable macro. You can add steps to switch you from table to table or from one view to another, or to pick menu items. In fact, there are commands you can include in your macros to copy, delete, navigate, and do virtually anything Access can do. For example, this example uses the SendKeys command to tell Access to send the equivalent of a TAB keystroke (notice how it is enclosed in braces):

Action	Comment
OpenQuery	Opens the Old Tapes Query Dynaset
DoMenuItem	Open the Replace dialog box
SendKeys	Type "No" in the Find What: box
▶ SendKeys	Tab to the Replace With: box

Regular keystrokes (like No or Yes) are simply typed as action arguments. Key *combinations* like (ALT+A) are sent using special characters. For example, ALT is represented by the percent sign, so to specify ALT+A, you'd enter the argument **%A**. (See online Help and the bigger books for details.)

5. When you've finished entering steps, save the macro with the File | Save command (CTRL+S), and test it. The following screen illustrates a completed (but imperfect) macro.

Action	Comment
OpenQuery	Opens the Old Tapes Query, Dynaset contains only tapes > 1 year old
DoMenuItem	Open the Replace dialog box
SendKeys	Type "No" in the Find What: box
SendKeys	Tab to the Replace With: box
SendKeys	Type "Yes" in the Replace With: box
SendKeys	Type Alt+W to turn off Match Whole Field option
SendKeys	Type Alt+E to turn off the Search Only Current Field option
▶ SendKeys	Type Alt+A to press the Replace All button

Approve Sale of Old Tapes : Macro

warning   *Do us all a favor. If you work at a nuclear power plant, don't just read this chapter and then try automating your workplace. Marketing hoopla notwithstanding, when you create macros you are* **programming***. Test your work on* **copies** *of your important databases rather than the original. Dig into the big books, and get help from experienced Access Basic macro writers, at least for your first few important projects.*

Troubleshooting Macros

It is often difficult to spot potential problems with macros. The strangest things can happen. For instance, in the sample macro, you asked Access to search for all occurrences of "No" in the Dynaset, and then replace "No" with "Yes." Since the Dynaset contains only old tapes, you might think that a safe move, but look at what happened to the film titles *No Holds Barred* and *No Way Out.*

Old Tapes : Select Query

Movie Title	Date Acquired	Sell Used
12 Angry Men	1/5/95	Yes
20,000 Leagues Beneath the Sea	3/4/94	Yes
▶ Yes Holds Barred	3/3/94	Yes
Yes Way Out	1/2/95	Yes
101 Dalmations	10/12/92	Yes
1492: Conquest of Paradise	2/2/93	Yes

Record: |◀ ◀ | 3   ▶ ▶| ▶*| of 6

Ho, boy; it's drawing-board time. Remember—computers are very unimaginative, and often (under the guise of being helpful) a little quirky. For instance, you might regularly get away with that "Swap Yes for No" trick you pulled in the Replace dialog box as long as the Match Whole Field box option is selected, since it would only change things in fields where it found only the word "No" all by itself.

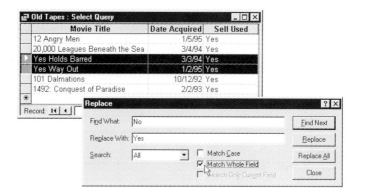

But the Replace dialog box, and some others, remember settings from their prior uses. So if after you create your macro, you or a coworker use the Replace dialog box for some other task and change the options, new settings may be retained; these could affect the outcome the next time you run your macro, which will use the altered dialog box.

That's what happened here. Access was never told to look just in the Sell Used? field, but it worked anyway because the other occurrences of "No" in the database were not exact. That is to say, the occurrences of "No" in the Movie Title field had other words with them. But later, with the *Match Whole Field* option cleared, Access felt justified—*compelled,* actually—to replace all occurrences of "No" with "Yes."

The moral? When in doubt, include instructions in your macro to specify all important options. Or better yet—unless you have the time and disposition to become a programmer, keep your day job and leave the programming to a pro. Next stop, something fun: graphics in Access.

CHAPTER 37

Graphics in Databases

I'T'S a graphical world, and Access has some of the tools you need to live in it. You've already seen examples of clip art embellishing Access forms and reports. You can also insert or link charts, drawings, photos, and other graphics into records, reports, and forms. It's even possible to link multimedia files.

You'll spot many similarities between the use of graphics in Access and in the rest of the Office suite, but there are significant differences. Let's dig in.

Objects: Linked, Embedded, Bound, and Unbound

Let's get this out of the way up front. In Access, graphics are *objects,* so you'll need to brush up on the object linking and embedding concepts explored in Chapter 3 of this book. You'll also need to know a few more terms.

All Access graphics are placed in *object frames.* Think of frames as containers for graphics and other objects. You manipulate a frame to change the size, shape, location, and cropping of the graphic it contains. Some of the techniques will seem familiar. Others won't work as you'd expect. For example, to switch between cropping and resizing a graphic, you'll have to modify the frame's *properties* (characteristics), as you will see in a moment.

Bound Versus Unbound

There are two types of object frames: *bound* object frames and *unbound* object frames. When graphics are stored in a *table,* they are referred to as *bound objects.* For example, in Figure 37-1, the promotional photo for each film in the Tape Inventory database is a bound image.

The three pictures that make up the logo art in Figure 37-1 are examples of unbound objects.

Embedded Versus Linked

An Access graphic (object) can be *embedded,* meaning that it is stored within the Access database; or it can be *linked,* meaning that the object is stored in some other file, but used by Access. That should sound familiar.

As you embed photos, the size of your database file (the .mdb file) increases significantly, telling you that the graphic objects are being stored within the file itself. That is, embedded objects are stored with (stored within) the main database file.

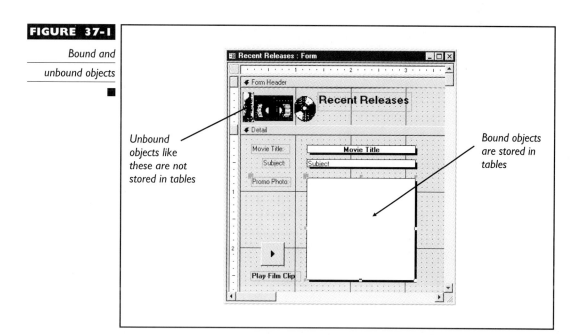

FIGURE 37-1

Bound and unbound objects

Unbound objects like these are not stored in tables

Bound objects are stored in tables

Linked objects are stored outside of the Access main database file. Because Access supports OLE, you can edit both embedded and linked graphics by using the general techniques discussed in Chapter 3.

Unbound Graphics as Form and Report Embellishments

You can round up graphics from the usual sources (Office's ClipArt Gallery, art disks, and so on) and use them in Access. Graphics can be inserted either from your Clipboard or with the Insert Object command, then resized, moved, piled one on top of the other, and so on.

Here are the general steps taken to create unbound graphics on a form or report:

1. Open the form or report of interest and switch to Design view.

2. If necessary, make room for the new graphics in the appropriate section (header, detail, and so on). In this example the art will be added to the Detail section of the form, but it is also common to place art in headers and footers.

3. To add an unbound object, click on the Unbound Object Frame button as shown here:

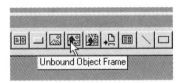

4. Note that the mouse pointer changes shape. Drag to define the desired location, size, and shape of the frame.

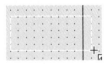

5. When you release the mouse button, Access will insert the frame and display the Insert Object dialog box, listing a choice of object sources.

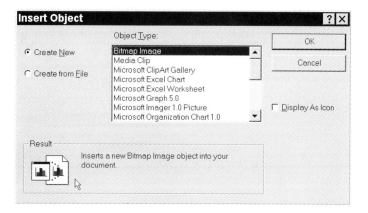

MANAGING YOUR DATA WITH ACCESS

6. Pick one (Microsoft ClipArt Gallery in this example).

7. Select or create the desired image and return to Access. The exact steps vary with the graphic source. Check Chapter 3 and other documentation as required to see how best to insert the finished image—various techniques will work. For example, selecting and then clicking OK, or double-clicking both work in the Microsoft ClipArt Gallery:

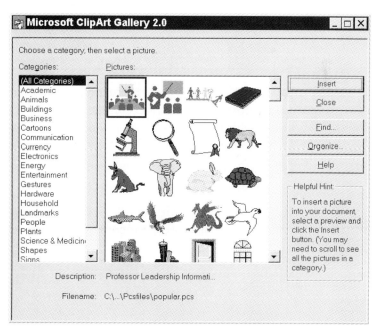

8. Back in the Access Design View window, you'll see all or part of your graphic surrounded by the frame handles. The function of the handles changes based on the frame's Size Mode selection in the Frame's Layout Properties dialog box. Reach the dialog box by choosing Properties from the View menu with the frame selected:

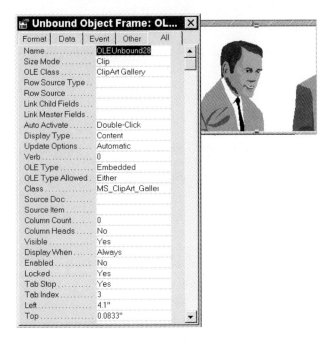

Clip displays as much of the object as will fit in the frame. *Stretch* makes the graphic fit the frame's shape and size, distorting the graphic in the process. *Zoom* resizes the image proportionally to fit either the height or width, sometimes leaving part of the frame empty.

9. If necessary, change the Size Mode property and drag the frame handles to get the desired effect.

10. Switch to Form view (or Print Preview when working with reports) to see how the project is coming. Switch back to Design view to

alter your work or to continue designing. For example, to reposition a graphic, switch to Design view, select the graphic, move the mouse pointer until it turns into a hand, and then use it to move the frame.

Bound Graphics in Records

Sometimes it's useful to have graphics for each record. The promotional photos and film clips are examples in the Video Tape database. Employee databases sometimes contain photos. Real estate databases can contain photos, floor plans, videotape walkthroughs, and so on.

The technical realities of using this capability are sometimes lost by the folks marketing the products—it's not quite as simple as it may seem from the demos—so you'll want to experiment to see if you're ready for big graphics-intensive databases and vice versa. There are some pitfalls. For starters, collections of photos and multimedia "show" files consume *acres* of disk space, and they can slow even the most enthusiastic Pentium machine to a crawl. Moreover, the OLE links required to pull this off can be a little funky at times. They might hang your machine or produce unexpected formatting results, for example. But if you are in the mood to experiment, come along on this short journey. The steps are very similar to those used to include unbound graphics.

Suppose you want to collect and display promotional photos in a video tape database.

1. Start by opening a table that will contain the bound graphic or other element (the Video Store Tape Inventory table in this example).

2. Switch to Design view.

3. Add the necessary field or fields (three fields in the following example—one for video clips, one for photos, and a third for Excel charts).

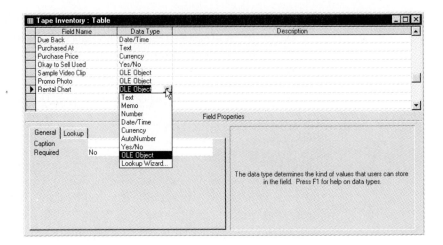

4. Switch to Table view, and select the record and field where you want to insert your first bound graphic. For example, here a photo is inserted into the Promo Photo field of the *Hot Enough for June* record in the Tape Inventory table:

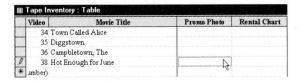

5. Get thee to a graphic of interest. You can use the Access Insert Object command, or launch another application like Paintbrush, and then copy the image to the Clipboard. One or another (or many) of the techniques described in Chapter 3 will work, depending upon the mood of the "Different Way to Work" gods.

6. Switch to the Access table, if you are not already there, and insert the graphic (this will happen for you automatically in some cases, other times you'll need to use Paste Special).

7. You'll know you are on the right track if a description of the item you've attempted to insert appears in the table. You might see the words "Bitmap Image," for instance, as seen here:

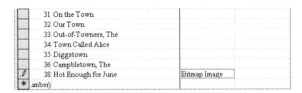

8. Since you can't see graphics in Table view, you'll need to switch to a form or report containing a frame for the graphic—or you can create one. For instance, this Form design has a bound field frame for the Promo Photo:

9. In Form or Report view, your graphics should appear, all cropped or zoomed or whatever, depending on how you've set the Picture Properties back in Design view. Here's a typical record containing a bound graphic in both Table and Form views.

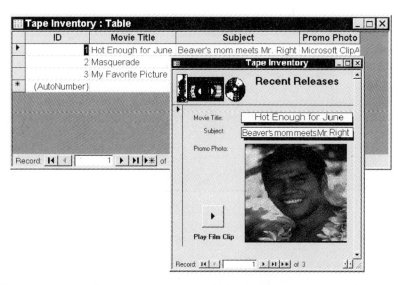

You can use similar techniques to include charts, movies, or other objects from various applications. For example, the following illustration shows a collection of Excel charts bound to Access records:

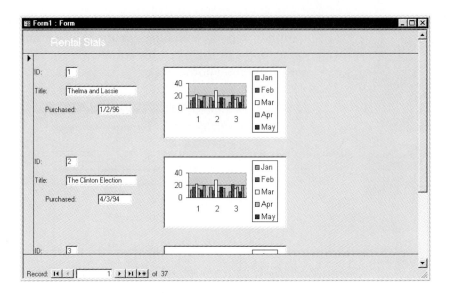

In this case Excel chart objects were inserted into Access records. Again, your mileage may vary. Combining object linking, embedding, and Access is going to take some experimenting. Even the big books can't cover all of the possible approaches and pitfalls, but take a look at them for more coverage.

Adding Graphics to Buttons

Here's a quick trick you can use to spruce-up buttons on your Access screens. Remember the Play Film Clip command button in the Recent Releases form?

It started out life as a boring Command button labeled "Button 24."

To change its face, all you need to do is

1. Select the button in Design view.

2. Visit the button's properties and click the ellipsis button to the right of Picture.

3. Scroll through the resulting list of button names, clicking once on those that sound interesting and watching the sample as you work:

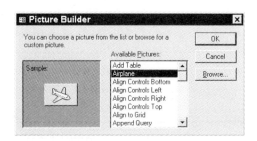

4. When you see a button you like, click OK.

5. The graphic will appear on the button's face.

If you don't like the stock selection of button faces, you can roam your hard disk looking for other bitmap graphics (the extension for these is .BMP) by using the Browse button. For instance, you can use the bitmap graphics in your Windows directory as button faces, or you can create your own bitmap graphics in a paint program. Then follow the preceding steps 1 through 5.

Chart Wizard: Charting Your Data

The Access Chart Wizard lets you use Microsoft Graph to create graph objects that can be included in Access reports. Once created, the charts can be further embellished using Microsoft Graph itself.

Suppose, for instance, that you wanted to create a new form containing a graph depicting customers by region. Here are the general steps. (Check online Help, the other information on Microsoft Graph in Chapter 18, and the big books for more details on using this powerful feature.)

1. Select the table you want to base the form on, and then choose New Form from the toolbar.

2. Click on Chart Wizard and then click the OK button.

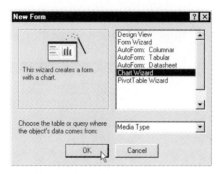

3. You'll see the Chart Wizard dialog box. Double-click to select the fields you want to include in your graph (Customer ID and Region in the example).

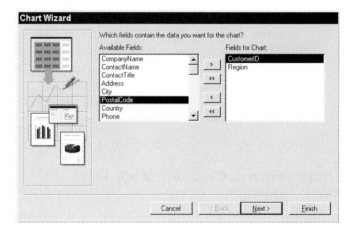

4. Click Next > to move forward. Choose the type of chart you want to create, then choose Next > again.

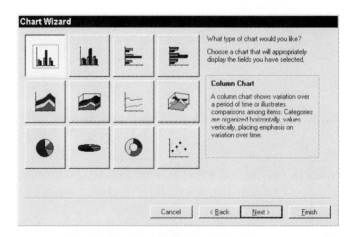

5. Watch the sample develop as you work. Use the < Back button if you want to try different approaches.

6. When you click Finish, the Wizard will insert a graph object in your report, like the one shown here:

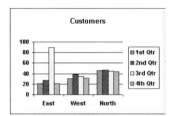

7. To modify the graph, double-click on it and you will see a Chart window like this one.

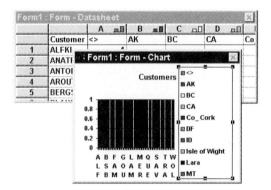

8. Use Chart's options to change the appearance of the finished graph object. For instance, this uses the Chart Type command and the Options button to change to a pie chart:

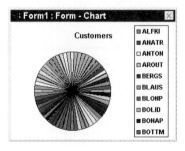

CHAPTER 38

Linking, Importing, and Exporting Records

F R E Q U E N T L Y , the biggest consumer of your time when you're creating a new database is data entry—just typing in all the information for each record. Access provides ways to minimize this if you've already put the data on disk for some other purpose. For example, if you've already typed a parts list in Word, you might be able to avoid rekeying all those part numbers and descriptions. With Access you can *import* data from other databases, spreadsheets, and word processing documents; or you can *link* non-Access files as tables.

Moreover, you'll sometimes want to *export* all or some of your Access records for use by some other program. For example, you might want to export names and mailing addresses to be used in a Word Print Merge project, or export financial transaction details for an Excel budgeting project. Here are some examples of data sources and destinations:

- Other Microsoft Access database files
- Microsoft FoxPro versions 2.0, 2.5, 2.6, and 3.0 database files
- Paradox version 3.*x*, 4.*x*, and 5.0 tables
- dBASE III, III+, IV, and V files
- Btrieve 5.1*x* and 6.0 tables
- SQL database files
- Microsoft Excel 2.0, 3.0, 4.0, 5.0, and 7.0
- Lotus 1-2-3 .wks, .wk1, and .wk3 spreadsheets
- Fixed-width and delimited text files
- Microsoft Word for Windows mail-merge data files (export only)
- Most other applications that can create or read fixed-length records

■ Most other applications that can create or read comma-separated or tab-separated records

While Access makes this all pretty easy, there are some potential "gotchas." Welcome to Chapter 38.

warning   *Once you upgrade an Access database—for example, with a newer version—the database will not be usable as-is with older versions. That is to say, you can't simply open a version 7 database with Access version 2.x. You'll have to export the tables from version 7 to the older versions. (Access will convert the tables in the course of exporting.) To avoid confusion and inconvenience, you might need to purchase new software for your home and coworkers. Test before making the commitment, and **always make backup copies of your old databases** and store them in a safe place before you attempt any kind of conversion, importing, or exporting.*

Using Records from Earlier Access Versions

If you or your coworkers have created Access version 2.*x* database files, you will probably want to convert them to Access 7 database files. This will make it possible for you to use the new features in version 7 and probably will improve the overall performance of the database. Conversion will not affect linked tables. Evey linked table you intend to use will need to be converted separately. The steps for converting from Access version 2.*x* to version 7 are pretty straightforward:

1. Back up your old database file and confirm that the backup was successful.

2. Quit the old version of Access (thereby closing the old database file).

3. If you are on a network, make sure no one else is using the database you plan to convert. (Access will display a message alerting you if there is another user; when this happens, you will need to either ask the other user to close the file, or wait until he or she is finished with it.)

4. Run the new version of Access (7).

5. Choose Tools | Database Utilities | Convert Database.

6. Select the database file you want to convert and click Convert.

7. Give the database file a new name or, if you choose to keep the old name, specify a new location (different subfolder) for it to occupy once it's converted.

8. Click Save to save the new version.

9. Convert related database files as well if that's part of the plan.

10. Test the converted database.

Testing After Conversion

It is important to test your converted database file(s). Access version 7 does some things differently than earlier versions. Look for the obvious. Are all of your records there? Do the queries work properly? How about reports, buttons, macros, and so on? Do they run properly and match earlier results with the old database? Can other networked users access the new database? (Did you move it to a new subfolder on the server and forget to tell them?) Poke at the security features and make certain only users with a need to know have access.

If you are an advanced user/tester, pay particular attention to the more advanced issues:

- Linked tables
- Validation rules for data entry and integrity checking
- Fields containing null characters and zero-length text strings
- The Visible property
- Fields containing the back-quote character (')
- List boxes
- Subforms

Importing Versus Linking

If you have data that was created with other programs (like dBASE, Paradox, or Microsoft Word), you can convert (import) the data to Access tables, or you can *link* the unconverted tables so that Access can use them without converting. (This is a good idea if some users will be working with the data in Access, while others will be working with the data in the original program—dBASE, Paradox, or Word, perhaps.) In choosing whether to import or link, there are important trade-offs to consider.

Importing definitely has its advantages. Converted databases generally run faster than linked ones. There will be fewer compatibility issues once the data has been converted. Some changes that you can make to Access tables can't be made to linked tables. For instance, you can't create Access primary keys in linked tables (although you can sometimes use keys from the creating database application).

Linking, however, lets you keep the data in its old format for use with the old tools. For example, if you link a Word file, you can still use Word to make changes to the file. Or, if most of the people in your company still use dBASE, you can share the data with them and even alter it without them needing to purchase Access.

Consider testing the same database using both converted and linked tables to see which suits you.

t i p *If possible, test with a few hundred or even a few thousand records. Smaller samples will not give you a good indication of how quickly the database will perform in the real world. If you test with tens-of-thousands or millions of records and the design is such that the thing runs slowly, the wait will seem endless.*

Linking Other Databases as Tables

Let's look at the general steps for linking a non-Access database as a table, then turn to importing as an alternative. To link,

1. Open the Access database to which you plan to link the non-Access database. (Or open a new Access database if you are starting from scratch.) In either case, bring the Tables tab forward and choose File | Get External Data | Link Tables.

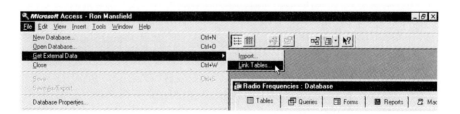

2. Tell Access the type and version of the source file (Paradox 3.*x*, dBASE IV, and so on):

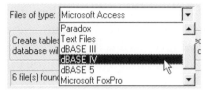

3. Locate the file you want to link:

4. If the file has an index (built by its application), sometimes Access can use it. Locate the index file if there is one and attempt to link it, as shown here:

5. Click Link. Faster than you can recite the Academy Awards voting rules, you'll have it—a linked non-Access database, usable as an Access table. In this case you've linked 307,659 FCC radio frequency assignment records.

CITY	STATE	FREQUENCY	SERVICE	CALLSIGN	LICENSEE
HALF MOON BA	CA	468.275	IB	KNET237	MULLER, JOHN:MULLER, EDA
HALF MOON BA	CA	463.275	IB	KNET237	MULLER, JOHN:MULLER, EDA
SAN RAFAEL	CA	468.2875	IB	WNYL606	BRUNO S GROCERY CO
SAN RAFAEL	CA	464.1375	IB	WNYL606	BRUNO S GROCERY CO
OAKLAND	CA	466.525	IB	KRW654	RONALD L DAY TRANSPORTATI
CUPERTINO	CA	461.525	IB	KRW654	RONALD L DAY TRANSPORTATI
CUPERTINO	CA	466.525	IB	KRW654	RONALD L DAY TRANSPORTATI
WALNUT CREEK	CA	461.525	IB	KRW654	RONALD L DAY TRANSPORTATI
WALNUT CREEK	CA	466.525	IB	KRW654	RONALD L DAY TRANSPORTATI
NOVATO	CA	461.525	IB	KRW654	RONALD L DAY TRANSPORTATI
NOVATO	CA	466.525	IB	KRW654	RONALD L DAY TRANSPORTATI
KETTLEMAN CI	CA	33.16	IB	WNYC645	JACK IN THE BOX JB3263
KETTLEMAN CI	CA	154.515	IB	WNYC645	JACK IN THE BOX JB3263
NORTH HIGHLA	CA	468.475	IB	KJ9580	HANDY ANDY TV & APPLIANCE
SANTA PAULA	CA	151.925	IB	WPBW867	MERCO CONSTRUCTION ENGIN
SAN MARCOS	CA	33.16	IB	WPBW819	RALLYS 109

6. Notice the listing for this linked table in the Tables tab of the Database window. The arrow with the "dB" preceding the table name (FREQUENC) tells you that this table is a linked database.

Working with Linked Tables

You can do a surprising number of things to a linked table. You can add, change, and delete records. Remember this when you are experimenting, particularly when working with someone else's database (or when permitting someone else to link *your* data to *their* Access databases). Normally, Access will obey security rules if they've been properly established. But again—back up and test.

tip *To make certain that Access will not make your existing databases unusable with their original applications, **test** by using backup copies. After using them with Access (deleting, adding, and modifying records, for example), try to reuse the altered databases with their original program (dBASE, or whatever). As long as you're doing this with backup copies, if and when something goes wrong, you'll be covered—you'll still have the original.*

There are, naturally, things you cannot do with a linked database. For example, you cannot change certain of the table's properties. Access warns you of this whenever you switch to Design view while in a linked table:

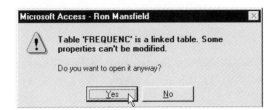

You cannot change field names (although you can add captions for your own use. And you can't change field types (from Text to Number, for instance).

But you can do things like change the appearance of numbers in the table. For example, in some circles, it's considered fashionable to display radio frequencies rounded to four decimal places. This you can do:

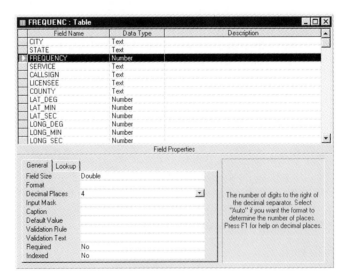

Watch the note box to the right of properties as you select them. Red notes tell you that you can't make property changes, blue notes tell you that you can. (Users of monochrome displays and the color-blind will need to break down and actually *read* the onscreen notes.)

Incidentally, when Access warns that you can't make many specific property changes, it often lets you enter your illegal desires in the various property boxes, then scolds you and ignores the forbidden requests when you attempt to switch back to Table view.

Importing Data from dBASE and Other DBMS Programs

As you read earlier, Access almost always performs more quickly when using imported (as opposed to linked) data. Let's look at the general steps for importing a non-Access database as a table. The steps vary somewhat based on the database that created the original database, so let's leave those intricacies to online Help and the bigger books.

1. Make sure you have enough extra room on your hard disk for a new version of the database file, since the Import feature makes a completely new copy of all your records.

2. Open the Access database to which you plan to import the non-Access database. (Or open a new Access database if you are starting from scratch.) With the Tables tab topmost, choose File | Get External Data | Import.

3. Tell Access the type and version of source file (Paradox 3.*x*, dBASE 5, and so on).

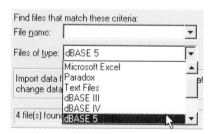

4. Locate the file you want to link, changing the Files of type entry, if necessary. For instance, to see just dBase files, pick dBase 5 files (*.DBF).

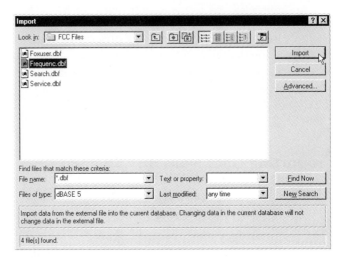

5. Click Import. In a while, perhaps a *long* while, Access will convert the database and place its name in the Tables list.

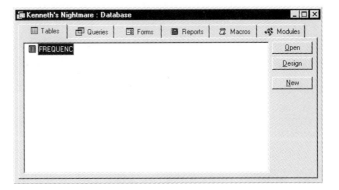

6. Notice the listing for this converted table in the Tables tab of the Database window. There is no arrow or "dB" preceding the table name (FREQUENC) because you've created a real Access table.

7. Examine the table, create indexes if necessary (see Chapter 39), and set up desired queries, forms, reports, and so on.

8. Once satisfied with the conversion (and only then, and only if you've backed up the old database), you can delete the old database from your hard disk or the server, unless you will need it again with the original application (dBASE, or whatever).

Importing Delimited and Fixed-Length Records

The computer industry has established a number of data format standards. The intent has been to enable transfer of data between competitive systems. Even antique programs and scientific instruments usually offer ways to export their data as *comma-separated* or *tab-separated* or *fixed-length* records.

Tab- and comma-separated records use tab marks or commas to separate fields. For instance, tab-separated records might look like this:

```
Mickey{Tab}Springer{Tab}Handbiters, Inc.{CR}

Bob{Tab}Wernikowski{Tab}U. S. Department of Redundancy Dpt.{CR}
```

A *comma-separated* record almost always includes quotation marks around text so that commas used in the data aren't confused with the commas used for separation. So comma-separated records might look like this:

```
"Mickey","Springer","Handbiters, Inc." {CR}

"Bob","Wernikowski","U. S. Department of Redundancy Dpt."{CR}
```

Fixed-length records store the same number of characters for each record, even if this means filling with spaces. You can specify desired field lengths in the Import/Export Setup dialog box. There are usually no separators as such. Here's an example of fixed-length records. Notice what happens when an entry is too long to fit the fixed width:

```
MickeySpringer Handbiters, Inc.  {CR}

BobWernikowski U. S. Department o{CR}
```

Access can import data using any of these standards. You can use this imported data to create new tables, or you can append it to existing tables. Here are the general steps:

1. Open the database to which you want to add the records (or create a new one).

2. Choose File | Get External Data | Import.

3. Select Text Files.

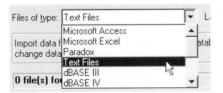

4. Locate the file to be imported and click the Import button:

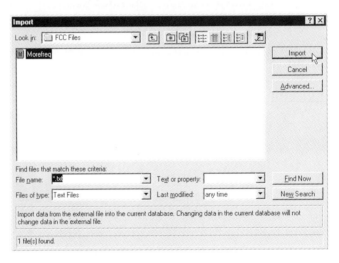

5. Next you'll see the first dialog box of the Text Import Wizard. It usually makes pretty good guesses as to how your data is arranged, and it shows a preview of what it intends to do. Here it has correctly guessed that the data is in tab-delimited format. When you are ready to move on, click Next >.

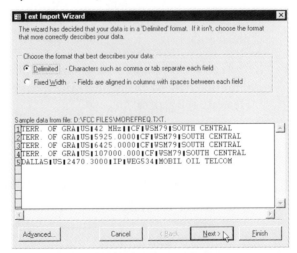

6. In the next box, you tell Access how your data is delimited if it didn't guess right. Also, some programs export field names as the first row of an exported file. If you want to import that first row and have Access use it to create field names for a new table, click to place a check in the First Row Contains Field Names box. Choose the appropriate delimiter character (usually comma or tab).

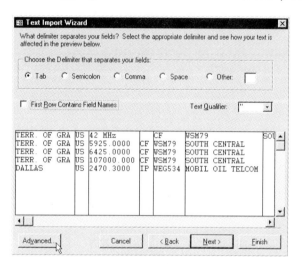

7. Notice that you can click Advanced at any time to get to the advanced features dialog box. Here you can tell Access how incoming dates and times are organized (whether there will be leading zeros, and so on).

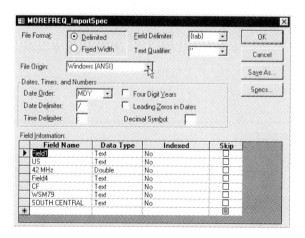

8. When you are ready to move on, click Next > (or OK and then Next >, if you are visiting the advanced dialog box). In this box,

you tell access if you want to create a new file or append the records being imported to an existing table. (Sometimes it is easier to troubleshoot before the import step, then append the cleaned-up data after inspecting it.)

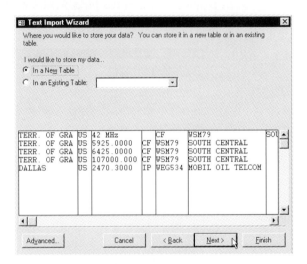

9. Click Next > to go on. You will be given a chance to specify information about the fields you are importing. You will also, at this time, have a chance to exclude fields from importing. Click Next > when you've finished here.

10. Finally, Access will ask you if you want to specify a primary key, or if you want to let the program do the dirty work. Click Next > to reach the final dialog box.

11. If you would like Access to analyze the structure of your table after importing, check the option box. Then click Finish.

12. Inspect the imported records.

Import Error Tables

If all goes well, you will be notified that the import was successful. But if any of the data you imported is flawed, you'll get an alert. For example, if there is text in a numeric field, Access will spot it. Data that shouldn't be duplicated in a field will also cause an alert. There are many potential problems. Here's a typical dialog box:

Access used to create an error report for you when it spotted a mistake; now it just tells you it can't import the data and you're screwed. Don't panic, though. It's often useful to look at the actual file you tried to import. This shows it opened in Microsoft Word:

```
TERR.·OF·GRA →US   →  42·MHz·CF  →   WSM79·SOUTH·CENTRAL¶
TERR.·OF·GRA →US   →  5925.0000  →   CF  →  WSM79·SOUTH·CENTRAL¶
TERR.·OF·GRA →US   →  6425.0000  →   CF  →  WSM79·SOUTH·CENTRAL¶
TERR.·OF·GRA →US   →  107000.000 →   CF  →  WSM79·SOUTH·CENTRAL¶
DALLAS   →   US   →  2470.3000  →   IP  →   WEG534   →   MOBIL·OIL·TELCOM¶
¶
```

The first potential error in this file is that there is text ("MHz") in what should be a numeric field. Another error might be that there is an unwanted paragraph mark at the end of the data being imported—Access probably confused this with an empty record. Fix errors such as these and try reimporting; there's no other way.

mporting Data from Spreadsheet Files

Access will attempt to import data from a variety of spreadsheet formats including Excel, Lotus 1-2-3, and clones thereof. Use the same importing techniques just described, except choose the appropriate spreadsheet file type when given the opportunity. (You can specify just a range to be imported if you don't want the whole spreadsheet.) Access attempts to name fields and pick appropriate data types based on the spreadsheet's contents and specifications. If you don't like the results, you can always change the data types later, by altering the appropriate Access table properties.

Importing Data from Word Files

To import Word files, either save the files as text and use the text-importing techniques described earlier in this chapter, or take the following steps.

1. Place the Word data in Word tables organized in the same way as tables in your Access database file.

2. Copy from the Word table to your Clipboard.

3. Switch to the Access table window.

4. Select the first field in the "new" record at the end of your Access table.

5. Select Paste Append from the Edit menu. Access will import each Word table row as a record.

Exporting Access Data

Exporting is much like importing in reverse. Here are the general steps:

1. Open the Access database file containing the data you want to export.

2. Choose File | Save As | Export.

3. Specify whether you want to save the file to the current database or to an external file (the default):

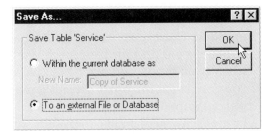

4. Specify a name, location, and file type for the new file Access will create when it exports. Here, the file Service will be exported to FoxPro 3.0 format.

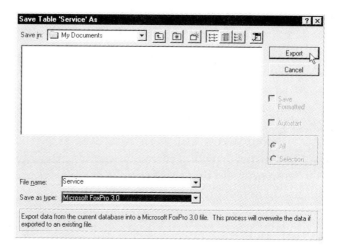

5. Click Export.

6. Check the finished file with an application that can read it, such as FoxPro.

Access Records as Word Merge Source Data

You can use Access records as Microsoft Word Merge data sources, making it possible to create personalized Word form letters and other documents containing Access data. Word has a Wizard that you can use for this purpose. It is described in Chapter 12. Alternatively, you can use the Merge It toolbar button. Consult online Help and the bigger books for details.

Analyze with Excel

There are times when it might be helpful to export Access records to create Excel worksheets. You can export the contents of a data sheet, form, or report. The resulting file will have a filename that ends in .xls, and you'll be able to open the file with Excel. Use the Output To MS Excel toolbar button to create Excel files. See the bigger books for details.

Access and SQL

Access is SQL savvy; it can both use and create SQL-style data. That is, if your computer is properly connected to a network, Access can work with external, compatible Structured Query Language databases like those resident on Microsoft SQL or Oracle servers. Not all SQL servers are Microsoft Access compatible.

Before Access can work with SQL server data, you or your network administrator will need to run the Open Database Connectivity (ODBC) Setup program that came with Microsoft Access. Moreover, ODBC drivers are required. Again, you'll probably need assistance from your network support people to install the appropriate driver software on your computer. Finally, you will need to be granted permission to use the appropriate SQL databases.

Unfortunately, space does not permit full coverage of this topic, so you will need to check with the big books and your network administrator if you plan to use Access for SQL tasks.

CHAPTER 39

Troubleshooting, Maintaining, and Protecting Databases

S

ETTING up a database is just the beginning. You must maintain it, protect it, and occasionally fix it. Welcome to the real world, and the last chapter on database ownership.

You will learn about ways to speed up database operations, troubleshoot common problems, and set up security restrictions. This chapter will start with some general troubleshooting tips first, and then turn to speed and security issues.

Troubleshooting

Kaaboom!...Always when you are in a hurry, some cryptic message fills your screen. "Can't do this. Can't do that. Inappropriate data type." Relational databases are perhaps the most complex computer organisms that average users are permitted to alter, and that means you're as likely to run into trouble as to have things go smoothly.

First, realize that keeping your database designs simple is often better. If you design a complex, show-offish, gee-whiz database and then spend the rest of your life trying to make it work or explaining the missing data and faulty reports, you are not a more productive worker. (And you know what happens to even the marginally unproductive these days.) So step 1 is to *keep it simple*. If things don't work well when they're automated, rethink them. Imagine a peaceful Japanese rock garden, and create the computer equivalent.

Getting Help in a Hurry

OK, you can't simplify things any further. You are going about your business and up jumps the devil—an alert box like the example in the middle of Figure 39-1.

FIGURE 39-1

Read error message carefully; you can get help if you need it

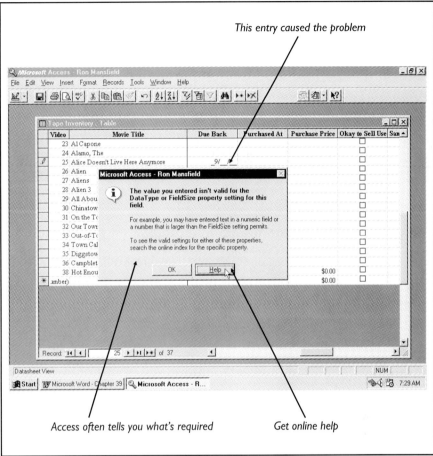

This entry caused the problem

Access often tells you what's required

Get online help

In Figure 39-1 the date entered does not match the required format for the field. If you click OK and then try to do anything other than fix the date at this point, you'll probably see the error message again, as if you're trapped in a vicious cycle. Read error messages carefully; they're there to help you. And don't forget to check the online Help, where you can click on underlined words for more information.

Common Error Messages and What They Mean

There are a few messages that you'll see so often that it is worth reading about them here. They are particularly common when you're designing new queries, forms, and reports, but you'll see some of them at other times.

Referential Integrity Warnings

Referential integrity messages vary, but they are all telling you something similar: "You can't do that because of forced integrity relationships that you or the database designer have specified."

For instance, in the Pirates database, if you try to delete a player from the roster (the 1997 Buellton Pirates table) and the player has records in the Game Stats table, and *if you've specified referential integrity*, Access won't let you delete the player. You'll get a message like this one:

That's because if you delete the record for a player, the reports and queries that look up players' names won't find a name for the deleted player. You have perhaps three choices at this point: don't delete the player, turn off referential integrity, or rethink the design of your database so it doesn't do this type of lookup.

Can't Edit or Save Changes to a Record

You'll get various messages like this one about not being able to make or save changes to records:

The reason might be any of several. The changes you are attempting may break Access' rules (like trying to type text in a numeric field), for example, or you may not have permission to change the record in question. Contact the owner of the database or your network administrator if you think you should be able to make changes to shared records and you can't.

Can't Change a Property Data Type or Field Size

There are many things that stand in the way of changing established properties, data types, and field designs. If a field is related to others, you'll often see messages like this:

Your best bet is to delete the offending relationships, change the data type and/or size, then reestablish the relationships.

Can't Change a Table, Form, or Query Design

If you try to switch to Design view and you see a message like the one that follows (offering read-only access), there can be a number of reasons.

Perhaps the most common problem is that you have a query or form open that is bound to the table. Simply close your Query or Form window, and you can try again. If you share this database with others over a network, perhaps someone else is using the table, or a form or query that is bound to the table. Try to make design changes when others are not using the database. Finally, in a secured database, you may not have permission to make design changes. Contact the database owner or network administrator for help.

The Database Documentor

There is a Database Documentor in Access that will print a description of your database, including field names, properties, relationships, and more. You reach it by choosing Tools | Analyze | Documentor.

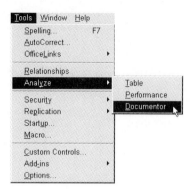

If you don't see this choice on your menu, run the Access Installer again and add it. Documentor reports can get quite long; so to avoid having to read through a lot of stuff you don't care about, you can specify which items you'd like to document:

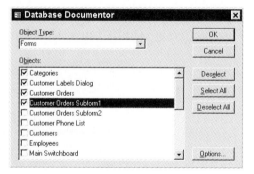

Use the Options button to fine-tune the report. When you run the report, it may span many pages (the sample report was 10 pages long). Figure 39-2 shows a typical page.

It's a good idea to run a final version of the report and store it after your database is up, running, and tested. Then you can refer back to it if future changes foul things up. The finished report may be displayed in Print Preview, giving you the option to print or not to print, or even *what* to print.

Recovering a Damaged Database

If you do not close your database and Access properly (because a power failure has crashed your system, for example), there may be damage to the

FIGURE 39-2

A typical

report page

■

Form: Categories

Tuesday, October 24, 1995
Page: 1

Properties

Allow Additions:	Yes	Allow Deletions:	Yes
Allow Edits:	Yes	Allow Filters:	Yes
Allow Updating:	No	Auto Center:	Yes
Auto Resize:	Yes	Border Style:	Sizable
Caption:	Categories	Close Button:	Yes
Control Box:	Yes	Count:	7
Cycle:	Current Record	Data Entry:	No
Datasheet Back Color:	16777215	Datasheet Cells Effect:	Flat
Datasheet Font Height:	10	Datasheet Font Italic:	No
Datasheet Font Name:	MS Sans Serif	Datasheet Font Underline	No
Datasheet Font Weight:	400	Datasheet Fore Color:	0
Datasheet Gridlines Beha	No Gridlines	Datasheet Gridlines Color	8421504
Date Created:	9/13/95 10:51:50 AM	Default View:	Single Form
Description:	Add and edit product categories. Main form displays category information; subform displays limited product information.	Dividing Lines:	Yes
Fast Laser Printing:	Yes	Filter On:	No
Frozen Columns:	1	Grid X:	10
Grid Y:	12	Help Context Id:	0
InsideHeight:	4260	InsideWidth:	8745
Key Preview:	No	Last Updated:	9/13/95 10:51:50 AM
Layout for Print:	Yes	LogicalPageWidth:	9360
Max Button:	Yes	Min Button:	Yes
Min Max Buttons:	Both Enabled	Modal:	No
Navigation Buttons:	Yes	Order By On:	-1
Order By:	CategoryName	Owner:	admin
Palette Source:	(Default)	Picture Alignment:	Top-left
Picture Size Mode:	Clip	Picture Tiling:	Yes
Picture:	(bitmap)	PicturePalette:	˙•
PictureType:	0	Pop Up:	No
Record Locks:	No Locks	Record Selectors:	No
Record Source:	Categories	Recordset Type:	Dynaset
Row Height:	Default	Scroll Bars:	Neither
Shortcut Menu:	Yes	Show Grid:	Yes
Timer Interval:	0	Views Allowed:	Form
Visible:	No	Whats This Button:	No
Width:	8928	Window Height:	5010
Window Width:	9180		

Objects

Section: Detail

Back Color:	12632256	Can Grow:	Yes
Can Shrink:	No	Display When:	Always
Event Proc Prefix:	Detail	Force New Page:	None
Height:	4560	In Selection:	No

database. Usually, Access detects this damage the next time you attempt to open the database and automatically attempts to repair it. If this does not happen, you can choose Tools | Database Utilities | Repair Database with no database open. Choose the database of interest from the list that appears, and then click Repair.

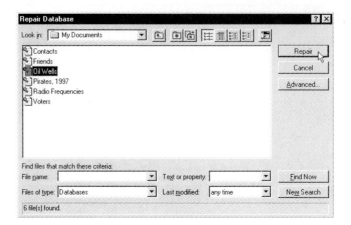

With luck, the computer gods will give you back your data. On rare occasions you might need to revert to your most recent backup of the database (you *do* have a backup, right?) and reenter or reedit changes made since the last backup.

tip *Shared databases have an important file called the System.mda file. This is where security settings live. It's a good idea to back up this file regularly. Otherwise, you'll need to reinstall Access and reestablish security privileges if the file gets damaged or lost.*

Maintaining Your Databases

Databases are like gardens. They need care and attention. Besides the obvious task of keeping records up to date (changing people's phone numbers, and so on), there are some other things you can do to tune up your masterpiece.

Indexing

If you've ever waited endlessly while Access slogs through 10,000 records looking for Mr. Right, it may be because the database has grown to the point where one or more fields need *indexing*. The process helps Access keeps track of where records are stored in a way that speeds searches and other tasks.

For example, the radio frequency database has a number of text fields and contains over 300,000 records.

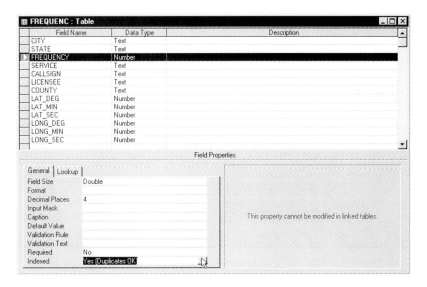

CITY	STATE	FREQUENCY	SERVICE	CALLSIGN	LICENSEE
HALF MOON BA	CA	468.275 IB		KNET237	MULLER, JOHN:MULLER, ED
HALF MOON BA	CA	463.275 IB		KNET237	MULLER, JOHN:MULLER, ED
SAN RAFAEL	CA	468.2875 IB		WNYL606	BRUNO S GROCERY CO
SAN RAFAEL	CA	464.1375 IB		WNYL606	BRUNO S GROCERY CO
OAKLAND	CA	466.525 IB		KRW654	RONALD L DAY TRANSPORT
CUPERTINO	CA	461.525 IB		KRW654	RONALD L DAY TRANSPORT
CUPERTINO	CA	466.525 IB		KRW654	RONALD L DAY TRANSPORT
WALNUT CREEK	CA	461.525 IB		KRW654	RONALD L DAY TRANSPORT
WALNUT CREEK	CA	466.525 IB		KRW654	RONALD L DAY TRANSPORT

Record: 61538 of 307659

Searching for a text string in an *unindexed* field using a 60MHz Pentium machine takes about two minutes, while doing the same search on the same field after *indexing* takes less than two *seconds....*

Here are the steps for indexing a field:

1. Open the database file.

2. Select the table containing the field to be indexed.

3. Switch to Design view.

4. Select the field to be indexed (Frequency in this example).

FREQUENC : Table

Field Name	Data Type	Description
CITY	Text	
STATE	Text	
FREQUENCY	Number	
SERVICE	Text	
CALLSIGN	Text	
LICENSEE	Text	
COUNTY	Text	
LAT_DEG	Number	
LAT_MIN	Number	
LAT_SEC	Number	
LONG_DEG	Number	
LONG_MIN	Number	
LONG_SEC	Number	

Field Properties

General | Lookup

Field Size	Double
Format	
Decimal Places	4
Input Mask	
Caption	
Default Value	
Validation Rule	
Validation Text	
Required	No
Indexed	Yes (Duplicates OK)

This property cannot be modified in linked tables.

5. In the Field Properties area of the dialog box, click in the Indexed area and choose the desired indexing option—Yes or No (duplicates permitted or not).

6. Change other field properties (index other fields by repeating steps 1 through 5, for instance).

7. Save the table (CTRL+S).

8. Switch back to Datasheet view and test the results. Remember, you can always "unindex" a field if you like.

Index Strategies

Since indexes take extra disk space, and slow down some data entry and importing tasks, don't get carried away. Experiment on a field or two, and only add indexes to fields that you regularly search in or sort. Sorting and searching speed should improve noticeably.

Compacting a Database

Over time, databases get flabby. As you delete, add, and modify records, the data gets fragmented. Compacting makes a smaller, leaner, better-performing database; but the process requires enough disk space for the old file and the new one, at least temporarily. (Some software makers call this process "packing" the database.) Here are the steps:

1. Close the database file.

2. Make sure there is enough disk space for an additional copy of the .mdb file nearly the size of your existing database file.

3. In a multiuser environment, make sure others have closed the database file.

4. Consider backing up the database file to a separate medium (tape or whatever) just in case.

5. Choose Tools | Database Utilities | Compact Database.

6. Pick the database file you want to compact.

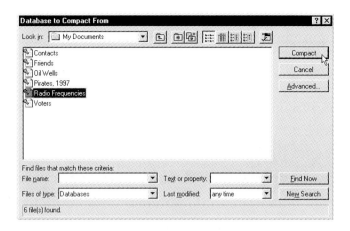

7. Choose a destination name (and location) for the compacted database file. It can be the same name as the old database, in which case, Access will delete the old database file automatically after compacting. You'll be asked to confirm the overwriting. (Unless you have made a backup of the database, it's a good idea to use a new name for the new file.)

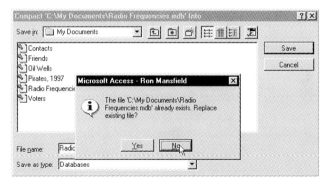

8. Unless Access has done so for you in step 7, delete the old database file.

Security: Protecting Your Information

Some information needs to be kept private. If you doubt this, post a list of employees and their salaries on a bulletin board and see what happens. The very things that make Access easy to use make it possible for inquiring minds to know things they shouldn't. You'll need different levels of security for different situations. Typical security requirements include

- Preventing others from opening your Access databases with Access whether sitting at their computer or yours

- Preventing others from opening your Access databases with other programs (like Word or dBASE)

- Preventing others from changing or deleting data

- Preventing others from changing or deleting database design elements (forms, relationships, and so on)

note *Check with your network administrator if you have questions about Microsoft Access security levels. Also be aware that some organizations have policies regarding passwords. Make certain that you understand your organization's policies.*

A Security Overview

When you create a new database, it starts out life available to everyone. You secure a database by removing permission to do various things (like open tables, change records, and so on). There are five concepts you'll need to understand if you want to use the various possible levels of Access security:

- Workgroups
- User accounts
- Group accounts
- Administrator and owner accounts
- Permission assignments

Jeez. More buzzwords and concepts. Complexity is the price of privacy. Workgroups, user accounts, and group accounts let you specify which information can be seen and changed by various people in your organization. While normally associated with network operations, these security tools can also be used if different people share your computer, or if you are afraid that people might sit at your desk for the electronic equivalent of after-hours Dumpster-diving.

Workgroups

Access Workgroup information lets you specify which people can potentially work with your database. When you installed Access, the installation program created a default Workgroup with some generic entries (accounts, actually) with names like Admins and Guest. You can add more specific accounts, as you'll see in a moment. While it is possible to create and use Workgroups other than the default one (the one created by the installation program), let's leave those gory details to the bigger books.

User Accounts

Users are people who can have access to your database. You are a user. Different users can have different levels of security clearance. The information about a specific user's privileges is stored in a *user account*. You will see how to create these in a moment.

Group Accounts

Groups make it easy to set up and change specific security levels for more than one person simultaneously. For instance, you might let everyone in accounting *see* employee payroll information, but only let accounting managers *change* pay rates. The quick way to do this is to split accounting people into two groups (managers and bookkeepers, for instance), then assign different security levels to the two *groups* instead of to each individual user. The information about a group's privileges is stored in a *group account*.

When you install Access, some group accounts are automatically set up. These include

- Admins
- Users
- Guests

Permission Assignments

Permission assignments are stored with your database. They collect the nitty-gritty details like who gets to see and change what. Different permissions can be granted to individual users, but it is often better to grant permissions to groups, then add selected people to the appropriate group(s). See the big books for more information on personalizing permission.

Owners and Administrators

By default, the person who creates a new database is its *owner*. The owner can always have complete run of the database, and is free to make changes, deletions, redesign things, and so on. By default, the Admin account is the owner of each database when it is created, and remains the owner unless you change ownership. Unless you want the administrator of your system to be able to modify the database *you* have created, you should change the ownership of the database to yourself. Remember, as a matter of policy, some organizations require that multiple people know passwords. This way, if you get hit by a commuter train or win the lottery, your fellow employees will be able to pick up where you left off. Be certain you understand and adhere to your organization's policies in this regard.

warning   *Since the initial Admin account is exactly the same for each copy of Access shipped by Microsoft, it is important that you change the Administrator (owner) for your system, and create unique passwords for these accounts. Until you do this, everyone will have access to your data. You'll see how to change Admin and ownership information next.*

Creating and Changing an Administrator Account

To change the Administrator account, follow these steps:

1. Open any Access database file.

2. Choose Tools | Security | User and Group Accounts.

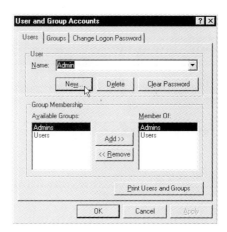

3. Click the New button.

4. Type a new account name and a personal ID. Account names can be 20 characters long and can include most characters, except for " ? | [ ] : < > + = ; , ? * or '. The personal ID can contain a minimum of four and a maximum of 20 characters:

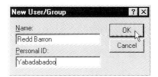

5. Click OK.

6. When you see the Users dialog box again, it will contain the new account name. Select Admins from the Available Groups list, click Add >>, and then click Close.

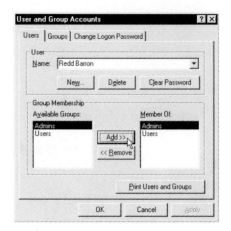

warning   *Write down exact account names and personal ID numbers and store them in a safe place. Remember: **capitalization counts!***

Now that you've activated security, you can start to take *real* control.

Forcing Logon Challenges

Until you activate the Logon feature, anybody can run Access just by starting it, thanks to the Admin account. The default password for the Admin account is—well, there is no password.

You need to change that next.

1. Open a database file if there isn't one open already.

2. Choose Tools | Security | User and Group Accounts.

3. In the User And Group Accounts dialog box, click the Change Logon Password tab to bring it forward, but don't type anything in the Old Password portion of the dialog box.

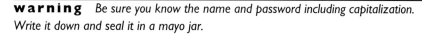

4. Instead, tab to move to the New Password blank (or click on it), and enter the desired password, which can be up to 14 characters long and include anything except the Null character. (Most people don't know how to type that, anyway.) Incidentally, Access cares about capitalization here.

5. Tab to the Verify box (or click on it) and reenter the new password, using identical spelling and capitalization.

6. Click OK.

7. If all goes well, the dialog box will disappear and not much else that is visible will happen. If you get a dialog box telling you "No permission for (account name)", you mistyped either the password or verification, or someone else got there first and changed the password from nothing to something.

8. Quit Access to test the logon feature.

warning   *Be sure you know the name and password including capitalization. Write it down and seal it in a mayo jar.*

note   *To remove password protection, repeat steps 1 through 8 in the preceding exercise, clicking the Clear Password button instead of entering a new password.*

Logging On After Protecting Access

Once you've established a password for the Admin account, you'll need to supply the name and password whenever you run Access.

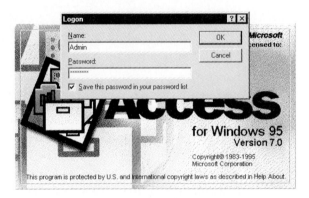

The password created is for the Admin account. You need to type **Admin** and the password, or your new user name and no password. Once you are in Access, open a database and select Security, Change Password, type in a password for the new user, and check that User Name shows the correct name.

Creating and Deleting Groups

Since it's a good idea to store users in groups (to minimize the need to redefine the same security parameters over and over again), you'll want to set up some groups. Here are the general steps:

1. Open a database file.

2. Choose Tools | Security | User and Group Accounts.

3. Click on the Groups tab to bring it forward. Type a meaningful group name and personal ID.

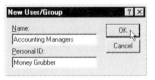

4. Add other groups if you like.

Deleting a Group

If you find it necessary to delete a group (when a project is completed, or a department disbanded, for example), follow these simple steps.

1. Open a database file.

2. Choose Tools | Security | User and Group Accounts.

3. Click on either the Users or Groups tab to bring it forward.

4. Pick a group name from the drop-down list.

5. Click the Delete button.

6. Confirm the deletion.

Creating Users

The steps for adding users will remind you of adding groups. The difference is you'll probably want to assign users to groups as you go:

1. Open a database file.

2. Choose Tools | Security | User and Group Accounts.

3. Click New.

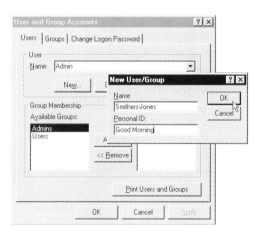

4. Type a meaningful user name and personal ID in the resulting dialog box.

5. Click OK.

6. Add other users if you like, and then click Close.

Assigning Users to Groups

1. Open a database file.

2. Choose Tools | Security | User and Group Accounts.

3. Pick a user from the drop-down name list.

4. Pick a group name from the scrollable Available Groups list.

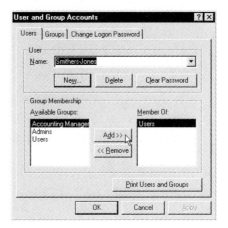

5. Click the Add >> button (or just double-click on the group name).

6. Add the user to other groups if you like.

7. Pick a new user and perform steps 4 through 6, if you like, and then click Close when you've finished.

Granting Permission

Once you've set up users (and probably groups), you can specify what they can and cannot do. Here are the general steps:

1. Open a database file.

2. Choose Tools | Security | User and Group Permissions.

3. Pick a user or group from the User/Group Name list. You will need to click the appropriate list button (Users or Groups) to display lists of either users or groups. Here you see groups:

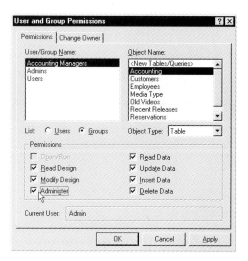

4. Click to add or remove permission for things like reading and updating data.

5. Click the Apply button when you've finished specifying permission.

6. Change permission for other users and groups if you like.

7. Click Close when you've finished.

8. Test to verify that security is what you expect.

Protecting Forms, Tables, and Data

You can choose who gets to see and use each table, query, form, and so on. Here are the general steps:

1. In the Database window, select the item you want to secure.

2. Choose Tools | Security | User and Group Permissions.

3. Choose names or groups from the User/Group Name list and grant the level of permissions.

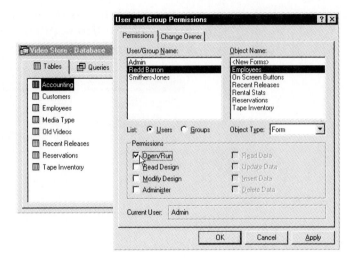

4. Click Apply.

5. Grant permission to others, if you like; then click Close when you've finished.

Encryption

After you've done all that security defining and assigning, some wonk down the hall can *still* open your database without even the electronic equivalent of a crowbar; a program as mundane as a word processor can do it. For example, here's part of an Employee table opened in Microsoft Word:

HealthIssues
Photograph□□𝔖𝔶ỹ□ỹ□ỹ□ỹ□ỹ□ỹ□ỹ□)□□+𝔖𝔥𝔖𝔥𝔖𝔥ỹ□ỹ□ỹ□ỹ□)□□,□□𝔖𝔥·□□□□□□□𝔖□□
ÿÿÿÿ□□□□𝔰𝔥𝔥□F
PrimaryKey□□□)□□□)□𝔰□□□□□𝔥□□□□𝔥𝔥□𝔟□□¼
8Fô□Þ•-ÆÂ¾
□Ê6□𝔏𝔞𝔏¼˜□ñÎ>òÙ˜ü¾$JœgoJ"ÊMú
ÿ汯1 $¶§5-8˜ÉNN bμBù V□¾ÿ汥J±
Randall Scott ÅZë˜Ý□¾U=üˢ¸ ¾·
ÿ5HG]□ý(ˢ§©□¾ÄD(§□wCñNÜₓ□□8□₰₰□G₄□$·-œ,,Ä□Æw#□6□‡□¾Ẑ²⁵·-"□Ç̃Ẽ□Ý f□-P>Ç□□Q
«L-'>ıÓ¾M—É□□ₓ'oˢ□§²f⁻□5⁻□₰₰₰ˢ ¶E˜—]ÅhB(
This employee has repeatedly threatened his boss, once even brandishing a large wrench. Consult lawyer on possible dismissal and risks.

You don't need to be a litigation genius to see that you are looking at a possible termination. If Randall Scott were to see this—well, you figure it out. Sure there's lots of garbage in there, but there's plenty of interesting information, too.

So to be really paranoid—that is, "secure," *encrypt* your important stuff. This scrambles the contents of your database (.mdb file) so that only you and folks you authorize (and perhaps Bill Gates) can make any sense of it. Here are the steps:

1. Close the database file if it is open.

2. Make sure you have room on the hard disk for a second copy of this database file, albeit an encrypted one.

3. Back up, then hide the backup copy of the original database (the .mdb file) in a very secure place—your bank safe-deposit box, perhaps.

4. Choose Tools | Security | Encrypt/Decrypt Database.

5. Locate the database you want to encrypt and select it:

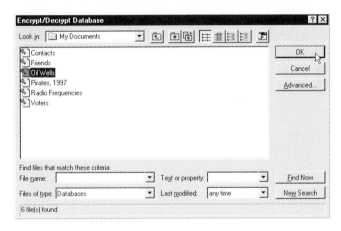

6. Click OK and pick a name for the new encrypted database.

7. Click OK and let 'er rip.

8. Test the encrypted database.

9. Delete the old database file. (You'll need to use something like Norton Utilities to *really* wipe it out. The DOS and Windows file deletion commands don't really wipe things from your hard disk.)

Does it work? You be the judge. Here's the same employee entry *after* encryption. Can you figure out what it says or who it talks about?

ýÖ—¡5FB—ŒmW‚a f› 2 Ib à DþA\Ÿ Aráz÷æ‘å ̄ufo ðn}á W ÇÙ°7
   -ƒ4,,1+Þ¾¾O-"'q8 y X 09 K¾Aœõ% Û ̈ ËO‚w~} O , Sg
~`4Ð ̄ƒGj+ _ F÷ Ã éfüx~»• H»«× Æ‚7AÎ× ËVp O-F<®MÁ(... ËÃ"‹/
-----------------------------------Page Break-----------------------------------
ªé2g Cùü ‘yçDæ†Ö±¿ Œ 0h°è`< 6 2í "å Œ 4@géz3Ë ̃ l¾ ̃ Fõjáx¿£Þ°OFŸÎ.Ð
Â ̄Ì ̃ OBh" FÐ X $Uç > VG—+rAY 5 ̃ Òj   ª?-S?Sw PT ̃ $Áv Ë V &2\
 PñÂOªý Y ̃ ÆÉw},'"N "È Xi E Q t s ̈ ̈ tÙ[Ø)6DÚõ   E YÍDue+.i)´Î ̧ÀÓ"ñ qæ `-
D"é ̈üwÁ µ‾•" • ̈"¢ƒ"xKƒ†F—Ü Šý ̄
 Ø IÐ$Çõ"¾]á Æ uÓ@u +·µ ̀ú— I"YwÐ=?g("‘Ÿ ́4 ®6\É±T®Ë$Ç¥SÎGSñíé Ù ÞÐ+ Þ ̈wB U¶
 Óõ &U-<o'%/aRÐ Ý ® ¶ ƒ"A≈F®KDÓJ¡ ́½«Å£Y3¡®ÌEK1½<]þÆ™×X ...õ ñF
y
—#
-----------------------------------Page Break-----------------------------------
x µ}Fp±Üe

PART 6

Organizing Your Life with Schedule+

Even if you have a PDA (personal data assistant), you're going to find Schedule+ a wonderful assistant in organizing your busy life. Schedule+ lets you quickly keep track of all meetings and appointments you have for the day, week, or month. You can coordinate with other people's schedules, set alarm reminders, automate entry of recurring events, and even devise project schedules. To make getting hold of people easier, Schedule+ comes complete with a Contacts utility. A To Do list lets you note down odds and ends that you haven't gotten around to scheduling formally. If you are a gadget addict, you can even use Schedule+ to program your Timex Data Link watch!

CHAPTER 40

Making Appointments in Schedule+

S

$C H E D U L E +$ is what is known as a *PDA* (personal data assistant). You can use it for simple tasks, such as writing down appointments; but the more you play with it, the more you will discover its power and flexibility. In this chapter, you will first learn how to make simple entries in the calendar section of Schedule+ and add unscheduled obligations to the To Do list. Then you'll go on to some more advanced tasks, such as planning meetings and using the Timex Watch Wizard. So, as Vin Scully likes to say, pull up a chair, we're just getting started . . .

Starting Schedule+

Schedule+ works like all the other Windows programs you've been reading about. To start Schedule+, you can:

- Choose it from the Programs submenu on the Start menu.

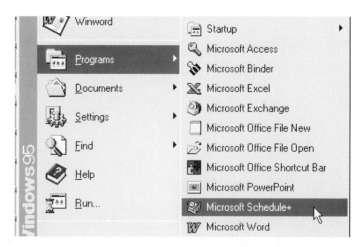

■ Click the Schedule+ icon in the Office Shortcut Bar.

■ Double-click on the Schedule+ program icon or a Schedule+ document icon (it will have the extension .SCD if you are showing extensions) in Windows Explorer or anyplace on the Windows desktop.

Microsoft
Schedule+

Any of these will start Schedule+. If you are connected to a network, the first thing you will probably see is the Group Enabling dialog box.

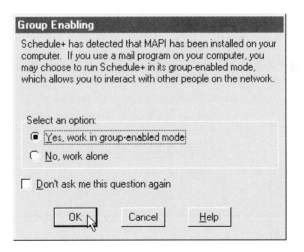

 tip *If you run Schedule+ every day, consider putting a shortcut for it in the Windows Startup folder.*

This dialog box lets you specify whether you want to run Schedule+ in such a way that others on the network can access your data. If you do want to share your data, choose "Yes, work in group-enabled mode"; otherwise, choose "No, work alone." If you know you're always going to want to be connected, click to check the "Don't ask me this question again" option. You might see a Microsoft Mail message; just click OK. If all goes according to Hoyle, the Schedule+ window will appear, in all its glory, as discussed next.

The Schedule+ Window

When you start Schedule+, the first *interesting* thing you'll see will be the Schedule+ application window, shown in Figure 40-1.

You'll notice a few familiar elements, notably the menu bar, toolbar, and status area. But much of the Schedule+ window is new to Windows users.

FIGURE 40-1

The cockpit of a 767 . . . oops! . . . the main Schedule+ window

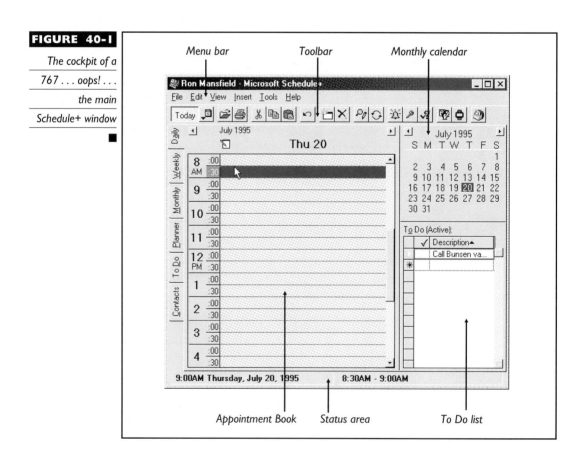

Appointment Book   Status area   To Do list

First, there is the Appointment Book. You enter your appointments, meetings, and other tasks here, as explained later in the section "Scheduling Appointments in the Appointment Book." Notice that you can look at your daily, weekly, or monthly schedule. You move from one tab to the next by clicking, as you're used to doing in other Windows applications.

note   *The Contacts tab of the Appointment Book is covered in more detail in Chapter 41.*

The monthly calendar is a great way to move to a specific day of the month. You can also use it to look ahead to other months.

tip   *You can often get a better sense of your schedule if you maximize the Schedule+ window, which is somewhat smaller than full screen by default. Do so by clicking the Maximize button.*

The To Do list is a handy place to note down your tasks that have no specific date or deadline. It is also a good place to write in little things that need doing but that might not relate to work, such as taking your snake to the vet. You'll look at the To Do list in more detail later in the section Using the To Do List.

Navigating and Working in the Schedule+ Window

Getting around in Schedule+ is pretty straightforward:

- Click in the Appointment Book to add an entry.

- Use the scroll bars, boxes, and arrows to see other parts of your Appointment Book or To Do list that are hidden.

- Click the left- and right-pointing arrows of the Appointment Book to see the next or previous day.

- Click the left- and right-pointing arrows in the monthly calendar to see the next or previous month.

- Click one of the tabs running along the left edge of the Appointment Book to see your daily, weekly, or monthly schedule, or your To Do or Contact lists.

Apart from these idiosyncrasies, you can use any of the usual Windows techniques for menu commands or for minimizing, maximizing, or closing the Schedule+ window.

Getting Help

Schedule+ comes complete with help features similar to those of Word, Excel, Access, and PowerPoint. For example, if you choose Help | Microsoft Schedule+ Help Topics, you will see the Help Topics window.

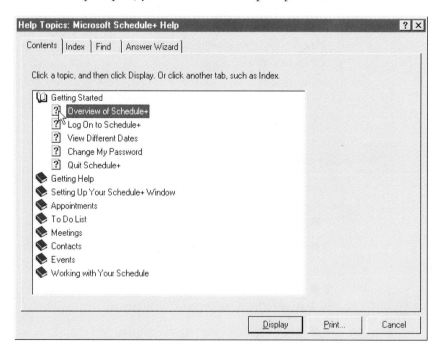

Here you can double-click on items to read them or click on one of the other tabs. Click Index to get an alphabetical list of Schedule+ topics. Click Answer Wizard to reach the keyword searching utility.

tip *Choosing Help | Answer Wizard will take you directly to the Answer Wizard tab of the Help Topics dialog box.*

There is another choice on the Help menu in Schedule+ that you won't find anywhere else. It is Help | Seven Habits Help Topics. It brings up the Seven Habits Tools Help, which is essentially the text from the best-selling book *The Seven Habits of Highly Effective People* by Stephen R. Covey. This is a hypertext document, which means you can click on highlighted terms and topics to go directly to related sections. Reading this text, in whole or in part, can make you a more effective person, too! (Well, at least a better-read person . . .)

Finally, there is the About Microsoft Schedule+ choice on the Help menu, which gives you systems information, and so forth.

Printing Schedules

Printing in Schedule+ is quite easy; deciding what to print might not be, though. Follow these steps:

1. It is always a good idea to get to roughly what you want to print—the specific day, week, or month, for example—using the navigation techniques discussed earlier.

2. Choose File | Print, click the Print button on the toolbar, or use the CTRL+P keyboard shortcut to bring up the Print dialog box.

3. You'll notice you have many choices about what to print in the Print Layout section of the Print dialog box. They include

   - All text
   - Your contact list
   - Your daily schedule (fixed or dynamic)
   - Your monthly schedule (regular or tri-fold graphical)
   - Your To Do list (choice of three formats)
   - Your weekly schedule (five or seven day)

4. Make a decision about what you want to print, as well as how many copies, the page format, what printer to use, and so on.

ORGANIZING YOUR LIFE WITH SCHEDULE+

5. Very important: Be sure you specify the range of dates you want printed. Don't assume that Schedule+ will know! For instance, if you want *tomorrow's* schedule, don't just blithely print away—chances are, Schedule+ will just print out today's schedule again. That's the default, at any rate.

6. When you are satisfied with your choices, click OK.

tip *If you want to see how things will look before you actually print, click the Preview button in the Print dialog box. This is just like Print Preview in the other Office programs.*

Using the Backup Command

There is no File | Save command in Schedule+, as such. Schedule+ saves your work whenever you click the close box; but if you're doing a lot of entries and you don't want to lose your data, one way to save your work is to use the File | Backup command. This works pretty much the same as the File | Save command does in other Office programs, it just has a different name. To back things up, follow these steps:

1. Choose File | Backup.

2. In the Backup dialog box that appears, specify a drive and folder for your backup. It will probably list the My Documents folder by default, but you can place it anywhere you like. After you've backed up once, Schedule+ will remember where to back up in the future.

3. Click Save.

4. You'll get a message asking if you want to overwrite the existing file.

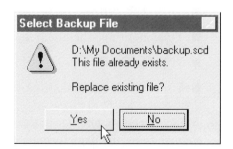

5. Click Yes. Schedule+ will back up all your data, making the world once again safe for democracy. You will be returned to Schedule+, where you can continue working.

Quitting Schedule+

You quit Schedule+ just as you would any other Office program:

■ Click the close box in the upper-right corner.

■ Choose File | Exit or File | Exit and Log Off.

■ Press ALT+F4.

n o t e   *The difference between File | Exit and File | Exit And Log Off is that you can quit Schedule+ (with File | Exit) and leave other message-receiving programs logged on to receive messages. The latter command logs off entirely. You can close an Appointment Book window by double-clicking the icon (or control) menu.*

Scheduling Appointments in the Appointment Book

Ah, now for the fun stuff! Entering, deleting, and moving appointments around in Schedule+ is as easy as entering, deleting, and moving text in Word or data in Access. Furthermore, many of your entries will be *dynamic*. In other words, they will appear in more than one place and be connected, just like fields in Word. Furthermore, Schedule+ features many time-saving devices to make mundane tasks like entering recurring events a snap.

t i p   *The Undo button on the toolbar or the Edit | Undo command both work in Schedule+ as you'd expect them to in a well-behaved Office program.*

Entering Appointments

You can enter appointments in one of two ways. To enter an appointment directly into the Appointment Book, follow these steps:

1. Find the day for which you want to schedule the appointment.

2. Click on the time slot where you want the appointment to go.

3. Type in the text of the appointment.

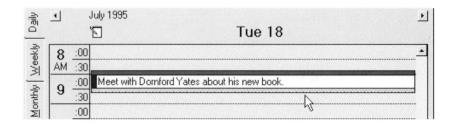

4. Use any of the special toolbar buttons or other features to mark the appointment, if appropriate. This can include setting it to recurring (a weekly meeting with your boss, perhaps), marking it private or tentative, or setting a reminder alarm to go off.

tip *You can schedule appointments for longer than the half-hour time slots by dragging to select as much time as you'll need. You can also expand or contract the allotted time by selecting the appointment, clicking the bottom of the time slot, and dragging it up or down.*

You can enter information in more detail by using the Insert New Appointment button on the toolbar. You can click the button from anywhere (that is, the desired day does not have to be visible in the Appointment Book).

tip *You reach this dialog box, with some of the information already filled in, by double-clicking on a time slot in the Appointment Book. As you might expect, the Date and Time fields will already be filled in for you if you use this method.*

When you click this button, the Appointment dialog box appears.

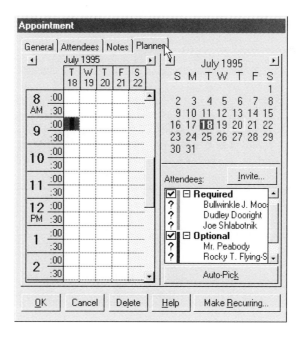

As you can see, you can enter a lot of detail here. For instance, you can type in the location, click the option boxes to set reminders, make the appointment private, note if it is going to take all day, and so on. You can even click the Make Recurring button if it is going to be repeated periodically.

Click any of the other tabs to reach them and more levels of detail.

This might look complicated now—but when you see how easy it is to add names to the Required and Optional lists, you'll be scrounging high and low for meetings to plan! There are a number of options in the Appointment dialog box (and touched upon earlier) that are worth going into in some detail. Let's do so now.

Recurring Events

What could be more of a nuisance than having to type in the same recurring events every month. Or every week. Or every day. (You are getting sleepy . . .) Wake up! There's none of that in Schedule+, not with the handy Make Recurring command. To make an event recurring:

- Click the Recurring button on the toolbar.
- Choose Insert | Make Recurring.
- In the Appointment dialog box, click Make Recurring.

However you give the command, the Appointment Series dialog box will appear, with the When tab foremost.

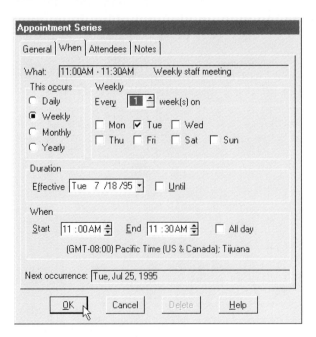

This example sets a weekly staff meeting for every Tuesday at 11:00 A.M. Notice that if staff meetings were held biweekly (or semimonthly), you could enter 2 in the Every box. You can also specify the start and end times and the duration (not how long *individual* meetings are supposed to run, but how long you plan to hold this *series* of meetings), as well as see when the next meeting is scheduled for. When you are satisfied, click OK.

Setting Reminders

If you're one of those people who forgets to look at your computer for appointments—and let's face it, who isn't?—you'll love Schedule+'s reminder feature. As you might expect, it pops up a dialog box, along with a beep, to remind you of your appointments. It has all the expected details:

Reminder for 4:00PM Thu, Jul 20, 1995	[X]

Where: [ ]

Project meeting with Hal.

(Notify me again (in): [5 ÷] [minute(s) ▼] [ ] Beforehand
(•) Don't notify me again

[OK]   [Edit...]   [Help]

Notice that you can have Schedule+ notify you again in a few minutes if you're not ready for the appointment, or you can tell it to go fly a kite. What's nice is that you'll see the reminder regardless of what program you're using. Schedule+ does have to be running, though. Reminders won't come if you haven't started the program.

You set reminders for selected appointments in one of the following ways:

- Click the Reminder button on the toolbar.
- Choose Edit | Set Reminder.
- Click the Set Reminder option box in the Appointment dialog box.

ORGANIZING YOUR LIFE WITH SCHEDULE+

Tentative Appointments

Sometimes, you're just not sure. Everyone can make Wednesday at 10:00 except Bill, who's having his otter spayed. Only three people can make it on Friday at 4:00, because of the annual fax-off. How do you ever get anything scheduled? Well, you can always schedule meetings and so forth and then mark them as tentative. It's easy to make the selected appointment tentative:

- Click the Tentative button on the toolbar.
- Choose Edit | Tentative.
- Click the Tentative option box in the Appointment dialog box.

The appointment you've so marked will be distinguished by having a darker background than other appointments. Also, an icon with a check mark and a question mark will appear next to it.

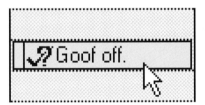

Privacy

Let's face it: there are some reminders you just don't want other people to see. These can range from not forgetting your spouse's birthday to a clandestine meeting with Bill's otter, which might, come to think of it, be related. Anyway, the way to keep prying eyes from seeing certain appointments is to mark them as private. You do so in one of the following ways:

- Click the Private button on the toolbar.
- Choose Edit | Private.
- Click the Private option box in the Appointment dialog box.

note *While using the Private command is a good way to keep people from seeing individual events, it won't prevent their perusing your Appointment Book. To make your entire Appointment Book inaccessible to others, you might want to set a password for opening it in the first place. You can also set Access Preferences for any other users you wish.*

The Private entry will be marked with a key.

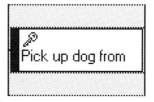

Entries marked as private will not be seen by others accessing your schedule.

Deleting Appointments

Piece of cake. Just select the doomed appointment and click the Delete button on the toolbar.

Moving Appointments

Another piece of cake. You just select the appointment, and then click and drag it. This works just like drag-and-drop in Word, Excel, and so on. At first you will see the now-familiar four-headed arrow (not to be confused with the two-headed snake), and then you will see the usual drag-and-drop box and cursor.

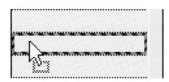

Ho hum. You're getting pretty good at this, eh? Alternatively, you can double-click an item, and set a new time and date in the Appointment dialog box, discussed earlier.

Daily, Weekly, or Monthly

You've probably noticed that along the left side of the Appointment Book, there are a number of tabs, including Daily, Weekly, and Monthly. (The To Do tab will be covered later in this chapter, and the Contacts and Planner tabs, in Chapter 41.)

These tabs allow you to get an overview of your schedule. Daily, of course, shows the current day's workaday toil.

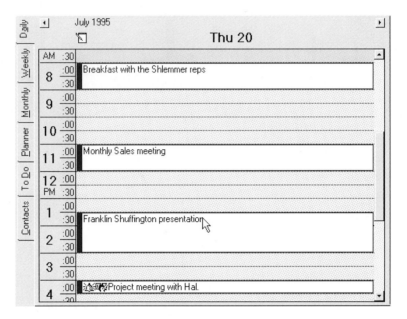

You can click to go backward or forward to see what other days' schedules are like.

Click the Weekly tab to get a sense of how your week's shaping up.

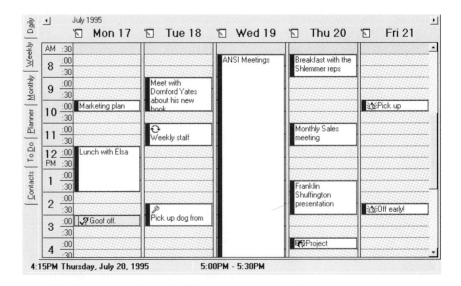

The advantage of this view of your schedule is that you can move things around and rearrange your work, moving things from day to day. This can be quite handy if, for instance, someone decides they can't meet with you this afternoon, but would like to meet first thing in the morning.

Finally, there is the Monthly view:

	July 1995					
Sunday	Monday	Tuesday	Wednesday	Thursday	Friday	Saturday
Jun 25	26	27	28	29	30	**Jul 1**
2	3	4	5	6	7	8
9	10	11	12	13	14	15
16	17 10AM Marketin... 12PM Lunch wi... 3PM Goof off.	18 9AM Meet with ... 11AM Weekly s... 2:30PM Pick up...	19 8AM ANSI Mee...	20 8AM Breakfast ... 11AM Monthly ... 1:30PM Frankli...	21 10AM Pick up p... 2:30PM Off early!	22
23	24 10AM Marketin... 3PM Goof off.	25 8AM Breakfast ... 11AM Weekly s...	26 12PM Lunch wi...	**27** 4PM Project me...	28	29
30	31 10AM Marketin... 3PM Goof off.	**Aug 1** 11AM Weekly s...	2	3 4PM Project me...	4	5

Makes you feel rather regal, eh? The advantages of seeing the month's tasks will be obvious. You can move appointments from one week to another and plan projects pretty far in advance. Clicking on Monthly gives you the big picture. The disadvantage, though, is that you can't see much detail. Click in any darkened square to move to that day's schedule.

Using the To Do List

Ah, what to do with those odds and ends: pick up some milk on the way home; reconcile that travel expense report (particularly the $300 for that night on the town); sort through your phone list and throw out old contacts; write a thank-you note to Kamiar for the baklava; call about the house insurance; look into buying a new modem; pick up fresh fish and flowers for Bill's otter. Your list is probably similar. Everyone has miscellaneous tasks to do, some for work, some for themselves. It is precisely this flotsam and jetsam of your life that always seem to get lost in the shuffle. Hence, the To Do list in Schedule+.

The To Do feature was probably intended as a list of tasks for projects, for which it works wonderfully. It can be just as useful for your personal errands, though. There are two ways you can view the To Do list.

- If you click on the Daily tab, you'll see a list of that day's tasks.

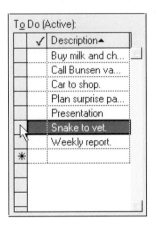

- If you click the To Do tab, you'll see a list of all your tasks, nicely separated out into today's, tomorrow's, next week's, and so on.

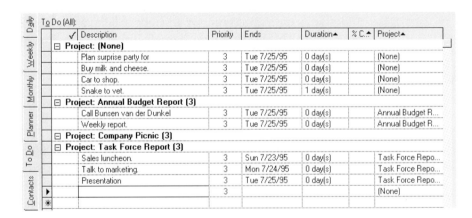

Adding Tasks to the To Do List

Adding tasks to the To Do list is very similar to adding appointments to the Appointment Book. There are two ways to add a task: using the Task dialog box, and typing directly into the list. Let's look at the Task dialog box first.

1. Either in the Daily tab or in the To Do tab, double-click in the first cell of the last row. This will bring up the Task dialog box.

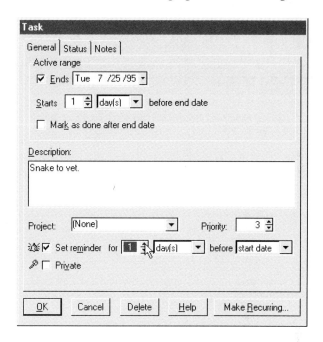

2. Type in your task. In this example, it is **Snake to vet.**

3. Set other parameters, including a reminder if you want one. If this were part of a project, you could indicate that by choosing a project from the Project list.

4. When you are satisfied, click OK. Your entry will appear in your To Do list.

note   *If you started out in the To Do tab, you'll have to specify the date range yourself.*

Entering a task directly into the To Do list is simple. Just select the second cell in the last column and begin typing. When you move to another cell, your entry is saved to that cell.

Deleting Items from the To Do List

Deleting items on the To Do list works the same way as deleting items from the Appointment Book. Simply select the hapless victim, and click the Delete button on the toolbar.

Manipulating Tasks on the To Do List

Following are a number of ways you might want to manipulate your To Do list.

Crossing Out Items on the To Do List

Often it is better to cross something out (or check it off) from the To Do list, rather than simply deleting it. To cross out an item, simply click in the blank cell to the left of it. It will be stricken through and through.

Moving Items on the To Do List

Moving items around on the To Do list is analogous to moving them around in your Appointment Book. You just select the item to be moved and drag to where you want it to go.

	Call Bunsen van der Dunkel		3
	Weekly report.		3
	⊟ **Project: Company Picnic (3)**		
	⊟ **Project: Task Force Report (3)**		
	Sales luncheon.		3
	Talk to marketing.		3
	Presentation		3

Assigning Tasks to Projects

You can assign a Task to a particular project in one of two ways:

■ In the To Do tab, click in the Project column on the row of the task you want to reassign. In the drop-down list, choose the project you want to assign the task to.

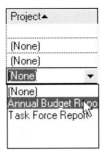

■ In the Task dialog box, choose a project from the Project drop-down list.

Go Mobile with the Timex Watch Wizard!

The Timex Data Link watch is amazing. This gadget is essentially a PDA in watch form. Sure, you wear it on your wrist, but you ain't seen nuthin' like this before

Why you should care about the Timex Data Link watch is that you can download your schedule and contacts list to the watch. This actually works. What happens is that your watch scrolls across reminders, and so on, throughout the day, just as Schedule+ might flash reminders on your screen. Anyway, let's check it out.

What You Need to Make It Work

You do, of course, need the Timex Data Link watch. Sorry, that old Bulova that your grandmother gave you just won't cut it. Of course, you need Schedule+. And you'll need a computer with a regular CRT display. You *cannot* program the watch from laptop LCD screens. (Bummer!)

Exporting Data to Your Timex Data Link Watch

To export data to your Timex Data Link watch, follow these steps.

1. Make sure all your scheduling information is up to date.

2. Choose File | Export | Timex Data Link Watch, or click the Timex Watch Wizard button on the toolbar. This will bring up the Timex Data Link Watch Wizard dialog box, which recently won an award for the dialog box with the longest name.

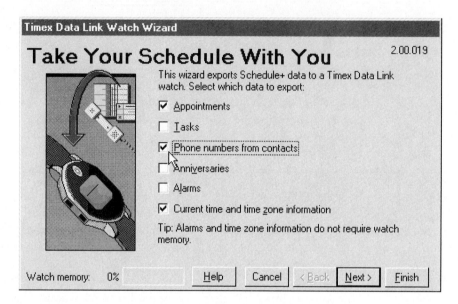

3. Click to select the information you want exported and click Next >.

t i p *If you know that the information in the remaining dialog boxes is what you want it to be (Schedule+ saves any changes you make to the settings), just click Finish and go straight to step 7.*

4. In the next dialog box, you'll be given a chance to specify how many days' worth of information you want downloaded. Also, you can click options boxes to set reminders, and so on. Click Next > when you've finished.

5. If you chose to export contacts in the first dialog box, the next dialog box has a list of all your contacts. Choose the ones you want exported along with your scheduling information. When you have finished, click Next >.

6. Finally, you will be given a chance to change the watch's time zone. Make the desired changes and click Next >. (You might get a message saying that your screen is being configured; usually

you just have to wait a few seconds while Schedule+ handles a few details.)

warning   *If you ask Schedule+ to adjust the time (or the time zone) of your watch and your computer's internal clock and calendar are wrong, your watch will be wrong, too!*

7. Two dialog boxes will appear. One is a summary of the data you have indicated you want to download to the watch. The other is the Export To Watch dialog box.

Timex Data Link Watch Wizard

Data Summary

	Number of items	Watch memory used
Appointments	11	20%
Tasks	0	0%
Phone numbers	0	0%
Anniversaries	0	0%
Alarms	0	
Time zone data	2	
--- Total data ---		20%

Watch memory: 20%   Help

Export To Watch

C O M M
R E A D Y

Make sure the watch is COMM READY, hold the watch face to the screen, and choose OK.

OK   Cancel

8. Repeatedly press the brown button on your watch until the watch face says COMM MODE and changes to COMM READY.

warning   *If you are sensitive to serial data, take off the watch! Every year, hundreds of people suffer the tragedy of having their entire schedule electronically stuffed into their brains by forgetting to take off their Data Link watches. What happens is that the information enters through the capillaries in your wrist and passes through the autonomic nervous system straight to your brain. The only way to get rid of it is to have a lobotomy or watch a whole bunch of old Ronald Reagan movies. If you are not serial-data-phobic, it's okay to leave the watch on your wrist while programming it.*

9. Be sure you're holding the face of the watch about six inches from the center of the screen and click OK with your mouse.

10. The data you have requested will be exported to your watch. (You'll hear a series of short beeps.) Be sure to hold the watch near the screen, keeping it as still as possible, until you hear a final, long, plaintive beep. You'll also get a message asking whether the data transfer was successful.

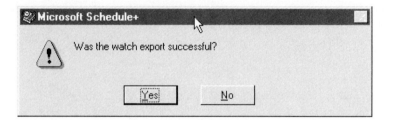

11. Test the watch to see if it was. If so, click Yes to dismiss the dialog box. You're done! If not, click No and retry the download.

tip As you are specifying information to be exported, keep an eye on the Watch Memory box in the lower-left corner of the Wizard dialog box. It will inform you about how much free space remains on your watch.

CHAPTER 41

Using Your Contact List and Planning Projects

IN addition to helping you plan your schedule, Schedule+ has a powerful contacts database you can use to keep track of all business and personal connections. You can use your Contact list to plan meetings and projects, to schedule appointments, and much more.

In addition, Schedule+ comes with many features for planning meetings and organizing projects. Let's look at them in some detail, including the powerful and all-knowing Meeting Wizard. After all, what would an Office program be without a Wizard or two?!

An Overview of the Contact List

As with any index, your Schedule+ Contact list is only going to be useful to you if you are scrupulous about keeping it up to date and accurate. This section looks at these tasks and other aspects of the Contact list.

The Contacts Tab

First, though, lets get acquainted with the Contacts tab. To see it, click on the Contacts tab in the Appointment Book.

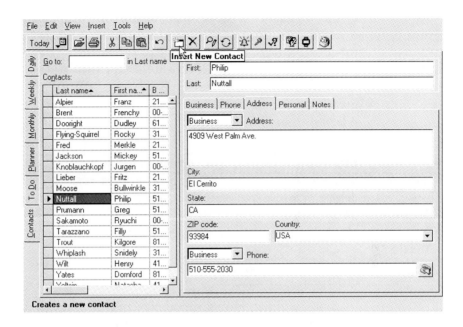

The Contact list is a database, much like Mail Merge databases in Word or tables in Access. What you see in the Contacts tab is a list of all the records on the left, and information specific to the current record on the right. To see more information about the current record, click one of the other tabs (Business, Phone, Address, Personal, or Notes):

You can enter a staggering amount of information into these tabs. Ironically, though, among all these fields, some of them bizarre or irrelevant to most contacts (including *seven*—count 'em—seven telephone fields), Microsoft forgot to include a field for an e-mail address. Well, it's nice to know that, collectively, they do have feet of clay. You'll just have to enter e-mail addresses and other information that doesn't fit a particular field into one of the Notes fields.

tip *Many of the fields in your Contact list are dynamic. Two really great examples of this are the Birthday and Anniversary boxes on the Personal tab. These are linked dynamically to your Appointment Book, and on the special day, whatever it might be, you will be reminded of the event! Now you'll never forget another birthday or anniversary, provided you remember to turn on your computer.*

Viewing Other Records

To see information about another record, just click on the name you want. If you don't see the name you're trying to find or you have a huge contacts database, try typing the name into the Go To box near the top of the screen.

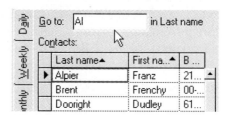

As you can see, this is a dynamic box. In other words, you don't have to type the whole name.

Finding Information

If you're still having trouble finding what you want, you might try using the Find command. Here's how:

1. Choose Edit | Find or use the CTRL+F shortcut. The Find dialog box will appear.

2. Type the name or address or phone number you are trying to find in the Find What box.

3. Click Start Search. The Find utility will locate what you have asked it to, and display information about its location in the status area at the bottom of the dialog box.

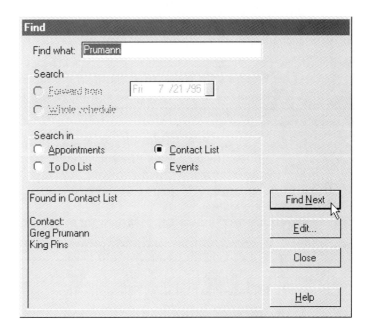

4. If the entry found is not the one you were looking for, click Find Next, and the Find utility will locate the next entry that matches what you're looking for.

5. Continue doing this until you have found what you want.

note *You can use the Find dialog box elsewhere in Schedule+; it is not limited to just the Contact list.*

Entering Contacts

There are several ways to place new entries in the Contact list: importing them, using the Contact dialog box, and entering data directly into the Contacts tab. Let's look at them.

Importing Contacts

Chances are you can't import all your contacts, but it's a great way to quickly enter all of your company's sales representatives or all of the customers in a region, or other information that a company is likely to keep in a nice, up-to-date database somewhere. Here's how to import contacts.

1. Be sure you have some idea of where the information you want to import is. If you don't, the computer will once again succeed in its single-minded task of making you look like an idiot.

2. You now want to choose one of the options from the File | Import submenu. Depending upon which one you choose, the steps from here on in will branch in one of three directions, so let's look at each one.

SCHEDULE+ INTERCHANGE   If you want to import data that has already been saved in Schedule+ format, you're in luck, because this is probably the surest method of getting things in the right places.

1. Choose File | Import | Schedule+ Interchange. The Import Schedule+ Interchange dialog box will appear.

2. Use the usual Windows 95 techniques to locate the Schedule+ file you want to import. It will have the extension *.SCH or *.SC2.

3. When you have found the desired file, double-click it to import the information.

If any records being imported overlap with or duplicate records you already have, you will be advised of this potential conflict and given the chance to either import the records anyway or only import those records that don't conflict with existing records. Use caution when importing records wholesale, because you might have more pieces of information that are more up to date than those in the incoming records.

TEXT   You probably won't be importing text for contacts; it is really intended for your schedule. Still, if you can think of a way to do it, here's how.

1. Choose File | Import | Text. The Text Import Wizard will magically appear and offer to grant three wishes, provided that all of them involve importing a text-based document into Schedule+.

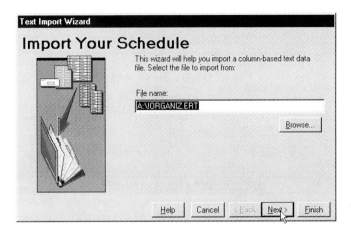

2. Follow the prompts (you'll be asked to find the file you want, how the information is delimited, and so on), clicking Next > when you've answered the questions and indicated the desired settings in each successive Wizard dialog box.

3. When everything is copacetic, click Finish to import the text.

OTHER SYSTEMS The third way to import data into Schedule+ is to grab it from other systems. These can include other scheduling programs such as Lotus Organizer and ACT, or even pocket PDAs such as the Sharp 5000, 6500, 7600, 8000, or 8600 series personal organizers. If you'd been storing your contacts on the Windows Cardfile, you can also use the Other Systems option to import that data into Schedule+. Let's see how.

1. Make sure your system is properly hooked up to your computer and is ready to receive data.

2. Choose File | Import | Other Systems. The Select Source System dialog box will appear.

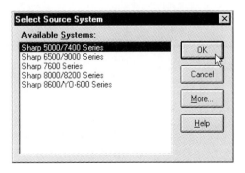

3. Choose one of the listed available systems or click the More button to see other systems.

4. When you click OK, the Schedule+ 7.0 dialog box appears. Use its three tabs to make decisions about your import and then click Import.

Typing in Contacts

Importing contacts is the easy way to do it, and is the way to go when you can do it. However, for your own personal contacts, or the new ones you probably make constantly, you'll have to enter the data by typing it in. There are two ways to enter data by typing: using the Contact dialog box and typing directly onto the Contacts tab.

USING THE CONTACT DIALOG BOX   The major advantage of using the Contact dialog box over just entering data directly into the Contacts tab is that you can use it anywhere in Schedule+ (you don't have to be using the Contact list). To enter a contact by using the Contact dialog box, follow these steps:

1. Choose Insert | Contact, or, if you are in the Contact list already, click the Insert New Contact button on the toolbar. The Contact dialog box will appear.

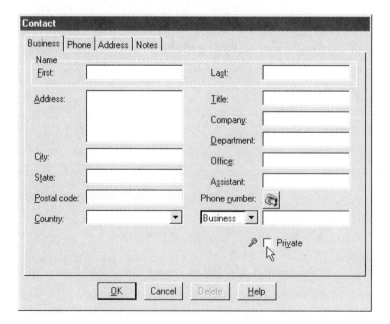

2. Enter a first name, last name, address, and other information that you would like to keep on your new contact. Tabbing will move you from field to field.

3. When you have finished with the Business tab, click on the Phone or Notes tabs to enter more information there. (The Address information also appears on the Business tab.)

4. If you like, you can click the Private button to keep others from seeing this contact when they access your Contact list.

5. When you've finished, click OK. The new contact will be added to your list.

USING THE CONTACTS TAB Entering information directly into the Contacts tab might be more convenient than using the Contact dialog box if you are already there. Here's how:

1. Move to the Contacts tab if you're not already there.

2. Click in the Last Name cell of the last row. You can always tell where this is, because there is a super-asterisk in the gray area next to it:

3. Type in the Last Name. Press TAB, type in the First Name, and then do the same to enter the Business phone. At this point, if you wish, you can simply click in the various fields of the Business tab and add more information about your new entry. Click on other tabs to enter more information.

Grouping

You might be wondering if there are ways of organizing this data in your Contact list. This would be especially useful if you have a large Contact list. Schedule+ allows you to *group* records in just about any way imaginable. Follow along to learn how.

1. Choose View | Group By to bring up the Group By dialog box.

2. In the first Group Contacts By drop-down list, choose the first category that you want to group by. This example shows Business Country chosen.

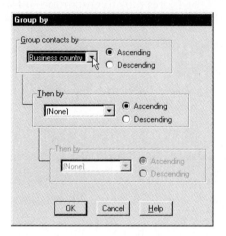

3. If you like, choose additional grouping keys (perhaps Business City and Business phone).

4. When you are happy with your choices, click OK.

If you want to remove any sorting, just choose View | Group By again, and choose None from the drop-down list. Then click OK.

Private Text

If you mark any text as private, it will not appear to others who are looking at your schedule. To mark text as private, follow these steps:

1. Select the text you wish to keep from prying eyes.

2. Choose Edit | Private.

To unmark private text, just select the entry and choose Edit | Private again to remove the check from the command.

Viewing Contacts

You've learned about grouping contacts to make them easier to find and keep track of. In this section, let's look at other handy features of Schedule+ that make managing your data easier. These include sorting and filtering, as well as rearranging and adjusting the size of the columns.

Sorting

Similar to grouping, Schedule+ also allows you to *sort* records in just about any way imaginable. Here are the steps to do this:

1. Choose View | Sort to bring up the Sort dialog box. It will remind you of the Group By dialog box.

2. In the first Sort Contacts By drop-down list, choose the first category that you want to group by. In this example, Business Address is chosen.

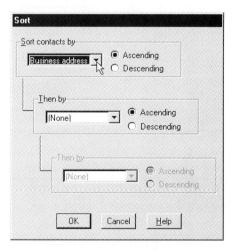

3. If you like, choose additional sorting keys (perhaps Business Phone).

4. When you are happy with your choices, click OK.

If you want to remove any sorting, just choose View | Sort again, and choose None from the drop-down list. Then click OK.

Columns

Obviously, everyone has different needs with respect to what they want to see onscreen. Sometimes you just want to see phone numbers, for example, while other times you might want to view a wide field (such as an address). Let's look at several ways to manipulate columns in the Contacts tab of Schedule+.

ADJUSTING COLUMN WIDTH Adjusting the width of columns in Schedule+ will remind you of how you do it in other Office programs. Essentially, you place the pointer at the top-left edge of the column's width you wish to change:

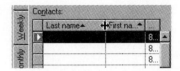

Then just click and drag the column until it is the size you want.

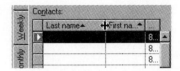

tip *You can automatically make a column wide enough to fit the longest data field by double-clicking the top-left corner of it.*

You can also type in column widths in the Columns dialog box, discussed next.

REARRANGING COLUMNS Perhaps *rearranging* columns is a misleading heading for this section. It should really be something like "deciding what columns to display and the order in which to display them." But that's too long for a heading! Anyway, you do all of these wonderful things in the Columns dialog box. Here's how.

1. Choose View | Columns | Custom to bring up the Columns dialog box.

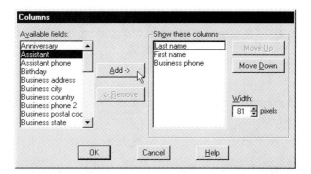

2. There's a lot going on here! You can do any number of things in this box:

   ■ To add fields you want to appear as columns, choose them and click Add.

   ■ To remove fields that you don't want to see, choose them and click Remove.

   ■ To specify the order in which columns appear, select them in the Show These Columns list, and click either Move Up or Move Down.

   ■ To change a column's width, select it and type in a new width.

3. When you are happy with your choices, click OK to register your desires.

Editing Contact Information

Naturally, when a contact changes his or her address or phone number, you'll want to bring your entry on that person up to date. Schedule+ makes this very easy. Click on the Contacts tab and then follow these steps:

1. Either double-click next to the name of the entry you want to edit, or click the Edit button on the toolbar. Either way, the Contact dialog box will appear.

2. Edit the information using the usual Windows techniques.

3. When you have finished, click OK.

ORGANIZING YOUR LIFE WITH SCHEDULE+

note *You can use the Edit button on the toolbar anywhere in Schedule+. Its use is not limited to the Contact list.*

You can also make simple changes (such as correcting the spelling of someone's name) by clicking on the information you want to change and retyping it.

Printing Contacts

There will be times when you want to print records from your Contact list, either all of them or some select portion. You'll also want to make decisions about the format, and preview your records before they print, to save trees. This section explores printing in some detail. The basics of printing Contacts information are

1. Choose File | Print to bring up the Print dialog box.

2. Select Contacts List in the Print Layout area.

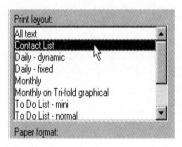

3. Choose a format from the Paper Format list.

4. Make other necessary choices.

5. Click OK.

Choosing a Paper Size

Paper size and paper format are not the same thing, so pay attention. To choose a paper size, follow these steps:

1. Choose File | Print to bring up the Print dialog box.

2. Click on Setup to bring up the Print Setup dialog box.

3. Choose the desired paper size from the Form drop-down list.

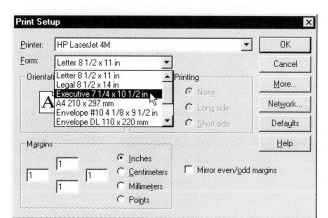

4. When you have finished, click OK twice to print the data on the size paper you have chosen.

t i p *Be sure all the settings are what you want when you get back to the Print dialog box (after clicking OK the first time). If you just click OK a second time, your document will print without giving you a chance to adjust anything.*

Choosing What to Print

You might not care what prints, but if you don't consider this carefully, you might print hidden entries as well, and everyone who walks past the printer will know you frequent Buffy's House of Rubber Chickens. Not so good. So before you print, be sure to check the Private Items list to ensure that you'll be printing only what you want to print. You can do any of the following with entries marked as Private:

■ Show them.

■ Hide them.

■ Hide only their text.

Choosing a Format

When you print contacts, you have a number of choices about the format of the printout. You have the staid, expected, full-page choice, but then you also have several label formats. While you might prefer to print your labels in Word, Schedule+ might end up being more handy if the data is all there and you don't want to muck about with Word. At any rate, all your choices are on the Paper Format list. Just choose the one you want.

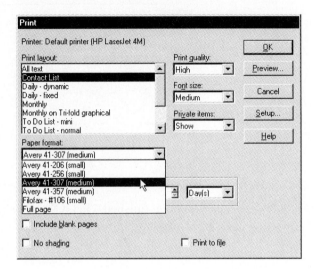

Sorting

As mentioned earlier, you can sort the information in the columns of your Contact list. When you print the Contact list, the printout reflects the settings you have made. For instance, if you have only the Last Name, First Name, and Business Phone columns showing, those columns will show up on your printout, in that order. In other words, if you want things to print differently, you'll have to change the sorting of your columns, the order, or what's showing.

Previewing

As always, it's a good idea to preview a printout before sending it to the printer and killing more trees. To do so, click the Preview button in the Print dialog box. You'll see something like the following illustration.

If you don't like what you see (and you can zoom in to get an idea of the details), close the Print Preview dialog box, click Cancel in the Print dialog box, and fix things before printing.

Dialing Your Phone from the Contacts Tab

Here's a really slick feature! You can actually have Schedule+ call people for you. That's right, if you have someone's phone number in your Contact list, you can dial the number with a click of the mouse. Here's how.

1. First make sure that your modem is ready.

2. Find the contact you wish to call, and find the number you wish to call.

3. Click the Dial Phone button next to the phone number, and Schedule+ will dial the number.

 note *This all assumes that your computer is hooked up to your phone in some way. Just because your computer and phone are right next to each other on your desk doesn't mean they can actually communicate. See the big books or consult your Network Administrator to learn how to hook up your computer to a phone line.*

Exporting from Contacts

You saw in Chapter 40 how to export data (including your Contact list) to a Timex Data Link watch. Let's now look at a few other ways you can export your contact information.

Exporting to Text Files

To export your Contact list data to a text file,

1. Choose File | Export | Text. The Text Export Wizard will make a grand appearance.

2. Click on Contact List and then click Next >.

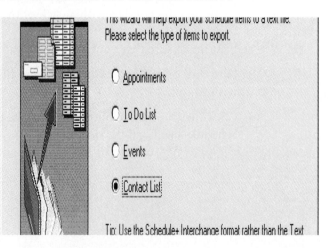

3. You'll see several more dialog boxes asking you for information about the format of the export and whether you want to include field names. Eventually you'll reach this dialog box:

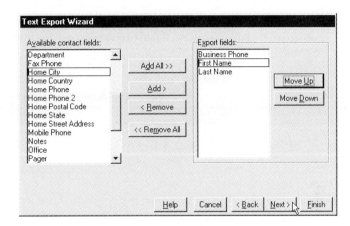

4. Here you specify which contact fields you want to export. You might need to export only names and phone numbers, for example. Or if you're making a birthday list, you might export only names and birthdays. You get the idea. When you've finished, click Next >.

5. You'll be asked to name your file. When you have done so, click Finish.

Exporting to Other Systems and PDAs

Exporting your Contact list to other systems and PDAs works the same as exporting it to a text file. Follow these steps:

1. Choose File | Export | Other Systems. The Select Target System dialog box will appear.

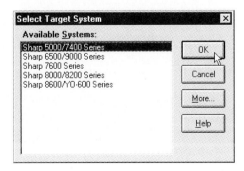

2. Choose one and click OK. The Schedule+ 7.0 Export dialog box will appear.

3. Choose Contacts in the Main tab.

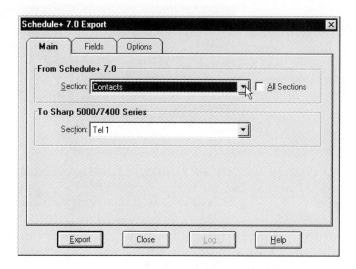

4. Use the Fields tab to map your export, and the Options tab to make other settings. What appears in these will vary, depending upon what kind of system you're exporting to.

5. When you're finished, click Export.

Using the Contact List to Schedule Appointments

This feature is really slick: you can schedule appointments directly from your contact list. Here's how:

1. Click on the name of the person with whom you want to meet.

2. Choose Insert | Appointment. The Appointment dialog box will appear.

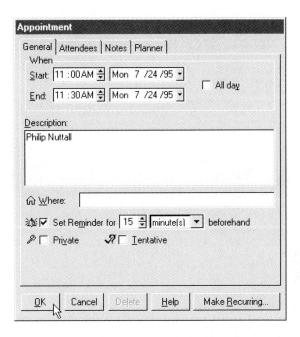

3. Schedule+ automatically inserts the person's first and last names in the Description box. Enter other information here as you learned in Chapter 40.

4. When you have finished, click OK.

5. If you're curious to see whether it worked, visit the day you've assigned the meeting for on the Daily or Weekly tabs to double-check.

Deleting Contacts

Unfortunately, you will find yourself having to delete people from your Contact list periodically. Either they will move on to other jobs, or they will annoy you, or they will die. To remove an entry from the Contact list, click on it and then click the Delete button on the toolbar. You will be asked if you really want to delete the subject.

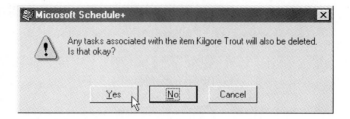

Click Yes.

tip *This is sort of a morbid subject, but it's good to think about: if you want to keep up with someone's family after he or she dies, you might only have that information in the person's record. So think twice before deleting a record. Consider marking the person "deceased" or some such.*

Organizing Projects

Schedule+ offers you a number of handy features to help you organize your projects. You create and name projects so you'll have an aegis under which to group related tasks, meetings, and appointments. Let's take a look.

Inserting Projects

Before you can assign things to a project, you have to insert (create) the project. To do so, follow these steps:

1. Choose Insert | Project. The Project dialog box will appear.

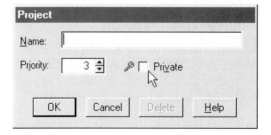

2. Type in a name for the project.

3. Assign a priority (3 is the default) for the project, and click to indicate whether you want it to be private.

4. When you are satisfied, click OK.

Now that you've created the project, you can assign tasks to it.

Assigning Tasks to Projects

To assign a task to a project, follow these steps.

1. Double-click the gray box next to the task you want to assign. This will bring up the Task dialog box.

2. Click on the Project list and choose a project to which to assign the task.

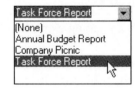

3. You can change other settings and information about the task at this time, if you wish.

4. When you are finished, click OK.

Deleting Projects

When you have finished with a project and you're sure you want to get rid of it, do the following:

1. Go to the To Do tab.

2. Click on the project you want to delete.

3. Click the Delete button on the toolbar.

4. You will be asked if you want to delete the project. Click Yes to delete it or No to cancel.

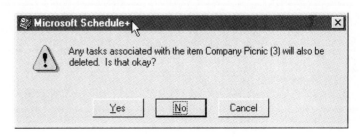

Planning Meetings

Schedule+ makes it easy to plan meetings. In Schedule+, meetings are appointments you set up and invite people to. Since you can download other people's Appointment Books, you'll know their schedules and can use the Planner to figure when people have free time in common. What's really slick is that you can use Meeting Wizard to automate the whole job, from deciding whom to invite to the meeting to sending them requests over e-mail. Read on to learn how.

Using the Meeting Wizard

To plan a meeting using Meeting Wizard, follow these steps:

1. Choose Tools | Make Meeting or click the Meeting Wizard button on the toolbar to bring up the Meeting Wizard dialog box.

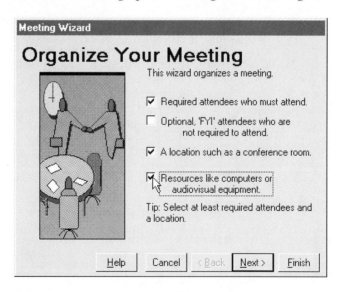

2. The options for required attendees and a location are automatically checked. You can also choose to invite people who aren't required to attend, or assign resources necessary for the meeting.

3. When you are ready to move on, click Next >. The next dialog box is where you specify attendees. You can type these in, but it's just as easy to display the list and choose from it. Let's do that now.

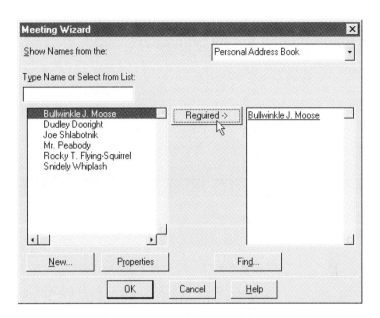

4. Select the names of people who are required to attend, and click the Required button to add them to the required list. Then click OK.

5. If you clicked to have optional attendees notified, you'll have a chance to do the same thing with them as you did in step 4 with required attendees. When you have finished, click Next >.

6. The next two dialog boxes (if you selected the options) will be for the location and necessary resources. They work exactly as the attendee lists worked. When you have finished with these two, click Next >.

7. You will then be asked how long the meeting will last. Change the default (1 hour) if you wish. You can also specify how long it will take people to get to the meeting. This is important if your complex comprises a number of far-flung offices, or if the meeting is off-site. Again, click Next > when you're ready to move on.

8. This next dialog box is pretty important, because this determines when the meeting is likely to be held. You use this box to specify acceptable dates and times for the meeting.

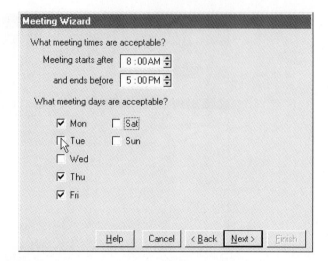

9. When you click Next >, you might get another dialog box asking if nonrequired attendees should have their schedules checked. Once you've specified what you want, click Finish.

10. You might get one or more messages like this one, explaining the status of several of your requests:

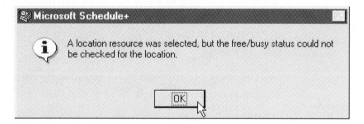

11. Just click OK (there's not much else you can do), and the Wiz will display its handiwork.

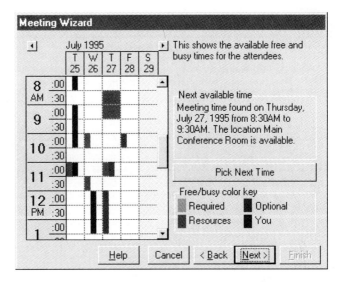

12. This dialog box shows busy times for you and for the attendees. It also picks out a time for the meeting (in dark green). Click on Pick Next Time to see other possible meeting times. You'll be able to see when the location and resources are free, as well.

13. When you click Next >, you'll get a screen that tells you what the next screen is going to be. But why wait? Click Finish and let's see! What you'll see is an e-mail invitation with all the attendees names filled in. You can add additional notes if you wish.

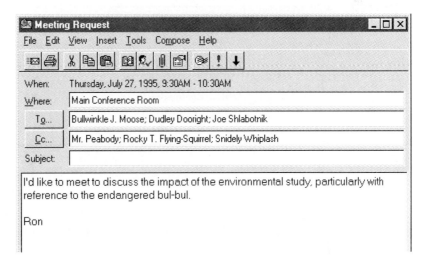

14. When you have finished, click the Send button on the toolbar to send the messages on their merry ways.

That's about it. You'll notice that there are now a bunch of icons next to the meeting notice in the Daily tab of your Appointment Book.

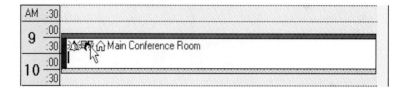

If you double-click on any of these icons, the Appointment dialog box will appear, and you can amend or review the information in it. For instance, you might click the Attendees tab to see who you invited and to make sure you've arranged for a room:

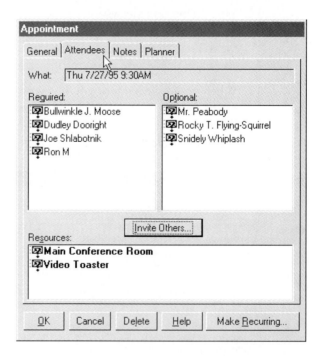

You could even use the opportunity to invite people you forgot to invite the first time by clicking on the Invite Others button and following the prompts.

Using the Planner

You've already seen the Planner at work, in the section entitled "Using the Meeting Wizard." That thing you saw at the end showing everyone's schedules was the Planner. Use the Planner to see others' schedules, as well as your own. It is a great tool for organizing projects and tasks. Here is the planner again, for those of you who miss it already.

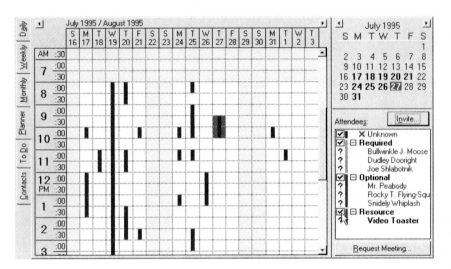

It's pretty much self-explanatory. You just look to see who's busy when. That way, you can plan meetings and such for times when everyone can attend. Click on the boxes in the Attendees area to see individual's schedules.

n o t e *You and the others with whom you are coordinating must all be running Schedule+ in Group Activated mode to take advantage of the Planner's features.*

Part 7

Delivering Information with Microsoft Exchange

Microsoft Exchange makes it possible for networked users to exchange messages and files. Depending on your network, you can communicate with other users in the same department, the same building, or even worldwide. Here you will find out how to use Exchange to join the e-mail revolution.

CHAPTER 42

Exchange Basics

W

ITH all the wires being strung everywhere, this truly is the decade of networking. Even small businesses are entangling their computers. E-mail is replacing in-house memos, "While You Were Out" notes, and even office supply order forms. Let's take a look at how a network might work for you.

What's Microsoft Exchange?

Microsoft Exchange is a collection of programs that makes it possible for coworkers to exchange messages and files over computer networks. Networked users can be in the same room, the same building, or stretched worldwide. Who you can exchange mail with depends on your network setup and decisions made by the person in charge of your network and mail services.

What's Required to Get Started?

At least one of the computers on the network acts as a mail server. Microsoft calls these *postoffices*. The postoffice is where the mail server and related administration software have been installed by the mail administrator. It is also where lists of authorized users and groups are stored. (And it may or may not be where your messages are stored.) Check with your administrator for details.

Your mail administrator will need to set up *access rights* for you and your *mailbox* in the postoffice or postoffices you'll access. You will also need to know the security procedures and probably will need to set up a password.

Your computer needs Exchange, which comes with Office but is *not* installed automatically when you install Office. Also, your computer will need to be connected to the same network with the postoffice or postoffices you wish to access.

tarting Exchange from the Office Shortcut Bar

Once everything is properly set up, you can start Microsoft Exchange by clicking on the Exchange button in the Office Shortcut Bar. The button's shown at the left.

To start mail from Explorer, double-click on the Microsoft Exchange icon in the Office 95 folder. You can also start Exchange by selecting it from the Programs submenu, found on the Start menu.

ogging On and Off

You will be asked to enter your name and password (unless Exchange has been set up to do this automatically for you—this process will be described later in the chapter).

1. Type your mailbox name exactly as you and the administrator agreed to set it up.

2. Press TAB.

3. Enter the mail password. Capitalization counts. *HoHoHo*, *hohoho*, and *HOHOHO* are all different passwords.

4. Click OK or press ENTER.

To quit Exchange, either choose File | Exit (which maintains your network connection with the postoffice), or choose File | Exit and Log Off, which disconnects you from the postoffice.

Getting Online Help

Exchange, like the other Office programs, has context-sensitive online Help. Reach it from Exchange's Help menu or with F1.

Getting an Overview

There is a nice introduction to Exchange in the Help utility. It is worth looking at now:

1. Start Exchange.

2. Choose Help | Microsoft Exchange Help Topics.

3. Click to bring the Contents tab foremost if it isn't already. Then double-click on the Overview of Microsoft Exchange icon, as shown next.

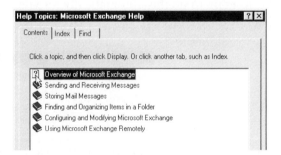

4. This will bring up the aforementioned overview, which you can print if you wish by choosing Options | Print Topic:

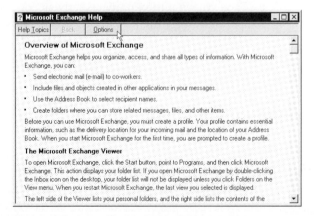

Sending Mail

There are a few basic steps to sending mail:

- Bring up the New Message dialog box.
- Pick the intended recipient(s) and address your message.
- Type the text of the message.
- Spell-check if you like (optional).
- Attach a file if you wish to send one along (optional).
- Send away.

Let's look at those steps in more detail. Specific procedures at your site may vary, so don't be afraid to ask for help if things go wrong.

Sending a Message

Begin by opening Microsoft Exchange and clicking on the New Message button, shown at left. You will see the New Message dialog box, illustrated in Figure 42-1.

FIGURE 42-1

The New Message dialog box is where you compose, address, and send mail

■

Click to send a finished message ──

Click to see names in your Address Book

Type your message here ──

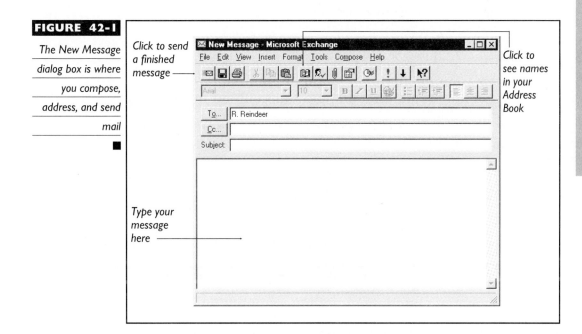

Addressing Mail

Microsoft Exchange needs to know where to send your message. You can either type the name of the recipient in the To box, or look it up by clicking on the Address Book button in the New Message dialog box. If you click the Address Book button, you'll see the Address Book dialog box.

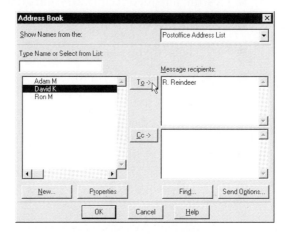

Pick a name in any of the following ways:

- Type the first few characters of a name to scroll the list into "the right neighborhood," and then use the up or down arrow to find the desired name and press ENTER, *or*

- Double-click on the name in the list, *or*

- Select a name and click the To -> button

tip *Click the down arrow of the "Show Names from the" list to see other address lists. If you work in a large company, individuals might be listed by department in separate mailing lists.*

In any case, the name will be added to the To list. You can place more than one name in the To box this way.

To place names in the Cc (carbon copy) list, tab or click to move the insertion point there, and then pick names as before.

When you've finished adding names to the To and Cc lists, click OK.

tip *Send mail to yourself—it's a good way to practice, and a way to confirm that the postoffice is working properly.*

Composing Mail

You compose mail in the large white box illustrated in Figure 42-1.

1. Begin by adding a subject in the Subject box (tab or click to move the insertion point there).

2. When you've finished typing the subject, tab again or click in the message area.

3. Type and edit text as you would in any good Windows program. Be aware of the following.

   ■ Text will wrap, so only press ENTER when you want to start a new paragraph.

   ■ You can embellish text with attributes like bold and italics just as you would in any other Office program. You can even make the text different colors.

   ■ You can indent with TAB (or the indent keys on the Formatting toolbar) and change fonts by choosing from the Font drop-down list in the Formatting toolbar.

   ■ When text fills the screen, it will scroll. Use PAGEUP, PAGEDOWN, and the arrow keys to navigate.

   ■ To delete text, select it and press DEL.

   ■ Move text by cutting and pasting or using drag-and-drop.

   ■ You can even have bulleted or numbered lists.

Spell-Checking Messages

To spell-check messages before sending them, press F7 or choose Spelling from the Edit menu. Your entire message, including the subject line, will be checked. To check just a word or just part of your text, select it first. Exchange's Spell Checker is a lot like Word's, described in Chapter 10 (see the "Spelling Checker" section).

Attaching Files

You can attach a file that will be sent along with your message by clicking the Insert button in the New Message dialog box. This will reveal an Insert File dialog box that will remind you of most Windows Open dialog boxes.

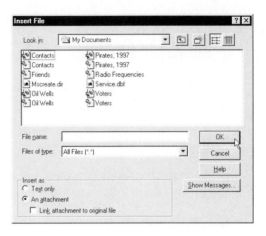

Chapter 43 will explore variations on this process.

Sending Messages

Once the message is addressed and typed, click on the Send button, or use the keyboard shortcut ALT+S, to send it.

Sending Urgent Messages

The High and Low importance buttons in the New Message dialog box set the priority of the message. Importance is set to Normal by default. If you click one of these buttons and then decide you want to reset the importance to Normal, choose Tools | Options to bring up the Options dialog box, and click the Send tab to bring it forward:

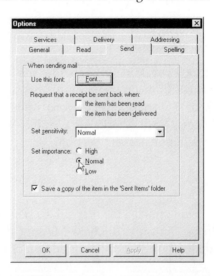

Change the priority as desired and click OK.

note *Messages sent as High importance appear with an ! next to them in recipients' mail lists.*

Requesting a Return Receipt

To learn if and when a recipient read your message, either click on the Read Receipt button in the Standard toolbar, or choose one of the Return Receipt options in the Options dialog box:

1. Create the message.

2. Click on the Read Receipt button in the Standard toolbar. Alternatively, you can choose Tools | Options and click on the Send tab to bring it forward.

3. Choose one of the Return Receipt options. You can ask Exchange to notify you when

   ■ The item has been read

   ■ The item has been received

4. Click OK.

5. Click Send to send the message. When the recipient(s) read your message or when it is delivered (depending upon which option you chose), you will receive a receipt detailing the time and date the message was read or delivered, even if your recipient(s) do not reply.

Saving Copies of Messages You Send

To save copies of messages you send, choose the Save A Copy option on the Send tab of the Options dialog box:

1. Create the message.

2. Choose Tools | Options and click the Send tab to bring it to the front.

3. Choose the Save A Copy option.

4. Click OK.

DELIVERING INFORMATION
WITH MICROSOFT EXCHANGE

5. Click Send to send the message. A copy of the message will be placed in your Sent Items folder.

Aborting a Message Before Sending

If you have a change of heart before sending a message, close the New Message window (CTRL+F4) and answer No to the Save Changes? prompt.

Receiving and Reading Mail

Incoming mail is stored in your *inbox*. How you are alerted to incoming mail depends on which options you've specified. (See the section "Personalizing Microsoft Exchange Settings," later in this chapter.)

To look inside your inbox, open Exchange and double-click on the icon shown at left. You'll see an inbox like the one in Figure 42-2.

The Exchange inbox tells you what mail you've received and its status. Unread messages have unopened envelopes next to them, like those shown in Figure 42-2. Urgent messages have exclamation points to the left of the envelope icons.

To read a message, double-click anywhere on its listing in the inbox. The message will appear onscreen, complete with a header describing the sender, date, subject, and so on.

Scroll if necessary to read the entire message.

FIGURE 42-2

The Exchange inbox

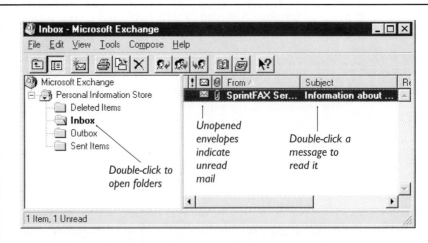

tip   *If you have a lot of mail in your inbox, you can sort it by sender's name, subject, or time and date received. Simply click on the headings "From," "Subject," or "Received" above the list of mail.*

Printing Mail

To print a message or messages:

1. Select a message name in the message list by clicking on it, or select multiple names by holding down CTRL while you click.

2. Choose File | Print, click the Print button on the Standard toolbar, or use the usual CTRL+P shortcut. You'll be given a chance to print attachments as well.

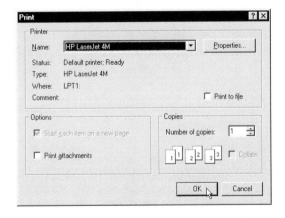

3. Click OK to print the message(s).

Responding to Mail

To reply to a message, click on the Reply button in the message window. To reply to all messages, use the Reply To All button:

DELIVERING INFORMATION WITH MICROSOFT EXCHANGE

Microsoft Exchange will automatically address the reply message, but you can add or delete names from the address lists if you like.

The subject box will contain the subject of the original message preceded by "RE:" This can also be edited.

You'll see the original message in the text area with the reply area separated by a solid line. Type the reply and click Send, or use the ALT+S shortcut.

tip *You can also forward messages to other people. Click the Forward button. The original message will appear, along with a field for you to fill in an addendum to the message.*

Saving and Deleting Mail

You'll want to delete unwanted messages to remove the clutter from your inbox. There may also be times when you want to save copies of messages on your disk. Here's how to do both.

Saving Messages

To save messages:

1. Select the message name in the message list by clicking on it, or select multiple names by holding down CTRL while you click.

2. Choose File | Save As to bring up a standard Windows Save As dialog box.

3. Give the file a new name, or accept the default and click Save.

Deleting Messages

To delete messages:

1. Select a message name in the message list by clicking on it, or select multiple names by holding down CTRL while you click.

2. Press DEL, choose Delete from the File menu, or click the Delete button on the Standard toolbar.

Personalizing Microsoft Exchange Settings

You have some control over how Exchange behaves. For instance, you can choose whether to be alerted to incoming mail with a chime. To see and select mail options, choose Tools | Options. You'll see the Options dialog box, where you can change the settings to your liking.

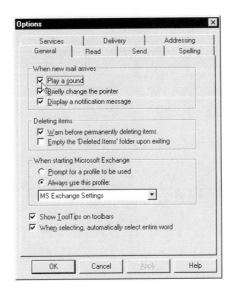

Click on the other tabs to see other options.

Working Offline

While you'll usually want to work with Microsoft Exchange while connected to the network and postoffice, there are times when that won't be possible—for instance, if you have a portable computer and take it out of the office, or if the network or mail server is inoperative.

Under these conditions, it is sometimes possible to accomplish some mail tasks—like composing mail. You may also be able to read some unread mail and review saved mail. Check with online Help and your mail administrator for details.

CHAPTER 43

Microsoft Mail and Office Applications

T HIS chapter looks at Word, Excel, and PowerPoint features for both *mailing* and *routing* files on a network. Mailing simply sends copies of files to recipients, while routing lets you control who gets the copy when, and then lets you collect and include the work of others in your finished project. Typically, you'll mail *multiple* copies of files to many people at once or route a *single* copy of a document from one person to another and often back to you.

To exchange and work with documents this way, you and the recipients must have the Office applications used to create the documents and Microsoft Mail, or a compatible mail program installed on your computers.

The exact steps for mailing and routing vary slightly from application to application. Let's look at Microsoft Word first, since it has some annotation and merging features not found in the other applications.

Word Documents and E-Mail

Word offers two menu commands (File | Add Routing Slip and File | Send) that you can use to send and return copies of Word documents. You can also add toolbar buttons for some mail and routing tasks.

note *If the Add Routing Slip and Send commands do not appear on your File menu or if they are dim, contact your Mail manager or network administrator. You may have an improperly installed mail program, an incompatible mail program, or network problems.*

Sending Word documents via electronic mail is pretty simple:

1. Open the document you want to send. If the document's already open because you've just created or altered it, make sure it's saved.

2. Select File | Add Routing Slip. The Routing Slip dialog box will appear.

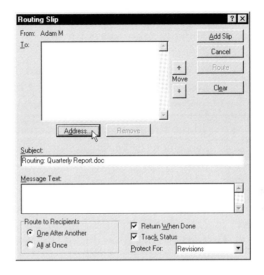

3. Click the Address button. In the Address Book dialog box, select the names of the people you want to send the document to and choose the To button.

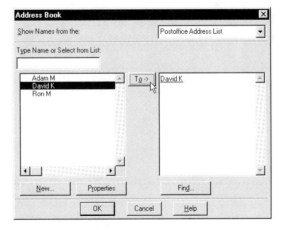

To route the document to one recipient after another (covered in a minute), arrange the names in the appropriate order by using the arrow buttons.

4. Click OK to return to the Routing Slip dialog box. The names you entered will appear in the To box.

5. Type the subject of your communiqué in the Subject box and any message in the Message Text box. Each recipient will get the same subject and message, so don't get too personal.

If the To box shows you that you've added someone you shouldn't have, click the Remove button and remove that person from the list.

Word automatically will add to your message the instructions that tell the recipients to select File | Send when finished with the document you send; you don't need to write that in your message.

6. In the Route To Recipients area, choose whether you want the document to be sent to the recipients One After Another or All At Once.

7. If you're ready to send your document, choose the Route button. The document will be sent to recipients as an attached Word file.

To further edit your document before you send it, click the Add Slip button again, do your editing, and then select File | Send to send the document. Click Yes in the confirmation dialog box.

tip *If you send a document to the recipients One After Another, each successive recipient will see his or her predecessors' comments. This way, you may be able to avoid duplicate comments. If you send multiple copies All At Once, everyone's comments will be between them and you (until you put them in the ultimate document and attribute them to their maker!). You'll probably also get quicker answers this way.*

Let's look quickly at three further options in the Routing Slip dialog box: Return When Done, Track Status, and Protect For.

Return When Done	Check this box to have the document sent back to you when the last recipient finishes with the document and chooses File | Send.
Track Status	Check this box to keep track of where your document has been routed. Word will send you a message each time the document is sent to the next person in the To list.
Protect For	Select protection for your document from the drop-down list: *Annotations* allows recipients to add only annotations to the document; *Revisions* allows them to make changes (forcibly marked with revision marks) and add annotations; and *Forms* lets recipients enter information only in form fields.

Revising and Returning a Mailed Document

If you're the target of an e-mailed Word document, here's how you do your bit:

1. Retrieve the document from your mail program in the usual way for that program, and open the document in Word.

2. Revise the document depending on how the sender has protected it:

    ■ If the document allows annotations only, select Insert | Annotation, type your annotation into the annotation pane, and click Close when you've finished.

    ■ If the document allows both revisions and annotations, just go ahead and make your revisions. Word will use revision marks to mark your revisions.

    ■ If the document is protected as a form, you're wearing a straitjacket. Fill in the fields (*all* the fields—be good) and don't try to do anything else.

3. Choose File | Send. The Send dialog box will appear (see the following), asking if you want to use the routing slip or send the document without using the routing slip. To send it, choose the Route Document option and click OK.

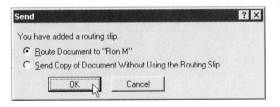

    ■ If the original sender chose to route the document to recipients All At Once, this will return the document to the sender.

    ■ If the original sender chose to route the document to recipients One After Another, this will pass the document on to its next victim—unless you're the last, in which case the document will be returned to the sender.

    ■ If the original sender checked Track Status, Word will let the sender know when you send the document to its next recipient. Yup, Big Brother is e-mailing about you.

note *If you choose the Send Copy Of Document Without Using The Routing Slip option, all protection the original sender chose remains in effect.*

Merging Annotations and Revisions

So you sent out—all at once—seven copies of your latest marketing proposal for industrial-strength deodorant, "Hang-Gliding off Power Pylons," and everyone got back to you with helpful comments. Well, sort of helpful. Most of them, anyway. Bunch of cynics, the lot of them. Now you need to merge the annotations and revisions into one copy so that you can pick out the best and trash the rest.

tip *You can't merge annotations and revisions back into the original document unless they're marked. Makes sense if you think about it. This is another good reason for protecting your document for revisions or annotations before sending it out. If you forget to protect your document, try using Tools | Revisions and using the Compare Versions feature.*

To merge all those pesky revision marks and annotations:

1. Retrieve your returned document from your mail program. Word will automatically ask you if you want to merge revisions with the original document.

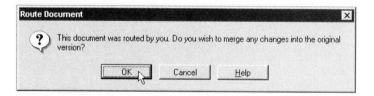

2. Click OK. The Merge Revisions dialog box will appear (well, what did you expect?).

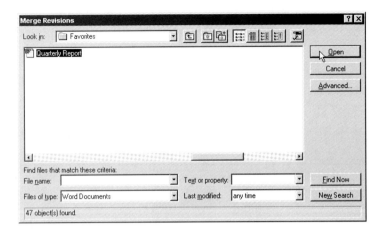

3. Select the original file and click OK. The original document will open, and the revisions will be merged into it.

4. Repeat as necessary with the other six copies of the report.

note *When you merge revisions or annotations from multiple documents into the original, Word will use a different color for each reviewer (up to eight—after that, Word will cycle through the colors again).*

For Additional Help with Mail in Word

Mail and network connections can be confusing, particularly on the complex networks that have been proliferating recently. Read your mail program's user guide to glean further information, or go harass your friendly network administrator or hallway guru.

Network Security Considerations

Networks can be a source of security problems. While there's no way that you can absolutely safeguard all your work, remember to take the following obvious precautions:

- Protect your documents from changes.

- Save your documents frequently, and back them up to a safe medium frequently.

- If you store your documents on a network drive, be careful whom you give access. If necessary, make your documents read-only.

If you're sharing documents a lot, here are a few things to think about first:

- Don't use templates that the other people in the group don't have.

- If you share templates, keep them clean. Don't redefine built-in key combinations—you may confuse your coworkers, or worse.

- Don't use fonts that the other people in the group don't have. (But remember that you can embed TrueType fonts in shared documents so that other users who don't have the fonts installed can see the fonts and print them. Select Tools | Options, click the Save tab in the Options dialog box, and check the Embed TrueType Fonts check box.)

- Don't lose your file-protection password.

Excel and Mail

Excel lets you both mail and route *workbooks* (collections of worksheets). The process is virtually the same as that described for mailing and routing Word documents. You can use File | Add Routing Slip and File | Send on Excel's File menu, or the Routing Slip and Send Mail buttons, shown at left, on the WorkGroup toolbar.

Remember: When you mail someone a copy of a workbook (or route a workbook copy), the original file stays in your possession. It is not modified. The copy or copies and original are not linked.

PowerPoint and Mail

As with Word and Excel, you can mail or route copies of PowerPoint presentation files over the network to others who have Mail and PowerPoint installed. As with Word and Excel, PowerPoint will display File | Add Routing Slip and File | Send choices on your File menu if you have a compatible mail program installed and running.

You can add Mail buttons to your PowerPoint toolbars if you wish. The process is illustrated in Figure 43-1.

Here are the steps:

1. Choose Tools | Customize.

2. Highlight the File category if it isn't already highlighted.

3. Point to the button you want to add (the Send Mail button, for instance).

4. Hold down the primary mouse button and drag the button to the desired location on a PowerPoint toolbar.

5. When you release the mouse button, the toolbar will make room for the new button. For instance, here's the PowerPoint Standard toolbar with the Send Mail and Routing Slip buttons inserted:

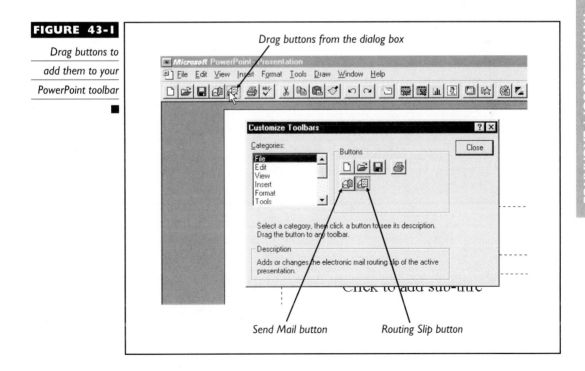

FIGURE 43-1

Drag buttons to add them to your PowerPoint toolbar

Drag buttons from the dialog box

Send Mail button

Routing Slip button

PART 8

Sharing Information with OLE

Object linking and embedding (OLE) are perhaps the two most powerful ways to share information between documents and programs. These techniques are available to all of the components of Microsoft Office. With OLE you can create a graph in Excel or Graph and then insert it in a Word document. In your PowerPoint slides, you can include items from Word, Excel, and other OLE-savvy applications. You can even have the inserted data updated automatically or have it remain static. All this and more is available with the OLE capabilities of Office.

CHAPTER 44

An Overview of Object Linking and Embedding

O
BJECT linking and embedding let you share information between applications. With OLE you can cause information to be updated automatically whenever the source is changed, updated only when you want it updated, or left forever as it was when you inserted it.

For example, suppose you publish a monthly newsletter in Word that shows company safety statistics, new product lists, and so on, that you're getting from other files or objects. Let's call the newsletter the *destination* document. The other files or objects are called *source* documents. Since the information in the source documents just mentioned is being updated regularly, you probably want your newsletter to use the most recently updated version of that information. You could *link* a framed area in the newsletter with information kept in an Excel spreadsheet and an Access database. Word can automatically *update* the newsletter each month to include changes made to the linked source documents.

Other types of information that you might want to put into your newsletter would not fall into the update category. Photographs, cartoons, the news stories themselves—these are used only once, and hence do not need to be linked. They can simply be *embedded*. And if you have an application that can open the embedded object separately (don't worry, if it was created in Office, you've got the application), you can also *edit* the embedded object—you can touch up a dark photograph, or correct a mistake in your lead story.

Technical Requirements for OLE

To *link* an object created in another application to another file, you need to be running both applications in Windows 95. Both applications must support either object linking and embedding (OLE) or dynamic data exchange (DDE—an earlier form of linking). If your setup doesn't match these requirements, you won't be able to link. All of the Office programs support some kind of OLE, although actual capabilities vary.

The following illustrations contain a sample newsletter created with Word, version 7. In this and the next chapter, you'll see how the linked and embedded objects in that newsletter were created.

The *Thicker* Gazette

Volume 12 Issue 7	A Thicker Publication Production	December 1996

SAFETY CORNER

Editorial Still Riskier Than Shipping

Hernias led last month's list of on-the-job injuries at Thicker, followed by head trauma, mostly among editors.

Here are the departmental breakdowns:

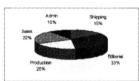

"I must have hit my bloody forehead on my bloody desk six times in the last ten days," observed editor Guy Friendly.

Deadlines, tedium, and lack of sleep were most often cited as causes of head injuries, with "I can't believe he/she/I wrote that!" syndrome a close fourth. This month's safety slogan is:

> **LIFT OUR BOOKS WITH YOUR KNEES— NEVER WITH YOUR BACK!**

Inside This Issue

1	Our older authors recall a time when books had no pictures and weighed less than computers!
2	Cafeteria now open all night. (Coin changer fixed.)
3	How Crown Books converted the entire *Grand Canyon* into "the world's first GigaSuperStore".

JUST HIRED

OUR NEW MAJOR ACCOUNTS REP

Our new major accounts rep will be on-board starting Monday.

"We've got a *lot* of preachin' to do," smiled the Rev. Al B. Shure. "People just need to get the word about how bigger is better, and it's gonna take a really big effort."

The former child-preacher turned sales rep will soon call upon accounts from coast to coast. A special bus has been added to the Thicker Publishing, Inc. fleet to make life easier away from home for the Reverend and regional reps who will accompany him on major accounts visits.

> **PRAISE THE LORD AND FIRE UP THE FORKLIFT!**

COMING SOON

Obsession Series Ships!

The new Thicker Publications, Inc. Obsession series will soon buckle bookshelves everywhere, starting with a 2,000 page book titled:

Obsessing Over Word 12 for the Power Mac Cray Emulator

Starting with the history of writing (cuneiform to Gutenburg), our new, 18-pound reference covers all 6,000 Microsoft Word commands; 12,000 keyboard shortcuts (including those elusive four-fingered ones), and much, much more. History buffs will find a 600-page appendix of Word's programmers *and* all their children's names.

"Finding the names of those kids was the hard part," confessed Q. Group. "Fortunately, there weren't many. *Very few* Microsoft employees have time to procreate. In fact, it's discouraged," Group confided.

OTHER FORTHCOMING TITLES:

Title	Due
Windows for Buttheads	Spring
DOS Boot: Jetz Gut!	Spring
Mastering BIOS ROM	Spring
Upgrading Commodore 101 Computers	Whenever
Pervert's Guide to Internet	Summer
Stay Home and Vacation on Internet	Summer

SHARING INFORMATION WITH OLE

2   The Thicker Gazette

Slide Show Ballyhoos Bulky Books

When the good Reverend hits the road, he'll be taking along a new slide show created by A. V. Handy in PowerPoint. Here are highlights:

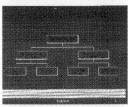

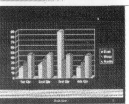

Weigh-In

Well, the results are in. The heaviest book in our current catalog is *Why Smart Women Buy Dumb Books*, by G. Allrad. Here are our seven most corpulent creations:

Title	Author	Weight	Pages	Price	Cost/Lb
Why Smart Women Buy Dumb Books	G. Allrad	18.00	2,800	$ 45.95	$ 2.55
Windows for Gluttons	W. Gates	13.00	1,875	$ 44.50	$ 3.42
Top 10,000 WordPerfect Commands	A. Wonk	12.60	2,565	$ 29.95	$ 2.38
Novell Trilogy	Mr. Spock	12.50	1,850	$ 22.18	$ 1.77
Using Computer Books for Step Aerobics	J. Fonda	12.22	25	$ 16.29	$ 1.33
OS/2 in a Gig or Less	T. Watson	4.70	2,100	$ 38.75	$ 8.24
DOS Big and Beautiful	W. Gates	2.50	2,000	$ 39.50	$ 15.80
Average		10.79	1,888	$ 33.87	$ 5.07

New Logo

Those funky looking people in the art department have fired up their incense burner and are designing a new logo. Of the top three contenders, which do you like?

3   The Thicker Gazette

Our Readers Write

We always love getting letters from our readers and booksellers. Sometimes we even learn things. Check out this great idea from the Book Heap in Stinking Bog, California:

The Book Heap

1425 Foothill Lane

Stinking Bog, CA 95555

```
June 9, 1996

Thicker Publications, Inc.
2323 Fifth Avenue
New York, NY  14567

Dear Thickeners:

Thanks for the swell shipment of new Thick books. We've run
out of shelf space, but we find that, when stacked, your
hefty books make swell room dividers, sales counters, and
couches. The Special Editions are particularly useful.

We are wondering how high the books can be piled in
earthquake country. Any advice would be much appreciated
(the sooner the better).


Sincerely,

S. I. Jest

Shirley I. Jest
SIJ/mos
```

What Is Linking?

Linking is a way of attaching information. For example, when you *link* an object to a Word document, the Word document stores the *location* of the object and its source application in a *field* in the document. Linking leaves the source document available to be used or updated on its own, by you or another user. Your Word document, to which is attached the linked object, can then be updated at your convenience to include the latest information in the source document—you can choose to update it manually (just when you want to update it), or to have it updated automatically (whenever the source changes). You can lock the links when the document and the object it contains are finalized, and you can break the links so that objects cannot be updated any further.

In the newsletter example, the injuries graph from Excel, the weigh-in worksheet from Excel, and the slides from PowerPoint are all linked. (The "Book Heap" letter is also linked to the newsletter, just to show that it's possible to link Word documents with *other* Word documents.)

What Is Embedding?

Embedding, like linking, is a way of attaching information. When you *embed* information, the information becomes part of the destination document and is stored in that destination document. You can double-click on the information in the destination document to open the source object in its original application, ready for editing if you so desire.

Embedded objects in the newsletter example include the photo-image (originally a multimedia video frame, turned into a Word Picture object), the "Forthcoming Titles" list (from an Access table), and the logos in the "New Logo" section of the newsletter.

Oh yes, there's one more embedded item—the logo in the Book Heap letter. Yes, you can have embedded items *within* linked items, and the embedded items can still be edited.

warning *Embedding an object increases the size of the destination file considerably. If you embed a whole bunch of big objects (TIFF true-gray files, for example), your files will bloat. This can slow down editing, scrolling, and other tasks.*

To Link or to Embed?

If you link objects in documents to their sources, you can either update the objects whenever it suits you, or have them update automatically whenever the source objects change. When your document is finalized or ready for distribution, you can lock or break the links and freeze the document in final form.

If you embed objects in documents, you can enjoy the quality of the originals within the destination documents *and* have the convenience of being able to edit the objects in the original application (by double-clicking on them). No need to remember which object came from which source application—OLE keeps track of that information for you.

Remember that whereas *linked* information is still stored in the *source* file in the source application, *embedded* information becomes part of the *destination* document (and is stored in it). When you link, OLE records the location of the information in the source file and displays a picture of the information in the destination document. So here's the bottom line:

- Link when you will need to share information with another file. Embed when you know you will not need to share information with another file.

Here are a couple of other considerations to keep in mind:

- Linking is a complicated operation, even with the constant improvements in OLE. Although your computer may be a thundering P-6 with more RAM than you can count, updating large, linked files will take a while. If you have a slow computer, plan a few coffee breaks.

- Linking creates a number of temporary files (for example, ~wrf001f.tmp). Check your computer every now and then for stray temp files and erase them (see the following tip). You're most likely to have leftover temp files if your computer crashes while you're working with linked files.

tip   *Temp files (~dft064f.tmp and the like) are files created by Windows applications for temporary storage. They're supposed to be deleted automatically when you exit the application that produced them or when you quit Windows (depending on what produced them). Every now and then, check your disk for stray temp files **after** loading Windows and **before** running any Windows applications—that is, before your applications get a chance to create new temp files. Run Find File looking for ***.tmp**. This will round up the usual suspects. Don't trash temp files unless you know what you are doing, however.*

OLE Tips and Techniques

Here are some OLE suggestions to keep in mind:

- Experiment on *copies* of the source and destination documents! Check both documents regularly as you work.

- The exact keystrokes and menu choices for OLE vary from program to program. Some OLE-capable programs don't even have menu bars. So you will need to consult online help and maybe even experiment a little.

- Whereas the Undo command often works, it may not work completely. For instance, if you use drag-and-drop to move information from an Excel cell to a Word document, Undo in Word may remove the insertion, but it won't necessarily restore the item to its original location in the source document. Check for this!

- Get in the habit of clicking on the Office Shortcut Bar buttons to switch back and forth when setting up links. Consider adding other OLE-savvy programs (like CorelDRAW!) to the Office Shortcut Bar if you link with them regularly.

With that said, let's get to specifics. Linking is the topic of Chapter 45. Embedding is the topic of Chapter 46.

CHAPTER 45

Linking

Y

O U can either link an existing object, or you can create a new object and then link it. Start by learning to link the easy way. Later you can graduate to the more sophisticated way if you wish.

Establishing a Link the Easy Way

The simplest way to link an object to a destination file is as follows:

1. Open the documents you want to link.

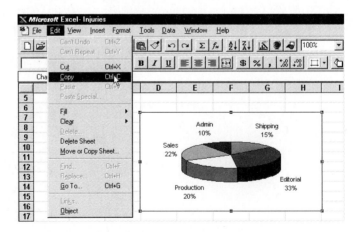

2. Select the object you want to link and copy it to the Clipboard (select Edit | Copy, press CTRL+C or CTRL+INS, or click on any Copy button the application offers).

3. Switch back to the destination application by pressing ALT+TAB, by clicking in the appropriate window, or by clicking in the Taskbar

(press CTRL+ESC, or click the appropriate button in the Office Manager toolbar).

4. Put the insertion point at a suitable place in your destination document, and select Edit | Paste Special to open the Paste Special dialog box:

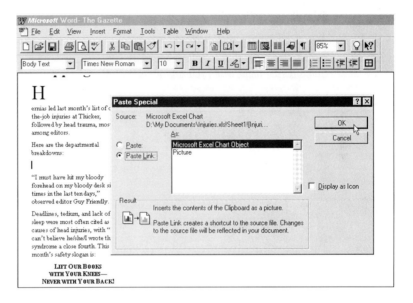

5. In the Paste Special dialog box, select the Paste Link option button to link the object to your Word file. (The Paste Link option button description will be dimmed if it's not available—that is, if the object copied to the Clipboard is in an application that doesn't support OLE.)

6. In the As box, select the form in which you want the linked object to appear. The Result box explains the effect of the option selected in the As box.

7. Leave the Display As Icon check box unchecked for now. It will be discussed in a moment.

8. Click OK. The object will be paste-linked into your document.

9. If necessary, reformat the pasted item, frame it, change its border, and otherwise work with it using Word techniques.

Notice how, since the chart was pasted into a narrow column, Word automatically resized it to fit. Alas, life is not often that easy. Sometimes you'll need to crop, resize, change table settings, change font sizes, and so on. In fact, one point of space had to be added above the chart to make the border show properly. So it goes in the OLE jungle. Save your destination document *before* inserting new objects; then, if things get too frustrating, close the destination document without saving. Then you can reopen and try again.

tip   *Give your destination application (Word, or whatever) a moment to digest new objects after you insert them. On slower computers, in particular, things will look pretty bad immediately after inserting. Sometimes all it takes is some repagination time to fix things. Experiment when you are not in a hurry.*

To Link an Existing Object

Here's how to link an existing object to a document:

1. In your destination document, put the insertion point where you want to insert the linked object.

2. Choose Insert | Object. The Object dialog box will appear.

3. As you're linking an existing object, choose the Create From File tab.

4. Locate the file that contains the object you want to link.

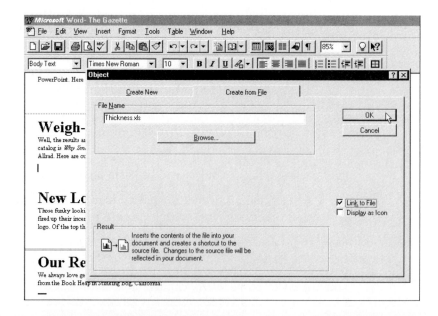

5. Leave the Display As Icon check box unchecked for now. It will be discussed in a moment.

6. Check the Link To File check box and choose the OK button. The selected object will be inserted and linked to your destination file.

7. Reformat if necessary.

The primary advantage of this technique is that you don't have to open the source application. The primary disadvantage is that the whole business can be so slow that you hardly save any time over opening the source application yourself and editing manually.

Displaying the Linked Object as an Icon

You can save display space by displaying the linked object as an *icon* in the destination document. Your readers can then decide on their own whether they want to see the information or not, by clicking on it or not.

To display the linked object as an icon, check the Display As Icon check box in whichever dialog box you are using to link the object (the Paste Special dialog box or one of the Create tabs in the Insert | Object dialog box). The standard icon for the source application will appear below the check box, along with a Change Icon button, should you want to use a different one.

If you want to display a different icon for your object, select the Change Icon button in the Program Manager. In the Change Icon dialog box, select one of the icons the application offers, or click the Browse button to check out the icons from different applications. When you've finished browsing, click OK to return to the Change Icon dialog box, and OK again to accept the icon you chose. That icon will now appear in the Object dialog box.

When Are Linked Documents Updated?

Links can be updated in any of three ways:

Automatically	The default. Links are created with automatic updating; you'll have to change them to one of the following if you want something else.
Manually	You update any or all links only when you want to.
On Printing	All links will be updated at the point that you print the document.

The following sections explain these three options and how to choose them.

Updating a Link

Updating a link is straightforward and intuitive:

1. Select Edit | Links.

2. In the Links dialog box, select the link or links that you want to update:

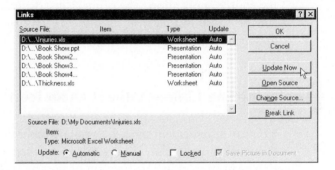

3. Choose how you want the selected links to be updated:

   ■ Choose the *Automatic* option button to update linked information every time the source file is changed.

   ■ Choose the *Manual* option button to update links only when you choose to do so.

4. Choose OK to close the Links dialog box and accept the changes you've made.

tip   *To update several links, hold down* CTRL *while you click on each link, or hold down* SHIFT *and click on the first and last links of the desired range to select all the links in between.*

To Update a Link Manually

To retain the most control over your document and its linked objects, you can update your links manually. Here's how:

1. Select Edit | Links.

2. In the Links dialog box, select the link or links that you want to update.

3. Choose the Update Now button to update the links.

tip   *To update links quickly, select the links you want to update and press F9.*

To Update Links Every Time You Print

To make sure your documents are up-to-date whenever you print them, arrange for their links to be updated each time you print.

1. Select Tools | Options.

2. In the Options dialog box, select the Print tab.

3. Choose the Update Links check box.

4. Click the OK button to close the dialog box. Links in your documents will now be updated whenever you print.

Editing Linked Information

You're best off editing linked information in its source file so that your changes will be reflected in both the source file and the destination documents. To edit linked information, follow these steps:

1. In the destination document, right-click the linked information to edit.

2. Select Edit | Object (this menu item will vary depending on what kind of object you have selected). Choose Edit from the mini-menu that appears. The source application will open with the selected information displayed.

3. Make the changes you want in the source file.

4. Select File | Exit or click the close box to get back to your destination document. The edits you made in the source file will be reflected in the destination file.

Breaking Links—Careful Here!

To prevent linked information from being updated ever again, you can break a link. Before you do this, though, make sure that's what you want to do. Once you've broken a link, the only way to reconnect it is by choosing the Undo command, and that only works if you haven't done anything else since you broke the link. So you only get one chance to fix your mistake—and you have to fix it *pronto!*

> **tip** If you only want to **temporarily** prevent linked information from being updated, you need only to **lock** a link, not break it. Locking is the topic of the following section.

To break a link, follow these steps:

1. Select Edit | Links.

2. In the Link dialog box, select the link or links that you want to break.

3. Choose the Break Link button. A dialog box will appear, asking for confirmation.

4. Choose Yes. The link or links will be broken.

> **tip** To break a link quickly by using the keyboard, press CTRL+SHIFT+F9.

Locking and Unlocking Links

You can *temporarily* prevent linked information from being updated by *locking* links. When you want to update the information again, you just unlock the links. Here's how it works:

1. Select Edit | Links.

2. In the Links dialog box, select the link or links that you want to lock or unlock.

3. To lock a link or links, check the Locked check box. To unlock a link or links, uncheck the Locked check box.

4. Choose OK to leave the Links dialog box and save your changes.

tip   *To lock links quickly by using the keyboard, first select the links and press CTRL+FII. To unlock links, press CTRL+SHIFT+FII.*

Reconnecting Lost Links

It's pretty easy to lose a link. For instance, you might rename or move the source file, forgetting that information in it was linked to another file. Someone else might even do this and forget to tell you.

note   *You'll have to do a pretty good job of renaming things to confuse OLE. It's remarkably adept at tracking files that you move or rename. Most likely you'll have to follow these steps if you move the file to another disk or some such.*

If you lose links in a document, don't despair—you *can* reconnect lost links. Here's how:

1. Choose Edit | Links.
2. In the Links dialog box, choose the link you want to reconnect.
3. Choose the Change Source button.
4. In the File Name box of the Change Source dialog box, select the file to which you want to reconnect the link. Then click OK. If your document contains other links to the same source file, you will be asked whether you want to change all links from the previous source file to the new source file. Choose Yes or No.

Troubleshooting Links

Following are a number of potential problems you might encounter in your linking, along with ways of fixing them.

SHARING INFORMATION WITH OLE

Problem: Linked Items Don't Update

If you get this message, check to see that you've actually established links, and that they are set to update when you expect. For example, if you choose Locked as a link option, changes in the source will not be reflected in the destination document.

Make sure that the source document still exists. Then make sure it hasn't been moved. If the document exists, you can reestablish the link by doing the following:

1. Switch to the destination document (a Word document, perhaps).

2. Choose Links from the Edit menu.

3. Select the troublesome link from the Source File list.

4. Click on the Change Source button.

5. Use the resulting Change Source dialog box to find the source document, and click OK.

Problem: Object Types Not Available

If you don't see an object type that you think should be available in the Object Type list used to insert objects, try reinstalling the application that generates the object type. For instance, if you expect to see Microsoft WordArt objects listed and you don't, try reinstalling Microsoft Word from the original Microsoft disks; if you do a custom installation, make certain that WordArt is one of the items specified.

CHAPTER 46

Embedding

A s you should remember by now, *embedding* actually puts objects into your destination documents, as opposed to *linking,* which only keeps track of objects in other files, in order to position them in a frame in the document you're viewing or printing. The difference between the two is borne out by the difference in file size: embedding objects into a file adds considerably to the destination document's size. Examples of embedded objects in the sample newsletter (see Chapter 44) include the logos, the "Book Heap" letter, and the photo image. Many of the other objects (like the Excel "Weigh-In" worksheet) *could* have been embedded but they were not.

note *Remember that embedded objects are only "updated" when you choose to edit them or replace them with more recent versions. Also remember that when you edit embedded objects, you need to have the application or applications that created them loaded on the computer you're using.*

How to Embed

You can choose either to embed an existing object or to create an object and then embed it. There's a simple way to embed objects, and then there's a more complicated way. We'll look at the simple way first.

Embedding with the Insert Object Command

Here are the steps to follow to create, then embed an object:

1. Position the insertion point where you want to insert the new object.

2. Use the Insert | Object command to select an object type. (Here, Microsoft WordArt 2.0 was chosen from the list in the Create New tab in the Object dialog box.)

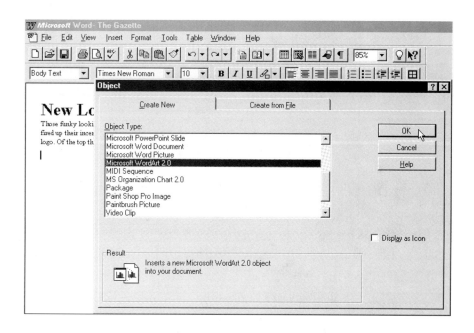

3. Create the object by use of the appropriate techniques for the application you are using.

4. Close the finished object, and return to the destination document. (Sometimes you'll use a Close command on the File menu, other times just clicking in the destination document will close the source application and insert the new object, as is the case with WordArt 2.0.)

Embedding Existing Objects

1. Position the insertion point where you want to insert the new object.

2. Choose Insert | Object.

3. Click on the Create From File tab to bring it frontmost if it isn't already.

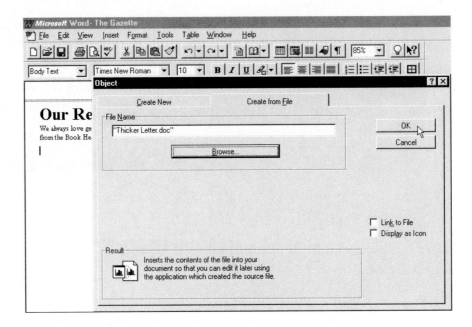

4. Locate the desired file and double-click on it.

5. The source document will be embedded in your destination.

The results can be a little frustrating, particularly if the destination document's margins can't accommodate the source document. You'll need to experiment.

Editing Embedded Objects

You edit embedded objects just as you would edit them in their original applications. Suppose, for example, that you had embedded that Excel worksheet instead of linking it, and wanted to make some changes:

1. Click the object to select it. Selection handles and a frame will appear around the object, as shown next.

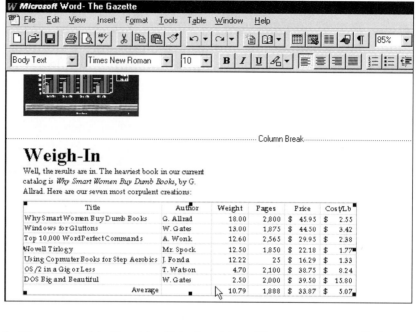

2. You guessed it. Double-click the object. Your computer will chug and whir for a while (quite a while if your object is something complicated, like a drawing). Then the application in which the object was created will open, with the object ready for editing. Notice how the window is titled "Microsoft Word," but Excel's menus and toolbars are available:

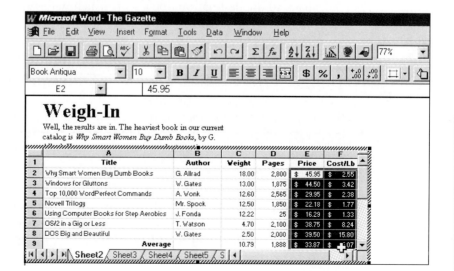

3. Edit the object, as you wish.

4. Select File | Exit or click the close box to quit the source application and return to the destination document, which will reappear with the object updated to reflect your changes. (You may need to use different techniques for different object types. Pressing ESC often works, too.)

Editing Sound and Video Clips

If you've been using sound and video clips, you will have spotted the fallacy in the preceding section. If you double-click a sound or video clip, you'll run it. These objects object to being edited this way. They wanna play instead.

In such cases (and in others, if you like), you can edit the embedded objects by using the Object command:

1. Select the object you want to edit.

2. Select Edit | Object; the command might be Edit | Linked Presentation Object | Edit or some such if you've chosen the object first. Choose the name of the object you want to edit, and then choose Edit. (If you are offered the choice of Edit or Open, choose Edit if you want to edit the object in the destination application window, or choose Open to open the application to which the object belongs and edit it there.)

3. When you've finished editing the object, select File | Exit to get back to the destination document, which will reappear with the edited object in place.

Converting an Embedded Object to a Different Format

You may run into situations in which you need to convert an embedded object to a different format. You might want to do this if you receive a file containing an embedded object that was created in an application you do not have, or if you take a file that contains embedded objects to a colleague who does not have the relevant application.

To change an embedded object's source application, follow these steps:

1. Select the object you want to change.

2. Select Edit | Object, choose the object you want to convert, and select Convert from the extension menu. This may read Edit | Linked Presentation Object | Convert or some such if you've chosen the object first.

3. In the Convert dialog box, specify the format to which you want to convert the file.

   ■ Select the Convert To button to *permanently* convert the embedded object to the format you specify.

   ■ Select the Activate As button to *temporarily* convert the embedded object to the format you specify. You can then edit the object in that format; but when you save it, it will be saved in its original format.

4. Click OK.

Converting an Embedded Object to a Graphic

If you've been embedding objects and you want to save some space, you can reduce the size of your file by converting the embedded objects to graphics. Any text in the object will no longer actually exist as text, so its readability may suffer at smaller sizes, and you will no longer be able to edit the object except with graphics editing tools. Also, you cannot convert the graphic back to an embedded object.

Still want to do it? Here's how:

1. Select the object you want to convert to a graphic.

2. Select Edit | Object and select the object in the Object dialog box. See the preceding caveats as to the actual command.

3. Choose Convert.

4. In the Object Type box, select Picture. Click OK. The object will be displayed as a picture.

tip *If you have field codes displayed, you will also see the field {Embed Word Drawing}. This is helpful when you're sharing documents with people who may not have the same graphics applications.*

Removing Embedded Objects

This being the end of the chapter, it seems like the natural place to mention how to start over. If your embedded object has served its purpose and is no longer needed, you can get rid of it, greatly reducing the size of your file.

Removing an embedded object is easy. Select it and press DEL. Or right-click on the object to pop up the shortcut menu, and choose Cut.

Index